Spanish
ALL-IN-ONE
FOR
DUMMIES®

Spanish
ALL-IN-ONE
FOR
DUMMIES®

**by Cecie Kraynak
with Gail Stein, Susana Wald,
Jessica M. Langemeier, Berlitz**

John Wiley & Sons, Inc.

Spanish All-in-One For Dummies®

Published by
John Wiley & Sons, Inc.
111 River St.
Hoboken, NJ 07030-5774
www.wiley.com

WILEY

About the Authors

Cecie Kraynak, MA has taught and tutored Spanish at the junior high, high school, and college levels for more than 25 years. She is a frequent traveler to Spanish-speaking countries and has studied abroad at the University of the Americas in Cholula, Mexico and the Universidad Complutense in Madrid, Spain. She earned her bachelor's degree in Spanish and secondary education in 1980 and her master's degree in Spanish literature from Purdue University. Cecie authored *Spanish Verbs For Dummies* and has edited numerous books on learning Spanish. She is currently the ESL coordinator for the South Montgomery Schools in New Market, Indiana.

Gail Stein, MA is a retired language instructor who taught in New York City public junior and senior high schools for more than 33 years. She has authored several French and Spanish books, including *Intermediate Spanish For Dummies*, *CliffsQuickReview French I* and *II*, *CliffsStudySolver Spanish I* and *II*, *575+ French Verbs*, and *Webster's Spanish Grammar Handbook*. Gail is a multiple-time honoree in *Who's Who Among America's Teachers*.

Susana Wald is a writer and a simultaneous and literary translator in Hungarian, Spanish, English, and French. As a publisher, she has been working with books and authors for many years. She has been a teacher in Chile and Canada and has known the joy of learning from her students and their untiring enthusiasm and tolerance. She is also an artist and has had her work shown in many countries in North, Central, and South America and in Europe.

Jessica M. Langemeier received her BA in education, with a second major in Spanish, from the University of Northern Iowa in 1998. After moving to Indianapolis, Indiana, in 1999, she taught Spanish, English as a Second Language (ESL), and general education in multilingual communities and schools. She also has developed ESL and Spanish language programs for individuals and companies. She received her MS in language education from Indiana University in 2004. She has lived and worked in Mexico and Japan and has taught students of all ages and nationalities.

Berlitz has meant excellence in language services for more than 120 years. At more than 400 locations and in 50 countries worldwide, Berlitz offers a full range of language and language-related services, including instruction, cross-cultural training, document translation, software localization, and interpretation services. Berlitz also offers a wide array of publishing products, such as self-study language courses, phrase books, travel guides, and dictionaries.

The world-famous Berlitz Method® is the core of all Berlitz language instruction. From the time of its introduction in 1878, millions have used this method to learn new languages. For more information about Berlitz classes and products, please consult your local telephone directory for the Language Center nearest you or visit the Berlitz Web site at www.berlitz.com, where you can enroll in classes or shop directly for products online.

Dedication

To my children, Nick and Ali, who have opened my eyes anew through their explorations of Spanish language and culture and who make great travel companions. — Cecie Kraynak

Author's Acknowledgments

Thanks to Michael Lewis for choosing me to write this book and working closely with me during the initial stages to formulate the vision. Thanks also go to project editor Tim Gallan for carefully shaping the manuscript and shepherding the text through production, and to Megan Knoll, copy editor, for purging the manuscript of any typos and ugly grammatical errors. Last but not least, thanks to my husband, Joe, who assisted in preparing the numerous manuscript submissions. — Cecie Kraynak

Publisher's Acknowledgments

We're proud of this book; please send us your comments through our Dummies online registration form located at http://dummies.custhelp.com. For other comments, please contact our Customer Care Department within the U.S. at 877-762-2974, outside the U.S. at 317-572-3993, or fax 317-572-4002.

Some of the people who helped bring this book to market include the following:

Acquisitions, Editorial, and Media Development

Senior Project Editor: Tim Gallan

Acquisitions Editor: Mike Lewis

Copy Editor: Megan Knoll

Technical Reviewer: Language Training Center

Editorial Program Coordinator: Joe Niesen

Editorial Manager: Michelle Hacker

Editorial Assistants: Jennette ElNaggar, David Lutton

Cartoons: Rich Tennant (www.the5thwave.com)

Composition Services

Project Coordinator: Kristie Rees

Layout and Graphics: Carl Byers, Reuben W. Davis, Melissa K. Jester, Christin Swinford, Christine Williams

Proofreaders: ConText Editorial Services, Inc., Caitie Copple

Indexer: BIM Indexing & Proofreading Services

Publishing and Editorial for Consumer Dummies

    Kathleen Nebenhaus, Vice President and Executive Publisher

    David Palmer, Associate Publisher

    Kristin Ferguson-Wagstaffe, Product Development Director

Publishing for Technology Dummies

    Andy Cummings, Vice President and Publisher

Composition Services

    Debbie Stailey, Director of Composition Services

Contents at a Glance

Table of Contents

Introduction

Gaining mastery over your first language is as easy as learning to walk. One day it's all goo-goo ga-ga, and the next you're stringing together words like a born orator. Picking up a second language, particularly when you're not immersed in it, is quite a bit more challenging. You have to set aside the conventions of your own language and get up to speed on new rules, structures, and vocabulary all at the same time.

Sure, you can pick up a handful of phrases overnight and perhaps recite the alphabet and count to ten by the end of the week, but that's not going to get you through a normal dinner conversation or enable you to understand foreign soap operas. You need some serious training to reach that point. Fortunately, *Spanish All-in-One For Dummies*, along with some practice, can get you there.

About This Book

Spanish All-in-One For Dummies is a comprehensive guide to acquiring Spanish as a second (or third or fourth or fifth) language that delivers the information and instruction in easily digestible, bite-sized chunks. It's the closest thing to a Spanish language immersion program you can get off a bookshelf — addressing both spoken and written Spanish and presenting it in the context of real-life situations. Think of it as your own personal tutor, reference book, and workbook all rolled into one.

This book is not a class that you have to drag yourself to twice a week for a specified period of time. You can use *Spanish All-in-One For Dummies* however you want to, whether your goal is to pick up a few common words and phrases, write a Spanish-speaking pen pal, or travel to a Spanish-speaking country. We set no timetable, so proceed at your own pace, reading as much or as little at a time as you like. You don't have to trudge through the chapters in order, either; just read the sections that interest you.

And don't forget to practice by using the CD at the back of this book for help in pronunciation. The only way to really know and love a language is to speak it. Throughout the book, we give you lots of words, phrases, and dialogues, complete with pronunciations. Only a sampling of them are on the CD, but we've provided a broad selection that should serve most of your basic needs.

Conventions Used in This Book

To make this book easy for you to navigate, we've set up a couple of conventions:

- ✏ Spanish terms are set in **boldface** to make them stand out.
- ✏ English pronunciations, set in *italics*, accompany the Spanish terms.
- ✏ Whenever we include the phonetic pronunciation of a Spanish word, we also use italics to denote any stress you add to that word. (See Book 1, Chapter 1 for more on pronunciation and stress.)
- ✏ As you begin to use this book, you will no doubt notice that we chose a rather conventional method to introduce the different verb conjugations — a *conjugation box*, which looks like this:

pedir (e to i) (*to ask for*)	
pido	pedimos
pides	pedís
pide	piden

This handy little tool acts like a mental billboard. It displays the Spanish verb, its English meaning, and then conjugates the verb, presenting the three singular conjugations in the left column (for I; you informal singular; and he, she, it/you formal singular) and the three plural conjugations (we, you informal plural, and they/you formal plural) in the right column. Some even include an example sentence below the conjugations at no extra charge.

- ✏ **Vocabulary chart:** Vocabulary charts provide a quick rundown of common words or expressions, typically providing the Spanish word in the left column with its English equivalent in the right column. In some cases, the charts contain additional columns to illustrate different forms, such as a present participle.

Language learning is a peculiar beast, so this book includes a few elements that other *For Dummies* books don't, such as the Talkin' the Talk dialogue. One of the best ways to learn a language is to see and hear how it's used in conversation, so we include dialogues throughout Books I and IV. The dialogues come under the heading "Talkin' the Talk" and show you the Spanish phrases, the pronunciation, and the English translation.

Also note that because each language has its own ways of expressing ideas, the English translations that we provide for the Spanish terms may not be exactly literal. We want you to know the gist of what's being said, not just the words that are being said. For example, you can translate the Spanish phrase **de nada** (deh *nah*-dah) literally as *of nothing,* but the phrase really means *you're welcome.* This book gives the *you're welcome* translation.

Foolish Assumptions

To write this book, we had to make some assumptions about who you are and what you want from a book called *Spanish All-in-One For Dummies.* Here are the assumptions we've made about you:

- ✔ You know little or no Spanish — or if you took a Spanish class some years ago, you don't recall much of what you knew.

- ✔ You're looking for more than your average conversational Spanish lesson, but you want that, too.

- ✔ You want to have fun and pick up a little bit of Spanish at the same time.

If these statements apply to you, you've found the right book!

How This Book is Organized

This book is actually six books in one, each of which tackles Spanish and Spanish language acquisition in a different way. In the following sections, we provide a brief description of what you can expect to find in each book.

Book 1: Speaking in Everyday Settings

This book focuses on the spoken word and allows you to get your feet wet and wade in slowly. We begin with the bare basics, including some guidance on proper pronunciation; introduce words for numbers, colors, dates, and time; show you how to initiate conversations with greetings and small talk; and then place you in various situations where you pick up Spanish in every-day settings, including grocery stores, restaurants, department stores, and even in emergency situations.

Book II: Grasping Basic Grammar Essentials

In Book II, we get more formal as we introduce you to the various rules and regulations that govern the Spanish language. Don't worry, we start out very slowly with the building blocks — the parts of speech, including nouns, verbs, adjectives, and adverbs — before moving on to slightly more involved topics like conjugating verbs in the simple past, present, and future tenses. In very short order, you'll be constructing your own original expressions in complete sentences! You also discover how to ask questions, spice up your expressions with adjectives and adverbs, and build your own prepositional phrases.

Book III: Mastering More Advanced Grammar Essentials

Consider this book a more advanced course in Spanish grammar than Book 2. Here, you discover how to issue commands with the imperative mood, take action on object pronouns, talk about yourself with the reflexive, wish and hope with the subjunctive, and double the number of verb tenses with the helping verb **haber**.

Book IV: Spanish at Work

Even if you're fairly fluent in everyday Spanish, you may have trouble communicating with customers or colleagues at work because the words and phrases you need so specific to your line of work. To assist you with your Spanish on the job, we've included several chapters that deal with various professions and workplace scenarios:

- Healthcare workers
- Law enforcement professionals
- Educators and administrators
- Banking and financing professionals
- Office workers
- Hotel and restaurant managers
- Builders, mechanics, and factory workers
- Real estate professionals
- Gardeners and landscapers

Book V: Appendixes

At the very back of this book, just before the index, we provide four appendixes for quick reference:

- ✔ **Appendix A:** Verb conjugations for regular and irregular verbs
- ✔ **Appendix B:** Spanish-to-English dictionary
- ✔ **Appendix C:** English-to-Spanish dictionary
- ✔ **Appendix D:** About the CD

Icons Used in This Book

You may be looking for particular information while reading this book. To make certain types of information easier for you to find, we've placed the following icons in the left-hand margins throughout the book:

This icon highlights tips that can make learning Spanish easier.

Languages are full of quirks that may trip you up if you're not prepared for them. This icon points to discussions of these weird grammar rules.

If you're looking for information and advice about culture and travel, look for these icons. They draw your attention to interesting tidbits about the countries in which Spanish is spoken.

The audio CD that comes with this book gives you the opportunity to listen to real Spanish speakers so that you can get a better understanding of what Spanish sounds like. This icon marks the Talkin' the Talk dialogues you can find on the CD.

Remember icons call your attention to important information about the language — something you shouldn't neglect or something that's out of the ordinary. Don't ignore these paragraphs.

Where to Go from Here

Like all *For Dummies* books, this one is designed for a skip-and-dip approach. You can skip to any chapter or section that catches your eye and find a mini-lesson on the topic du jour. If you've never had any instruction in Spanish or much exposure to it, we encourage you to begin with the first four chapters of Book I. These chapters form the foundation on which you can start building your knowledge.

Books I and IV present a more conversational, situational approach, for when you need to know a few key words and phrases and you don't have time for the rules or you need some specialized vocabulary you can't find anywhere else.

When you do have time for the rules, spend some time cozying up to Books II and III, where true Spanish mastery is laid and hatched. This stuff is the meat-and-potatoes Spanish . . . or should we say rice and beans?

Book I
Speaking in Everyday Settings

In this book . . .

When you're just getting started with a new language, sampling a few appetizers can whet your appetite for more. In this book, we warm you up with some basics, including rules on pronunciation and stress (without stressing you out too much). We cover numbers, colors, dates, and time; engage you in some Spanish small talk; and then place you in common situations in which you pick up the language quite naturally.

Here are the contents of Book I at a glance:

Chapter 1

Warming Up with the Bare Basics

In This Chapter

- Recognizing the little Spanish you know
- Pronouncing the Spanish alphabet
- Adding stress to the correct syllables
- Utilizing Spanish punctuation and pause-fillers

*T*he learning curve for Spanish is steep enough to give most people vertigo and convince some people to throw in the towel before their first conversation. The key to success in acquiring any language, even your first language, is to take baby steps. Start slowly and try to gain some momentum.

This chapter starts you out very gradually, introducing you to the Spanish language by pointing out some words and phrases you're probably already, familiar with, leading you through the process of reciting your Spanish ABCs and then encouraging you to stretch your abilities by reaching for some words and phrases that may not be so familiar.

Starting with What You Already Know

The English language is ever evolving. It evolved from other older languages and continues to be influenced by other languages old and new. As a result, English has many words that are identical or very similar to foreign words. These words can cause both delight and embarrassment. The delight comes in the words that look and sound alike and have similar meanings. The embarrassment comes from words that have the same roots but mean completely different things.

Among the delightful similarities are words like **soprano** (soh-*prah*-noh) (*soprano*), **pronto** (*prohn*-toh) (*right away; soon*), and thousands of others that differ by just one or two letters such as **conclusión** (kohn-kloo-see-*ohn*) (*conclusion*), **composición** (kohm-poh-see-see-*ohn*) (*composition*), **invención** (een-bvehn-see-*ohn*) (*invention*), and **presidente** (preh-see-*dehn*-teh) (*president*).

Don't let the false cognates fool ya

False cognates are words in different languages that look very similar and even have the same root yet mean completely different things. One that comes to mind is the word *actual*. In English, *actual* means *real*; *in reality*; or *the very one*. Not so in Spanish. **Actual** (ahk-too*ahl*) in Spanish means *present*; *current*; *belonging to this moment, this day, or this year*. When you say *the actual painting* in English, you're referring to the real one — the very one people are looking at or want to see. But, when you say **la pintura actual** (lah peen-*too*-rah ahk-too*ahl*) in Spanish, you're referring to the painting that belongs to the current time, the one that follows present day trends — a modern painting.

Another example is the adjective *embarrassed*. In English, *embarrassed* means *ashamed*. In Spanish, **embarazada** (ehm-bvah-rah-*sah*-dah) comes from the same root as the English word, but it's almost exclusively used to mean *pregnant*. So you can say in English that you're a little *embarrassed*, but in Spanish you can't be just a little **embarazada**. Either you're pregnant or you're not.

Noting common similarities

Word trouble ends at the point where a word originating in English is absorbed into Spanish or vice versa. The proximity of the United States to Mexico produces a change in the Spanish spoken there. An example is the word *car*. In Mexico, people say **carro** (*kah*-rroh). In South America, on the other hand, people say **auto** (*ahoo*-toh). In Spain, people say **coche** (*koh*-cheh). Here are just a few examples of Spanish words that you already know because English uses them, too:

- ✔ You've been to a **rodeo** (roh-*deh*-oh) or a **fiesta** (fee-*ehs*-tah).

- ✔ You've probably taken a **siesta** (see-*ehs*-tah) or two.

- ✔ You probably know at least one **señorita** (seh-nyoh-*ree*-tah), and you surely have an **amigo** (ah-*mee*-goh). Maybe you'll see him **mañana** (mah-*nyah*-nah).

- ✔ You already know the names of places like **Los Angeles** (lohs *ahn*-Heh-lehs) (*the angels*), **San Francisco** (sahn frahn-*sees*-koh) (*St. Francis*), **La Jolla** (la *Hoh*-yah) (*the jewel*), and **Florida** (floh-*ree*-dah) (*the blooming one*).

✔ You've had a **tortilla** (tohr-*tee*-yah), **taco** (*tah*-koh), or **burrito** (bvoo-*rree*-toh).

✔ You fancy the **tango** (*tahn*-goh), **bolero** (bvo-*leh*-roh), or **rumba** (*room*-bvah).

Reciting Your ABC's

Correct pronunciation is key to avoiding misunderstandings. The following sections present some basic guidelines for proper pronunciation.

Next to the Spanish words throughout this book, the pronunciation is in parentheses (*pronunciation brackets*). Within the pronunciation brackets, we separate all the words that have more than one syllable with a hyphen, like this: (*kah*-sah). An italicized syllable within the pronunciation brackets tells you to stress that syllable. We say much more about stress later in this chapter.

In the following section we comment on some letters of the alphabet from the Spanish point of view. The aim is to help you to understand Spanish pronunciations. Here is the basic Spanish alphabet and its pronunciation:

a (ah)	**b** (bveh)	**c** (seh)	**d** (deh)
e (eh)	**f** (*eh*-feh)	**g** (Heh)	**h** (*ah*-cheh)
i (ee)	**j** (*Hoh*-tah)	**k** (kah)	**l** (*eh*-leh)
m (*eh*-meh)	**n** (*eh*-neh)	**ñ** (*eh*-nyeh)	**o** (oh)
p (peh)	**q** (koo)	**r** (*eh*-reh)	**s** (*eh*-seh)
t (teh)	**u** (oo)	**v** (bveh)	**w** (*doh*-bleh bveh) (oo-bveh *doh*-bvleh) (Spain)
x (*eh*-kees)	**y** (ee-gree-*eh*-gah)	**z** (*seh*-tah)	

Spanish also includes some double letters in its alphabet: **ch** (cheh), **ll** (*eh*-yeh or ye), and **rr** (a trilled *r*).

We don't go through every letter of the alphabet in the sections that follow, only those that you use differently in Spanish than in English. The differences can lie in pronunciation or the way they look, or in the fact that you seldom see the letters/don't pronounce them at all.

Consonants

Consonants tend to sound the same in English and Spanish. Only a few consonants in Spanish differ from their English counterparts. The following sections look more closely at the behavior and pronunciation of these consonants.

Inside the Spanish-speaking world, consonants may be pronounced differently than in English. For example, in Spain the consonant **z** is pronounced like the *th* in the English word *thesis*. (Latin Americans don't use this sound; in all other Spanish-speaking countries, **z** and **s** sound the same.)

In the Spanish speaker's mind, a consonant is any sound that needs a vowel next to it when you pronounce it. For example, saying the letter **t** by itself may be difficult for a Spanish speaker. To the Spanish ear, pronouncing **t** sounds like "*te*" (teh). Likewise, the Spanish speaker says **ese** (*eh*-seh) when pronouncing the letter **s**.

The letter K

In Spanish, the letter **k** is used only in words that have their origin in foreign languages. More often than not, this letter is seen in **kilo** (*kee*-loh), meaning "thousand" in Greek. An example is **kilómetro** (kee-*loh*-meh-troh) (*kilometer*) — a thousand-meter measure for distance.

The letter H

In Spanish, the letter **h** is always mute unless it follows **c** as in **ch** (cheh), discussed earlier in this chapter. Following are some examples of the Spanish **h**:

  ✔ **hada** (*ah*-dah) (*fairy*)

  ✔ **hola** (*oh*-lah) (*hello*)

  ✔ **huevo** (ooeh-bvoh) (*egg*)

The letter J

The consonant **j** sounds like a guttural **h**. Normally, you say **h** quite softly, as though you were just breathing out. Now, say your **h** but gently raise the back of your tongue as if you were saying **k**. Push the air out real hard, and you get the sound. Try it! There — it sounds like you're gargling, doesn't it?

To signal that you need to make this sound, we use a capital letter **H** within the pronunciation brackets. Now try the sound out on these words:

  ✔ **Cajamarca** (kah-Hah-*mahr*-kah) (the name of a city in Peru)

  ✔ **cajeta** (kah-*Heh*-tah) (a delicious, thick sauce made of milk and sugar)

  ✔ **cajón** (kah-*Hohn*) (*big box*)

- ✔ **jadeo** (Hah-*deh*-oh) (*panting*)
- ✔ **Jijón** (Hee-*Hohn*) (the name of a city in Spain)
- ✔ **jota** (*Hoh*-tah) (the Spanish name for the letter **j**; also the name of a folk dance in Spain)
- ✔ **tijera** (tee-*Heh*-rah) (*scissors*)

The letter C

The letter **c**, in front of the vowels **a**, **o**, and **u**, sounds like the English **k**. We use the letter **k** in the pronunciation brackets to signal this sound. Following are some examples:

- ✔ **acabar** (ah-kah-*bvahr*) (*to finish*)
- ✔ **café** (kah-*feh*) (*coffee*)
- ✔ **casa** (*kah*-sah) (*house*)
- ✔ **ocaso** (oh-*kah*-soh) (*sunset*)

When the letter **c** is in front of the vowels **e** and **i**, it sounds like the English **s**. In the pronunciation brackets, we signal this sound as **s**. Following are some examples:

- ✔ **acero** (ah-*seh*-roh) (*steel*)
- ✔ **cero** (*seh*-roh) (*zero*)
- ✔ **cine** (*see*-neh) (*cinema*)

In much of Spain — primarily the northern and central parts — the letter **c** is pronounced like the **th** in thanks when placed before the vowels **e** and **i**.

The letters S and Z

In Latin American Spanish, the letters s and z always sound like the English letter **s**. We use the letter **s** in the pronunciation brackets to signal this sound. Following are some examples:

- ✔ **asiento** (ah-see*ehn*-toh) (*seat*)
- ✔ **sol** (sohl) (*sun*)
- ✔ **zarzuela** (sahr-soo*eh*-lah) (*Spanish-style operetta*)

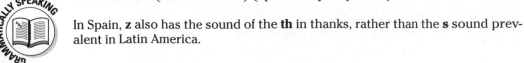

In Spain, **z** also has the sound of the **th** in thanks, rather than the **s** sound prevalent in Latin America.

The letters B and V

The letters **b** and **v** are pronounced the same, the sound being somewhere in-between the two letters. This in-between is a fuzzy, bland sound — closer to **v** than to **b**. If you position your lips and teeth to make a **v** sound, and then try to make a **b** sound, you have it. To remind you to make this sound, we use **bv** in our pronunciation brackets, for both **b** and **v**. Here are some examples:

- ✔ **cabeza** (kah-*bveh*-sah) (*head*)
- ✔ **vida** (*bvee*-dah) (*life*)
- ✔ **violín** (bveeoh-*leen*) (*violin*)

The letter Q

Spanish doesn't use the letter **k** very much; when the language wants a **k** sound in front of the vowels **e** and **i**, it unfolds the letter combination **qu**. So when you see the word **queso** (*keh*-soh) (*cheese*), you immediately know that you say the **k** sound. Here are some examples of the Spanish letter combination **qu**, which we indicate by the letter **k** in pronunciation brackets. Check out these examples:

- ✔ **Coquimbo** (koh-*keem*-bvoh) (the name of a city in Chile)
- ✔ **paquete** (pah-*keh*-teh) (*package*)
- ✔ **pequeño** (peh-*keh*-nyoh) (*small*)
- ✔ **tequila** (teh-*kee*-lah) (Mexican liquor, spirits)

The letter G

In Spanish the letter **g** has a double personality, like the letter **c**. When you combine the letter **g** with a consonant or when you see it in front of the vowels **a**, **o**, and **u**, it sounds like the **g** in goose. Here are some examples:

- ✔ **begonia** (bveh-*goh*-neeah) (*begonia*)
- ✔ **gato** (*gah*-toh) (*cat*)
- ✔ **gracias** (*grah*-seeahs) (*thank you*)

The **g** changes personality in front of the vowels **e** and **i**. It sounds like the Spanish **j**, which we signal with the capital **H** in our pronunciation brackets.

- ✔ **agenda** (ah-*Hehn*-dah) (*agenda; date book*)
- ✔ **gerente** (Heh-*rehn*-teh) (*manager*)

To hear the sound **g** (as in *goat*) in front of the vowels **e** and **i**, you must insert a **u**, making **gue** and **gui**. To remind you to make the goat sound (**g**, not "mmehehe") we use **gh** in our pronunciation brackets. Some examples:

- ✔ **guía** (*ghee*-ah) (*guide*)
- ✔ **guiño** (*ghee*-nyoh) (*wink*)
- ✔ **guerra** (*gheh*-rrah) (*war*)

Double consonants

Spanish has two double consonants: **ll** and **rr**. They're considered singular letters, and each has a singular sound. Because these consonants are considered singular, they stick together when you separate syllables. For example, the word **calle** (*kah*-yeh) (*street*) appears as **ca-lle**. And **torre** (*toh*-rreh), (*tower*) separates into **to-rre**.

The letter LL

The **ll** consonant sounds like the **y** in the English word *yes*, except in Argentina and Uruguay.

Argentineans and Uruguayans pronounce this consonant as the sound that happens when you have your lips pursed to say **s** and then make the **z** sound through them. Try it. Fun, isn't it? But really, the sound isn't that difficult to make, because you can find the English equivalent in words like *measure* and *pleasure*. The way you say those *s* sounds is exactly how **ll** is pronounced in Argentina and Uruguay.

Throughout this book, we use the sound like the English **y** in the word *yes*, which is how **ll** is pronounced in 18 of the 20 Spanish-speaking countries. In the pronunciation brackets, we use **y** to signal this sound.

Now try the **ll** sound, using the **y** sound, in the following examples:

- ✔ **brillo** (*bvree*-yoh) (*shine*)
- ✔ **llama** (*yah*-mah) (*flame; also the name of an animal in Peru*)
- ✔ **lluvia** (*yoo*-bveeah) (*rain*)

The letter RR

The **rr** sounds like a strongly rolled **r**. In fact, every **r** is strongly rolled in Spanish, but the double one is the real winner. To roll an **r**, curl your tongue against the roof of your mouth as if you were pronouncing the double *d* in the word *ladder* and direct your outward airflow over the top of your tongue. This should cause the tongue to vibrate against the roof of your mouth, making the trill sound.

An easy way to make this sound is to say the letter **r** as though you were pretending to sound like an outboard motor. There. You have it!

Spanish speakers take special pleasure in rolling their **rr**s. One fun fact about **rr** is that no words begin with it. Isn't that a relief! In pronunciation brackets, we simply signal this sound as **rr**.

Play with these words:

- **carrera** (kah-*rreh*-rah) (*race; profession*)
- **correo** (koh-*rreh*-oh) (*mail, post*)
- **tierra** (tee*eh*-rrah) (*land*)

The letter y

This letter represents sounds that are very similar to those of **ll**. The people of both Argentina and Uruguay pronounce this sound differently from the rest of Latin America. We advise that you pronounce it as the English **y** in *yes* and *you*. In the pronunciation brackets, we signal this sound as **y**. Following are some examples:

- **playa** (*plah*-yah) (*beach*)
- **yema** (*yeh*-mah) (*yolk*; also *fingertip*)
- **yodo** (*yoh*-doh) (*iodine*)

In Spanish, the letter **y** is never a vowel, always a consonant.

The letter Ñ

When you see a wiggly line on top of the letter **n** that looks like **ñ**, use the **ny** sound that you use for the English word *canyon*. The wiggly line is called a *tilde* (*teel*-deh). In pronunciation brackets, we show this sound as **ny**. Here are some examples:

- **cuñado** (koo-*nyah*-doh) (*brother-in-law*)
- **mañana** (mah-*nyah*-nah) (*tomorrow*)
- **niña** (*nee*-nyah) (*girl*)

Vowels

If you want your Spanish to sound like a native's, you have to concentrate on your vowels. The biggest difference between English and Spanish is almost certainly in the way the vowels are written and pronounced. By now, you may be well aware that one vowel in English can have more than one sound.

Look, for instance, at *fat* and *fate*. Both words have the vowel **a**, but they're pronounced much differently from each other. The good news is that in Spanish, you always say the vowels one way and one way only.

The upcoming sections discuss the five vowels — which are the only vowel sounds in Spanish. They're **a** (ah), **e** (eh), **i** (ee), **o** (oh), and **u** (oo). Spanish sees each of these vowels by itself and makes other sounds by combining the vowels in pairs.

The Spanish vowels **a**, **e**, **i**, **o**, and **u** are pronounced staccato, as in the music notation that requires you to hit a note with a short, hard stroke with no trailing sound. For example, although English speakers would pronounce *trail* almost like "tray-ill," Spanish speakers would never draw out the vowel sound. They would still pronounce the long **a**, but it would stop short, more like *trehl*.

The vowel A

As children, almost everybody sings the ABC's. In Spanish, the English **a** that starts off the song is pronounced *ah*. The easiest way to remember how to pronounce the letter **a** in Spanish is to sing the chorus of the Christmas carol "Deck the Halls" to yourself. You remember the chorus, don't you? Fa la la la la, la la, la la. We write this sound as **ah** in the pronunciation brackets.

Following are some sample words to practice. Remember that you pronounce each and every **a** exactly the same way.

- **Caracas** (kah-*rah*-kas) (a city in Venezuela)
- **mapa** (*mah*-pah) (*map*)
- **Guadalajara** (gooah-dah-lah-*Hah*-rah) (a city in Mexico)

The vowel E

To get an idea of how the Spanish **e** sounds, smile gently, open your mouth a bit and say "eh." The sound should be like the **e** in the English word *pen*. In our pronunciation brackets, this vowel appears as **eh**. Try these:

- **pelele** (peh-*leh*-leh) (*rag doll; puppet*)
- **pelo** (*peh*-loh) (*hair*)
- **seco** (*seh*-koh) (*dry*)

The vowel I

In Spanish the vowel **i** sounds like the **ee** in *seen*, but just a touch shorter. To give you an example, when English speakers say *feet* or *street*, the Spanish speaker hears what sounds like almost two **i**'s. We signal this sound as **ee** in our pronunciation brackets. Following are some examples:

✔ **irritar** (ee-rree-*tahr*) (*to irritate*)

✔ **piña** (*pee*-nyah) (*pineapple*)

✔ **pintar** (peen-*tahr*) (*to paint*)

The vowel O

The Spanish put their mouths in a rounded position, as if to breathe a kiss over a flower, and keeping it in that position, say **o**. It sounds like the **o** in *floor*, but a bit shorter. We signal this sound as **oh** in the pronunciation brackets. Try practicing the sound on these words:

✔ **coco** (*koh*-koh) (*coconut*)

✔ **Orinoco** (oh-ree-*noh*-koh) (a river in Venezuela)

✔ **Oruro** (oh-*roo*-roh) (a city in Bolivia)

✔ **toronja** (toh-*rohn*-Hah) (*grapefruit*)

The vowel U

The fifth and last vowel in Spanish is the **u**, and it sounds like the **oo** in *moon* or *raccoon*, but just a touch shorter. **Oo**, we think you've got it! We write this sound as **oo** in the pronunciation brackets. Here are some examples of the **u** sound:

✔ **cuna** (*koo*-nah) (*cradle*)

✔ **cuñado** (koo-*nyah*-doh) (*brother-in-law*)

✔ **cúrcuma** (*koor*-koo-mah) (*turmeric*)

✔ **curioso** (koo-ree*oh*-soh) (*curious*)

✔ **fruta** (*froo*-tah) (*fruit*)

✔ **luna** (*loo*-nah) (*moon*)

✔ **tuna** (*too*-nah) (*prickly pear*)

Diphthongs

Diphthong comes from Greek, where **di** means *two*, and **thong** comes from a very similar word meaning *sound* or *voice*. (Don't worry, we had to look it up in the dictionary ourselves.) Very simply, it means "double sound." There. That's easier.

The Spanish word is **diptongo** (deep-*tohn*-goh). **Diptongos** are the combination of two vowels, from the Spanish-speaking point of view. For instance, **i** and **o** combine to make **io** as in **patio** (*pah*-teeoh) (*courtyard* or *patio*.)

Joining the weak to the strong

Diptongos are always made up of a weak and a strong vowel. Calling vowels "weak" or "strong" is a convention of the Spanish language. To the Spanish-speaker, **i** and **u** are weak vowels, leaving **a**, **e**, and **o** as strong ones. The convention comes from the fact that the so-called strong vowel is always dominant in the diphthong.

To visualize this weak or strong concept, consider a piccolo flute and a bass horn. The sound of the piccolo is definitely more like the Spanish **i** and **u**, and the base horn sounds more like the Spanish **a**, **e**, and especially **o**.

Any combination of one strong and one weak vowel is a **diptongo** (deep-*tohn*-goh), which means that they belong together in the same syllable. In fact, they're not only together, they're stuck like superglue; they can't be separated.

In the **diptongo**, the stress falls on the strong vowel (more about stress later in this chapter). An accent mark alerts you when the stress falls on the weak vowel. In the combination of two weak vowels, the stress is on the second one. Try these examples of diphthongs:

- **bueno** (bvoo*eh*-noh) (*good*)
- **cuando** (koo*ahn*-doh) (*when*)
- **fiar** (fee*ahr*) (*to sell on credit*)
- **fuera** (foo*eh*-rah) (*outside*)
- **suizo** (soo*ee*-soh) (*Swiss*)
- **viudo** (bvee*oo*-doh) (*widower*)

Separating the strong from the strong

When two strong vowels are combined, they don't form a diphthong. Instead, the vowels retain their separate values, so you must put them into separate syllables. Here are some examples:

- **aorta** (ah-ohr-tah) (*aorta*) (See! Just as in English!)
- **feo** (*feh*-oh) (*ugly*)
- **marea** (mah-*reh*-ah) (*tide*)
- **mareo** (mah-*reh*-oh) (*dizziness*)

Did you notice in the previous list how changing one letter, in **marea** and **mareo**, for example, can change the meaning of a word? This letter phenomenon occurs in Spanish, just as in English. Finding such words is fun. In the case of the previous list, at least the two words come from the same root **mar** (mahr) (*sea*). And, associating the tide to one's dizziness isn't all that difficult. But in other places you can have oceans of difference. Here are some more examples: **casa** (*kah*-sah) (*house*) and **cosa** (*koh*-sah) (*thing*); and **pito** (*pee*-toh) (*whistle*), **pato** (*pah*-toh) (*duck*), and **peto** (*peh*-toh) (*bib* or *breastplate*.)

Honing Your Pronunciation Skills

In Spanish, one syllable always gets more stress — that is, you say it louder than the others. In single-syllable words, finding the stress is easy. But many words have more than one syllable, and that's when the situation becomes . . . well, stressful.

Looking for stress in the usual places

Can you believe that you're looking for stress? In Spanish, the right stress at the right time is a good thing, and fortunately, stress in Spanish is easy to control. If you have no written accent, you have two rules to follow:

✔ You stress the word on the next to last syllable if it ends in a vowel, an **n**, or an **s**. Here are some examples:

- **camas** (*kah*-mahs) (*beds*)
- **mariposas** (mah-ree-*poh*-sahs) (*butterflies*)
- **pollo** (*poh*-yoh) (*chicken*)

✔ You stress the word on the last syllable when it ends in a consonant that isn't an **n** or **s**. Look at these examples:

- **cantar** (kahn-*tahr*) (*to sing*)
- **feliz** (feh-*lees*) (*happy*)

If a word doesn't follow one of these two rules, it has an accent mark on it to indicate where you place the stress.

Adverbs ending in -**mente** (equivalent to the English *-ly*) have two stressed syllables, because they keep the stress of the root word and the stress in the suffix, -**mente**; for example, **generalmente** (*hehn*-ehr-ahl-*mehn*-teh). Many compound words also have two stressed syllables, as in the case of **eléctromagnético** (ee-*lehk*-troh-mag-*neh*-tee-coh).

Scouting out accented syllables

Book I

Speaking in Everyday Settings

One good point about having the accent mark on a syllable is that you can tell immediately where the stress is just by looking at the word.

The accent mark doesn't affect how you pronounce the vowel, just which syllable you stress. Here are some examples of words with accent marks:

- ✔ **balcón** (bvahl-*kohn*) (*balcony*)
- ✔ **carácter** (kah-*rahk*-tehr) (*character, personality*)
- ✔ **fotógrafo** (foh-*toh*-grah-foh) (*photographer*)
- ✔ **pájaro** (*pah*-Hah-roh) (*bird*)

The accent mark isn't always an indication of stress on a syllable. It's also used in some single-syllable words to distinguish the meanings of two words that are otherwise identical; Table 1-1 gives you some examples:

Table 1-1	One-Syllable Words That Change Meaning Under Stress		
Accented	**Means**	**Unaccented**	**Means**
dé	give (subjunctive of **dar**)	de	of/from
él	he, him	el	the
más	more	mas	but
mí	me	mi	my
sé	I know, be	se	one's self
sí	yes	si	if
té	tea	te	you
tú	you	tu	your
¡vé!	go!	ve	sees

Discovering accents on diphthongs

An accent in a diphthong shows you which vowel to stress. Take a look at these examples:

> ✔ **¡Adiós!** (ah-dee*ohs*) (*Good-bye!*)
>
> ✔ **¡Buenos días!** (bvoo*eh*-nohs *dee*-ahs) (*Good morning!*)
>
> ✔ **¿Decía?** (deh-*see*-ah) (*You were saying?*)
>
> ✔ **tía** (*tee*-ah) (*aunt*)

See "Diphthongs" earlier in this chapter for more on these vowel combos.

Getting Familiar with Punctuation Rules

You may notice unfamiliar punctuation in phrases like **¡Buenos días!**, **¿Decía?**, and **¡Adiós!**? Spanish indicates the mood (or tone) of what you're saying both at the beginning and at the end of the phrase that is a question or an exclamation, as in **¿Decía?** (deh-*seeah*) (You were saying?) or **¡Decía!** (deh*see*-ah) (You were saying!).

As far as we know, Spanish is the only language that provides this sort of punctuation. However, this punctuation is very useful when you have to read something aloud because you know beforehand how to modulate your voice when the phrase is coming up. This punctuation is the verbal equivalent of making gestures, which you can see in the following examples:

> ✔ **¿Dónde está?** (*dohn*-deh ehs-*tah*) (*Where is it?*)
>
> ✔ **¡Qué maravilla!** (keh mah-rah-*bvee*-yah) (*How wonderful!*)

Brushing Up on Basic Phrases

The following phrases can get you through a number of awkward pauses as you think of the right word:

> ✔ **¡Olé!** (oh-*leh*) (*Great!/Superb!/Keep going!*) This very Spanish expression is used during bullfights in Mexico and Peru.
>
> ✔ **¿Quiubo?** (kee-*oo*-bvoh) (*Hello, what's happening?*)
>
> ✔ **¿De veras?** (deh *bveh*-rahs) (*Really?*) This phrase signals slight disbelief.
>
> ✔ **¡No me digas!** (noh meh *dee*-gahs) (*You don't say!*) This phrase also indicates disbelief.

Chapter 2

Uno, Dos, Tres: Numbers, Colors, Dates, and Time

Functioning in any language requires that you be able to recite your ABC's, count to ten, describe items in very basic terms, and deal with schedules and appointments.

Though Book I, Chapter 1 covers the ABC's, this chapter deals with all the other basics, including counting, naming your colors, naming the days of the week and months of the year, and telling time.

Counting with Ordinal and Cardinal Numbers

One of the first skills you acquire, usually long before you tackle kindergarten, is to count in your native language — it's one of the few skills that falls in both the language and math categories. Likewise, one of the first skills you need to pick up in Spanish is the ability to count, at least up to ten.

The following sections show you how to count in Spanish — both with cardinal numbers (*one, two, three*) and ordinal numbers (*first, second, third*).

Cardinal numbers

You can get by with asking for one thing, or more than one thing, or even some things . . . for a while. But eventually you'll want to ask for two things, or ten things, or even more. When numbers are important, you need to know how to say them, so we show you how to count from one to two million in Spanish:

Number	Spanish	Number	Spanish
0	**cero** (*seh*-roh)	17	**diecisiete** (deeeh-see-see*eh*-teh)
1	**uno** (*oo*-noh)	18	**dieciocho** (deeeh-see-*oh*-choh)
2	**dos** (dohs)	19	**diecinueve** (deeeh-see-noo*eh*-bveh)
3	**tres** (trehs)	20	**veinte** (bveh*een*-teh)
4	**cuatro** (koo*ah*-troh)	21	**veintiuno** (bveheen-tee-*oo*-noh)
5	**cinco** (*seen*-koh)	22	**veintidós** (bveheen-tee-*dohs*)
6	**seis** (*seh*ees)	23	**veintitrés** (bveheen-tee-*trehs*)
7	**siete** (see*eh*-teh)	24	**veinticuatro** (bveheen-tee-coo*ah*-troh)
8	**ocho** (*oh*-choh)	25	**veinticinco** (bveheen-tee-*seen*-koh)
9	**nueve** (noo*eh*-bveh)	26	**veintiséis** (bveheen-tee-*seh*ees)
10	**diez** (dee*eh*s)	27	**veintisiete** (bveheen-tee-see*eh*-teh)
11	**once** (*ohn*-seh)	28	**veintiocho** (bveheen-tee-*oh*-choh)
12	**doce** (*doh*-seh)	29	**veintinueve** (bveheen-tee-noo*eh*-bveh)
13	**trece** (*treh*-seh)	30	**treinta** (*treh*een-tah)
14	**catorce** (cah-*tohr*-seh)	40	**cuarenta** (kooah-*rehn*-tah)
15	**quince** (*keen*-seh)	50	**cincuenta** (seen-koo*ehn*-tah)
16	**dieciséis** (deeeh-see-*seh*ees)	60	**sesenta** (seh-*sehn*-tah)

Book I

Speaking in Everyday Settings

70	**setenta** (seh-*tehn*-tah)	900	**novecientos** (noh-bveh-see*ehn*-tohs)
80	**ochenta** (oh-*chehn*-tah)	1.000	**mil** (meel)
90	**noventa** (noh-*bvehn*-tah)	2.000	**dos mil** (dohs meel)
100	**cien (ciento)** (see*ehn*) (see*ehn*-toh)	100.000	**cien mil** (see*ehn* meel)
101	**ciento uno** (see*ehn*-toh *oo*-noh)	1.000.000	**un millón** (oon mee-*yohn*)
200	**doscientos** (doh-see*ehn*-tohs)	2.000.000	**dos millones** (dohs mee-*yoh*-nehs)
500	**quinientos** (kee-nee*ehn*-tohs)	1.000.000.000	**mil millones** (meel mee-*yoh*-nehs)
700	**setecientos** (seh-teh-see*ehn*-tohs)	2.000.000.000	**dos mil millones** (dohs meel mee-*yoh*-nehs)

English speakers generally write the number 1 in one short, downward stroke. In the Spanish-speaking world, however, the number 1 has a little hook on top, which makes it look like a 7. So, in order to distinguish a 1 from a 7, you put a line through the 7, which makes it look like this: 7̶.

Remember the following rules when using cardinal numbers in Spanish:

✔ **Uno** (*one*), used only when counting, becomes **un** before a masculine noun and **una** before a feminine noun, whether the noun is singular or plural (for more about gender issues, check out Book II, Chapter 2):

   • **uno, dos, tres** (*one, two, three*)

   • **un niño y una niña** (*a boy and a girl*)

   • **sesenta y un dólares** (*61 dollars*)

   • **veintiuna (veinte y una) personas** (*21 people*)

✔ You use the conjunction **y** (*and*) only for numbers between 16 and 99. You don't use it directly after hundreds:

   • **ochenta y ocho** (*88*)

   • **doscientos treinta y siete** (*237*)

✔ You generally write the numbers 16 through 19 and 21 through 29 as one word. The numbers 16, 22, 23, and 26 have accents on the last syllable:

   • 16: **dieciséis**

   • 22: **veintidós**

- 23: **veintitrés**
- 26: **veintiséis**

✔ When used before a masculine noun, **veintiún** (*21*) has an accent on the last syllable:

- **veintiún días** (*21 days*)
- **veintiuna semanas** (*21 weeks*)

✔ **Ciento** (*100*) becomes **cien** before nouns of either gender and before the numbers **mil** and **millones**. Before all other numbers, you use **ciento**. **Un** (*one*), which you don't use before **cien(to)** or **mil,** comes before **millón.** When a noun follows **millón,** you put the preposition **de** between **millón** and the noun. **Millón** drops its accent in the plural (**millones**):

- **cien sombreros** (*100 hats*)
- **cien blusas** (*100 blouses*)
- **cien mil millas** (*100,000 miles*)
- **cien millones de dólares** (*100 million dollars*)
- **ciento noventa acres** (*190 acres*)
- **mil posibilidades** (*1,000 possibilities*)
- **un millón de razones** (*1,000,000 reasons*)

✔ In compounds of **ciento** (**doscientos, trescientos**), there must be agreement with a feminine noun:

- **cuatrocientos pesos** (*400 pesos*)
- **seisientas pesetas** (*600 pesetas*)

With numerals and decimals, Spanish uses commas where English uses periods, and vice versa:

English	Spanish
6,000	6.000
0.75	0,75
$14.99	$14,99

Ordinal numbers

You may identify what you did during the day by reciting what you did first, second, third, and so on. Those very words *first*, *second*, and *third* are *ordinal numbers*. They tell you order and sequence.

When given directions, you hear a lot of phrases describing locations like the third block to the left or the fourth floor. So ordinal numbers are extremely useful. Here are the first ten:

- **primero** (pree-*meh*-roh) (*first*)
- **segundo** (seh-*goon*-doh) (*second*)
- **tercero** (tehr-*seh*-roh) (*third*)
- **cuarto** (koo*ahr*-toh) (*fourth*)
- **quinto** (*keen*-toh) (*fifth*)
- **sexto** (*sehks*-toh) (*sixth*)
- **séptimo** (*sehp*-tee-moh) (*seventh*)
- **octavo** (ohk-*tah*-bvoh) (*eighth*)
- **noveno** (noh-*bveh*-noh) (*ninth*)
- **décimo** (*deh*-see-moh) (*tenth*)

Here are some phrases to help you practice using ordinal numbers:

- **Vivo en el octavo piso.** (*bvee*-bvoh ehn ehl ohk-*tah*-bvoh *pee*-soh) (*I live on the eighth floor.*)
- **En la tercera calle hay un museo.** (ehn lah tehr-*seh*-rah *kah*-yeh ahy oon moo-*seh*-oh) (*At the third street there is a museum.*)
- **Este es el cuarto cine que veo aquí.** (*ehs*-teh ehs ehl koo*ahr*-toh *see*-neh keh *bveh*-oh *ah*-kee) (*This is the fourth cinema I've seen here.*)
- **En el primer piso hay una florería.** (ehn ehl pree-*mehr pee*-soh ahy *oo*-nah floh-reh-*ree*-ah) (*On the first floor there is a flower shop.*)
- **Voy a bajar al segundo piso.** (bvohy ah bvah-*Hahr* ahl seh-*goon*-doh *pee*-soh) (*I'm going down to the second floor.*)
- **La terraza está en el décimonoveno piso.** (lah teh-*rrah*-sah ehs-*tah* ehn ehl *deh*-see-moh-noh-*bveh*-noh *pee*-soh) (*The terrace is on the nineteenth floor.*)

The following list outlines everything you must remember when using ordinal numbers in Spanish:

- ✔ Spanish speakers rarely use ordinal numbers after 10th. After that, they usually use cardinal numbers in both the spoken and written language:

  - **el séptimo mes** (*the seventh month*)

  - **el siglo quince** (*the 15th century*)

- ✔ Ordinal numbers must agree in gender (masculine or feminine) with the nouns they modify. You can make ordinal numbers feminine by changing the final **-o** of the masculine form to **-a:**

  - **el cuarto día** (*the fourth day*)

  - **la cuarta vez** (*the fourth time*)

  Primero and **tercero** drop the final **-o** before a masculine singular noun:

  - **el primer muchacho** (*the first boy*)

  - **el tercer hombre** (*the third man*)

- ✔ The Spanish ordinal numbers may be abbreviated. You use the superscript ^{o} for masculine nouns and the superscript ^{a} for feminine nouns. And you use ^{er} only for the abbreviations of **primer** and **tercer:**

  - **primero(a):** $1^{o(a)}$

  - **segundo(a):** $2^{o(a)}$

  - **tercero(a):** $3^{o(a)}$

  - **cuarto(a):** $4^{o(a)}$

  - **primer:** 1er

  - **tercer:** 3er

- ✔ A cardinal number that replaces an ordinal number above 10th is always masculine, because the masculine word **número** (*number*) is understood:

  la calle (número) ciento y dos (*102nd Street*)

- ✔ In dates, **primero** is the only ordinal number you use. All other dates call for the cardinal numbers:

  - **el primero de mayo** (*May 1st*)

  - **el doce de enero** (*January 12th*)

- ✔ In Spanish, cardinal numbers precede ordinal numbers:

  las dos primeras escenas (*the first two scenes*)

- ✔ You use cardinal numbers when expressing the first part of an address:

  mil seiscientos Avenida Pennsylvania (*1600 Pennsylvania Avenue*)

Adding a Touch of Color

The colors in Spanish-speaking countries are sun-warmed and vibrant. Whether you're describing something or shopping for an item and need to express a color preference, you need to be able to name at least the basic colors. Table 2-1 gives you a handle on the Spanish color palette:

Table 2-1	Selecting Your Colors	
Color	*Pronunciation*	*Translation*
blanco	*bvlahn*-koh	white
negro	*neh*-groh	black
gris	grees	grey
rojo	*roh*-Hoh	red
azul	ah-*sool*	blue
verde	*bvehr*-deh	green
morado	moh-*rah*-doh	purple
violeta	bveeoh-*leh*-tah	violet, purple
café	kah-*feh*	brown
marrón	mah-*rrohn*	brown (Argentina)
amarillo	ah-mah-*ree*-yoh	yellow
naranja	nah-*rahn*-Hah	orange
rosado	roh-*sah*-doh	pink
celeste	seh-*lehs*-teh	sky blue
claro	*klah*-roh	light
oscuro	ohs-*koo*-roh	dark

Making Dates

Dates are important parts of everyday life (in more ways than one!). If you're writing a paper with a strict due date, leaving on vacation and need flight confirmations, or scheduling appointments for your clients and customers, you need to know how to express dates. To write out dates in Spanish, which you see how to do later in this section, you have to practice the days of the week, the months of the year, and numbers (see the previous section).

Days

If you hear **¿Qué día es hoy?** (keh *dee*-ah ehs ohy) someone must have forgotten what day of the week it is. You should respond with **Hoy es . . .** (ohy ehs) (*Today is . . .*) and then provide the name of one of the days listed here:

English	*Spanish*
Monday	**lunes** (*loo*-nehs)
Tuesday	**martes** (*mahr*-tehs)
Wednesday	**miércoles** (mee*ehr*-koh-lehs**)**
Thursday	**jueves** (hoo*eh*-bvehs)
Friday	**viernes** (bvee*ehr*-nehs)
Saturday	**sábado** (*sah*-bvah-doh)
Sunday	**domingo** (doh-*meen*-goh)

Unlike the English calendar, the Spanish calendar starts with Monday. Here are two more guidelines for talking about days of the week in Spanish:

- ✔ Unless you use them at the beginning of a sentence, you don't capitalize the days of the week in Spanish:

  - **Lunes es un día de vacaciones.** (*loo*-nehs ehs oon *dee*-ah deh bvah-kah-see*oh*-nehs) (*Monday is a vacation day.*)

  - **Lunes y martes son días de vacaciones.** (*loo*-nehs ee *mahr*-tehs sohn *dee*-ahs deh bvah-kah-see*oh*-nehs) (*Monday and Tuesday are vacation days.*)

- ✔ You use **el** to express *on* when referring to a particular day of the week and **los** to express *on* when the action occurs repeatedly:

  - **No trabajo el sábado.** (noh trah-*bvah*-Hoh ehl *sah*-bvah-doh) (*I'm not working on Saturday.*)

  - **No trabajo los sábados.** (noh trah-*bvah*-Hoh lohs *sah*-bvah-dohs) (*I don't work on Saturdays.*)

With the exception of **sábado** and **domingo**, the plural forms of the days of the week are the same as the singular forms:

Singular	*Plural*
lunes	lunes
martes	martes
miércoles	miércoles
jueves	jueves
viernes	viernes
sábado	sábados
domingo	domingos

Months

If you hear **¿En qué mes . . .?** (ehn keh mehs), someone is asking you in what month a certain event takes place. The curious person may be asking about the beginning or end of the school year, a special holiday celebration, the occurrence of a business meeting, or expected travel plans. The following table provides the names of the months in Spanish:

English	*Spanish*
January	**enero** (eh-*neh*-roh)
February	**febrero** (feh-*bvreh*-roh)
March	**marzo** (*mahr*-soh)
April	**abril** (ah-*bvreel*)
May	**mayo** (*mah*-yoh)
June	**junio** (*hoo*-neeoh)
July	**julio** (*hoo*-leeoh)
August	**agosto** (ah-*gohs*-toh)
September	**septiembre** (sehp-tee*ehm*-bvreh) or **setiembre** (seh-tee*ehm*-bvreh)
October	**octubre** (ohk-*too*-bvreh)
November	**noviembre** (noh-bvee*ehm*-bvreh)
December	**diciembre** (dee-cee*ehm*-bvreh)

Like days of the week, the months aren't capitalized in Spanish:

> **Junio es un mes agradable.** (*hoo*-neeoh ehs oon mehs ah-grah-*dah*-bvleh) (*June is a nice month.*)
>
> **Junio y julio son meses agradables.** (*hoo*-neeoh ee *hoo*-leeoh sohn *meh*-sehs ah-grah-*dah*-bvlehs) (*June and July are nice months.*)

In Spanish, the seasons are masculine except for **la primavera** (lah pree-mah-*bveh*-rah) (*the spring*):

> **el invierno** (ehl een-bvee*ehr*-noh) (*the winter*)
>
> **la primavera** (lah pree-mah-*bveh*-rah) (*the spring*)
>
> **el verano** (ehl bveh-*rah*-noh) (*the summer*)
>
> **el otoño** (ehl oh-*toh*-nyoh) (*the autumn/fall*)

Writing dates

If you want to ask a passerby or an acquaintance about the date, politely inquire **¿Cuál es la fecha de hoy?** (koo*ahl* ehs lah *feh*-chah deh ohy) (*What is today's date?*) The person should respond with **Hoy es . . .** (ohy ehs . . .) (*Today is . . .*) and then use the following formula to express the correct date:

> day + (**el**) + cardinal number (except for **primero**) + **de** + month + **de** + year

The following is an example translation, using this formula:

> Sunday, April 15, 2008: **Hoy es domingo, el quince de abril de dos mil ocho.** (ohy ehs doh-*meen*-goh ehl *keen*-seh deh ah-*bvreel* dohs meel *oh*-choh)

Now that you have a handy formula, you need to know a few more details about writing dates in Spanish:

- ✔ You express the first day of each month with **primero** (pree-*meh*-roh). You use cardinal numbers for all other days:
  - **el primero de enero** (ehl pree-*meh*-roh deh eh-*neh*-roh) (*January 1st*)
  - **el siete de enero** (ehl see*eh*-teh deh eh-*neh*-roh) (*January 7th*)
  - **el treinta de octubre** (ehl *treh*een-teh deh ohk-*too*-bvreh) (*October 30th*)
- ✔ Use **el** (ehl) to express *on* with Spanish dates: **Partimos el once de octubre.** (pahr-*tee*-mohs ehl *ohn*-seh deh ohk-*too*-bvreh) (*We are leaving on October 11th.*)

✔ In Spanish, you express years in thousands and hundreds, not only in
hundreds:

1492: **mil cuatrocientos noventa y dos** (meel koo*ah*-troh-see*ehn*-tohs
noh-*bvehn*-tah ee dohs) (*fourteen hundred ninety-two*)

In Spanish, when dates are written they follow the sequence day/month/
year. So when dates are written in Spanish as numbers, they also follow the
sequence day/month/year, which may prove confusing to English speakers —
especially for dates below the 12th of the month:

You write *February 9th* as 2/9 in English, but in Spanish it's **el 9 de
febrero** or **9/2.**

When speaking of dates in everyday language, the words and expressions
that follow may come in handy:

English	*Spanish*	*English*	*Spanish*
a day	**un día** (oon *dee*-ah)	day before yesterday	**anteayer** (ahn-teh-ah-*yehr*)
a week	**una semana** (*oo*-nah seh-*mah*-nah)	yesterday	**ayer** (ah-*yehr*)
a month	**un mes** (oon mehs)	today	**hoy** (ohy)
a year	**un año** (oon *ah*-nyoh)	tomorrow	**mañana** (mah-*nyah*-nah)
in	**en** (ehn)	tomorrow morning	**mañana por la mañana** (mah-*nyah*-na pohr lah mah-*nyah*-nah)
ago	**hace** (*ah*-seh)	tomorrow afternoon	**mañana por la tarde** (mah-*nyah*-nah pohr lah *tahr*-deh)
per	**por** (pohr)	tomorrow night	**mañana por la noche** (mah-*nyah*-nah pohr lah *noh*-cheh)
during	**durante** (doo-*rahn*-te)	day after tomorrow	**pasado mañana** (pah-*sah*-doh mah-*nyah*-nah)
next	**próximo(a)** (*prohk*-see-moh)	from	**desde** (*dehs*-deh)

last	**pasado(a)** (pah-*sah*-doh/dah)	a week from today	**de hoy en una semana** (deh ohy ehn *oo*-nah seh-*mah*-nah)
last (in a series)	**último(a)** (*ool*-tee-moh/mah)	two weeks from tomorrow	**de mañana en dos semanas** (deh mah-*nyah*-nah ehn dohs seh-*mah*-nahs)
eve	**la víspera** (lah *bvees*-peh-rah)	within one (two) week(s)	**dentro de una (dos) semana(s)** (*dehn*-troh deh *oo*-nah/dohs seh-*mah*-nah/nahs)

Spanish holidays

Spanish-speaking countries celebrate many holidays and feasts that have their origin in Christian religion and mythology. These Christian myths, together with those of pre-Columbian times and the ones brought from Africa, are the origin of the new and peculiar ones that have shaped what nowadays make the great holidays, including the following:

- **Año Nuevo:** Throughout the Spanish-speaking world, people celebrate the **Fiesta de Año Nuevo** (fee*ehs*-tah deh *ah*-nyoh noo*eh*-bvoh) (*New Year's Eve Party*). Wherever you go during the night of December 31, and into the morning of January 1, parties and revelers surround you, helping you cheer in the New Year in Spanish. People sing and shout **¡Salud!, ¡Feliz Año Nuevo!** (sah-*lood* feh-*lees ah*-nyoh noo*eh*-bvoh) (*Cheers, happy New Year!*).

- **La Fiesta de Reyes:** In Spain and most of Latin America, children get their holiday presents on January 6, which is **La Fiesta de Reyes** (lah fee-*ehs*-tah deh *reh*-yehs) (*The Kings' Holiday*). In Spain, this holiday is called **la epifanía** (lah eh-pee-fah-*nee*-ah) (*the epiphany*). January 6th celebrates the Three Kings' visit to Bethlehem. Because the Kings brought presents to the infant Jesus, children participate in the celebration by getting their own presents. All business and normal endeavors stop, and families spend the holiday with their children. It's good to be a child at the time of Reyes. Adults don't get gifts.

- **Paradura del Niño:** In many parts of Spanish-speaking America, the fun times surrounding the birth of Jesus start at Christmas and don't end until the beginning of February. In the Andean Region of Venezuela, people have a special way of enjoying this time by celebrating **La Paradura, Robo, y Búsqueda del Niño** (lah pah-rah-*doo*-rah *roh*-bvoh ee *bvoos*-keh-dah dehl *nee*-nyoh) (*The Hosting, Stealing, and Searching for the Child*). The figure of Jesus as a Child is "stolen" from the manger representation in someone's house, instigating a search. Of course, the person "stealing" the Child is some neighbor, and the place the Child is hidden in is a secret, the same way hide-and-seek is played. The neighbor or family member that finds the Child has to host a party on February 2nd, on the **Fiesta de la Candelaria** (fee-*ehs*-tah deh lah kahn-deh-*lah*-reeah) (*Candelmas*) also called **Fiesta de la Purificación** (fee-ehs-tah deh lah poo-ree-fee-kah-see*ohn*) (*The Feast of Purification*).

✔ **Carnaval:** Countless places in the Spanish-speaking world — from Oruro (oh-*roo*-roh) in Bolivia and Cartagena (kahr-tah-*Heh*-nah) in Colombia, on to Veracruz (bveh-rah-*kroos*) in Mexico and Ciudad Real (thiu-*dahd* reh-*ahl*) and Santa Cruz de Tenerife (teh-neh-*ree*-feh) in Spain — celebrate **Carnaval** (kahr-nah-*bvahl*) (*Shrovetide*, or *Mardi Gras*) just before the arrival of Lent. **Carnaval** is a feast of dancing, singing, and excess before the time of moderation and fasting.

✔ **Viernes Santo: Viernes Santo** (bvee*ehr*-nehs *sahn*-toh) is *Good Friday*. On this day, many Spanish-speaking communities in Latin America and Spain display exceptional ceremonies and events. This remembrance of the crucifixion of Jesus is accompanied in some places by real enactments of the event. Whole communities reenact the Biblical Story like one large play, in which all participate. One person is chosen to take the part of Jesus and is "crucified" while other village actors recite the New Testament texts.

✔ **Día de la Madre:** *Mother's Day*, **Día de la Madre** (*dee*-ah deh lah *mah*-dreh) isn't celebrated anywhere quite like the way it's celebrated in Mexico on May 10. People travel thousands of miles to come home, because on this day they must be there. Nothing is more sacred to Mexicans than their mothers, and they show it abundantly on this day. Mothers are feasted, toasted, and showered with presents. If a woman is also a mother, she is celebrated — even by people outside her family. People send each other's mothers gifts and greetings. And the family itself gathers for this day, the way families in the United States and Canada gather for Christmas.

✔ **Día de los Muertos:** On November 2, in the Andean countries and in Mexico, people celebrate **El Día de los Muertos** (ehl *dee*ah deh lohs moo*ehr*-tohs) (*the Day of the Dead*), an event also celebrated in Spain. People in these countries believe that deceased family members come to visit on this day. They receive these relatives with offerings of all the things the departed liked during their lifetimes. This remembrance of the dead is also a celebration of the harvests and of plenty. (Imagine inviting dead relatives to your Thanksgiving dinner and you have the right idea.)

Telling Time

Knowing how to understand, speak, and write time-related words and phrases is a must for anyone who's studying a foreign language and planning to put these studies to use (to do some traveling one day, for instance).

If you hear **¿Qué hora es?** (keh *oh*-rah ehs), someone wants to know the time. You should start by responding with the following:

> **Es la una** (ehs lah *oo*-nah) (for the 1:00 hour) or **Son las** (sohn lahs) + any other time

To express the time after the hour (but before half past the hour), use **y** (ee) (*and*) and the number of minutes. Use **menos** (*meh*-nohs) (*less*) + the number of the following hour to express the time before the next hour (after half past the hour).

You can also express time numerically (as shown in the third example here):

> **Es la una y media.** (ehs lah *oo*-nah ee *meh*-deeah) (*It's 1:30.*)
>
> **Son las cinco menos veinte.** (sohn lahs *seen*-koh *meh*-nohs bveh*een*-teh) (*It's 4:40.*)
>
> **Son las cuatro y cuarenta.** (sohn lahs koo*ah*-troh ee kooah-*rehn*-tah) (*It's 4:40.*)

If you want to discuss *at* what time a particular event will occur, you can use a question — **¿A qué hora . . . ?** (ah keh *oh*-rah . . .) — or answer with **A la una** (ah lah *oo*-nah) or **A las** (ah lahs) + any time other than 1:

> **¿A qué hora vienen?** (ah keh *oh*-rah bvee*ehn*-ehn) (*At what time are they coming?*)
>
> **A la una.** (ah lah *oo*-nah) (*At 1:00.*)
>
> **A las tres y cuarto.** (ah lahs trehs ee koo*ahr*-toh) (*At 3:15.*)

The following chart shows how to express time after and before the hour:

Time	Spanish
1:00	**la una** (lah *oo*-nah)
2:05	**las dos y cinco** (lahs dohs ee *seen*-koh)
3:10	**las tres y diez** (lahs trehs ee dee*ehs*)
4:15	**las cuatro y cuarto** (lahs koo*ah*-troh ee koo*ahr*-toh) or **las cuatro y quince** (lahs koo*ah*-troh ee *keen*-seh)

5:20	**las cinco y veinte** (lahs *seen*-koh ee *bveh*een-teh)
6:25	**las seis y veinticinco** (lahs *seh*ees ee bveheen-tee-*seen*-koh)
7:30	**las siete y media** (lahs see*eh*-teh ee *meh*-deeah) or **las siete y treinta** (lahs see*eh*-teh ee *treh*een-teh)
7:35	**las ocho menos veinticinco** (lahs *oh*-choh *meh*-nohs bveheen-tee-*seen*-koh) or **las siete y treinta y cinco** (lahs see*eh*-teh ee *treh*een-tah ee *seen*-koh)
8:40	**las nueve menos veinte** (lahs noo*eh*-veh *meh*-nohs *bveh*een-teh) or **las ocho y cuarenta** (lahs *oh*-choh ee kooah-*rehn*-tah)
9:45	**las diez menos cuarto** (lahs dee*ehs meh*-nohs koo*ahr*-toh) or **las nueve y cuarenta y cinco** (lahs noo*eh*-veh ee kooah-*rehn*-tah ee *seen*-koh)
10:50	**las once menos diez** (lahs *ohn*-seh *meh*-nohs dee*ehs*) or **las diez y cincuenta** (lahs dee*ehs* ee seen-koo*ehn*-tah)
11:55	**las doce menos cinco** (lahs *doh*-seh *meh*-nohs *seen*-koh) or **las once y cincuenta y cinco** (lahs *ohn*-seh ee seen-koo*ehn*-tah ee *seen*-koh)
noon	**el mediodía** (ehl *meh*-deeoh-*dee*-ah)
midnight	**la medianoche** (lah meh-deeah-*noh*-cheh)

Exploring Common Expressions of Time

When expressing time, the words and expressions in the following table may come in handy:

English	*Spanish*
a second	**un segundo** (oon seh-*goon*-doh)
a minute	**un minuto** (oon mee-*noo*-toh)
a quarter of an hour	**un cuarto de hora** (oon koo*ahr*-toh deh *oh*-rah)
an hour	**una hora** (*oo*-nah *oh*-rah)
a half hour	**una media hora** (*oo*-nah *meh*-deeah *oh*-rah)
in the morning (a.m.)	**por la mañana** (pohr lah mah-*nyah*-nah)
in the afternoon (p.m.)	**por la tarde** (pohr lah *tahr*-deh)
in the evening (p.m.)	**por la noche** (pohr lah *noh*-cheh)
at what time?	**¿a qué hora?** (ah keh *oh*-rah)
at exactly 9:00	**a las nueve en punto** (ah lahs noo*eh*-bveh ehn *poon*-toh)

at about 2:00	**a eso de las dos** (ah *eh*-soh deh lahs dohs)
in an hour	**en una hora** (ehn *oo*-nah *oh*-rah)
in a while	**dentro de un rato** (*dehn*-troh deh oon *rah*-toh)
until 10:00	**hasta las diez** (*ahs*-tah lahs dee*ehs*)
before 9:00	**antes de las nueve** (*ahn*-tehs deh lahs noo*eh*-bveh)
after 7:00	**después de las siete** (dehs-poo*ehs* deh lahs see*eh*-teh)
since what time?	**¿desde qué hora?** (*dehs*-deh keh *oh*-rah)
since 8:00	**desde las ocho** (*dehs*-deh lahs *oh*-choh)
one hour ago	**hace una hora** (*ah*-seh *oo*-nah *oh*-rah)
early	**temprano** (tehm-*prah*-noh)
late	**tarde** (*tahr*-deh)
late (in arriving)	**de retraso** (deh reh-*trah*-soh)

Chapter 3

Greetings, Salutations, and Farewells

In This Chapter

- Mastering formal and informal greetings
- Getting a handle on the Spanish naming system
- Knowing the difference between **ser** (sehr) (*to be*) and **estar** (ehs-tahr) (*to be*)
- Waving good-bye

Meeting and greeting go hand in hand! This chapter shows you how to greet both friend and stranger, as well as address folks with complicated-looking names. You also discover the difference between the *be* verbs **ser** and **estar.** When you're ready to end the conversation, we give you several ways to say "sayonara" (okay, **adiós**).

In Latin America especially, how you greet people matters a great deal. Latin Americans tend to be very respectful of each other and of strangers. So as a rule, when you greet someone for the first time in Latin America, it's best not to say "Hello!" — a greeting that is quite informal.

Greetings in Formal or Friendly Settings

As you begin a relationship, Latin Americans believe that keeping a certain distance is best. Only when you already know the person should you use the friendlier, informal phrases. Because Latinos look at building relationships this way, try to respect that view when you're in Spanish-speaking countries or with Latinos in the United States. It's just being polite, Latin-style. A relationship with a customer in a business situation, however, is always formal.

Latinos don't use **tú** (too), the informal *you* (refer to Book II, Chapter 1) when addressing someone they respect and have never met. And they don't greet each other informally on the first occasion they meet.

Latin Americans know that people in the States tend to treat each other very informally, so some may treat you as someone they already know. You may feel a bit leery of this behavior, though: The uncharacteristic informality may make you wonder whether there's some special reason for treating you with such familiarity. On the other hand, an overly friendly Spanish-speaker may simply be trying to put you at ease.

The following sections give you the lowdown on all sorts of Spanish greetings.

Meeting on formal terms

Introducing yourself formally means that you don't talk in a chummy, informal way to a person with whom you have no relationship as yet. It's a way of showing respect toward a new acquaintance and should not be considered cold or distant.

People who don't know each other use **usted** (oos-*tehd*) — the formal form of *you* — and its verb form when addressing one another. The following dialogue shows you just such an encounter.

Talkin' the Talk

In a more formal situation, people introduce each other differently. Listen to Pedro García Fernández as he approaches a table at a sidewalk cafe with a person already sitting there.

Pedro: **¿Me permite?**
           meh pehr-*mee*-teh
           May I?

Jane: **Sí, ¡adelante!**
           see, ah-deh-*lahn*-teh
           Yes, [go] ahead!

Pedro: **Buenas tardes. Me llamo Pedro García Fernández.**
           bvooeh-nahs *tahr*-dehs meh *yah*-moh *peh*-droh
           gahr-*see*-ah fehr-*nahn*-dehs
           Good afternoon. My name is Pedro García Fernández.

Capitalize abbreviations

Only in abbreviations (as well as proper names) do Spanish-speakers use capitals. Here's how it goes:

Señor (*seh*-nyohr)	**Sr.**	Mr.
Señora (seh-*nyoh*-rah)	**Sra.**	Mrs.

Señorita (seh-nyoh-*ree*-tah)	**Srta.**	Miss or Ms.
Usted (*oos*-tehd)	**Ud.**	you (formal)
Ustedes (oos-*teh*-dehs)	**Uds.**	you (plural formal)

Jane:	**Mucho gusto, señor García.**	
	moo-choh *goos*-toh seh-*nyohr* gahr-*see*-ah	
	Nice to meet you, Mr. García.	
Pedro:	**Y usted, ¿cómo se llama?**	
	ee *oos*-tehd *koh*-moh seh *yah*-mah	
	And you, what's your name?	
Jane:	**Me llamo Jane Wells.**	
	meh *yah*-moh Jane Wells	
	My name is Jane Wells.	
Pedro:	**Mucho gusto.**	
	moo-choh *goos*-toh	
	A pleasure.	

When you're talking to a child, you speak less formally. The adult speaker may be identified by the insertion of **don** (dohn) in front of his name. Calling someone **don** (or the feminine form, **doña** [*doh*-nyah]) can be a way of showing that you're addressing an older and respected person. (To the child, the adult looks old.)

The dialogue that follows demonstrates how various groups of people greet each other depending on their relationships.

Talkin' the Talk

 Sr. Rivera and Sra. Salinas work in the same building. Here's how they might greet each other in the hallway.

Sra. Salinas: **Buenos días, Sr. Rivera. ¿Cómo está?**
bvoo*eh*-nohs *dee*-ahs seh-*nyohr* ree-*veh*-rah *koh*-moh ehs-*tah*
Good morning, Mr. Rivera. How are you?

Sr. Rivera: **Muy bien. ¿Y Ud.?**
moo-ee bvee*eh*n ee oos-*tehd*
Very well. And you?

Sra. Salinas: **Bien, gracias.**
bvee*eh*n, *grah*-seeahs
Well, thank you.

Recent acquaintances John and Julia meet again by accident a few days later while on their way to school.

John: **Buenos días. ¿Qué tal?**
bvoo*eh*-nohs *dee*-ahs keh tahl
Good morning. How are things?

Julia: **¡Ah, hola, John! ¿Cómo estás?**
ah *oh*-lah john *koh*-moh ehs-*tahs*
Ah, hello, John! How are you?

John: **Bien. ¿Y tú?**
bvee*eh*n ee too
Well. And you?

Julia: **Bien.**
Bvee*eh*n
Well.

This dialogue presents a sample introduction.

Talkin' the Talk

 In this conversation, Pepe is formally introducing Lucía and
Fernando to Mr. Kendall.

Pepe:	**Buenas tardes. ¿El señor Kendall?** bvoo*eh*-nahs *tahr*-dehs ehl seh-*nyohr* Kendall *Good afternoon. Mr. Kendall?*
Mr. Kendall:	**Sí, me llamo Kendall.** see meh *yah*-moh Kendall *Yes, my name is Kendall.*
Pepe:	**Permítame que le presente al señor Fernando Quintana Martínez.** pehr-*mee*-tah-me keh leh preh-*sehn*-teh ahl seh-*nyohr* fehr-*nahn*-doh keen-*tah*-nah mahr-*tee*-nehs *Allow me to introduce Mr. Fernando Quintana Martínez.*
Mr. Kendall:	**Mucho gusto.** *moo*-choh *goos*-toh *A pleasure.*
Pepe:	**Esta es la señora de Kendall.** *ehs*-tah ehs lah seh-*nyoh*-rah deh Kendall *This is Mrs. Kendall.* **Esta es la señora Lucía Sánchez de Quintana.** *ehs*-tah ehs lah seh-*nyoh*-rah loo-*see*-ah *sahn*-ches deh keen-*tah*-nah *This is Mrs. Lucía Sánchez de Quintana.*
Mrs. Kendall:	**Mucho gusto, señora.** *moo*-choh *goos*-toh seh-*nyoh*-rah *A pleasure, ma'am.*

Making more solemn introductions

Some situations call for a certain level of solemnity. An example is when
you're being introduced to a very important or famous person.

Like English, a few, specific phrases signal this formality, as the following examples demonstrate:

- ✔ **¿Me permite presentarle a . . . .?** (meh pehr-*mee*-teh preh-sehn-*tahr*-leh ah) (*May I introduce. . . .?*)

- ✔ **Es un gusto conocerle.** (ehs oon *goos*-toh koh-noh-*sehr*-leh) (*It's a pleasure to meet you.*)

- ✔ **El gusto es mío.** (ehl *goos*-toh ehs *mee*-oh) (*The pleasure is mine.*)

Getting chummy: Informal greetings

When you're greeting someone you're familiar with (or you're being introduced to a child), you can use a more informal greeting without fear of offending the other person.

This dialogue shows you how young people meeting for the first time interact.

Talkin' the Talk

 Listen to how John and Julia, two teenagers, greet each other informally.

John: **¡Hola! ¿Cómo te llamas?**
   oh-lah! *koh*-moh teh *yah*-mahs
   Hi! What's your name?

Julia: **Me llamo Julia. ¿Y tú?**
   meh *yah*-moh *Hoo*-leeah ee too
   My name is Julia. And yours?

John: **Yo me llamo John.**
   yoh meh *yah*-moh John
   My name is John.

Addressing Others by Name or Surname

Latin Americans are generally easygoing people who love to converse. Feel free to initiate contact with them, using the greetings we present in this chapter. If you feel interest on both your part and theirs to keep the contact going, you can introduce yourself, but wait for your acquaintance to give you his or her name. Only if the other person doesn't give you his or her name should you ask what it is. In some specific situations, a third person introduces you, but usually you're expected to introduce yourself. In this chapter, we show you several ways that introductions can happen.

As we get into the names issue, we need to clear up one little thing. When you meet someone, he or she probably will tell you just his or her first name, or maybe only part of it — Carmen (*kahr*-mehn), rather than María del Carmen (mah-*ree*-ah dehl *kahr*-mehn). But, as you get to know people better, you'll learn their surnames, as well.

A new acquaintance usually expresses some caution in the beginning by giving you only a partial name. When you receive the full name and the two surnames, you know you have a complete introduction.

These little maneuvers take place because, in the Spanish-speaking world, it isn't customary to wait to be introduced to someone before you talk to him or her. An introduction as such isn't necessary. When a third party does introduce you, it's just meant to make your contact with the new acquaintance much faster.

Deconstructing Spanish names

Suppose that you meet a woman named María del Carmen Fernández Bustamante (mah-*ree*-ah dehl *kahr*-mehn fehr-*nahn*-dehs bvoos-tah-*mahn*-teh). You can tell that you may call her **señorita** (seh-nyoh-*ree*-tah), or *Miss* Fernández (fehr-*nahn*-dehs) because of the three-part structure of her name. (In an English-speaking country, she would rearrange her name to María del Carmen Bustamante Fernández because English speakers put the father's name at the end and use the person's last name as a reference.)

So far, so good. But if Miss Fernández marries, she adds on more names. In our example, she marries **señor** (seh-*nyohr*) (*Mr.*) Juan José García Díaz (Hoo*ahn* Hoh-*seh* gahr-*see*-ah *dee*ahs). She is still called Fernández, but after her father's name she adds **de** (deh) (*of*) and her husband's surname, which is García. Now, she is **señora** (seh-*nyoh*-rah María del Carmen Fernández de García (mah-*ree*ah dehl *kahr*-mehn fehr-*nahn*-dehs deh gahr-*see*-ah).

Note that Spanish-speakers capitalize **señor** or **señora** when abbreviated the way people in the States capitalize Mr. and Mrs.

Within the social circles of some countries, the surname of a married woman's husband gets more emphasis; in other places, her father's surname is stressed. For example, you hear the husband's surname used more often in Argentina than in Mexico.

The effect of these conventions is that women keep their family names, which are considered very important and meaningful. A child's surnames indicate both his or her father and mother. **Señor** García, in our example, has a child, Mario, by a previous marriage to a woman whose surname was Ocampo. Because children carry the surnames of both parents, Mario is called Mario García Ocampo. And when **señor** García and María del Carmen Fernández de García's daughter, Ana, is born, her name is Ana García Fernández. Ana and Mario are siblings, having the same father and different mothers. The Spanish use of both the father's and mother's surnames immediately indicates the relationship between the siblings.

Among Spanish-speaking peoples, using both parents' first names for their same-sex children is customary. So, in a family where the mother, Marta Inés, has three daughters, she may call one Marta Julieta, another Marta Felicia, and the third Marta Juana. When the father's name is used for the son, the two are called identical names, because *Jr.* isn't used in Spanish. But you can tell the men apart because their mother's surnames are different.

Introducing yourself with the verb llamarse

Now is a good time to include the conjugation of **llamarse** (yah-*mahr*-seh), the equivalent of *name is*, which you use when you introduce yourself.

The verb **llamar** is a regular **-ar** verb; however, the **se** at the end of it tells you that the verb is reflexive. A *reflexive* verb is one that acts on the noun (or subject) of the sentence. For instance, the sentence **yo me llamo** (yo meh *yah*-moh) literally means *I call myself*. In this case, "I" is the subject of the sentence and "call myself" reflects back to "I." Anytime you see the **se** at the end of a verb, you simply put the reflexive pronoun (**me** in the example sentence) in front of the verb. For more on reflexive verbs, see Book III, Chapter 3.

Take a look at the following table for the conjugation of **llamarse** in the present tense. Pay attention to the reflexive pronouns — they stay the same for all reflexive verbs.

My name is Is, isn't it?

When, in English, you say, *I introduce myself*, you're using a reflexive form of the verb *introduce*, and so you say *myself*. Likewise, when Pedro says **me llamo Pedro** (meh *yah*-moh *peh*-droh), the word **me** (meh) means *myself*. (See Book III, Chapter 3 for details about reflexive verbs.)

Often, beginning Spanish-speakers say, **Me llamo es**, using a mistakenly literal translation of *My name is*. But, note that **me** in Spanish means "to me" or "myself" — it never means "I." **Llamo** is the first person of the singular of a verb, so **me llamo** can be translated as *I call myself*. Even in English, you don't add *is* to that.

Conjugation	Pronunciation
yo me llamo	yoh meh *yah*-moh
tú te llamas	too teh *yah*-mahs
él, ella, ello, uno, usted se llama	ehl, eh-yah, eh-yoh, oo-noh, oos-*tehd* seh *yah*-mah
nosotros nos llamamos	noh-*soh*-trohs nohs yah-*mah*-mohs
vosotros os llamáis	bvoh-*soh*-trohs ohs yah-*mah*ees
ellos, ellas, ustedes se llaman	*eh*-yohs, *eh*-yahs, oos-*teh*-dehs seh *yah*-mahn

Asking "How Are You?"

In Spanish, you have two ways to ask, *To be or not to be?* You can say **¿Ser o no ser?** (sehr oh noh sehr), when the state of being is unlikely to change (you'll always be a person, for example). You use **¿Estar o no estar?** (ehs-*tahr* o no ehs-*tahr*) if the state of being is changeable (you won't always be tired).

Being in a permanent way with ser

Ser refers to a kind of being that is permanent, like the fact that you're you. The word also refers to all things that are expected to be permanent, such as places, countries, and certain conditions or states of being, such as shape, profession, nationality, and place of origin. This permanent "to be" in Spanish is **ser** (sehr):

✔ **Soy mujer.** (sohy moo-*Hehr*) (*I'm a woman.*)

✔ **Soy Canadiense.** (sohy kah-nah-dee-*ehn*-seh) (*I'm Canadian.*)

✔ **Soy de Winnipeg.** (sohy de Winnipeg) (*I'm from Winnipeg.*)

✔ **Ellos son muy altos.** (*eh*-yohs sohn mooy *ahl*-tohs) (*They're very tall.*)

✔ **¿Ustedes son Uruguayos?** (oos-*teh*-dehs sohn oo-roo-*gooah*-yohs) (*Are you [formal] Uruguayan?*)

✔ **Ella es maestra.** (*eh*-yah ehs mah-*ehs*-trah) (*She's a teacher.*)

✔ **Eres muy bella.** (*eh*-rehs mooy *bveh*-yah) (*You're very beautiful.*)

✔ **Eres muy gentil.** (*eh*-rehs mooy Hehn-*teel*) (*You're very kind.*)

The verb **ser** (sehr) (to be) is the one most frequently used in Spanish. And, of course, just like the English "to be," it's an irregular verb. (We discuss irregular verbs in Book II, Chapter 3.) The following table shows how **ser** is conjugated.

Conjugation	*Pronunciation*
yo soy	yoh sohy
tú eres	too *eh*-rehs
él, ella, ello, uno, usted es	ehl, *eh*-yah, *eh*-yoh, *oo*-noh, oos-*tehd* ehs
nosotros somos	noh-*soh*-trohs *soh*-mohs
vosotros sois	bvoh-*soh*-trohs *soh*ees
ellos, ellas, ustedes son	*eh*-yohs, *eh*-yahs, oos-*teh*-dehs sohn

Being right now with estar

Remember that Spanish is a very precise language. In Spanish, you have two forms of "to be," each with a different meaning, to supply more precision to your statements. Unlike in English, when you talk about *being* in Spanish, the verb you use removes any guesswork about what your meaning is.

As we discuss in the preceding section, when you speak of permanently being someone or something in Spanish, you use the verb **ser** (sehr). But when you're talking about a state of being that isn't permanent — such as being someplace (you won't be there forever), or being some temporary way (being ill, for instance) — you use the verb **estar** (ehs-*tahr*). The following table conjugates the present tense of the verb **estar**:

Conjugation	*Pronunciation*
yo estoy	yoh ehs-*tohy*
tú estás	too ehs-*tahs*
él, ella, ello, uno, usted está	ehl, *eh*-yah, *eh*-yoh, *oo*-noh, oos-*tehd* ehs-*tah*
nosotros estamos	noh-*soh*-trohs ehs-*tah*-mohs
vosotros estáis	bvoh-*soh*-trohs ehs-*tahees*
ellos, ellas, unos, ustedes están	*eh*-yohs, *eh*-yahs, *oo*-nohs, oos-*teh*-dehs ehs-*tahn*

We use this verb a great deal in this book, so we give you the simple past and future tenses, also. The following table provides conjugation of the past (preterit) tense:

Conjugation	*Pronunciation*
yo estuve	yoh ehs-*too*-bveh
tú estuviste	too ehs-too-*bvees*-teh
él, ella, ello, uno, usted estuvo	ehl, *eh*-yah, *eh*-yoh, *oo*-noh, oos-*tehd* ehs-*too*-bvoh
nosotros estuvimos	noh-*soh*-trohs ehs-too-*bvee*-mohs
vosotros estuvisteis	bvoh-*soh*-trohs ehs-too-*bvees*-tehees
ellos, ellas, unos, ustedes estuvieron	*eh*-yohs, *eh*-yahs, *oo*-nohs, oos-*teh*-dehs ehs-too-bvee*eh*-rohn

Here's how you conjugate the future tense of **estar**:

Conjugation	*Pronunciation*
yo estaré	yoh ehs-tah-*reh*
tú estarás	too ehs-tah-*rahs*
él, ella, ello, uno, usted estará	ehl, *eh*-yah, *eh*-yoh, *oo*-noh, oos-*tehd* ehs-tah-*rah*
nosotros estaremos	noh-*soh*-trohs ehs-tah-*reh*-mohs
vosotros estaréis	bvoh-*soh*-trohs ehs-tah-*reh*ees
ellos, ellas, unos, ustedes estarán	*eh*-yohs, *eh*-yahs, oos-*teh*-dehs ehs-tah-*rahn*

The following dialogue shows you how to use **estar.**

Talkin' the Talk

Here's a dialogue to help you practice this new way of being, the one that isn't forever. While having a cup of coffee in a neighborhood café, you overhear the following conversation.

Guillermo: **¿Cómo están ustedes?**
koh-moh ehs-*tahn* oos-*teh*-dehs
How are you?

Sra. Valdés: **Estamos muy bien, gracias.**
ehs-*tah*-mohs mooy bvee*ehn* grah-seeahs
We're very well, thank you.

Guillermo: **¿Están de paseo?**
ehs-*tahn* deh pah-*seh*-oh
Are you talking a walk?

Sra. Valdés: **Estamos de vacaciones.**
ehs-*tah*-mohs deh bvah-kah-see*oh*-nehs
We're on vacation.

Guillermo: **¿Están contentos?**
ehs-*tahn* kohn-*tehn*-tohs
Are you content?

Sra. Valdés: **Estamos muy felices.**
ehs-*tah*-mohs mooy feh-*lee*-sehs
We're very happy.

Guillermo: **¿Cómo está su hija?**
koh-moh ehs-*tah* soo ee-Hah
How is your daughter?

Sra. Valdés: **Más o menos, no está muy feliz.**
mahs oh *meh*-nohs noh ehs-*tah* mooy feh-*lees*
So-so, she's not very happy.

Americans all

You probably like to tell people where you're from, and you like to know where the people you meet are from, too.

Almost everyone likes to talk about nationalities. And when you talk about nationalities with Latin Americans, you're wise to remember one crucial point: Latin Americans are Americans, too. So to say **americano** (ah-meh-ree-*kah*-noh) when you mean someone from the United States doesn't quite cover the ground. You make yourself better understood if you say **norteamericano** (nohr-teh-ah-meh-ree-kah-noh), meaning *North American* or **estadounidense** (eh-stah-doh-oo-nee-*dehn*-seh), meaning *U.S. citizen*.

The dialogue that follows demonstrates how to use **estar** in a very important situation.

Talkin' the Talk

Everyone, at one time or another, needs to find a bathroom. Here's a sample of how such a conversation might sound. You are again at the cafe, this time in the back, near the bathroom.

Renata: **¿Está libre este baño?**
             ehs-*tah* lee-bvreh *ehs*-teh *bvah*-nyoh
             Is the bathroom free?

Elena: **No, está ocupado.**
             noh ehs-*tah* oh-koo-*pah*-doh
             No, it's occupied.

Renata: **¿Está libre el otro baño?**
             ehs-*tah* lee-bvreh ehl *oh*-troh *bvah*-nyoh
             Is the other bathroom free?

Elena: **Sí, está libre.**
             see ehs-*tah* lee-bvreh
             Yes, it's free.

Saying "¡Adios!"

Whenever you're done talking and are ready to part company, you want to have a few good-byes or see-ya-laters. Here are some common ways to say *good-bye* in Spanish:

- **Adiós.** (ah-dee*ohs*) (*Goodbye.*)
- **Chau.** (*chah*oo) (*Goodbye,* informal)
- **Hasta luego.** (*ahs*-tah loo*eh*-goh) (*See you later.*)
- **Hasta pronto.** (*ahs*-tah *prohn*-toh) (*See you soon.*)
- **Hasta mañana.** (*ahs*-tah mah-*nyah*-nah) (*See you tomorrow.*)
- **Hasta viernes.** (*ahs*-tah bvee*ehr*-nehs) (*See you on Friday.*)
- **¡Que tenga un buen día!** (keh *tehn*-gah oon bvoo*ehn* dee*ah) (*Have a good day!*)
- **¡Buena suerte!** (bvoo*eh*-nah soo*ehr*-teh) (*Good luck!*)
- **¡Cuídate/Cuídense!** (koo*ee*-dah-teh/coo*ee*-dehn-seh) (*Take care!* singular/plural)

Chapter 4

Engaging in a Little Chitchat

Meeting new people and getting to know them can be stressful, especially when you have to converse in a language that isn't your own. Small talk is the universally recognized means of joining a new situation by discussing common, easily understood interests and concerns. Through small talk, you can better understand how the people you come to know live and go about their lives.

This chapter helps you make small talk with your Spanish-speaking neighbors so that you can begin to achieve a better understanding all around.

Sparking Conversations with Questions

You may have heard about "The Five Ws," which represent the questions that you need to ask to cover the basic information about a situation (who, what, where, when, and why). We've added three more questions to this group that you may find useful when you meet someone. Here are the key questions:

- **¿Quién?** (kee*ehn*) (*Who?*)
- **¿Qué?** (keh) (*What?*)
- **¿Dónde?** (*dohn*-deh) (*Where?*)

- **¿Cuándo?** (koo*ahn*-doh) (*When?*)
- **¿Por qué?** (pohr keh) (*Why?*)
- **¿Cómo?** (*koh*-moh) (*How?*)
- **¿Cuánto?** (koo*ahn*-toh) (*How much?*)
- **¿Cuál?** (koo*ahl*) (*Which?*)

The following are examples of how to use these words:

- **¿Quién es él?** (kee*ehn* ehs ehl) (*Who is he?*)
- **¿Qué hace usted?** (keh *ah*-seh oos-*tehd*) (*What do you do?*)
- **¿Dónde viven?** (*dohn*-deh *bvee*-bvehn) (*Where do you [plural]/they live?*)
- **¿Cuándo llegaron?** (koo*ahn*-doh yeh-*gah*-rohn) (*When did you [plural]/they arrive?*)
- **¿Por qué está aquí?** (pohr keh ehs-*tah* ah-*kee*) (*Why are you [formal] here? Why is he/she/it here?*)
- **¿Cómo es el camino?** (*koh*-moh ehs ehl kah-*mee*-noh) (*What's the road like?*)
- **¿Cuánto cuesta el cuarto?** (koo*ahn*-toh koo*ehs*-tah ehl koo*ahr*-toh) (*How much is the room?*)
- **¿Cuál hotel es mejor?** (koo*ahl* oh-*tehl* ehs meh-*Hohr*) (*Which hotel is better?*)

You may notice that some of the words have accent marks. Why did those words, which were used in questions, have an accent? The reason is to help you, and readers of Spanish in general, distinguish how the word is being used. For example,

You can use a word such as **quien** (kee*ehn*), which means *who*, in two ways:

- In a sentence to refer to someone who did this or that. **Quien** has no accent when you use it this way.
- As a question — *Who did it?* — or as an exclamation — *Who could have said that?* To call your attention to the fact that who is being used as a question or an exclamation, it carries an accent, as in **¡quién!** or **¿quién?**

The treatment is the same for other words you use to make a question or an exclamation, such as *when?* **¿cuándo?** (koo*ahn*-doh); *what!* **¡qué!** (keh); *where?* **¿dónde?** (*dohn*-deh); *why?* **¿por qué?** (pohr keh); *how?* **¿cómo?** (*koh*-moh); and *which?* **¿cuál?** (koo*ahl*).

Three useful sentences amid all the other talk

Sometimes, you may not understand what someone is saying. Or you may bump into someone and need to excuse yourself. The following courtesy phrases can come in handy:

✔ **No entiendo.** (noh ehn-tee*ehn*-doh) (*I don't understand.*)

✔ **Lo lamento.** (loh lah-*mehn*-toh) (*I regret it; I'm sorry.*)

✔ **¡Perdone!** (pehr-*doh*-neh) (*Excuse me!*) Say this when you bump into someone.

The accents don't change the way the words sound; you use them only in the written form of the language. When speaking, your *inflection,* or tone of voice, tells listeners how to interpret these words.

The following dialogue shows you an example of someone making small talk with an unfamiliar person.

Talkin' the Talk

Carlos is on Flight Number 223, from Mendoza to Buenos Aires. He has introduced himself to his seatmates, so he knows their names, but he wants to make small talk about himself. Here's how such a conversation might go.

Carlos: **¡Qué vuelo tan agradable!**
keh bvoo*eh*-loh tahn ah-grah-*dah*-bvleh
Such a pleasant flight!

Juan: **Sí, es un viaje tranquilo.**
see ehs oon bvee*ah*-Heh trahn-*kee*-loh
Yes, it's a peaceful trip.

Carlos: **¿Viaja a menudo en avión?**
bvee*ah*-Hah ah meh-*noo*-doh ehn ah-bvee*ohn*
Do you fly often?

Juan: **No, éste es mi primer vuelo.**
noh, *ehs*-teh ehs mee pree-*mehr* bvoo*eh*-loh
No, this is my first time flying.

Carlos: **¿De dónde es usted?**
deh *dohn*-deh ehs oos-*tehd*
Where are you from?

Juan: **Soy de Buenos Aires. ¿Y usted?**
sohy deh bvoo*eh*-nohs *ahee*-rehs ee oos-*tehd*
I'm from Buenos Aires. And you?

Carlos: **Yo soy de Nueva York . . .**
yoh sohy deh noo*eh*-bvah yohrk
I'm from New York . . .
. . . ¿cómo es Buenos Aires?
koh-moh ehs bvoo*eh*-nohs *ahee*-rehs
. . . what's Buenos Aires like?

Juan: **Es una ciudad grande y maravillosa.**
ehs *ooh*-nah seeoo-*dahd grahn*-deh ee
mah-rahbvee-*yoh*-sah
It's a large and wonderful city.

Chatting about the Weather

Weather is an obsession in temperate countries where conditions vary a great deal, and where it often gets to be, as Canadians like to say, "inclement." In warmer climates, weather is much less of an issue. Some cities in southern Mexico, for example, don't even do weather reports. Even so, the weather is always a relatively safe topic of conversation, wherever your travels take you. The following dialogue presents a sample weather-based conversation.

Talkin' the Talk

 Mario has just returned from a six-month assignment in Argentina. Now back at his home office, Mario and his co-worker Rosa talk about the weather in Buenos Aires.

Rosa: **¿Cómo es el clima de Buenos Aires?**
koh-moh ehs ehl *klee*-mah deh bvoo*eh*-nohs
ahee-rehs
What's Buenos Aires' climate like?

Mario: **Es muy agradable y templado.**
ehs mooy ah-grah-*dah*-bvleh ee tehm-*plah*-doh
It's very pleasant and temperate.

Rosa: **¿Llueve mucho?**
yoo*eh*-bveh *moo*-choh
Does it rain a lot?

Mario: **Sí, llueve todo el año, pero no mucho.**
see, yoo*eh*-bveh *toh*-doh ehl *an*-nyoh, *peh*-roh noh *moo*-choh
Yes, there's rain all year round, but not too much.

Rosa: **¿Y también hay sol?**
ee tahm-bvee*ehn* ahy sohl
And is it also sunny?

Mario: **Sí, hay sol casi todos los días.**
see ahy sohl *kah*-see *toh*-dohs lohs *dee*-ahs
Yes, it's sunny almost every day.

Rosa: **¿No nieva nunca?**
noh nee*eh*-bvah *noon*-kah
Does it ever snow?

Mario: **No, en Buenos Aires nunca nieva.**
noh ehn bvoo*eh*-nohs *ahee*-rehs *noon*-kah nee*eh*-bvah
No, in Buenos Aires it never snows.

Discussing Work, Hobbies, and Activities

Work and professions are always useful subjects for small talk. And when discussing these topics, you want to be sure that you understand each other, so you use the irregular verb **entender** (ehn-tehn-*dehr*) (*to understand*). Because **entender** is irregular, you conjugate it in the present tense as shown in the following table:

Conjugation	*Pronunciation*
yo entiendo	yoh ehn-tee*ehn*-doh
tú entiendes	too ehn-tee*ehn*-dehs
él, ella, ello, uno, usted entiende	ehl, *eh*-yah, eh-yoh, *oo*-noh,oos-*tehd* ehn-tee*ehn*-deh
nosotros entendemos	noh-*soh*-trohs ehn-tehn-*deh*-mohs
vosotros entendéis	bvoh-*soh*-trohs ehn-tehn-*deh*ees
ellos, ellas, ustedes entienden	*eh*-yohs, *eh*-yahs, oos-*teh*-dehs ehn-tee*ehn*-dehn

CULTURAL WISDOM

An understanding proverb

A buen entendedor, pocas palabras. (ah bvoo*ehn* ehn-tehn-deh-*dohr* poh-kahs pah-*lah*-bvrahs.) (*Who knows, knows. [Literally: To the one who understands, few words.]*)

This proverb comes in handy when you assume that the other person already knows about the issue you're discussing.

If we had to explain it with body language, we would say it's the equivalent of a knowing wink.

Here are some examples to help you use the irregular verb **entender**:

- **Yo entiendo de enfermería.** (yoh ehn-tee*ehn*-doh deh ehn-fehr-meh-*ree*-ah) (*I know about nursing.*)

- **Francisca entiende de cocina.** (frahn-*sees*-kah ehn-tee*ehn*-deh deh koh-*see*-nah) (*Francisca knows about cooking.*)

- **Nosotros entendemos el problema.** (noh-*soh*-trohs ehn-tehn-*deh*-mohs ehl proh-*bvleh*-mah) (*We understand the problem.*)

- **Pedro no entiende.** (*peh*-droh noh ehn-tee*ehn*-deh) (*Pedro doesn't understand.*)

- **Ellos entienden lo que decimos.** (*eh*-yohs ehn-tee*ehn*-dehn loh keh deh-*see*-mohs) (*They understand what we are saying.*)

The following dialogue follows two strangers chatting about their work.

Talkin' the Talk

Listen to Jane and Pedro in a café talking about their jobs.

Jane: **¿Dónde trabaja usted?**
dohn-deh trah-*bvah*-Hah oos-*tehd*
Where do you work?

Pedro: **Trabajo en México; soy ingeniero.**
trah-*bvah*-Hoh ehn *meh*-Hee-koh sohy
een-Heh-nee*eh*-roh
I work in Mexico [City]; I'm an engineer.

Jane:	**¿Para qué compañía trabaja?**
	pah-rah keh kohm-pah-*nyee*-ah trah-*bvah*-Hah
	What company do you work for?

Pedro:	**Soy empresario independiente.**
	sohy ehm-preh-*sah*-reeoh een-deh-pehn-dee*ehn*-teh
	I'm an independent entrepreneur.

Jane:	**¿Cuántos empleados tiene?**
	koo*ahn*-tohs ehm-pleh-*ah*-dohs tee*eh*-neh
	How many employees do you have?

Pedro:	**Tengo nueve empleados. ¿Y usted qué hace?**
	tehn-goh noo*eh*-bveh ehm-pleh-*ah*-dohsee oos-*tehd* keh *ah*-seh
	I have nine employees. What do you do?

Jane:	**Soy dentista.**
	sohy dehn-*tees*-tah
	I'm a dentist.

Pedro:	**¿Y dónde tiene su consultorio?**
	ee *dohn*-deh tee*eh*-neh soo kohn-sool-*toh*-reeoh
	And where do you work?

Jane:	**En Puebla.**
	ehn poo*eh*-bvlah
	In Puebla.

Discussing Family Matters and Relatives

The individual is the basic element of U.S. and Canadian societies. In Latin America, on the other hand, the family is the basic unit. People work, live, and function in consonance with their families. When visiting your Spanish-speaking neighbors, therefore, you'll be more comfortable if you pay attention to the way that Latinos stress the importance of the family and of family relationships.

The following list gives basic names for family members:

- ✔ **padre** (*pah*-dreh) (*father*)
- ✔ **madre** (*mah*-dreh) (*mother*)
- ✔ **hijo** (*ee*-Hoh) (*son*)

- **hija** (*ee*-Hah) (*daughter*)
- **hermano** (ehr-*mah*-noh) (*brother*)
- **hermana** (ehr-*mah*-nah) (*sister*)
- **yerno** (*yeh*r-noh) (*son-in-law*)
- **nuera** (noo*eh*-rah) (*daughter-in-law*)
- **nieto** (nee*eh*-toh) (*grandson*)
- **nieta** (nee*eh*-tah) (*granddaughter*)
- **cuñado** (koo-*nyah*-doh) (*brother-in-law*)
- **cuñada** (koo-*nyah*-dah) (*sister-in-law*)
- **primo** (*pree*-moh) (*cousin [male]*)
- **prima** (*pree*-mah) (*cousin [female]*)
- **padrino** (pah-*dree*-noh) (*godfather*)
- **madrina** (mah-*dree*-nah) (*godmother*)
- **tío** (*tee*-oh) (*uncle*)
- **tía** (*tee*-ah) (*aunt*)
- **abuelo** (ah-bvoo*eh*-loh) (*grandfather*)
- **abuela** (ah-bvoo*eh*-lah) (*grandmother*)

You may notice a certain amount of ceremony in the way people invite others into their homes; the following dialogue shows you how one friend invites another to his family's house.

Talkin' the Talk

Shirley is visiting a family at their home for the first time.

Juan Carlos: **Mire, le invito a que conozca mi casa.**
mee-reh leh een-*bvee*-toh ah keh koh-*nohs*-kah mee *kah*-sah
Look, I'm inviting you to see my house.

Shirley: **Por favor, no quiero molestarle.**
pohr fah-*bvohr* noh kee*eh*-roh moh-lehs-*tahr*-leh
Please, I don't want to bother you.

Juan Carlos: **No es ninguna molestia, y así le presento mi familia.**
noh ehs neen-*goo*-nah moh-*lehs*-teeah ee ah-*see* leh preh-*sehn*-toh mee fah-*mee*-leeah

It's no bother, and this way I can introduce you to my family.

Shirley: **Pues si no le parece un abuso . . .**
poo*ehs* see noh leh pah-*reh*-seh oon ah-*bvoo*-soh
Well, if you don't think I'm abusing [your hospitality] . . .

Juan Carlos: **No, para nada, le insisto . . .**
noh *pah*-rah *nah*-dah leh een-*sees*-toh
Not at all, I insist . . .

Talking about Where You Live

It's natural after you've been invited to someone's house to invite them back to yours. And "where do you live?" is as frequent a question as "where do you work?" when making small talk. The verb **vivir** (bvee-*bveer*) is a regular verb, and it means *to live*. You can see how to conjugate its present tense in the following table.

Conjugation	*Pronunciation*
yo vivo	yoh *bvee*-bvoh
tú vives	too *bvee*-bvehs
él, ella, ello, uno, usted vive	ehl, *eh*-yah, *eh*-yoh, *oo*-noh, oos-*tehd* *bvee*-bveh
nosotros vivimos	noh-*soh*-trohs bvee-*bvee*-mohs
vosotros vivís	bvoh-*soh*-trohs bvee-*bvees*
ellos, ellas, ustedes viven	*eh*-yohs, *eh*-yahs, oos-*teh*-dehs *bvee*-bvehn

In the following dialogue, a friend remarks on another friend's house as she sees it for the first time.

Talkin' the Talk

Shirley has been invited into a beautiful, middle-class family house.

Juan Carlos: **Bueno, ya llegamos a la casa de mis padres.**
bvoo*eh*-noh yah yeh-*gah*-mohs ah lah *kah*-sah deh mees *pah*-drehs
Well, we're at my parents' house.

Shirley:	**¡Qué bella casa! Parece muy antigua.** keh *bveh*-yah *kah*-sah pah-*reh*-seh mooy ahn-*tee*-gooah *What a beautiful house! It seems very old.*
Juan Carlos:	**Sí, es una casa del siglo diecisiete.** see ehs *oo*-nah *kah*-sah dehl *see*-gloh deeeh-see-see*eh*-teh *Yes, it's a seventeenth-century house.*
Shirley:	**¡Qué patio tan bello!** keh *pah*-teeoh tahn *bveh*-yoh *What a beautiful patio!*
Juan Carlos:	**Sí, el patio es muy tradicional.** see ehl *pah*-teeoh ehs mooy trah-dee-seeoh-*nah*l *Yes, it's very traditional.*

This dialogue follows new acquaintances as they chat about living arrangements and make plans for tomorrow.

Talkin' the Talk

After Shirley is introduced to the family, they will want to know where she lives, and they will invite her to come again.

Family member:	**¿Dónde vives?** *dohn*-deh *bvee*-bvehs *Where do you live?*
Shirley:	**Busco un departamento pequeño.** *bvoos*-koh oon deh-pahr-tah-*mehn*-toh peh-*keh*-nyoh *I'm looking for a small apartment.*
Family member:	**A la vuelta, arriendan un departamentito.** ah lah bvoo*ehl*-tah ah-rree*ehn*-dahn oon deh-pahr-tah-mehn-*tee*-toh *Around the corner, they rent a little apartment.*
Shirley:	**Bueno, voy a verlo.** bvoo*oeh*-noh bvoy ah *bvehr*-loh *Good, I'm going to see it.*

Family member: **Te va a gustar.**
teh bvah ah *goos*-tahr
You'll like it.

Shirley: **Bueno, no quiero molestar más, tengo que irme.**
bvoo*eh*-noh noh kee*eh*-roh moh-lehs-*tahr* mahs
tehn-goh keh *eer*-meh
Well, I don't want to bother you any more, I have to go.

Family member: **Aquí tienes tu casa.**
ah-*kee* tee*eh*-nehs too *kah*-sah
This is your home.

Shirley: **Muchas gracias.**
moo-chahs *grah*-seeahs
Thanks a lot.

Family member: **Te invito a que vengas mañana a tomar el tecito con nosotros.**
teh een-*bvee*-toh ah keh *bvehn*-gahs mah-nyah-*nah* ah toh-*mahr* el teh-*see*-toh kohn noh-*soh*-trohs
I invite you to come tomorrow for [a small] tea [with us].

Shirley: **Lo haré con mucho gusto.**
loh ah-*reh* kohn *moo*-choh *goos*-toh
I'd love to.

Engaging in "Small" Talk with Diminutives

In English when you want to say that something is small, you have to add the adjective *small* or *little* in front of the noun. Not so in Spanish. In Spanish, you add a few letters to the noun, called a *suffix*, meaning that you paste it to the end of the word. With that suffix, you create a diminutive, and people know that you're talking about something or someone small. The suffixes you add to the words are **-ito** (*ee*-toh) or **-ita** (*ee*-tah). A **niño** (*nee*-nyoh) (*boy/child*) turns little when you add the suffix **niñito** (nee-*nyee*-toh) (*little boy/child*).

Diminutives are used in Spain and other Spanish-speaking countries, but not as profusely as in some Latin American countries — especially the ones near the Andes Mountain range, such as Chile, Peru, and Ecuador.

In all Latin American countries, children are an important part of the family. See how Shirley takes this fact into consideration in the following dialogue.

Talkin' the Talk

Shirley chats about kids with her hosts.

Florencia:	**Dime Shirley, ¿tienes hijos?** *dee*-meh Shirley tee*eh*-nehs ee-Hohs *Tell me Shirley, do you have children?*
Shirley:	**Tengo un hijo. Aquí está su foto.** *tehn*-goh oon ee-Hoh ah-*kee* ehs-*tah* soo *foh*-toh *I have a son. Here's his photo.*
Florencia:	**A ver . . . Un muchacho muy buen mozo.** ah bvehr oon moo-*chah*-choh mooy booehn *moh*-so *Let's see . . . A good-looking boy.*
Shirley:	**Sí. ¿Y tú?** see ee too *Yes. And you?*
Florencia:	**Yo tengo una hija y un hijo.** yoh *tehn*-goh *oo*-nah ee-Hah ee oon ee-Hoh *I have a daughter and a son.*
Shirley:	**¿Cuántos años tienen?** koo*ahn*-tohs *ah*-nyohs tee*eh*-nehn *How old are they?*
Florencia:	**Mi hija tiene seis años y mi hijo tres. Allí viene mi hija.** mee ee-Hah tee*eh*-neh se*hees* *ah*-nyohs ee mee ee-Hoh trehs ah*ee* bvee*eh*-neh mee ee-Hah *My daughter is six and my son three. There comes my daughter.*
Shirley:	**Hola, ¿cómo te llamas?** *oh*-lah *koh*-moh teh *yah*-mahs *Hello, what's your name?*

Rosita:	**Me llamo Rosita.** meh *yah*-moh roh-*see*-tah *My name is Rosita.*
Shirley:	**¡Qué bello nombre, me gusta mucho!** keh *bveh*-yoh *nohm*-breh meh *goos*-tah *moo*-choh *What a beautiful name, I like it very much!*

Brushing Up on Common Expressions

When you're engaged in small talk, you can often get by with a few standard expressions, such as the following:

✔ **Muchas gracias.** (*moo*-chahs *grah*-seeahs) (*Thank you very much.*)

✔ **No, gracias.** (no *grah*-seeahs) (*No, thank you.*)

✔ **Nada, gracias.** (*nah*-dah *grah*-seeahs) (*Nothing, thanks.*)

✔ **Lo siento.** (loh see*ehn*-toh) (*I'm sorry.*)

✔ **Mi culpa.** (mee *kool*-pah) (*My fault.*)

✔ **Con permiso.** (kohn pehr-*mee*-soh) (*Excuse me.* [in the way])

✔ **Discúlpeme.** (dees-*kuhl*-peh-meh) (*Excuse me.* [interrupt])

✔ **¿Qué necesita usted?** (keh neh-seh-*see*-tah oos-tehd) (*What do you need?*)

✔ **Quiero unas baterías.** (kee*eh*-roh *oo*-nahs bah-tehr-*ee*-ahs) (*I want some batteries.*)

✔ **¿Habla usted inglés?** (*ah*-bvlah oos-tehd een-*glehs*) (*Do you speak English?*)

✔ **Hablo inglés.** (*ah*-bvloh een-*glehs*) (*I speak English.*)

✔ **¿Habla usted español?** (*ah*-bvlah oos-tehd eh-spah-*nyohl*) (*Do you speak Spanish?*)

✔ **Hablo español.** (*ah*-bvloh eh-spah-*nyohl*) (*I speak Spanish.*)

✔ **No entiendo.** (noh ehn-tee*ehn*-doh) (*I don't understand.*)

✔ **No hablo mucho español.** (no *ah*-bvloh *moo*-choh eh-spah-*nyohl*) (*I don't speak much Spanish.*)

✔ **¿Repita, por favor?** (reh-*pee*-tah pohr fah-*bvohr*) (*Can you repeat that, please?*)

> ✔ **Necesito información, por favor.** (neh-seh-*see*-toh een-fohr-mah-see-*ohn* pohr fah-*bvohr*) (*I need information, please.*)
>
> ✔ **Necesito ayuda.** (neh-seh-*see*-toh ah-*yoo*-dah) (*I need some help.*)
>
> ✔ **¿Adónde va usted?** (ah-*dohn*-deh bvah oos-*tehd*) (*Where are you going?*)
>
> ✔ **No sé.** (noh seh) (*I don't know.*)

Use It or Lose It: Practicing What You Know

The best way to master any skill is to practice it until it becomes as natural as tying your shoelaces. The same is true when you're acquiring a new language. We encourage you to practice speaking Spanish as much as possible. The following list provides you with some suggestions to help you identify opportunities without necessarily traveling outside the country:

- ✔ **Visit Spanish-speaking places:** This information probably comes as no surprise, but the absolute best way, by far, to learn Spanish is to be in an environment where everybody speaks the language and no one speaks yours. Finding this sort of environment is pretty simple if you can afford to travel. Consider submerging yourself in the language by giving yourself a Spanish-speaking vacation. With Spanish-speaking places appearing just as you come across the southern border of the United States, travel by car, bus, or plane is generally inexpensive.

- ✔ **Scope out your neighborhood:** You may be able to find Spanish-speaking people in your own neighborhood or town. And among these people, you may find some who are willing to spend a few hours a week with you, doing everyday activities. You may join one of their clubs or volunteer in one of their community centers. In addition to honing your language skills, you can also explore a fascinating new culture.

- ✔ **Tune in to Spanish radio and TV:** Because so many people in North, Central, and South America speak Spanish, you may be lucky enough to find a radio station or a TV channel in your area that offers Spanish programming. By listening to and watching these programs, you add new vocabulary, gain an understanding of the body language and idioms of Spanish-speaking people, and gain insight into their idea of fun.

- ✔ **Rent Spanish-speaking video flicks:** Video centers in your area may offer films in Spanish. To get the effect of being in a Spanish-speaking country, choose a film that has no dubbing or subtitles. You'll be amazed at how much you understand even the first time you see the movie, but the good thing about video is that you can play the film as many times as your whim and time allow.

✔ **Check out your library's offerings:** Your local library may house books, tapes, and other materials about Spanish and Spanish-speaking countries. Every bit of information you get counts in building up your mental Spanish library. Here are some things you're looking for:

- Atlases and maps of Spanish-speaking North, Central, and South American countries.

- Travel guides and books that describe Spanish-speaking areas.

- Novels that describe Spanish places. Most of these are translations of texts by authors from countries that speak Spanish, but others are written in English.

✔ **Read the liner notes:** The liner notes you find in CDs and cassette tapes often have the song lyrics printed on them. Try buying albums by your favorite Spanish singer and then check the liner notes. Eventually, liner notes or not, you're bound to find yourself singing along — in Spanish!

✔ **Explore the Internet:** Look up your favorite Spanish-speaking countries, sample online tutorials and other offerings, and perhaps even strike up conversations with native speakers in online chat rooms and discussion forums. (You can even practice searching the Web in Spanish! Instead of going to www.google.com, try searching from www.google.es to browse Spanish Web sites.)

✔ **Make up games:** You can make up games of your own. For example, you may decide to make a game of learning a sentence a day:

1. Put the sentence with little stickers on your refrigerator, next to your phone, on your bathroom mirror, or other places you choose.

2. Every time you open the refrigerator, hang up your phone, or look into the mirror, read and repeat the sentence aloud. Use your imagination and have fun!

✔ **Label all your stuff in Spanish:** On little stickers, write the Spanish word for all the things in one room of your house. Put each sticker on the correct item. Say the Spanish word aloud every time you use the object. As you feel comfortable with the words, remove the stickers, but continue saying the name aloud. If you forget the name, replace the sticker. When the majority of stickers are gone, move to another room.

✔ **Practice your script:** You hear a Spanish phrase in a film, you sing a line in Spanish of a song, or you catch a Spanish sentence in an ad. These are treasures, and your goal is to use and polish them all the time. Several times a day, repeat those words and phrases aloud. So that you know what you're repeating, you may consult a dictionary, which can be the very one in Appendix B of Book V. Soon, the treasure is yours to keep.

✔ **Take a Spanish class:** Although *Spanish All-in-One For Dummies* contains everything you need to know to get started, it can't possibly replace the classroom experience, where you can obtain feedback from a teacher who knows the language. Consider signing up for a Spanish class at a nearby college or university. In addition to improving your Spanish language skills and pronunciation, you can receive credit for your studies that can help in future job searches.

Chapter 5

Speaking of Food . . .

Food is an important element of any culture. Each country and region in Latin America has different-tasting food, making restaurant hopping and trying new dishes there among the most diverse experiences possible. The same is true in sunny Spain, where deep-fried fish, mountain-cured ham, and a variety of other tasty treats await you.

In this chapter, we bring you up to speed on table talk, so you can order meals (and drinks) at your favorite Mexican restaurants and shop for food at the market, fairly confident that you're getting what you want.

Getting Up to Speed on Table Talk

To this day, food remains the universal language and one of the best tools for introducing students to new languages and cultures. Knowing some basic words and phrases before sitting down for a meal can make the experience more enjoyable and certainly improves the opportunities for engaging in stimulating dinner conversation.

When shall we eat what?

Sometimes the same word has a different meaning from country to country. **Desayuno** in Argentina is a light breakfast — what hotels call a Continental breakfast. In Mexico, a **desayuno** is even lighter, often just a cup of coffee or juice. So, in Mexico, around ten o'clock or so, people sit down to a meal that is a lot like breakfast in the United States: juice or fruit, eggs with sauces, steak, plus lots of tortillas. Mexicans call this meal **almuerzo**.

In South America, **almuerzo** is simply lunch, and it's eaten around noon or one o'clock. In Spain, **almuerzo** is a late breakfast. In Uruguay an **almuerzo** is soup, a main dish with meats or fish, and a dessert.

Comida in Chile is a meal that you eat in the evening, and may again be soup, a main dish, and dessert. The same word in Mexico signifies a meal taken between two and four o'clock in the afternoon. It's a hearty affair, with appetizers, soup, main dish, and dessert, and leads to an immediate siesta. In Spain, **comida** is lunch.

Cena is supper, eaten late, between eight and ten in the evening. In some countries, you have just fruit at this time, but some families do eat a main dish and dessert.

Table terms

You may find these phrases useful when you plan a meal:

- **¡A poner la mesa!** (ah poh-*nehr* lah *meh*-sah) (*Set the table!*)
- **Aquí están los platos y los vasos.** (ah-*kee* ehs-*tahn* lohs *plah*-tohs ee lohs *bvah*-sohs) (*Here are the dishes and glasses.*)
- **¿Qué cubiertos?** (keh koo-bvee*ehr*-tohs) (*What cutlery?*)
- **Cuchara, cuchillo, tenedor, y cucharita.** (koo-*chah*-rah koo-*chee*-yo teh-neh-*dohr* ee koo-chah-*ree*-tah) (*Spoon, knife, fork, and coffee or demitasse spoon.*)
- **Aquí están las servilletas.** (ah-*kee* ehs-*tahn* lahs sehr-bvee-*yeh*-tahs) (*Here are the napkins.*)
- **Más sal en el salero.** (mahs sahl ehn ehl sah-*leh*-roh) (*More salt in the salt shaker.*)

Phrases for food and drink

Here are some common terms connected with meals:

✔ **almuerzo** (ahl-moo*ehr*-soh) (*lunch*)

✔ **cena** (*seh*-nah) (*supper*)

✔ **comida** (koh-*mee*-dah) (*dinner*)

✔ **desayuno** (deh-sah-*yoo*-noh) (*breakfast*)

✔ **tengo sed** (*tehn*-goh sehd) (*I'm thirsty*)

✔ **tiene hambre** (tee*eh*-neh *ahm*-bvreh) (*he's/she's hungry*)

You may hear these phrases, or speak them yourself, when giving or receiving foods and beverages:

✔ **¡Buen provecho!** (bvoo*ehn* proh-*bveh*-choh) (*Enjoy your meal!* — the equivalent of the French *Bon appetit!*)

✔ **¿Con qué está servido?** (kohn keh ehs-*tah* sehr-*bvee*-doh) (*What does it come with?*)

✔ **Está caliente.** (ehs-*tah* kah-lee*ehn*-teh) (*It's hot [*temperature*].*)

✔ **Está frío.** (ehs-*tah* free*oh*) (*It's cold.*)

✔ **Está picante.** (ehs-*tah* pee-*kahn*-teh) (*It's hot [*flavor/spice*].*)

✔ **Es sabroso.** (ehs sah-*bvroh*-soh) (*It's tasty.*)

✔ **Lamento, no tenemos . . .** (lah-*mehn*-toh noh teh-*neh*-mohs) (*Sorry, we don't have . . .*)

✔ **¿Qué ingredientes tiene?** (keh een-greh-dee*ehn*-tehs tee*eh*-neh) (*What are the ingredients?*)

✔ **¿Qué más trae el plato?** (keh mahs *trah*-eh ehl *plah*-toh) (*What else is in the dish?*)

These words can help you when you're ordering something to drink:

✔ **Escoger un vino.** (ehs-koh-*Hehr* oon *bvee*-noh) (*Choose a wine.*)

✔ **¡Salud!** (sah-*lood*) (*Cheers!*)

✔ **Tomar un refresco.** (toh-*mahr* oon reh-*frehs*-koh) (*Drink a soda pop.*)

✔ **Tomar un trago.** (toh-*mahr* oon *trah*-goh) (*Have a drink [*alcoholic*].*)

✔ **Un vaso de agua.** (oon *bvah*-soh deh *ah*-gooah) (*A glass of water.*)

✔ **Un vaso de leche.** (oon *bvah*-soh deh *leh*-cheh) (*A glass of milk.*)

Eating and Drinking: Three Must-Know Verbs

In Spanish, you talk about drinking with two verbs. One is **tomar** (toh-*mahr*); the other is **beber** (bveh-*bvehr*).

Take and drink with tomar

Tomar (toh-*mahr*) means literally *to take* and often means exactly that. But when you say **tomar un refresco** (toh-*mahr* oon reh-*frehs*-koh), you're talking about *drinking a soda*, not literally taking one, and you know that's what you mean because **tomar** is followed by something you drink.

Tomar is a regular verb of the **-ar** (ahr) group. The root of the verb is **tom-** (tohm), as you can see from the table that follows:

Conjugation	Pronunciation
yo tomo	yoh *toh*-moh
tú tomas	too *toh*-mahs
él, ella, ello, uno, usted toma	ehl, *eh*-yah, *eh*-yoh, *oo*-noh, oos-*tehd* *toh*-mah
nosotros tomamos	noh-*soh*-trohs toh-*mah*-mohs
vosotros tomáis	bvoh-*soh*-trohs toh-*mah*ees
ellos, ellas, ustedes toman	*eh*-yohs, *eh*-yahs, oos-*teh*-dehs *toh*-mahn

Drink up with beber

In the case of the verb **beber**, you can have no doubts: This verb applies to drinking only.

Beber (bveh-*bvehr*) is also a regular verb; it's from the **-er** (ehr) group. The root of the verb is: **beb-** (bvehbv), as you can see in the following table:

Conjugation	Pronunciation
yo bebo	yoh *bveh*-bvoh
tú bebes	too *bveh*-bvehs

él, ella, ello, uno, usted bebe	ehl, *eh*-yah, *eh*-yoh, *oo*-noh oos-*tehd* *bveh*-bveh
nosotros bebemos	noh-*soh*-trohs bveh-*bveh*-mohs
vosotros bebéis	bvoh-*soh*-trohs bveh-*bve*hees
ellos, ellas, ustedes beben	*eh*-yohs, *eh*-yahs, oos-*teh*-dehs *bveh*-bvehn

Chow down with comer

Comer (kohm-*ehr*) means *to eat*. A regular verb from the **-er** (ehr) group, the root of this verb is com (kohm), as the following table shows:

Conjugation	*Pronunciation*
yo como	yoh *koh*-moh
tú comes	too *koh*-mehs
él, ella, ello, uno, usted come	chl, *eh*-yah, *eh*-yoh, *oo*-noh, oos-*tehd* *koh*-meh
nosotros comemos	noh-*soh*-trohs koh-*meh*-mohs
vosotros coméis	bvoh-*soh*-trohs koh-*meh*ees
ellos, ellas, ustedes comen	*eh*-yohs, *eh*-yahs, oos-*teh*-dehs *koh*-mehn

Sampling the Exotic Cuisine

A menu in a foreign language can be intimidating. But Latin America has many tasty and exotic foods that you don't want to miss. This list identifies the most popular ones:

- **Agua** (*ah*-gooah) in Mexico can mean *water*, which is its exact translation, but it can also be a beverage made with water, fruit, and sugar. All fruits, and even some vegetables, make refreshing **aguas** (*ah*-gooahs).

- In Chile, **aguita** (ah-goo*ee*-tah) (*little water*) can be an herb tea served after a meal.

- **Empanada** (ehm-pah-*nah*-dah) actually means *in bread*. In Mexico, an **empanada** is a folded and stuffed corn tortilla. You can get **empanadas** made out of wheat dough, which is then folded and stuffed, in Argentina and Chile. Argentinians like theirs small. Chileans make theirs big. Either way, they're delicious!

✔ In Spain, a **tortilla** (tohr-*tee*-yah) is a potato, onion, and egg omelette that's often served at room temperature.

✔ In Mexico, **elote** (eh-*loh*-teh) is the name of tender corn, the kind you eat from the cob. The same thing in Argentina, Chile, Peru, and Bolivia is called **choclo** (*choh*-kloh).

✔ Green beans in Mexico are called **ejotes** (eh-*Hoh*-tehs). In South America, you find them under names like **porotos verdes** (poh-*roh*-tohs *bvehr*-dehs), or **porotitos** (poh-roh-*tee*-tohs). When the beans are dry, they're called **porotos** (poh-*roh*-tohs) in most of Spanish-speaking America, except in Mexico, where they're known as **frijoles** (free-*Hoh*-lehs). Nowhere else can you see as great a variety of beans as in a Peruvian market. They come in enough colors and shapes and sizes to make your mouth water. You may want to try them all.

✔ In Chile, **filete** (fee-*leh*-teh) is the cut of beef called *sirloin* in the United States. In Argentina, the same cut is called **lomo** (*loh*-moh).

✔ The basic Argentinean meal is **bife, con papas y ensalada** (*bvee*-feh kohn *pah*-pahs ee ehn-sah-*lah*-dah), which translates to *grilled steak, with potatoes and salad*. On an Argentinean grill, you're likely to find a number of meats familiar to you, along with others that you probably never have eaten. Among the more exotic are **chinchulín** (cheen-choo-*leen*), which is braided and grilled beef bowels. **¡Delicioso!** Another delicacy is **molleja** (moh-*yeh*-Hah), which is the thyroid gland of a cow.

✔ In Mexico, however, **molleja** (moh-*yeh*-Hah) is chicken gizzard. And in Chile, the same chicken gizzard is **contre** (*kohn*-treh).

✔ The liver that you eat in Chile is called **pana** (*pah*-nah); in most other places in Latin America, liver is **hígado** (*ee*-gah-doh).

✔ In Spain, **jamón serrano** (Ha-*mohn* seh-*rran*-oh), salt cured ham typical of the mountain regions, is a great delicacy.

If you love fish and seafood, the places to go are Chile and Peru. The best fish in the world swim in the Humboldt Current, coming from Antarctica.

✔ You find delights such as **loco** (*loh*-koh), a truly gigantic scallop, and **congrio** (*kohn*-greeoh), or *conger eel*, a type of fish.

✔ You can also find **albacora** (ahl-bvah-*koh*-rah) (*swordfish*), **cangrejo** (kahn-*greh*-Hoh) (*giant crab*), **jaiba** (*Hah*ee-bvah) (*small crab*), **langosta** (lahn-*gohs*-tah) (*lobster*); **langostino** (lahn-gohs-*tee*-noh) (*prawn*), **camarón** (kah-mah-*rohn*) (*shrimp*), and other delights to crowd your **sopa marinera** (*soh*-pah mah-ree-*neh*-rah) (*fish soup*).

✔ In Peru, they make **ceviche** (seh-*bvee*-cheh) out of raw fish or raw seafood. **Ceviches** come in many varieties. One commonality is that Latinos like their **ceviche** very hot. In **ceviche**, raw fish or seafood is marinated in lemon juice, salt, and hot peppers. The fish or seafood is still raw after this treatment, but it looks less transparent, as though it were cooked. Sensational!

You also may want to order some of these specialties:

- Called **aguacate** (ah-gooah-*kah*-teh) in Mexico and **palta** (*pahl*-tah) in Argentina, Uruguay, and Chile, it's still the same *avocado*.

- In the south of Mexico, when you say **pan** (pahn), meaning *bread*, people usually think of something that the baker made to taste sweet. In South America, **pan** is closer to what you eat in the States.

- **Torta** (*tohr*-tah) in Mexico is a sandwich in a bun (a **sandwich** is made with bread baked in a mold and sliced.) But most everywhere else in Latin America, **torta** (*tohr*-tah) means *cake*, and **sandwich** means *sandwich* (no matter how it's served).

- **Memelas** (meh-*meh*-lahs) in Mexico are tortillas that are pinched on the side to form a hollow, which is filled with pastes and delicacies.

- **Gazpacho** (gahs-*pah*-choh), is a chilled vegetable soup from Spain flavored with olive oil, garlic, and vinegar.

- In Spain, **paella** (pah-*eh*-yah) is a favorite dish made of seafood and saffron rice.

How do you like your salsa?

Some people say that what's truly special about Latin American foods is the sauce. This statement is especially true of the sauces served in Mexico, which have an infinite variety of flavors and textures.

Mole: Truly hot sauces

Mole (*moh*-leh), a word used in Mexico, means *sauce*. These Mexican moles are served hot with meats and chicken:

- **Mole negro** (*moh*-leh *neh*-groh) (*black mole*) looks black — naturally! — and is made with all toasted ingredients: cocoa, chilies, almonds, onions, garlic, and bread. It can be very spicy or less so.

- **Mole colorado** (*moh*-leh koh-loh-*rah*-doh) (*red mole*) looks red and is made with chilies. It's spicy hot! The sauce is also called **coloradito** (koh-loh-rah-*dee*-toh).

- **Mole amarillo** (*moh*-leh ah-mah-*ree*-yoh) (*yellow mole*) is orangy yellow. You make it with almonds and raisins, among other ingredients. Generally, it's only mildly spicy.

- **Mole verde** (*moh*-leh *bvehr*-deh) (*green mole*) is made with green tomatoes, green chilies (hot peppers), and coriander (cilantro) and looks green. It can be very spicy or mildly hot.

Mexicans don't eat moles every day. These delicacies are served only on special occasions. Tourists are luckier — they can find them all the time.

Chilled hot sauces

Mexicans bring some cold sauces to the table to add more spice to your food.

- **Pico de gallo** (*pee*-koh deh *gah*-lyoh), which translates as *rooster's beak*, is made totally with vegetables. It looks red, green, and white, because it's made with tomatoes, jalapeño peppers, coriander, and onions. Hot!

- **Guacamole** (gooah-kah-*moh*-leh) needs no translation. It's the dip made with avocado, chili (*chee*-lee) "hot pepper," coriander (cilantro), lemon, and salt. It's sometimes spicy hot.

- **Salsa verde** (*sahl*-sah *bvehr*-deh) green sauce is made with green tomatoes, chilies, and coriander. Hot!

- **Salsa roja** (*sahl*-sah *roh*-Hah) red sauce is made with red tomatoes and chilies. Hot!

Making a restaurant reservation

The following dialogue provides the terminology typically needed to make a restaurant reservation.

The vast majority of restaurants in Latin America don't require reservations.

Talkin' the Talk

Señor Porter wants to take his wife to a nice restaurant on her birthday. Listen in as he calls the restaurant to make reservations.

Señor Porter:	**Quiero reservar una mesa para dos personas.**
	keee*eh*-roh reh-sehr-*bvahr* oo-nah *meh*-sah *pah*-rah dohs pehr-*soh*-nahs
	I want to reserve a table for two people.
Waiter:	**¡Cómo no! ¿Para qué hora será?**
	koh-moh noh *pah*-rah keh *oh*-rah seh-*rah*
	Of course! At what time?
Señor Porter	**Para las ocho de la noche.**
	pah-rah lahs *oh*-choh deh lah *noh*-cheh
	At eight o'clock in the evening.

Waiter:	**¿A nombre de quién?**
	ah *nohm*-bvreh deh kee*ehn*
	Under what name?

Señor Porter:	**El señor Porter.**
	ehl *seh*-nyohr Porter
	Mr. Porter.

Waiter:	**Bien, les esperamos.**
	bvee*ehn* lehs ehs-peh-*rah*-mohs
	Good, we'll look forward to seeing you.

Señor Porter:	**Muchas gracias.**
	moo-chahs *grah*-seeahs
	Many thanks.

Ordering up some grub with the verb querer

The verb **querer** (keh-*rehr*) is often used to convey *to want* or *to wish*.

Querer is an irregular verb. Notice that the root **quer-** (kehr) is transformed into **quier-** (keeehr) with most subject pronouns.

Conjugation	*Pronunciation*
yo quiero	yoh kee*eh*-roh
tú quieres	too kee*eh*-rehs
él, ella, ello, uno, usted quiere	ehl, *eh*-yah, *eh*-yoh, *oo*-noh, oos-*tehd* kee*eh*-reh
nosotros queremos	noh-*soh*-trohs keh-*reh*-mohs
vosotros queréis	bvoh-*soh*-trohs keh-*reh*ees
ellos, ellas, ustedes quieren	*eh*-yohs, *eh*-yahs, oos-*teh*-dehs kee*eh*-rehn

The following dialogue shows you **querer** in action.

Calling a waiter

A waiter in Argentina is a **mozo** (*moh*-soh) or *young man*.

But, calling someone **mozo** in Chile is offensive. In Chile, you say **garzón** (gahr-*sohn*), which is derived from the French word for *young man*— the similarly spelled and identically pronounced **garçon**.

If you call the waiter by either of these terms in Mexico, he may not react. You can better get his attention by saying **joven** (*Hoh*-bvehn), meaning *young*, even if he isn't so young.

In Spain, a *waiter* is a **camarero** (kah-mah-*reh*-roh).

When a woman is serving you, call her simply **señorita** (seh-nyoh-*ree*-tah), *Miss*, no matter where you are.

Talkin' the Talk

If you want to order a beverage to drink with your food, you may participate in a conversation similar to this one.

Waiter: **¿Quieren algo para beber?**
keee*eh*-rehn *ahl*-goh *pah*-rah bveh-*bvehr*
Do you want anything to drink?

¿Se sirven un agua de frutas?
seh *seer*-bvehn oon *ah*-gooah deh *froo*-tahs
Would you like a diluted fruit juice?

Señora **No, yo quiero un vaso de vino tinto.**
Porter: noh yoh keee*eh*-roh oon *bvah*-soh de *bvee*-noh
teen-toh
No, I want a glass of red wine.

Waiter: **Muy bien, ¿y usted?**
mooy bveee*ehn* ee oos-*tehd*
Very well, and you?

Señor **Yo quiero una cerveza.**
Porter: yoh keee*eh*-roh *oo*-nah sehr-*bveh*-sah
I want a beer.

Waiter: **¿Lager o negra?**
lah-*gehr* oh *neh*-grah
Lager or dark?

Señor Porter:	**Prefiero negra.**
	preh-fee*eh*-roh *neh*-grah
	I prefer dark.

The following dialogue shows you a sample restaurant order exchange.

Talkin' the Talk

Now for great eating! You can use the following conversation as an example to order some soup or salad.

Waiter:	**¿Están listos para ordenar?**
	ehs-*tahn lees*-tohs *pah*-rah ohr-deh-*nahr*
	Are you ready to order?

Señora Porter:	**Yo quiero una ensalada mixta.**
	yoh kee*eeh*-roh *oo*-nah ehn-sah-*lah*-dah *meeks*-tah
	I want a mixed [several vegetables] salad.

Señor Porter:	**Y para mí una sopa de mariscos.**
	ee *pah*-rah mee *oo*-nah *soh*-pah deh mah-*rees*-kohs
	And for me, seafood soup.

Waiter:	**¿Y de plato fuerte?**
	ee deh *plah*-toh foo*ehr*-teh
	And as the main course?

Señor Porter:	**¿Qué nos recomienda?**
	keh nohs reh-koh-mee*eh*-dah
	What do you suggest?

Waiter:	**Tenemos dos platos especiales: mole amarillo con carne de res y huachinango a la veracruzana.**
	teh-*neh*-mohs dohs *plah*-tohs ehs-peh-see*ah*-lehs *moh*-leh ah-mah-*ree*-yoh kohn *kahr*-neh deh rehs ee ooah-chee-*nahn*-goh ah lah bveh-rah-kroo-*sah*-nah
	We have two specials: yellow mole with beef and red snapper Veracruz style.

Señora Porter:	**¿Qué es el huachinango a la veracruzana?**
	keh ehs ehl ooah-chee-*nahn*-goh ah lah bveh-rah-kroo-*sah*-nah
	What is red snapper Veracruz style?

Waiter:	**Es pescado con tomates, chile, cilantro, y cebolla.** ehs pehs-*kah*-doh kohn toh-*mah*-tehs *chee*-leh see-*lahn*-troh ee seh-*bvoh*-yah *It's fish with tomatoes, hot peppers, coriander (cilantro), and onions.*
Señora Porter:	**Yo quiero pollo frito.** yoh kee*eh*-roh *poh*-yoh *free*-toh *I want fried chicken.*
Waiter:	**No tenemos pollo frito. Tenemos pollo asado en salsa de mango.** noh teh-*neh*-mohs *poh*-yoh *free*-toh teh-*neh*-mohs *poh*-yoh ah-*sah*-doh ehn *sahl*-sah deh *mahn*-goh *We don't have fried chicken. We have broiled chicken with mango sauce.*
Señora Porter:	**¿Con qué está acompañado?** kohn keh ehs-*tah* ah-kohm-pah-*nyah*-doh *What does it come with?*
Waiter:	**Con elotes frescos, y calabazas entomatadas.** kohn eh-*loh*-tehs *frehs*-kohs ee kah-lah-*bvah*-sahs ehn-toh-mah-*tah*-dahs *With fresh corn, and zucchini in tomato sauce.*
Señora Porter:	**Bueno, voy a probar el pollo con mango.** bvoo*eh*-noh, bvohy ah proh-*bvahr* ehl *poh*-yoh kohn *mahn*-goh *Good, I'll try the chicken with mango.*

Paying the bill

When paying the bill, one typically asks the waiter for **la cuenta** (lah koo*ehn*-tah) or check. The following dialogue covers getting the check and leaving a tip.

Talkin' the Talk

You may have an exchange like the following as you pay your bill.

Señor Porter:	**Joven, ¿nos trae la cuenta por favor?** *Hoh*-bvehn nohs *trah*-eh lah koo*ehn*-tah pohr fah-*bvohr* *Waiter, will you bring us the check please?*

Taking a bathroom break

Inevitably, you want to wash your hands, freshen your makeup, or do something else that requires the use of a public bathroom. Bathrooms in Latin America are very similar to those in the States and Canada — the more expensive the restaurant, the more elegant the bathroom. The following phrases can help you find the room you need.

✔ **¿Dónde están los baños?** (_dohn_-deh ehs-_tahn_ lohs _bvah_-nyohs) (_Where are the bathrooms?_)

✔ **Los baños están al fondo, a la derecha.** (lohs _bvah_-nyohs ehs-_tahn_ ahl _fohn_-doh ah lah deh-_reh_-chah) (_The bathrooms are at the back, to the right._)

✔ **¿Es este el baño?** (ehs _ehs_-teh ehl _bvah_-nyoh) (_Is this the bathroom?_)

✔ **No, este no es el baño. Es ese.** (noh _ehs_-teh noh ehs ehl _bvah_-nyoh ehs eh-se) (_No, this isn't the bathroom. It's that one._)

Waiter:	**Ya vuelvo con la cuenta.** yah bvoo_ehl_-bvoh kohn lah koo_ehn_-tah _I'll be back with the check._
Señor Porter:	**¿Aceptan tarjetas de crédito?** ah-_sehp_-tahn tahr-_Heh_-tahs deh _kreh_-dee-toh _Do you accept credit cards?_
Waiter:	**No, lo lamento mucho, aquí no aceptamos tarjetas de crédito.** noh loh lah-_mehn_-toh _moo_-choh ah-_kee_ noh ah-sehp-_tah_-mohs tahr-_Heh_-tahs deh _kreh_-dee-toh _No, I'm very sorry; we don't take credit cards._
A bit later:	
Señora Porter:	**¿Ya pagamos la cuenta?** yah pah-_gah_-mohs lah koo_ehn_-tah _We paid the check already?_
Señor Porter:	**Ya la pagué.** yah lah pah-_gheh_ _I paid it already._
Señora Porter:	**¿Dejamos propina?** deh-_Hah_-mohs proh-_pee_-nah _Did we leave a tip?_
Señor Porter:	**Sí dejé propina.** see deh-_Heh_ proh-_pee_-nah _Yes, I left a tip._

Going to Market

In this section, you visit markets that may be open or under a roof, but are more informal than supermarkets. Also, vendors in these markets are salespeople, not just cashiers, and they may approach you to sell you goods you may or may not want. When you don't want something, you can simply say one of the following:

- ✔ **Ahora no, gracias.** (ah-*oh*-rah noh *grah*-seeahs) (*Not now, thank you.*)
- ✔ **Ya tengo, gracias.** (yah *tehn*-goh *grah*-seeahs) (*I already have some [or it], thanks.*)
- ✔ **No me interesa, gracias.** (no meh een-teh-*reh*-sah *grah*-seeahs) (*It doesn't interest me, thank you.*)
- ✔ **Más tarde, gracias.** (mahs *tahr*-deh *grah*-seeahs) (*Later, thank you.*)
- ✔ **No me gusta, gracias.** (noh meh *goos*-tah *grah*-seeahs) (*I don't like it, thanks.*)
- ✔ **No me moleste, ¡por favor!** (noh meh moh-*lehs*-teh pohr fah-*bvohr*) (*Don't bother me, please!*)

When you go to the market, it's a good idea to bring your own shopping bags or baskets to carry away the stuff you buy. Supermarkets provide bags, of course, but at the more informal markets, the vendor simply packs the stuff you buy but doesn't provide a larger container to carry it away. Wherever this is the rule, you can find stalls that sell bags or baskets of all sizes. More often than not, you want to take these bags home with you — many of them are handmade and quite beautiful.

Shopping with the verb comprar

Comprar (kohm-*prahr*) means *to shop*, and **ir de compras** (eer deh *kohm*-prahs) means *to go shopping*. **Comprar** is a regular verb of the **-ar** (ahr) group. The root of the verb is **compr-** (kohmpr). Here's how you conjugate **comprar** in the present tense:

Conjugation	Pronunciation
yo compro	yoh *kohm*-proh
tú compras	too *kohm*-prahs
él, ella, ello, uno, usted compra	ehl, *eh*-yah, *eh*-yoh, *oo*-noh, oos-*tehd* *kohm*-prah

nosotros compramos	noh-*soh*-trohs kohm-*prah*-mohs
vosotros compráis	bvoh-*soh*-trohs kohm-*prah*ees
ellos, ellas, ustedes compran	*eh*-yohs, *eh*-yahs, oos-*teh*-dehs *kohm*-prahn

These phrases, based on **ir de compras** (eer deh *kohm*-prahs) (*to go shopping*), can help you at the market.

✔ **Fue de compras.** (fooeh deh *kohm*-prahs) (*She or he is out shopping.*)

✔ **¡Voy de compras!** (bvoy deh *kohm*-prahs) (*I'm going shopping!*)

✔ **¡Vamos de compras al mercado!** (*bvah*-mohs deh *kohm*-prahs ahl-mehr-*kah*-do) (*Let's go shopping at the market!*)

Selecting fruit

Here are the names of fruits you find at the market:

✔ **la cereza** (lah seh-*reh*-sah) (*the cherry*)

✔ **la ciruela** (lah see-ro-*eh*-lah) (*the plum*)

✔ **el durazno** (ehl doo-*rahs*-noh) (*the peach*)

✔ **la fresa** (la *freh*-sah) (*the strawberry*) [Mexico, Central America, and Spain]

✔ **la frutilla** (lah froo-*tee*-yah) (*the strawberry*) [from Colombia to the South Pole]

✔ **la guayaba** (lah gooah-*yah*-bvah) (*the guava*)

✔ **el higo** (ehl *ee*-goh) (*the fig*)

✔ **la lima** (lah *lee*-mah) (*the lime*)

✔ **el limón** (ehl lee-*mohn*) (*the lemon*)

✔ **el mango** (ehl *mahn*-goh) (*the mango*)

✔ **la manzana** (lah mahn-*sah*-nah) (*the apple*)

✔ **el melocotón** (ehl meh-loh-koh-*tohn*) (*the peach*) [in Spain]

✔ **el melón** (ehl meh-*lohn*) (*the melon*)

✔ **la mora** (lah *moh*-rah) (*the blackberry*)

✔ **la naranja** (lah nah-*rahn*-Hah) (*the orange*)

✔ **la papaya** (lah pah-*pah*-yah) (*the papaya*)

- **la pera** (lah *peh*-rah) (*the pear*)
- **el plátano** (ehl *plah*-tah-noh) (*the banana*)
- **el pomelo** (ehl poh-*meh*-loh) (*the grapefruit*) [in Mexico]
- **la sandía** (lah sahn-*dee*-ah) (*the watermelon*)
- **la toronja** (lah toh-*rohn*-Ha) (*the grapefruit*) [in Mexico]
- **la tuna** (lah *too*-nah) (*the prickly pear*)
- **la uva** (lah *oo*-bvah) (*the grape*)

Picking out veggies

Fresh vegetables are always tasty. You can easily find the following:

- **las acelgas** (lahs ah-*sehl*-gahs) (*the swiss chard*)
- **el aguacate** (ehl ah-gooah-*kah*-teh) (*the avocado*)
- **el ají** (el ah-*Hee*) (*the hot pepper*) [in South America]
- **el ajo** (ehl *ah*-Hoh) (*the garlic*)
- **el brócoli** (ehl *bvroh*-koh-lee) (*the broccoli*)
- **la calabacita** (lah kah-lah-bvah-*see*-tah) (*the zucchini*) [in Mexico]
- **las cebollas** (lahs seh-*bvoh*-yahs) (*the onions*)
- **el chile** (ehl *chee*-leh) (*the hot pepper*) [in Mexico and Guatemala]
- **el chile morrón** (ehl *chee*-leh moh-*rrohn*) (*the sweet pepper*) [in Mexico]
- **la col** (lah kohl) (*the cabbage*) [in Mexico]
- **la coliflor** (lah koh-lee-*flohr*) (*the cauliflower*)
- **la espinaca** (lah ehs-pee-*nah*-kah) (*the spinach*)
- **la lechuga** (lah leh-*choo*-gah) (*the lettuce*)
- **las papas** (lahs *pah*-pahs) (*the potatoes*); **patatas** (pah-*tah*-tahs) [in Spain]
- **la palta** (lah *pahl*-tah) (*the avocado*) [in South America]
- **el pimentón** (ehl pee-mehn-*tohn*) (*the sweet pepper*) [in Argentina, Chile, and Uruguay]
- **el repollo** (ehl reh-*poh*-yoh) (*the cabbage*) [in Argentina and Chile]
- **la zanahoria** (lah sah-nah-*oh*-reeah) (*the carrot*)
- **el zapallito** (ehl sah-pah-*yee*-toh) (*zucchini*) [in Uruguay and Argentina]

Fishing for seafood

These terms can help you when you're selecting seafood:

- ✔ **el camarón** (ehl kah-mah-*rohn*) (shrimp); *gambas* (*gahm*-bahs) in Spain
- ✔ **el huachinango** (ehl ooah-chee-*nahn*-goh) (*red snapper*)
- ✔ **el langostino** (ehl lahn-gohs-*tee*-noh) (*prawn*)
- ✔ **el marisco** (ehl mah-*rees*-koh) (*seafood*)
- ✔ **el pescado** (ehl pehs-*kah*-doh) (*fish*)
- ✔ **la trucha** (lah *troo*-chah) (*trout*)

The following dialogue shows you how to get what you need at the fish market.

Talkin' the Talk

Latin Americans prepare fish and seafood in a variety of ways, all of them delicious. Here's how Amalia shops for fish.

Amalia: **¿Cuánto cuesta el pescado?**
koo*ahn*-toh koo*ehs*-tah ehl pehs-*kah*-doh
How much is the fish?

Vendor: **Treinta pesos el kilo.**
tre*heen*-tah *peh*-sohs ehl *kee*-loh
Thirty pesos per kilo.

Amalia: **Lo quiero fileteado, sin espinas.**
loh kee*eh*-roh fee-leh-teh-*ah*-doh seen *ehs*-pee-nas
I want it filleted, boneless.

Vendor: **¿Se lleva la cabeza para la sopa?**
seh *yeh*-bvah lah kah-bveh-sah *pah*-rah lah *soh*-pah
Will you take the head for soup?

Amalia: **Sí, aparte, por favor.**
see ah-*pahr*-teh pohr *fah*-bvohr
Yes, separately, please.

Knowing your weights and volumes

The United States is one of the few countries that hasn't fully adopted the metric system, so you need to get up to speed on metric weights and volumes before you go to market. A **kilo** (kee-loh) is a bit more than two pounds. *Kilo* actually comes from the word **kilogram**, which means one thousand grams. One gram is **un gramo** (oon *grah*-moh) — roughly equivalent to the weight of the water filling a thimble. A **litro** (lee-troh) or *liter*, is a bit more than a quart or exactly half as much as you get in one of those two-liter soda bottles. Here's a list of other quantities:

- **una docena** (*oo*-nah doh-*seh*-nah) (*a dozen*)

- **media docena** (*meh*-deeah doh-*seh*-nah) (*a half dozen*)

- **una cincuentena** (*oo*-nah seen-kooehn-*teh*-nah) (*fifty*; *50*)

- **una centena** (*oo*-nah sehn-*teh*-nah) (*one hundred*; *100*)

- **un millar** (oon mee-*yahr*) (*one thousand*; *1,000*)

The following dialogue demonstrates how you discuss these measures with vendors at the market.

Talkin' the Talk

 Listen as Amalia bargains with a vendor over oranges at a fruit and vegetable stand.

Amalia:	**¿A cuánto las naranjas?**
	ah koo*ahn*-toh lahs nah-*rahn*-Hahs
	How much for the oranges?

Vendor:	**A diez pesos las veinticinco.**
	ah dee*ehs peh*-sohs lahs bveheen-tee-*seen*-koh
	Ten pesos for twenty five.

Amalia:	**¿A cuánto los aguacates?**
	ah koo*ahn*-toh lohs ah-gooah-*kah*-tehs
	How much for the avocados?

Vendor:	**Quince pesos el kilo.**
	keen-seh *peh*-sohs ehl *kee*-loh
	Fifteen pesos for one kilo.

Amalia:	**¡Es muy caro!** ehs mooy *kah*-roh *It's very expensive.*
Vendor:	**Es más barato que ayer.** ehs mahs bvah-*rah*-toh keh ah-*yehr* *It's cheaper than yesterday.*
Amalia:	**¿Tiene plátanos?** teee*h*-neh *plah*-tah-nohs *Do you have bananas?*
Vendor:	**¿Sí, de cuáles?** see deh koo*ah*-lehs *Yes, which kind?*
Amalia:	**De esos. ¿Cuánto cuestan?** deh *eh*-sohs koo*ahn*-toh koo*ehs*-tahn *Those. How much do they cost?*
Vendor:	**Tres pesos el kilo.** trehs *peh*-sohs ehl *kee*-loh *Three pesos per kilo.*
Amalia:	**Medio kilo, por favor. Los ajos, ¿a cuánto?** *meh*-deeoh *kee*-loh porh fah-*bvohr*. lohs *a*-Hos ah koo*ahn*-toh *A half kilo please. How much is the garlic?*
Vendor:	**A cinco pesos el ramillete.** ah *seen*-koh *peh*-sohs ehl rah-mee-*yeh*-teh *5 pesos per bunch [of heads.]*

Shopping at the Supermercado

Of course, you can also buy groceries at the **supermercado** (soo-pehr-mehr-*kah*-doh) (*supermarket*), where you proceed very much as you do in the United States. You may also find food there that you're more accustomed to. The supermarket is a good place to go for things like cereals and canned goods.

Following are some words and phrases that can help you at the supermarket:

- ✔ **el arroz** (ehl ah-*rrohs*) (*the rice*)
- ✔ **el atún** (ehl ah-*toon*) (*the tuna*)
- ✔ **el fideo** (ehl fee-*deh*-oh) (*the pasta*)
- ✔ **los cereales** (lohs seh-reh-*ah*-lehs) (*the cereals*)
- ✔ **las galletas** (lahs gah-*yeh*-tahs) (*the cookies* or *crackers*)
- ✔ **la leche** (lah *leh*-cheh) (*the milk*)
- ✔ **pagar** (pah-*gahr*) (*to pay*)
- ✔ **el pasillo** (ehl pah-*see*-yoh) (*the aisle*)
- ✔ **las sardinas** (lahs sahr-*dee*-nahs) (*the sardines*)
- ✔ **el vino** (ehl *bvee*-noh) (*the wine*)
- ✔ **el vuelto** (ehl bvoo*ehl*-toh) (*change* [as in money back]); **la vuelta** (lah bvoo*ehl*-tah) in Spain
- ✔ **las ollas** (lahs *oh*-yas) (*pots*)
- ✔ **el tercer pasillo** (ehl tehr-*sehr* pah-*see*-yoh) (*the third aisle*)
- ✔ **al fondo** (ahl *fohn*-doh) (*at the back*)
- ✔ **Gracias, aquí está su vuelto.** (*grah*-seeahs ah-*kee* ehs-*tah* soo bvoo*ehl*-toh) (*Thanks, here's your change.*)

Chapter 6

Going Shopping

Even experienced shoppers can enjoy new ways to shop and new stores to shop at. Shopping beyond the borders of the United States can be entertaining, and you can find some great bargains. But whether shopping is fun or hard work for you, in this chapter, we explain how to go about it Latin style!

In Latin American cities, you are likely to find that the shopping process resembles what you're used to. A worldwide trend seeks to make shopping faster, more abundant, and more varied. In larger cities like **Buenos Aires** (bvoo*eh*-nohs a*hee*-rehs), **Caracas** (kah-*rah*-kahs), and **Santiago de Chile** (sahn-tee*ah*-goh deh *chee*-leh), stores and marketplaces have clothes and objects in styles that may be new and different from what you have already seen. And if you like to shop the way you're used to, you usually find department stores and supermarkets that carry merchandise that feels exotic but is still familiar.

In smaller places, or in villages and other areas where traditional ways of exchanging goods at an open-air market are still in use, you enter a new kind of shopping world — one full of surprises. At times, the merchandise may seem unfamiliar to the point of making it difficult to recognize what an item is and what it's used for. And the shopping style also differs from what you're used to. This is what we call a fun time!

Checking Out the Local Department Stores

When you daydream about traveling to foreign lands, you probably imagine the locals doing most of their shopping in open-air markets or small boutiques. The fact of the matter, however, is that in larger cities all around the world, people shop in department stores much as they do in the United States. When visiting foreign lands, consider scheduling a shopping trip to a major department store. This excursion is a great way to see how and where the locals get their clothes and other necessities. In department stores, you also find the prices clearly posted and labeled. And you can surely find items that have local flavor.

By contrast, if you want exotic items sold the old-fashioned way, a department store isn't the best place to go. Exotic clothes and objects are sold in markets where the whole shopping operation is different. We cover traditional markets later in this chapter.

Labels aren't taken as seriously in all countries as they are in Canada or the States. Often, you may find merchandise that doesn't have all the information you need. Information the salesperson gives you may be just as fuzzy, simply because the United States and Canada put more emphasis on certain things than other countries do. Trust your senses and your experience.

These phrases can help you at a department store:

- ✔ **¿Dónde está la entrada?** (*dohn*-deh ehs-*tah* lah ehn-*trah*-dah) (*Where's the entrance?*)

- ✔ **¿Dónde está la salida?** (*dohn*-deh ehs-*tah* lah sah-*lee*-dah) (*Where's the exit?*)

- ✔ **empuje** (ehm-*poo*-Heh) (*push*)

- ✔ **tire** (*tee*-reh) (*pull*)

- ✔ **jale** (*Hah*-leh) (*pull [in Mexico]*)

- ✔ **el ascensor** (ehl ah-sehn-*sohr*) (*the elevator*)

- ✔ **la escalera mecánica** (lah ehs-kah-*leh*-rah meh-*kah*-nee-kah) (*the escalator*)

- ✔ **el vendedor** (ehl bvehn-deh-*dohr*) or la vendedora (lah bvehn-deh-*doh*-rah) (*the salesperson [male and female]*)

- ✔ **la caja** (lah *kah*-Hah) (*the check out stand*)

The vocabulary in Table 6-1 can help you as you shop.

Table 6-1	Shopping Terms	
Spanish	*Pronunciation*	*English*
ayudar	ah-yoo-*dahr*	to help
probar	proh-*bvahr*	to try
medir	meh-*deer*	to measure
más	mahs	more
menos	*meh*-nohs	less
liso	lee-soh	plain; flat
apretado	ah-preh-*tah*-doh	tight
suelto	soo*ehl*-toh	loose
grande	*grahn*-deh	large
pequeño	peh-*keh*-nyoh	small
la talla	lah *tah*-yah	the size
el probador	ehl proh-bvah-*dohr*	the fitting room

Suppose you're planning your day and you want to know the store's hours. Here's how to ask for that information:

- ✔ **¿A qué hora abren?** (ah keh *oh*-rah *ah*-bvrehn) (*At what time do you [formal] open?*)

- ✔ **¿A qué hora cierran?** (ah keh *oh*-rah see*eh*-rrahn) (*At what time do you [formal] close?*)

In the United States and Canada, you are probably used to browsing and shopping by yourself. In some places in Latin America, the salesperson wants to help you as soon as you enter the department. If you find the person insistent, our advice is to let yourself be helped. The salespeople aren't trying to impose anything on you; quite to the contrary, they can be very involved and helpful. Let yourself feel like royalty, being pampered as you shop.

On the other hand, if you only want to browse, be firm about refusing help; the following dialogue shows you an example of just such a situation.

Talkin' the Talk

Here's how to tell a salesperson that you want just to browse around the store.

Salesperson: **¿Busca algo en especial?**
bvoos-kah ahl-goh ehn ehs-peh-seeahl
Looking for something special?

Silvia: **Quiero mirar, no más.**
keeeeh-roh mee-rahr noh mahs
I just want to look.

Salesperson: **Me llama cuando me necesita.**
meh yah-mah kooahn-doh meh neh-seh-see-tah
Call me when you need me.

Silvia: **Sí, le voy a llamar, gracias.**
see leh bvohy ah yah-mahr grah-seeahs
Yes, I'll call you, thank you.

Sampling the Goods with Probar (to Try)

The verb **probar** (proh-bvahr) (*to try, to try on,* or *to taste*) is one that you may use quite a lot when shopping.

Probar's root changes from **pro-** (proh) to **prue-** (prooeh) in some tenses, so it's an irregular verb. (For more about spelling-changing verbs, see Book II, Chapter 3 and Appendix A.) Here is the conjugation:

Conjugation	Pronunciation
yo pruebo	yoh prooeh-bvoh
tú pruebas	too prooeh-bvahs
él, ella, ello, uno, usted prueba	ehl eh-yah eh-yoh oo-noh oos-tehd prooeh-bvah
nosotros probamos	noh-soh-trohs proh-bvah-mohs
vosotros probáis	bvoh-soh-trohs proh-bvahees
ellos, ellas, ustedes prueban	eh-yohs eh-yahs oos-teh-dehs prooeh-bvahn

After you know how to use **probar**, you can ask to try on anything before you buy it, which is important to do when shopping in Latin America. Different people have different shapes, and some cuts may look different on Latinos than on you.

The following dialogue shows you how to find the store department you need.

Talkin' the Talk

You want the section of the store with the goods you are looking for. Here's how you can ask where it is:

Silvia:	**¿Dónde están los vestidos de señora?** *dohn*-deh ehs-*tahn* lohs bvehs-*tee*-dohs deh seh-*nyoh*-rah *Where are the ladies' clothes?*
Salesperson:	**En el quinto piso.** ehn ehl *keen*-toh *pee*-soh *On the fifth floor.*
Silvia:	**¿Dónde está la ropa de hombre?** *dohn*-deh ehs-*tah* lah *roh*-pah deh *ohm*-bvreh *Where are the men's clothes?*
Salesperson:	**En el cuarto piso.** ehn ehl koo*ahr*-toh *pee*-soh *On the fourth floor.*
Silvia:	**¿Dónde encuentro artículos de tocador?** *dohn*-deh ehn-koo*ehn*-troh ahr-*tee*-koo-lohs deh toh-kah-*dohr* *Where do I find toiletries?*
Salesperson:	**Al fondo, a la izquierda.** ahl *fohn*-doh ah lah ees-kee*ehr*-dah *At the back, to the left.*
Silvia:	**Busco la sección de ropa blanca.** *bvoos*-koh lah sehk-see*ohn* deh *roh*-pah *bvlahn*-kah *I'm looking for sheets and towels.*
Salesperson:	**Un piso más arriba.** oon *pee*-soh mahs ah-*rree*-bvah *One floor up.*

Silvia:	**¿Venden electrodomésticos?**
	bvehn-dehn eehl-*ehk*-troh-doh-*mehs*-tee-kohs
	Do you sell appliances?

Salesperson:	**Sí, en el último piso.**
	see ehn ehl *ool*-tee-moh *pee*-soh
	Yes, on the top floor.

Before heading out to the market, brush up on your numbers and colors, as covered in Book I, Chapter 2.

The following dialogue demonstrates how to ask a salesperson for help.

Talkin' the Talk

Silvia accidentally split her skirt bending down to pick up some boxes at work. She needs a new one quick — one with pockets to hold the art supplies she needs as a graphic designer. She asks a salesperson for help:

Silvia:	**¿Me ayuda por favor?**
	meh ah-*yoo*-dah porh fah-*bvohr*
	Will you help me, please?

	Busco una falda con bolsillos.
	bvoos-koh oo-nah *fahl*-dah kohn bvohl-*see*-yohs
	I'm looking for a skirt with pockets.

Salesperson:	**¿Qué talla tiene?**
	keh *tah*-yah tee*eh*-neh
	What's your size?

Silvia:	**Talla doce americana.**
	tah-yah *doh*-seh ah-meh-ree-*kah*-nah
	Size twelve, American.

Salesperson:	**¿Me permite medirla, para estar seguras?**
	meh pehr-*mee*-teh meh-*deer*-lah *pah*-rah ehs-*tahr* seh-*goo*-rahs
	May I take your measurements to be sure?

	Ah, su talla es treinta y ocho.
	ah soo *tah*-yah ehs *treh*een-tah ee *oh*-choh
	Ah, your size is 38.

¿Qué color busca?
keh koh-*lohr bvoos*-kah
What color are you looking for?

Silvia: **Rojo.**
roh-Hoh
Red.

Salesperson: **¿La quiere con flores?**
lah keee*eh*-reh kohn *floh*-rehs
Do you want it with flowers?

Silvia: **No, lisa, por favor.**
noh *lee*-sah pohr fah-*bvohr*
No, plain, please.

Shopping for clothes

A word of wisdom: Men's shirts seem to come in the same sizes in Spanish-speaking countries as they do in the United States and Canada. But just in case, checking the fit is a good idea.

In some areas, people are smaller and sizes vary; the medium there may be what you consider a small. Your best bet is to try on the shirt before you leave the store. The following dialogue presents a sample fitting-room exchange.

Talkin' the Talk

Here's how you may ask to try on pants:

Claudio: **¿Puedo probarme este pantalón?**
pooe*eh*-doh proh-*bvahr*-meh *ehs*-teh pahn-tah-*lohn*
May I try on these trousers?

Salesperson: **Cómo no, por aquí.**
koh-moh no pohr ah-*kee*
Of course, this way.

Claudio: **Me queda grande.**
meh *keh*-dah *grahn*-deh
They are too big. (Literally: It fits me large.)

Salesperson:	**Le busco otro.** leh *bvoos*-koh *oh*-troh *I'll find you another.*
Claudio:	**Este aprieta aquí.** *ehs*-teh ah-pree*eh*-tah ah-*kee* *This one is tight here.*
Salesperson:	**A ver este.** ah bvehr *ehs*-teh *Let's see this one.*
Claudio:	**¿Lo tiene en verde?** loh tee*eh*-neh ehn *bvehr*-deh *Do you have it in green?*
Salesperson:	**Este, ¿a ver?** *ehs*-teh ah bvehr *This one, let's see?*
Claudio:	**Queda muy bien.** *keh*-dah mooy bvee*ehn* *It fits very well.*

Discussing fibers and fabrics

When shopping, you may notice that poorer regions favor fabrics made with artificial fibers and that the prices for these fabrics aren't lower than those of natural fibers. These terms help you ask about the fibers (or fabrics) of which the garments are made:

- ✔ **pura** (*poo*-rah) (*pure*)
- ✔ **la lana** (lah *lah*-nah) (*the wool*)
- ✔ **el algodón** (ehl ahl-goh-*dohn)* (*the cotton*)
- ✔ **la fibra** (lah *fee*-bvrah) (*the fiber*)
- ✔ **por ciento** (pohr see*eh*-toh) (*percent; percentage*)

And here are typical questions you may ask about fabrics:

- ✔ **¿Este pantalón es de pura lana?** (*ehs*-teh pahn-tah-*lohn* ehs de *poo*-rah *lah*-nah) (*Are these pants made of pure wool?*)

  No, es de lana con nylon. (noh ehs deh *lah*-nah kohn *nahee*-lohn) (*No, they are made of wool and nylon.*)

✔ **¿La camisa es de puro algodón?** (lah kah-*mee*-sah ehs deh *poo*-roh ahl-goh-*dohn*) (*Is the shirt made of pure cotton?*)

   No, es de algodón con poliéster. (noh, ehs deh ahl-goh-*dohn* kohn poh-lee*ehs*-tehr) (*No, it's made of cotton and polyester.*)

✔ **¿Cuánto algodón tiene esta tela?** (koo*ahn*-toh ahl-goh-*dohn* tee*eh*-neh *ehs*-tah *teh*-lah?) (*How much cotton is there in this fabric?*)

   Tiene cuarenta por ciento. (tee*eh*-neh koo*ah*-*rehn*-tah pohr see*ehn*-toh) (*It has forty percent.*)

✔ **Busco ropa de fibras naturales.** (*bvoos*-koh *roh*-pah deh *fee*-bvrahs nah-too-*rah*-lehs) (*I'm looking for natural fiber clothes.*)

   También tenemos. (tahm-bvee*ehn* teh-*neh*-mohs) (*We have them also.*)

Take That! The Verb Llevar

Whenever you go shopping, be sure to take along the verb **llevar**.

In Spanish *to wear* and *to take with you* are the same verb — **llevar** (yeh-*bvahr*). Good news! This is a regular verb of the group ending in **-ar** (ahr); its root is **llev-** (yehbv-).

Conjugation	*Pronunciation*
yo llevo	yoh *yeh*-bvoh
tú llevas	too *yeh*-bvahs
él, ella, uno, usted lleva	ehl *eh*-yah oo-noh oos-*tehd yeh*-bvah
nosotros llevamos	noh-*soh*-trohs yeh-*bvah*-mohs
vosotros lleváis	bvoh-*soh*-trohs yeh-*bva*ees
ellos, ellas, ustedes llevan	*eh*-yohs *eh*-yahs oos-*teh*-dehs *yeh*-bvahn

Count on these examples to help you keep track of this dressing and tracking verb:

✔ **Me llevo esta camisa.** (meh *yeh*-bvoh *ehs*-tah kah-*mee*-sah) (*I'll take this shirt.*)

✔ **El vestido que llevas es bellísimo.** (ehl bvehs-*tee*-doh keh *yeh*-bvahs ehs bveh-*yee*-see-moh) (*The dress you have on is very beautiful.*)

✔ **Llevo un regalo para ti.** (*yeh*-bvoh ooh reh-*gah*-loh *pah*-rah tee) (*I'm taking a present for you.*)

- **Los llevo a la escuela todos los días.** (lohs *yeh*-broh ah lah ehs-koo*eh*-lah *toh*-dohs lohs *dee*-ahs) (*I take them to school every day.*)

- **Siempre llevo un uniforme en mi trabajo.** (see*ehm*-preh yeh-bvoh oon oo-nee-fohr-meh ehn mee trah-*bvah*-Hoh) (*I always wear a uniform at my job.*)

- **La llevo.** (lah *yeh*-bvoh) (*I'll take it.*)

Another way to say to wear is **vestir** (bvehs-*teer*) (*to dress*), which comes from **vestido** (bves-*tee*-doh) (*dress*).

In the following dialogue, a customer tries on a garment with help from a salesperson.

Talkin' the Talk

The skirt is the right color, so Silvia wants to try it on to be on the safe side before she makes a final decision.

Salesperson: **Pase al probador, por favor.**
pah-seh ahl proh-bvah-*dohr* pohr fah-*bvohr*
Please go into the fitting room.

Silvia: **¿Dónde está?**
dohn-deh ehs-*tah*
Where is it?

Salesperson: **Por aquí.**
pohr ah-*kee*
This way.

¿Le quedó bien?
leh keh-*doh* bvee*ehn*
Did it fit?

Silvia: **No, está muy apretada.**
noh ehs-*tah* mooy ah-preh-*tah*-dah
No, it's very tight.

¿Puede traer una de talla más grande?
poo*eh*-deh trah-*ehr* oo-nah *tah*-yah mahs *grahn*-deh
Can you bring a larger size?

Comparing Products: Good, Better, Best

When you compare one thing to another, you talk in comparatives and super-latives. In Spanish, most of the time you use the word **más** (mahs) (*more*) for comparisons and **el más** (ehl mahs), which literally means *the most*, for superlatives. An example is the word **grande** (*grahn*-deh), which means *large* in English. **Más grande** (mahs *grahn*-deh) means *larger*, and **el más grande** (ehl mahs *grahn*-deh) means *the largest*.

In English, you usually change the word's ending; in Spanish, you just add **más** or **el más**. English has a similar system of adding comparatives and superla-tives for longer words, such as expensive, where the comparative adds *more* before expensive, and the superlative adds *most*. For more about forming com-parisons, check out Book II, Chapter 7.

Here are some examples of Spanish comparatives and superlatives:

- **grande** (*grahn*-deh) (*big; large*)
  más grande (mahs *grahn*-deh) (*bigger; larger*)
  el más grande (ehl mahs *grahn*-deh) (*biggest; largest*)

- **pequeño** (peh-*keh*-nyoh) (*small*)
  más pequeño (mahs peh-*keh*-nyoh) (*smaller*)
  el más pequeño (ehl mahs peh-*keh*-nyoh) (*smallest*)

- **chico** (*chee*-koh) (*small; short; young*)
  más chico (mahs *chee*-koh) (*smaller; shorter; younger*)
  el más chico (ehl mahs *chee*-koh) (*smallest; shortest, youngest*)

- **apretado** (ah-preh-*tah*-doh) (*tight*)
  más apretado (mahs ah-preh-*tah*-doh) (*tighter*)
  el más apretado (ehl mahs ah-preh-*tah*-doh) (*tightest*)

- **suelto** (soo*ehl*-toh) (*loose*)
  más suelto (mahs soo*ehl*-toh) (*looser*)
  el más suelto (ehl mahs soo*ehl*-toh) (*loosest*)

- **caro** (*kah*-roh) (*expensive*)
  más caro (mahs *kah*-roh) (*more expensive*)
  el más caro (ehl mahs *kah*-roh) (*most expensive*)

- **barato** (bvah-*rah*-toh) (*cheap*)
  más barato (mahs bvah-*rah*-toh) (*cheaper*)
  el más barato (ehl mahs bvah-*rah*-toh) (*cheapest*)

Just as in English, a few exceptions exist, in which the comparative form doesn't require the word **más**, such as the following examples. Notice that the English translations are also exceptions to the English rules for forming comparatives and superlatives.

- ✔ **bueno** (bvoo*eh*-noh) (*good*)
  mejor (meh-*Hohr*) (*better*)
  el mejor (ehl meh-*Hohr*) (*best*)

- ✔ **malo** (*mah*-loh) (*bad*)
  peor (peh-*ohr*) (*worse*)
  el peor (ehl peh-*ohr*) (*worst*)

Adding Even More Emphasis

Spanish speakers love to exaggerate. What may seem to non-Spanish speakers to be an excessive way to talk simply adds a bit more emphasis in the Spanish-speaking mind.

Exaggeration is something you see everywhere, even in classical Spanish poetry. For example, **Francisco de Quevedo y Villegas** (frahn-*sees*-koh deh keh-*bveh*-doh ee bvee-*yeh*-gahs), the Spanish poet of the Golden Century (who lived from 1580 to 1645), says in his poem "**A una nariz**" (ah *oo*-nah nah-*rees*) (*to a nose*) to a person with a very large one:

> "**muchísima nariz**" (moo-*chee*-see-mah nah-*rees*) (*a whole lotta nose*)

So in Spanish, you can not only compare things but also express an exaggerated state of things.

To say that something is exaggeratedly this or that, you add **-ísimo** (*ee*-see-moh) or **-ísima** (*ee*-see-mah) to an adjective or an adverb. For example, to say that something *good*, **bueno** (bvoo*eh*-noh), is exaggeratedly so, you say **buenísimo** (bvoo*eh*-*nee*-see-moh) (*exceptionally good*).

Here are some examples:

- ✔ **La película es buenísima.** (lah peh-*lee*-koo-lah ehs bvoo*eh*-*nee*-see-mah) (*The film is exceptionally good.*)

- ✔ **La ciudad es grandísima.** (lah seeoo-*dahd* ehs grahn-*dee*-see-mah) (*The city is huge.*)

- ✔ **Los perros son bravísimos.** (los *peh*-rrohs sohn bvrah-*bvee*-see-mohs) (*The dogs are extremely fierce.*)

- ✔ **El hotel es malísimo.** (ehl oh-*tehl* ehs mah-*lee*-see-moh) (*The hotel is really bad.*)

✔ **El postre está dulcísimo.** (ehl *pohs*-treh ehs-*tah* dool-*see*-see-moh) (*The dessert is sickeningly sweet.*)

✔ **Los colores son vivísimos.** (losh koh-*loh*-rehs sohn bvee-*bvee*-see-mohs) (*The colors are exceedingly bright.*)

✔ **El bus andaba lentísimo.** (ehl bvoos ahn-*dah*-bvah lehn-*tee*-see-moh) (*The bus advanced extremely slowly.*)

✔ **La tienda cobraba carísimo.** (lah tee*ehn*-dah koh-*bvrah*-bvah kah-*ree*-see-moh) (*The shop was exorbitantly expensive.*)

Shopping in Specialty Stores

You may want to shop in the specialized stores or galleries generally located on the more elegant boulevards, streets, and avenues in all Latin American countries. Seeking the finest artistic, cultural, or fashion items may include buying original art or silver in **Lima, Peru** (*lee*-mah peh-*roo*) and Mexico City, or shopping for paintings, sculpture, fine shoes, leather objects, and exquisite collectibles in **Buenos Aires, Argentina** (bvoo*eh*-nohs *ah*ee-rehs ahr-Hehn-*tee*-nah).

Table 6-2 lists the types of specialty items you may be shopping for.

Table 6-2	Specialty Items	
Spanish	*Pronunciation*	*English*
el alfiler	ehl ahl-fee-*lehr*	the pin
los aretes	lohs ah-*reh*-tehs	the earrings
el broche	ehl *broh*-cheh	the brooch
el colgante	ehl kohl-*gahn*-teh	the pendant
el collar	ehl koh-*yahr*	the necklace
los diamantes	lohs dee-ah-*mahn*-tehs	the diamonds
la escultura	lah ehs-kool-*too*-rah	the sculpture
los gemelos	lohs heh-*meh*-lohs	the cuff links
el grabado	ehl grah-*bvah*-doh	the etching
los huaraches	lohs oo*ah*-rah-chehs	the leather sandals
el huipil	ehl oo*ee*-peel	the (traditional) sleeve-less blouse or dress
la joyaría de oro	lah Hoh-yah-*ree*-ah deh *oh*-roh	the gold jewelry

(continued)

Table 6-2 *(continued)*

Spanish	Pronunciation	English
la joyaría de plata	lah Hoh-yah-*ree*-ah deh *plah*-tah	the silver jewelry
las mascaras	lahs *mahs*-kah-rahs	the masks
la perla	lah *pehr*-lah	the pearl
la pintura	lah peen-*too*-rah	the painting
la pulsera	lah pool-*seh*-rah	the bracelet
el reloj	ehl reh-*loh*	the watch

You can use these phrases when shopping at a specialized store or gallery:

- **Busco grabados de Rufino Tamayo.** (*bvoos*-koh grah-*bvah*-dohs deh roo-*fee*-noh tah-*mah*-yoh) (*I'm looking for etchings by Rufino Tamayo.*)

- **¿Tiene broches de plata?** (tee*eh*-neh *bvroh*-chehs deh *plah*-tah) (*Do you have silver brooches?*)

- **¿Cuánto cuesta el collar que tiene en la ventana?** (koo*ahn*-toh koo*ehs*-tah ehl koh-*yahr* keh tee*eh*-neh ehn la bvehn-*tah*-nah) (*How much is the necklace you have in the window?*)

- **¿Y la pintura?** (ee lah peen-*too*-rah) (*And the painting?*)

- **¿Vende perlas del sur de Chile?** (*bvehn*-deh *pehr*-lahs dehl soor deh *chee*-leh) (*Do you sell pearls from the south of Chile?*)

- **¿De quién es la escultura en la vitrina?** (deh kee*ehn* ehs lah ehs-kool-*too*-rah ehn lah bvee-*tree*-nah) (*By whom is the sculpture in the display case?*)

- **¿Lo embalamos y mandamos a su domicilio?** (loh ehm-bvah-*lah*-mohs ee mahn-*dah*-mohs a soo doh-mee-*see*-leeoh) (*Shall we pack it and send it to your address?*)

Sticking with Traditional Markets

You can find typical clothes and objects in the traditional markets, many of which are open every day and all year round, where bargaining and haggling are the norm. In these markets, you probably won't find any labels stating the prices, because the prices aren't really fixed. (That's what the bargaining and haggling are all about.)

Sampling typical market items

As you travel around the marketplaces of Latin America, you can end up with treasures such as these:

✔ **Un bol de madera tropical de Asunción, Paraguay** (oon bvohl deh mah-*deh*-rah troh-pee-*kahl* deh ah-soon-see*ohn* pah-rah-goo*ahy*) (*A bowl made from tropical wood, from Asunción, Paraguay*)

✔ **Una alfombra de lana de Otavalo, Ecuador** (*oo*-nah ahl-*fohm*-bvrah deh *lah*-nah deh oh-tah-*bvah*-loh eh-kooah-*dohr*) (*A rug made of wool, from Otavalo, Ecuador*)

✔ **Una tabla con jeroglíficos de la Isla de Pascua, Chile** (*oo*-nah *tah*-bvlah kohn Heh-roh-*glee*-fee-kohs deh lah *ees*-lah deh *pahs*-kooah *chee*-leh) (*A wooden board covered with hieroglyphs, from Easter Island, Chile*)

✔ **Una chaqueta hecha de tela de lana tejida a mano y bordada con seda, de Antigua, Guatemala** (*oo*-nah chah-*keh*-tah *eh*-chah deh *teh*-lah deh *lah*-nah teh-*Hee*-dah ah *mah*-noh ee bvohr-*dah*-dah kohn *seh*-dah deh ahn-*tee*-gooah gooah-teh-*mah*-lah) (*A jacket made of handwoven wool embroidered in silk, from Antigua, Guatemala*)

In the markets, you find color in the merchandise, in the conversation, in the shopping style. You also find handcrafted goods, made in the manner of preindustrial times, where the human hand has left its mark unmatched in feeling by machine production. You find the informality that comes from the precariousness of open markets and which also makes for displays of the goods in original ways — without display cases or marketing tricks.

Like the bazaars of *A Thousand and One Nights*, the markets of **Otavalo** (oh-tah-*bvah*-loh), **Ecuador; Lima** (*lee*-mah), **Perú; Antigua** (ahn-*tee*-gooah) in **Guatemala;** or **Tlacolula** (tlah-koh-*loo*-lah) in the State of **Oaxaca** (oh-ah-*Hah*-kah) in Mexico, are really magical, fun places that put you in touch with life as it used to be and still is for many people in Latin America.

Haggling for a better deal

If you shop in traditional markets, getting there early is a good idea. Many merchants feel that they must make a first sale to kick off their day. If you find yourself in such a situation, you may notice that the merchant doesn't want you to leave without buying something and is therefore more willing to reduce the price to make a sale, and you can end up with a bargain.

CULTURAL WISDOM

Advice for the bargainer

In a traditional market or on the streets, when you're offered something you're interested in and price is mentioned, offer half. Of course, this is really outrageous and the merchant reacts to that price with outrage. And thus a social game begins.

So after offering half, you get an answer from the merchant stating a sum slightly less than what was first asked for. At this point you know the game is on. So you offer a bit more than your first amount. And the game goes on until you feel or believe that the merchant will go no further and the price is what you can afford.

Bargaining like this is a very satisfying activity for the seller and can also be so for the buyer. You establish a certain relationship while you bargain that shows your determination and that of the seller in addition to your ability to follow a certain rhythm in the operation.

The following phrases help you when you need to haggle in the market place:

- **¿Cuánto cuesta?** (koo*ahn*-toh koo*ehs*-tah) (*How much is it?*)
- **¿Cuánto vale?** (koo*ahn*-toh *bvah*-leh) (*How much is it worth?*)
- **¿A cuánto?** (ah koo*ahn*-toh) (*How much?*)
- **Es barato.** (ehs bvah-*rah*-toh) (*It's cheap/inexpensive.*)
- **Es caro.** (ehs *kah*-roh) (*It's expensive.*)

Use these phrases to provide emphasis. You won't be using these all the time, especially the second and third ones, yet they are fun to use and help you express a certain level of emotion:

- **¡Una ganga!** (*oo*-nah *gahn*-gah) (*A bargain!*)
- **¡Un robo!** (oon *roh*-bvoh) (*A rip-off!*)
- **¡Un asalto!** (oon ah-*sahl*-toh) (*An insult!*)

The following dialogue shows you haggling in action.

Talkin' the Talk

Bargaining is sometimes a little difficult in a department store, but in traditional market places in Latin America, it is part of the deal. Listen to how Sylvia haggles over a nice rug that she's spotted at an outdoor market.

Sylvia: **Este tapete, ¿cuánto cuesta?**
ehs-teh tah-*peh*-teh koo*ahn*-toh koo*ehs*-tah
How much is this rug?

Merchant: **Quinientos pesos.**
kee-nee*ehn*-tohs *peh*-sohs
500 pesos.

Sylvia: **¿Tiene otros más baratos?**
tee*eh*-neh *oh*-trohs mahs bvah-*rah*-tohs
Do you have cheaper ones?

Merchant: **Tengo este, más pequeño.**
tehn-goh *ehs*-teh mahs peh-*keh*-nyoh
I have this smaller one.

Sylvia: **No me gusta el dibujo.**
noh meh *goos*-tah ehl dee-*bvoo*-Hoh
I don't like the pattern.

Merchant: **Este en blanco y negro, a trescientos.**
ehs-teh ehn *bvlahn*-koh ee *neh*-groh ah
trehs-see*ehn*-tohs
This black and white one, for 300.

Sylvia: **Me gusta. ¿A doscientos?**
meh *goos*-tah ah dohs-see*ehn*-tohs
I like it. 200?

Merchant: **No puedo. Doscientos cincuenta. Último precio.**
noh *pooeh*-doh dohs-see*ehn*-tohs seen-koo*ehn*-tah
ool-tee-moh *preh*-seeoh
I can't. 250. Last price.

Sylvia: **Bueno, me lo llevo.**
bvoo*eh*-noh meh loh *yeh*-bvoh
Good. I'll take it.

Shopping for copper, glass, clay, and wood goods

Latin American artisans are well known for their fine work in copper, glass, wood, textiles, and clay, and items made of these substances are highly sought after by collectors and lovers of their typical beauty. Here's some vocabulary worth knowing:

✔ **el cobre** (ehl *koh*-bvreh) (*the copper*)

✔ **el vidrio** (ehl *bvee*-dreeoh) (*the glass*)

✔ **soplar** (soh-*plahr*) (*to blow*)

✔ **hecho a mano** (*eh*-choh ah *mah*-noh) (*handmade*)

✔ **la cerámica** (lah seh-rah-mee-kah) (*the ceramic*)

Copper is beautiful and lasting but heavy to carry. However, you can't resist these beautiful pieces . . . or the delicate glass . . . or the colorful but breakable clay pot. You see wooden spoons, and these intricately painted darling things aren't as fragile as glass or clay, nor as heavy as the copper. What to buy?

These phrases can help you when you shop for these specialty items:

✔ **¿Dónde venden objetos de cobre?** (*dohn*-deh *bvehn*-dehn ohbv-*Heh*-tohs deh *koh*-bvreh) (*Where do they sell copper objects?*)

✔ **Busco objetos de vidrio.** (*bvoos*-koh ohbv-*Heh*-tohs deh *bvee*-dreeoh) (*I'm looking for glass objects.*)

✔ **Allí hay cerámica hecha a mano.** (ah-*yee* ahy seh-*rah*-mee-kah *eh*-chah ah *mah*-noh) (*There are some handmade ceramics.*)

✔ **Estas ollas de barro sirven para cocinar.** (*ehs*-tahs oh-yahs deh *bvah*-rroh *seer*-bvehn *pah*-rah koh-see-*nahr*) (*These clay pots are suitable for cooking.*)

Shopping for embroidered clothes

Who has time to embroider any more? Well, in Latin America, you can find some wonders of embroidery skill. Here are some phrases that can help you make a good selection:

✔ **¡Qué bello este bordado!** (keh *bveh*-yoh *ehs*-teh bvohr-*dah*-doh) (*What beautiful embroidery!*)

✔ **¿Tiene blusitas para niña?** (tee*eh*-neh bloo-*see*-tahs *pah*-rah *nee*-nyah) (*Do you have little blouses for a girl?*)

✔ **¿Tiene vestidos para mujer?** (tee*eh*-neh bvehs-*tee*-dohs *pah*-rah moo-*Hehr*) (*Do you have ladies' dresses?*)

Shopping for baskets

Actually, you can pack everything you buy in one of those large, colorful baskets and then use them at home for storage and as decorative accents. Because baskets come in so many materials, shapes, and sizes and are generally quite long lasting, they make a beautiful addition to any home. The following sentences help you purchase baskets:

✔ **Estos son canastos de mimbre.** (*ehs*-tohs sohn kah-*nahs*-tohs deh *meem*-bvreh) (*These are wicker baskets.*)

✔ **¿Tiene canastos para la ropa?** (tee*eh*-neh kah-*nahs*-tohs *pah*-rah lah *roh*-pah) (*Do you have laundry baskets?*)

✔ **Estos canastos son de totora.** (*ehs*-tohs kah-*nahs*-tohs sohn de toh-*toh*-rah) (*These baskets are made from a reed [found in the Andean Region].*)

✔ **Estos canastos son de totomoztle.** (*ehs*-tohs kah-*nahs*-tohs sohn deh toh-toh-*mohs*-tleh) (*These baskets are made from corn leaves. [Mexico]*)

Chapter 7

Conversing Over the Phone

In This Chapter

⬤ Describing common phone activities

⬤ Answering the phone and delivering your greeting

⬤ Encouraging fast talkers to slow down and spell it out

⬤ Conjugating common phone-related verbs

*T*alking on the phone, arranging things over the phone, and even having social lives on the phone are activities that people in the United States and Canada often take for granted.

In the United States and Canada, you can get and place phone calls quite easily, with practically no delay. This isn't the case everywhere in Latin America. In larger cities, a good deal of business is done on the phone, and people use it frequently. But in smaller places, where getting a phone can take years and cost heaps of money, people aren't used to relying on them. In those places, you use the phone mostly to set up appointments, and then you conduct your business in person.

If you travel to a Latin American country, you may notice that some places still primarily have rotary dial phones instead of touch tone ones. Nevertheless, talking on the phone hasn't changed much in the last half century, and this chapter gives you a pretty accurate idea of what you may say and hear no matter what kind of phone you use.

Placing a Call

Before you even think about talking on the phone in Spanish, you need to know how to talk about placing a phone call.

These terms are relevant when using the phone:

⬤ **llamar** (yah-*mahr*) (*to call*)

⬤ **marcar** (mahr-*kahr*) (*to dial*)

- ✔ **colgar** (kohl-*gahr*) (*to hang up*)

- ✔ **responder** (rehs-pohn-*dehr*) (*to answer*)

- ✔ **hablar** (ah-*bvlahr*) (*to talk*)

- ✔ **escuchar** (ehs-koo-*chahr*) (*to listen to; to hear*)

- ✔ **preguntar** (preh-goon-*tahr*) (*to ask [a question]*)

- ✔ **el número** (ehl *noo*-meh-roh) (*the number*)

- ✔ **la línea** (lah *lee*-neh-ah) (*the line*)

- ✔ **libre** (*lee*-bvreh) (*free*)

- ✔ **ocupada** (oh-koo-*pah*-dah) (*busy [as in "the line is busy"]*)

The following phone use phrases can come in handy when you need to place a call:

- ✔ **llamar por teléfono** (yah-*mahr* pohr teh-*leh*-foh-noh) (*make a phone call*)

- ✔ **marcar el número** (mahr-*kahr* ehl *noo*-meh-roh) (*dial/punch in the number*)

- ✔ **colgar** (kohl-*gahr*) (*hang up*)

- ✔ **la línea está libre** (lah *lee*-nehah ehs-*tah lee*-bvreh) (*The line is open.*)

- ✔ **la línea está ocupada** (lah *lee*-neh-ah ehs-*tah* oh-koo-*pah*-dah) (*The line is busy.*)

- ✔ **el teléfono no responde** (ehl teh-*leh*-foh-noh noh rehs-*pohn*-deh) (*There's no answer.*)

Delivering an Effective Opening Line

So you punch in or dial a phone number — now what? Now, the person you called needs to answer the phone and deliver a greeting. Following are typical greetings you're likely to hear depending on the country. Respond in kind before introducing yourself and explaining why you called:

- ✔ Argentineans say **¡Holá!** (oh-*lah*).

- ✔ Chileans say **¡Aló!** (ah-*loh*).

- ✔ Mexicans say **¡Bueno!** (bvoo*eh*-noh).

- ✔ In Spain, you hear **¡Sí!**

These words all mean *Hello!* Most Spanish-speaking countries use **aló**, in the Chilean way.

Slowing Down and Spelling It Out

When you're conversing with a Spanish-speaker over the phone, you need to make adjustments not only for the differences in language but also for the *way* you speak. You don't see the person and she can't see you, so you don't get the gist of the communication from body language or facial expressions.

In the following sections, we show you how to slow down and spell out certain words or names to avoid confusion.

Slowing down fast talkers

When learning a language, you may find that some people you talk to speak too quickly for you. You can't make out the words; everything seems mushy, like porridge. On the phone, fast talking is even more of a problem.

Don't be too hard on yourself. Gently request that the other person repeat the sentence more clearly. You're not being rude in the least; you simply didn't get the whole message, so you're asking for a repeat. No harm there.

The person you're talking to may have similar difficulties, even if the language is his own, so please be just as patient with him as you'd like him to be with you. The following dialogue gives you some handy phrases you can use when the conversation turns to porridge.

Talkin' the Talk

Clarisa tries to contact Juanita.

Clarisa:	**¡Bueno! ¿Hablo con Juanita?** bvoo*eh*-noh *ah*-bvloh kohn Hooah-*nee*-tah *Hello! Am I speaking to Juanita?*
Voice on other side:	**Mzfg utrc eeruet.** *(Not intelligible.)*
Clarisa:	**Perdone, no le escucho.** pehr-*doh*-neh noh leh ehs-*koo*-choh *Excuse me, I can't hear you.*
Voice on other side:	**N st mmet o st.** *(Not intelligible.)*

Clarisa:	**Está muy mala la línea, ¿lo repita por favor?**
	ehs-*tah* mooy *mah*-lah lah *lee*-neh-ah loh reh-*pee*-tah pohr fah-*bvohr*
	The line is very bad, will you please repeat what you said?
Voice on other side:	**En este momento no está.**
	ehn *ehs*-teh moh-*mehn*-toh noh ehs-*tah*
	She's not here at the moment.
Clarisa:	**Llamo más tarde, gracias.**
	yah-moh mahs *tahr*-deh *grah*-seeahs
	I'll call later, thanks.

The word **tarde** (tahr-deh), without the article **la**, means (*late*). But when you hear the article **la** (*the*) in front of it, as in **la tarde**, you know that the speaker is talking about *the afternoon*.

Spelling it out for clarity's sake

Because English spelling is erratic, you may automatically spell out your name or other information you give out. Spanish has more regular spelling rules, however, so generally no one asks to have a Spanish name like Rodríguez spelled out — the spelling is obvious. As a result, many Spanish speakers aren't used to spelling out information or taking down information that is being spelled out. Therefore, if asked to spell your name, try to do so veeeery slooowly so that people can absorb the unusual situation.

The following dialogue lets you practice spelling out names. Book I, Chapter 1 has the complete Spanish alphabet, so head that way if you need it. (And for numbers, days, hours, months, and other date and calendar words, refer to Book I, Chapter 2).

Talkin' the Talk

Sheryl wants to leave a message and spells out her name to avoid miscommunication.

Sheryl Lyons:	**Quisiera dejar un mensaje.**
	kee-seeeh-rah deh-*Hahr* oon mehn-*sah*-Heh
	I'd like to leave a message.

**El mensaje es que la señora Lyons va a llegar hoy a
las cinco de la tarde.**
ehl mehn-*sah*-Heh ehs keh lah seh-*nyoh*-rah *lee*-ohns
bvah ah yeh-*gahr* ohy ah lahs *seen*-koh deh lah
tahr-deh
*The message is that Mrs. Lyons will arrive today at
five in the afternoon.*

Voice: **¿Me puede repetir su apellido, por favor?**
meh poo*eh*-deh reh-peh-*teer* soo ah-peh-*yee*-doh
pohr fah-*bvohr*
Can you repeat your last name, please?

Sheryl Lyons: **Me llamo Lyons.**
meh *yah*-moh *lee*-ohns
My name is Lyons.

Voice: **¿Cómo se escribe?**
koh-moh seh ehs-*kree*-bveh
How do you spell it?

Sheryl Lyons: **Ele, i griega, o, ene, ese.**
eh-leh ee gre*ceh*-gah oh *eh*-neh *eh*-seh
L-Y-O-N-S.

Voice: **Ah, Lyons. Gracias. ¿Cómo es su nombre?**
ah *lee*-ohns *grah*-seeahs *koh*-moh ehs soo
nohm-bvreh
Ah, Lyons, thank you. What's your first name?

Sheryl Lyons: **Es Sheryl. Ese, hache, e, ere, i griega, ele.**
ehs *sheh*-reel *eh*-seh *ah*-cheh eh *eh*-reh ee gree*eh*-gah
eh-leh
It's Sheryl. S-H-E-R-Y-L.

Voice: **Ah, Sheryl, gracias. Diré que llamó la señora Sheryl
Lyons, y que va a llegar a las cinco de la tarde.**
ah *sheh*-reel *grah*-seeahs dee-*reh* keh yah-*moh* lah
seh-*nyoh*-rah *sheh*-reel *lee*-ohns ee keh bvah a yeh-
gahr ah lahs *seen*-koh deh lah *tahr*-deh
*Ah, Sheryl, thanks. I'll say Mrs. Sheryl Lyons phoned,
and that she'll arrive at 5 p.m.*

In some countries, calling long-distance can cost twice as much as the same
call in the United States or Canada. If you travel in Spanish-speaking America,
remember that collect calls can save you quite a bit of money. The following
dialogue shows you how.

Talkin' the Talk

 Lucy wants to make a collect call to her parents because she's short on change.

Lucy: **¡Bueno!, operadora, quisiera hacer una llamada por cobrar.**
bvoo*eh*-noh oh-peh-rah-*doh*-rah kee-see*eh*-rah *ah*-sehr oo-nah yah-*mah*-dah pohr koh-*bvrahr*.
Hello, operator, I'd like to make a collect call.

Operator: **¿A qué número?**
ah keh *noo*-meh-roh
To what number?

Lucy: **Al 4372-2351.**
ahl koo*ah*-troh trehs see*eh*-teh dohs dohs trehs *seen*-koh oo-noh
To 4372-2351.

Operator: **¿Y el código del área?**
ee ehl *koh*-dee-goh dehl *ah*-reh-ah
And the area code?

Lucy: **El 11.**
ehl *ohn*-seh
11.

Operator: **¿Cómo se llama usted?**
koh-moh seh *yah*-mah oos-*tehd*
What's your name?

Lucy: **Lucy Sánchez.**
Lucy Sánchez.

Operator: **Muy bien, un momento . . . .**
mooy bvee*ehn* oon moh-*mehn*-toh
Very well, one moment . . . .

La línea no responde. Llame más tarde, por favor.
lah *lee*-neh-ah noh rehs-*pohn*-deh *yah*-meh mahs *tahr*-deh pohr fah-*bvohr*
The line doesn't answer. Call later, please.

This dialogue demonstrates how you can discuss your weekend activities with a friend:

Talkin' the Talk

Jorge and Felipe discuss Felipe's weekend.

Jorge: **Hola Felipe, ¿cómo te fue en el fin de semana?**
oh-lah feh-*lee*-peh *koh*-moh teh fooeh ehn ehl feen deh seh-*mah*-nah
Hello, Felipe, how was your weekend?

Felipe: **Ahora, pienso que muy bien. Ayer todavía no sabía.**
ah-*oh*-rah peee*ehn*-soh keh mooy bveee*ehn* ah-*yehr* toh-dah-*bvee*-ah noh sah-*bvee*-ah
Now, I think it went very well. Yesterday I wasn't sure.

Jorge: **¿No sabías qué?**
noh sah-*bvee*-ahs keh
You weren't sure about what?

Felipe: **Quién era la persona que encontré en el club.**
keee*ehn* eh-rah lah pehr-*soh*-nah keh ehn-kohn-*treh* ehn ehl kloobv
Who the person was that I met at the club.

Jorge: **¿Y quién era?**
ee keee*ehn* eh-rah
And who was it?

Felipe: **Gonzalo Ramírez, el director del diario.**
gohn-*sah*-loh rah-*mee*-rehs ehl dee-rehk-*tohr* dehl dee*ah*-reeoh
Gonzalo Ramírez, the manager of the newspaper.

Jorge: **¿Qué dijo?**
keh *dee*-Hoh
What did he say?

Felipe: **Que iba a dejar el diario.**
keh ee-bvah ah deh-*Hahr* ehl dee*ah*-reeoh
That he's going to leave the newspaper.

Jorge: **¿Quién va a reemplazarlo?**
keee*ehn* bvah a rehehm-plah-*sahr*-loh
Who will replace him?

Felipe:	**Me dijo que me recomendaría, y hoy me llamaron para una entrevista.**
	meh *dee*-Hoh keh meh reh-koh-mehn-dah-*ree*-ah ee ohy meh yah-*mah*-rohn *pah*-rah oo-nah ehn-treh-*bvees*-tah
	He said he would recommend me, and today they called me for an interview.
Jorge:	**¡Muy buena noticia!**
	mooy bvoo*eh*-nah noh-*tee*-seeah
	Very good news!

Calling Listening, Hearing, and Other Phone-y Verbs

The verb **llamar** (yah-*mahr*) means *to call*. So why is that verb in Book I, Chapter 3, which covers names? Because when asked for their names, Spanish speakers respond with me **llamo** (meh *yah*-moh), which literally means, *I call myself* or *I give myself the name.*

In this section, however, we talk about calling as a way of trying to reach someone with words and messages. We also talk about calling someone on the phone. Llamar also means *to phone.*

Here are some examples:

✔ **Mañana te llamo por teléfono.** (mah-*nyah*-nah teh *yah*-moh pohr teh-*leh*-foh-noh) (*Tomorrow, I'll call you.*)

✔ **Hoy no nos llamó nadie.** (ohy noh nohs yah-*moh nah*-deeeh) (*Nobody called us today.*)

✔ **Ella llama a su madre todos los días.** (*eh*-yah *yah*-mah ah soo *mah*-dreh *toh*-dohs lohs *dee*-ahs) (*She phones her mother every day.*)

✔ **Llamamos para saber el horario.** (yah-*mah*-mohs *pah*-rah sah-*bvehr* ehl oh-*rah*-reeoh) (*We're calling to ask about the schedule.*)

See Book I, Chapter 3 for more about the verb **llamar**.

In Spanish as in English, phone calls involve some standard activities, such as placing a call, leaving a message, and listening to what the other person has to say. The good news is that in Spanish, the verbs for all these activities are regular, belonging to the **-ar** group. If you take off the **-ar**, you get the root of each verb. And, when you conjugate **llamar**, **dejar** (deh-*Har*) (*to leave*), and

escuchar (ehs-koo-*char*) (*to listen to; to hear*), the words end the same way for each pronoun. So, if we give you the conjugation for **llamar**, you can also conjugate **dejar** and **escuchar**.

Conjugation	*Pronunciation*
yo llamo	yoh *yah*-moh
tú llamas	too *yah*-mahs
él, ella, ello, uno, usted llama	ehl *eh* yah *eh*-yoh *oo*-noh oos-*tehd yah*-mah
nosotros llamamos	noh-*soh*-trohs yah-*mah*-mohs
vosotros llamáis	bvoh-*soh*-trohs yah-*mah*ees
ellos, ellas, ustedes llaman	*eh*-yohs, *eh*-yahs, oos-*tehd*-es *yah*-mahn

Don't forget to try your own conjugation. Check the verb tables in Appendix A of Book V if you're stumped.

Of course, when you're on the phone, you're not always talking about what's happening right now. You may need to discuss past and possible future events. The following sections show you how to form the past tense of **llamar**, **dejar**, and **escuchar**. For more about conjugating verbs in all tenses, check out Books II and III and Appendix A.

You called? The past tense of llamar

Use the root of **llamar** (yah-*mahr*), which is **llam-**, to conjugate for the past tense.

Conjugation	*Pronunciation*
yo llamé	yoh yah-*meh*
tú llamaste	too yah-*mahs*-teh
él, ella, ello, uno, usted llamó	ehl *eh*-yah *eh*-yoh *oo*-noh oos-*tehd* yah-*moh*
nosotros llamamos	noh-*soh*-trohs yah-*mah*-mohs
vosotros llamásteis	bvoh-*soh*-trohs yah-*mahs*-tehees
ellos, ellas, ustedes llamaron	*eh*-yohs *eh*-yahs oos-*teh*-dehs yah-*mah*-rohn

If you missed a call, you may hear the following:

✔ **Te llamaron por teléfono.** (teh yah-*mah*-rohn pohr teh-*leh*-foh-noh) (*You had a phone call.*)

✔ **Le llamé ayer.** (leh yah-*meh* ah-*yehr*) (*I called you [formal] yesterday.*)

✔ **Ayer no me llamaste.** (ah-*yehr* noh meh yah-*mahs*-teh)
(*Yesterday you [informal] didn't call me.*)

✔ **Cuando te llamé me colgaron.** (koo*ahn*-doh teh yah-*meh* meh
kohl-*gah*-rohn) (*When I called you [informal], they hung up on me.*)
(Literally: *they hung me up*)

✔ **Si hoy me llamaste, no me enteré.** (see ohy meh yah-*mahs*-teh noh meh
ehn-teh-*reh*) (*If you called me today, I didn't know about it.*)

A popular book title that uses the verb **llamar** is Jack London's *The Call of the
Wild*, which in Spanish reads *El llamado de la selva* (ehl yah-*mah*-doh deh
lah *sehl*-bvah).

Did you leave a message? The past tense of dejar

Here is the past tense of **dejar** (deh-*Hahr*), that "leaving and allowing" verb.
The root is **dej-** (deh).

Conjugation	Pronunciation
yo dejé	yoh deh-*Heh*
tú dejaste	too deh-*Hahs*-teh
él, ella, ello, uno, usted dejó	ehl *eh*-yah *eh*-yoh *oo*-noh oos-*tehd* deh-*Hoh*
nosotros dejamos	noh-*soh*-trohs deh-*Hah*-mohs
vosotros dejásteis	bvoh-*soh*-trohs deh-*Hahs*-tehees
ellos, ellas, ustedes dejaron	*eh*-yohs *eh*-yahs oos-*teh*-dehs deh-*Hah*-rohn

These examples use forms of the verb **dejar**:

✔ **Te dejé un recado.** (teh deh-*Heh* oon reh-*kah*-doh) (*I left you a message.*)

✔ **¿Dejaste un mensaje largo?** (deh-*Hahs*-teh oon mehn-*sah*-Heh *lahr*-goh)
(*Did you [informal] leave a long message?*)

✔ **El mensaje que dejaron es breve.** (ehl mehn-*sah*-Heh keh deh-*Hah*-rohn
ehs *bvreh*-bveh) (*The message they left is brief.*)

✔ **Dejamos tres mensajes.** (deh-*Hah*-mohs trehs mehn-*sah*-Hehs) (*We left
three messages.*)

✔ **Dejó el número de teléfono.** (deh-*Hoh* ehl *noo*-meh-roh deh
teh-*leh*-foh-noh) (*He/She left the telephone number.*)

Have you heard? The past tense of escuchar

In the case of the verb **escuchar** (ehs-koo-*chahr*) (*to listen to*), the conjugation is very similar to the previous two verbs because they're all regular verbs with **-ar** endings. For **escuchar**, the root is **escuch-** (ehs-kooch).

Conjugation	*Pronunciation*
yo escuché	yoh ehs-koo-*cheh*
tú escuchaste	too ehs-koo-*chahs*-teh
él, ella, ello, uno, usted escuchó	ehl *eh*-yah *eh*-yoh *oo*-noh oos-*tehd* ehs-koo-*choh*
nosotros escuchamos	noh-*soh*-trohs ehs-koo-*chah*-mohs
vosotros escuchásteis	bvoh-*soh*-trohs ehs-koo-*chahs*-tehees
ellos, ellas, ustedes escucharon	*eh*-yohs *eh*-yahs oos-*teh*-dehs ehs-koo-*chah*-rohn

Test your hearing-verb abilities with the following phrases:

✔ **Aló, ¿me escuchaste, Juan?** (ah-*loh* me ehs-koo-*chahs*-teh Hoo*ahn*) (*Hello, did you hear me, Juan?*)

✔ **No te escuché nada.** (noh teh ehs-koo-*cheh nah*-dah) (*I didn't hear anything.*)

✔ **¿Así escuchó bien?** (ah-*see* ehs-koo-*choh* bvee*ehn*) (*Did he/she hear well this way?*)

✔ **Así te escuchamos un poco mejor.** (ah-*see* teh ehs-koo-*chah*-mohs oon *poh*-koh meh-*Hohr*) (*This way we heard you [informal] a little better.*)

✔ **Así escucharon muy bien.** (ah-*see* ehs-koo-*chah*-rohn mooy bvee*ehn*) (*This way they heard very well.*)

Chapter 8

Asking Directions

. . . .

In This Chapter

- Pinpointing locations
- Receiving directions
- Gettin' in gear with **¡Vamos!** (*bvah*-mohs!) (*Let's go!*)
- Heading up with **subir** (soo-*bveer*) and down with **bajar** (bvah-*Hahr*)
- Expressing distance with **cerca** (*sehr*-kah) (*near*) and **lejos** (*leh*-Hohs) (*far*)

. . . .

When you're exploring foreign lands, "Let's go!" becomes your call to action. But before you head out, you need to know two things — where you're going and how to get there. In Spanish, the only way to figure out where you're going and how to get there is by asking questions, and that means asking *"Where?"* **¿Dónde?** (*dohn*-deh).

In this chapter, you discover how to use **¿Dónde?** and other common Spanish words and phrases to figure out where you're going and how to get there. Yep, you're about to get directions on how to ask for directions. Even more importantly, as you become familiar with these words and phrases, you understand not only the questions but also the answers that people provide.

Going Places with ¿Dónde?

Consider the question **¿A dónde va?** (ah *dohn*-deh bvah?) (*Where are you going?*)

Where? is one of the big questions — the wandering question, the question that expresses your need to experience places that can give you a sense of wonder or a sense of the new.

Where? is the question that makes searchers and explorers conquer the planet and unravel its mysteries. For example, the question, "Where do I go for pepper?" has led seafarers to travel around Africa, cross the oceans, and discover the American continent. Likewise, the question "Where do these people come from?" is the question that creates new connections between nations.

Of course, most times asking *Where?* simply helps you find what you're look-ing for and takes you to a place quite ordinary but most necessary. Where would you be without *Where?* The following sections help you practice using *Where?* in Spanish-speaking countries.

Where Is . . . ? Where Are . . . ?

In its most basic application, the *Where?* question helps you determine where something is. When you're lost, for example, you probably wonder *Where am I?* When you're looking for a particular place, such as a theater, you may ask *Where is the dinner theater?* When you misplace something, like a pen, you may ask *Where is the pen?*

Because you're asking where things *are* (where they *be*), you pair the Spanish word **donde** with the verb expressing being in a temporary sense — **estar** (ehs-*tahr*), covered in Book I, Chapter 3.

When you use **¿dónde?** in a question, you add an accent over the **o**, but when you use it in a phrase such as **el pueblo donde ellos viven** (ehl poo-*eh*-bvloh *dohn*-deh eh-yohs *bvee*-bvehn) (*the town where they live*), the **o** doesn't get an accent mark.

Sample the following sentences that use **¿dónde?** and **estar:**

- ✔ **¿Dónde está el Museo de Larco?** (*donh*-deh ehs-*tah* ehl moo-*seh*-oh deh *lahr*-koh (*Where is the Larco Museum?*)

- ✔ **¿Dónde estamos ahora?** (*dohn*-deh ehs-*tah*-mohs ah-*oh*-rah) (*Where are we now?*)

- ✔ **¿Dónde está el Hotel del Camino?** (*dohn*-deh ehs-*tah* ehl oh-*tehl* dehl kah-*mee*-noh) (*Where is the Hotel del Camino?*)

- ✔ **¿Dónde estuviste anoche?** (*dohn*-deh ehs-too-*bvees*-teh ah-*noh*-cheh) (*Where were you last night?*)

And here is a sentence for the person who wants to know everything:

¡Quiero saber el cómo, el cuándo, y el dónde! (keee*eh*-roh sah-*bvehr* ehl *koh*-moh ehl kooo*ahn*-doh ee ehl *dohn*-deh) (*I want to know the how, the when, and the where!*)

You can use another line to express your determination to find that special place:

¡Dondequiera que esté, lo encontraremos! (donh-deh-keee*eh*-rah keh ehs-*teh*, loh ehn-kohn-trah-*reh*-mohs) (*Wherever it is, we'll find it!*)

Using Yourself as a Reference Point

You can identify the space around your body in six ways:

- **delante** (deh-*lahn*-teh) (*in front*):

  Paula camina delante de Clara. (*pah*oo-lah kah-*mee*-nah deh-*lahn*-teh deh *klah*-rah) (*Paula walks in front of Clara.*)

- **detrás** (deh-*trahs*) (*behind*):

  Clara va detrás de Paula. (*klah*-rah bvah deh-*trahs* deh *pah*oo-lah) (*Clara goes behind Paula.*)

- **a la derecha** (ah lah deh-*reh*-chah) (*to the right*):

  A la derecha de Paula está Felipe. (ah lah deh-*reh*-chah deh *pah*oo-lah ehs-*tah* feh-*lee*-peh) (*To the right of Paula is Felipe.*)

- **a la izquierda** (ah lah ees-kee*ehr*-dah) (*to the left*):

  José se pone a la izquierda de Clara. (Hoh-*seh* seh *poh*-neh ah lah ees-kee*ehr*-dah deh *klah*-rah) (*José sits [Literally: he puts himself] to the left of Clara.*)

- **debajo** (deh-*bvah*-Hoh) (*beneath*; *under*):

  Hay pasto debajo de los pies de José. (ahy *pahs*-toh deh-*bvah*-Hoh deh lohs pee*ehs* deh Hoh-*seh*) (*There's grass under Jose's feet.*)

- **encima** (ehn-*see*-mah) (*above*):

  La rama está encima de la cabeza de Paula. (lah *rah*-mah ehs-*tah* ehn-*see*-mah deh lah kah-*bveh*-sah deh *pah*oo-lah) (*The branch is above Paula's head.*)

Before you go any farther, you need to understand the distinction between two very similar words: **derecho** (deh-*reh*-choh) (*straight*) and **derecha** (deh-*reh*-chah) (*right*).

What was that; you say? Look again. The only difference between the words is that one word ends in **o** and the other in **a**, and the meaning is no longer the same!

- **derecho** (deh-*reh*-choh) (*straight; straight ahead*):

  Siga derecho por esta calle. (*see*-gah deh-*reh*-choh pohr *ehs*-tah kah-yeh) (*Keep going straight on this street.*)

- **derecha** (deh-*reh*-chah) (*right*):

  En la esquina doble a la derecha. (ehn lah ehs-*kee*-nah *doh*-bvleh ah lah deh-*reh*-chah) (*At the corner, turn to the right.*)

The following dialogue demonstrates asking for and understanding directions; if you need a crash course in ordinal numbers to describe building floors or levels, head to Book I, Chapter 2.

Talkin' the Talk

 After checking in at her hotel, Catalina asks the hotel receptionist for directions to the restaurant and the pool.

Catalina: **¿Dónde está el restaurante?**
dohn-deh ehs-*tah* ehl rehs-tahoo-*rahn*-teh
Where's the restaurant?

Receptionist: **Está arriba, en el segundo piso.**
ehs-*tah* ah-*rree*-bvah ehn ehl seh-*goon*-doh *pee*-soh
It's upstairs, on the second floor.

Catalina: **¿En qué piso está la piscina?**
ehn keh *pee*-soh ehs-*tah* lah pee-*see*-na
On what floor is the pool?

Receptionist: **Está en el quinto piso.**
ehs-*tah* ehn ehl *keen*-toh *pee*-soh.
It's on the fifth floor.

Puede tomar el ascensor.
poo*eh*-deh toh-*mahr* ehl ah-sehn-*sohr*
You may take the elevator.

Catalina: **¿Y cómo llego al ascensor?**
ee *koh*-moh *yeh*-goh ahl ah-sehn-*sohr*
How do I get to the elevator?

Receptionist: **El ascensor está ahí, a la izquierda.**
ehl ah-sehn-*sohr* ehs-*tah* ah-*ee* ah lah ees-kee*ehr*-dah
The elevator is here, to the left.

Space Travel: Grasping Spatial Directions

You often use words to tell where people or things are in relation to other people and things. You can use these terms to describe the relationships:

✔ **al lado** (ahl *lah*-doh) (*beside*, *next to*, *at the side of*)

✔ **al frente** (ahl *frehn*-teh) (*in front of*)

✔ **dentro** (*dehn*-troh) (*inside*)

✔ **adentro** (ah-*dehn*-troh) (*inside*; because **dentro** also means *inside*, **adentro** may express movement, as when someone or something moves toward an interior)

✔ **fuera** (foo*eh*-rah) (*outside*)

✔ **afuera** (ah-foo*eh*-rah) (*outside*; can express movement, as in the case of **adentro** — the fourth bullet point in this list)

✔ **bajo** (*bvah*-Hoh) (*under, below*)

✔ **debajo** (deh-*bvah*-Hoh) (*underneath*)

✔ **arriba** (ah-*ree*-bvah) (*above*)

Practicing these directions comes in handy. The sentences that follow use spatial-direction terms:

✔ **La pastelería está al lado del banco.** (lah-pahs-teh-leh-*ree*-ah ehs-*tah* ahl *lah*-doh dehl *bvahn*-koh) (*The pastry shop is next to the bank.*)

✔ **Al frente del banco hay una zapatería.** (ahl *frehn*-teh dehl *bvahn*-koh ahy *oo*-nah sah-pah-teh-*ree*-ah) (*In front of the bank there is a shoe store.*)

✔ **Las mesas del café están afuera.** (lahs *meh*-sahs dehl kah-*feh* ehs-*tahn* ah-foo*eh*-rah) (*The tables of the cafe are outside.*)

✔ **Cuando llueve ponen las mesas adentro.** (koo*ahn*-doh yoo*eh*-bveh *poh*-nehn lahs *meh*-sahs ah-*dehn*-troh) (*When it rains they put the tables inside.*)

✔ **Arriba hay cielo despejado.** (ah-*ree*-bvah ahy see-*eh*-loh dehs-peh-*Hah*-doh) (*Above, the sky is clear.*)

✔ **Hay agua bajo los pies de Carlos.** (ahy *ah*-gooah *bvah*-Hoh lohs pee*ehs* de *kahr*-lohs) (*There's water under Carlos's feet.*)

✔ **Debajo de la calle corre el tren subterráneo.** (deh-*bvah*-Hoh deh lah *kah*-yeh *koh*-rreh ehl trehn soobv-teh-*rrah*-neh-oh) (*The subway runs under the street.*)

✔ **Este ascensor va arriba.** (*ehs*-teh ah-sehn-*sohr* bvah ah-*rree*-bvah) (*This elevator goes up.*)

✔ **Hay un gato dentro de la caja.** (ahy oon *gah*-toh *dehn*-troh deh lah *kah*-Hah) (*There's a cat inside the box.*)

Referring to a Map When All Else Fails

Some directions are used throughout the world to explain how to get some-where or find something by using the points on a compass. The following terms help you specify north from south and east from west:

- **el norte** (ehl *nohr*-teh) (*the north*)

- **el sur** (ehl soor) (*the south*)

- **el este** (ehl *ehs*-teh) (*the east*)

- **el oriente** (ehl oh-ree*ehn*-teh) (*the east [Literally: where the sun originates]*)

- **el oeste** (ehl oh-*ehs*-teh) (*the west*)

- **el poniente** (ehl poh-nee*ehn*-teh) (*the west [Literally: where the sun sets]*)

Maps are your keys to your getting around. The first thing you should ask for at your car rental office, or the first thing to buy on arrival in a city, is a map. You can get around more easily if you find your way on a map or if someone can show you on the map how to get to the place you're looking for.

Here are some mapping phrases to practice:

- **La avenida Venus está al este de aquí.** (lah ah-bveh-*nee*-dah *bveh*-noos ehs-*tah* ahl *ehs*-teh deh ah-*kee*) (*Venus Avenue is east of here.*)

- **Al oeste se encuentra la calle Las Violetas.** (ahl oh-*ehs*-teh seh ehn-koo*ehn*-trah lah *kah*-yeh lahs bveeoh-*leh*-tahs) (*To the west is Violetas Street.*)

- **El parque está al norte.** (ehl *pahr*-keh ehs-*tah* ahl *nohr*-teh) (*The park is to the north.*)

- **Al sur se va hacia el río.** (ahl soor seh bvah *ah*-see-ah ehl *ree*-oh) (*To the south is the river. [Literally: To the south, one goes toward the river.]*)

- **El oriente es donde el sol se levanta.** (ehl oh-ree*ehn*-teh ehs *dohn*-deh ehl sohl seh leh-*bvahn*-tah) (*The east is where the sun rises.*)

- **El poniente es donde el sol se pone.** (ehl poh-nee*ehn*-teh ehs *dohn*-deh ehl sohl seh *poh*-neh) (*The west is where the sun sets.*)

- **Jordania está en el Cercano Oriente.** (Hohr-*dah*-neeah ehs-*tah* ehn ehl sehr-*kah*-noh oh-ree*ehn*-teh) (*Jordan is in the Near East.*)

- **China está en el Lejano Oriente.** (*chee*-nah ehs-*tah* ehn ehl leh-*Hah*-noh oh-ree*ehn*-teh) (*China is in the Far East.*)

✔ **América está al oriente del Océano Pacífico.** (ah-*meh*-ree-kah ehs-*tah* ahl oh-ree*ehn*-teh dehl oh-*seh*-ah-noh pah-*see*-fee-koh) (*America is east of the Pacific Ocean.*)

✔ **Asia está al poniente del océano.** (*ah*-seeah ehs-*tah* ahl poh-nee*ehn*-teh dehl oh-*seh*-ah-noh) (*Asia is west of the ocean.*)

The following phrases are helpful when asking or giving general directions:

✔ **la calle** (lah *kah*-yeh) (*the street*)

✔ **la avenida** (lah ah-bveh-*nee*-dah) (*the avenue*)

✔ **el bulevar** (ehl bvoo-leh-*bvahr*) (*the boulevard*)

✔ **el río** (ehl *ree*-oh) (*the river*)

✔ **la plaza** (lah *plah*-sah) (*the square*)

✔ **el parque** (ehl *pahr*-keh) (*the park*)

✔ **el jardín** (ehl Hahr-*deen*) (*the garden; sometimes a small park*)

✔ **el barrio** (ehl *bvah*-rreeoh) (*the neighborhood*)

✔ **la cuadra** (lah koo*ah*-drah) (*the block*)

✔ **la manzana** (lah mahn-*sah*-nah) (*the block*)

✔ **izquierda** (ees-kee*ehr*-dah) (*left*)

✔ **derecha** (deh-*reh*-chah) (*right*)

✔ **derecho** (deh-*reh*-choh) (*straight*)

✔ **doblar** (doh-*bvlahr*) (*to turn*)

✔ **seguir** (seh-*gheer*) (*to follow*)

Asking for directions is always a bit problematic. The people who answer your questions know the city and the answers seem so obvious to them! So to keep you going and sharpen your ear, here are some phrases to practice:

✔ **En el barrio hay una avenida ancha.** (ehn ehl *bvah*-rreeoh ahy *oo*-nah ah-bveh-*nee*-dah *ahn*-chah) (*In the neighborhood, there is a wide avenue.*)

✔ **Nuestra calle va de norte a sur.** (noo*ehs*-trah *kah*-yeh bvah deh *nohr*-teh ah soor) (*Our street runs north to south.*)

✔ **Mi tía vive en la Cerrada del Olivo.** (mee *tee*-ah *bvee*-bveh ehn lah seh-*rrah*-dah dehl oh-*lee*-bvoh) (*My aunt lives at the Cerrada* [street with no exit] *del Olivo* [olive tree].)

✔ **Junto al río hay un gran parque.** (*Hoon*-toh ahl *ree*-oh ahy oon grahn *pahr*-keh) (*On the riverside there is a large park.*)

- **La plaza está en el centro de la ciudad.** (lah *plah*-sah ehs-*tah* ehn ehl *sehn*-troh deh lah seeoo-*dahd*) (*The square is in the center of the city.*)

- **En el jardín hay juegos para niños.** (ehn ehl Hahr-*deen* ahy Hoo*eh*-gohs *pah*-rah *nee*-nyohs) (*In the small park, they have a children's playground.*)

- **El Zócalo de México es una plaza enorme.** (ehl *soh*-kah-loh deh *meh*-Hee-koh ehs *oo*-nah *plah*-sah eh-*nohr*-meh) (*The Zocalo in Mexico is an immense square.*)

- **Esa avenida se llama La Alameda.** (*eh*-sah ah-bveh-*nee*-dah seh *yah*-mah lah ah-lah-*meh*-dah) (*The name of that avenue is La Alameda.*)

The following dialogue shows you a sample direction-giving situation.

Talkin' the Talk

Ana Luisa is an artist who's anxious to visit the Graphics Museum. She plans to walk there from her hotel so she can avoid the heavy traffic.

Ana Luisa:	**Disculpe, ¿cómo llego al Museo de la Estampa?** dees-*kool*-peh *koh*-moh *yeh*-goh ahl moo-*seh*-oh deh lah ehs-*tahm*-pah *Excuse me, how do I get to the Graphics Museum?*
Receptionist:	**Muy fácil. Está muy cerca.** mooy *fah*-seel esh-*tah* mooy *sehr*-kah *Very easy. It's very close.*
	Sale del hotel. *sah*-leh dehl *oh*-tehl *You go out of the hotel.*
Ana Luisa:	**¿Dónde está la salida?** *dohn*-deh ehs-*tah* lah sah-*lee*-dah *Where is the exit?*
Receptionist:	**La salida está a la derecha.** lah sah-*lee*-dah ehs-*tah* ah lah deh-*reh*-chah *The exit is to the right.*
	Al salir va hacia la izquierda ahl sah-*leer* bvah *ah*-seeah lah ees-kee*ehr*-dah *As you get out, you go to the left*
	camina hasta la segunda calle kah-*mee*-nah *ahs*-tah lah seh-*goon*-dah *kah*-yeh *walk to the second street*

> **da vuelta a la derecha, una cuadra**
> dah bvoo*ehl*-tah ah lah deh-*reh*-chah oo-nah
> koo*ah*-drah
> *turn to the right, go one block*
>
> **y llega al museo.**
> ee *yeh*-gah ahl moo-*seh*-oh
> *and you arrive at the museum.*

Ana Luisa: **Gracias por su ayuda.**
grah-seeahs pohr soo ah-*yoo*-dah
Thanks for your help.

Dealing with the Normal Ups and Downs: Subir and Bajar

Usually when you're getting or giving directions, you're dealing with two dimensions, as on a map. In some cases, however, you need to navigate the third dimension by going up and down hills, ascending or descending stairs, riding the elevator up or down, and so on. In situations such as these, you need to know how to use the verbs **subir** (soo-*bveer*) (*to ascend; to go up*) and **bajar** (bvah-*Hahr*) (*to descend; to go down*). The following sections show you how to conjugate these two verbs in the present tense and use them in sentences.

Going up with subir

The following minitable shows you how to conjugate the present tense of the verb **subir** (soo-*bveer*) (*to go up; to ascend*) — a very useful regular verb when you want to go up! Its root is **sub-** (soobv).

Conjugation	*Pronunciation*
yo subo	yoh *soo*-bvoh
tú subes	too *soo*-bvehs
él, ella, ello, uno, usted sube	ehl, *eh*-yah, *eh*-yoh, *oo*-noh, oos-*tehd soo*-bveh
nosotros subimos	noh-soh-trohs soo-*bvee*-mohs
vosotros subís	bvoh-*soh*-trohs soo-*bvees*
ellos, ellas, ustedes suben	*eh*-yohs, *eh*-yahs, oos-*teh*-dehs *soo*-bvehn

Practicing verb conjugations is essential; that way, they soon become second nature. But until they do become second nature, here are some phrases to help you:

- ✔ **Suben por esa escalera.** (*soo*-bvehn pohr *eh*-sah ehs-kah-*leh*-rah) (*They go up that staircase.*)

- ✔ **Subes por esa calle, a la izquierda.** (*soo*-bvehs pohr eh-sah *kah*-yeh, ah lah ees-kee*ehr*-dah) (*You [informal] go up on that street, to the left.*)

- ✔ **Nosotros vamos a subir con ustedes.** (noh-*soh*-trohs *bvah*-mohs ah soo-*bveer* kohn oos-*teh*-dehs) (*We're going to go up with you.*)

- ✔ **El ascensor de la derecha sube.** (ehl ah-sehn-*sohr* deh lah deh-*reh*-chah soo-bveh) (*The elevator to the right goes up.*)

- ✔ **Yo subo allí todos los días.** (yoh *soo*-bvoh ah-*yee toh*-dohs lohs *dee*-ahs) (*I go up there every day.*)

Going down with bajar

What goes up must come down, right? The descending verb is **bajar** (bvah-*Hahr*) (*to descend; to go down*).

Bajar is a regular verb, and its root is **baj-** (bvahH). Here's how you conjugate **bajar** in the present tense:

Conjugation	Pronunciation
yo bajo	yoh *bvah*-Hoh
tú bajas	too *bvah*-Hahs
él, ella, ello, uno, usted baja	ehl, *eh*-yah, *eh*-yoh, *oo*-noh, oos-*tehd*, *bvah*-Hah
nosotros bajamos	noh-*soh*-trohs bvah-*Hah*-mohs
vosotros bajáis	bvoh-*soh*-trohs bvah-*Hah*ees
ellos, ellas, ustedes bajan	*eh*-yohs, *eh*-yahs, oos-*teh*-dehs *bvah*-Hahn

When you need to go down, right down you go! Practice, practice, practice!

- ✔ **Ella baja por la escalera.** (*eh*-yah *bvah*-Hah pohr lah ehs-kah-*leh*-rah) (*She goes down the stairs.*)

- ✔ **Bajamos por esta calle.** (bvah-*Hah*-mohs pohr *ehs*-tah *kah*-yeh) (*We go down this street.*)

- ✔ **Tú bajas del auto con el perro.** (too *bvah*-Hahs dehl *ahoo*-toh kohn ehl *peh*-rroh) (*You [informal] get out of the car with the dog.*)

- ✔ **Dicen que ya van a bajar.** (*dee*-sehn keh yah bvahn ah *bvah*-Hahr) (*They say they're going to go down [to the lobby or some other lower area].*)

Being Here, There, and Everywhere

An old saying has the confused person never knowing whether he's *here* or *there*. In Spanish, whether you're here or there doesn't matter — just choose the word you like and end the confusion.

In Spanish, you can indicate here and there in two ways. Native Spanish speakers interchange *here* and *there* often, with no distinction between the two words. *Here* and *there* are adverbs; they always work in the vicinity of a verb and words that talk about space:

- ✔ **allá** (ah-*yah*) (*there*)
- ✔ **allí** (ah-*yee*) (*there*)
- ✔ **acá** (ah-*kah*) (*here*)
- ✔ **aquí** (ah-*kee*) (*here*)

To show that it makes no difference whether you use one of these pairs of words or the other, the following sentences enable you to practice situations in which you may use *here* or *there*:

- ✔ **Allí, en la esquina, está el banco.** (ah-*yee* ehn lah ehs-*kee*-nah ehs-*tah* ehl *bvan*-koh) (*There, on the corner, is the bank.*)
- ✔ **Allá van los turistas.** (ah-*yah* bvahn lohs too-*rees*-tahs) (*There go the tourists.*)
- ✔ **Aquí se come muy bien.** (ah-*kee* seh *koh*-meh mooy bvee*ehn*) (*Here one eats very well.*)
- ✔ **Acá está el museo.** (ah-*kah* ehs-*tah* ehl moo-*seh*-oh) (*Here is the museum.*)
- ✔ **¡Ven acá!** (bvehn ah-*kah*) (*Come here!*)
- ✔ **¡Corre allá!** (*koh*-rreh ah-*yah*) (*Run there!*)

Sometimes you talk about no-places and all-places: *nowhere* and *everywhere*, along with *anywhere*. You can use the following phrases to express the idea of all places or no particular places in Spanish:

- ✔ **en todas partes** (ehn *toh*-dahs *pahr*-tehs) (*everywhere*)
- ✔ **en ninguna parte** (ehn neen-*goo*-nah *pahr*-teh) (*nowhere, anywhere*)

The following sentences can help you practice using these phrases:

- ✔ **En todas partes hay gente simpática.** (ehn *toh*-dahs *pahr*-tehs ahy *Hehn*-teh seem-*pah*-tee-kah) (*There are nice people everywhere.*)
- ✔ **Busqué mis llaves por todas partes.** (bvoos-*keh* mees *yah*-bvehs pohr *toh*-dahs *pahr*-tehs) (*I searched for my keys everywhere.*)

✔ **En ninguna parte encuentro mis llaves.** (ehn neen-*goo*-nah *pahr*-teh ehn-koo*ehn*-troh mees *yah*-bvehs) (*I can't find my keys anywhere.*)

✔ **Mira por todas partes cuando busca algo.** (m*ee*-rah pohr *toh*-dahs pahr-tehs koo*ahn*-doh *bvoos*-kah *ahl*-goh) (*He/She looks everywhere when searching for something.*)

Knowing How Far to Go with Cerca and Lejos

In this section, you can explore the words **cerca** (*sehr*-kah) (*near, close*) and **lejos** (*leh*-Hohs) (*far*). Use these two words when you want to discuss how great the distance, and the possible size of the effort, required to arrive at a specific place. The following dialogue gives you a look at **cerca** and **lejos** in action.

Talkin the Talk

Ines is deciding how to spend her day. Should she attend the cinema, visit a museum, or do both? First, she needs to find out how near these places are to her and to each other.

Ines:	**¿Está lejos el cine Las Flores?** ehs-*tah leh*-Hohs ehl *see*-neh lahs *floh*-rehs *Is the Las Flores cinema far?*
Martine:	**No, está muy cerca . . .** noh ehs-*tah* mooy *sehr*-kah . . . *No, it's quite near . . .*
	. . . a sólo dos cuadras. ah *soh*-loh dohs koo*ah*-drahs *. . . only two blocks away.*
Ines:	**¿Y el Teatro Bolívar?** ee ehl teh-*ah*-troh bvoh-*lee*-bvahr *And the Bolivar Theater?*
Martine:	**El teatro Bolívar sí está lejos . . .** ehl teh-*ah*-troh bvoh-*lee*-bvahr see ehs-*tah leh*-Hohs *The Bolivar Theater is really far . . .*
	tiene que tomar el subte. tee*eh*-neh keh toh-*mahr* ehl *soobv*-teh *you have to take the subway.*

Chapter 9

Dealing with Emergencies

- -

In This Chapter

- Asking for help
- Communicating at the hospital
- Talking with the doctor
- Dealing with the police
- Protecting your rights abroad

- -

*B*e prepared. That's the Boy Scout motto, and it's not a bad idea for any situation. You should always be prepared for emergencies, especially in areas where residents don't speak your native language. The language difference can complicate the emergency if no one can understand you, or if you don't understand what is being said.

This chapter looks at two main areas where you may experience an emergency. The first part of the chapter looks at health concerns — breaking an arm or experiencing stomach flu; the second part deals with legal emergencies — car accidents and other law infractions that may require the help of your consulate or a lawyer. But before you start preparing for these emergencies, you need to know a few important words that will quickly get you the help you need.

Hollering for Help

You may find yourself in a situation where you need to cry for help. Thumbing through your dictionary isn't going to be quick enough, so you may want to memorize these words. You can use the first two interchangeably.

When the pot falls

You see a flower pot falling from a balcony while someone is passing by. What do you shout? All Spanish speakers, with the exception of Mexicans, react to

¡Cuidado! (kooee-*dah*-doh) (*Watch out!*) (Literally: *Care!*)

When the flower pot is falling in Mexico, however, you have to say

¡Aguas! (*ah*-gooahs) (*Watch out!*) (Literally: *Waters!*)

This habit most likely comes from the times when drains were nonexistent, so people in colonial cities simply tossed their dirty water out the second-floor window. They shouted **¡Aguas!** to warn passersby that dirty water was coming their way. Eventually, the habit of shouting **¡Aguas!** extended to all danger.

Following are basic distress-signaling words:

- ✔ **¡Socorro!** (soh-*koh*-rroh) (*Help!*)
- ✔ **¡Auxilio!** (ahoo-*ksee*-leeoh) (*Help!*)
- ✔ **¡Ayúdeme!** (ah-*yoo*-deh-meh) (*Help me!*)
- ✔ **¡Incendio!** (een-*sehn*-deeoh) (*Fire!*)
- ✔ **¡Inundación!** (ee-noon-dah-see*ohn*) (*Flood!*)
- ✔ **¡Temblor!** (tehm-*bvlohr*) (*Earth tremor!*)
- ✔ **¡Terremoto!** (teh-rreh-*moh*-toh) (*Earthquake!*)
- ✔ **¡Maremoto!** (mah-reh-*moh*-toh) (*Tidal wave!*)

You can help speed up your request by using one of these two words:

- ✔ **¡Rápido!** (*rah*-pee-doh) (*Quick!*)
- ✔ **¡Apúrense!** (ah-*poo*-rehn-seh) (*Hurry!*)

Dealing with Medical Issues

When an illness or an accident jeopardizes your health, losing your head is a common and understandable reaction. We try to guide you through these potential problems in a calm and prudent manner. *Note:* Most of the information in this section is for English-speaking patients who are seeking care from Spanish-speaking healthcare providers. If you're an English-speaker providing healthcare to Spanish-speaking patients, some of the words and phrases presented here may be very useful to you, but we provide additional guidance in Book IV, Chapter 1.

In our experience, most native Spanish speakers are caring, gentle people who are tolerant of faulty pronunciation and very ready to help a foreigner. In fact, they may even be overly helpful, leaving you with the difficult task of being firm and level-headed about your needs without damaging their feelings and being negative about their good will.

Here are some sentences to help you be just as caring and kind, but at the same time firm, with your refusal for help when you don't want any. Suppose the person trying to be helpful says things like

- ✔ **¡Pobrecito!, ¿le ayudo?** (poh-breh-*see*-toh leh ah-*yoo*-doh) (*Poor little you [male], can I help you?*)

- ✔ **¡Vengan todos, a ayudar!** (*bvehn*-gahn *toh*-dohs ah ah-yoo-*dar*) (*Come, everybody, let's help!*)

In which case, you can answer with things like

- ✔ **Por favor, estoy bien, no me ayude.** (pohr fah-*bvohr* ehs-*tohy* bvee*en* noh meh ah-*yoo*-deh) (*Please, I'm fine, don't help me.*)

- ✔ **Muchas gracias, le agradezco, prefiero estar solo.** (*moo*-chahs *grah*-seeahs leh ah-grah-*dehs*-koh preh-fee*eh*-roh ehs-*tahr soh*-loh) (*Thank you very much; I prefer to be alone.*)

- ✔ **Estoy muy bien, gracias, no necesito ayuda.** (ehs-*tohy* mooy bvee*ehn grah*-seeahs noh neh-seh-*see*-toh ah-*yoo*-dah) (*I'm fine, thanks; I don't need help.*)

- ✔ **Usted es muy gentil, gracias; no me ayude, por favor.** (oos-*tehd* ehs mooy Hehn-*teel grah*-seeahs noh meh ah-*yoo*-deh pohr fah-*bvohr*) (*You're very kind, thanks; don't help me, please.*)

- ✔ **Ustedes son muy amables, pero estoy bien.** (oos-*teh*-dehs sohn mooy ah-*mah*-bvlehs *peh*-roh ehs-*tohy* bvee*ehn*) (*You [formal, plural] are very kind, but I'm fine.*)

If you ask for a doctor who speaks English, and you're introduced to one, try to make sure that the doctor's English is better than your Spanish before you get involved with him or her. If you're having trouble being understood in English or Spanish, ask for another doctor whose language skills more nearly match your own.

Remember that if you have to speak in Spanish to the Spanish-speaking person you're addressing, you want to speak s-l-o-w-l-y and keep in mind that in an emergency people are generally eager to assist. Don't worry about money when those around you want to help. You'll have time for that when you've recovered or are out of the mess. Also, let people help you if at all possible; that makes them feel good. As to procedures relating to emergency rooms or hospitals, let those things work themselves out, and simply be a patient patient. Remember that all those concerned are doing the best they can. Finally, keep in mind that procedures can vary from place to place in relation to the availability of people and equipment.

If you get sick while traveling, ask for advice at your hotel's reception desk.

Table 9-1 lists some common terms you may need to know in a medical emergency. For additional terms relating to body parts and medical lingo, check out Book IV, Chapter 1. That chapter is intended more for healthcare professionals but provides plenty of Spanish that's also useful for patients.

Table 9-1	Medical Terms	
Spanish	**Pronunciation**	**English**
el médico	ehl *meh*-dee-koh	the doctor
el/la enfermo/a	ehl/lah ehn-*fehr*-moh/mah	the sick person
la camilla	lah kah-*mee*-yah	the stretcher; the trolley; the gurney
la fractura	lah frahk-*too*-rah	the fracture/broken bone
la radiografía	lah rah-deeoh-grah-*fee*-ah	the x-ray picture
el yeso	ehl *yeh*-soh	the plaster (either in casts or walls)
enyesar	ehn-yeh-*sahr*	to set in a cast
el dolor	ehl doh-*lohr*	the pain
el analgésico	ehl ah-nahl-*Heh*-see-koh	the painkiller
el corte	ehl *kohr*-teh	the cut
la anestesia	lah ah-nehs-*teh*-seeah	the anesthesia
sangrar	sahn-*grahr*	to bleed
la herida	lah eh-*ree*-dah	the wound
el mareo	ehl mah-*reh*-oh	the dizziness
los puntos	lohs poon-tohs	the stitches (surgical)

Helping out with the verb ayudar

The verb **ayudar** (ah-yoo-*dahr*) (*to help*), is, as you would expect, a very helpful word to know. It's a regular verb of the **-ar** variety, so it's very easy to conjugate. Here it is in the present tense:

Conjugation	Pronunciation
yo ayudo	yoh ah-*yoo*-doh
tú ayudas	too ah-*yoo*-dahs
él, ella, ello, uno, usted ayuda	ehl *eh*-yah *eh*-yoh *oo*-noh oos-*tehd* ah-*yoo*-dah
nosotros ayudamos	noh-*soh*-trohs ah-yoo-*dah*-mohs
vosotros ayudáis	bvoh-*soh*-trohs ah-yoo-*dah*ees
ellos, ellas, ustedes ayudan	*eh*-yos *eh*-yas oos-*teh*-dehs ah-*yoo*-dahn

What follows are phrases that are helpful in cases when you're talking to people you haven't met — like a doctor, or some passerby. We also give you phrases for situations when those around you are closely related to you, or when they're children.

We begin with some phrases you can use when you want to be formally helpful. The formal way of speech is more normal to use both on your part and on the part of those who are helping. It shows respect on your part to the doctor, for example, and on his part to you. Neither of you has an intimate or informal relationship with the other:

- ✔ **¿Le ayudo?** (leh ah-*yoo*-doh) (*Can I help you?*)

- ✔ **Sí, ayúdeme a pedir una ambulancia.** (see ah-*yoo*-deh-meh ah peh-*deer* oo-nah ahm-bvoo-*lahn*-seeah) (*Yes, help me get an ambulance.*)

- ✔ **Espere. Le van a ayudar a cargar al herido.** (ehs-*peh*-reh leh bvahn ah ah-*yoo*-dahr ah kahr-*gahr* ahl eh-*ree*-doh) (*Wait. They'll help you carry the injured person.*)

- ✔ **Usted ayude al enfermo a bajar de la camilla.** (oos-*tehd* ah-*yoo*-deh ahl ehn-*fehr*-moh ah bvah-*Hahr* deh lah kah-*mee*-yah) (*You [formal] go help the sick person get off the stretcher.*)

- ✔ **¡Apúrese!** (ah-*poo*-reh-seh) (*Hurry up!*)

The following phrases are for informal situations. Remember, informality is appropriate when you talk to a child, or if the person helping you is someone you know.

- ✔ **¿Te ayudo?** (teh ah-*yoo*-doh) (*Can I help you?*)

- ✔ **Sí, ayúdame.** (see ah-*yoo*-dah-meh) (*Yes, help me.*)

- ✔ **Te busco un médico.** (teh *bvoos*-koh oon *meh*-dee-koh) (*I'll get a doctor for you.*)

- ✔ **¡Apúrate!** (ah-*poo*-rah-teh) (*Hurry up!*)

- ✔ **¡Sujétame!** (soo-*Heh*-tah-meh) (*Hold onto me!*)

Ouch! and other expressions of pain

When you're hurt, you want to be able to tell people about it so that they can help ease your pain. The following sentences tell you how to talk about pain — and, just as carrying an umbrella can prevent rain, perhaps practicing talking about pain can prevent you from getting hurt (in Spanish, anyway)!

- **Me duele la espalda.** (meh doo*eh*-leh lah ehs-*pahl*-dah) (*My back hurts.*)

- **¿Le duele la cabeza?** (leh doo*eh*-leh lah kah-*bveh*-sah) (*Does your head hurt? [formal]*)

- **Les duele todo.** (lehs doo*eh*-leh *toh*-doh) (*They hurt all over.*)

- **Nos duelen las manos.** (nohs doo*eh*-lehn lahs *mah*-nohs) (*Our hands hurt.*)

- **¿Te duele aquí?** (teh doo*eh*-leh ah-*kee*) (*Does it hurt you [informal] here?*)

The ways you express pain in English and Spanish differ very little. In English, for example, you may say something like *My toe hurts*; in Spanish, you would add the equivalent of *to me* — with *to* acting as a preposition, and *me* acting as an indirect pronoun. (See Book II, Chapter 1 to brush up on your parts of speech.) Table 9-2 lists the indirect object pronouns.

Table 9-2	Indirect Object Pronouns
Pronoun	*Translation*
me (meh)	me
te (teh)	you (informal, singular)
le (leh)	him, her, you (formal, singular)
nos (nohs)	us
os (ohs)	you (informal, plural)
les (lehs)	them, you (formal, plural)

The following dialogue shows you some of these pain-describing expressions at work.

Talkin' the Talk

After a collision, Nancy is taken to a hospital and is being looked after to see whether she's broken anything.

Doctor: **¿Tiene dolor en la pierna?**
tee-*eh*-neh doh-*lohr* ehn lah pee-*ehr*-nah
Does your leg hurt? [Literally: Do you have any pain in the leg?]

Nancy: **Sí doctor, ¡duele mucho!**
see dohk-*tohr* doo*eh*-leh *moo*-choh
Yes, doctor, it hurts a lot!

Doctor: **Vamos a sacarle rayos X.**
bvah-mohs ah sah-*kahr*-leh *rah*-yohs *eh*-kees
We'll take an x-ray.

X-ray
technician: **Aquí, súbanla a la mesa.**
ah-*kee*, *soo*-bvahn-lah ah lah *meh*-sah
Here, get her on the table.

No se mueva por favor.
noh seh moo*eh*-bvah pohr fah-*bvor*
Don't move, please.

Doctor: **Ya está la radiografía.**
yah ehs-*tah* lah rah-deeoh-grah-*fee*-ah
The x-ray picture is ready.

Aquí tiene la fractura.
ah-*kee* tee*eh*-neh lah frahk-*too*-rah
You have a fracture here.

Vamos a tener que enyesar su pierna.
bvah-mohs ah teh-*nehr* keh ehn-yeh-*sahr* soo
pee*ehr*-nah
We're going to have to put your leg in a cast.

Le voy a dar un analgésico.
leh bvohy a dahr oon ah-nahl-*Heh*-see-koh
I'll give you a painkiller.

Dealing with a bleeding wound

Following are some examples of how to get medical help for someone who's bleeding:

- **¡Hay una emergencia!** (ahy *oo*-nah eh-mehr-*Hehn*-seeah) (*There's an emergency!*)
- **¡Traigan un médico!** (*trah*ee-gahn oon *meh*-dee-koh) (*Bring a doctor!*)
- **¡Traigan una ambulancia!** (*trah*ee-gahn *oo*-nah ahm-bvoo-*lahn*-seeah) (*Bring an ambulance!*)
- **Lo más rápido posible.** (loh mahs *rah*-pee-doh poh-*see*-bleh) (*As fast as possible.*)
- **Tiene un corte.** (tee*eh*-neh oon *kohr*-teh) (*You [formal] have a cut.*)
- **Necesita puntos.** (neh-seh-*see*-tah *poon*-tohs) (*You [formal] need stitches.*)

Closing the wound

If you ever need to get stitches, here are some useful phrases:

- **Me duele mucho.** (meh doo-*eh*-leh *moo*-choh) (*It hurts me a lot.*)
- **Le vamos a poner anestesia local.** (leh *bvah*-mohs a poh-*nehr* ah-nehs-*teh*-seeah loh-*kahl*) (*We'll use local anesthesia.*)
- **Ya se pasó el dolor.** (yah seh *pah*-soh ehl doh-*lohr*) (*The pain is gone.*)

Telling where it hurts

Here, we give you several phrases that may be useful in telling someone what the problem is. (Later, we provide some vocabulary words that may also come handy.)

- **Me sangra la nariz.** (meh *sahn*-grah lah nah-*rees*) (*My nose is bleeding.*)
- **No puedo ver.** (noh poo*eh*-doh bvehr) (*I can't see.*)
- **Me entró algo en el ojo.** (meh ehn-*troh ahl*-goh ehn ehl *oh*-Hoh) (*Something got into my eye.*)
- **Me torcí el tobillo.** (meh tohr-*see* ehl toh-*bvee*-yoh) (*I twisted my ankle.*)
- **Se quebró el brazo derecho.** (seh keh-*broh* ehl *bvrah*-soh deh-*reh*-choh) (*He broke his right arm.*)
- **La herida está en el antebrazo.** (lah eh-*ree*-dah ehs-*tah* ehn ehl ahn-teh-*bvrah*-soh) (*The wound is on the forearm.*)
- **Le duele la muñeca izquierda.** (leh doo*eh*-leh lah moo-*nyeh*-kah ees-kee*ehr*-dah) (*Her left wrist hurts.*)

✔ **Se cortó el dedo índice.** (seh kohr-*toh* ehl *deh*-doh *een*-dee-seh) (*He cut his index finger.*)

✔ **Se torció el cuello.** (seh tohr-see*oh* ehl koo*eh*-yoh) (*She twisted her neck.*)

✔ **Ahora ya no sale sangre.** (ah-*oh*-rah yah noh *sah*-leh *sahn*-greh) (*It stopped bleeding. [Literally: Now there is no more blood coming out.]*)

✔ **Usted tiene la presión muy alta.** (oos-*tehd* tee*eh*-neh lah preh-see*ohn* mooy *ahl*-ta) (*You have very high blood pressure.*)

✔ **He sentido náuseas.** (eh sehn-*tee*-doh *nahoo*-seh-ahs) (*I felt nauseated.*)

The following dialogue shows you how someone uses the information in this chapter to get in to the doctor.

Talkin' the Talk

Julia just can't get rid of her headache, and she decides to see her doctor. She's at her doctor's office, talking to the receptionist.

Julia: **¿Está el doctor Díaz?**
ehs-*tah* ehl dohk-*tohr* dee-ahs
Is Dr. Díaz in?

Receptionist: **Sí, está. ¿Tiene cita?**
see ehs-*tah* tee*eh*-neh *see*-tah
Yes, he's in. Do you have an appointment?

Julia: **No tengo cita, pero necesito verle.**
noh *tehn*-goh *see*-tah *peh*-roh neh-seh-*see*-toh *bvehr*-leh
I don't have an appointment, but I need to see him.

Tengo mucho dolor de cabeza.
tehn-goh *moo*-cho doh-*lohr* deh kah-*bveh*-sah
I have a bad headache.

Receptionist: **Muy bien, ¿cómo se llama?**
mooy bvee*ehn* *koh*-moh seh-*yah*-mah
Very well, what's your name?

Julia: **Soy Julia Frank.**
sohy *Hoo*-leeah frahnk
I'm Julia Frank.

Receptionist: **Un momento, por favor. Tome asiento en la sala de espera.**
oon moh-*mehn*-toh pohr fah-*bvohr* *toh*-meh ah-see-*ehn*-toh ehn lah *sah*-lah deh ehs-*peh*-rah
One moment, please. Take a seat in the waiting room.

In this dialogue, a patient describes her problem to the doctor.

Talkin' the Talk

 After waiting a few minutes, Julia is ushered into the doctor's office and begins to explain her symptoms.

Julia:	**Me duele la cabeza.** meh doo*eh*-leh lah kah-*bveh*-sah *My head hurts.*
Dr. Díaz:	**¿Desde cuándo?** *dehs*-deh koo*ahn*-doh *Since when?*
Julia:	**Desde ayer. Me golpeé la cabeza.** *dehs*-deh ah-yehr meh gohl-peh-*eh* lah kah-*bveh*-sah *Since yesterday. I banged my head.*
Dr. Díaz:	**¿Cómo se golpeó?** *koh*-moh seh gohl-peh-*oh* *How did you bang [it]?*
Julia:	**Me caí en la calle.** meh kahee ehn lah *kah*-yeh *I fell on the street.*
Dr. Díaz:	**¿Tiene mareos?** tee-*eh*-neh mah-*reh*-ohs *Do you get dizzy?*
Julia:	**Sí, tengo mareos.** see *tehn*-goh mah-*reh*-ohs *Yes, I get dizzy.*
Dr. Díaz:	**Vamos a tenerle en observación durante dos días.** *vah*-mohs ah teh-*nehr*-leh ehn ohbv-sehr-bvah-see*ohn* doo-*rahn*-teh dohs *dee*-ahs *We'll keep you under observation for two days.*

When speaking with a doctor and describing your symptoms, it helps to be able to tell the doctor which body part(s) are affected. Check out Book IV, Chapter 1 for a list of body parts and their Spanish names.

When you sneeze among native Spanish-speakers, you never get a chance to excuse yourself. The moment you sneeze, someone immediately says: **¡Salud!** (sah-*lood*) (*Health!*) And you immediately answer: **¡Gracias!** (*grah*-seeahs) (*Thanks!*).

Seeing the dentist

If you have a dental problem while you're in a Spanish-speaking country, you'll probably discover that dental care is a lot less expensive in Spanish-speaking America than it is in English-speaking America. Part of the reason may be that dental offices in Mexico, Central, South, and Latin America aren't as jazzy as they usually are in the United States and Canada; just be sure to find a dentist with the proper equipment to take care of your problem.

You may find the following phrases helpful when you go to a Spanish-speaking dentist:

- ✔ **Necesito un dentista.** (neh-seh-*see*-toh oon dehn-*tees*-tah) (*I need a dentist.*)

- ✔ **¿Me puede recomendar un dentista?** (meh poo*eh*-deh reh-koh-mehn-*dahr* oon dehn-*tces*-tah) (*Can you recommend a dentist?*)

- ✔ **Doctor, me duele el diente.** (dohk-*ohr* meh doo*eh*-leh ehl dee*ehn*-teh) (*Doctor, I have a toothache.*)

- ✔ **Tiene una caries.** (tee-*eh*-neh oo-nah kah-ree*ehs*) (*You have a cavity.*)

- ✔ **Quebré una muela.** (keh-*bvreh* oo-nah moo*eh*-lah) (*I broke a molar.*)

- ✔ **Le pondré anestesia.** (leh pohn-*dreh* ah-nehs-*teh*-seeah) (*I'll give you anesthesia.*)

- ✔ **Le taparé la caries.** (leh tah-pah-*reh* lah *kah*-reeehs) (*I can fill the cavity.*)

- ✔ **Le sacaré la muela.** (leh sah-kah-*reh* lah moo*eh*-lah) (*I'll [have to] pull the molar out.*)

- ✔ **Le pondré un puente.** (leh-pohn-*dreh* oon poo*ehn*-teh) (*I'll put in a bridge.*)

- ✔ **Le pondré una corona.** (leh-pohn-*dreh* oo-nah koh-*roh*-nah) (*I'll put on a crown.*)

Here's a summary of terms you typically hear in a dentist's office:

- ✔ **el/la dentista** (ehl/lah dehn-*tees*-tah) (*the dentist*)

- ✔ **el diente** (ehl dee*ehn*-teh) (*the tooth*)

- ✔ **la muela** (lah moo*eh*-lah) (*the molar*)

- ✔ **la caries** (lah kah-ree*ehs*) (*the cavity*)

- ✔ **dolor de muelas** (doh-*lohr* deh moo*eh*-lahs) (*toothache*)

Talking about insurance

If you need to visit a dentist, or any other professional, while you're traveling, be sure you get a receipt to give to your insurance carrier at home. The following phrases are useful in dealing with insurance questions:

- ✔ **¿Tiene seguro dental?** (tee*eh*-neh seh-*goo*-roh dehn-*tahl*) (*Do you have dental insurance?*)

- ✔ **¿Tiene seguro de salud?** (tee*eh*-neh seh-*goo*-roh deh sah-*lood*) (*Do you have health insurance?*)

- ✔ **¿Me puede dar un recibo para el seguro?** (meh poo*eh*-deh dahr oon reh-*see*-bvoh *pah*-rah ehl seh-*goo*-roh) (*Can you give me a receipt for my insurance?*)

Calling the Police

Most people obey the laws and usually don't engage in activities that involve the police or other aspects of the legal system. But accidents happen, and you can break a law that you know nothing about. If that's the case, you need help from your consulate or a lawyer to make sure that your rights are protected. ***Note:*** Most of the information in this section is for travelers who experience legal issues in Spanish-speaking countries. If you're a law enforcement officer in an English-speaking country needing to interact with Spanish-speakers, check out Book IV, Chapter 2.

If you have legal dealings in a Spanish-speaking country, take into account that the legal system is likely to be completely different from the one you're familiar with, and the laws of the country you're in override the laws of the country you hold citizenship in. Be aware, too, that the philosophy behind the legal system applies to many of the institutions you may encounter. Probably the most important difference is that in the United States and Canada, you're innocent until proven guilty, whereas in all Latin American countries, you're guilty until proven innocent.

In an emergency of any kind, but particularly in a situation involving legal officials, try to be patient, and above all, firm. Keep in mind that just as you're unfamiliar with the practices and procedures of a foreign system, the officers and administrators of that system are unaware of your legal expectations.

If you get involved in a Spanish-speaking country's legal system, try to get someone from your consulate to help you handle the situation — he or she will take your interests much more to heart than a local lawyer or the local police. In fact, after you set the dates for a visit to a Spanish American area, find out where your country's closest consulate is — and when you arrive, register there in case you need emergency assistance.

You may also ask when you arrive:

- ✔ **¿Hay aquí un Consulado de Estados Unidos?** (ahy ah-*kee* oon kohn-soo-*lah*-doh deh ehs-*tah*-dohs oo-*nee*-dohs) (*Is there an American consulate here?*)

- ✔ **¿Hay un abogado que hable inglés?** (ahy oon ah-bvoh-*gah*-doh keh *ah*-bvleh een-*glehs*) (*Is there a lawyer who speaks English?*)

If Spanish isn't your first language, and you're in a Spanish-speaking area, ask for a lawyer who speaks English and make sure the lawyer's English is better than your Spanish before you get involved with him or her. Don't accept just anyone. If you have trouble making yourself understood, get another lawyer.

The following dialogue shows you an extreme case of legal trouble abroad. We doubt you'll be involved in a situation like Silverio's, but we want to cover all your bases, and just in case, these few sentences may be useful.

Talkin' the Talk

Silverio has been detained by the police and is trying to get to the bottom of the situation.

Police officer:	**Usted va detenido.** oos-*tehd* bvah deh-teh-*nee*-doh *You're under arrest.*
Silverio:	**¿Por qué?** pohr keh *Why?*
Police officer:	**Está circulando ebrio.** ehs-*tah* seer-koo-*lahn*-doh *eh*-bvreeoh *For impaired driving.*
Silverio:	**Oficial, yo no tomo alcohol.** oh-fee-see*ahl* yoh noy *toh*-moh ahl-koh-*ohl* *Officer, I don't drink alcohol.*
Police officer:	**Vamos a la comisaría.** *bvah*-mohs ah lah koh-mee-sah-*ree*-ah *We're going to the police station.*
Silverio:	**Creo que usted se equivoca.** kreoh keh oos-*tehd* seh eh-kee-*bvoh*-kah *I believe you're mistaken.*

Police officer:	**Va preso conmigo.**
	bvah *preh*-soh kohn-*mee*-goh
	Come with me. (Literally: You go prisoner with me.)

Silverio:	**Quiero hablar con un abogado.**
	keee*eh*-roh ah-*bvlahr* kohn oon ah-bvoh-*gah*-doh
	I want to talk to a lawyer.

Quiero hablar con mi cónsul.
keee*eh*-roh ah-*bvlahr* kohn mee *kohn*-sool
I want to talk to my consulate.

Quiero hablar por teléfono.
keee*eh*-roh ah-*bvlahr* pohr teh-*leh*-foh-noh
I want to talk on the phone.

Reporting a robbery

If someone robs you while you're in a Spanish-speaking area, you can attract the help you need by using these phrases.

- ✔ **¡Un robo!** (oon *roh*-bvoh) (*A burglary!*)
- ✔ **¡Un asalto!** (oon ah-*sahl*-toh) (*A holdup!*)
- ✔ **¡Atrápenlo!** (ah-*trah*-pehn-loh) (*Catch him!*)
- ✔ **¡Policía!** (poh-lee-*see*-ah) (*Police!*)

We hope you never need to use them, but if you're ever robbed or attacked in a Spanish-speaking area, these phrases are important to know:

- ✔ **¡Llamen a la policía!** (*yah*-mehn ah lah poh-lee-*see*-ah) (*Call the police!*)
- ✔ **¡Me robó la billetera!** (meh roh-*bvoh* lah bvee-yeh-*teh*-rah) (*[She/He] stole my wallet!*)
- ✔ **Haga una denuncia a la policía.** (*ah*-gah *oo*-nah deh-*noon*-seeah ah la poh-lee-*see*-ah) (*Report it to the police. [Literally: Make an accusation to the police.]*)

Describing the crime and suspect

If you do have an unpleasant encounter with a thief, here are some words that can be helpful in describing the culprit to the police:

- **Era un hombre bajo, corpulento.** (*eh*-rah oon *ohm*-bvreh *bvah*-Hoh kohr-poo-*lehn*-toh) (*He was a short man, heavyset.*)

- **Tenía cabello oscuro y barba.** (teh-*nee*-ah kah-*bveh*-yoh ohs-*koo*-roh ee *bvahr*-bvah) (*He had dark hair and a beard.*)

- **Vestía pantalón de mezclilla y camisa blanca.** (bvehs-*tee*-ah pahn-tah-*lohn* deh mehs-*klee*-yah ee kah-*mee*-sah *bvlahn*-kah) (*He wore jeans and a white shirt.*)

- **Tendrá unos cuarenta años.** (tehn-*drah* oo-nohs kooah-*rehn*-tah *ah*-nyos) (*He's around 40 years old.*)

- **Iba con una mujer delgada.** (*ee*-bvah kohn oo-nah moo-*Hehr* dehl-*gah*-dah) (*He was with a thin woman.*)

- **Era alta, rubia, de ojos claros.** (*eh*-rah *ahl*-tah *roo*-bveeah deh *oh*-Hohs *klah*-rohs) (*She was tall, blond, with light-colored eyes.*)

The following verbs can help you describe a crime:

- **atacar** (ah-tah-*kahr*) (*to attack*)

- **robar** (roh-*bvahr*) (*to steal; to rob*)

In the following dialogue, you can see how various people interact after an accident.

Talkin' the Talk

Crash! Bang! A collision. Julieta doesn't need it, but here she is. What does she do?

Julieta:	**¡Rápido, vengan!**
	rah-pee-doh *bven*-gahn
	Quickly, come here!

Passerby:	**Hubo un choque.**
	oo-bvoh oon *choh*-keh
	There was a collision.

Julieta:	**Paré porque cambió la luz.**
	pah-*reh pohr*-keh kahm-*bveeoh* lah loos
	I stopped because the light changed.

Police officer:	**¿A qué velocidad iba?**
	ah keh bveh-loh-see-*dahd* ee-bvah
	How fast were you going?

Julieta:	**Iba lento, a menos de cuarenta kilómetros.**
	ee-bvah *lehn*-toh ah *meh*-nohs deh kooah-*rehn*-tah
	kee-*loh*-meh-trohs
	I was going slowly, less than 40 kilometers.

Police officer:	**¿Tiene usted seguro para el auto?**
	tee*eh*-neh oos-*tehd* seh-*goo*-roh *pah*-rah ehl *ahoo*-toh
	Do you have car insurance?

Julieta:	**Sí, quiero avisar a mi compañía de seguros.**
	see, kee*eh*-roh ah-bvee-*sahr* ah mee
	kohm-pah-*nyee*-ah deh seh-*goo*-rohs
	Yes, I want to notify my insurance company.

Looking for Help with Buscar

Buscar (bvoos-*kahr*) is a much-used regular verb with a number of meanings: *to look for*, *to try to find*, or *to search for*.

Conjugation	*Pronunciation*
yo busco	yoh *bvoos*-koh
tú buscas	too *bvoos*-kahs
él, ella, ello, uno, usted busca	ehl *eh*-yah *eh*-yoh *oo*-noh oos-*tehd* *bvoos*-kah
nosotros buscamos	noh-*soh*-trohs bvoos-*kah*-mohs
vosotros buscáis	bvoh-*soh*-trohs bvoos-*kah*ees
ellos, ellas buscan	*eh*-yohs *eh*-yahs *bvoos*-kahn

Practice using buscar with these phrases:

- ✔ **Buscan un mecánico.** (*bvoos*-kahn oon meh-*kah*-nee-koh) (*They're looking for a mechanic.*)

- ✔ **Ellos buscan un médico.** (*eh*-yohs *bvoos*-kahn oon *meh*-dee-koh) (*They're looking for a doctor.*)

- ✔ **Buscas un lugar donde descansar.** (*bvoos*-kahs oon loo-*gahr* dohn-deh dehs-kahn-*sahr*) (*You're looking for a place where you can rest.*)

- ✔ **Ya no busca, encontró un abogado.** (yah noh *bvoos*-kah ehn-kohn-*troh* oon ah-bvoh-*gah*-doh) (*He/She isn't searching any more, he/she found a lawyer.*)

- ✔ **Buscan un espacio y no encuentran.** (*bvoos*-kahn oon ehs-*pah*-seeoh ee noh ehn-koo*ehn*-trahn) (*They're looking for a space and can't find one.*)

Book II

Grasping Basic Grammar Essentials

In this book . . .

Every language is governed by rules and regulations to ensure mutual understanding between the person doing the talking and the person being spoken to. Spanish is no different in this regard. In this book, we introduce you to the basic rules and regulations that govern the Spanish language. We start slowly by introducing the various parts of speech before moving on to slightly more advanced topics like conjugating verbs.

Here are the contents of Book II at a glance:

Chapter 1

Getting to Know Your Parts of Speech

. . . .

In This Chapter

- Differentiating among the various parts of speech
- Starting out right with subject pronouns
- Selecting the correct subject pronoun for every situation

. . . .

Years ago, diagramming sentences was an essential skill covered in English grammar class. Students would sit in class, pen (and sometimes ruler) in hand, dissecting sentences; labeling the nouns, verbs, modifiers, and elusive direct and indirect objects; and creating schematics showing how all the words related to one another.

Though many students felt that these exercises were utterly useless, those who took them seriously developed a deeper understanding of language and how it worked. They also developed a stronger aptitude for acquiring new languages. Those who didn't grasp these basics of English grammar usually require a brief primer before embarking on the study of a new language — a primer like the one provided in this chapter. If you've already mastered English grammar, your job's much easier, but you're still likely to benefit by observing the similarities and differences between Spanish and English.

This chapter provides a quick course on identifying and using the parts of speech that make Spanish sentences grammatically correct. Specifically, you discover how to recognize nouns, verbs, adjectives, adverbs, pronouns (especially subject pronouns), and the supporting cast — articles, prepositions, and conjunctions — that stitch everything together.

Before you begin to examine the basic building blocks of a sentence, familiarize yourself with the two essential components of every sentence — subject and predicate. The *subject* is the entity performing the action along with anything that describes the subject. The *predicate* is everything else — the action (or verb) and everything related to that action.

Unveiling the Parts of Speech

You may be questioning why knowing your Spanish grammar is so important. Can't you just grab a dictionary when you want to find a word or phrase? Nope. Language is more complex than that. Sure, memorizing vocabulary is essential, but equally important is understanding the various forms those words can take, where they need to appear in a sentence, and how they function in relation to one another. You can't build an airplane simply by dumping all the parts in the center of a production plant, nor can you speak or understand a language without knowing how the words are assembled to form meaningful expressions. Grammar consists of the rules that govern a particular language.

This chapter introduces the essentials of Spanish grammar by anchoring them to what you already know about English grammar. In the following sections, you discover the basic building blocks that go into making sentences so that you have a solid foundation upon which to understand all the other concepts explained in Books 2 and 3.

Nouns

A *noun* is the part of speech that refers to a person, place, thing, quality, idea, or action. Here are some examples of nouns in action:

- **Person:** *The boy is friendly.* (**El muchacho es amable.**)
- **Place:** *I want to go home.* (**Quiero ir a casa.**)
- **Thing:** *I would like to see that book.* (**Quisiera ver ese libro.**)
- **Quality:** *I admire her courage.* (**Admiro su coraje.**)
- **Idea:** *Communism is a political theory.* (**El comunismo es una teoría política.**)
- **Action:** *The plane's departure is imminent.* (**La partida del avión es inminente.**)

In everyday speaking/writing, you use nouns (in this case, Mary) most often in the following forms:

- As the subject of a verb:

  Mary speaks Spanish. (**Mary habla español.**)
- As the direct object of a verb:

  I see Mary. (**Yo veo a Mary.**)

✔ As the indirect object of a verb:

I speak to Mary. (**Yo le hablo a Mary.**)

✔ As the object of a preposition:

I went out with Mary. (**Yo salí con Mary.**)

Unlike English nouns, all Spanish nouns have a gender: masculine or feminine. All words you use to qualify or describe a noun must agree with the noun with respect to gender. This topic is discussed in more detail in Book II, Chapter 2.

The Spanish language classifies nouns as common or proper, collective, or concrete or abstract. A *common noun* refers to a general class of persons, things, places, and so on:

> **El hombre es alto.** (*The man is tall.*)
>
> **Los edificios son modernos.** (*The buildings are modern.*)
>
> **Me gustan los deportes.** (*I like sports.*)

A *proper noun* is the specific name of a person, thing, place, and so on:

> **George Washington fue un presidente.** (*George Washington was a president.*)
>
> **Guernica es una pintura por Picasso.** (*Guernica is a painting by Picasso.*)
>
> **España es un país en Europa.** (*Spain is a country in Europe.*)

A *collective noun* is used singularly and refers to a group:

> **Mi familia es pequeña.** (*My family is small.*)

A *concrete noun* refers to something that you can perceive with your senses; an *abstract noun* refers to an idea:

> Concrete: **El agua es azul.** (*The water is blue.*)
>
> Abstract: **El odio es un vicio.** (*Hate is a vice.*)

Articles

Articles are the tiny words that introduce nouns. Most people know them by name: *the, a, an.* In English, you simply need to know the articles and a couple of rules for choosing the right one. For example, when you first introduce something, you generally use an *indefinite article* (*a* or *an*). When you refer

Book II

Grasping Basic Grammar Essentials

to it again, you can then use a *definite article,* such as *the.* English divides the articles into two groups:

- ✔ **Definite article:** the
- ✔ **Indefinite articles:** a, an

Spanish uses two different types of articles, too, but selecting an article is further complicated by the fact that the article's gender (masculine or feminine) and number (singular or plural) must agree with the noun's gender and number. As a result, Spanish uses four definite articles (see Table 1-1):

Table 1-1	Spanish Definite Articles	
Number	**Masculine**	**Feminine**
Singular	el	la
Plural	los	las

To say *the boy* in Spanish, you say **el muchacho.** To say *the girl*, you say **la muchacha.**

Because articles are so dependent on gender, they're covered in Book II, Chapter 2, which provides an in depth discussion of gender issues and how they affect all articles in Spanish.

Spanish also uses two singular indefinite articles — which are the equivalent of *a* or *an* in English and two plural indefinite articles — which are translated as "some" (see Table 1-2).

Table 1-2	Spanish Indefinite Articles	
Number	**Masculine**	**Feminine**
Singular	un	una
Plural	unos	unas

Whereas all the definite articles translate as *the*, the singular indefinite articles translate as *a* or *an,* and the plural forms translate as *some.*

To say *a boy* in Spanish, you say **un muchacho.** To say *a girl*, you say **una muchacha.** And to say *some boys and girls,* you say **unos muchachos.**

Pronouns

A *pronoun* is a part of speech used in place of a noun. The following list outlines the pronouns discussed in this book:

- *Demonstrative pronouns* (see Book II, Chapter 2) express *this, that, these,* and *those:*

  Show me *that*. (**Muéstreme éso.**)

- *Subject pronouns* (discussed later in this chapter) are followed by the verb expressing the main action in the sentence (*I, you, he, she, it, we, they*):

  You are nice. (**Ud. es simpático.**)

- *Possessive pronouns* (see Book II, Chapter 2) indicate that something belongs to a specific person (*mine, yours, his, hers, its, ours, theirs*):

  That is *mine*. (**Es mío.**)

- *Interrogative pronouns* (see Book II, Chapter 4) ask a question (*who, which, what,* and so on):

  Who is it? (**¿Quién es?**)

- *Direct object pronouns* (see Book III, Chapter 2) replace direct object nouns; they answer whom or what the subject is acting upon. The direct object pronouns are **me, te, lo, la** (**le** in Spain), **nos,** (**os** in Spain), **los,** and **las** (**les** in Spain):

  I'll be seeing you. (**Te veo.**)

- *Indirect object pronouns* (see Book III, Chapter 2) replace indirect object nouns; they explain to or for whom something is done. They include **me, te, le, nos,** (**os** in Spain), and **les:**

  He wrote to *me*. (**Me escribió.**)

- *Reflexive pronouns* (see Book III, Chapter 3) show that the subject is acting upon itself (**me, te, se, nos,** [**os** in Spain]):

  They wake [themselves] up early. (**Ellos se despiertan temprano.**)

- *Prepositional pronouns* (see Book II, Chapter 8) are used after prepositions (**mí, ti, él, ella, Ud., nosotros, vosotros** (in Spain), **ellos, ellas, Uds.**):

  They're going to the movies without *me*. (**Van al cine sin mí.**)

  The prepositional pronouns **mí** and **ti** become **migo** and **tigo,** respectively, after the preposition **con** (with):

  Is he going to school with *you*? (**¿Va a la escuela contigo?**)

Book II

Grasping Basic Grammar Essentials

Verbs

A verb is a part of speech that shows an action or a state of being. In Spanish, as in English, verbs change from their infinitive form (they're *conjugated*, in other words) as follows:

- ✔ To agree with the person performing the action (I, you, he, she, it, we, they)

- ✔ To indicate the time when the action was performed (past, present, future)

- ✔ To indicate the mood of the action — for example, whether you're simply making a statement (indicative), issuing a command (imperative), or expressing desire (subjunctive)

The infinitive of form of a verb is its "raw" form — its "to" form before it's conjugated. It represents a situation where the action is stated, but no one is *doing* the action. Infinitives in Spanish have three different endings, and you conjugate them according to these endings (**-ar, -er,** and **-ir**) when a subject is present or is implied. The following presents a sample conjugation of the verb to swim:

nadar (to swim)

He likes to swim.	**Le gusta nadar.**

Note that in the above example the sentence states that "He likes to swim." But it doesn't state that he is actually swimming. Therefore, the verb is used in its infinitive form both in English and Spanish.

He swims rather well.	**Él nada bastante bien.**
We swim well, too.	**Nosotros nadamos bien también.**

Verbs are classified as transitive or intransitive. A *transitive* verb must be followed by a direct object to complete its meaning:

> *I opened the door.* (**Yo abrí la puerta.**)

An *intransitive* verb doesn't require an object:

> *I understand.* (**Yo comprendo.**)

You can use some verbs both transitively and intransitively:

> *She speaks Spanish.* [direct object] (**Ella habla español.**)

> *She speaks well.* [no direct object] (**Ella habla bien.**)

Also, a verb may be used reflexively or reciprocally to show that the subject is acting upon itself (see Book III, Chapter 3):

I washed myself. (**Yo me lavé.**)

They love each other. (**Ellos se aman.**)

Adjectives

An adjective is a part of speech that describes a noun:

The house is <u>white</u>. (**La casa es <u>blanca</u>.**)

A Spanish adjective can have other applications, too, which we outline in the following list:

Book II

Grasping
Basic
Grammar
Essentials

✔ A *possessive adjective* tells to whom the noun belongs:

   It's <u>my</u> book. (**Es mi libro.**)

✔ A *demonstrative adjective* shows this, that, these, or those:

   <u>That</u> film is good. (**<u>Esa</u> película es buena.**)

✔ An *interrogative adjective* asks the question whose, which, or what:

   <u>Whose</u> car is that? (**¿<u>De quién</u> es ese coche?**)

✔ An *indefinite adjective* shows an indefinite amount:

   He has <u>many</u> friends. (**Él tiene <u>muchos</u> amigos.**)

✔ A number (cardinal or ordinal; see Book I, Chapter 2) is an adjective that gives a specific amount:

   I need <u>two</u> pens. (**Necesito <u>dos</u> bolígrafos.**)

   It's his <u>tenth</u> birthday. (**Es su <u>décimo</u> cumpleaños.**)

To find out more about adjectives, check out Book II, Chapter 7.

Adverbs

An *adverb* is a part of speech that modifies a verb, an adjective, or another adverb:

✔ Modifying a verb: *You speak <u>quickly</u>.* (**Ud. habla <u>rápidamente</u>.**)

✔ Modifying an adjective: *Her grandmother is <u>very</u> old.* (**Su abuela es <u>muy</u> vieja.**)

✔ Modifying an adverb: *They eat <u>too</u> slowly.* (**Ellos comen <u>demasiado</u> despacio.**)

In English, many adverbs end in -ly: calmly, certainly, and so on. In Spanish, many adverbs end in **-mente: tranquilamente** (*calmly*), **ciertamente** (*certainly*), and so on. For more about adverbs, check out Book II, Chapter 7.

Prepositions

You can find almost as many definitions of *preposition* as prepositions themselves, because these words serve so many functions. One of the best ways to look at prepositions, however, is to understand that they don't tell who does what but rather where, when, how, and why something's done. Jenny may hit the ball, but the preposition tells you where she hit it — *through* the window, *across* the street, *into* the pot of soup.

Following are some examples of common Spanish prepositions in action:

> **Yo puse los libros <u>en</u> mi mochila.** (*I put the books <u>in</u> my backpack.*)

> **Él habló <u>por</u> teléfono <u>con</u> su novia.** (*He talked <u>on</u> the phone <u>with</u> his girlfriend.*)

> **Este regalo es <u>para</u> mi abuela.** (*This gift is <u>for</u> my grandmother.*)

Although prepositions seem basic and straightforward, choosing the right preposition for the right job can be quite a challenge. In addition, Spanish further complicates the use of prepositions by making certain prepositions mandatory in the presence of certain verbs. For all you need to know about prepositions, see Book II, Chapter 8.

Conjunctions

As in English, Spanish uses *conjunctions* to connect related or contrasting thoughts within the same sentence. Conjunctions can also be used at the beginning of a sentence to connect it to a thought expressed in a previous sentence. The most commonly used conjunctions are

> *and* (**y**)

> *but* (**pero, sino**)

> *nor* (**ni**)

> *or* (**o**)

Here are some examples of conjunctions in use in Spanish:

✔ **Siempre voy con Juan y Susana.** (*I always go with Juan and Susana.*)

Replace **y** with **e** in front of a word beginning with **i** or **hi**. For example: **Visitamos Francia e Inglaterra.** (*We visited France and England.*)

✔ **Nos encanta comer en este restaurante pero es muy caro.** (*We love to eat at this restaurant, but it's very expensive.*)

Use **sino** instead of **pero** when the meaning is *but on the contrary*. For example: **Ella no era aburrida sino muy divertida.** (*She wasn't boring but on the contrary very amusing.*)

Ni is very often used in cases of double negation. For example: **No tienen ni casa ni comida.** (*They have neither a house nor any food.*)

✔ **¿Quisiera mayonesa o mostaza para su sandwich?** (*Would you like mayonnaise or mustard for your sandwich?*)

Use **u** is used in place of **o** in front of a word beginning with **o** or **ho**. For example: **Creo que tengo siete u ocho de sus libros.** (*I believe that I have seven or eight of his books.*)

Complex conjunctions can be formed by adding **que** to an adverb or a preposition, such as in these examples:

although (**aunque**)

because (**porque**)

since (**puesto que, desde que**)

until (**hasta que**)

without (**sin que**)

Here are some examples of complex conjunctions in use in Spanish:

✔ **Vamos al cine porque tiene la película que queremos ver.** (*We're going to the cinema because it has the movie that we want to see.*)

✔ **Vamos a ir a su casa aunque es muy tarde.** (*We're going to go to his house although it's very late.*)

✔ **Él trabajó hasta que terminó.** (*He worked until he finished.*)

Spanish commonly uses conjunctions in sentences with phrases requiring the subjunctive mood, so be sure to check out Book III, Chapter 6, where we cover the subjunctive.

Book II

Grasping Basic Grammar Essentials

Meeting Subject Pronouns Face to Face

A *subject pronoun* is a word used in place of a subject noun. Instead of saying "Lucy fried an egg," for example, you would say, "She fried an egg." *She* (the subject pronoun) takes the place of *Lucy* (the subject noun). This pronoun identifies who or what is performing the action (verb).

In English, you use subject pronouns all the time in place of, or to avoid, repeating subject nouns. It's much simpler to write "They left" than "Mr. Anthony Bolavolunta and Miss Cleopatra Johnson left." The subject pronouns *I, you, he, she, we,* and *they* enable you to write clear, concise sentences. Subject nouns and pronouns alike are followed by the appropriate forms of the verbs expressing particular actions. (Book II, Chapter 3 introduces verbs in the present tense.)

You don't use Spanish subject pronouns as frequently as their English counterparts, because a Spanish verb ending generally indicates the subject. You use Spanish subject pronouns, therefore, mainly to be polite, to emphasize or stress the subject, or to be perfectly clear as to who the subject is.

Just like in English, Spanish subject pronouns have a person (first, second, or third) and a number (singular or plural), as you can see in Table 1-3.

Table 1-3	Spanish Subject Pronouns			
Person	*Singular*	*Meaning*	*Plural*	*Meaning*
1st person	yo	I	nosotros (nosotras)	we
2nd person informal	tú	you	vosotros (vosotras)	you (familiar)
2nd person formal	usted (Ud.)	you	ustedes (Uds.)	you (polite)
3rd person	él	he	ellos	they
	ella	she	ellas	they

Unlike the English subject pronoun *I,* which is always capitalized, the Spanish pronoun **yo** is capitalized only at the beginning of a sentence. You always write the abbreviations **Ud.** and **Uds.** with capital letters, even though you write the English equivalent you with a lowercase letter unless it appears at the beginning of a sentence. When **usted** and **ustedes** aren't abbreviated, they're capitalized only at the beginning of a sentence. Here are some examples:

Yo me voy. (*I'm leaving.*)

Eduardo y yo salimos. (*Eduardo and I are going out.*)

¿Busca Ud. (usted) algo? (*Are you looking for something?*)

¿Uds. (Ustedes) necesitan ayuda? (*Do you need help?*)

Applying subject pronouns

The use of certain subject pronouns can be confusing for many reasons. Two different Spanish pronouns may have the same English meaning. Some Spanish subject pronouns are used primarily in Spain or in Latin America. Finally, some Spanish subject pronouns refer only to females, whereas others refer to males or to a mixed group of males and females. The following sections help you select the correct subject pronouns for all circumstances in all parts of the Spanish-speaking world.

Book II

Grasping Basic Grammar Essentials

Tú versus Ud.

You use the informal (familiar) subject pronoun **tú** to address one friend, relative, child, or pet, because it's the informal, singular form of **you.** Basically, you use **tú** to express **you** when you really like the person or pet:

Tú eres mi mejor amigo. (*You're my best friend.*)

You use **Ud.** to show respect to an older person or when speaking to a stranger or someone you don't know well, because **Ud.** is the formal, singular form of *you.* You may also use **Ud.** when you want to get to know the person better:

¿Es Ud. español? (*Are you Spanish?*)

Vosotros (vosotras) versus Uds.

Vosotros and **vosotras** are informal plural subject pronouns expressing *you.* The **vosotros** (**vosotras**) form is used primarily in Spain to address more than one friend, relative, child, or pet — the informal, plural form of *you.* You use **vosotros** when speaking to a group of males or to a combined group of males and females. You use **vosotras** only when speaking to a group of females. Basically, you only use **vosotros** (**vosotras**) in Spain when speaking to a group of people you really like!

¿Vosotros me comprendís? (*Do you understand me?*)

Uds. is a plural subject pronoun that also expresses *you.* **Uds.** is used throughout the Spanish-speaking world to show respect to more than one older person or when speaking to multiple strangers or people you don't know well. **Uds.** is the formal, plural form of *you* and replaces **vosotros (vosotras)** in Spanish (Latin, Central, and South) America. Basically, you're playing it safe if you use **Uds.** when speaking to a group of people:

> **Uds. son muy simpáticos.** (*You're very nice.*)

You don't express the English pronoun *it* as a subject in Spanish; it can be understood from the meaning of the sentence:

> **¿Qué es?** (*What is it?*)
>
> **Es una herramienta.** (*It's a tool.*)

Él versus ella

Él (*he*) refers to one male person; **ella** (*she*) refers to one female person:

> **Él toca la guitarra mientras ella baila.** (*He plays the guitar while she dances.*)

Ellos versus ellas

Ellos (*they*) refers to more than one male or to a combined group of males and females, no matter the number of each gender present. **Ellas** refers to a group of females only:

> **Juan y Jorge (Ellos) escuchan.** (*Juan and Jorge [They] listen.*)
>
> **Luz y Susana (Ellas) escuchan.** (*Luz and Susana [They] listen.*)
>
> **Juan y Luz (Ellos) escuchan.** (*Juan and Luz [They] listen.*)
>
> **El niño y mil niñas (Ellos) escuchan.** (*The boy and 1,000 girls [They] listen.*)

Nosotros (nosotras)

When you're talking about someone else and yourself at the same time, you must use the "we" (**nosotros/nosotras**) form of the verb. Nosotros refers to more than one male or to a combined group of males and females, no matter the number of each gender present. **Nosotras** refers to a group of females only:

> **Jorge y yo (Nosotros) jugamos al tenis.** (*Jorge and I [We] play tennis.*)
>
> **Luz y yo (Nosotras) jugamos al tenis.** (*Luz and I [We] play tennis.*)

Omitting subject pronouns

In English, you use subject pronouns all the time to explain who's doing what. In Spanish, however, you use subject pronouns a lot less frequently because the verb ending generally indicates the subject. No matter the infinitive ending of the verb (**-ar, -er, -ir**), if the verb form ends in **-o**, the subject must be **yo** because no other present-tense verb conjugation has an **-o** ending. **Hablo español**, for instance, can only mean *I speak Spanish.*

If, on the other hand, you see **Habla español,** you can't know whether the subject is **él** (*he*), **ella** (*she*), or **Ud.** (*you*) if the sentence is taken out of context. When given the context, you usually omit the subject pronoun **él** or **ella**: **Le presento a mi amiga, Marta. Habla español.** (*Let me introduce you to my friend, Marta. She speaks Spanish.*)

To avoid confusion, you regularly use the subject pronoun **Ud.** to differentiate between *he, she,* and *you*:

> **¿Habla español?** (*Do you [Does he/she] speak Spanish?*)
>
> **Mi novio habla español. Habla bien.** (*My boyfriend speaks Spanish. He speaks well.*)
>
> **¿Habla Ud. español?** (*Do you speak Spanish?*)

You regularly use the subject pronoun **Uds.** for sentences in the plural to differentiate between *they* and *you*:

> **Cantan bien.** (*They [You] sing well.*)
>
> **Mis primos están en el coro. Cantan bien.** (*My cousins are in the chorus. They sing well.*)
>
> **Uds. cantan bien también.** (*You sing well, too.*)

Book II

Grasping Basic Grammar Essentials

Chapter 2

Addressing Gender Issues

· ·

In This Chapter

✏ Getting specific with definite articles

✏ Keeping it general with indefinite articles

✏ Applying demonstrative adjectives and pronouns correctly

✏ Determining the gender of nouns

✏ Forming the plural and showing possession

· ·

Gender is a battle that English-speakers don't fight. In English, a noun is simply a noun; you don't have to worry about a noun having a gender (masculine or feminine). In Spanish, however, a noun has a gender, and the gender of a noun very often determines the spelling of other words in the sentence. What determines this gender? Certainly not what you may perceive to be masculine or feminine.

Don't assume anything. For instance, *a tie* (**una corbata**) is feminine in Spanish, but *lipstick* (**un lápiz de labios**) is masculine! Don't ask why. We can't explain it. Gender in language is something you have to accept. Take heart, though, because in Spanish, many word endings help you to determine the gender of certain nouns.

This chapter helps you to correctly mark the gender of a noun by using definite articles (which express *the*), indefinite articles (which express *a, an,* or *some*), or demonstrative adjectives (which express *this, that, these,* or *those*). You find out how you can avoid repetition of the noun by using demonstrative pronouns. This chapter also demystifies the gender of nouns by showing you noun endings that tend to be masculine or feminine. You discover the tricks to making nouns plural. Finally, after you've built some confidence with nouns, you can read up on the three different ways to show possession.

Expressing Gender with Definite Articles

A *definite article* expresses the English word *the* and indicates a specific person or thing, such as "the boy" or "the book." When you know whether a noun is masculine or feminine in Spanish (or singular or plural), you must choose the correct definite article to "match" that noun in order to say *the*. Choosing the right definite article is easy after you know the noun's gender.

The definite article precedes the noun it modifies and agrees with that noun in number and gender. For example, **El muchacho es rubio y las muchachas son morenas.** (*The boy is blond and the girls are brunette.*)

Identifying the definite articles

Spanish features four distinct definite articles that correspond to *the* in English:

	Masculine	Feminine
Singular	el	la
Plural	los	las

Here are some examples of these definitive articles in action:

El muchacho es grande. (*The boy is big.*)

Los libros son interesantes. (*The books are interesting.*)

La muchacha es alta. (*The girl is tall.*)

Las casas son blancas. (*The houses are white.*)

Using the definite articles

In Spanish you often use the definite article even though you may or may not use it in English. Study the rules in the following list; they show how you use the definite articles in Spanish in many different situations:

✔ With nouns in a general or abstract sense:

El amor es divino. (*Love is divine.*)

✔ With nouns in a specific sense:

La tía María trae regalos. (*Aunt María brings gifts.*)

✔ With names of languages (except after the verb **hablar** and after the prepositions **de** and **en**):

Me gusta el español. (*I like Spanish.*)

¿Dónde está mi libro de español? (*Where's my Spanish book?*)

✔ With parts of the body (when the possessor is clear) in place of the possessive adjective:

Me duelen los pies. (*My feet hurt.*)

✔ With titles and ranks when you aren't addressing the person:

La señora Rivera está aquí. (*Mrs. Rivera is here.*)

Siéntese, Señora Rivera. (*Have a seat, Mrs. Rivera.*)

✔ With last names:

Los Gómez viven en Colombia. (*The Gómezes live in Colombia.*)

✔ With days of the week (except after the verb **ser**):

El domingo voy a México. (*On Sunday I'm going to Mexico.*)

Hoy es miércoles. (*Today is Wednesday.*)

✔ With seasons (you may omit the article after **en**):

Me gusta el verano. (*I like summer.*)

No trabajo en (el) verano. (*I don't work in the summer.*)

✔ With dates:

Es el cinco de mayo. (*It's May 5th.*)

✔ With the hour of the day and other time expressions:

Son las once y media. (*It's 11:30.*)

Salgo por la tarde. (*I'm going out in the afternoon.*)

✔ With the names of many cities and countries (in current usage, speakers tend to omit the article):

el Brasil, el Ecuador, el Japón, el Paraguay, el Perú, El Salvador, el Uruguay, la Argentina, la China, La Habana, la India, los Estados Unidos

Visitamos (el) Brasil. (*We visited Brazil.*)

Vivo en los Estados Unidos. (*I live in the United States.*)

Capitalized articles are actually parts of the names of the countries, whereas articles in lowercase aren't. For example, **Yo nací en El Salvador pero pasé muchos años en la Argentina.** (*I was born in El Salvador but I spent many years in Argentina.*)

Book II

Grasping Basic Grammar Essentials

✔ With rivers, seas, and other geographical locations:

El Orinoco es un río. (*The Orinoco is a river.*)

✔ With the names of boats or ships:

El Titanic se hundió. (*The Titanic sank.*)

✔ With adverbs and infinitives used as nouns (this is optional when the infinitive serves as the subject of the sentence):

Lo hizó por el bien común. (*He did it for the common good.*)

(El) decir la verdad es una virtud. (*Telling the truth is a virtue.*)

✔ With weights and measures to express *a, an,* and *per:*

Cuestan seis dólares la media docena. (*They cost six dollars per half dozen.*)

✔ With clothing used in a general sense:

Al entrar él se quitó el sombrero. (*Upon entering, he removed his hat.*)

Omitting definite articles

You omit the definite articles in the following situations in Spanish:

✔ Before nouns *in apposition* (when one noun explains another):

Madrid, capital de España, es una ciudad popular. (*Madrid, the capital of Spain, is a popular city.*)

✔ Before numerals that express the title of rulers:

Carlos Quinto (*Charles the Fifth*)

Using contractions with definite articles

Spanish features only two contractions. They occur when the definite article **el** is joined with the preposition **a** (**a** + **el** = **al**) or **de** (**de** + **el** = **del**). The only exception to the rule is when the definite article is part of the title or name; for example:

Voy al Uruguay. (*I'm going to Uruguay.*) **Voy a El Salvador.** (*I'm going to El Salvador.*)

Soy del Uruguay. (*I'm from Uruguay.*) **Soy de El Salvador.** (*I'm from El Salvador.*)

Remaining neutral with lo

Neuter, in language, means that a word has no gender. You can identify a few neuter words in Spanish. One of them is the article **lo,** which you use only in the singular. The following list presents some examples of how you use **lo:**

✔ Before an adjective used as a noun to express an abstract idea or a quality:

Lo normal es dormir de noche. (*It's normal to sleep at night.*)

✔ **Lo** + an adjective (or adverb) + **que,** which means *how:*

¿Ves lo serio que es? (*Do you see how serious it is?*)

Es increíble lo rápidamente que él corre. (*It's incredible how fast he runs.*)

✔ **Lo** preceded by **a,** which means *in the manner of* or *like:*

Ella habla a lo loco. (*She talks like crazy.*)

Indicating Gender with Indefinite Articles

An *indefinite article,* which expresses the English words *a, an,* or *some,* refers to persons or objects not specifically identified (such as "a boy" or "some books"). As with definite articles, when you know whether a noun is masculine or feminine (and singular or plural), you can choose the correct indefinite article to "match."

As with definite articles, the indefinite article precedes the noun it modifies and agrees with that noun in number and gender.

Recognizing the indefinite articles

Four Spanish indefinite articles correspond to *a,* and *an* in the singular and *some* in the plural. The following table presents these articles:

	Masculine	Feminine
Singular	un	una
Plural	unos	unas

Here are a couple of examples of the indefinite articles in action:

Compró un abrigo. (*She bought an overcoat.*)

Necesito unos limones y unas limas. (*I need some lemons and some limes.*)

Omitting indefinite articles

You omit the indefinite article in the following situations:

✔ Before unmodified nouns that express nationality, profession, or religious or political affiliation:

El señor Robles es professor. (*Mr. Robles is a teacher.*)

When the noun is modified, you use the indefinite article, however:

El señor Robles es un profesor liberal. (*Mr. Robles is a liberal teacher.*)

✔ Before unmodified nouns in apposition (unless you're referring to a family or business relationship):

Cervantes, escritor español, escribió Don Quijote. (*Cervantes, a Spanish writer, wrote Don Quixote.*)

✔ Before the following words:

- **cien** (*one hundred*) — **cien niños** (*one hundred children*)
- **cierto** (*certain*) — **ciertos idiomas** (*certain languages*)
- **mil** (*one thousand*) — **mil dólares** (*one thousand dollars*)
- **otro** (*other*) — **otra clase** (*another class*)
- **qué** (*what a*) — **qué lástima** (*what a pity*)
- **semejante** (*similar*) — **problema semejante** (*a similar problem*)
- **tal** (*such a*) — **tal cosa** (*such a thing*)

Getting Particular with Demonstrative Adjectives and Pronouns

Although it's not polite to point with your finger, pointing with words is often necessary with the use of demonstrative adjectives and pronouns — words including *this, that, these,* or *those.* You can use these words in three ways: 1) like a kid in a candy store to point to specific items when you don't know their names; 2) to separate one or more items from a group, such as *these* people as opposed to *those* people; or 3) to refer to a person, place, or thing you already identified.

The following sections bring you up to speed on demonstrative adjectives and pronouns used in Spanish and show you how to use them in sentences.

Demonstrative adjectives

Demonstrative adjectives indicate or point out the person, place, or thing to which a speaker is referring. For instance, "this shirt" or "that pair of pants." Demonstrative adjectives precede and agree in number and gender with the nouns they modify. In Spanish, you select the demonstrative adjective according to the distance of the noun from the speaker (see Table 2-1).

Book II

Grasping
Basic
Grammar
Essentials

Table 2-1		Demonstrative Adjectives		
Number	*Masculine*	*Feminine*	*Meaning*	*Distance*
Singular	**este**	**esta**	this	Near to or directly concerned with speaker
Plural	**estos**	**estas**	these	
Singular	**ese**	**esa**	that	Not particularly near to or directly concerned with speaker
Plural	**esos**	**esas**	those	
Singular	**aquel**	**aquella**	that	Far from and not directly concerned with speaker
Plural	**aquellos**	**aquellas**	those	

The following list shows these demonstrative adjectives in action:

- **Estos pantalones son cortos y esta camisa es larga.** (*These pants are short and this shirt is long.*)
- **Aquellos países son grandes y aquellas ciudades son pequeñas.** (*Those countries are large and those cities are small.*)

Here's what you need to know about demonstrative adjectives in Spanish:

- You use them before each noun:

    este abogado y ese cliente (*this lawyer and that client*)
- You can use adverbs to reinforce location:

    esta casa aquí (*this house here*)

    esas casas ahí (*those houses there*)

Demonstrative pronouns

A *demonstrative pronoun* replaces a demonstrative adjective and its noun. You use it to make the language flow more naturally in writing and in conversation. Demonstrative pronouns express *this (one), that (one), these (ones),* or *those (ones).* The only difference between a demonstrative adjective and a demonstrative pronoun in writing is the addition of an accent to the pronoun (see Table 2-2).

Table 2-2		Demonstrative Pronouns		
Number	*Masculine*	*Feminine*	*Meaning*	*Distance*
Singular	**éste**	**ésta**	this (one)	Near to or directly concerned with speaker
Plural	**éstos**	**éstas**	these (ones)	
Singular	**ése**	**ésa**	that (one)	Not particularly near to or directly concerned with speaker
Plural	**ésos**	**ésas**	those (ones)	
Singular	**aquél**	**aquélla**	that (one)	Far from and not directly concerned with speaker
Plural	**aquéllos**	**aquéllas**	those (ones)	

The following list presents some examples of demonstrative pronouns in action:

- ✔ **Mire éstos y ésta también.** (*Look at these and this one, too.*)

- ✔ **Quiero ése y ésas.** (*I want that and those.*)

- ✔ **Aquél es viejo y aquélla es moderna.** (*That one is old and that one is modern.*)

Here's what you need to know about demonstrative pronouns in Spanish:

- ✔ They agree in number and gender with the nouns they replace:

  Me gusta este coche y ésos. (*I like this car and those.*)

- ✔ You use a form of **aquél** to express *the former* and a form of **éste** to express *the latter:*

  Patricia es la hermana de Francisco; éste es rubio y aquélla es morena. (*Patricia is the sister of Francisco; Francisco [the latter] is blond and Patricia [the former] is brunette.*)

Sorting Out Masculine and Feminine Spanish Singular Nouns

Spanish nouns are either masculine or feminine. Nouns that refer to males are always masculine, and nouns that refer to females are feminine, no matter their endings. You can't always be sure when it comes to places or things, though. In Spanish, certain endings are good indications as to the gender (masculine or feminine designation) of nouns. For instance, nouns that end in **-o** (except **la mano** [*the hand*] and **la radio** [*the radio*]) usually are masculine. Nouns that end in **-a, -ad** (**la ciudad** [*city*]), **-ie** (**la serie** [*the series*]), **-ción** (**la canción** [*the song*]), **-sión** (**la discusión** [*discussion*]), **-ud** (**la salud** [*health*]), and **-umbre** (**la costumbre** [*custom*]) generally are feminine.

Book II

Grasping Basic Grammar Essentials

Here are more rules that deal with gender in Spanish:

- Certain nouns belonging to a theme are masculine. These include

  - Numbers: **cuatro** (*four*)

  - Days of the week: **el jueves** (*Thursday*)

  - Compass points: **el norte** (*north*)

  - Names of trees: **el manzano** (*apple tree*)

  - Compound nouns: **el mediodía** (*noon*)

  - Names of rivers, lakes, mountains, straits, and seas: **el Mediterráneo** (*the Mediterranean*)

- Certain nouns belonging to a theme are feminine. These groups include

  - Many illnesses: **la gripe** (*the flu*), **la apendicitis** (*appendicitis*)

  - Islands and provinces: **la Córsega** (*Corsica*)

The following sections dive into some more detail with respect to noun gender in Spanish, including some special cases you must consider.

Gender benders: Reverse-gender nouns

Some Spanish nouns are tricky because they end in **-a** but are masculine, and others end in **-o** but are feminine. These nouns may be referred to as *reverse-gender nouns*. For instance, some nouns that end in **-ma** and **-eta** (words that are derived from the Greek language) are masculine, as are the words **el día** (*the day*) and **el mapa** (*the map*). The following table outlines these masculine words:

-ma	-eta
el clima (*the climate*)	**el planeta** (*the planet*)
el drama (*the drama*)	
el idioma (*the language*)	
el poema (*the poem*)	
el problema (*the problem*)	
el telegrama (*the telegram*)	
el tema (*the theme*)	

Here are a couple of nouns that end in **-o** and are feminine:

- ✔ **la mano** (*the hand*)
- ✔ **la radio** (*the radio*)

Note that **la foto** is the abbreviation for **la fotografía** (*the photgraph*) and **la moto** is the abbreviation for **la motocicleta** (*the motorcycle*).

Transgender nouns: The same for both genders

Some nouns have the same spelling for both genders. For these nouns, all you have to do is change the article to reflect whether the person in question is male or female. The following table presents the most common of these nouns:

Masculine	Feminine	Translation
el artista	**la artista**	the artist
el dentista	**la dentista**	the dentist
el periodista	**la periodista**	the journalist
el telefonista	**la telefonista**	the operator
el joven	**la joven**	the youth
el estudiante	**la estudiante**	the student

The following nouns, however, always remain feminine, regardless of the gender of the person being described:

la persona (*the person*)

la víctima (*the victim*)

Meaning-changing nouns

Some nouns change meaning according to their gender. Knowing the proper usage is the difference between praying to the Pope or to a potato! You simply must memorize nouns in this category. The following table presents some of the high-frequency Spanish words whose meanings change according to gender:

Masculine	Meaning	Feminine	Meaning
el capital	the capital (money)	la capital	the capital (country)
el cura	the priest	la cura	the cure
el frente	the front	la frente	the forehead
el guía	the male guide	la guía	the female guide; the guidebook
el Papa	the Pope	la papa	the potato
el policía	the police officer	la policía	the police force; the policewoman

Rule breakers: Special cases

You can always find some exceptions to the rule. In Spanish, for instance, masculine nouns that refer to people and end in **-or, -és,** or **-n** require the addition of a final **-a** to get the female equivalent. And if the masculine noun has an accented final syllable, you drop that accent in the feminine form. Here are some examples:

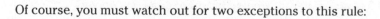

> **el professor** ⇨ **la profesora** (*the teacher*)
>
> **el francés** ⇨ **la francesa** (*the French person*)
>
> **el alemán** ⇨ **la alemana** (*the German person*)

Of course, you must watch out for two exceptions to this rule:

> **el actor** (*the actor*) ⇨ **la actriz** (*the actress*)
>
> **el emperador** (*the emperor*) ⇨ **la emperatriz** (*the empress*)

Some nouns have distinct masculine and feminine forms. The following table presents a list of these nouns, which you must simply memorize. *Note:* Spanish does have a masculine equivalent to **la esposa** (*wife*) — **el esposo** (*husband*).

Masculine	Meaning	Feminine	Meaning
el héroe	the hero	**la heroína**	the heroine
el hombre	the man	**la mujer**	the woman
el marido	the husband	**la esposa**	the wife
el príncipe	the prince	**la princesa**	the princess
el rey	the king	**la reina**	the queen
el yerno	the son-in-law	**la nuera**	the daughter-in-law

To prevent the clash of two vowel sounds, the Spanish language uses the masculine singular article **el** (**un**) with feminine singular nouns that begin with a stressed a sound (**a-** or **ha-**). In the plural, you use las (**unas**) for these nouns; for example:

> **el agua** (*the water*); **las aguas** (*the waters*)
>
> **un alma** (*a soul*); **unas almas** (*some souls*)
>
> **el ave** (*the bird*); **las aves** (*the birds*)
>
> **un hacha** (*an ax*); **unas hachas** (*some axes*)
>
> **el hambre** (*the hunger*); **las hambres** (*the hungers*)

Pluralizing Your Nouns

You use plural nouns to refer to more than one person, place, thing, quality, idea, or action. Not surprisingly, just as you do in English, you use the letters **-s** and **-es** to form the plurals of Spanish nouns. The following list outlines the many plural variations you see in Spanish nouns and the rules for forming plurals:

- ✔ You add **-s** to form the plural of nouns ending in a vowel:

    el mango (*the mango*); **los mangos** (*the mangoes*)

    la manzana (*the apple*); **las manzanas** (*the apples*)

- ✔ You add **-es** to form the plural of nouns ending in a consonant (including **-y**):

    el emperador (*the emperor*); **los emperadores** (*the emperors*)

    el rey (*the king*); **los reyes** (*the kings*)

- ✔ You add or delete an accent mark in some nouns ending in **-n** or **-s** to maintain the original stress:

    el joven; los jóvenes (*the youths*)

    el examen; los exámenes (*the tests*)

    la canción; las canciones (*the songs*)

    el francés; los franceses (*the Frenchmen*)

    el limón; los limones (*the lemons*)

    el melón; los melones (*the melons*)

    el melocotón; los melocotones (*the peaches*)

✔ Nouns that end in **-z** change **z** to **-c** before you add **-es:**

    la luz (*the light*); **las luces** (*the lights*)

✔ Nouns that end in **-es** or **-is** don't change in the plural, except for **el mes** (*the month*), which becomes **los meses** (*the months*):

    el lunes (*Monday*); **los lunes** (*Mondays*)

    la crisis (*the crisis*); **las crisis** (*the crises*)

✔ Compound nouns (nouns composed of two nouns that join together to make one) don't change in the plural:

    el abrelatas (*can opener*); **los abrelatas** (*can openers*)

✔ You express the plural of nouns of different genders (where one noun is masculine and the other[s] is feminine) with the masculine plural:

    el rey y la reina (*the king and queen*); **los reyes** (*the kings or the king[s] and the queen[s]*)

    el muchacho y la muchacha (*the boy and the girl*); **los muchachos** (*the boys or the boy[s] and the girl[s]*)

✔ Some nouns are always plural, such as

    las gafas/los espejuelos (*eyeglasses*)

    las matemáticas (*mathematics*)

    las vacaciones (*vacation*)

Book II

Grasping Basic Grammar Essentials

Becoming Possessive

The majority of people in the world are possessive of their loved ones and their things. You have several ways to express possession in Spanish: by using the preposition **de** (*of*), by using possessive adjectives before the persons or things, or by using possessive pronouns to take the place of possessive adjectives and their nouns. The sections that follow guide you through the ways you can stake your claims.

Using de

Expressing possession by using the preposition **de** (*of*) is quite unlike what people are accustomed to in English. English speakers put an apostrophe + *s* after the noun representing the owner: *John's family,* for instance. Spanish nouns have no apostrophe + *s,* so you must use a reverse word order joined by the preposition **de** (instead of saying *John's car,* you say *the car of John*). The following list presents the rules of using **de:**

- ✔ You use the preposition **de** between a noun that's possessed and a proper noun representing the owner:

    Es el coche de Julio. (*It's Julio's car.*)

- ✔ You use **de** + a definite article between the noun that's possessed and a common noun representing the owner:

    Tengo el abrigo de la muchacha. (*I have the girl's coat.*)

- ✔ **De** contracts with the definite article **el** to form **del** (*of the*) before a masculine singular common noun:

    Necesito el libro del profesor. (*I need the teacher's book.*)

- ✔ If the sentence contains more than one owner, you need to repeat **de** before each noun:

    Voy a la casa de Roberto y de Marta. (*I'm going to Roberto and Marta's house.*)

- ✔ You use a construction that's the reverse of English to answer the question "**¿De quién es . . .?**":

    ¿De quién(es) es la idea? (*Whose idea is it?*)

    Es la idea de Julia y del hermano de Julia. (*It's Julia's and her brother's idea.*)

Showing possession with adjectives

You use a *possessive adjective* before the noun that's possessed in order to express *my, your, his, her, its, our,* or *their.* Possessive adjectives must agree in gender (masculine or feminine) and number (singular or plural) with the objects that are possessed; they never agree with the possessors. Table 2-3 outlines the possessive adjectives, and the following examples illustrate the previous points:

Julia escribe a sus amigas. (*Julia writes to her friends.*)

Yo perdí mis gafas. (*I lost my glasses.*)

Nosotros escuchamos a nuestro profesor. (*We listen to our teacher.*)

Table 2-3	Possessive Adjectives			
English word	**Masculine singular**	**Masculine plural**	**Feminine singular**	**Feminine plural**
my	**mi**	**mis**	**mi**	**mis**
your (informal)	**tu**	**tus**	**tu**	**tus**
his/her/your (formal)	**su**	**sus**	**su**	**sus**
our	**nuestro**	**nuestros**	**nuestra**	**nuestras**
your (informal, plural)	**vuestro**	**vuestros**	**vuestra**	**vuestras**
their/your (formal, plural)	**su**	**sus**	**su**	**sus**

Book II

Grasping Basic Grammar Essentials

Because **su** can mean _his, her, your_ (singular or plural) or _their_, you can clarify who the possessor really is by replacing the possessive adjective (**su**) with the corresponding definite article (**el, la, los,** or **las**) + noun + **de** + (**él, ella, Ud., Uds., (ellos, ellas.**):

> _I need his help._
>
> **Necesito su ayuda.**
>
> **Necesito la ayuda de él.**

With parts of the body or clothing, when the possessor is clear, you replace the possessive adjective with the correct definite article:

> **Me cepillo los dientes dos veces al día.** (_I brush my teeth twice a day._)

Making your pronouns possessive

A _possessive pronoun_ replaces a noun. For instance, **Tu coche y el mío son deportivos** (_Your car and mine are sporty._) To form a possessive pronoun, you select the definite article corresponding in number and gender to the noun being possessed and then add the corresponding possessive pronoun (see Table 2-4). Here are some examples:

> **Tu hermana y la mía son pelirrojas.** (_Your sister and mine are redheads._)

Note the contraction with **a** and **él**:

> **A tu hermano le encanta la ópera; al mío también.** (_Your brother likes the opera; mine, too._)

El coche de tu primo es viejo; el del mío es nuevo. (*Your cousin's car is old; my cousin's is new.*)

Table 2-4	Possessive pronouns			
English word	*Masculine singular*	*Masculine plural*	*Feminine singular*	*Feminine plural*
mine	**mío**	**míos**	**mía**	**mías**
yours (informal)	**tuyo**	**tuyos**	**tuya**	**tuyas**
his, hers, its, yours (formal)	**suyo**	**suyos**	**suya**	**suyas**
ours	**nuestro**	**nuestros**	**nuestra**	**nuestras**
yours (informal, plural)	**vuestro**	**vuestros**	**vuestra**	**vuestras**
theirs, yours (formal, plural)	**suyo**	**suyos**	**suya**	**suyas**

After the verb **ser** (*to be*), you generally omit the definite article:

Este asiento es mío, no es suyo. (*This seat is mine, not yours.*)

For more about the verb **ser,** see Book I, Chapter 3.

Chapter 3

Dealing with the Here and Now: Present Tense Verbs

In This Chapter

- Getting started with present tense **-ar, -er,** and **-ir** verb conjugations
- Discovering the personal **a** and the passive voice
- Wrestling with a few irregular verbs
- Expressing likes and dislikes with **gustar**

*V*erbs are action words. They're the movers and the shakers of the world. They describe the action that is taking place, has taken place, or will take place. They command, they question, they conjecture, and they describe states of being. No sentence is complete without one.

In this chapter, you wade into the pool of Spanish verbs slowly, beginning with the conjugation of regular verbs in the present tense.

You can then wander out to the deep end to explore the *personal a* and the passive voice and take on the challenge of conjugating a few irregular verbs in the present tense.

Regular verbs in the present tense are the bread and butter (or beans and rice) of mastering Spanish verb conjugations. What you pick up in this chapter is the basis for all other skills related to conjugating Spanish verbs, so take your time to make sure you fully grasp one topic before moving on to the next. For the bare basics of Spanish verbs (and verbs in general), check out Book II, Chapter 1.

Conjugating Verbs in the Present Tense

Most verbs are fairly well-behaved. They follow the rules. They're predictable, especially in the present tense, which makes them fairly easy to master. The regular Spanish verbs come in three flavors — **-ar, -er,** and **-ir** — and you won't find anything tricky about conjugating them. Regular verbs, therefore, are a great place to start your warm-up with the present tense.

In the following sections, you discover the three regular verb forms in the present tense. You find out how to conjugate all three by using a subject pronoun chart. In these sections, you also meet a host of commonly used regular -ar, -er, and -ir verbs so you can begin using them in your everyday conversations.

Conjugating -ar verbs

Conjugating regular **-ar** verbs is a snap. You take the infinitive form of the verb, which ends in **-ar,** chop off the **-ar** ending, and replace it with the ending for the appropriate subject pronouns: *I, you, he, she, we,* or *they*. If you need to review subject pronouns and how they influence verb conjugations, refer to Book II, Chapter 1. We're going to present all verb conjugations in these three-row, two-column boxes until you're sick and tired of seeing them, so master the concept of subject pronouns before you go any further.

The subject pronoun dictates the verb form that you use in a sentence. If you start a sentence with *I,* for example, and you use a present tense **-ar** verb, that verb must end in **-o.**

Regular present tense -ar verb endings	
yo -o	nosotros/as -amos
tú -as	vosotros/as -áis
él, ella, Ud. -a	ellos/as, Uds. -an

So the present-tense conjugations for a regular **-ar** verb such as **hablar** (to speak) are . . .

hablar *(to speak)*	
hablo	hablamos
hablas	habláis
habla	hablan
Yo hablo español. (I speak Spanish.)	

Now we bet you want a few more **-ar** verbs to play with, so Table 3-1 shows some commonly used regular **-ar** verbs that you can throw around at your next dinner party.

Table 3-1	Common Regular -*ar* Verbs
-*ar* Verb	*Translation*
andar	to walk
anunciar	to announce
arreglar	to fix
ayudar	to help
bailar	to dance
caminar	to walk
cantar	to sing
celebrar	to celebrate
cenar	to eat supper
cepillar	to brush
charlar	to chat
cocinar	to cook
comprar	to buy
cortar	to cut
dibujar	to draw
escuchar	to listen (to)
estudiar	to study
ganar	to win, to earn
lavar	to wash
limpiar	to clean
mirar	to look (at)

Book II

Grasping Basic Grammar Essentials

 Unlike English, which keeps its verbs and prepositions separate, some verbs in the Spanish language include a preposition (like *to* or *at*). The chart above includes two such verbs: **escuchar** and **mirar.** As an English-speaker, you may be tempted to toss in an extra preposition. Avoid the temptation.

Conjugating -er verbs

The **-ar** verbs set the pattern for all the regular verbs, including the **-er** and **-ir** verbs. To conjugate **-er** verbs, you chop the **-er** off the end of the verb and add the appropriate verb endings so that the verb agrees with its subject pronoun. If you can etch the following conjugation chart on your gray matter, you'll have everything you need to conjugate any **-er** verb you may encounter.

Regular present tense **-er** verb endings:	
yo -o	nosotros/as -emos
tú -es	vosotros/as -éis
él, ella, Ud. -e	ellos/as, Uds. -en

So the present-tense conjugations for a regular **-er** verb such as **comprender** (to understand) are

comprender (*to understand*)	
comprendo	comprendemos
comprendes	comprendéis
comprende	comprenden
Nosotros comprendemos. (We understand.)	

Understanding is certainly important, but you don't want to restrict all of your actions to such a passive activity, so Table 3-2 gives you some additional **-er** verbs that are a little more exciting.

Table 3-2	Common Regular -er Verbs
Term	*Translation*
aprender	to learn
barrer	to sweep
beber	to drink
comer	to eat
correr	to run
creer	to believe
deber	to owe, must, ought
depender	to depend
leer	to read
poseer	to possess, own
prometer	to promise

Term	Translation
responder	to respond
romper	to break
socorrer	to help
sorprender	to surprise
tañer	to pluck, play a stringed musical instrument
temer	to fear, dread
vender	to sell

Conjugating -ir verbs

The **-ar** and **-er** verbs make up the bulk of the regular verbs, but a small number of **-ir** verbs round out the collection. You conjugate these verbs the same as the **-er** verbs, except for the **nosotros** and the **vosotros** forms. The following conjugation chart shows just what we mean.

Regular present tense -ir verb endings:	
yo -o	nosotros/as -imos
tú -es	vosotros/as -ís
él, ella, Ud. -e	ellos/as, Uds. -en

The present tense conjugations for a regular **-ir** verb such as **escribir** (to write) are

escribir (*to write*)	
escribo	escribimos
escribes	escribís
escribe	escriben
Ella escribe. (She writes.)	

Getting chummy with the personal "a"

In Spanish, the preposition *to* is **a**. If you want to say "to the store," for example, you say "**a la tienda.**"

Spanish has a very important use for **a** that doesn't even translate to English, and that's the personal **a**. Whenever the direct object of the verb is a person or a pet, the direct object *must* be preceded by the Spanish personal **a**.

This rule is sometimes hard to remember because it has no English equivalent, but a few examples can help drive home the point:

Ellos ayudan a los estudiantes mucho. *They help the students a lot.*

Yo ayudo a mi mamá en la cocina todos los días. *I help my mom in the kitchen every day.*

Él camina a su perro en el parque. *He walks his dog in the park.*

Although the collection of regular **-ir** verbs is relatively small, it includes a respectable number of verbs that you simply can't live without. Here, in Table 3-3, are some commonly used regular **-ir** verbs to give you some additional examples to work with.

Table 3-3	Common Regular *-ir* Verbs
Spanish	*Translation*
abrir	to open
cubrir	to cover
imprimir	to impress, to imprint
aburrir	to annoy, to bore
cumplir	to fulfill
cumplir ___ años	to complete ___ years
inscribir	to inscribe, to record
admitir	to admit
decidir	to decide
permitir	to permit
añadir	to add
describir	to describe
prohibir	to prohibit
aplaudir	to applaud
descubrir	to discover

Spanish	Translation
recibir	to receive
assistir	to attend
discutir	to discuss, to debate
repartir	to distribute, to deal cards

Speaking of the Passive Voice . . .

With the passive voice, you never know who's performing the action, which sometimes is exactly how you want to present certain information, especially if you're a scientist or a politician. Following are some examples:

✔ No swimming *is allowed* after 10 p.m.

✔ No eating *is allowed* outside of the dining room.

✔ English and Spanish *are spoken* here.

✔ French *is spoken* in France.

In Spanish, you form the passive voice with **se** and either the third-person singular or the third-person plural of the verb in question. The noun or nouns that follow the conjugated verb determine whether the verb is singular or plural in form. In other words, a singular noun is preceded by a verb in its singular form, and a plural noun or multiple nouns are preceded by a verb in its plural form.

The following list provides translations of the English statements in the preceding bulleted list:

✔ **No se permite nadar después de las 10 p.m.**

✔ **No se permite comer fuera del comedor.**

✔ **Se hablan inglés y español aquí.**

✔ **Se habla francés en Francia.**

Dealing with Irregulars

Some verbs refuse to conform to the rules of proper conjugations. In Spanish, these irregular verbs huddle into the following six categories:

- ✔ Spelling-changing verbs
- ✔ Stem-changing verbs
- ✔ Spelling- and stem-changing verbs
- ✔ Verbs irregular only in the **yo** form
- ✔ Verbs irregular in all forms except **nosotros** and **vosotros**
- ✔ Incredibly irregular verbs

In the following sections, you encounter these exceptional verbs and find out how to deal with them.

Spelling-changing verbs

Some Spanish verbs undergo spelling changes for pronunciation purposes (usually to preserve the original sound of a verb after you add a new ending). This change is nothing to be overly concerned about, because it occurs only in the first-person singular (**yo**) form of the verb. In the present tense, verbs with the endings listed in Table 3-4 undergo spelling changes.

Table 3-4		Spelling Changes in the Present Tense	
Infinitive Ending	*Spelling Change*	*Verb Examples*	*Present Conjugation*
vowel + -**cer/-cir**	c ⇨ zc	ofre**cer** (to offer)	yo ofre**zco**
		tradu**cir** (to translate)	yo tradu**zco**
consonant + -**cer/-cir**	c ⇨ z	conven**cer** (to convince)	yo conven**zo**
		espar**cir** (to spread out)	yo espar**zo**
-**ger/-gir**	g ⇨ j	esco**ger** (to choose)	yo esco**jo**
		exi**gir** (to demand)	yo exi**jo**
-**guir**	gu ⇨ g	distin**guir** (to distinguish)	yo distin**go**

The majority of the verbs that undergo spelling changes in the present tense end in vowel + -**cer** or vowel + -**cir**. Only a few high-frequency verbs fall under the other categories (-**ger**, -**gir**, -**guir**); in all likelihood, you'll see them rarely, if at all.

Here are the verbs with spelling changes in the present tense that you can expect to encounter most often:

Spanish Verb	Translation
aparecer	to appear
conocer	to know (to be acquainted with)
merecer	to deserve, merit
nacer	to be born
obedecer	to obey
parecer	to seem
producir	to produce
reconocer	to recognize
reducir	to reduce
reproducir	to reproduce

Book II

Grasping Basic Grammar Essentials

Stem-changing verbs

Some Spanish verbs undergo *stem changes* — changes to a vowel in the stem of the verb. (The *stem* of the verb is what remains when the **-ar, -er,** or **-ir** ending has been taken off.) In the present tense, all stem changes occur in all of the conjugated forms except for the **nosotros** and **vosotros** forms.

-ar stem changes

Many Spanish verbs with an **-ar** ending undergo stem changes in all forms except **nosotros** and **vosotros.** The following list details these changes:

✔ **e ➪ ie:** For instance, **empezar** (*to begin*) changes to yo emp**ie**zo (nosotros emp**e**zamos). Here are the most frequently used Spanish verbs that fit into this category:

- cerrar (*to close*)
- comenzar (*to begin*)
- despertar (*to wake up*)
- negar (*to deny*)
- nevar (*to snow*)
- pensar (*to think*)
- recomendar (*to recommend*)

✔ **o/u ➪ ue:** For instance, **mostrar** (*to show*) changes to yo m**ue**stro (nosotros m**o**stramos), and j**u**gar (*to play*) changes to yo j**ue**go (nosotros ju**g**amos). Here are the most frequently used Spanish verbs that fit into this category:

- ac**o**rdar (*to agree*)
- ac**o**star (*to put to bed*)
- alm**o**rzar (*to eat lunch*)
- c**o**lgar (*to hang up*)
- c**o**ntar (*to tell*)
- c**o**star (*to cost*)
- enc**o**ntrar (*to meet*)
- pr**o**bar (*to try [on]*)
- rec**o**rdar (*to remember*)

- **Jugar** is the only common **-ar** verb whose stem vowel changes from **u** to **ue**:

  - **Yo juego al fútbol.** (*I play soccer.*)
  - **Julio y yo jugamos al golf.** (*Julio and I play golf.*)

-er stem changes

Many Spanish verbs with an **-er** ending undergo stem changes in all forms except **nosotros** and **vosotros**. The following list details these changes:

- **e ⇨ ie:** For instance, querer (*to wish, want*) changes to yo qu**ie**ro (nosotros qu**e**remos). Here are the most frequently used Spanish verbs that fit into this category:

  - def**e**nder (*to defend*)
  - enc**e**nder (*to light*)
  - ent**e**nder (*to understand*)
  - p**e**rder (*to lose*)

- **o ⇨ ue:** For instance, v**o**lver (*to return*) changes to yo v**ue**lvo (nosotros v**o**lvemos). Here are the most frequently used Spanish verbs that fit into this category:

  - dev**o**lver (*to return*)
  - d**o**ler (*to hurt*)
  - env**o**lver (*to wrap up*)
  - ll**o**ver (*to rain*)
  - p**o**der (*to be able to, can*)

Some verbs with stem changes in the present tense are used impersonally in the third-person singular only:

> **Llueve.** (*It's raining.*) (**llover; o ⇨ ue**)
>
> **Nieva.** (*It's snowing.*) (**nevar; e ⇨ ie**)
>
> **Hiela.** (*It's freezing.*) (**helar; e ⇨ ie**)
>
> **Truena.** (*It's thundering.*) (**tronar; o ⇨ ue**)

-ir stem changes

Many Spanish verbs with an **-ir** ending undergo stem changes in all forms except **nosotros** and **vosotros**. The following list outlines these changes:

✔ **e ⇨ ie:** For instance, preferir (*to prefer*) changes to yo pref**ie**ro (nosotros preferimos). Here are the most frequently used Spanish verbs that fit into this category:

- advertir (*to warn*)
- consentir (*to allow*)
- divertir (*to amuse*)
- mentir (*to lie*)
- sentir (*to feel, regret*)
- sugerir (*to suggest*)

✔ **o ⇨ ue:** For instance, dormir (*to sleep*) changes to yo d**ue**rmo (nosotros dormimos). Another verb conjugated like **dormir** is **morir** (*to die*).

✔ **e ⇨ i:** For instance, servir (*to serve*) changes to yo s**i**rvo (nosotros servimos). Here are the most frequently used Spanish verbs that fit into this category:

- despedir (*to say goodbye to*)
- expedir (*to send*)
- medir (*to measure*)
- pedir (*to ask for*)
- repetir (*to repeat*)
- vestir (*to clothe*)

Stem change for verbs ending in -iar

Some Spanish verbs with an **-iar** ending undergo a stem change in all forms except **nosotros** and **vosotros**. This stem change is **i ⇨ í**. For instance, guiar (*to guide*) changes to yo gu**í**o (nosotros guiamos). Here are the most frequently used Spanish verbs that fit into this category:

Book II

Grasping Basic Grammar Essentials

- ✔ enviar (*to send*)
- ✔ esquiar (*to ski*)
- ✔ fotografiar (*to photograph*)
- ✔ vaciar (*to empty*)

Stem change for verbs ending in -uar

Some Spanish verbs with a **-uar** ending undergo a stem change in all forms except **nosotros** and **vosotros.** This stem change is **u ⇨ ú.** For instance, continuar (*to continue*) changes to yo continúo (nosotros continuamos). Here are the most frequently used Spanish verbs that fit into this category:

- ✔ habituar (*to accustom someone to*)
- ✔ valuar (*to value*)
- ✔ evaluar (*to evaluate*)

Stem change for verbs ending in -uir (not -guir)

Some Spanish verbs with a **-uir** ending (but not a **-guir** ending) undergo a stem change in all forms except **nosotros** and **vosotros.** This stem change is adding a **y** after the **u.** For instance, concluir (*to conclude*) changes to yo concluyo (nosotros concluimos). Here are the most frequently used Spanish verbs that fit into this category:

- ✔ construir (*to build*)
- ✔ contribuir (*to contribute*)
- ✔ destruir (*to destroy*)
- ✔ distribuir (*to distribute*)
- ✔ incluir (*to include*)
- ✔ sustituir (*to substitute*)

Verbs with spelling and stem changes

A few Spanish verbs have both a spelling change and a stem change in the present tense. You must conjugate these verbs to accommodate both changes. Table 3-5 provides a listing of these verbs.

Verb	English	Conjugation
Table 3-5	**Verbs with Spelling and Stem Changes in the Present**	
corregir	to correct	corri**jo**, corri**ges**, corri**ge**, corre**gimos**, corre**gís**, corri**gen**
elegir	to elect	eli**jo**, eli**ges**, eli**ge**, ele**gimos**, ele**gís**, eli**gen**
conseguir	to get, obtain	consi**go**, consi**gues**, consi**gue**, conse**guimos**, conse**guís**, consi**guen**
seguir	to follow	si**go**, si**gues**, si**gue**, se**guimos**, se**guís**, si**guen**

Book II

Grasping
Basic
Grammar
Essentials

Common verbs with irregular yo forms

In the present tense, some verbs are irregular only in the first-person singular (**yo**) form. You conjugate the other verb forms in the regular fashion:
by dropping the infinitive ending (**-ar, -er,** or **-ir**) and then adding the ending
that corresponds to the subject. The following table presents the irregular **yo**
forms of these verbs:

Spanish Verb	Translation	Present-tense yo Form
caber	to fit	**quepo**
caer	to fall	**caigo**
dar	to give	**doy**
hacer	to make, to do	**hago**
poner	to put	**pongo**
saber	to know a fact, to know how to	**sé**
salir	to go out	**salgo**
traer	to bring	**traigo**
valer	to be worth	**valgo**
ver	to see	**veo**

The following examples show these irregular forms in action:

Yo le **doy** un reloj y él le **da** aretes. (*I give her a watch and he gives her earrings.*)

Yo me **pongo** un abrigo y él se **pone** un suéter. (*I put on a coat and he puts on a sweater.*)

Yo **salgo** a la una y él **sale** a las tres. (*I go out at 1:00 and he goes out at 3:00.*)

The irregular yo, tú, él (ella, Ud.), and ellos (ellas, Uds.) forms

In the present tense, the verbs listed in Table 3-6 are irregular in all forms except **nosotros** and **vosotros**.

Table 3-6	Irregular Verbs in All Forms Except nosotros and vosotros						
Verb	*Translation*	*yo*	*tú*	*él*	*nosotros*	*vosotros*	*ellos*
decir	to say, to tell	digo	dices	dice	decimos	decís	dicen
estar	to be	estoy	estás	está	estamos	estáis	están
oler	to smell	huelo	hueles	huele	olemos	oléis	huelen
tener	to have	tengo	tienes	tiene	tenemos	tenéis	tienen
venir	to come	vengo	vienes	viene	venimos	venís	vienen

Tener followed by **que** means *to have to* and shows obligation:

> **Yo tengo que trabajar ahora.** (*I have to work now.*)
>
> **Nosotros tenemos que partir.** (*We have to leave.*)

A couple of really irregular verbs

Do you ever get that feeling that you don't know whether you're coming or going? Well, in the following sections, you get to do both with the Spanish verbs **venir** (*to come*) and **ir** (*to go*). Although these verbs are two of the tiniest in the Spanish language, they're also two of the most commonly used and irregular verbs, and they demand special attention. In the following sections, we take on the challenge of conjugating these verbs.

Going the distance with ir

The verb **ir** is definitely the smallest **-ir** verb, and that's really all it is — an **i** and an **r**. Actually, it looks like a verb without a verb stem, an end with no beginning. It's also one of the most irregular verbs in the Spanish language, as you can see from its conjugation chart.

ir (*to go*)	
voy	vamos
vas	vais
va	van
Nosotros vamos. (We go.)	

Coming around with venir

As the saying goes, what goes around comes around, and in Spanish, you can't come around without the verb **venir.** Although **venir** isn't quite as irregular as **ir,** it's still irregular, as the following conjugation chart shows.

venir (*to come*)	
vengo	venimos
vienes	venís
viene	vienen
Uds. vienen. (You [formal, plural] come.)	

Another notable exception: gustar

When it comes to liking and disliking something, English and Spanish have slightly different ways of expressing what's going on. In English, the subject of the sentence is in charge of liking or disliking something. You may say "I like vanilla ice cream," or "I don't like red sports cars." In Spanish, the object of your desire, or lack of desire, is more responsible for pleasing you. Instead of saying "I like vanilla ice cream," you say "Vanilla ice cream is pleasing to me" or **"Me gusta el helado de vainilla."**

In these constructions, you look to the end of the sentence to determine the verb form instead of looking for the subject at the beginning of the sentence. That's because in Spanish, the object (not the subject) is at the beginning of the sentence. The whole sentence order is in complete reverse, but of course the verb stays in the middle. Before tackling **gustar** and verbs like it, get a handle on object pronouns, as explained in the following section. (For more about object pronouns, consult Book III, Chapter 2.)

A word about indirect object pronouns

An *indirect object* is anything or anyone that the action of a sentence affects in an indirect way. If you kick your friend Sally the ball, for example, *the ball* is the *direct object* because it's getting kicked, and *Sally* is the *indirect object* (the object receiving the ball).

A *pronoun* is a word that stands in for a specific name or noun. Think of it as the generic brand. So if instead of saying you "kicked your friend Sally the ball," you said you "kicked her the ball," you'd be using an indirect object pronoun — *her.* The indirect object pronoun usually implies the word *to* or *for.* Spanish uses the indirect object pronouns in the table that follows.

Indirect Object Pronoun	Translation
me	to me
te	to you (informal)
le	to him, her, you (formal)
nos	to us
os	to you (informal, plural)
les	to them, you (formal, plural)

When you use one of these indirect-object pronouns in a Spanish sentence, be sure to place it *in front of* the conjugated verb.

Gusta or gustan?

In Spanish, expressions of like and dislike are completely flip-flopped when compared to English. You use the verb **gustar** for the verb *to like* in English, but **gustar** really means *to be pleasing to.* When you form a sentence, then, whatever is doing the pleasing becomes the subject and determines the form of the verb **gustar.** Use the following rules as your guide:

- ✔ If you like a single thing, use the third-person singular form, **gusta.**

- ✔ If you like two or more things, use the third-person plural form, **gustan.**

- ✔ If you like to do activities and you're using verbs to describe those activities, use the third-person singular form. Stick with the third-person singular, even if you like multiple activities.

- ✔ Use indirect-object pronouns to clarify to whom the thing (subject) is pleasing. If you need further clarification, place a clause with **a** and the name of the person at the beginning of your sentence.

To see how these rules play out in real life, check out the following example:

> *Sentence:* **A Juan le gusta el restaurante mexicano.**
>
> *Literal translation:* *To Juan, to him, is pleasing the Mexican restaurant.*
>
> *Real-life translation:* *Juan likes the Mexican restaurant.*

A Juan is used here to clarify who is indicated by the pronoun **le.** Sometimes you need prepositional phrases only for emphasis rather than clarity. For example, if we were telling you about something that we liked, you'd know that the Spanish indirect-object pronoun **nos** was us, but we can emphasize that we *really* liked it by adding **A nosotros** at the front of our sentence.

Here's a sentence with a plural subject. Remember, the subject is at the end of the sentence.

> *Sentence:* **A ellos les gustan las películas.**
>
> *Literal translation:* *To them, to them, are pleasing movies.*
>
> *Real-life translation:* *They like movies.*

You simply put a **no** in front of the indirect-object pronoun — after the clarifying clause — to make a negative statement with the verb **gustar** and other similar verbs. So for example:

> **A él no le gusta pescar.** *He doesn't like to fish.*

You can add **mucho** after the verb to say that you *really* like something. For example:

> **A ella le gusta mucho bailar.** *She really likes dancing.*

Other verbs like gustar

You have to admit that **gustar** is out of the norm as far as Spanish verbs go, but it isn't a one-of-a-kind wonder. The verb **gustar** is a member of an exclusive organization of verbs that include verbs that mean *repugnant to, fascinating to,* and *interesting to.*

Conjugating these verbs is a snap. All these verbs conjugate just like **gustar,** using indirect-object pronouns. Table 3-7 shows the most commonly used **gustar** look-alikes along with their meanings.

Book II

Grasping Basic Grammar Essentials

Table 3-7	Verbs Conjugated in the Third Person with Indirect Objects
Spanish Verb	*Translation*
disgustar	to be repugnant to
encantar	to be enchanting to
faltar	to be lacking to

(continued)

Table 3-7 *(continued)*

Spanish Verb	Translation
fascinar	to be fascinating to
importar	to be important to
interesar	to be interesting to
molestar	to bother
parecer	to seem; to appear to

The **-ar** verbs in Table 3-7 generally use either the endings **-a** or **-an.** The verb **parecer,** which is the only **-er** verb, generally uses the endings **-e** or **-en.**

Some common, though irregular, expressions

The irregular verbs **dar** (*to give*), **hacer** (*to make, to do*), and **tener** (*to have*), as well as a few other irregular verbs, are commonly used in everyday Spanish as part of expressions. If you want to sound like you really know the language well, you need to devour the expressions in this section and commit them to memory.

Verbs ending in **-se** are reflexive verbs; we discuss these in Book III, Chapter 3.

High-frequency expressions that use **dar** include the following:

Expression	Translation
dar un abrazo (a)	to hug, to embrace
dar las gracias (a)	to thank
dar recuerdos (a)	to give regards to
dar un paseo	to take a walk
dar una vuelta	to take a stroll
darse cuenta de	to realize
darse prisa	to hurry

Here are some examples of **dar** expressions:

> **Yo le doy un abrazo a mi novio.** (*I hug my boyfriend.*)

> **Ellos dan un paseo por el parque.** (*They take a walk in the park.*)

High-frequency expressions that use **hacer** include the following:

Expression	*Translation*
hacer buen (mal) tiempo	to be nice (bad) weather
hacer frío (calor)	to be cold (hot) weather
hacer una pregunta	to ask a question
hacer una visita	to pay a visit
hacer un viaje	to take a trip
hacer viento	to be windy

Here are some examples of **hacer** expressions:

> **Hace mal tiempo hoy.** (*The weather is bad today.*)
>
> **Hacemos un viaje a Puerto Rico.** (*We are taking a trip to Puerto Rico.*)

High-frequency expressions that use **tener** include the following:

Expression	*Translation*
tener calor (frío)	to be warm (cold)
tener celos de	to be jealous of (someone)
tener cuidado	to be careful
tener dolor de ___	to have a(n) ___ ache
tener éxito	to succeed
tener ganas de	to feel like
tener hambre (sed)	to be hungry (thirsty)
tener lugar	to take place
tener miedo de	to be afraid of
tener prisa	to be in a hurry
tener razón	to be right
tener sueño	to be sleepy
tener suerte	to be lucky

Here are some examples of **tener** expressions:

> **Tengo un dolor de cabeza.** (*I have a headache.*)
>
> **Ellos tienen razón.** (*They're right.*)

Book II

Grasping
Basic
Grammar
Essentials

What follows is a perfect example of how you can easily make a mistake in Spanish if you try to translate your English thoughts word for word. Although the verb **tener** means to have, Spanish speakers often use it with a noun to express a physical condition. In English, however, you follow the verb with an adjective to express the same physical condition:

> **Tengo sed.** (*I am thirsty. Literally: I have thirst.*)

> **Ellos tienen miedo de los perros.** (*They're afraid of dogs. Literally: They have fear of dogs.*)

Common expressions that use other verbs that have a spelling change or stem change in the present tense or in another tense include the following:

Expression	Translation
dejar caer	to drop
llegar a ser	to become
oír decir que	to hear that
pensar + infinitive	to intend
querer decir	to mean
volverse + adjective	to become

Here are some examples of these expressions in action:

> **¡Cuidado! No dejes caer el vaso.** (*Be careful! Don't drop the glass.*)

> **Pensamos hacer un viaje.** (*We intend to take a trip.*)

Chapter 4

¿Qué? Asking Questions

In this chapter, you find out how to obtain all the information you need — from easy yes/no questions to more detailed inquiries about *Who? What? When? Where? How?* or *Why?* This chapter helps you become proficient at not only asking questions but also giving appropriate answers to the questions others ask you.

Spanish Inquisitions

Curious people ask a lot of questions. There's nothing wrong with that. Fortunately for you, asking questions in Spanish is a rather simple task.

You certainly need to use two main types of questions in Spanish: those that call for a yes-or-no answer and those that ask for more detailed information. We cover these questions in the sections that follow.

Asking yes/no questions

You can easily form a Spanish question that requires a yes-or-no answer. You use three simple methods:

✏ Intonation

✏ The tag ¿**(No es) verdad?** (*Isn't that so?*) or ¿**Está bien?** (*Is that all right?*)

✏ Inversion

The following sections break down these methods.

Unlike in English, when you want to write a question in Spanish, you put an upside-down question mark — ¿ — at the beginning of the sentence and a standard question mark — ? — at the end:

¿Tiene Ud. sed? (*Are you thirsty?*)

Also, the words *do* and *does* and sometimes *am*, *is*, and *are* don't translate from English into Spanish. In Spanish, these words are part of the meaning of the conjugated verb:

¿Te gusta este restaurante? (*Do you like this restaurant?*)

¿Vienen hoy? (*Are they coming today?*)

To form a negative question, you put **no** before the conjugated Spanish verb:

¿Ud. no quiere tomar algo? (*Don't you want to drink something?*)

Adjusting your intonation

Intonation is by far the easiest way to ask a question in Spanish. If you're speaking, all you need to do is raise your voice at the end of what was a statement and add an imaginary question mark at the end of your thought. When writing, you just write down your thought and put question marks before and after it. It's that simple. Here's an example:

¿Ud. quiere tomar algo? (*Do you want to drink something?*)

Deciphering the tags "¿No es verdad?" and "¿Verdad?"

¿No es verdad? and **¿Verdad?** are tags that can have a variety of meanings:

- ✔ Isn't that so?
- ✔ Right?
- ✔ Is(n't)/does(n't) he/she?
- ✔ Are(n't)/do(n't) they?
- ✔ Are(n't)/do(n't) we?
- ✔ Are(n't)/do(n't) you?

You generally place **¿No es verdad?**, **¿Verdad?**, or **¿Está bien?** at the end of a statement — especially when "yes" is the expected answer:

Ud. quiere tomar algo. ¿No es verdad? (*You want to drink something, don't you?*)

Tenemos jugo. ¿Está bien? (*We have juice. Is that all right?*)

Flipping the word order

When forming a "yes" or "no" question in Spanish, you may invert (flip) the word order of a statement and put the pronoun or the subject noun after its accompanying verb form. Here are a couple of examples:

- ✔ **Ud. tiene sed.** (*You are thirsty.*) **¿Tiene Ud. sed ?** (*Are you thirsty?*)

- ✔ **Ella va a tomar té.** (*She is going to drink tea.*) **¿Va ella a tomar té?** (*Is she going to drink tea?*)

The following list details some considerations when using inversion:

- ✔ If the subject noun or pronoun is followed by two consecutive verbs, put the subject noun or pronoun after the phrase containing the second verb (remember to keep the meaning of the phrase intact):

  - Incorrect: **¿ Quieren Uds. comer?** (*Do you want to eat?*)

  - Correct: **¿Quieren comer Uds.?** (*Do you want to eat?*)

  In most instances, the subject pronoun is omitted in Spanish when the subject is obvious:

  ¿Quieres comer algo ahora? (*Do you want to eat something now?*)

- ✔ To ask a negative inverted question, put **no** before the inverted verb and noun or pronoun. For verbs preceded by a direct or indirect object pronoun (see Book III, Chapter 2) or for reflexive verbs (see Book III, Chapter 3), the pronoun should remain before the conjugated verb:

  - **¿No toma frutas tu amigo?** (*Doesn't your friend eat fruit?*)

  - **¿No las toma tu amigo?** (*Doesn't your friend eat them?*)

  - **¿No se desayuna temprano Alberto?** (*Doesn't Albert eat breakfast early?*)

Probing for information

When a simple "yes" or "no" won't satisfy your curiosity, you need to know how to ask for more information in Spanish. Although the names sound a bit formidable, interrogative adjectives, interrogative adverbs, and interrogative pronouns are the tools that allow you to get all the facts you want and need. Find out how in the following sections.

Using interrogative adjectives

You use the interrogative adjectives **¿cuánto/a?** (*how much?*) and **¿cuántos/as?** (*how many?*) before a noun when that noun may be measured or counted. These interrogatives must agree in number and gender with the noun they describe:

	Masculine	*Feminine*
Singular	¿cuánto?	¿cuánta?
Plural	¿cuántos?	¿cuántas?

Here are some examples:

> **¿Cuánto dinero necesitas?** (*How much money do you need?*)

> **¿Cuántos dólares ganan por hora?** (*How many dollars do they earn per hour?*)

> **¿Cuánta moneda tiene Ud.?** (*How much change [How many coins] do you have?*)

> **¿Cuántas horas trabajan?** (*How many hours do they work?*)

Note that **cuánto, cuánta, cuántos,** and **cuántas** may also be used as interrogative pronouns, discussed later in this section.

The interrogative adjective **¿qué?,** on the other hand, is invariable (it doesn't change) and refers to a noun that isn't being counted. This word is equivalent to the English interrogative adjectives *what* or *which:*

> **¿Qué idiomas sabes hablar?** (*What [Which] languages do you know how to speak?*)

You may use a preposition before an interrogative adjective where logical:

> **¿A qué hora sale el tren?** (*At what time does the train leave?*)

> **¿Con cuánta frecuencia vas al cine?** (*[With how much frequency] How often do you go to the movies?*)

> **¿De cuántos hombres hablan?** (*How many men are you speaking about?*)

Using interrogative adverbs

You use interrogative adverbs when you need an adverb to ask a question. You often use the interrogative adverbs that follow with inversion to form questions (see the earlier section "Inversion"):

English Adverb	*Spanish Interrogative Adverb*
How?	**¿cómo?**
When?	**¿cuándo?**
Where (to)?	**¿(a)dónde?**
Why? (for what reason)	**¿por qué?**
Why? (for what purpose)	**¿para qué?**

Here are a couple of these interrogative adverbs at work:

> **¿Cómo va Ud. a la oficina?** (*How do you get to work?*)
>
> **¿Dónde vive tu hermana?** (*Where does your sister live?*)

You may use a preposition before an interrogative adverb where logical (note that the preposition **a** is attached to the interrogative adverb in the first example):

> **¿Adónde quieren ir los niños?** (*Where do the children want to go?*)
>
> **¿Para qué sirve esta herramienta?** (*What purpose does this tool serve?*)

The interrogative adverb **¿Para qué?** asks about a purpose and, therefore, requires an answer with **para** (*for, to*):

> **¿Para qué usa Ud. esa brocha?** (*Why [For what purpose] do you use that brush?*)
>
> **Uso esa brocha para pintar.** (*I use that brush to paint.*)

¿Por qué? asks about a reason and, therefore, requires an answer with **porque** (*because*):

> **¿Por qué llora el niño?** (*Why [For what reason] is the child crying?*)
>
> **Llora porque está enfermo.** (*He's crying because he is sick.*)

Using interrogative pronouns

You use an interrogative pronoun when a pronoun is used to ask a question. The following table presents the Spanish equivalents to English pronouns:

English Pronoun	Spanish Interrogative Pronoun
Who?	**¿quién(es)?**
What? (Which one[s]?)	**¿cuál(es)?**
What?	**¿qué?**
How much?	**¿cuánto(a)?**
How many?	**¿cuántos(as)?**

The following list breaks down the characteristics of the interrogative pronouns in the previous list:

✔ The interrogative pronouns **¿quién(es)?** and **¿cuál(es)?** are variable pronouns and change to agree in number with the noun they replace:

- **¿Quién(es) llega(n)?** (*Who is arriving?*)
- **Raquel llega.** (*Raquel is arriving.*)

- **Raquel y Domingo llegan.** (*Raquel and Domingo are arriving.*)

- **¿Cuál(es) de estas blusas prefieres?** (*Which one(s) of these blouses do you prefer?*)

- **Prefiero la roja.** (*I prefer the red one.*)

- **Prefiero las rojas.** (*I prefer the red ones.*)

✔ **¿Cuál?** means *what* or *which* (*one/s*) and asks about a choice or a selection:

- **¿Cuál es tu número de teléfono?** (*What is your phone number?*)

- **¿Cuál de los dos es el mejor?** (*Which [one] of the two is better?*)

- **¿Cuáles son los días de la semana?** (*What are the days of the week?*)

✔ **¿Cuántos/as?** (*How many?*) agrees in both number and gender with the noun being replaced:

- **¿Cuántos toman el examen?** (*How many are taking the test?*)

✔ **¿Cuánto/a?** (*How much?*) only has to agree in gender because it's used exclusively with singular nouns, and **¿qué?** (*What?*) remains invariable:

- **¿Cuánto vale ese coche?** (*How much is that car worth?*)

- **¿Qué significa esto?** (*What does that mean?*)

✔ A preposition + **quién** refers to people. A preposition + **que** refers to things:

- **¿De quiénes habla Ud.?** (*About whom are you speaking?*)

- **¿De qué habla Ud.?** (*About what are you speaking?*)

- **¿A quién se refiere él?** (*To whom is he referring?*)

- **¿A qué se refiere él?** (*To what is he referring?*)

✔ **¿Qué?** means *what* when it precedes a verb and asks about a definition, description, or an explanation. When **¿qué?** precedes a noun, it expresses *which*:

- **¿Qué hacen durante el verano?** (*What are they doing during the summer?*)

- **¿Qué película quieres ver?** (*Which film do you want to see?*)

Hay (*there is/are*) or **¿Hay?** (*is/are there?*) is a present-tense form of the auxiliary verb **haber** (*to have*). You use this verb impersonally both to ask and to answer the question you ask. You can use **hay** by itself or with a preceding question word:

¿(No) Hay un buen restaurante por aquí? (*Is[n't] there a good restaurant nearby?*)

¿Dónde hay un buen restaurante por aquí? (*Where is there a good restaurant nearby?*)

Yes, Sir/No, Ma'am: Answering Questions in Spanish

All speakers of a new language spend a lot of time asking questions, but many struggle to answer them. Where you can really shine and impress others is by providing information properly. You undoubtedly know how to answer "yes" in Spanish, because the word for "yes" is common in pop culture. Answering "no" requires a bit more work, because a simple "no" doesn't always suffice. Sometimes you need to express *nothing, nobody,* or other negative ideas. The following sections cover these topics in detail. We also explain how to answer questions that seek specific information.

Book II

Grasping Basic Grammar Essentials

Answering yes

Saying *yes* in Spanish is really quite easy. You use **sí** to answer *yes* to a question:

> **¿Quieres salir counigo?** (*Do you want to go out with me?*)
>
> **Sí, con mucho gusto.** (*Yes, with pleasure.*)

Saying no in oh so many ways

The most common negative response to a question is a plain and simple no (no, not). Other common negatives, which you may or may not use in conjunction with no, include the following:

Spanish	Negative English Equivalent
ni . . . ni	neither . . . nor
tampoco	neither, not either
jamás, nunca	never, (not) ever
nadie	no one, nobody
ninguno(a)	no, none, (not) any
nada	nothing

Here's a list that details some general considerations to ponder when answering negatively in Spanish:

✔ In Spanish, you generally place negative words before the conjugated verb:

> **Nunca comprendo lo que Miguel dice.** (*I never understand what Miguel says.*)

Unlike in English, it's perfectly acceptable — and sometimes even necessary in common usage — for a Spanish sentence to contain a double negative. Some sentences may even contain three negatives! For example, **No le creo ni a él ni a ella.** (*I don't believe either him or her.*) If **no** is one of the negatives, it precedes the conjugated verb. When **no** is omitted, the other negative precedes the conjugated verb. Here are some examples of both:

- **No lo necesito tampoco./Tampoco lo necesito.** (*I don't need it either.*)

- **No fumo nunca./Nunca fumo.** (*I never smoke.*)

- **No viene nadie./Nadie viene.** (*No one is coming.*)

- **No tengo ninguna idea./Ninguna idea tengo.** (*I don't have any idea.*)

- **No le escucha a nadie nunca./Nunca le escucha a nadie.** (*He never listens to anyone.*)

✔ When you have two verbs in the negative answer, place **no** before the conjugated verb and put the other negative word after the second verb:

- **No puedo comer ninguna comida picante.** (*I can't eat any spicy food.*)

✔ You may also place negative words before the infinitive of the verb:

- **¿Por qué quieres no comer nada?** (*Why don't you want to eat anything?*)

- **Él prefiere no ver a nadie.** (*He doesn't want to see anyone.*)

✔ You may use negatives alone (without **no**):

- **¿Qué buscas?** (*What do you want?*)

- **Nada.** (*Nothing.*)

- **¿Dice mentiras ese muchacho?** (*Does that boy tell lies?*)

- **Nunca.** (*Never.*)

✔ A negative preceded by a preposition (see Chapter 8) retains that preposition when placed before the verb:

- **No habla de nadie./De nadie habla.** (*He doesn't speak about anyone.*)

Just plain "no"

To make a sentence negative, you can put **no** before the conjugated verb. If the conjugated verb is preceded by a pronoun, put **no** before the pronoun. **No** often is repeated for emphasis:

¿**Tocas la guitarra?** (*Do you play the guitar?*)

(**No,**) **No toco la guitarra.** (*[No,] I don't play the guitar.*)

¿**Debe estudiar los verbos ella?** (*Should she study the verbs?*)

(**No,**) **Ella no los debe estudiar.** (*[No,] She shouldn't study them.*)

Ni . . . ni

In a **ni . . . ni** construction (*neither . . . nor*), the sentence usually begins with the word **no.** Each part of the **ni . . . ni** construction precedes the word or words being stressed. Each **ni,** therefore, may be used before a noun, an adjective, or an infinitive:

> **No nos gusta ni el café ni el té.** (*We don't like coffee or tea.*)
>
> **Su coche no es ni grande ni pequeño.** (*His car is neither big nor little.*)
>
> **No puedo ni cocinar ni coser.** (*I can neither cook nor sew.*)

Book II

Grasping
Basic
Grammar
Essentials

Nada and friends

You use the negatives **nadie, nada, nunca,** and **jamás** after comparisons (see Book II, Chapter 7). Note that the English translation of a Spanish negative equivalent may have an opposite meaning:

> **Mi madre cocina mejor que nadie.** (*My mother cooks better than anyone.*)
>
> **Ella conduce mejor que nunca.** (*She drives better than ever.*)
>
> **Quieren visitar España más que nada.** (*They want to visit Spain more than anything.*)

Ninguno

Ninguno (*no, none [not] any*), when used before a masculine singular noun, drops the final **-o** and adds an accent to the **u** (**ningún**). The feminine singular form is **ninguna.** No plural forms exist. Here's an example of its usage:

> ¿**Tiene algunos problemas?** (*Do you have any problems?*)
>
> **No tengo problema ninguno.** (*I don't have a problem.*)
>
> **No tengo ningún problema.** (*I don't have a problem.*)

When used as an adjective, **ninguno/a** may be replaced by **alguno/a,** which is a more emphatic negative. This construction then follows the noun:

> **No tiene ninguna mascota./No tiene mascota alguna.** (*He doesn't have a pet.*)

Answering a positive question with a negative answer

When used in questions, some words require that you use negative words of opposite meaning in the responses. The following table presents these words:

If the question contains	The negative answer should contain
alguien (*someone, anyone*)	**nadie** (*no one, nobody*)
siempre (*always*)	**jamás/nunca** (*never*)
algo (*something*)	**nada** (*nothing*)
también (*also*)	**tampoco** (*neither, either*)
alguno(a) (*some, any*)	**ninguno(a)** (*none, [not] any*)

Here's an example sentence:

> **¿Ves algo?** (*Do you see something?*)
>
> **No veo nada.** (*I don't see anything.*)

Answering information questions

This section is chock full of tips on how to answer questions that ask you for information in Spanish. Carefully consider what's being asked so you answer each question in an appropriate manner.

✔ When you see a question with **¿Cómo?** (*how, what*), give the information or the explanation that's requested:

- **¿Cómo te llamas?** (*What's your name?*)
- **Susana.** (*Susana.*)
- **¿Cómo estás?** (*How are you?*)
- **Muy bien, gracias.** (*Very well, thank you.*)
- **¿Cómo prepara Ud. ese plato?** (*How do you prepare that dish?*)
- **Con mantequilla y crema.** (*With butter and cream.*)

✔ When you see a question with **¿Cuánto(a)(s)** (*how much, many*), you answer with a number, an amount, or a quantity (see Book I, Chapter 2 for more on numbers):

- **¿Cuánto cuesta este coche?** (*How much does this car cost?*)

- **Diez mil dólares.** (*$10,000.*)

- **¿Hace cuántas horas que está esperando Ud.?** (*How long have you been waiting?*)

- **Dos horas.** (*Two hours.*)

- **¿Cuántos huevos necesitas?** (*How many eggs do you need?*)

- **Una docena.** (*A dozen.*)

✔ When you see a question with **¿Cuándo?** (*when*), you answer with a specific time or an expression of time (see Book I, Chapter 2):

- **¿Cuándo empieza la película?** (*When does the film begin?*)

- **En diez minutos.** (*In ten minutes.*)

- **A las tres y media.** (*At 3:30.*)

- **En seguida.** (*Immediately.*)

✔ When you see a question with **¿Dónde?** (*where*), you answer with the name of a place. You use the preposition **en** to express *in:*

- **¿Dónde vive Ud.?** (*Where do you live?*)

- **En Nueva York.** (*In New York.*)

You must use the preposition **a** (**al, a la, a los, a las**) + the name of a place in your answer to the question **¿adónde?** (which translates literally as *to where*):

- **¿Adónde van?** (*Where are they going?*)

- **Van al estadio.** (*They're going to the stadium.*)

You must use the preposition **de** (**del, de la, de los, de las**) + the name of a place in your answer to the question **¿de dónde?** (which translates literally as *from where*):

- **¿De dónde es Ud.?** (*Where are you from?*)

- **Soy de San Juan.** (*I'm from San Juan.*)

For more on prepositions, head to Chapter 8.

Book II

**Grasping
Basic
Grammar
Essentials**

↳ When you see a question with **¿Por qué?** (*why*), answer with **porque** (*because*) + a reason:

  • **¿Por qué no trabaja ella?** (*Why isn't she working?*)

  • **Porque está enferma.** (*Because she's sick.*)

↳ When you see a question with **¿Quién?** (*who, whom*), answer with the name of a person.

  If the question contains a preposition — **a, de, con, para,** and so on — you must use that same preposition in the answer:

  • **¿Quién te acompaña al espectáculo?** (*Who is going with you to the show?*)

  • **Isabel.** (*Isabel.*)

  • **¿A quién espera Ud.?** (*Whom are you waiting for?*)

  • **A mi novio.** (*For my boyfriend.*)

  • **¿Con quién vives?** (*With whom do you live?*)

  • **Con mis abuelos.** (*With my grandparents.*)

↳ When you see a question with **¿Qué?** (*what*), answer according to the situation. As with the previous bullet, if the question contains a preposition, you must use that same preposition in the answer:

  • **¿Qué haces?** (*What are you doing?*)

  • **Escribo algo.** (*I'm writing something.*)

  • **¿Qué escribes?** (*What are you writing?*)

  • **Una carta.** (*A letter.*)

  • **¿Con qué escribes?** (*With what are you writing?*)

  • **Con un bolígrafo.** (*With a ballpoint pen.*)

Chapter 5

What's Happen*ing*: Present Participles and the Present Progressive Tense

. . . .

In This Chapter

↙ Reviewing the different uses of present participles

↙ Forming the present participles of regular, stem-changing, and irregular verbs

↙ Discussing the present progressive with **estar**

↙ Using other verbs with a present participle to express an ongoing action

. . . .

***P**resent participles* are the "happen*ing*" parts of speech — the -ing forms of verbs. Spanish and English both use present participles to express ongoing or continuous action; for example, "One can learn a lot while *traveling*."

In this chapter, you discover how to form the present participles of Spanish verbs, as well as to use a Spanish present participle to translate the English *-ing* ending. We also show you how to form the present progressive tense by using the verb **estar** (*to be*) with present participles.

Using Present Participles: It's an "ing" Thing

A Spanish present participle is called **un participio de presente** and, as in English, is derived from a verb. A Spanish present participle can be used in the following ways:

✔ As an adverb to modify the action of another verb in the same sentence; for example:

Gasté todo mi dinero comprando monedas raras. (*I spent all of my money buying rare coins.*)

Viajando por Europa, vimos muchos sitios hermosos. (*While traveling through Europe, we saw many beautiful places.*)

✔ To express continuous or ongoing action when used with verbs such as **andar** (*to walk*), **ir** (*to go*), and **seguir** (*to continue*); for example:

Anda buscando su carro. (*He is walking around looking for his car.*)

Vas mejorando todos los días. (*You're gradually improving everyday.*)

Juan sigue trabajando allí. (*Juan keeps working there.*)

✔ In an adjective clause to describe a noun mentioned in the same sentence; for example:

El hombre quien está hablando es muy famoso. (*The man who is talking is very famous.*)

✔ To form the *present progressive tense* when used with a present tense conjugation of the verb **estar** (*to be*). This tense describes an action that is ongoing at the present time; for example:

Ella está bailando. (*She is dancing.*)

Ellos están explicando los verbos. (*They're explaining the verbs.*)

In English, the –ing form of a verb can function as a noun. In this instance, it is called a *gerund*; for example, "*Seeing is believing.*" In Spanish, the –ing forms aren't used as nouns. Instead, Spanish uses the infinitive (the **-ar, -er,** or **-ir**) form of the verb, as in **"Ver es creer."** Another example: **Nadar es mi pasatiempo favorito.** (*Swimming is my favorite pastime. Literally: To swim is my favorite pastime.*)

Spanish also uses the infinitive form of the verb rather than the -ing form when using verbs as adjectives:

Necesito nuevos zapatos de correr. (*I need new running shoes.*)

Although English describes a future event by using the present progressive tense, Spanish uses the present or future tense:

Vendremos mañana. (*We'll be coming tomorrow.*)

Llegamos el domingo. (*We are arriving on Sunday.*)

Turning Regular Verbs into Present Participles

Forming present participles of regular verbs — infinitives that conjugate without spelling or stem changes or other irregularities — is quite easy, because present participles have only one form. Here's all you have to do:

✔ Drop the **-ar** from **-ar** verb infinitives and add **-ando** (the equivalent of the English *-ing*).

✔ Drop the **-er** or **-ir** from **-er** or **-ir** verb infinitives, respectively, and add **-iendo** (the equivalent of the English *-ing*).

The following table shows these changes for some example verbs:

Ending	Verb	Meaning	Present Participle	Meaning
-ar	**hablar**	*to speak*	habl**ando**	*speaking*
-er	**aprender**	*to learn*	aprend**iendo**	*learning*
-ir	**escribir**	*to write*	escrib**iendo**	*writing*

Be careful! Watch out for the following changes.

If an **-er** or **-ir** verb stem ends in a vowel, you must drop the ending and add **-yendo** (the Spanish equivalent of *-ing*) to form the present participle:

caer (*to fall*): ca**yendo**

construir (*to build*): constru**yendo**

creer (*to believe*): cre**yendo**

leer (*to read*): le**yendo**

oír (*to hear*): o**yendo**

traer (*to bring*): tra**yendo**

If an **-er** or **-ir** verb stem ends in **ll** or **ñ**, you must drop the ending and add only **-endo** to get the *-ing* ending. (This is because **ll** and **ñ** already create the **i** sound.) Here are some examples:

bullir (*to bubble*): bull**endo**

engullir (*to gobble up*): engull**endo**

escabullirse (*to slip away*): escabull**endo**

gruñir (*to grumble*): gruñ**endo**

reñir (*to tell off*): reñ**endo**

teñir (*to dye*): teñ**endo**

The Present Participle of Stem-Changing and Irregular Verbs

Generally, but not always, the stem change of a verb is indicated in parentheses after the verb. For example, **mentir** (**i**) means that the stem **e** changes to **i** in certain forms and in certain tenses. However, you'll come to recognize these verbs after you work with them often enough.

You form the present participle of a stem-changing **-ir** (**-e** to **-i** or **-o** to **-u**) verb by changing the vowel in the stem from **-e** to **-i** or from **-o** to **-u**, dropping the **-ir** infinitive ending, and adding the proper ending (see the previous section). (For more about stem-changing verbs, see Book II, Chapter 3.)

From **e** to **i**:

d**e**cir (*to say, to tell*) ➪ d**i**ciendo (*saying, telling*)

m**e**ntir (*to lie*) ➪ m**i**ntiendo (*lying*)

p**e**dir (*to ask*) ➪ p**i**diendo (*asking*)

rep**e**tir (*to repeat*) ➪ rep**i**tiendo (*repeating*)

s**e**ntir (*to feel*) ➪ s**i**ntiendo (*feeling*)

s**e**rvir (*to serve*) ➪ s**i**rviendo (*serving*)

v**e**nir (*to come*) ➪ v**i**niendo (*coming*)

From **o** to **u**:

d**o**rmir (*to sleep*) ➪ d**u**rmiendo (*sleeping*)

m**o**rir (*to die*) ➪ m**u**riendo (*dying*)

Only three Spanish verbs have irregular present participles. You don't use them very frequently, but you should still be aware of their forms and memorize them:

- ✔ **ir** (*to go*): **yendo**
- ✔ **poder** (*to be able*): **pudiendo**
- ✔ **reír** (*to laugh*): **riendo**

Expressing Progress with the Present Progressive

For people who speak English as a first language, the concept of two present tenses — the present and the present progressive — can be very confusing. How do you determine when to use the present or the present progressive in Spanish? Good news: The choice really isn't that difficult.

You use the present tense when you want to express an action or event that the subject generally does at a given time, or that's habitual:

> **Él va a la oficina a las siete de la mañana.** (*He goes [does go] to the office at seven in the morning [every day].*)

You use the *present progressive* tense to express an action or event that's in progress or that's continuing at a given time — which calls for the use of present participles:

> **Él está trabajando.** (*He is working [at the present time].*)

The following sections show the most common way to form the present progressive — by using the present tense of the verb **estar** (*to be*) and a present participle.

Forming the present progressive with estar

To form the Spanish present progressive tense, use the present tense conjugation of the verb **estar** (*to be*) + a present participle. The following table gives you the present tense conjugation of this irregular verb, which you must commit to memory:

estar (*to be*)	
estoy	estamos
estás	estáis
está	están

To form the present progressive with this verb, you simply include a present participle after the proper form of **estar**. Here are some examples:

> **El niño está durmiendo.** (*The child is sleeping.*)

> **Estamos escuchando.** (*We are listening.*)

Expressing ongoing action with other verbs

You can use the present tense of several other verbs to describe an ongoing or continuous action in Spanish. Use the present tense of the verbs **seguir** or **continuar**, or verbs of motion — such as **salir, ir, andar, entrar,** and **llegar** — to show that an action or event is ongoing.

The following tables list the conjugations of these verbs in the present tense:

seguir (*to continue, keep*)	
sigo	seguimos
sigues	seguís
sigue	siguen

continuar (*to continue*)	
continúo	continuamos
continúas	continuáis
continúa	continúan

salir (*to leave, go out*)	
salgo	salimos
sales	salís
sale	salen

ir (*to go*)	
voy	vamos
vas	vais
va	van

andar (*to walk*)	
ando	andas
andas	andáis
anda	andan

Just as you do with the verb **estar,** you include a present participle with the proper present tense verb form. Here are some examples:

¿Por qué sigues interrumpiendo a los demas? (*Why do you continue interrupting others?*)

La muchacha continúa leyendo. (*The girl continues reading.*)

Yo salgo sonriendo. (*I leave smiling.*)

Su humor va cambiando. (*Your mood is changing.*)

Ellos andan hablando. (*They walk while speaking.*)

Book II

Grasping Basic Grammar Essentials

Chapter 6

Two More Simple Tenses: Future and Conditional

. . . .

In This Chapter

- Using the present tense of **ir** + **a** to talk about the future
- Conjugating regular and irregular forms of the future
- Understanding the uses of the future tense
- Playing "What if?" with the conditional tense

. . . .

In this chapter, we explore a two tenses that can leave you feeling a little uncertain — the future and the conditional.

This chapter can remove some of your uncertainty by showing you a simple way to express upcoming events, using the verb **ir** (in the present tense) + **a** + a verb infinitive. It also presents the basics of forming and using the future tense to describe actions and events that will occur. You also discover how to use the conditional tense to talk about things that you *would* do *if* conditions were right.

Peering into the Future

You may not be planning to write a futuristic novel in Spanish, but you still need to know how to describe actions that are likely to occur at some future time. In the following sections, we show you a couple of ways to describe the future or "near future" by using what you already know. These are sort of mock future tenses. We then show you how to form the future tense with regular and irregular verbs.

Implying future with the present

You use the present tense to imply the future when asking for instructions or when the proposed action will take place in the not-so-distant or near future. Here are two examples of these usages:

>¿**Dejo de hablar?** (*Shall I stop talking?*)

>**Ellos pasan por nuestra casa.** (*They'll be stopping by our house.*)

Expressing the near future with ir + a

You use the present tense of the verb **ir** (*to go*) + the preposition **a** (which, in this case, has no meaning) + the infinitive of the verb to express an action that will be taking place rather soon or that's imminent. Here are some examples that express what the subject is going to do:

>**Voy a salir.** (*I'm going to go out.*)

>**Vamos a esperarlos.** (*We are going to wait for them.*)

The present tense of **ir** is irregular, and you conjugate it as follows:

ir (*to go*)	
voy	vamos
vas	vais
va	van

Futurizing regular verbs

The future tense in Spanish is one of the easiest tenses to form because all verbs — regular and irregular — have the same future endings. For regular future tense verbs you simply take the entire **-ar, -er,** or **-ir** verb in its infinitive form and add the appropriate ending (depending on the subject.) So after you've memorized these endings, you have most of the battle won!

Future endings for all verbs	
yo -é	nosotros -emos
tú -ás	vosotros -éis
él, ella, Ud. -á	ellos, ellas, Uds. -án

Time for some examples. The tables that follow show how you form the future of some regular verbs with the endings from the previous table:

trabajar (*to work*)	
trabajaré	trabajaremos
trabajarás	trabajaréis
trabajará	trabajarán

vender (*to sell*)	
yo venderé	nosotros venderemos
tú venderás	vosotros venderéis
él, ella, Ud. venderá	venderán

discutir (*to discuss, argue*)	
yo discutiré	nosotros discutiremos
tú discutirás	vosotros discutiréis
él, ella, Ud. discutirá	discutirán

Book II

Grasping
Basic
Grammar
Essentials

Now check out some example sentences utilizing the future tense:

Yo no los invitaré a mi fiesta. (*I won't invite them to my party.*)

Ellos no beberán alcohol. (*They won't drink alcohol.*)

¿Abrirás una cuenta bancaria pronto? (*Will you open a bank account soon?*)

Verbs such as **oír** (*to listen*) and **reír** (*to laugh*) — whose infinitives contain an accent mark over the **i** — drop their accent in the future tense:

Yo no oiré esas mentiras. (*I won't listen to those lies.*)

Ellos no reirán de él. (*They won't laugh at him.*)

Futurizing irregular verbs

Certain Spanish verbs are irregular in the future tense. These verbs have irregular future stems, which always end in **-r** or **-rr** — an easy way to remember them! To form the future of these irregular verbs, you do one of three things:

✔ Add an **r** to the stem of the verb before adding the future ending given in the previous section "Futurizing regular verbs":

Infinitive	Meaning	Future Stem
caber	to fit	cabr-
poder	to be able	podr-
querer	to want	querr-
saber	to know	sabr-

Here are some example sentences:

¿Cabrá esa máquina en el gabinete? (*Will that machine fit in the cabinet?*)

No podremos venir. (*We won't be able to come.*)

Querré verlo. (*I'll want to see it.*)

¿Sabrá hacerlo? (*Will he know how to do it?*)

✔ Add the letters **dr** to the verb stem before adding the proper future ending:

Infinitive	Meaning	Future Stem
poner	to put	pondr-
salir	to leave	saldr-
tener	to have	tendr-
valer	to be worth	valdr-
venir	to come	vendr-

These verbs are illustrated in the following example sentences:

Yo pondré los papeles en la mesa. (*I'll put the papers on the table.*)

¿Cuándo saldrán? (*When will they leave?*)

> **Ella no tendrá bastante dinero.** (*She won't have enough money.*)
>
> **¿Cuánto valdrá ese coche?** (*How much will that car be worth?*)
>
> **¿No vendrás mañana?** (*Won't you be coming tomorrow?*)

✔ The verbs in the third group of future irregulars have irregular stems that you must simply memorize and then add the proper future endings:

Infinitive	Meaning	Future Stem
decir	to say	dir-
hacer	to make, to do	har-

> Observe these verbs in action:
>
> **Yo diré lo que pienso.** (*I'll say what I think.*)
>
> **¿Qué harán para resolver el problema?** (*What will they do to solve the problem?*)

Book II

Grasping
Basic
Grammar
Essentials

Foretelling, predicting, and wondering with the future tense

Using the future to express future time seems kind of obvious. However, you must be aware of other instances in Spanish when you may use the future, too. For instance, you use the future

✔ To express what will happen:

> **Yo te ayudaré.** (*I'll help you.*)

✔ To predict a future action or event:

> **Lloverá pronto.** (*It will rain soon.*)

✔ To express wonder, probability, conjecture, or uncertainty in the present.

The Spanish future, in this case, is equivalent to the following English phrases: "I wonder," "probably," or "must be." Here are a few examples:

> **¿Cuánto dinero tendrán?** (*I wonder how much money they have.*)
>
> **Serán las seis.** (*It's probably [It must be] six o'clock.*)
>
> **Alguien viene. ¿Quién será?** (*Someone is coming. I wonder who it is.*)
>
> **¿Será mi esposo?** (*I wonder whether it's my husband.*)
>
> **¿Irá a darme un anillo mi novio?** (*I wonder whether my boyfriend is going to give me a ring.*)

✔ To express something that you expect and that's due to or caused by a present action or event:

Si viene a tiempo el jefe no se quejará. (*If you come on time, the boss won't complain.*)

Si sigues la receta prepararás una buena comida. (*If you follow the recipe, you'll prepare a good meal.*)

As If: The Conditional Tense

I would've if. . . . That's what the conditional tense is all about. If the conditions were appropriate, the action would have resulted . . . theoretically speaking. Simply put, you use the *conditional tense* to express a conditional action. But you can also use it to make a polite request or to subtly, or not so subtly, suggest that someone perform a certain action.

In the following sections, you investigate the regular and irregular conjugations of the conditional tense. You find out how to form the conditional tense and how to use it in a sentence.

Waffling with the conditional tense

The conditional tense is great for waffling on issues. You can state any impossible condition or set of conditions you like and then say you would've done something if only that condition or set of conditions had been in place. It works in every language — English, Spanish, Italian, you name it — and you don't even have to be a politician to use it.

You often use the conditional tense in a sentence with two verbs. One verb states the condition or problem, and then the second verb states, in the conditional, what you'd do under that condition or if faced with that problem. For example, in the sentence, "If I had a million dollars, I'd travel around the world," the first verb states a situation or condition, and the second verb expresses what you *would* do if that situation or condition existed.

A sentence with an *if clause* requires the subjunctive mood (See Book 3, Chapter 6).

Forming the regular conditional

In English, the key word to forming the conditional tense is *would*. You or somebody else *would* do something *if* the conditions were right. In Spanish, you actually change the form of the verb to build the sense of *would* right into it. When conjugating Spanish verbs in the regular conditional tense, keep the following points in mind:

- ✔ The regular conditional tense is a combination of the imperfect and future tenses.

- ✔ The regular conditional tense requires no spelling or stem changes.

When conjugating regular **-ar, -er,** and **-ir** verbs in the conditional tense, you simply take the entire verb infinitive (don't drop anything) and then add the imperfect verb endings you use for **-er** and **-ir** verbs.

Book II

**Grasping
Basic
Grammar
Essentials**

Conditional endings for all verbs	
yo -ía	**nosotros/as -íamos**
tú -ías	**vosotros/as -íais**
él, ella, usted -ía	**ellos/as, ustedes -ían**

Check out the following conjugation charts for each verb type.

preparar (*to prepare*)	
prepararía	**prepararíamos**
prepararías	**prepararíais**
prepararía	**prepararían**
Ud. prepararía. (*You [formal] would prepare.*)	

vender (*to sell*)	
vendería	**venderíamos**
venderías	**venderíais**
venderías	**venderían**
Vosotras venderíais. (*You [informal, plural, female] would sell.*)	

escribir (*to write*)	
escribiría	escribiríamos
escribirías	escribiríais
escribiría	escribirían
Ella escribiría. (*She would write.*)	

Forming the irregular conditional

The future-tense irregulars can show you everything you need to know about forming the irregular conditional, because the two share the same stems. In other words, the irregular conditional verbs can be divided into three groups based on their formation:

✔ **Group 1:** Add an **r** to their infinitive stem and then add the corresponding verb ending (according to the subject of the sentence).

✔ **Group 2:** Add **dr** to the infinitive stem and then add the corresponding verb ending.

✔ **Group 3:** Memorize the irregular stems in this group and then add the corresponding verb ending:

   • **hacer** (*to do, make*) becomes **har**

   • **decir** (*to say, tell*) becomes **dir**

Table 6-1 summarizes the irregular conditional stems.

Table 6-1	Irregular Conditional Stems	
Infinitive	**English**	**Irregular Conditional Stem**
caber	to fit	cabr-
decir	to say, to tell	dir-
haber	(helping verb) to have	habr-
hacer	to do, to make	har-
poder	to be able to	podr-
poner	to put	pondr-
querer	to want	querr-

Infinitive	English	Irregular Conditional Stem
saber	to know a fact; to know how	sabr-
tener	to have	tendr-
valer	to be worth	valdr-
venir	to come	vendr-

Here are some examples of irregular conditional verbs in sentences:

- ✔ **Yo podría hacerlo el viernes.** (*I'd be able to do it on Friday.*)
- ✔ **Nosotros pondríamos los libros en la mesa.** (*We'd put the books on the table.*)
- ✔ **Yo siempre diría la verdad.** (*I'd always tell the truth.*)

Book II

Grasping Basic Grammar Essentials

Chapter 7

Spicing Up Your Talk with Adjectives and Adverbs

In This Chapter

✏ Seasoning your descriptions with adjectives

✏ Using adverbs to describe actions

✏ Comparing nouns and actions

*W*hether you're writing or speaking, communication is only as clear and engaging as it is descriptive, and this is what adjectives and adverbs are all about.

This chapter illustrates how adjectives in Spanish differ from adjectives in English and presents all you need to know to use them properly. You also discover how to make your actions more descriptive with the use of adverbs. Finally, we include an explanation on how to compare and contrast people, places, things, ideas, and activities so that you can speak and write more descriptively and precisely in Spanish.

Describing Stuff with Adjectives

An adjective's sole purpose is to describe a noun or pronoun so that your audience can form a clearer mental image of it. Mention *tree* to a roomful of people from 20 different places, and each of them forms a different mental image depending on the trees they've seen and experienced. Narrow it down to *palm tree,* and you instantly slash the number of variations. Everyone has a clearer idea of the type of tree you're describing.

In English, adding adjectives is easy. You just plop it down in front of the noun you want to modify. In Spanish, the process is more complex. You have to make sure the adjective agrees with the noun in gender and number and make sure you position it in the correct location relative to the noun. The following sections show you how to use adjectives properly.

Changing an adjective's gender

Unlike in English, in which adjectives have only one form, Spanish adjectives change form to agree with the nouns they modify in gender (masculine or feminine) and number (singular or plural). The following sections bring you up to speed on the rules for assigning an adjective a gender.

Adjective endings

Most Spanish adjectives end in **-o** in their masculine form or **-a** in their feminine form. Adjectives that end in **-o,** like most nouns, are masculine. (In some instances, however, masculine adjectives end in another vowel and maybe even in a consonant; see the following section.) As you may expect, a masculine, singular adjective ending in **-o** forms its feminine counterpart by changing **-o** to **-a.**

Table 7-1 lists many common adjectives that you may find especially useful in Spanish.

Table 7-1	Common Spanish Adjectives	
Masculine	*Feminine*	*Meaning*
aburrido	aburrida	boring
afortunado	afortunada	fortunate
alto	alta	tall
atractivo	atractiva	attractive
bajo	baja	short
bonito	bonita	pretty
bueno	buena	good
delgado	delgada	thin
delicioso	deliciosa	delicious
divertido	divertida	fun
enfermo	enferma	sick
enojado	enojada	angry
famoso	famosa	famous
feo	fea	ugly
flaco	flaca	thin

Masculine	Feminine	Meaning
generoso	generosa	generous
gordo	gorda	fat
guapo	guapa	pretty, good-looking
listo	lista	ready
magnífico	magnífica	magnificent
malo	mala	bad
moderno	moderna	modern
moreno	morena	dark-haired
necesario	necesaria	necessary
negro	negra	black
nuevo	nueva	new
ordinario	ordinaria	ordinary
orgulloso	orgullosa	proud
pardo	parda	brown, drab
peligroso	peligrosa	dangerous
pequeño	pequeña	small
perezoso	perezosa	lazy
perfecto	perfecta	perfect
rico	rica	rich
romántico	romántica	romantic
rubio	rubia	blond
serio	seria	serious
simpático	simpática	nice
sincero	sincera	sincere
tímido	tímida	shy
todo	toda	all
viejo	vieja	old

Book II

Grasping Basic Grammar Essentials

Here's an example of an adjective in action:

Mi primo Jaime es tímido, y mi prima Francisca es tímida también.
(My cousin Jaime is shy, and my cousin Francisca is shy, too.)

Exceptions to the rules

There are some exceptions to every rule. In Spanish, masculine, singular adjectives may end in **-a, -e,** or a consonant (other than **-or**). The adjectives in Table 7-2 don't change in their feminine form.

Table 7-2	Adjectives that End in -a or -e	
Masculine	*Feminine*	*Meaning*
egoísta	egoísta	selfish
materialista	materialista	materialistic
optimista	optimista	optimistic
pesimista	pesimista	pessimistic
realista	realista	realistic
alegre	alegre	happy
amable	amable	nice
eficiente	eficiente	efficient
elegante	elegante	elegant
excelente	excelente	excellent
grande	grande	big
horrible	horrible	horrible
importante	importante	important
inteligente	inteligente	intelligent
interesante	interesante	interesting
pobre	pobre	poor
responsable	responsable	responsible
sociable	sociable	sociable
triste	triste	sad
valiente	valiente	brave

And the adjectives in Table 7-3 end in consonants and undergo no change for gender.

Table 7-3	Adjectives that End in Consonants	
Masculine	*Feminine*	*Meaning*
cortés	cortés	courteous
azul	azul	blue
débil	débil	weak
fácil	fácil	easy
fiel	fiel	loyal
genial	genial	pleasant
leal	leal	loyal
puntual	puntual	punctual
tropical	tropical	tropical
joven	joven	young
popular	popular	popular
feroz	feroz	ferocious
sagaz	sagaz	astute
suspicaz	suspicaz	suspicious

Book II

Grasping Basic Grammar Essentials

Here's an example of one of these adjectives at work:

> **Mi padre es joven, y mi madre es joven también.** (*My father is young, and my mother is young, too.*)

In Spanish, some adjectives of nationality with a masculine form ending in a consonant add **-a** to form the feminine. The adjectives **inglés** (and other adjectives of nationality that end in **-és**) and **alemán** also drop the accent on their final vowel to maintain their original stresses:

Masculine	*Feminine*	*Meaning*
español	española	Spanish
inglés	inglesa	English
alemán	alemana	German

And some adjectives with a masculine form ending in **-or** add **-a** to form the feminine:

Masculine	Feminine	Meaning
encantador	encantadora	enchanting
hablador	habladora	talkative
trabjador	trabajadora	hard-working

Here are some examples:

Fritz es alemán, y Heidi es alemana también. (*Fritz is German, and Heidi is German, too.*)

Carlota es trabajadora, pero su hermano no es trabajador. (*Carlota is hard-working, but her brother isn't hard-working.*)

Making adjectives plural

You have three basic rules to follow to form the plural of adjectives in Spanish. These are the same rules that you follow when forming the plural form of nouns in Spanish. (See Book II, Chapter 3.)

▮ ✔ First, you add **-s** to singular adjectives ending in a vowel:

Singular	Plural	Meaning
alto	altos	tall
rubia	rubias	blond
interesante	interesantes	interesting

▮ ✔ Second, you add **-es** to singular adjectives ending in a consonant:

Singular	Plural	Meaning
fácil	fáciles	easy
trabajador	trabajadores	hard-working

▮ ✔ Third, if a singular adjective ends in **-z** change **-z** to **–c**, add **-es**:

Singular	Plural	Meaning
feliz	felices	happy

Some adjectives add or drop an accent mark to maintain original stress:

joven ⇨ **jóvenes** (*young*)

inglés ⇨ **ingleses** (*English*)

alemán ⇨ **alemanes** (*German*)

Just like with some nouns and pronouns, when speaking about mixed company (males and females, with no mind to number) make sure to use the masculine form of the adjective:

> **Mi hermana y mis hermanos son rubios.** (*My sister and my brothers are blond.*)

Placing adjectives in the right spots

In Spanish, adjectives may precede or follow the nouns they modify. The placement depends on the type of adjective being used, the connotation the speaker wants to convey, and the emphasis being used. Sometimes, when more than one adjective describes a noun, the rules for placement vary according to the type of adjectives being used. For example, possessive adjectives, demonstrative adjectives, and adjectives of quantity precede the nouns they modify, whereas descriptive adjectives generally follow the nouns they modify. The following sections delve deeper into these topics.

Book II

Grasping Basic Grammar Essentials

Adjectives that follow the noun

In Spanish, most descriptive adjectives follow the nouns they modify. The descriptive adjectives **feos, querido, delgado,** and **interesantes** follow the noun:

> **dos gatos feos** (*two ugly cats*)
>
> **mi padre querido** (*my dear father*)
>
> **ese hombre delgado** (*that thin man*)
>
> **algunas cosas interesantes** (*some interesting things*)

Adjectives that precede the noun

Adjectives that impose limits — numbers, possessive adjectives, demonstrative adjectives, and adjectives of quantity — usually precede the noun they modify. The possessive adjective **su** and the number **una** precede the noun:

> **su novia francesa** (*his French girlfriend*)
>
> **una compañía próspera** (*one successful company*)

Descriptive adjectives that emphasize qualities or inherent characteristics appear before the noun:

> **Tenemos buenos recuerdos de su fiesta.** (*We have good memories of her party.*)

In this example, the speaker is emphasizing the quality of the memories.

Abbreviating your adjectives

Some Spanish adjectives get shortened in certain situations. The following list details when this occurs:

- ✔ The following adjectives drop their final **-o** before a masculine, singular noun. **Alguno** and **ninguno** add an accent to the **-u** when the **-o** is dropped:

    - **uno** (*one*) ⇨ **un coche** (*one car*)
    - **bueno** (*good*) ⇨ **un buen viaje** (*a good trip*)
    - **malo** (*bad*) ⇨ **un mal muchacho** (*a bad boy*)
    - **primero** (*first*) ⇨ **el primer acto** (*the first act*)
    - **tercero** (*third*) ⇨ **el tercer presidente** (*the third president*)
    - **alguno** (*some*) ⇨ **algún día** (*some day*)
    - **ninguno** (*no*) ⇨ **ningún hombre** (*no man*)

When a preposition separates the adjective from its noun, you use the original form of the adjective (don't drop the **-o**):

uno de tus primos (*one of your cousins*)

- ✔ **Grande** becomes **gran** (*great, important, famous*) before a singular masculine or feminine noun (note the change of its meaning, depending on where it's placed):

    - **un gran profesor** (*a great teacher [male]*)
    - **una gran profesora** (*a great teacher [female]*)

But it remains **grande** (*large*) after the noun:

    - **un escritorio grande** (*a large desk*)
    - **una mesa grande** (*a large table*)

- ✔ **Ciento** (*one hundred*) becomes **cien** before nouns and before the numbers **mil** and **millones**:

    - **cien hombres y cien mujeres** (*one hundred men and one hundred women*)
    - **cien mil habitantes** (*one hundred thousand inhabitants*)
    - **cien millones de euros** (*one hundred million euros*)

Describing Actions with Adverbs

The function of an adverb is to describe a verb, another adverb, or an adjective so that your audience has a better understanding of how or to what degree or intensity an action is performed. Does a person run (very) quickly? Is his or her house very big? You use adverbs frequently when you write to express the manner in which things are done. The following sections work on helping you form adverbs and position them correctly in sentences.

Forming adverbs

Book II

Grasping
Basic
Grammar
Essentials

Many English adverbs end in **-ly;** the equivalent Spanish ending is **-mente.** To form an adverb in Spanish, you add **-mente** to the feminine singular form of an adjective. If the adjective has the same masculine and feminine form (for example, those adjectives that end in **-e** or a consonant), you simply use the singular form. Table 7-4 illustrates how it's done.

Unlike adjectives, which require agreement in gender and number with the noun they describe, adverbs require no agreement because they modify a verb and not a noun or pronoun.

Table 7-4	Forming Various Types of Adverbs		
Masc. Adj.	*Fem. Adj.*	*Adverb*	*Meaning*
completo	**completa**	**completamente**	completely
lento	**lenta**	**lentamente**	slowly
rápido	**rápida**	**rápidamente**	quickly
alegre	**alegre**	**alegremente**	happily
breve	**breve**	**brevemente**	briefly
frecuente	**frecuente**	**frecuentemente**	frequently
especial	**especial**	**especialmente**	especially
final	**final**	**finalmente**	finally
feroz	**feroz**	**ferozmente**	ferociously

The following example shows an adverb in action:

> **Él entra rápidamente, y ella sale rápidamente.** (*He enters quickly, and she leaves quickly.*)

Adverbial phrases

Sometimes, it's quite awkward to form an adverb in Spanish by using the feminine singular form of the adjective. When writing, you may find the spelling tricky. And at other times, you may not recall the feminine form of the adjective. Luckily, you have an easy way out. You can use the preposition **con** (*with*) + the noun to form an adverbial phrase, which functions in the same way as an adverb.

For instance, if you have trouble remembering or writing **cuidadosamente** (*carefully*), you can substitute con **cuidado** (*with care*), and your Spanish will be perfect. Here are some examples of how this works:

con + noun	*Adverb*	*Meaning*
con alegría	**alegremente**	happily
con claridad	**claramente**	clearly
con cortesía	**cortésmente**	courteously
con energía	**enérgicamente**	energetically
con habilidad	**hábilmente**	skillfully
con paciencia	**pacientemente**	patiently
con rapidez	**rápidamente**	quickly
con respeto	**respetuosamente**	respectfully

Here's an example of this construction:

> **Ella habla con respeto** (**respetuosamente**). (*She speaks with respect [respectfully].*)

Simple adverbs

Some adverbs and adverbial expressions aren't formed from adjectives; they're words or phrases in and of themselves. Table 7-5 lists some of the most frequently used expressions that fit this description.

Table 7-5	Frequently Used Unique Phrases		
Adverb	*Meaning*	*Adverb*	*Meaning*
a menudo	often	**menos**	less
a veces	sometimes	**mientras**	meanwhile
ahora	now	**más tarde**	later
ahora mismo	right now	**mejor**	better

Adverb	Meaning	Adverb	Meaning
al fin	finally	muy	very
allá	there	peor	worse
aquí	here	poco	little
bastante	quite, rather, enough	por consiguiente	consequently
casi	almost	por supuesto	of course
cerca	near	pronto	soon
de buena gana	willingly	pues	then
de nuevo	again	siempre	always
de repente	suddenly	sin embargo	however, nevertheless
de vez en cuando	from time to time	también	also, too
demasiado	too	tan	as, so
despacio	slowly	tarde	late
después	afterward	temprano	soon, early
en seguida	immediately	todavía	still, yet
hoy día	nowadays	todos los días	everyday
lejos	far	ya	already
más	more	ya no	no longer

Book II

Grasping
Basic
Grammar
Essentials

Here's an example of one of these phrases in use:

Él acepta la responsabilidad de buena gana. (*He willingly accepts the responsibility.*)

Adjectives versus adverbs: Choose wisely

The use of certain adjectives and adverbs can require some thought and an understanding of the function of the parts of speech in English. Alas, their use in Spanish can be just as tricky. The following list presents some adjective/adverb situations that can trip you up when learning how to use these tools in Spanish:

✔ **Buen(o/a)(s)** (*good*) and **mal(o/a)(s)** (*bad*) are adjectives; **bien** (*well*) and **mal** (*badly/poorly*) are adverbs.

   • **Ellas tienen muchas buenas (malas) ideas.** (*They have many good [bad] ideas.*)

   • **Elena juega bien (mal).** (*Elena plays well [poorly].*)

✔ The Spanish words **más** (*more*), **menos** (*less, fewer*), **mejor** (*better*), **peor** (*worse*), **mucho** (*much, many*), **poco** (*little, few*), and **demasiado** (*too much, too many*) may be used as adjectives or adverbs.

As adjectives, **más** and **menos** remain invariable; **mejor** and **peor** add **-es** to agree only with noun plurals that they modify; and **mucho, poco,** and **demasiado** agree in number and gender with the nouns they modify. As adverbs, all these words remain invariable. Look at the following sentences where adjectives appear in the first examples and adverbs are used in the second examples:

- **Samuel tiene más (menos) energía.** (*Samuel has more [less] energy.*)

  Samuel trabaja más (menos) enérgicamente. (*Samuel works more [less] energetically.*)

- **Teodoro tiene mejores (peores) notas.** (*Teodoro has better [worse] grades.*)

  Teodoro se aplica mejor (peor). (*Teodoro applies himself better [worse].*)

- **Da muchas (pocas, demasiadas) excusas.** (*He gives many [few, too many] excuses.*)

  Piensa mucho (poco, demasiado). (*He thinks a lot [a little, too much].*)

Keeping an eye on adverb placement

You generally place adverbs directly after the verbs they modify. Sometimes, however, the position of the adverb is variable and comes where you'd logically put an English adverb:

¿Hablas español elocuentemente? (*Do you speak Spanish eloquently?*)

Afortunadamente, yo recibí el paquete. (*Fortunately, I received the package.*)

Comparing Stuff

You generally make comparisons by using adjectives or adverbs. You can make comparisons of equality or inequality, and you can use superlatives. The information present in the previous sections of this chapter, along with the following sections, present you with all the tools you need.

In English, comparatives usually end in **-er:**

> She is tall**er** than I.
>
> He runs fast**er** than they.

In Spanish, things are a little more complicated.

Comparing equals

Comparisons of equality show that two things or people are the same. In Spanish, whether you're using an adjective or an adverb, you make the comparison the same way. You use **tan** + adjective or adverb + **como,** to express "*as* + adjective or adverb + *as*"; check out these examples:

> **Dolores es tan consienzuda como Jorge.** (*Dolores is as conscientious as Jorge.*)
>
> **Ella estudia tan diligentemente como él.** (*She studies as diligently as he does.*)

Remember that when you use an adjective, it must agree in number and gender with the noun or pronoun that it's modifying.

You can make negative comparisons by putting **no** before the verb:

> **Tú no eres tan trabajadora como él.** (*You aren't as hard-working as he is.*)
>
> **Tú no escuchas tan atentamente como Juan.** (*You don't listen as attentively as Juan.*)

Comparing inequalities

Comparisons of inequality show that two things or people aren't the same. As with comparisons of equality, whether you're using an adjective or an adverb, you make the comparison the same way. You create the comparison of inequality with **más** (*more*) or **menos** (*less*) + adjective or adverb + **que** (*than*). So

> **más** + adjective or adverb + **que** = more + adjective or adverb + than

and

> **menos** + adjective or adverb + **que** = less + adjective or adverb + than

Book II

Grasping Basic Grammar Essentials

Here are two examples:

> **Diego es más hablador que yo.** (*Diego is more talkative than I.*)
>
> **Diego habla menos que yo.** (*Diego talks less than I.*)

The best: The superlative

The superlative shows that something (or someone) is the best or worst of its (or his or her) kind. You form the superlatives of adjectives as follows:

> Subject + verb + **el (la, los, las)** + **más/menos** (*more/less*) + adjective + **de** (*in*)

Here's an example:

> **Ella es la más alta de su clase.** (*She is the tallest in her class.*)

If the superlative is describing a direct object, you form the superlative by inserting the noun being described after **el (la, los, las)**:

> **Ella prepara la paella más deliciosa del mundo.** (*She prepares the best paella in the world.*)

English superlatives usually end in **-est**:

> She is the tall**est** in her class.
>
> He runs the fast**est** of them all.

Now we come to adverbs. Superlatives of adverbs aren't distinguished from their comparative forms (see the previous sections):

> **Él acepta críticas menos pacientemente que los otros.** (*He accepts criticism less patiently than others.*)

Even better: The absolute superlative

The absolute superlative expresses the ultimate; you use it when no comparison is made. To form this basic construction, you add **-ísimo** (masc.), **-ísima** (fem.), **-ísimos** (masc. plural), or **-ísimas** (fem. plural) to the adjective according to the gender and number of the noun being described. The meaning is the same as **muy** (*very*) + adjective:

> **La catedral es muy bella. La catedral es bellísima.** (*The cathedral is very beautiful.*)

Los edificios son muy altos. Los edificios son altísimos. (*The buildings are very tall.*)

Here are some more things you need to know to form the absolute superlative:

✔ You drop the final vowel of an adjective before adding **-ísimo** (**-a, -os, -as**):

La casa es grande. La casa es grandísima. (*The house is very large.*)

✔ You use **muchísimo** to express *very much:*

Te adoro muchísimo. (*I adore you very much.*)

✔ Adjectives ending in **-co** (**-ca**), **-go** (**-ga**), or **-z** change **c** to **qu, g** to **gu,** and **z** to **c,** respectively, before adding **-ísimo:**

- **La torta es muy rica. La torta es riquísima.** (*The pie is very tasty.*)

- **El juez es muy sagaz. El juez es sagacísimo.** (*The judge is very shrewd.*)

Book II

Grasping Basic Grammar Essentials

Checking out the irregular comparatives

As adjectives, **bueno** (*good*), **malo** (*bad*), **grande** (*big*), and **pequeño** (*small*) have irregular forms in the comparative and superlative. Note that **grande** and **pequeño** each have two different meanings in their comparative and superlative forms. Table 7-6 highlights the changes.

Table 7-6 Irregular Adjectives in the Comparative and Superlative

Adjective	Comparative	Superlative
bueno/buena (*good*)	**mejor** (*better*)	**el/la mejor** (*the best*)
buenos/buenas	**mejores**	**los/las mejores**
malo/mala (*bad*)	**peor** (*worse*)	**el/la peor** (*the worst*)
malos/malas	**peores**	**los/las peores**
grande(s) (*great, big*)	**mayor(es)** (*older, greater in age or status*)	**el/la (los/las) mayor(es)** (*the oldest, greatest*)
	más/menos grande(s) (*larger/less large in size*)	**el/la (los/las) más/menos grande(s)** (*the largest/the least large*)
pequeño(s)/ pequeña(s) (*small*)	**menor(es)** (*minor, lesser, younger in age or status*)	**el/la (los/las) menor(es)** (*the least, the youngest*)
	más/menos pequeño(s)/ pequeña(s) (*smaller/less small in size*)	**el/la (los/las) más pequeño(s)/ pequeña(s)** (*the smallest/least small*)

The adverbs **bien** (*well*) and **mal** (*poorly*) become **mejor** (*better*) and **peor** (*worse*), respectively, in their comparative forms and follow the verb or verb phrase they modify:

> **Tomás juega al fútbol mejor que Javier.** (*Tomás plays soccer better than Javier.*)

> **Ella cocina peor que yo.** (*She cooks worse than I do.*)

Chapter 8

Defining Relationships with Prepositions

. . . .

In This Chapter

- Incorporating common Spanish prepositions
- Selecting the appropriate preposition
- Identifying Spanish verbs that do and don't require prepositions
- Knowing when to use a prepositional pronoun

. . . .

Prepositions are words typically used in front of nouns and pronouns to form phrases that describe a relationship of time or space. Common prepositions in English include *at, below, in, out, to, under, until,* and *with.*

This chapter introduces you to common Spanish prepositions and shows you how to use them in sentences. Certain Spanish verbs require a preposition before the infinitive form, so being familiar with them enhances your speaking and writing skills. Also, you find out about the pronouns that follow prepositions.

Meeting the Most Common Spanish Prepositions

Prepositions should be followed by objects to create prepositional phrases. *Prepositions* relate elements in a sentence: noun to noun, verb to verb, or verb to noun/pronoun. Prepositions also may contract with articles: **a** + **el** = **al** and **de** + **el** = **del**. The following examples show how prepositions work in different sentences:

- Noun to noun: **Necesito esa hoja <u>de</u> papel.** (*I need that piece <u>of</u> paper.*)
- Verb to verb: **El niño empieza <u>a</u> reír.** (*The child begins <u>to</u> laugh.*)
- Verb to noun: **Ella estudia <u>con</u> sus amigas.** (*She studies <u>with</u> her friends.*)
- Verb to pronoun: **¿Qué piensas <u>de</u> ellos?** (*What do you think <u>about</u> them?*)

You use prepositions before the names of geographical locations to refer to travel and location:

> **Mi familia está en Puerto Rico.** (*My family is in Puerto Rico.*)
>
> **Voy a España.** (I'm going <u>to</u> Spain.)

We list the Spanish prepositions that you'll find most useful in your sentences in Table 8-1.

Table 8-1	Common Spanish Prepositions		
Preposition	*Meaning*	*Preposition*	*Meaning*
a	to; at	**detrás de**	behind
a eso de (+ time)	about (time)	**durante**	during
a fuerza de	by persevering	**en**	in; on; at; by
a pesar de	in spite of	**en cambio**	on the other hand
a tiempo	on time	**en casa de**	at the house of
a través (de)	across; through	**en lugar de**	instead of
acerca de	about	**en vez de**	instead of
además de	besides	**encima de**	above; on top of
alrededor de	around	**enfrente de**	opposite; in front of
antes (de)	before	**entre**	between
cerca de	near	**frente a**	in front of
con	with	**fuera de**	outside of
contra	against	**hacia**	toward
de	of; from; about	**hasta**	until
de otro modo	otherwise	**lejos de**	far
debajo de	beneath; under	**por**	for; by
delante de	in front of	**para**	for
dentro de	inside; within	**según**	according to
desde	since	**sin**	without
después (de)	after	**sobre**	over; above; on; upon

Here are more examples to show you prepositions at work in Spanish:

> **La farmacia está cerca del supermercado.** (*The pharmacy is near the supermarket.*)
>
> **A fuerza de estudiar Ud. saldrá bien.** (*By studying you will succeed.*)

Telling the Difference between Prepositions

Sometimes, selecting the correct preposition to use in a sentence can be tricky, because some prepositions have more than one meaning. Take **a,** for example, which can mean *to* or *at;* **en,** which can mean *in, on, at,* or *by;* and **por** and **para,** which can both mean *for.* Fortunately, Spanish has some rules that can help you understand when the more common prepositions are appropriate.

A

Start with the preposition **a** (which contracts with the definite article **el** to become **al**). You use **a** to show

- ✔ Time: **Te llamo a las tres.** (*I'll call you at 3:00.*)
- ✔ Movement: **Vamos a la playa.** (*We're going to the beach.*)
- ✔ Location: **Espere a la entrada.** (*Wait at the entrance.*)
- ✔ Means/manner: **Hágalo a mano.** (*Do it by hand.*) **Se prepara a la española.** (*It's prepared the Spanish way.*)
- ✔ Price: **Puede comprarlo a cien pesos.** (*You can buy it for 100 pesos.*)
- ✔ Speed: **Iba a cien kilómetros por hora.** (*He was going 1,000 kilometers per hour.*)

You use the preposition **a** before a direct object alluding to a person; this is referred to as the *personal a* (see Book II, Chapter 3):

Buscamos al señor Nuñez. (*We are looking for Mr. Nuñez.*)

De

Another preposition with several meanings is **de** (which contracts with the definite article **el** to become **del**). You use **de,** which means *of, from,* or *about,* to show:

- ✔ Possession: **Es el coche de Julio.** (*It's Julio's car.*)
- ✔ Origin: **Soy de Panamá.** (*I'm from Panama.*)
- ✔ Time: **No duerme de noche.** (*He doesn't sleep at night.*)

✔ Cause: **Fracasa de no estudiar.** (*He is failing from not studying.*)

✔ Material: **Es un anillo de oro.** (*It's a gold ring.*)

✔ Characteristics: **Es de buena calidad.** (*It's of a good quality.*)

✔ Contents: **Bebo una taza de café.** (*I'm drinking a cup of coffee.*)

✔ Relationship: **Madrid es la capital de España.** (*Madrid is the capital of Spain.*)

✔ Part of a whole: **Toma un trozo de pan.** (*She's taking a piece of bread.*)

✔ Subject: **No encuentro mi libro de arte.** (*I can't find my art book.*)

✔ A superlative: **Es el más alto de todos.** (*He's the tallest of them all.*) (Check out Book II, Chapter 7 for more on superlatives.)

En and hasta

The preposition **en** can mean *in, on, at,* or *by.* You use **en** to show

✔ Time: **Estamos en el otoño.** (*It's [We're in the] fall.*)

✔ Location: **Está en esa calle.** (*It's on that street.*) **Estamos en casa.** (*We are at home.*)

✔ Means/manner: **Hable en voz baja.** (*Speak in a low voice.*) **Está escrita en español.** (*It's written in Spanish.*)

✔ Movement: **Entran en el banco.** (*They enter the bank.*)

✔ Means of transport: **Viajan en avión.** (*They're traveling by plane.*)

The preposition **hasta,** which means *until* (but also can have the meaning *to*), shows the following:

✔ Place/location: **Conduzca hasta el semáforo.** (*Drive to the traffic light.*)

✔ Time: **Hasta luego.** (*See you later./Until then.*)

Por and para

Now you come to two prepositions that can cause much confusion. **Por** and **para** both mean *for* in English, which is what causes the problem. In Spanish, however, the two prepositions serve different purposes.

The preposition **para** shows the following:

✔ Destination/place: **Salimos para Madrid.** (*We are leaving for Madrid.*)

✔ Destination/person: **Esto es para Ud.** (*This is for you.*)

- A future time limit: **Es para mañana.** (*It's for tomorrow.*)
- Purpose/goal: **Nado para divertirme.** (*I swim to have fun.*)
- Use/function: **Es un cepillo para el pelo.** (*It's a hair brush.*)
- Comparisons: **Para su edad, lee bien.** (*For her age, she reads well.*)
- Opinion: **Para mí es demasiado crudo.** (*For me it's too rare.*)

The preposition **por** shows the following:

- Motion/place: **Caminan por las calles.** (*They walk through the streets.*)
- Means/manner: **Lo envío por correo aéreo.** (*I'm sending it by air-mail.*)
- In exchange for/substitution: **Voy a hacerlo por tí.** (*I'm going to do it for you.*)
- Duration of an action: **Trabajo por una hora.** (*I'm working for an hour.*)
- Indefinite time period: **Duerme por la tarde.** (*He sleeps in the afternoon.*)
- On behalf of: **La firmo por Ud.** (*I am signing it on your behalf.*)
- Per: **Me pagan por día.** (*They pay me per day.*)

If you're speaking about a means of transportation for a passenger, use **en** rather than **por** to express *by:*

> **Van a la capital en tren.** (*They're going to the capital by train.*)

You use **por** to express *for* after the verbs **enviar** (*to send*), **ir** (*to go*), **mandar** (*to order, send*), **preguntar** (*to ask*), **regresar** (*to return*), **venir** (*to come*), and **volver** (*to return*). Here are two examples:

> **Voy por la factura.** (*I am going for the bill.*)
>
> **Ven por tu libro.** (*Come for your book.*)

You also use **por** in the following adverbial expressions:

- **por eso** (*therefore; so*)

  Trabaja mucho y por eso gana mucho dinero. (*He works a lot and therefore he earns a lot of money.*)

- **por lo general** (*generally*)

  Por lo general me acuesto a las diez. (*Generally, I go to bed at 10:00.*)

- **por supuesto** (*of course*)

  ¿Puede Ud. ayudarme? ¡Por supuesto! (*Can you help me? Of course!*)

Combining Prepositions with Infinitives

The only verb form in the Spanish language that may follow a preposition is an infinitive. When a Spanish sentence combines a conjugated verb with an infinitive, there are certain verbs that require the preposition **a, de, en,** or **con** before the infinitive verb form. Other Spanish verbs are followed immediately by the infinitive and don't require a preposition. The following sections break down all the categories for you.

A + infinitive

How can you tell which verbs require the preposition **a** before the infinitive? Generally, verbs that express beginning, motion, teaching, or learning take **a.** Many other verbs, however, use this preposition before their infinitive form, so you have to memorize these verbs. Table 8-2 shows which Spanish verbs call for the use of **a** before the infinitive. (Stem changes are shown in parentheses.)

Table 8-2	Spanish Verbs Requiring a		
Infinitive	*Meaning*	*Infinitive*	*Meaning*
acercarse	to approach	empezar (ie)	to begin to
acostumbrarse	to become accustomed to	enseñar	to teach to
aprender	to learn to	ir	to go
apresurarse	to hurry to	llegar	to succeed in
aspirar	to aspire to	negarse (ie)	to refuse to
atreverse	to dare to	obligar	to force to
ayudar	to help to	ponerse	to begin to
comenzar (ie)	to begin to	regresar	to return to
convidar	to invite	resignarse	to resign oneself to
correr	to run to	salir	to go out to
decidirse	to decide to	venir (ie)	to come to
dedicarse	to devote oneself to	volver (ue)	to return (again) to
disponerse	to get ready to		

Here are some examples that show how you use the preposition **a:**

Los niños se apresuran a llegar a tiempo. (*The children hurry to arrive on time.*)

No empieza a llorar. (*Don't start to cry.*)

De + infinitive

The list of verbs requiring **de** before an infinitive is much shorter than the list for verbs requiring **a.** We can't give you any hard and fast rules to help you with these. You simply have to memorize them. Table 8-3 lists the Spanish verbs that are followed by **de** before an infinitive.

Table 8-3	Spanish Verbs Requiring de
Infinitive	*Meaning*
acabar	to have just done something
acordarse (ue)	to remember to
alegarse	to be glad
cesar	to stop
dejar	to stop
encargarse	to take charge of
olvidarse	to forget
tratar	to try to

Book II

Grasping Basic Grammar Essentials

These examples show you how to use **de** before an infinitive:

> **Mi mejor amiga dejó de fumar.** (*My best friend stopped smoking.*)
>
> **Mi esposo siempre olivida de sacar la basura.** (*My husband always forgets to take out the garbage.*)

En + infinitive

The list of verbs that require **en** before an infinitive is even shorter than the others. Again, you must commit them to memory to know when to use them. Table 8-4 lists the Spanish verbs that are followed by **en** before an infinitive.

Table 8-4	Spanish Verbs Requiring en
Infinitive	*Meaning*
consentir (ie)	to agree to
consistir	to consist of
convenir (ie)	to agree to
insistir	to insist on
tardar	to delay in

These examples illustrate how you use **en** before an infinitive:

> **Yo consiento en ir al teatro con Ramón.** (*I agree to go to the theater with Ramón.*)

> **¿Por qué insistes en partir ahora?** (*Why do you insist on leaving now?*)

Con + infinitive

The good news? As you move through all the preposition tables, your memorization duties get shorter and shorter! Table 8-5 shows the Spanish verbs that use **con** before an infinitive.

Table 8-5	Spanish Verbs Requiring con
Infinitive	*Meaning*
contar (ue)	to count on
soñar (ue)	to dream of
amenazar	to threaten

Here are examples with verbs that require **con** before the infinitive:

> **Él cuenta con trabajar con nosotros.** (*He is counting on working with us.*)

> **Yo sueño con salir con él.** (*I am dreaming about going out with him.*)

Spanish verbs that can stand alone

What's that? You thought your memorization duties were over? Actually, you have one more important list to study. Table 8-6 presents a list of verbs that don't require a preposition and are followed by the infinitive.

Table 8-6	Verbs That Require No Preposition
Infinitive	*Meaning*
deber	to have to
dejar	to allow to
desear	to want, wish to
esperar	to hope to

Infinitive	Meaning
hacer	to make (have something done)
lograr	to succeed in
necesitar	to need to
oír	to hear
pensar (ie)	to intend to
poder (ue)	to be able to
preferir (ie)	to prefer to
pretender	to attempt to
prometer	to promise to
querer (ie)	to want; to wish to
saber	to know how to
ver	to see

Book II

Grasping Basic Grammar Essentials

Example sentences containing verbs that require no preposition before the infinitive follow:

Pensamos hacer un viaje pronto. (*We plan to take a trip soon.*)

Sé tricotar. (*I know how to knit.*)

Brushing Up on Prepositional Pronouns

You must use certain special Spanish pronouns after prepositions. The prepositional pronoun is used as the object of a preposition and always follows the preposition. Table 8-7 presents these prepositional pronouns.

Table 8-7	Prepositional Pronouns
Singular	*Plural*
mí (me)	**nosotros/as** (us)
ti (you informal)	**vosotros/as** (you informal)
él (him; it masculine)	**ellos** (them masculine or mixed group)
ella (her; it feminine)	**ellas** (them feminine)
Ud. (you formal)	**Uds.** (you formal)
sí (yourself; himself; herself; itself)	**sí** (yourselves; themselves)

Here are some examples that show how you use these pronouns:

> **Esta carta es para mí, no es para ella.** (*This letter is for me, not for her.*)
>
> **Juego al tenis con él, no con ella.** (*I play tennis with him, not with her.*)

Perhaps you've noticed that most of the pronouns that follow prepositions are the same as the subject pronouns we discuss in Book II, Chapter 1. The exceptions are **mí, ti,** and **sí.** (Good for you!) Here are some examples of these prepositional pronouns in use:

> **Puedes sentarte detrás de mí.** (*You can sit behind me.*)
>
> **Yo no quiero salir sin ti.** (*I don't want to leave without you.*)
>
> **Logró preparar la comida por sí sola.** (*She was able to prepare the meal by herself.*)

You use the reflexive prepositional pronoun **sí** both in the singular to express *yourself, himself, herself,* or *itself* and in the plural to express *themselves* or *yourselves.* They're only used when the subject of the sentence and the object of the preposition are the same person(s).

The prepositional pronouns **mí, ti,** and **sí** combine with the preposition **con** as follows:

- ✔ **conmigo** (*with me*)
- ✔ **contigo** (*with you*)
- ✔ **consigo** (*with him/her/you/them*)

The following list presents some examples of these words:

> **¿Puedes ir al cine conmigo?** (*Can you go to the movies with me?*)
>
> **No puedo ir contigo.** (*I can't go with you.*)
>
> **Siempre lleva una cartera consigo.** (*She always carries a wallet with her.*)

To emphasize that the subject of the sentence and the object of the preposition are the same person(s) when you use **sí** (*himself; herself; yourself; yourselves;* and *themselves*), you may add the adjective **mismo** (**misma, mismos, mismas**) to your sentence:

> **Él habla consigo mismo.** (He is talking with himself.)

Book III

Mastering More Advanced Grammar Essentials

The 5th Wave   By Rich Tennant

"I didn't know they had mimes here in Madrid.
I don't speak Spanish — what's he saying?"

In this book . . .

Book III is Book II's sequel, introducing you to more advanced grammatical rules and regulations, but still in a very straightforward way. Here, you discover how to issue commands with the imperative, take action on object pronouns, talk about yourself with reflexive verbs, recall the past with the preterit and imperfect tenses, wish and hope with the subjunctive, and double the number of verb tenses with the helping verb **haber**. As soon as you wrap your brain around Books II and III, you have the fundamental framework in place for both speaking and writing in Spanish.

Here are the contents of Book III at a glance:

Chapter 1

Getting Bossy with the Imperative Mood

In This Chapter

- Expressing formal commands
- Giving informal commands

*W*hen you tell a waiter to bring you water, ask a dinner guest to please pass the salt, or tell your dog to lie down, you're using the *imperative mood*. You're giving a command — telling someone, or sometimes yourself, to do something. The imperative is called a *mood* rather than a *tense* because it deals with wants and desires, and the time is always *now*.

In this chapter, you discover how to issue various kinds of commands in the imperative mood so that whatever needs to get done gets done.

English has only one form of *you,* and in commands, the *you* is often implied rather than stated. Spanish has four forms of *you* — the singular and plural of the formal and informal.

	Singular	*Plural*
Informal (familiar)	**tú**	**vosotros**
Formal (polite)	**Ud.**	**Uds.**

In English, you may put an exclamation mark at the end of a command. In Spanish, you must place an *inverted exclamation mark* (¡) at the beginning of an emphasized command and a *regular exclamation mark* (!) at the end:

¡Abra la ventana! (*Open the window!*)

¡No discuten! (*Don't argue!*)

Issuing Formal Commands

You give formal commands to people who are older and wiser or are unfamiliar to you. Of course, in a formal situation you don't want to be rude, so you use the Spanish words for *please:* **por favor.** Giving a formal command can also mean that you're asking a person to help you or to do a favor for you.

The subjects of formal commands are **Ud.** (if you're addressing only one person) and **Uds.** (if you're addressing more than one person):

> **Abra (Ud.) la puerta, por favor.** (*Open the window, please.*)
>
> **Por favor, hablen (Uds.) más despacio.** (*Please speak more slowly.*)

In English, you never actually say the word *you* when you give a command or make a request. In Spanish, the use of a subject pronoun (**Ud., Uds., tú,** or **vosotros**) in a command is optional and not used all that frequently. You can identify the subject by a quick look at the verb form being used:

> **Pase (Ud.) la sal, por favor.** (*Pass the salt, please.*)
>
> **Presten (Uds.) atención.** (*Pay attention.*)

Commandeering regular verbs

To form either an affirmative or negative formal command:

1. **Drop the final -o from the** yo **form of the present tense.**
2. **For infinitives ending in** -ar, **add -e for** Ud. **and -en for** Uds. **For infinitives ending in** -er **or** -ir, **add -a for** Ud. **and -an for** Uds.
3. **To form the negative, simply put** no **before the verb created in Step 2.**

Here's a chart to help you see these changes in action:

-ar verbs	*-er verbs*	*-ir verbs*
firmar (*to sign*)	**comer** (*to eat*)	**subir** (*to go up*)
yo firmo (*I sign*)	**yo com**o (*I eat*)	**yo sub**o (*I go up*)
[No] Firme (Ud.)	**[No] Coma (Ud.)**	**[No] Suba (Ud.)**
(*[Don't] Sign.*)	(*[Don't] Eat.*)	(*[Don't] Go up.*)
[No] Firmen (Uds.)	**[No] Coman (Uds.)**	**[No] Suban (Uds.)**
(*[Don't] Sign.*)	(*[Don't] Eat.*)	(*[Don't] Go up.*)

The following list shows some regular verbs in action in commands:

Trabajen cuidadosamente. (*Work carefully.*)

No trabajen tan despacio. (*Don't work so slowly.*)

Lea en voz alta. (*Read aloud.*)

No lea esa carta. (*Don't read that letter.*)

Escriba cómo se llega a su casa. (*Write how to get to your house.*)

No escriba nada. (*Don't write anything.*)

Commandeering other verbs

Watch for those verbs with irregular **yo** forms or stem and/or spelling changes, because these irregularities affect how you conjugate their command forms. Also, some verbs have irregular command forms that you have to memorize. Fortunately for you, there are very few of these verbs.

Verbs with irregular yo forms

Table 1-1 starts you off by helping you navigate verbs with irregular **yo** forms.

Table 1-1	Verbs with Irregular yo Forms	
Spanish Verbs	*Commands*	*Meaning*
decir	(no) diga(n)	(don't) tell
conducir	(no) conduzca(n)	(don't) drive
conocer	(no)conozca(n)	(don't) meet
hacer	(no) haga(n)	(don't) do
oír	(no) oiga(n)	(don't) hear
poner	(no) ponga(n)	(don't) put
salir	(no) salga(n)	(don't) leave
tener	(no) tenga(n)	(don't) have (be)
traer	(no) traiga(n)	(don't) bring
valer	(no) valga(n)	(don't) be worth (cost)
venir	(no) venga(n)	(don't) come

The examples that follow show you how to use these verbs in the imperative:

Siempre digan la verdad. (*Always tell the truth.*)

No tenga miedo. (*Don't be afraid.*)

Verbs with spelling changes in the imperative

Table 1-2 highlights Spanish verbs with spelling changes in the imperative. For **-ar** verbs, the following changes occur: **c ⇨ qu**, and **g ⇨ gu** when preceeding an **e**. For **-er** and **-ir** verbs, you change **g ⇨ j, gu ⇨ g**, and **c ⇨ z** when preceding an **a**.

Table 1-2	Verbs with Spelling Changes in the Imperative	
Spanish Verbs	*Commands*	*Meaning*
-ar verbs		
sa**car**	(no) sa**que**(n)	(don't) take out
pa**gar**	(no) pa**gue**(n)	(don't) pay
organi**zar**	(no) organi**ce**(n)	(don't) organize
-er and **-ir** verbs		
esco**ger**	(no) esco**ja**(n)	(don't) choose
espar**cir**	(no) espar**za**(n)	(don't) scatter, spread
exi**gir**	(no) exi**ja**(n)	(don't) demand
distin**guir**	(no) distin**ga**(n)	(don't) distinguish

These examples show how to use verbs with spelling changes in commands:

> **Saque su tarjeta de crédito.** (*Take out your credit card.*)

> **Paguen la cuenta por favor.** (*Pay the bill, please.*)

If a verb has a stem change in the present tense, it also has the same stem change in the command forms. Here are some examples of stem changing verbs in commands:

> **Cierre la puerta.** (*Close the door.*)

> **Cuente los libros.** (*Count the books.*)

> **Pida perdón.** (*Apologize.*)

Verbs with spelling and stem changes in the imperative

Some Spanish verbs undergo both spelling and stem changes when used in commands. Table 1-3 presents these verbs.

Table 1-3	Verbs with Spelling and Stem Changes in the Imperative	
Spanish Verbs	*Commands*	*Meaning*
colgar (**o** to **ue/g** to **gu**)	(no) **cuelgue**(n)	(don't) hang
jugar (**u** to **ue/g** to **gu**)	(no) **juegue**(n)	(don't) play
comenzar (**e** to **ie/z** to **c**)	(no) **comience**(n)	(don't) begin
empezar (**e** to **ie/z** to **c**)	(no) **empiece**(n)	(don't) begin
almorzar (**o** to **ue/z** to **c**)	(no) **almuerce**(n)	(don't) eat lunch
corregir (**e** to **i/g** to **j**)	(no) **corrija**(n)	(don't) correct
seguir (**e** to **i/gu** to **g**)	(no) **siga**(n)	(don't) follow

Here are some sample commands containing verbs with both spelling and stem changes:

> **No jueguen allá.** (*Don't play there.*)

> **Empiecen inmediatamente.** (*Begin immediately.*)

Irregular verbs that you have to memorize for commands

Finally, Table 1-4 presents irregular verbs that you have to memorize in order to use them in commands.

Table 1-4	Irregular Verbs	
Spanish Verbs	*Commands*	*Meaning*
estar	(no) **esté**(n)	(don't) be
ir	(no) **vaya**(n)	(don't) go
saber	(no) **sepa**(n)	(don't) know
ser	(no) **sea**(n)	(don't) be

Here's how you include these irregular verbs in commands:

> **Estén listos a las siete.** (*Be ready at 7:00.*)

> **Vaya a la tienda ahora.** (*Go to the store now.*)

Book III

Mastering More Advanced Grammar Essentials

Delivering Informal Commands

You give informal commands to people you know: friends, peers, family members, or pets. The subject of an informal Spanish command is **tú** (if you're addressing one person) or **vosotros** (if you're addressing more than one person).

The **vosotros** (second person plural) command is used primarily in Spain. In Spanish American countries, people use the **Uds.** form for plural informal commands.

The sections that follow explain how to create singular and plural informal commands with both regular and irregular verbs.

Issuing singular commands with tú

To form the affirmative informal (**tú**) commands you simply use the present tense **Ud.** form of the verb. This rule holds true for all verbs except for a handful of irregular verbs that you just have to memorize.

To form a negative informal (**tú**) command, you follow the same rule as you do to form an **Ud.** command, and then add an **-s** and put **no** in front of the verb. The following steps show you how to form an **Ud.** command:

1. **Drop the final** -o **from the** yo **form of the present tense.**
2. **For infinitives ending in** -ar, **add** -es. **For infinitives ending in** -er **or** -ir, **add** -as.
3. **Put** no **before the verb.**

Using regular verbs

The following conjugations illustrate the difference between singular familiar commands in their affirmative and negative forms:

Infinitive	Affirmative	Negative	Meaning
firm**ar**	firm**a**	no firm**es**	(don't) sign
com**er**	com**e**	no com**as**	(don't) eat
sub**ir**	sub**e**	no sub**as**	(don't) go up

Here are some examples that show how singular familiar commands should look with regular verbs:

Usa (No uses) este libro. (*[Don't] Use this book.*)

Corre (¡No corras!) (*¡[Don't] Run!*)

Cubre (No cubras) los ojos. (*[Don't] Cover your eyes.*)

Using other verb types

Here are some examples of verbs with irregular **yo** forms:

Infinitive	Affirmative	Negative	Meaning
oír	oye	**no oigas**	(don't) hear
traer	trae	**no traigas**	(don't) bring

Two examples show how to use these verbs in their imperative forms:

¡Oye lo que digo! (*Hear what I am saying!*)

Trae (No traiga) el periódico. (*[Don't] Bring the newspaper.*)

Here are some examples of verbs that have spelling changes. As you can see, these verbs only have changes in the negative form.

Infinitive	Affirmative	Negative	Meaning
-ar verbs			
sacar	saca	no sa**ques**	(don't) take out
pagar	paga	no pa**gues**	(don't) pay
organizar	organiza	no organi**ces**	(don't) organize
-er and **-ir** verbs			
escoger	escoge	no esco**jas**	(don't) choose
esparcir	esparce	no espar**zas**	(don't) scatter, spread
exigir	exige	no exi**jas**	(don't) demand
distinguir	distingue	no distin**gas**	(don't) distinguish

The following examples show how to use these verbs:

Paga (No pagues) la cuenta. (*[Don't] Pay the bill.*)

Escoge (No escojas) la respuesta. (*[Don't] Choose the answer.*)

Here are some examples of verbs with stem changes. These verbs experience changes in both their affirmative and negative forms:

Book III

Mastering More Advanced Grammar Essentials

Infinitive	Affirmative	Negative	Meaning
-ar verbs			
cerrar (e to ie)	cierra	**no cierres**	(don't) close
mostrar (o to ue)	muestra	**no muestres**	(don't) show
enviar (i to í)	envía	**no envíes**	(don't) send
continuar (u to ú)	continúa	**no continúes**	(don't) continue
-er and **-ir** verbs			
perder (e to ie)	pierde	**no pierdas**	(don't) lose
volver (o to ue)	vuelve	**no vuelvas**	(don't) return
mentir (e to ie)	miente	**no mientas**	(don't) lie
dormir (o to ue)	duerme	**no duermas**	(don't) sleep
pedir (e to i)	pide	**no pidas**	(don't) ask (for)
destruir (add y)	destruye	**no destruyas**	(don't) destroy

Here are some examples of these verbs in action:

> **Continúa (No continúes) hablando.** (*[Don't] Continue speaking.*)

> **Pide (No pidas) la verdad.** (*[Don't] Ask for the truth.*)

Here are some examples of verbs with both spelling and stem changes. Notice that the stem change occurs in both the affirmative and the negative forms but the spelling changes occur only in the negative.

Infinitive	Affirmative	Negative	Meaning
colgar (o to ue/g to gu)	**cuelga**	**no cuelgues**	(don't) hang
jugar (u to ue/g to gu)	**juega**	**no juegues**	(don't) play
comenzar (e to ie/z to c)	**comienza**	**no comiences**	(don't) begin
empezar (e to ie/z to c)	**empieza**	**no empieces**	(don't) begin
almorzar (o to ue/z to c)	**almuerza**	**no almuerces**	(don't) eat lunch
corregir (e to i/g to j)	**corrige**	**no corrijas**	(don't) correct
seguir (e to i/gu to g)	**sigue**	**no sigas**	(don't) follow

The examples here show these verbs in the singular, familiar command form:

> **Cuelga. (No cuelgues.)** (*Hang up. [Don't hang up.]*)

> **Almuerza (No almuerces) conmigo.** (*[Don't] Eat lunch with me.*)

The following verbs are irregular in their singular, familiar affirmative and negative command forms. You must memorize these verbs and the changes they undergo.

Infinitive	Affirmative	Negative	Meaning
decir	di	no digas	(don't) say, tell
hacer	haz	no hagas	(don't) do, make
ir	ve	no vayas	(don't) go
poner	pon	no pongas	(don't) put
salir	sal	no salgas	(don't) leave
ser	sé	no seas	(don't) be
tener	ten	no tengas	(don't) have
valer	val or vale	no valgas	(don't) be worth
venir	ven	no vengas	(don't) come

Here are a couple of examples of these irregular verbs in commanding action:

Pon (No pongas) tu abrigo. (*[Don't] Put on your coat.*)

Ven (No vengas) aquí. (*[Don't] Come here.*)

The verb **estar** is irregular in its negative familiar command form, because it requires an accent on the **e.** The negative form of **estar** in the **tú** command form is **no estés.** Here is an example of a command with this form:

No estés triste. (*Don't be sad.*)

Book III

Mastering More Advanced Grammar Essentials

Issuing plural commands with vosotros

Forming plural, affirmative, informal commands is a cinch. You just drop the final **-r** of the infinitive and add **-d.** This rule holds true for regular verbs, verbs with irregular **yo** forms, verbs with spelling or stem changes, verbs with both spelling and stem changes, and all irregular verbs. To form all plural, negative, informal commands, follow these rules:

1. **Drop the final -o from the** yo **form of the present tense.**

2. **For infinitives ending in -ar, add -éis for the vosotros form. For infinitives ending in -er or -ir, add -áis for the vosotros form.**

3. **To form the negative, put** no **before the verb.**

Using regular verbs

The following conjugations illustrate the difference between plural, familiar commands in their affirmative and negative forms for regular verbs:

Regular Verbs	Affirmative	Negative	Meaning
firmar	firm**ad**	no firm**éis**	(don't) sign
comer	com**ed**	no com**áis**	(don't) eat
subir	sub**id**	no sub**áis**	(don't) go up

Here's how your **vosotros** commands should look when using regular verbs:

> **Tirad (No tirèis) la cuerda.** (*[Don't] Pull the cord.*)
>
> **Bebed (No bebáis) café.** (*[Don't] Drink coffee.*)
>
> **Resistid (No restistáis).** (*Resist. [Don't resist.]*)

Using other verb types

Verbs with irregular **yo** forms, verbs with spelling changes, verbs with stem changes, and verbs with both spelling and stem changes follow the same rules for forming plural commands as regular verbs. You must remember to make any necessary changes (described in the following tables), though. Here are a couple of verbs with irregular **yo** forms in the plural, informal command form:

Infinitive	Affirmative	Negative	Meaning
conducir	**conducid**	**no conduzcáis**	(don't) drive
conocer	**conoced**	**no conozcáis**	(don't) meet
oír	**oíd**	**no oigáis**	(don't) hear
traer	**traed**	**no traigáis**	(don't) bring

Here are these verbs shown in examples:

> **Oíd (No oigáis) esto.** (*[Don't] Hear this.*)
>
> **Traed (No tragáis) el libro.** (*[Don't] Bring the book.*)

Here are some verbs that require spelling changes in the negative plural command form:

Infinitive	Affirmative	Negative	Meaning
-ar verbs			
sacar	saca**d**	no sa**quéis**	(don't) take out
pagar	paga**d**	no pa**guéis**	(don't) pay
organizar	organiza**d**	no organi**céis**	(don't) organize
-er and **-ir** verbs			
escoger	escoge**d**	no esco**jáis**	(don't) choose
exigir	exigi**d**	no exi**jáis**	(don't) demand
distinguir	distingui**d**	no distin**gáis**	(don't) distinguish

The following examples show these verbs with spelling changes:

> **Organizad (No organicéis) una reunión.** (*[Don't] Organize a meeting.*)

> **Exigid (No exijáis) esto.** (*[Don't] Demand that.*)

The following verbs require stem changes in the negative, plural, informal command form. Stem changes occur only in verbs that end in **-ir** in their original infinitive form, and the only changes to occur are from **e** to **i** and **o** to **u**.

Book III

Mastering More Advanced Grammar Essentials

Infinitive	Affirmative	Negative	Meaning
-ir verbs			
mentir (**e** to **ie**)	menti**d**	no mint**áis**	(don't) lie
dormir (**o** to **ue**)	dormi**d**	no **durmáis**	(don't) sleep
pedir (**e** to **i**)	pedi**d**	no **pidáis**	(don't) ask (for)
destruir (add **y**)	destrui**d**	no **destruyáis**	(don't) destroy

Only **-ir** verbs have stem changes in the negative plural informal commands, and only **e** to **i** and **o** to **u**.

Here are two examples of these stem-changing verbs in the affirmative and negative plural informal:

> **Mentid (No mintáis).** (*[Don't] Lie.*)

> **Dormid (No durmáis) hasta el mediodía.** (*[Don't] Sleep until noon.*)

For the plural, informal command construction, when a verb has both a spelling change and a stem change, only the spelling change occurs, and it occurs only in the negative form. Here are some verbs that show you this construction.

Infinitive	Affirmative	Negative	Meaning
colgar (**o** to **ue**/**g** to **gu**)	col**gad**	no col**guéis**	(don't) hang
jugar (**u** to **ue**/**g** to **gu**)	ju**gad**	no ju**guéis**	(don't) play
comenzar (**e** to **ie**/**z** to **c**)	comen**zad**	no comen**céis**	(don't) begin
empezar (**e** to **ie**/**z** to **c**)	empe**zad**	no empe**céis**	(don't) begin
almorzar (**o** to **ue**/**z** to **c**)	almor**zad**	no almor**céis**	(don't) eat lunch
corregir (**e** to **i**/**g** to **j**)	corre**gid**	no corri**jáis**	(don't) correct
seguir (**e** to **i**/**gu** to **g**)	segu**id**	no si**gáis**	(don't) follow

The following examples show these verbs in action:

> **Colgad (No colguéis) la noticia aquí.** (*[Don't] Hang the notice here.*)

> **Comenzad (No comencéis).** (*[Don't] Begin.*)

Finally, Table 1-5 lists the irregular verbs that you must simply memorize in order to give plural, informal commands in Spanish.

Table 1-5   Irregular Verbs for Plural Informal Commands

Spanish Verbs	Affirmative	Negative	Meaning
decir	decid	**no digáis**	(don't) say, tell
hacer	haced	**no hagáis**	(don't) do
ir	id	**no vayáis**	(don't) go
poner	poned	**no pongáis**	(don't) put
salir	salid	**no salgáis**	(don't) leave
ser	sed	**no seáis**	(don't) be
tener	tened	**no tengáis**	(don't) have, be
valer	valed	**no valgáis**	(don't) be worth
venir	venid	**no vengáis**	(don't) come

Here are two examples of these irregular verbs in commands:

> **Id (No vayáis) allá.** (*[Don't] Go there.*)

> **Sed (No seáis) optimista.** (*[Don't] Be optimistic.*)

Chapter 2

Getting Object Pronouns Involved

In This Chapter

- Utilizing direct and indirect object pronouns
- Choosing and placing the proper object pronoun
- Using double object pronouns

Most languages, including English and Spanish, use pronouns in place of nouns as a matter of convenience and efficiency and to reduce repetition. Instead of saying "My grandfather likes ice cream. My grandfather likes ice cream best with chocolate syrup," you can use pronouns in place of some of the nouns: "My grandfather likes ice cream. **He** likes **it** best with chocolate syrup on **it.**"

Languages distinguish between subject pronouns (doing the action) and object pronouns (recipients of the action). In English:

	Subject Pronoun	*Object Pronoun*
First person singular	I	me
Second person singular	you	you
Third person singular	he, she, it	him, her, it
First person plural	we	us
Second person plural	you	you
Third person plural	they	them

Book I, Chapter 1, introduces the subject pronouns because they're so important in starting sentences. When you're ready to start crafting more complex expressions, you need to know about object pronouns.

This chapter introduces you to the direct and indirect object pronouns and the differences between them. It also shows you how to use the object pronouns correctly in a sentence and how to select which one to use.

Acting Directly on Direct Object Pronouns

A *direct object pronoun* plays two roles:

- ✔ As a *pronoun*, it takes the place of a noun.

- ✔ As a *direct object*, it's on the receiving end of the verb; for example, if I break *it,* the *it* is what is being broken. In other words the direct object receives the action of the verb directly.

Table 2-1 lists the direct object pronouns in Spanish.

Table 2-1	Spanish Direct Object Pronouns		
Singular Pronouns	*Meaning*	*Plural Pronouns*	*Meaning*
me	me	**nos**	us
te	you (informal)	**os**	you (informal)
lo	him, it, you (formal)	**los**	them, you (formal)
la	her, it, you (formal)	**las**	them, you (formal)

Direct object pronouns are much easier to deal with than subject pronouns, because you don't have to worry about subject-verb agreement. However, the direct-object pronoun does need to agree in number and gender with the noun it's replacing.

In both English and Spanish, the direct object follows the subject and its verb:

Veo la casa. (*I see the house.*)

Unlike in English, however, you usually place a Spanish direct-object pronoun *before* the conjugated verb:

La veo. (*I see it.*)

Here are some example sentences that show how you use Spanish direct object pronouns:

Él me comprende. (*He understands me.*)

¿Nos ve Ud.? (*Do you see us?*)

¿Los periódicos? Yo los leo cada día. (*The newspapers? I read them every day.*)

People often use **le** rather than **lo** in Spain to express *you* (masculine) or *him*. **Lo** is used as a direct object pronoun in Spanish America. The plural of **lo** and **le** is **los,** which means *them* or *you*. Here are some examples:

> **Cuido al niño.** (*I watch the child.*)
>
> **Lo [Le] cuido.** (*I watch him.*)
>
> **Cuido a los niños.** (*I watch the children.*)
>
> **Los cuido.** (*I watch them.*)
>
> **Miro el programa.** (*I watch the program.*)
>
> **Lo miro.** (*I watch it.*)
>
> **Miro los programas.** (*I watch the programs.*)
>
> **Los miro.** (*I watch them.*)

Using Indirect Object Pronouns

Indirect object nouns or *pronouns* refer only to people (and to beloved pets); they answer the question "To or for whom is the subject doing something?" An indirect object pronoun can replace an indirect object noun but is also used in Spanish when the indirect object noun is mentioned specifically. The indirect object pronoun agrees with the noun it refers to. And just like with direct object pronouns, indirect object pronouns generally are placed before the conjugated verb. For example:

> **Le escribo un e-mail.** (*I'm writing an e-mail to him.*)
>
> **Le escribo a Gloria un e-mail.** (*I'm writing an e-mail to Gloria.*)

Table 2-2 presents the indirect object pronouns in Spanish.

Table 2-2	Spanish Indirect Object Pronouns		
Singular Pronouns	**Meaning**	**Plural Pronouns**	**Meaning**
me	to/for me	**nos**	to/for us
te	to/for you (informal)	**os**	to/for you (informal)
le	to/for him, her, you (formal)	**les**	to/for them, you (formal)

The following sentences show how you use indirect object pronouns:

> **¿Me dices la verdad?** (*Are you telling me the truth?*)

> **La mujer nos ofrece un refresco.** (*The lady offers us a drink.*)
>
> **Les doy un abrazo.** (*I give them a hug.*)

A clue that may indicate that you need an indirect object pronoun is the use of the preposition **a** (**al, a la, a los,** or **a las**), which means *to* or *for* (unlike the personal **a,** which has no meaning [see Book II, Chapter 3]), followed by the name of or reference to a person. You may use **a él, a ella,** or **a Ud.** or the person's name to clarify whom you're referring to:

> **Yo le escribo a Rosa.** (*I write to Rosa.*)
>
> **Yo le escribo.** (*I write to her.*)
>
> **Ella le habla al muchacho.** (*She speaks to the boy.*)
>
> **Ella le habla.** (*She speaks to him.*)
>
> **Ella le habla a él.** (*She speaks to him.*)
>
> **Ella le habla a Juan.** (*She speaks to Juan.*)

Although you may use the prepositions *to* and *for* in English, you omit these prepositions in Spanish sentences before an indirect object pronoun:

> **Te compro un regalo.** (*I'm buying a present for you./ I'm buying you a present.*)
>
> **Me escriben.** (*They're writing to me./ They're writing me.*)

Picking the Right Object Pronoun for the Job

Sometimes people get confused when trying to figure out whether to use a direct object pronoun or an indirect object pronoun. The good news is you'll have absolutely no problem with **me, te, nos,** and **os** because they act as both direct and indirect object pronouns. (You may also recognize them as reflexive pronouns [see Book III, Chapter 3]:

> **Me respeta.** (*He respects me.*)
>
> **Me dice un secreto.** (*He tells me a secret.*)
>
> **Nos visita.** (*She visits us.*)
>
> **Nos trae flores.** (*She brings us flowers.*)

If you can use the word *to* or *for* in an English sentence before a reference to a person — no matter how awkward the construction may seem — you must use an indirect object pronoun in your Spanish sentence:

> **Quiero mostrarte esta foto.** (*I want to show [to] you this photo.*)

The following sections give you some more insider tips to help you decide between direct and indirect object pronouns.

Direct object verbs

Verbs that require an indirect object in English may require a direct object in Spanish because *to* or *for* is included in the meaning of the infinitive. (Remember that any **a** you see will be the personal **a;** see Book II, Chapter 3.) Some of these high-frequency verbs include the following:

- ✔ **buscar** (*to look for*)
- ✔ **escuchar** (*to listen to*)
- ✔ **esperar** (*to wait for*)
- ✔ **llamar** (*to call*)
- ✔ **mirar** (*to look at*)

The following examples illustrate how you use these verbs:

> **Nosotros esperamos a nuestros amigos.** (*We are waiting for our friends.*)
>
> **Nosotros los esperamos.** (*We are waiting for them.*)
>
> **Busco a mi perro.** (*I'm looking for my dog.*)
>
> **Lo busco.** (*I'm looking for it.*)

Indirect object verbs

Verbs that require a direct object in English don't necessarily require a direct object in Spanish. The verbs that follow take indirect objects in Spanish, regardless of the object used in English, because *to* or *for* is implied when speaking about a person or because the verb generally is followed by the preposition **a:**

acompañar (*to accompany*)

aconsejar (*to advise*)

contar (*to relate, tell*)

contestar (*to answer*)

dar (*to give*)

decir (*to say, tell*)

enviar (*to send*)

escribir (*to write*)

explicar (*to explain*)

llamar (*to call*)

mandar (*to send*)

obedecer (*to obey*)

ofrecer (*to offer*)

pedir (*to ask*)

preguntar (*to ask*)

presentar (*to introduce*)

prestar (*to lend*)

prohibir (*to forbid*)

prometer (*to promise*)

regalar (*to give a gift*)

telefonear (*to call*)

Here are a few examples:

Te aconsejo practicar más. (*I advise you to practice more.*)

Ella le pide disculpa a su amiga. (*She asks her friend for an apology.*)

Me regala un reloj. (*He is giving me a watch as a gift.*)

Putting Object Pronouns in Their Places

How do you decide where to place a direct or indirect object pronoun in a Spanish sentence? Generally, you place these pronouns before the conjugated verb:

Nosotros los necesitamos. (*We need them.*)

Siempre les cuentas chistes. (*You always tell them jokes.*)

In sentences with two verbs that follow one subject or in sentences with a present participle (the **-ando** or **-iendo** forms; see Book II, Chapter 5), you have the choice of placing the object pronoun before the conjugated verb or after and attached to the infinitive or the present participle. The following list provides some examples.

When you attach the pronoun to the present participle, you have to put an accent on the stressed vowel. In general, to correctly place the accent, you count back three vowels and add the accent. Also, remember that negatives go before the pronoun when it precedes the verb.

✔ With a present participle:

- **(No) Lo estoy haciendo.** (*I'm [not] doing it.*)

- **(No) Estoy haciéndolo.** (*I'm [not] doing it.*)

✔ With an infinitive:

- **(No) Lo quiero hacer.** (*I [don't] want to do it.*)

- **(No) Quiero hacerlo.** (*I [don't] want to do it.*)

In a negative command, the object pronoun precedes the verb. In an affirmative command, however, the object pronoun must follow the verb and be attached to it (for more on commands, refer to Book III, Chapter 1). An accent mark is normally required on the stressed vowel (if there are only two vowels, no accent is needed). To properly place the accent, count back three vowels and add it.

Here's what affirmative commands look like:

> **Prepárela.** (*Prepare it.*)
>
> **Hazlo.** (*Do it.*)

Now take a look at the negatives:

> **No la prepare.** (*Don't prepare it.*)
>
> **No lo hagas.** (*Don't do it.*)

Doubling Up with Object Pronouns

Spanish sentences often require both a direct and an indirect object pronoun. You have many rules to consider when creating these sentences, as the following list shows:

✔ When the verb has two object pronouns, the indirect object pronoun (a person) precedes the direct object pronoun (usually a thing):

- **Ella nos muestra las revistas.** (*She shows us the magazines.*)

- **Ella nos las muestra.** (*She shows them to us.*)

- **Nosotros te damos el boleto.** (*We give you the ticket.*)

- **Nosotros te lo damos.** (*We give it to you.*)

Book III

Mastering More Advanced Grammar Essentials

✔ When a sentence has two third-person object pronouns, the indirect object pronouns **le** and **les** change to **se** before the direct object pronouns **lo, la, los,** and **las:**

- **Él les lee la revista a sus abuelos.** (*He reads the magazine to his grandparents.*)

- **Él se la lee.** (*He reads it to them.*)

To clarify the meaning of **se** — because it can mean *to/for you, him, her,* and *them* — you may include the phrase **a Ud. (Uds.), a él (ellos),** or **a ella (ellas):**

Yo se los digo a él. (*I tell them to him.*)

✔ The same rules for the positioning of single object pronouns apply for double object pronouns (see the previous section). The following examples show how you use and place double object pronouns:

With an infinitive, you may place the two separate pronouns before the conjugated verb, or you may connect and attach them to the end of the infinitive:

- **(No) Te los quiero mostrar.** (*I [don't] want to show them to you.*)

- **(No) Quiero mostrártelos.** (*I [don't] want to show them to you.*)

With a participle, you may place the two separate pronouns before the conjugated form of **estar,** or you may connect and attach them to the end of the participle:

- **(No) Se la estoy leyendo a él.** (*I'm [not] reading it to him.*)

- **(No) Estoy leyéndosela a él.** (*I'm [not] reading it to him.*)

With commands:

- Formal:

  Affirmative: **Dígamelo.** (*Tell it to me.*)

  Negative: **No me lo diga.** (*Don't tell it to me.*)

- Informal:

  Affirmative: **Dímelo.** (*Tell it to me.*)

  Negative: **No me lo digas.** (*Don't tell it to me.*)

✔ When two pronouns appear in a sentence attached to an infinitive, you generally count back three vowels and add an accent:

Yo voy a escribírselo a Ud. (*I'm going to write it to you.*)

When you add two pronouns to a participle or an affirmative command, however, you generally count back four vowels when adding an accent:

- **Estamos comprándoselas a ellos.** (*We are buying it for them.*)

- **Muéstramelo.** (*Show it to me.*)

With a *diphthong* (two vowels blended together that stand for only one vowel sound — see Book I, Chapter 1), you may have to count back as many as five vowels:

Tráiganoslos. (*Bring them to us.*)

Book III

Mastering More Advanced Grammar Essentials

Chapter 3

Involving Yourself in the Action with the Reflexive

In This Chapter

- Understanding the purpose of reflexive verbs
- Exploring verbs that are reflexive by nature
- Adding reflexive pronouns to stress your point
- Making sure your reflexive pronouns are properly positioned

Reflexive constructions allow the subject of a sentence to act upon itself — like a dog chasing its own tail. Initially, you may feel just as frustrated when you begin working with reflexive verbs and pronouns in Spanish, but this chapter brings you up to speed in a hurry.

Here, you discover the basic concept of the reflexive and how to recognize and use reflexive verbs and pronouns in Spanish. You acquire the skills needed to match the right reflexive pronoun to the subject of a sentence. We also introduce you to special meanings of some reflexive verbs and show you how to use the reflexive to indicate passive action.

Grasping the Concept of Reflexive Verbs

Whenever you look at yourself, bathe yourself, or worry yourself silly, you're involved in a reflexive action. You, the subject, are doing something to yourself, the object. In English, reflexive actions become a little fuzzy, because so much is considered understood. Spanish, however, designates reflexive action by requiring the use of a reflexive verb *and* a reflexive pronoun, such as *myself, yourself,* or *herself.*

When creating a reflexive verb construction, you need a subject, a reflexive verb, and a reflexive pronoun, but not necessarily in that order. When you conjugate the reflexive verbs in English, you place the pronoun after the conjugated verb. In other words, you say, "You bathe yourself." But in Spanish, the order is *you yourself bathe*.

The following table shows a reflexive verb in all of its present tense conjugations.

bañarse (*to bathe one's self*)	
me baño	nos bañamos
te bañas	os bañáis
se baña	se bañan
Yo me baño. (*I bathe myself.*)	

Many of these reflexive verbs involve the mention of a body part, and because the owner of the body part is already clear (because of the reflexive verb), you don't use a possessive pronoun. Instead of saying, "I brush my hair," for example, you say, "I brush the hair," because the reflexive pronoun already signals that it's your hair.

Table 3-1 gives a list of some commonly used reflexive verbs; note that some have stem changes (see Book II, Chapter 3):

Table 3-1	Common Reflexive Verbs		
Spanish Verb (Used with a Reflexive Pronoun)	*Translation*	**Spanish Verb (Used with a Reflexive Pronoun)**	*Translation*
abrocharse	to fasten	**hacerse**	to become
aburrirse	to become bored	**irse**	to go away
acostarse (o to **ue)**	to go to bed	**lavarse**	to wash one's self
afeitarse	to shave one's self	**levantarse**	to stand up, get up
alegrarse (de)	to be glad	**llamarse**	to call one's self
aplicarse	to apply one's self	**maquillarse**	to put on makeup
apresurarse	to hurry	**marcharse**	to go away
asegurarse de	to make sure	**mirarse**	to look at one's self

Spanish Verb (Used with a Reflexive Pronoun)	Translation	Spanish Verb (Used with a Reflexive Pronoun)	Translation
bañarse	to bathe one's self	olvidarse (de)	to forget
burlarse (de)	to make fun of	pasearse	to go for a walk
callarse	to be silent	peinarse	to comb one's hair
cansarse	to become tired	ponerse la ropa	to put on (clothing)
casarse (con)	to get married; to marry (someone)	ponerse	to put on, become, place one's self
cepillarse el pelo	to brush one's hair	preocuparse por	to worry (about)
cepillarse los dientes	to brush one's teeth	quedarse	to remain
despedirse (e to i)	to say good-bye	quejarse (de)	to complain
despertarse (e to ie)	to wake up	quitarse	to take off, remove (clothing)
desvestirse (e to i)	to get undressed	refriarse	to catch a cold
divertirse (e to ie)	to have fun	reírse (de)	to laugh at
dormirse (o to ue)	to fall asleep	relajarse	to relax
ducharse	to take a shower	romperse	to break (a part of the body)
encontrarse (o to ue)	to be located, meet	secarse	to dry one's self
enfadarse (con)	to get angry	sentarse (e to ie)	to sit down
enfermarse	to get sick	sentirse (e to ie)	to feel
engañarse	to be mistaken	verse	to see one's self
enojarse	to become angry	vestirse (e to i)	to get dressed
equivocarse	to be mistaken	volverse (o to ue)	to become
fijarse (en)	to notice		

Book III

Mastering More Advanced Grammar Essentials

Doing More with Reflexive Verbs

Some situations in Spanish call for special reflexive constructions. For instance, you may use a plural reflexive construction to convey an English reciprocal action that expresses "one another" or "each other." Here's the simple way to create this kind of sentence:

> **Nos respetamos.** (*We respect one another [each other].*)
>
> **Se abrazan.** (*They hug one another [each other].*)

To clarify or reinforce the meaning of the reflexive pronoun in a reciprocal construction, you can add these singular forms: **uno a otro** (**una a otra**) or **el uno al otro** (**la una a la otra**) (*one another [each other]*). Or you can add these plural forms: **unos a otros** (**unas a otras**) or **los unos a los otros** (**las unas a las otras**) (*each other*). For example:

> **Las muchachas se miran.** (*The girls look at each other [at themselves].*)
>
> **Ellas se miran la una a la otra.** (*They look at each other.*)

You may use reflexive verbs in Spanish to express the *passive voice* (see Book II, Chapter 3) when the English subject is a thing (not a person) and when the person performing the action isn't indicated. To form the passive with a reflexive verb, use the third-person reflexive pronoun **se** and the third-person singular (**él, ella, Ud.**) or third-person plural (**ellos, ellas, Uds.**) form of the present tense. Note the reflexive construction in this first example:

> **Aquí se habla español.** (*Spanish is spoken here.*)
>
> **Se venden periódicos allá.** (*They sell newspapers over there.*)

Reflexivity Not Always Required

Keep in mind that the majority of the verbs in Table 3-1 can be used both reflexively and normally. Adding the reflexive pronoun merely indicates that the subject of the verb and the object of the verb are one and the same. When you use one of these verbs *nonreflexively*, the action of the verb is being received by someone (or something) other than the subject.

This isn't the case for all verbs, however. Table 3-2 shows how some verbs change meaning depending on whether you use them reflexively or nonreflexively:

Table 3-2	Spanish Verbs with Different Reflexive Meanings		
Nonreflexive Form	*Nonreflexive Meaning*	*Reflexive Form*	*Reflexive Meaning*
aburrir	to bore	**aburrirse**	to become bored
acordar (ue)	to agree	**acordarse de (ue)**	to remember
acostar (ue)	to put to bed	**acostarse (ue)**	to go to bed
bañar	to bathe (someone)	**bañarse**	to bathe one's self
cansar	to tire	**cansarse**	to become tired
colocar	to place (something)	**colocarse**	to place one's self; to get a job
dormir (ue)	to sleep	**dormirse (u)**	to fall asleep
enfadar	to anger, irritate	**enfadarse (con)**	to get angry, annoyed
engañar	to deceive	**engañarse**	to be mistaken
esconder	to hide (something)	**esconderse**	to hide one's self
ir	to go	**irse**	to go away
levantar	to raise (something)	**levantarse**	to get up
llamar	to call	**llamarse**	to be called; to call one's self
parar	to stop (something)	**pararse**	to stop one's self
poner	to put (something)	**ponerse**	to put (something on); to become; to place one's self
quitar	to remove	**quitarse**	to take off
sentar (ie)	to seat	**sentarse (ie)**	to sit down

Book III

Mastering More Advanced Grammar Essentials

Here are two examples that show you how the meanings of these verbs differ when you use them reflexively and nonreflexively:

La profesora se sienta después de sentar los alumnos por orden alfabético. (*The teacher sits after seating the students in alphabetical order.*)

Ella llama a su amiga que se llama Emilia. (*She calls her friend whose name is [who calls herself] Emilia.*)

A few Spanish verbs are always used reflexively:

- ✔ **arrepentirse (ie)** (*to repent*)
- ✔ **atreverse a** (*to dare*)
- ✔ **darse cuenta de** (*to realize*)
- ✔ **jactarse de** (*to boast about*)
- ✔ **quejarse de** (*to complain about*)
- ✔ **suicidarse** (*to commit suicide*)

Enlisting the Aid of Reflexive Pronouns

You always conjugate a reflexive verb with the reflexive pronoun that agrees with the subject. Generally, these pronouns, like the direct and indirect object pronouns in Book III, Chapter 2, precede the conjugated verbs. The verb conjugation isn't affected by the use of the pronoun. Table 3-3 demonstrates each reflexive pronoun with an example verb.

Reflexive pronouns are exactly the same as direct and indirect object pronouns except for the third-person singular and plural (**se**) forms.

Ella se llama Mariana. (*Her name is Mariana.*)

Table 3-3	Properly Using Reflexive Pronouns		
Infinitive	*Subject*	*Reflexive Pronoun*	*Verb*
dormirse (ue) (to fall asleep)	**yo**	**me**	**duermo**
despertarse (ie) (to wake up)	**tú**	**te**	**despiertas**
desvestirse (i) (to undress)	**él, ella, Ud.**	**se**	**desviste**
relajarse (to relax)	**nosostros**	**nos**	**relajamos**
callarse (to be silent)	**vosotros**	**os**	**calláis**
marcharse (to go away)	**ellos, ellas, Uds.**	**se**	**marchan**

Here are some examples that show you how to use these reflexive pronouns:

¿De qué se queja Ud? (*What are you complaining about?*)

Me quejo de los precios. (*I'm complaining about the prices.*)

¿A qué hora se acuestan los niños? (*At what time do the children go to bed?*)

Los niños se acuestan a las nueve. (*The children go to bed at 9:00.*)

To negate a reflexive verb, you put **no** or the proper negative word (see Book II, Chapter 4) before the reflexive pronoun:

¿Se enoja Ud. a menudo? (*Do you often get angry?*)

No, no me enojo a menudo. (*No, I don't get angry often.*)

Nunca me enojo. (*I never get angry.*)

No me enojo nunca. (*I never get angry.*)

Putting Reflexive Pronouns in Their Places

Just like with direct and indirect object pronouns (see Book III, Chapter 2), you generally place reflexive pronouns before the conjugated verbs:

Book III

Mastering More Advanced Grammar Essentials

Me aplico en la clase de español. (*I apply myself in Spanish class.*)

¿Por qué te pones enojado? (*Why are you becoming angry?*)

Ella no se siente bien. (*She doesn't feel well.*)

In sentences with two verbs that follow one subject (as in the first two examples that follow — see Book II, Chapter 3) or in sentences with a present participle (as in the second two examples that follow — see Book II, Chapter 5), you have the choice of placing the reflexive pronoun before the conjugated verb or after and attached to the infinitive or the present participle. When you attach the pronoun to a present participle, an accent is required on the stressed vowel:

Voy a maquillar<u>me</u>. (*I'm going to put on my make-up.*)

<u>Me</u> voy a maquillar. (*I'm going to put on my make-up.*)

Estoy maquillánd<u>ome</u>. (*I am putting on my make-up.*)

<u>Me</u> estoy maquillando. (*I am putting on my make-up.*)

In general, to correctly place the accent on a present participle-pronoun combo, count back three vowels and add the accent:

Ella (no) está peinánd<u>ose</u>. (*She [isn't] combing her hair.*)

If the statement is negative, **no** goes either directly in front of the verb (when the pronoun is attached to the present participle) or in front of the pronoun (when the pronoun precedes the conjugated verb). Any stated subject appears first.

- ✔ Without a stated subject:

    No voy a maquillar<u>me</u>. (*I'm not going to put on my make-up.*)

    No <u>me</u> voy a maquillar. (*I'm [not] going to put on my make-up.*)

- ✔ With a stated subject:

    Yo (no) voy a maquillar<u>me</u>. (*I'm [not] going to put on my make-up.*)

    Yo (no) <u>me</u> voy a maquillar. (*I'm [not] going to put on my make-up.*)

When used with a command, a reflexive pronoun (just like a direct or indirect object pronoun) precedes a negative command and follows (and is attached to) an affirmative command (formal or informal):

Láve<u>se</u>. (Láva<u>te</u>.) (*Wash yourself.*)

No <u>se</u> lave. (No <u>te</u> laves.) (*Don't wash yourself.*)

Keep these general rules about accentuation in mind:

- ✔ When one pronoun is attached, count back three vowels and add an accent:

    Acuésta<u>te</u> temprano. (*Go to bed early.*)

- ✔ When two pronouns are attached, count back four vowels and add an accent:

    Póngaselo. (*Put it on.*)

Chapter 4

Been There, Done That: Past (Preterit) Tense

In This Chapter

- Reminiscing about the past with the preterit tense
- Checking out verb charts for regular verbs in the preterit
- Conjugating verbs with spelling and stem changes
- Dealing with other irregularities in the preterit

*T*he *preterit tense* enables you to put the past behind you. It describes a completed past action — something that happened yesterday, last night, last week, last year, or at some other definite point in time. The action may have occurred a specific number of times or within an enclosed period of time, but it's done, finished. You can stick a fork in it.

To describe past actions such as these, you use the *preterit tense.* That's what this chapter is all about. It covers regular verbs and verbs with spelling changes, stem changes, and/or other conjugation irregularities in the preterit, and provides tips on memorizing common exceptions.

To express continuous, ongoing, or habitual action that "used to be happening" or "was happening" in the past, you use the imperfect tense (the "other" past tense), covered in Book III, Chapter 5.

Conjugating Regular Verbs in the Preterit

Forming the preterit for regular verbs is fairly straightforward. You drop the **-ar, -er,** or **-ir** infinitive ending and add the preterit endings to the verb stem. The regular **-ar** verbs conjugate with the following endings:

Regular preterit -ar verb endings	
yo -é	nosotros/as -amos
tú -aste	vosotros/as -asteis
él, ella, Ud. -ó	ellos/as, Uds. -aron

So here's what the verb **hablar** looks like in the preterit tense:

hablar (*to speak*)	
hablé	hablamos
hablaste	hablasteis
habló	hablaron
Yo hablé. (*I spoke.*)	

Regular **-er** and **-ir** verbs in the preterit tense share the same endings. You add the following endings to the verb stem:

Regular preterit -er and -ir verb endings	
yo -í	nosotros/as -imos
tú -iste	vosotros/as -isteis
él, ella, Ud. -ió	ellos/as, Uds. -ieron

Here's what the verb **comer** looks like in the preterit tense:

comer (*to eat*)	
comí	comimos
comiste	comisteis
comió	comieron
Él comió. (*He ate.*)	

And here's what the verb **vivir** looks like in the preterit tense:

vivir (*to live*)	
viví	vivimos
viviste	vivisteis
vivió	vivieron
Tú viviste. (*You [informal] lived.*)	

Notice that the **nosotros** forms of **-ar** and **-ir** verbs are the same in the preterit tense as they are in the present tense:

> **Nosotros hablamos.** (*We speak./ We spoke.*)

> **Nosotros subimos al ático.** (*We go up to the attic./ We went up to the attic.*)

When working with the preterit, you want to have some time words at your disposal so that you can describe specifically when a particular action took place. Table 4-1 lists time words commonly used with the preterit tense.

Table 4-1 Time-Related Words That Describe Completed Actions

Term	Translation
ayer	yesterday
ayer por la mañana	yesterday morning
ayer por la tarde	yesterday afternoon
ayer por la noche	yesterday evening (night)
anteayer	day before yesterday
la semana pasada	last week
el mes pasado	last month
el año pasado	last year
el otro día	the other day
esta mañana	this morning
esta tarde	this afternoon
entonces	then
anoche	last night
hace (dos días)	(two days) ago

Book III

Mastering More Advanced Grammar Essentials

Using the Preterit in a Sentence

Being able to use the preterit after learning how to form it often requires some additional practice. The key concept to wrap your brain around when it comes to the preterit tense is that the action is *completed in the past and shows no signs of continuing.* If you're looking to communicate this sense of finality, the preterit is the tense for you.

The following example shows you how to use the preterit to describe a typical morning, from the time you woke up to the time you arrived at work (all completed actions):

> **Me levanté a las siete y media.** (*I woke up at 7:30.*)
>
> **Me duché.** (*I took a shower.*)
>
> **Me cepillé los dientes y me peiné.** (*I brushed my teeth and combed my hair.*)
>
> **Me vestí.** (*I got dressed.*)
>
> **Desayuné.** (*I ate breakfast.*)
>
> **Salí de la casa a las ocho y media.** (*I left home at 8:30.*)
>
> **Llegué a mi trabajo a las nueve.** (*I arrived at work at 9:00.*)

Most of the sentences in the preceding list use reflexive verbs and pronouns, which you can read about in Book III, Chapter 3.

Facing Some Irregularities

Irregularities in the preterit tense can make your brain hurt. They're not all that confusing; they're simply more numerous and varied than in most tenses. To help you cope, the following sections group like verbs together to lend some order to the chaos. This grouping should help you understand and memorize the various formations so they become second nature.

Yo! Spelling changes in the preterit yo form

The preterit tense has several irregularities that are manifested as spelling changes or, if you prefer fancier terminology, *orthographic changes.* (Book II, Chapter 3 introduces the irregularities among Spanish verbs.) You need to remain aware of such spelling changes when dealing with irregularities in the preterit tense.

Spanish verbs experience the following three orthographic changes in the preterit, and they occur only in the first person singular, or **yo** form:

✔ Verbs ending in **-gar** change the **g** to **gu** in front of an **e**.

pagar becomes **yo pagué** (*I paid.*)

✔ Verbs ending in **-car** change the **c** to **qu** in front of an **e**.

buscar becomes **yo busqué** (*I looked for.*)

✔ Verbs ending in **-zar** change the **z** to **c** in front of an **e**.

comenzar becomes **yo comencé** (*I began.*)

Changing stems in the preterit

Some verbs experience stem changes when you conjugate them. In the present tense, stem changes occur in all three verbs types: **-ar, -er,** and **-ir.** In the preterit, however, only **-ir** verbs experience stem changes, and they occur only in the third-person/you (formal) singular (**él, ella, Ud.**) and plural (**ellos/as, Uds.**) forms of the verbs. Also, there are only two types of stem changes, from **o** to **u** and from **e** to **i**. These three factors narrow down preterit stem changes quite a bit.

Following are the three rules for stem changing verbs in the preterit:

✔ Stem changes only occur in **-ir** verbs.

✔ Stem changes only occur in the forms of **él, ella, Ud.** and **ellos/as, Uds.**

✔ Stem changes only occur from **o** to **u** and from **e** to **i**.

Table 4-2 lists some verbs that have these stem changes.

Book III

Mastering More Advanced Grammar Essentials

Table 4-2	Common Stem-Changing Verbs	
Spelling Change	*Infinitive*	*Translation*
o to **u**	**dormir**	to sleep
	morir	to die
e to **i**	**advertir**	to advise; to warn
	medir	to measure
	mentir	to lie
	pedir	to request; to ask for
	preferir	to prefer
	repetir	to repeat
	seguir	to follow; to continue
	sentirse	to feel
	servir	to serve

Sampling representative irregular verbs

When you're dealing with irregular verbs, sometimes the best way to proceed is to snatch a couple of representatives from the crowd, learn their irregularities, and then apply what you find out to similar verbs. This section introduces some sample irregular verbs that function as representatives for various small groups of verbs that behave in the same way.

Tagging along with traer, decir, and conducir

The verbs **traer** (*to bring*), **decir** (*to say; to tell*), and **conducir** (*to drive*), have a small group of followers, but when you're dealing with the preterit, you take any help you can get. These verbs all have the letter **j** in their preterit stems and share the same irregular endings. Here you can see how to conjugate these verbs and then apply the rules to similar verbs:

traer (*to bring*)	
traje	trajimos
trajiste	trajisteis
trajo	trajeron
Él trajo. (*He brought.*)	

Following are several verbs that conjugate in the preterit like **traer:**

- ✔ **atraer** (*to attract*)
- ✔ **distraer** (*to distract*)
- ✔ **extraer** (*to extract*)
- ✔ **retraer** (*to bring back*)
- ✔ **sustraer** (*to remove*)

decir (*to say; to tell*)	
dije	dijimos
dijiste	dijisteis
dijo	dijeron
Ella dijo. (*She said.*)	

conducir (*to drive*)	
conduje	condujimos
condujiste	condujisteis
condujo	condujeron
Ellos condujeron. (*They drove.*)	

Following is a list of verbs that conjugate like **conducir:**

- ✔ **deducir** (*to deduce*)
- ✔ **inducir** (*to induce; to infer*)
- ✔ **introducir** (*to introduce*)
- ✔ **producir** (*to produce*)
- ✔ **reducir** (*to reduce*)
- ✔ **traducir** (*to translate*)

Continuing the pattern with dar and ver

The verbs **dar** (*to give*) and **ver** (*to see*) have exactly the same preterit conjugated endings. What's interesting is that the verb **ver** actually follows the regular conjugation rules for **-er** preterit verbs *except* that it omits the accent marks on the first and third person singular (**yo** and **él, ella, Ud.**) forms. Here's what these two verbs look like in the preterit:

dar (*to give*)	
di	dimos
diste	disteis
dio	dieron
Yo di. (*I gave.*)	

ver (*to see*)	
vi	vimos
viste	visteis
vio	vieron
Nosotros vimos. (*We saw.*)	

Book III

Mastering More Advanced Grammar Essentials

Changing i to y in the preterit

In English, some words change the **y** to an **i** when they add **es.** Some Spanish verbs also change the **i** to **y.** Verbs that end in **-aer, -eer,** and **-oer** change the **i** to a **y** in the third-person singular (**él, ella, Ud.**) and plural (**ellos/as, Uds.**) forms and add a written accent over the letter **i** in all the other forms. Here's an example:

creer (to believe)	
creí	creímos
creíste	creísteis
creyó	creyeron
Nosotros creímos. (*We believed.*)	

Following are some other verbs that follow this pattern:

- **caerse** (*to fall [down]*)
- **leer** (*to read*)
- **oír** (*to hear*)
- **poseer** (*to possess*)
- **proveer** (*to provide*)

This rule has some exceptions. The verb **traer** (*to bring*) and the other verbs formed with **traer** (such as **atraer** (*to attract*) and **distraer** (*to distract*)) don't follow this conjugation pattern. See the earlier section "Tagging along with traer, decir, and conducir."

Constructing destructive verbs like destruir

When you feel like getting a little destructive with the verb **destruir** (*to destroy*) and other verbs that end in **-uir,** follow the **i**-to-**y** rule spelled out in the previous section, but be aware of one major exception. The written accent mark over the **i** is used only in the first-person singular (**yo**) form. Check out the following example:

destruir (to destroy)	
destruí	destruimos
destruiste	destruisteis
destruyó	destruyeron
Él destruyó. (*He destroyed.*)	

Following is a list of verbs that conjugate in the preterit according to the pattern shown here with **destruir:**

- ✔ **construir** (*to build; to construct*)
- ✔ **contribuir** (*to contribute*)
- ✔ **fluir** (*to flow*)
- ✔ **huir** (*to flee; to run away*)
- ✔ **incluir** (*to include*)
- ✔ **influir** (*to influence*)

The verb **seguir** (*to follow*) doesn't follow this conjugation pattern even though it ends in **-uir,** because the **u** is there to keep the hard *g* sound and doesn't create its own (vowel) sound.

Sharing irregularities: The verbs ser and ir

The verbs **ser** and **ir** are a couple of unique oddballs that form their own dysfunctional duet. They remain two distinct verbs, but in the preterit, they look exactly the same. The only way to tell the difference is to look at the context the verb is used in. Just look at the following conjugation chart to see what we mean:

ser (*to be*); ir (*to go*)	
fui	fuimos
fuiste	fuisteis
fue	fueron
Yo fui su amigo. (*I was his friend.*) **Yo fui al parque.** (*I went to the park.*)	

Eleven odd verbs that share their irregularities

Now here are some freaky verbs that look and behave more like a group! These 11 verbs *all* have irregular stems in the preterit, and they all share the same irregular preterit endings. Here are the endings that all 11 of these verbs use:

Endings for verbs with irregular preterit stems	
yo -e	nosotros/as -imos
tú -iste	vosotros/as -isteis
él, ella, Ud. -o	ellos/as, Uds. -ieron

Book III

Mastering
More
Advanced
Grammar
Essentials

These irregular preterit endings use no accent marks.

Table 4-3 lists the 11 verbs. Each verb is presented in its infinitive form, with the definition and then the irregular preterit stem.

Table 4-3	Verbs with Irregular Preterit Stems	
Verb	*Translation*	*Irregular Preterit Stem*
andar	to walk	**anduv-**
caber	to fit	**cup-**
estar	to be	**estuv-**
haber	to have (auxiliary verb)	**hub-**
hacer	to do; to make	**hic-/hiz-**
poder	to be able to	**pud-**
poner	to put	**pus-**
querer	to want	**quis-**
saber	to know	**sup-**
tener	to have	**tuv-**
venir	to come	**vin-**

The verb **hacer** changes the **c** to **z** in the third person singular form to avoid the *k* sound. Here is what this verb looks like in the preterit:

hacer (*to do; to make*)	
hice	hicimos
hiciste	hicisteis
hizo	hicieron
Ella hizo. (*She made.*)	

Verbs that change meanings in the preterit

Some verbs have the audacity to change their meaning slightly in the preterit, so be sure to get a handle on these subtle shifts in meaning. Table 4-4 introduces these meaning-shifters and provides their definitions in the present and preterit tenses so that you can compare them side-by-side.

Table 4-4	Verbs that Shift Meaning in the Preterit Tense	
Verb	*Present Tense Meaning*	*Preterit Tense Meaning*
conocer	to know (a person or place)	to meet
poder	to be able (to do something)	to manage (to do something)
no poder	not to be able (to do something)	to fail (to do something)
querer	to want	to try
no querer	not to want	to refuse
saber	to know (a fact/information)	to find out (learn)
sentir	to feel	to regret; to be sorry
tener	to have	to have (at a certain time)

Book III

Mastering More Advanced Grammar Essentials

Chapter 5

Continuing in the Past with the Imperfect Tense

he *imperfect tense* describes past actions that occurred in a vague or imprecise time frame. That's why it's called *imperfect*. When you're talking about something that happened in the past, but you're not really expressing a beginning or an end to the action, you use the imperfect tense. In English, you typically use the expressions *used to* or *always* to describe these actions:

> I used to golf every Sunday.

> My mom always made tamales for the holidays.

> Chico used to run five miles a day.

The imperfect is used to describe continuous, ongoing, or habitual past action.

In this chapter, you see how to form the imperfect of regular and irregular verbs. The chapter also includes plenty of explanations and clues to help you decide when the imperfect, rather than the preterit (see Book III, Chapter 4), is the tense of choice.

Preterit or Imperfect? You Decide

Now, the moment you've been waiting for — the moment that challenges you to choose the right tense for the right job. You're given a sentence that expresses or describes an action from the past, and it's up to you to decide which tense to use — preterit or imperfect. The following sections provide the guidelines necessary to select the appropriate tense.

Uses of the preterit

The *preterit* is a simple past tense to describe events that have been done and completed in the past — the sort of events that you need to get over, because you can't do anything about them. You use the preterit to

- ✔ Describe an action or series of actions that were completed in the past.
- ✔ Express an action, event, or state of mind that happened in the past and was completed at a specific moment or period.

Uses of the imperfect

The imperfect tense is more flexible than the preterit. With it, you can still talk about the past but in a way that doesn't sound so final. Use the imperfect tense to

- ✔ Describe ongoing, continuous, or habitual past actions without focusing on their beginnings or ends.
- ✔ Describe conditions in the past, such as the weather or characteristics of things or people.
- ✔ Tell the time or to tell one's age in the past.

After you've decided on the appropriate tense, you can then conjugate the verb and supply any necessary time phrases to complete the translation.

 When choosing between the imperfect and the preterit, watch for time words to use as clues and remember that the imperfect often translates to English as *used to.*

Conjugating Regular Verbs in the Imperfect

Forming the imperfect for regular verbs is fairly straightforward. You drop the **-ar, -er,** or **-ir** infinitive ending and add the imperfect endings to the verb stem. For **-ar** verbs you use the following endings:

Regular imperfect tense -ar verb endings	
yo -aba	nosotros/as -ábamos
tú -abas	vosotros/as -abais
él, ella, Ud. -aba	ellos/as, Ud. -aban

So the imperfect conjugations of **hablar** are

hablar (to speak; to talk)	
hablaba	hablábamos
hablabas	hablabais
hablaba	hablaban
Yo hablaba. (I used to speak.)	

To conjugate **-er** and **-ir** regular verbs into the imperfect tense, you add the following endings to the verb stem:

Regular imperfect tense -er and -ir verb endings	
yo –ía	nosotros/as -íamos
tú –ías	vosotros/as -íais
él, ella, Ud. -ía	ellos/as, Uds. -ían

So the imperfect conjugations of the verb **comer** are

comer (*to eat*)	
comía	comíamos
comías	comíais
comía	comían
Nosotros comíamos. (*We used to eat.*)	

And the imperfect conjugations of the verb **vivir** are

vivir (*to live*)	
vivía	vivíamos
vivías	vivíais
vivía	vivían
Ud. vivía. (*You [formal] used to live.*)	

In all of the imperfect verb formations whether *regular* or *irregular,* the first-person (**yo**) and third-person (**él, ella, Ud.**) singular forms are the same.

Practicing the Imperfect with Timely Expressions

When you're describing past actions with the imperfect tense, the following expressions can help you talk about when these actions *used to* occur:

Term	Translation
a menudo	often
a veces	sometimes
cada día	every day
cada semana	every week
cada mes	every month
cada año	every year
con frecuencia	frequently
de vez en cuando	from time to time

en aquella época	at that time
generalmente	usually
los lunes	on Mondays
los martes	on Tuesdays
los miércoles	on Wednesdays
los jueves	on Thursdays
los viernes	on Fridays
los sábados	on Saturdays
los domingos	on Sundays
muchas veces	many times
mucho	a lot
nunca	never
por un rato	for awhile
siempre	always
todas las semanas	every week
todos los fines de semana	every weekend
todos los días	every day
todo el tiempo	all the time
varias veces	several times

Book III

Mastering More Advanced Grammar Essentials

The imperfect is a very useful past tense for expressing background actions or actions that were going on when they were suddenly interrupted by a preterit tense action. The actions described by the imperfect tense are ongoing or habitual past actions that don't show their beginnings or their ends or any particular time limitations.

Meeting the Three Irregular Imperfect Verbs

The following three verbs are the only verbs in the Spanish language that are formed irregularly in the imperfect tense:

- ✔ **ir** (*to go*)
- ✔ **ser** (*to be*)
- ✔ **ver** (*to see*)

The conjugations of these verbs don't have anything in common with one another, but with only three verbs to remember, who's complaining? The tables that follow present the conjugations for these three verbs.

ir (*to go*)	
iba	íbamos
ibas	ibais
iba	iban
Nosotros íbamos. (*We used to go.*)	

ser (*to be*)	
era	éramos
eras	erais
era	eran
Tú eras. (*You [informal] used to be.*)	

ver (*to see*)	
veía	veíamos
veías	veíais
veía	veían
Nosotros veíamos. (*We used to see.*)	

Chapter 6

Getting That Subjunctive Feeling

In This Chapter

- Using the subjunctive mood with regular and irregular verbs
- Communicating wishes and desires
- Expressing doubt, uncertainty, opinions, and conditional actions
- Forming the imperfect subjunctive

*T*he subjunctive mood enables you to wish, desire, and suppose. It allows you to express your take on things and imagine that reality might be different if only certain conditions existed, "If only I were rich . . . ." The subjunctive mood also expresses doubt or uncertainty, offers impersonal opinions, and speculates on the outcome of a situation *if* certain actions were to occur.

In this chapter, you explore how to form the regular present tense subjunctive conjugations for **-ar, -er,** and **-ir** verbs, deal with irregularities, use the subjunctive for some unique expressions, and form the imperfect subjunctive.

 In previous verb-related chapters, we use the *indicative mood* for stating facts. The *subjunctive mood* expresses unreal, hypothetical, theoretical, imaginary, uncorroborated, or unconfirmed conditions or situations.

Conjugating Regular Verbs in the Present Subjunctive

Conjugating the present tense subjunctive mood is based on the system used to conjugate verbs in the present tense (see Book II, Chapter 3). By following those guidelines and adding a few new simple rules, you'll be ready to tackle conjugating regular verbs in the present subjunctive. Following are the two basic rules for conjugating **-ar, -er,** and **-ir** verbs in the present subjunctive:

✔ For **-ar** verbs, start with the **yo** form of the present indicative, drop the **-o**, then add the ending **-e, -es, -e, -emos, -éis,** or **-en.**

✔ For **-er** and **-ir** verbs, start with the **yo** form of the present indicative, drop the **-o,** and add then add the ending **-a, -as, -a, -amos, -áis,** or **-an.**

Except for the **yo** conjugations, the **-ar** verbs use regular present tense **-er** verb endings, and **-er** and **-ir** verbs use the regular present tense **-ar** verb endings. Following are the regular **-ar** present-tense subjunctive endings:

Regular subjunctive mood **-ar** verb endings	
yo -e	nosotros/as -emos
tú -es	vosotros/as -éis
él, ella, Ud. -e	ellos/as, Uds. -en

The verb **hablar** is a good example. Put **hablar** in the **yo** form, **hablo,** and then drop the **-o** and add the endings as specified. Here's what you get:

hablar (*to speak*)	
hable	hablemos
hables	habléis
hable	hablen
Ellos hablen. (*They may speak.*)	

Because the subjunctive mood expresses doubt, desire, uncertainty, and opinion, *may* is the best translation for the model verbs, but keep in mind that the word *may* may not always apply.

Following are the regular **-er** and **-ir** present-tense subjunctive endings:

Regular subjunctive mood **-er** and **-ir** verb endings	
yo -a	nosotros/as -amos
tú -as	vosotros/as -áis
él, ella, Ud. -a	ellos/as, Uds. -an

Using **comer** as the model **-er** verb, start with the **yo** form, drop the **-o,** and then add the appropriate endings as shown above. Here's what you get:

comer (*to eat*)	
coma	comamos
comas	comáis
coma	coman
Yo coma. (*I may eat.*)	

The **-ir** verbs follow the same routine. Using **vivir** as the model **-ir** verb, start with the **yo** form, drop the **-o,** and then add the appropriate endings:

vivir (*to live*)	
viva	vivamos
vivas	viváis
viva	vivan
Ud. viva. (*You [formal] may live.*)	

Confronting Irregularities

In the subjunctive, as in all verb conjugations, you encounter exceptions to the rules. In the following sections, we explain the various irregularities you encounter when conjugating verbs in the present subjunctive.

Verbs irregular in the yo form

You've met verbs that have irregular **yo** forms in the present tense indicative. Because conjugating verbs in the present subjunctive tense requires the use of this **yo** form, you need to keep these irregularities in mind. Table 6-1 lists verbs with irregular present tense **yo** forms.

Table 6-1 **Verbs with Irregular Present-Tense yo Forms**

Verb	Translation	yo Form	Subjunctive Forms
caber	to fit	quepo	quepa, quepas, quepa, quepamos, quepáis, quepan
caer	to fall	caigo	caiga, caigas, caiga, caigamos, caigáis, caigan
conocer	to know	conozco	conozca, conozcas, conozca, conozcamos, conozcáis, conozcan
decir	to say; to tell	digo	diga, digas, diga, digamos, digáis, digan
hacer	to make; to do	hago	haga, hagas, haga, hagamos, hagáis, hagan
oír	to hear	oigo	oiga, oigas, oiga, oigamos, oigáis, oigan
poner	to put	pongo	ponga, pongas, ponga, pongamos, pongáis, pongan
salir	to go out	salgo	salga, salgas, salga, salgamos, salgáis, salgan
tener	to have	tengo	tenga, tengas, tenga, tengamos, tengáis, tengan
traer	to bring	traigo	traiga, traigas, traiga, traigamos, traigáis, traigan
valer	to be worth	valgo	valga, valgas, valga, valgamos, valgáis, valgan
venir	to come	vengo	venga, vengas, venga, vengamos, vengáis, vengan
ver	to see	veo	vea, veas, vea, veamos, veáis, vean

Here are some examples of these types of verbs:

> **Es imposible que todo quepa en mi maleta.** (*It's impossible that everything will fit in my suitcase.*)

> **Es urgente que Uds. hagan todo este trabajo ahora.** (*It's urgent that you do all this work now.*)

Verbs with spelling changes

Several spelling changes come into play with the present-tense subjunctive conjugations. Note the following spelling changes:

✔ *z* to *c* in front of *e*:

> **empezar** (*to begin*) becomes **yo empiece** (*that I may begin*)

✔ hard *c* to *qu* in front of *e*:

> **buscar** (*to look for*) becomes **yo busque** (*that I may look for*)

✔ hard *g* to *gu* in front of *e*:

> **llegar** (*to arrive*) becomes **yo llegue** (*that I may arrive*)

✔ *gu* to *g* in front of *a*:

> **seguir** (*to follow*) becomes **yo siga** (*that I may follow*)

✔ soft *g* to *j* in front of *a*:

> **proteger** (*to protect*) becomes **yo proteja** (*that I may protect*)

✔ add *y* in front of *a* in verbs that end in -uir (with the exception of seguir):

> **huir** (*to flee; to escape*) becomes **yo huya** (*that I may flee*)

Verbs with stem changes

Verbs with stem changes in the present tense indicative have those same stem changes in the subjunctive. Indicative form **-ar** and **-er** verbs don't change stems in the **nosotros** or **vosotros** conjugations. However, **-ir** verbs have the following changes in the **nosotros** and **vosotros** forms:

✔ In -ir verbs with the stem change of *o* to *ue*, the *o* changes to *u*.

dormir (*to sleep*) becomes

> **nosotros durmamos** (*that we may sleep*)
>
> **vosotros durmáis** (*that you may sleep*)

✔ In -ir verbs with the stem change of *e* to *ie*, the *e* changes to *i*.

mentir (*to lie*) becomes

> **nosotros mintamos** (*that we may lie*)
>
> **vosotros mintáis** (*that you may lie*)

✔ In -ir verbs with the stem change of *e* to *i*, the *e* changes to *i*.

pedir (*to ask for*) becomes

> **nosotros pidamos** (*that we may become*)
>
> **vosotros pidáis** (*that you may become*)

Book III

Mastering More Advanced Grammar Essentials

Verbs with spelling and stem changes

Some very common Spanish verbs have both spelling and stem changes in the present subjunctive form, as shown in Table 6-2.

Table 6-2   Spelling and Stem Changes in the Present Subjunctive

Verb	Spelling Change	Stem Change	Present Subjunctive Forms
colgar (to hang)	g to gu	o to ue	cuelgue, cuelgues, cuelgue, colguemos, colguéis, cuelguen
jugar (to play)	g to gu	u to ue	juegue, juegues, juegue, juguemos, juguéis, jueguen
comenzar (to begin)	z to c	e to ie	comience, comiences, comience, comencemos, comencéis, comiencen
empezar (to begin)	z to c	e to ie	empiece, empieces, empiece, empecemos, empecéis, empiecen
almorzar (to eat lunch)	z to c	o to ue	almuerce, almuerces, almuerce, almorcemos, almorcéis, almuercen

The following examples show these changes in action:

> **María está contenta de que sus perros jueguen en el jardín.** (*Maria is happy that her dogs play in the backyard.*)

> **Estoy encantada que el espectáculo empiece ahora.** (*I am delighted that the show will begin now.*)

> **La madre no permite que sus hijos almuercen en la sala.** (*The mother doesn't permit her children to eat lunch in the living room.*)

Irregular verbs

Some verbs are completely irregular in the subjunctive mood, which means you can't follow any rules or patterns to form them. You can do nothing else but memorize them. Table 6-3 presents these verbs.

Table 6-3		Irregular Verbs in the Subjunctive
Spanish Verb	*Translation*	*Subjunctive Forms*
dar	to give	dé, des, dé, demos, deis, den
estar	to be	esté, estés, esté, estemos, estéis, estén
haber	to have (helping verb)	haya, hayas, haya, hayamos, hayáis, hayan
ir	to go	vaya, vayas, vaya, vayamos, vayáis, vayan
saber	to know	sepa, sepas, sepa, sepamos, sepáis, sepan
ser	to be	sea, seas, sea, seamos, seáis, sean

Here are some examples of irregular verbs in the subjunctive:

Estamos triste que tu abuela esté enferma. (*We are sad that your grandmother is sick.*)

Yo dudo que él sepa reparar la computadora. (*I doubt that he knows how to repair the computer.*)

Wishing in the Subjunctive

One of the coolest features of the subjunctive mood is that it enables you to express desire, hope, or preference; offer suggestions, recommendations, or advice; and even insist or beg for what you want. In other words, even though you may not get what you want, you can certainly ask for it, hope for it, and even insist on it. These expressions of desire, hope, and preference require a combination of two clauses:

✔ The main clause expresses the desire, doubt, or opinion in the indicative mood (statement of fact): for example, "I hope . . . ," "Sally advises . . . ," or "Pedro prefers. . . ."

✔ The subordinate clause describes whatever is being desired, doubted, or offered as an opinion, and you express it in the subjunctive mood. Using the first main clause from the previous bullet as an example: I hope "that my package arrives tomorrow."

This section introduces you to the most common expressions of desire used in main clauses that require the subjunctive in the subordinate clauses. These expressions of desire are verbs that relay hope, preference, or even a recommendation.

Keep in mind that these verbs (listed in Table 6-4) express what the subject wants or would like to happen, but the outcome is uncertain, so the subordinate clause requires the subjunctive. Stem changes are in parentheses.

Table 6-4	Verbs That Express Desire
Verb	**Translation**
aconsejar	to advise
esperar	to hope
insistir en	to insist on
mandar	to order
pedir (e to i)	to ask for; to request
preferir (e to ie)	to prefer
querer	to want
recomendar	to recommend
rogar (o to ue)	to pray; to beg
sugerir (e to ie)	to suggest

When the verb in the main clause expresses desire, the verb in the subordinate clause must be in the subjunctive. The conjunction **que** (*that*) connects the two clauses.

In the following bolded examples, the conjunction is <u>underlined</u>, and the subordinate clause is in *italics:*

- **Él <u>recomienda</u> que *yo llegue temprano*.** (*He recommends that I arrive early.*)

- **Ellos <u>prefieren</u> que *nosotros no paguemos*.** (*They prefer that we not pay.*)

Conveying Doubt, Opinion, or Incomplete Action

The subjunctive mood typically is positive, enabling subjects to hope, prefer, and insist, but it doesn't need to be positive. It simply needs to be uncertain, and uncertainty can take many forms, including

✔ **Doubt:** For the optimist, the subjunctive offers hope. For the pessimist, the subjunctive offers doubt. The subject doubts or can't imagine that something or other can happen.

✔ **Impersonal opinion:** When you want to put forth an opinion without taking credit or blame for it, you can use the subjunctive to express impersonal opinion. In English, the key word in expressing impersonal opinion is *it's*. For example, "It's important that . . . ," "It's necessary that . . . ," or "It's preferable that. . . ."

✔ **Incomplete action:** Some connecting words and phrases, such as *unless, before,* and *in case,* introduce subordinate clauses that express incomplete action. In such cases, the subjunctive mood expresses uncertainty, because the action hasn't yet been completed.

Expressing doubt and uncertainty

Like English, Spanish uses several words to express doubt, including the verb *doubt* itself. Each verb that expresses some form of doubt must be followed by the subjunctive in order to convey the sense of uncertainty. Table 6-5 presents common verbs that express doubt in Spanish.

Table 6-5	Verbs That Express Doubt
Verb	*Translation*
dudar	to doubt
no creer	to not believe
no estar convencido/a de	to not be convinced
no estar seguro/a de	to not be sure
no imaginarse	to not imagine
no parecer	to not seem
no pensar	to not think
no suponer	to not suppose
temer	to suspect; to fear

Book III

Mastering More Advanced Grammar Essentials

You can put together a sentence like this one to show that you're uncertain:

Yo dudo que ella llegue a tiempo. (*I doubt that she arrives on time.*)

Although the verbs listed in the negative use the subjunctive in their subordinate clauses, these verbs require the indicative in the affirmative.

Expressing impersonal opinion

When you want to express an opinion but don't necessarily want that opinion attributed to you, you can use the subjunctive to express impersonal opinion. The list of commonly used Spanish expressions in Table 6-6 state an impersonal opinion and require the subjunctive in the subordinate clause. These expressions convey impersonal opinion by expressing emotion, uncertainty, unreality, or an indirect or implied command.

Table 6-6	Common Expressions of Impersonal Opinion
Term	*Translation*
es fantástico	it's fantastic
es importante	it's important
es imposible	it's impossible
es increíble	it's incredible
es (una) lástima	it's a shame
es mejor	it's better
es necesario	it's necessary
es posible	it's possible
es probable	it's probable
es preferible	it's preferable
es ridículo	it's ridiculous
es terrible	it's terrible
ojalá	I hope; God willing
puede ser	it may be

Here's a sentence that expresses impersonal opinion:

Es necesario que ellos trabajen más. (*It's necessary that they work more.*)

Describing conditional actions

When one action is conditional upon another uncertain action, you use the subjunctive to convey that uncertainty. In the sentence "I'll clean their room as soon as they leave," the main clause, "I'll clean their room," is conditional upon the subordinate clause, "as soon as they leave." Several connecting phrases cue the use of the subjunctive, including the terms in Table 6-7.

Table 6-7	Connecting Phrases That Use the Subjunctive
Term	*Translation*
a menos que	unless
antes (de) que	before
con tal (de) que	provided that
cuando	when
después (de) que	after
en caso de que	in case
hasta que	until
mientras que	while
para que	so that; in order that
tan pronto como	as soon as

When the subordinate clause describes uncertain, incomplete action, the verb in the main clause is sometimes in the future tense. (For more information about the future tense, see Book II, Chapter 6.)

Here's a sentence that uses the future tense and the subjunctive mood:

> **Yo le hablaré tan pronto como llegue.** (*I'll speak with him as soon as he arrives.*)

Book III

Mastering More Advanced Grammar Essentials

Stepping Up to the Imperfect Subjunctive

In Spanish, you use the imperfect subjunctive to express uncertainty about the past. The good news is that unlike the indicative past tense, which gives you the choice between the preterit and the imperfect, the subjunctive uses only the imperfect. Whenever the verb in the main clause is in the past tense (whether preterit, imperfect, or past perfect), the subordinate clause uses the imperfect subjunctive.

In the following sections, you investigate how to form the imperfect subjunctive and then use it in various statements to express wishes, doubt, or opinions about the past.

Forming the imperfect subjunctive

Every tense and mood has its own quirky system for conjugating the verb. In the case of the imperfect subjunctive, here's what you do:

1. **Start with the third-person plural form of the preterit (found in Book III, Chapter 4).**

2. **Drop the -ron ending.**

   This rule applies to all verbs whether they're regular, irregular, stem-changing, or spelling-change verbs.

3. **Add the common endings from the list that follows:**

Imperfect subjunctive mood endings for all verbs	
yo -ra	nosotros/as -'ramos
tú -ras	vosotros/as -rais
él, ella, Ud. -ra	ellos/as, Uds. -ran

You can also use these alternate endings:

Alternate imperfect subjunctive endings	
yo -se	nosotros/as -'semos
tú -ses	vosotros/as -seis
él, ella, Ud. -se	ellos/as, Uds. -sen

The vowel that precedes the **nosotros** ending (in both charts) is always accented.

The following tables show examples of an **-ar, -er,** and **-ir** regular verb conjugated into the imperfect subjunctive.

hablar (to speak)	
hablara	habláramos
hablaras	hablarais
hablara	hablaran
Mi padre prohibió que yo hablara por teléfono después de las 11:00 por la noche. *(My father prohibited that I talk on the phone after 11:00 p.m.)*	

comer (*to eat*)	
comiera	comiéramos
comieras	comierais
comiera	comieran
Mi padre dudaba que nosotros comiéramos toda la pizza. (*My father doubted that we ate the whole pizza.*)	

abrir (*to open*)	
abriera	abriéramos
abrieras	abrierais
abriera	abrieran
Ellos deseaban que su padre abriera la puerta. (*They wished that his father would open the door.*)	

Wishing, doubting, and expressing opinions about the past

Whenever you express uncertainty about a past action, you use the imperfect subjunctive, but several key words and circumstances can also clue you in to the need for the imperfect subjunctive, like the following:

- Verbs, such as **desear** (*to wish*), **prohibir** (*to forbid*), and **creer** (*to believe*), when used to introduce a subordinate clause concerning an uncertain event that occurred in the past

- Expressions of personal opinion about past events that are introduced with **que** (*that*)

- The conjunctions **a fin de que** (*in order that; so that*) and **sin que** (*without*)

Exploring uncertain verbs

Some verbs naturally call for the subjunctive. Others always require the subjunctive when followed by a clause beginning with **que** (see Table 6-8).

Book III

Mastering More Advanced Grammar Essentials

Table 6-8	Verb Expressions That Require the Subjunctive
Term	**Translation**
alegrarse de que	to be happy about something
creer que (only in the affirmative)	to believe
desear que	to wish
impedir que	to prevent
negar que	to deny
pensar que (only in the affirmative)	to think
permitir que	to allow
prohibir que	to forbid
sentir que	to feel
suplicar que	to beg

Speaking in uncertain terms

Table 6-9 gives some additional expressions in the imperfect tense that require the imperfect subjunctive.

Table 6-9	Expressions That Require the Imperfect Subjunctive
Imperfect expression	**Translation**
era menester que	it was necessary that
era preciso que	it was mandatory that
era urgente que	it was urgent that
era natural que	it was natural that
era justo que	it was fair that
era interesante que	it was interesting that
era mejor que	it was better that
convenía que	it was suitable that
importaba que	it was important that
parecía mentira que	it was hard to believe that

Connecting with uncertain conjunctions

Conjunctions smooth the transition from the main clause to the subordinate clause. When these conjunctions express uncertainty, they must be followed by the subjunctive. Following are two conjunctions that always require the use of the subjunctive.

  ✔ **a fin de que** (*in order that; so that*)

  ✔ **sin que** (*without*)

Issuing polite requests

In polite society, you don't ask someone, "Can you do such and such?" Instead, you say something like, "Would you please do such and such?" Proper manners also are important in Spanish. To express yourself politely in Spanish, use the imperfect subjunctive with one of the following two words:

  ✔ **Querer,** which literally means *to want.* Instead of using the verb in the straight present tense, which would translate rather brusquely to "I want," use the imperfect subjunctive, which adds a much more subtle and polite sound to the request. **Quisiera una hamburguesa,** for example, translates as *I would like a hamburger.*

  ✔ **Poder,** which literally means *to be able to.* Rather than use the present tense (which translates as *Can you do such and such?*) or the future tense (which translates to *Will you do such and such?*) use the imperfect subjunctive. **¿Si pudieras, lavarías los platos?** for example, translates very politely as *If you could, would you wash the dishes?*

Dreaming of possibilities with "if"

The word *if* is packed to the gills with uncertainty; hence, it always calls for the use of the subjunctive.

> **Si yo fuera más inteligente, iría a la universidad.** (*If I were smarter, I would go to college.*)

In this example, you're starting the sentence with the subordinate clause, which requires that *were* be in the imperfect subjunctive. The main clause, *I would go to college,* is in the indicative.

Assuming with "as if" or "as though"

As if . . . has achieved slang status in the English language, essentially meaning *I can't believe what you're saying.* In Spanish, the phrase hasn't quite achieved that slang status, but it does imply a sense that you're assuming something is true. To say *as if* or *as though* in Spanish, you use the expression **como si.**

Book III

Mastering More Advanced Grammar Essentials

When a subordinate clause begins with **como si,** the verb is in the imperfect subjunctive. The main clause can either be in the present, past, or conditional.

Here are some examples of sentences that use *as if* and/or *as though*.

> **Ella actuaba como si ganara el premio.** (*She acted as though she had won the prize.*)

> **Él hablaba como si supiera todas las respuestas.** (*He talked as if he knew all the answers.*)

Chapter 7

Forming the Compound Tenses

The helping verb **haber** is like a turbocharger for other Spanish verbs. With the addition of **haber,** a verb in the past tense becomes more past, a present tense statement is already completed, and a future action is finished. **Haber** turns *did* into *had done, does* into *has done,* and *will* into *will have.* It's a helping verb that completes an action.

By adding **haber** to your toolbox, you equip yourself with a whole new set of tenses — the *compound tenses.* The sections in this chapter introduce you to the verb **haber** and show you how to use it to form the compound tenses.

Laying the Groundwork

Forming any compound tense in Spanish is essentially a two-step process:

1. **Begin with the helping verb** haber, **which translates as** *to have* **in the desired tense (the present tense in this section).**

2. **Tack on the past participle of the main verb.**

Voilá! You have the main verb expressed in the desired compound tense. In the following sections, we reveal the basic building blocks that go into forming the compound tenses.

Conjugating haber

The secret to conjugating verbs in any compound tense is discovering how to conjugate the verb **haber** (to have) in the desired tense. After you check that out, you simply tack on the past participle of the main verb, and you're done. Here's the verb **haber** conjugated in the present tense:

haber (helping verb *to have*)	
he	hemos
has	habéis
ha	han
Yo he hablado. (*I have spoken.*)	

Transforming -ar, -er, and -ir verbs into past participles

Every verb has a past participle that expresses a completed action, such as *taken, spoken,* and *danced.* Forming the past participle in English has probably become second nature to you. In Spanish, you simply need to observe the following two rules for forming the regular past participles of **-ar**, **-er**, and **-ir** verbs:

- For **-ar** verbs, drop the **-ar** of the infinitive form and add **-ado.**
- For **-er** and **-ir** verbs, drop the **-er** or **-ir** of the infinitive form and add **-ido.**

Forming and using the past participles is equivalent to using *-ed* or *-en* endings in English.

Infinitive	*Past Participle*
hablar (to speak)	**hablado** (spoken)
comer (to eat)	**comido** (eaten)
vivir (to live)	**vivido** (lived)

The past participles always end in **-o** when used in the compound tenses.

Brushing up on irregular past participles

If all verbs were as structured and disciplined as the regular **-ar, -er,** and **-ir** verbs, life as a student of the Spanish language would be a snap. But any set of grammar rules has exceptions, and the past participles are no different. Some Spanish verbs have irregular past participles. To make these verbs more memorable, I've broken them down into the following two groups:

✔ **Group 1** consists of **-er** and **-ir** verbs in which an **-a, -e,** or **-o** immediately precedes the infinitive ending. These verbs form their past participles regularly, *but* you must add an accent mark over the **i** in the **-ido** ending. Table 7-1 includes some Group 1 verbs:

✔ **Group 2** consists of verbs with irregular past participles that follow no particular pattern and thus must be memorized. Table 7-2 includes several common verbs whose past participles follow no rules:

Table 7-1	Group 1 (-a, -e, -o + -er/-ir ending) Irregular Past Participles	
Verb	*Translation*	*Past Participle*
atraer	to attract	atraído
caer	to fall	caído
creer	to believe	creído
leer	to read	leído
oír	to hear	oído
poseer	to possess	poseído
sonreír	to smile	sonreído
traer	to bring	traído

Table 7-2	Group 2 (No Pattern) Irregular Past Participles	
Verb	*Translation*	*Past Participle*
abrir	to open	abierto
cubrir	to cover	cubierto

(continued)

Table 7-2 (continued)

Verb	Translation	Past Participle
decir	to say, to tell	dicho
describir	to describe	descrito
descubrir	to discover	descubierto
devolver	to return (something)	devuelto
disolver	to dissolve	disuelto
envolver	to wrap (up)	envuelto
escribir	to write	escrito
freír	to fry	frito
hacer	to make, to do	hecho
morir	to die	muerto
oponer	to oppose	opuesto
poner	to put	puesto
proveer	to provide	provisto
resolver	to resolve	resuelto
romper	to break	roto
ver	to see	visto
volver	to return	vuelto

Forming the present perfect

Now that you know how to conjugate the verb **haber** in the present tense and form the past participle of some common verbs, you have everything you need to know to be able to form the present perfect. Put it all together and flex your muscles with your new compound tense. As you flex, keep the following rules and regulations in mind:

- ✔ Use the present perfect to talk about actions that have occurred (or not occurred) prior to the present time.
- ✔ Never separate the verb **haber** and the past participle with any other words.
- ✔ When you're using an object pronoun with the present perfect, the pronoun must precede the conjugated form of the verb **haber.**

The sample sentences in the list that follows show the use of the present perfect:

> **Yo he terminado la carta.** (*I have finished the letter.*)
>
> **Ellos han empezado la casa nueva.** (*They have started the new house.*)
>
> **Ella no ha leído aquella novela.** (*She hasn't read that novel.*)

Tackling the Pluperfect and Preterit Perfect

Because most people generally perceive time as a linear progression from one event to the next, some past actions can be more past than others. "After I had heard that grasshoppers were a delicacy in Mexico," for example, "I decided to try them." In English, the helping verb *had* is used along with the past participle of the main verb to form the *past perfect* or *pluperfect*. Spanish includes two past-perfect tenses:

✔ *Pluperfect* is commonly used in conversation. The pluperfect is formed with the imperfect tense of the verb **haber** followed by the past participle of the main verb.

✔ *Preterit perfect* is commonly used in formal writing and literature. The preterit perfect is formed with the preterit tense of the verb **haber** followed by the past participle of the main verb.

Book III

Mastering More Advanced Grammar Essentials

In most cases, you're going to use the pluperfect. You can pretty much ignore the preterit perfect, unless you're reading or writing a novel in Spanish or presenting a formal paper. If you're studying Spanish primarily to converse, be sure to skip the parts on the preterit perfect.

Forming the pluperfect tense

To form the pluperfect tense, you start with the imperfect conjugation of the verb **haber** and then tack on the past participle of the main verb. Fortunately, **haber** follows the rules of regular **-er** verbs in the imperfect tense dropping the infinitive verb ending and then adding the endings **-ía, -ías, -ía, -íamos, -íais,** and **-ían**. Following is the conjugation chart you need to etch on your brain cells.

haber (helping verb *to have*)	
había	habíamos
habías	habíais
había	habían
Él habia vivido. (*He had lived.*)	

Coming up with the right conjugation of **haber** is just the first step in forming your compound-verb conjugation. You must then add the past participle of the verb whose action is being described. See "Laying the Groundwork" earlier in this chapter for instructions on forming past participles.

Checking out the preterit perfect

Of the seven compound tenses, the preterit perfect is the one you're likely to use least often. It's a strictly formal tense that may come in handy for your reading or composition but won't come up in conversation.

To form the preterit perfect, you begin with the preterit tense of the verb **haber** and then add the past participle of the main verb. It just so happens that the preterit conjugations of **haber** are irregular, so you need to memorize the following conjugation chart.

haber (helping verb *to have*)	
hube	hubimos
hubiste	hubisteis
hubo	hubieron
Él hubo vivido. (*He had lived.*)	

Choosing the right tense at the right time

As you may notice, the pluperfect and preterit perfect tenses in Spanish have identical translations in English. Go figure! So what's the difference? Why do you use one rather than the other? Just as the imperfect and preterit tenses have subtle differences with regard to the past, so do the pluperfect and preterit perfect tenses. The differences in this case center less on conceptual distinctions and more on the contexts in which they're used:

✔ **Pluperfect:** The pluperfect is conversational and is used in everyday speech and writing to describe a past action that happened, or didn't happen, prior to another past action, as in the following examples:

> **Nosotros habíamos terminado con la cena antes de que ellos llegaron.** (*We had finished dinner before they arrived.*)

> **Ella no nos había llamado antes de visitar.** (*She hadn't called us before visiting.*)

> **Yo me había acostado después de mi programa favorito.** (*I had gone to bed after my favorite program.*)

✔ **Preterit perfect:** As we mention earlier in the chapter, the preterit perfect appears primarily in formal or literary Spanish. For everyday purposes you use the simple preterit tense. In the following examples you can see the use of the preterit perfect (more formal) followed by the more common use of the simple preterit tense.

> • **Después de que hubimos visto toda la película, salimos del cine.** (*After we had seen all of the movie, we left the theater.*)

> **Después de que vimos toda la película, salimos del cine.** (*After we saw all of the movie, we left the theater.*)

> • **Tan pronto como ellos hubicron terminado el trabajo, recibieron el dinero.** (*As soon as they had finished the work, they received the money.*)

> **Tan pronto como ellos terminaron el trabajo, recibieron el dinero.** (*As soon as they finished the work, they received the money.*)

> • **Tan pronto como ellos hubieron llegado, comimos.** (*As soon as they had arrived, we ate.*)

> **Tan pronto como ellos llegaron, comimos.** (*As soon as they arrived, we ate.*)

Book III

Mastering More Advanced Grammar Essentials

Table 7-3 includes conjunctions that call for the use of the preterit perfect or preterit in the subordinate clause.

Table 7-3	Words and Phrases That Require the Preterit Perfect or Preterit
Term	*Translation*
apenas	hardly
así que	so that
cuando	when
después de que	after

(continued)

Table 7-3 (continued)

Term	Translation
en cuanto	as soon as possible
ensiguida que	at once
tan pronto como	as soon as
una vez que	once

Forming the Future Perfect and Conditional Perfect

The compound tenses can be considered the *perfect tenses* in the sense that they express already completed actions. The future perfect tells about an action that will have been completed at some time in the future. The conditional perfect talks about an action that *would* have occurred in the past. The following sections introduce these two compound tenses:

✔ **Future perfect:** With the future perfect, you combine the future tense of the verb **haber** with the past participle of the main verb to express actions that *will have happened.*

✔ **Conditional perfect:** With the conditional perfect, you combine the conditional tense of the verb **haber** with the past participle of the main verb to express actions that *would have happened* if some specified condition had (or had not) existed.

Forming the future perfect tense

To form the future perfect, you follow the same two steps you take to form any of the compound tenses:

1. **Begin with the verb** haber **in the appropriate tense (in this case, future tense).**

2. **Add the past participle of the main verb.**

The only curve here is that the helping verb **haber** is formed irregularly in the future tense. The good news is that the future perfect and the conditional perfect tenses both share this same irregularity, which should make them easier to remember. To form the future perfect tense you start with the irregular verb stem **habr-** and add the regular future verb endings (check out Book II, Chapter 6 for a list of the regular future endings). The following chart shows the conjugation for the verb **haber** in the future tense:

haber (helping verb *to have*)	
habré	habremos
habrás	habréis
habrá	habrán
Nosotros habremos terminado el proyecto para el viernes. (*We will have finished the project by Friday.*)	

Giving yourself wiggle room with the conditional perfect

As we mention earlier in this section, the future perfect and conditional perfect share the same irregular verb stem. So to form the conditional perfect tense of the verb **haber,** you begin with the irregular verb stem **habr-** and then add the conditional endings, which you can find in Book II, Chapter 6. The following chart shows the verb **haber** conjugated in the conditional tense:

haber (helping verb *to have*)	
habría	habríamos
habrías	habríais
habría	habrían
Yo habría terminado la tarea pero estaba demasiado cansado. (*I would have finished the assignment but I was too tired.*)	

Book III

Mastering More Advanced Grammar Essentials

Future perfect or conditional perfect? You decide

Conceptually speaking, the future and conditional perfect tenses are similar because both of these tenses express an action that hasn't occurred — in the case of the conditional perfect, because a certain condition wasn't met, and in the case of the future perfect, because the future hasn't yet occurred. The similarities end there, however, because the future tense expresses an action that will have happened by a certain time in the future, whereas the conditional perfect talks about what would have occurred, but didn't. The following sections provide additional guidelines to help you distinguish between these two compound tenses and choose the tense that best suits your needs.

Choosing the future perfect

The future perfect is packed with promise. This tense lets you

- ✔ Express what will have happened by a given time in the future; for example:

    Nosotros habremos terminado para las dos. (*We will have finished by 2:00.*)

    Ellos habrán llegado para este fin de semana. (*They will have arrived by this weekend.*)

    Use **para** to introduce the time expressions in these sentences.

- ✔ Express probability or conjecture (when a slight doubt exists) of a recent past action; for example:

    Ella lo habrá terminado. (*She's probably finished it.*)

    Ellos habrán llegado. (*They must have [probably have] arrived.*)

Choosing the conditional perfect

Use the conditional perfect to express an action that would have happened but didn't. Such sentences typically contain a dependent clause explaining why the action didn't occur; that's your excuse clause — the one that gets you out of trouble.

When forming the dependent clause, keep the following two rules in mind (see Book III, Chapter 6):

- ✔ When the dependent clause begins with *but,* the verb in that clause is in the indicative.
- ✔ When the dependent clause begins with *if,* the verb in the clause is in the imperfect subjunctive.

Following are a couple of examples that show the conditional perfect at work in real, live sentences, complete with a dependent clause:

Nosotros habríamos ido, pero teníamos que trabajar. (*We would have gone, but we had to work.*)

Él habría hablado con ella, pero no entendía la situación. (*He would have talked with her, but he didn't understand the situation.*)

Ellos habrían ganado más dinero si hubieran trabajado más horas. (*They would have earned more money if they had worked more hours.*)

Tú habrías salido más temprano si ellos te hubieran llamado a tiempo. (*You would have left earlier if they had called you on time.*)

Encountering the Present Perfect Subjunctive

The present perfect is perfect for describing actions that *have* or *have not* already happened. The subjunctive mood is used in sentences that express a hope or wish, an opinion, doubt, emotion, or the unknown. Roll the two together and you get the present perfect subjunctive — a compound tense that describes actions that *may have* already happened.

The following sections show you how to form the present perfect subjunctive and use it in a sentence. (And see Book III, Chapter 6 for more on the subjunctive.)

Forming the present perfect subjunctive

Like the other compound tenses, you form the present perfect subjunctive by taking the following two steps:

1. **Begin with the verb** haber **conjugated in the appropriate tense (in this case, present subjunctive).**

2. **Add the past participle of the main verb.**

   (See "Laying the Groundwork" earlier in this chapter for instructions on how to form past participles.)

Book III

Mastering
More
Advanced
Grammar
Essentials

The following chart shows the verb **haber** conjugated in the present perfect.

haber (helping verb *to have*)	
haya	hayamos
hayas	hayáis
haya	hayan
Espero que ellos hayan terminado su trabajo a tiempo. (*I hope that they have finished their work on time.*)	

Notice that the first-person (**yo**), and the third-person (**él, ella, Ud.**) singular forms of the verb **haber** are the same in the present subjunctive.

Putting the present perfect subjunctive to good use

The subtle distinctions among different tenses can make deciding which tense to use tough for you. A case in point is the distinction between the present subjunctive and the present perfect subjunctive. The following guidelines should help you decide which tense is most appropriate:

✔ When the main clause of your sentence expresses doubt or desire in the present or present perfect tense, use the present subjunctive in the subordinate clause, as we discuss in Book III, Chapter 6.

Yo no supongo que tú leas los mismos libros que yo. (*I don't suppose that you [might] read the same books as I.*)

✔ When the main clause expresses doubt or desire in the present or present perfect tense and the subordinate clause refers to an action that *may have* taken place, use the present perfect subjunctive in the subordinate clause.

El profesor duda que todos los estudiantes hayan hecho la tarea. (*The teacher doubts that all of the students have done the homework.*)

✔ When the main clause of the sentence is in the future tense and depends on the completion of another action referred to in the subordinate clause that *may or will have* taken place, that subordinate clause will be in the present perfect subjunctive.

¿Qué harás después que hayas terminado con su trabajo? (*What will you do after you have finished with your work?*)

Doubting the Past with the Pluperfect Subjunctive

Have you ever hoped or wished that something *had* happened? If so, you probably did so in the pluperfect subjunctive and didn't even realize you were doing it. In modern spoken English, subjunctive use is more often implied than actually stated, as the following example shows:

I wished that I had (would have) slept before the party.

When the main clause *I wished* is in the past (preterit or imperfect) tense and refers to an action — *that I had slept before the party* — that is contrary to fact or that possibly had taken place, the subordinate clause is in the pluperfect subjunctive.

Before you get into the various uses of the pluperfect subjunctive, however, you need to find out how to form it. That's the subject of the following section.

Forming the pluperfect subjunctive

Like other compound tenses, you form the pluperfect subjunctive by taking the following two steps:

1. **Begin with the verb** haber **conjugated in the appropriate tense (in this case, imperfect subjunctive).**

2. **Add the past participle of the main verb.**

   (See "Laying the Groundwork" earlier in this chapter for instructions on forming past participles.)

As we explain in Book III, Chapter 6, the imperfect subjunctive has two possible sets of endings. The following chart shows the most commonly used endings. The rule for conjugating a verb into its imperfect subjunctive form is to take the third person plural form of the preterit tense of the verb, drop the **-ron,** and add the following endings:

Imperfect subjunctive endings for all verbs	
yo -ra	nosotros/as -'ramos
tú -ras	vosotros/as -rais
él, ella, Ud. -ra	ellos/as, Uds. -ran

Following this rule, the conjugation of the verb **haber** into the imperfect subjunctive is shown in the following chart.

haber (helping verb *to have*)	
hubiera	hubiéramos
hubieras	hubierais
hubiera	hubieran
Yo deseaba que hubiera dormido antes de la fiesta. (*I wished that I had slept before the party.*)	

Notice that the first-person **(yo)** and third-person (**él, ella, Ud.**) singular forms of this conjugation are the same.

Putting the pluperfect subjunctive to work

The pluperfect subjunctive expresses the same time frame as the pluperfect; that is, it expresses a past action that is more past than another past action. The difference is that the pluperfect subjunctive is used in sentences with a main clause that requires the use of the subjunctive mood in the subordinate clause.

The following sentences reveal the difference between the pluperfect indicative and the pluperfect subjunctive:

✔ **Pluperfect indicative**

> **Yo creía que ellos habían llegado a tiempo.** (*I believed that they had arrived on time.*)

> Note that this sentence is a statement of fact, which is why it uses the indicative.

✔ **Pluperfect subjunctive**

> **Yo dudaba que ella hubiera llamado.** (*I doubted that she had called.*)

> Note that this sentence expresses doubt, so it uses the subjunctive.

For basic information about the subjunctive mood, check out Book III Chapter 6.

Book IV
Spanish at Work

"Honey, can you look in the phrase book and tell me how 'scrambled' is pronounced in Spanish?"

In this book . . .

Whether you need to communicate in Spanish with customers or colleagues at work, you must master some highly specialized vocabulary — words and phrases specific to your industry and workplace. In this book, we provide specialized vocabulary, common fill-in-the-blank forms, and other tools to facilitate communication in a variety of workplace situations. Whether you're a teacher who needs to communicate with students and their parents or a construction supervisor who must delegate tasks to Spanish-speaking workers, you can find enough in this book to make it through a typical workday.

Here are the contents of Book IV at a glance:

Chapter 1

Spanish for Healthcare Workers

As a healthcare professional, you're dedicated to providing all your patients with the best treatment available, whatever language they happen to speak. Providing effective care, however, requires not only a thorough medical background but also an ability to clearly communicate with your patients. You need to be able to take your patients through the entire process — from meeting and greeting them to filling out paperwork, and from asking them questions to delivering your diagnosis, treatment plan, and instructions.

In the course of a single chapter, we can't possibly tell you everything you need to know to fully understand what your Spanish-speaking patients tell you or what you need to tell them, but we can bring you up to speed on the basics and show you how to communicate in the most common scenarios. Here, we cover the basics of gathering information from patients and explaining to patients the diagnosis and treatment.

Refer to the early chapters in Book I for basic coverage of conversational Spanish, including a pronunciation guide in Chapter 1. Book I, Chapter 3 leads you through the basics of meeting and greeting people, while Chapter 4 shows you how to engage in small talk — for when you're just getting to know your patients.

First Things First: Key Words and Emergency Lingo

Whatever your role is in serving patients — whether you're a receptionist meeting the patient for the first time or the doctor who ultimately provides diagnosis and treatment — you need to know some basic doctor's office vocabulary and how to communicate with patients in emergency situations. In the following sections, we introduce you to some general terminology along with Spanish names for body parts and internal organs. We also provide key phrases for dealing with accidents and emergencies.

Doctor-speak: Using basic terminology

When you're in a healthcare situation, whether in a doctor's office, pharmacy, or emergency room, you're likely to use many of the terms in Table 1-1.

Table 1-1	General Health-Related Words	
English	*Spanish*	*Pronunciation*
blood pressure	**la presión sanguínea**	lah preh-see*ohn* sahn-*ghee*-neh-ah
bowel movement (evacuation)	**la evacuación**	lah eh-bvah-kooah-see*ohn*
constipation	**el estreñimiento**	ehl ehs-treh-nyee-mee*ehn*-toh
doctor	**doctor/a**	dohk-*tohr*/rah
	médico/a	*meh*-dee-koh/kah
health	**la salud**	sah-*lood*
healthy	**sano/a**	*sah*-noh/nah
left	**izquierdo/a**	ees-kee*ehr*-doh/dah
medication; medicine	**la medicina**	lah meh-dee-*see*-nah
nausea; sickness	**la náusea**	lah *nah*oo-seh-ah
nurse	**enfermera**	ehn-fehr-*meh*-rah
pharmacist	**el farmacéutico**	ehl fahr-mah-*seh*oo-tee-koh
pharmacy	**la farmacia**	lah fahr-*mah*-seeah
prescription	**la receta**	lah reh-*seh*-tah
right	**derecho/a**	deh-r*eh*-choh/chah

English	Spanish	Pronunciation
sick	**enfermo/a**	ehn-*fehr*-moh/mah
sneeze	**el estornudo**	ehl ehs-tohr-*noo*-doh
surgery	**la cirugía**	lah see-roo-*Hee*-ah
syrup; elixir	**el jarabe**	ehl Hah-*rah*-bveh
urine	**la orina**	lah oh-*ree*-nah
wound	**la herida**	lah eh-*ree*-dah

Naming body parts

Fortunately, you and your patient can probably refer to body parts simply by pointing to them — although this method can get a bit tricky when it comes to internal organs. A more efficient way to communicate with your Spanish-speaking patients is to brush up your Spanish anatomy terminology. Table 1-2 brings you up to speed and acts as a quick reference.

Table 1-2	Spanish Terminology for Body Parts	
English	*Spanish*	*Pronunciation*
Head and Neck Words		
cheek	**la mejilla**	lah meh-*Hee*-yah
chin	**la barba**	lah *bvahr*-bvah
cranium	**el cráneo**	ehl *krah*-neh-oh
ear	**la oreja**	lah oh-*reh*-Hah
eye	**el ojo**	ehl *oh*-Hoh
eyeball	**el globo**	ehl *gloh*-bvoh
face	**el rostro**	ehl *rohs*-troh
forehead	**la frente**	lah *frehn*-teh
hair	**el pelo**	ehl *peh*-loh
head	**la cabeza**	lah kah-*bveh*-sah
jaw	**la mandíbula**	lah mahn-*dee*-bvoo-lah
lip	**el labio**	ehl *lah*-bveeoh
mouth	**la boca**	lah *bvoh*-kah
neck	**el cuello**	ehl koo*eh*-yoh

(continued)

Book IV

Spanish at Work

Table 1-2 *(continued)*

English	Spanish	Pronunciation
nose	**la nariz**	lah nah-*rees*
tongue	**la lengua**	lah *lehn*-gooah
tonsils	**las amígdalas**	lahs ah-*meeg*-dah-lahs
Arm and Hand Words		
arm	**el brazo**	ehl *bvrah*-soh
elbow	**el codo**	ehl *koh*-doh
finger	**el dedo**	ehl *deh*-doh
finger (forefinger)	**el dedo índice**	ehl *deh*-doh *een*-dee-seh
finger (little)	**el dedo meñique**	ehl *deh*-doh meh-*nyee*-keh
finger (middle)	**el dedo del medio**	ehl *deh*-doh dehl *meh*-deeoh
finger (ring)	**el dedo anular**	ehl *deh*-doh ah-noo-*lahr*
fist	**el puño**	ehl *poo*-nyoh
forearm	**el antebrazo**	ehl ahn-teh-*bvrah*-soh
hand	**la mano**	lah *mah*-noh
palm of the hand	**la palma de la mano**	lah *pahl*-mah deh lah *mah*-noh
shoulder	**el hombro**	ehl *ohm*-broh
thumb	**el pulgar**	ehl pool-*gahr*
wrist	**la muñeca**	lah moo-*nyeh*-kah
Leg and Foot Words		
ankle	**el tobillo**	ehl toh-*bvee*-yoh
calf	**la pantorrilla**	lah pahn-toh-*rree*-yah
foot	**el pie**	ehl pee*eh*
heel	**el talón**	ehl tah-*lohn*
knee	**la rodilla**	lah roh-*dee*-yah
leg	**la pierna**	lah pee*ehr*-nah
nail	**la uña**	lah *oo*-nyah
sole of the foot	**la planta del pie**	lah *plahn*-tah dehl pee*eh*
thigh	**el muslo**	ehl *moos*-loh
toe	**el dedo del pie**	ehl *deh*-doh dehl pee*eh*

English	Spanish	Pronunciation
Internal Organs and Other Stuff		
bladder	**la vejiga**	lah bve-*Hee*-gah
blood	**la sangre**	lah *sahn*-greh
bone	**el hueso**	ehl oo*eh*-soh
bowel; intestine; gut	**el intestino**	ehl een-tehs-*tee*-noh
brain	**el cerebro**	ehl seh-*reh*-bvroh
gallbladder	**la vesícula**	lah bveh-*see*-koo-lah
heart	**el corazón**	ehl koh-rah-*sohn*
joint	**la articulación**	lah ahr-tee-koo-lah-see*ohn*
kidney	**el riñón**	ehl ree-*nyohn*
liver	**el hígado**	ehl *ee*-gah-doh
lung	**el pulmón**	el pool-*mohn*
muscle	**el músculo**	ehl *moos*-koo-loh
nerve	**el nervio**	ehl *nehr*-bveeoh
pancreas	**el páncreas**	ehl *pahn*-kree-ahs
skin	**la piel**	lah pee*ehl*
spleen	**el vientre**	ehl bvee*ehn*-treh
stomach	**el estómago**	ehl ehs-*toh*-mah-goh
uterus	**el útero**	ehl *oo*-teh-roh

Dealing with emergencies

In emergency situations, you have very little time to establish rapport with the patient. You need to find out what's going on in a hurry and then issue whatever commands necessary to get the patient to cooperate. Here's a list of questions that can help you quickly ascertain what happened and evaluate the patient's condition:

✔ *Can you hear me?* **¿Me puede oír?** (meh poo*eh*-deh oh*eer*)

✔ *Can you talk?* **¿Puede hablar?** (poo*eh*-deh ah-*bvlahr*)

✔ *What is your name?* **¿Cómo se llama?** (*koh*-moh seh *yah*-mah)

- *Where does it hurt?* **¿Dónde le duele?** (*dohn*-deh leh doo*eh*-leh)

- *Do you know what day today is?* **¿Qúe día es hoy?** (keh *dee*-ah ehs ohy)

- *Do you know where you are?* **¿Sabe dónde está?** (*sah*-bveh *dohn*-deh ehs-*tah*)

- *We are going to put you on a stretcher.* **Vamos a ponerlo en una camilla.** (*bvah*-mohs ah poh-*nehr*-loh ehn *oo*-nah kah-*mee*-yah)

- *We are going in an ambulance.* **Vamos en la ambulancia.** (*bvah*-mohs ehn lah ahm-bvoo-*lahn*-seeah)

- *We are going to the hospital.* **Vamos al hospital.** (*bvah*-mohs ahl ohs-pee-*tahl*)

When you encounter an emergency situation, you need to take control and tell the patient exactly what you need her to do. These short commands are often all you need:

- *Try to calm down.* **Trate de calmarse.** (*trah*-teh deh kahl-*mahr*-seh)

- *Open your eyes.* **Abra los ojos.** (*ah*-bvrah lohs *oh*-Hohs)

- *Please, don't move!* **Por favor**, **¡No se mueva!** (pohr fah-*bvohr* noh seh moo*eh*-bvah)

- *Point to where it hurts.* **Apunte/señale donde le duele.** (ah-*poon*-teh/seh-*nyah*-leh *dohn*-deh leh doo*eh*-leh)

- *Sit down!* **¡Siéntese!** (see*ehn*-teh-seh)

- *Lie down!* **¡Acuéstese!** (ah-koo*ehs*-teh-seh)

- *Breathe slowly!* **¡Respire lentamente!** (rehs-*pee*-reh lehn-tah-*mehn*-teh)

- *Open!* **¡Abra!** (*ah*-bvrah)

- *Turn!* **¡Voltee!** (bvohl-*teh*-eh)

- *Listen!* **¡Oiga!** (*oh*ee-gah)

Admitting New Patients

The first encounter with a new patient is likely to be one of the most important, and it usually occurs with the receptionist who answers the phone and greets the patient when she arrives. This initial contact is when the patient first explains what's going on and why she needs to see a doctor, sets an appointment, completes the necessary paperwork, and discusses details relating to insurance and payments.

In the following sections, we reveal some basic terminology and phrases you need to know at this point and present you with dialogues of some common scenarios so you can begin to tune in to your Spanish-speaking patients.

A smile always conveys concern and compassion and makes a patient feel more at ease. This advice may seem trite, but people often forget how important body language can be, especially when they may be struggling with a language barrier.

One of the most common questions you're going to get is **¿Dónde está el baño?** (*dohn*-deh ehs-*tah* ehl *bvah*-nyoh) (*Where's the bathroom?*) You have two options here: You can escort the person to the nearest bathroom or give the person directions, as discussed in Book I, Chapter 8.

Setting appointments and asking initial questions

When a patient calls into the office, you need to gather some basic information — including the patient's complaint, name, and phone number — and then set up an appointment for the patient to see the doctor. The following dialogue leads you through a typical preliminary phone conversation.

Talkin' the Talk

Mrs. Cruz calls her doctor to set up an appointment. The receptionist, Janice, answers the call, obtains the necessary information from Mrs. Cruz, and then schedules the appointment. Here's how such a conversation is likely to go.

Janice:	**Bueno. Esta es la oficina de los Doctóres Smith, Rowe, y Cline.** bvooeh-noh *ehs*-tah ehs lah oh-fee-*see*-nah deh lohs dohk-*toh*-rehs smeeth, roh, ee kline *Hello. This is the office of Doctors Smith, Rowe, and Cline.*
Mrs. Cruz:	**Sí, necesito concertar una cita con el médico.** see, neh-seh-*see*-toh kohn-sehr-*tahr* oo-nah *see*-tah kohn ehl *meh*-dee-koh. *Yes, I need to make an appointment with the doctor.*

> **Mi doctór es el Doctór Rowe.**
> mee dohk-*tohr* ehs ehl dohk-*tohr* roh
> *My doctor is Dr. Rowe.*

Janice: **Él tiene una cita disponible hoy a las dos de la tarde.**
ehl teee*eh*-neh *oo*-nah *see*-tah dees-poh-*nee*-bvleh ohy
ah lahs dohs deh lah *tahr*-deh
He has an appointment available today at 2:00 p.m.

> **¿Está bien esta hora con usted?**
> ehs-*tah* bvee*ehn* ehs-tah *oh*-rah kohn oos-*tehd*
> *Is that time okay with you?*

Mrs. Cruz: **Sí, excelente.**
see ehk-seh-*lehn*-teh
Yes, excellent.

Janice: **¿Cómo se llama?**
koh-moh seh *yah*-mah
What's your name?

Mrs. Cruz: **Me llamo Sra. María Luisa Cruz.**
meh *yah*-moh seh-*nyoh*-rah mah-*ree*-ah looee-sah
kroos
My name is Mrs. María Luisa Cruz.

Janice: **¿Cuál es su fecha de nacimiento?**
koo*ahl* ehs soo *feh*-chah deh nah-see-mee*ehn*-toh
What is your birthdate?

Mrs. Cruz: **Es el veinte de mayo de mil novecientos setenta y cinco.**
ehs ehl bveh*een*-teh deh *mah*-yoh deh meel
noh-bveh-see*ehn*-tohs seh-*tehn*-tah ee *seen*-koh
It's May 20th, 1975.

Janice: **¿Qué es su número de teléfono?**
keh ehs soo *noo*-meh-roh deh teh-*leh*-foh-noh
What is your phone number?

Mrs. Cruz: **Mi número es 473-1205.**
mee *noo*-meh-roh ehs koo*ah*-troh see*eh*-teh trehs
oo-noh dohs *seh*-roh *seen*-koh
My number is 473-1205.

Janice: **¿Cuáles son sus síntomas?**
koo*ah*-lehs sohn soos *seen*-toh-mahs
What are your symptoms?

Mrs. Cruz: **Hace una semana que me duele la garganta mucho y tengo dolores en todas partes de mi cuerpo.**
ah-seh oo-nah seh-*mah*-nah keh meh doo*eh*-leh lah gahr-*gahn*-tah *moo*-choh ee *tehn*-goh doh-*loh*-rehs ehn *toh*-dahs *pahr*-tehs deh mee koo*ehr*-poh
For a week I have had a very bad sore throat and aches all over my body.

Janice: **¿Tiene Ud. fiebre?**
tee*eh*-neh oos-*tehd* fee*eh*-bvreh
Do you have a fever?

Mrs. Cruz: **De veras, no sé. No tengo termómetro en casa.**
deh *bveh*-rahs noh seh no *tehn*-goh tehr-*moh*-meh-troh ehn *kah*-sah
Honestly, I don't know. I don't have a thermometer at home.

Janice: **No hay problema. La enfermera tomará su temperatura durante la visita.**
no ahy proh-*bvleh*-mah lah ehn-fehr-*meh*-rah toh-mah-*rah* soo tehm-peh-rah-*too*-rah doo-*rahn*-teh lah bvee-*see*-tah
It's not a problem. The nurse will take your temperature during your visit.

Eso es toda la información que necesito. Gracias. Hasta las dos.
eh-soh ehs *toh*-dah lah een-fohr-mah-see*ohn* keh neh-seh-*see*-toh *grah*-seeahs *ahs*-tah lahs dohs
That is all the information that I need. Thanks. See you at 2:00.

Mrs. Cruz: **Gracias. Adiós.**
grah-seeahs ah-dee*ohs*
Thanks. Good-bye.

Book IV

Spanish at Work

At some point in your initial conversation, you need to find out why the person on the other end of the line needs to see the doctor. Here's the question you need to ask:

¿Por qué necesita Ud. consultar al médico? (pohr keh neh-seh-*see*-tah oos-*tehd* kohn-sool-*tahr* ahl *meh*-dee-koh) *(Why do you need to see the doctor?)*

Asking the question is the easy part (it always is); understanding the answer is the real challenge, because the patient can describe anything from the common cold to symptoms of a serious illness. Following are some of the more common reasons patients are likely to offer for needing to see a doctor:

- **Yo tengo un catarro/resfriado.** (yoh *tehn*-goh oon kah-*tah*-rroh/ rehs-free*ah*-doh) *(I have a cold.)*

- **Mi hijo/a tiene fiebre.** (mee *ee*-Hoh tee*eh*-neh fee*eh*-breh) *(My child has a fever.)*

- **Tengo un dolor de estómago.** (*tehn*-goh oon doh-*lohr* deh ehs-*toh*-mah-goh) *(I have a stomach ache.)*

- **Me duele la garganta.** (Fill in any body part.) (meh doo*eh*-leh lah gahr-*gahn*-tah) *(My throat hurts.)*

- **Estoy estreñido/a.** (ehs-*tohy* ehs-treh-*nyee*-doh/dah) *(I am constipated.)*

- **Tengo dolores en todas partes de mi cuerpo.** (*tehn*-goh doh-*loh*-rehs ehn *toh*-dahs *pahr*-tehs deh mee koo*er*-poh) *(I have aches all over my body.)*

- **Tengo un dolor de cabeza.** (*tehn*-goh oon doh-*lohr* deh kah-*beh*-sah) *(I have a headache.)*

- **Creo que me hubiera torcido el tobillo.** (Fill in any body part.) (*kreh*-oh keh meh oo-bvee*eh*-rah tohr-*see*-doh ehl toh-*bee*-yoh) *(I think I may have sprained my ankle.)*

- **Creo que me hubiera fracturado el brazo.** (Fill in any body part.) (*kreh*-oh keh meh oo-bvee*eh*-rah frahk-too-*rah*-doh ehl *bvrah*-soh) *(I think I may have fractured my arm.)*

- **Mi niño/a está vomitando desde hace dos días.** (mee *nee*-nyoh/nyah ehs-*tah* voh-mee-*tahn*-doh *dehs*-deh *ah*-seh dohs *dee*-ahs) *(My child has been vomiting for two days.)*

🗸 **Mi niño/a está quejando de un dolor de *estómago.*** (Fill in any body part.) (mee *nee*-nyoh/nyah ehs-*tah* keh-*Hahn*-doh deh oon doh-*lohr* deh ehs-*toh*-mah-goh) (*My child is complaining of a stomachache.*)

🗸 **Mi hijo/a tiene una tos muy persistente desde hace una semana.** (mee *ee*-Hoh/Hah tee*eh*-neh *oo*-nah tohs mooy pehr-sees-*tehn*-teh *dehs*-deh *ah*-seh *oo*-nah seh-*mah*-nah) (*My son/daughter has had a very persistent cough for a week.*)

🗸 **No consigo curarme esta tos.** (noh cohn-*see*-goh koo-*rahr*-meh *ehs*-tah tohs) (*I can't get rid of this cough.*)

🗸 **Mi esposo/a está quejando de dificultad en tragar.** (mee eh-*spoh*-soh/sah ehs-*tah* keh-*Hahn*-doh deh dee-fee-kool-*tahd* ehn trah-*gahr*) (*My husband/wife is complaining of difficulty swallowing.*)

🗸 **Estoy mareado/a cuando me pongo a pie.** (ehs-*tohy* mah-reh-*ah*-doh/dah koo*ahn*-doh meh *pohn*-goh ah pee*eh*) (*I am dizzy when I stand up.*)

🗸 **Me zumban los oídos.** (meh *soom*-bahn lohs oh*ee*-dohs) (*My ears are ringing.*)

Dealing with forms and other formalities

When a patient arrives at your office, you need to greet her and ask her to complete one or more forms. Book I, Chapter 3 offers everything you need to know about meeting and greeting people in Spanish. After dealing with the preliminaries, you need to have the patient sign in and then (if the person is a new patient) have her fill out the requisite forms.

The good news is that your Spanish-speaking patient's English may be better than your Spanish. Don't assume that because your patient enters the office speaking Spanish to her family that she doesn't speak English. Ascertain the patient's English language skills early on and her preferred language for dealing with the doctor. You may even want to note this information in the patient's records for future reference.

Having Spanish-language forms and other paperwork on hand (such as your privacy policy) is a big plus. Figure 1-1 provides a sample form for gathering basic information from new patients.

Información del paciente (Patient Information)

Fecha (Date): **Mes** (Month) _____ **Día** (Day) _____ **Año** (Year) _____

Nombre del paciente: Apellido, nombre, inicial del segundo nombre (Patient Name: Last, First, M.I.)

Dirección (Address)	**Ciudad/Estado/Código postal** (City/State/Zip Code)
Teléfono de casa (Home Telephone Number)	**Número de celular** (Cell Number)
Empleador (Employer)	**Teléfono de trabajo** (Work Telephone Number)
Fecha de nacimiento (Birthdate) **Mes** (Month) _____ **Día** (Day) _____ **Año** (Year) _____	**Número de Seguro Social** (Social Security Number) ____ ____ ____ - ____ ____ - ____ ____ ____ ____
Compañía de seguros de salud (Health Insurance Company Name)	**Número de póliza de seguro de salud** (Health Insurance Policy Number)

Información del responsable si es diferente que lo anotado arriba
(Information of the responsible party if different than that noted above)

Apellido, nombre, inicial del segundo nombre (Last Name, First Name, Middle Initial)

Dirección (Address)	**Ciudad/Estado/Código postal** (City/State/Zip Code)
Teléfono de casa (Home Telephone Number)	**Número de celular** (Cell Number)

Síntomas (Symptoms)

☐ **Toser** Coughing	☐ **Insomnio** Insomnia	☐ **Dolor de urinar** Pain when urinating	☐ **Hemorragia** Bleeding
☐ **Estornudar** Sneezing	☐ **Fatiga** Fatigue	☐ **Estreñimiento** Constipation	☐ **Dolor de músculo** Muscle ache
☐ **Dolor de garganta** Sore throat	☐ **Dolor de pecho** Chest pain	☐ **Flujo vaginal** Vaginal discharge	☐ **Dolor de articulación** Joint ache
☐ **Goteo nasal** Runny nose	☐ **Diarrea** Diarrhea	☐ **Picazón** Itching	☐ **Adormecimiento** Numbness
☐ **Dolor de oído** Earache	☐ **Dolor de estómago** Stomach ache	☐ **Piel seco** Dry skin	☐ **Hormigueo** Tingling
☐ **Dolor de cabeza** Headache	☐ **Náusea** Nausea	☐ **Sarpullido** Rash	☐ **Sudores por la noche** Night sweats
☐ **Dificultades con la respiración** Difficulty breathing	☐ **Vomitar** Vomiting	☐ **Magullar** Bruising	☐ **Otro** Other: _____
☐ **Mareos** Dizziness	☐ **Incontinencia** Incontinence	☐ **Corte** Cut	

Autorización, Consentimiento y Asignación de Beneficios
Authorization, Consent, and Benefit Allocation

Yo doy consentimiento a la atención del paciente a fin de incluir la evaluación, diagnóstico, consulta, y tratamiento de cuidado de salud. Doy mi permiso para que los beneficios del seguro a ser pagados directamente al proveedor de atención médica, y entiendo que soy financieramente responsable de los servicios no cubiertos.

I hereby give consent to patient care to include assessment, diagnosis, consultation, and healthcare treatment. I give permission for my insurance benefits to be paid directly to the healthcare provider, and I understand that I am financially responsible for services not covered.

Firma (Signature): _____ Fecha (Date): _____

Parentesco al paciente si es menor (Relationship to the patient if a minor) _____

Figure 1-1:
Spanish-language form for new patients.

The following dialogue illustrates the first meeting between a receptionist and a patient.

Talkin' the Talk

Janice greets Maria (a new patient), has her sign in, and asks her to fill out the new patient form.

Janice: **Buenas tardes. Por favor firme aquí con su nombre y apellido, el médico que va a ver, y la hora de su llegada.**
bvoo*eh*-nahs *tahr*-dehs pohr fah-*bvohr feer*-meh ah-*kee* kohn soo *nohm*-bvreh ee ah-peh-*yee*-doh ehl *meh*-dee-koh keh bvah ah bvehr ee lah *oh*-rah deh soo yeh-*gah*-dah
Good afternoon. Please sign in here with your first and last name, the doctor that you will see, and the time of your arrival.

María: **Está bien.**
ehs-*tah* bvee*ehn*
Fine.

Janice: **La enfermera la llamará cuando están listos.**
lah ehn-fehr-*meh*-rah lah yah-mah-*rah* koo*ahn*-doh ehs-*tahn lees*-tohs
The nurse will call you when they're ready.

Mientras tanto por favor llene este formulario.
mee*ehn*-trahs *tahn*-toh pohr fah-*bvohr yeh*-neh *ehs*-teh fohr-moo-*lah*-reeoh
Meanwhile, please fill out this form.

Necesitamos alguna información básica para su expediente.
neh-seh-see-*tah*-mohs ahl-*goo*-nah een-fohr-mah-see*ohn* bvah-see-kah *pah*-rah soo ehk-speh-dee*ehn*-teh
We need some basic information for your file.

María: **No es ninguna molestia.**
noh ehs neen-*goo*-nah moh-*lehs*-teeah
It's not a problem.

Book IV

Spanish at Work

Discussing insurance and payments

Discussing insurance and payments with patients upfront can help you steer clear of any confusion and potential disagreements later. You need to let the patient know your payment policy and how much you charge for a typical doctor's visit, as well as find out whether the person has health insurance (which may be included on the new patient form). In the following dialogue, the receptionist goes over these points with a patient.

Talkin' the Talk

 During María's first visit to Dr. Rowe's office, Janice informs María of their payment policy and gathers information about her insurance.

Janice: **Necesito establecer como pagará por la cita.**
Neh-seh-*see*-toh ehs-tah-bvleh-*sehr koh*-moh
pah-gah-*rah* pohr lah *see*-tah
I need to establish how you will pay for the appointment.

¿Tiene Ud. seguro?
teee*eh*-neh oos-*tehd* seh-*goo*-roh
Do you have insurance?

María: **Sí, tengo seguro.**
see *tehn*-goh seh-*goo*-roh
Yes, I have insurance.

Janice: **Entonces, por favor llene este formulario de seguro.**
ehn-*tohn*-sehs pohr fah-*bvohr yeh*-neh *ehs*-teh
fohr-moo-*lah*-reeoh deh seh-*goo*-roh
Well, then, please fill out this insurance form.

También necesito su tarjeta de seguro para hacer una fotocopia.
tahm-bveee*ehn* neh-seh-*see*-toh soo tahr-*Heh*-tah deh
seh-*goo*-roh *pah*-rah ah-*sehr* oo-nah
foh-toh-*koh*-peeah
I also need your insurance card to make a photocopy.

María: **Espere un momento, la tengo aquí en mi bolsa.**
ehs-*peh*-reh oon moh-*mehn*-toh lah *tehn*-goh ah-*kee*
ehn mee *bvohl*-sah
Wait a minute; I have it here in my purse.

Janice: **Gracias. Yo haré una fotocopia de la tarjeta mientras Ud. llena el formulario.**
grah-seeahs yoh ah-*reh* *oo*-nah foh-toh-*koh*-peeah de lah tahr-*Heh*-tah meee*ehn*-trahs oos-*tehd* yeh-nah ehl fohr-moo-*lah*-reeoh
Thank you. I will make a photocopy of the insurance card while you fill out the form.

Pregúntame si haya algo que no entienda.
preh-*goon*-tah-meh see *ah*-yah *ahl*-goh keh noh ehn-teee*ehn*-dah
Ask me if there is anything that you don't understand.

María: **Bien.**
bvee*ehn*
Fine.

Later when María returns with the insurance form completed:

Janice: **La información en su tarjeta indica que Ud. tiene que pagar veinte dólares de co-pago por la visita.**
lah een-fohr-mah-see*ohn* ehn soo tahr-*Heh*-tah een-*dee*-kah keh oos-*tehd* teee*eh*-neh keh pah-*gahr* *bveh*een-teh *doh*-lah-rehs deh koh *pah*-goh pohr lah bvee-*see*-tah
The information on your card indicates that you have to pay a $20 co-pay at the time of your visit.

¿Cómo desea pagar?
koh-moh deh-*seh*-ah pah-*gahr*
How do you want to pay?

María: **Lo pagaré en efectivo.**
loh pah-gah-*reh* en eh-fehk-*tee*-bvoh
I will pay in cash.

Janice: **Está bien. ¿Necesita un recibo?**
ehs-*tah* bvee*ehn* neh-seh-*see*-tah oon reh-*see*-bvoh
That's fine. Do you need a receipt?

María: **Sí, gracias.**
see *grah*-seeahs
Yes, thanks.

Book IV

Spanish at Work

Asking Questions: The Patient Interview

As a doctor, you very rarely have the opportunity to diagnose a patient's condition just by looking at her. You usually need to find out from the patient what's going on and why she came to see you. If you're lucky, your receptionist already obtained some general information about the patient's condition and passed it along to you. Chances are good, however, that you probably need to ask some additional questions, and you probably want to hear it from the patient yourself, anyway. The following dialogue presents just this kind of doctor-patient interview.

Talkin' the Talk

As you know, one of the best ways to figure out what's wrong with a patient is to ask questions — as many questions as needed to focus in on the problem. Here, Dr. Billess greets her patient, Mr. Manuel, and asks a series of common questions.

Dr. Billess: **Buenas tardes, Sr. Manuel. Me llamo Doctór Billess.**
bvooeh-nahs *tahr*-dehs seh-*nyohr* mah-nooehl meh *yah*-moh dohk-*tohr bee*-lehs
Good afternoon, Mr. Manuel. My name is Dr. Billess.

Mr. Manuel: **Mucho gusto.**
moo-choh *goo*-stoh
Pleased to meet you.

Dr. Billess: **¿Cómo puedo ayudar hoy?**
koh-moh pooeh-doh ah-yoo-*dahr* ohy
How may I help today?

Mr. Manuel: **He tenido un dolor de estómago por un tiempo.**
eh teh-*nee*-doh oon doh-*lohr* deh ehs-*toh*-mah-goh pohr oon teeehm-poh
I have had a stomachache for a while.

Dr. Billess: **¿Me puede decir específicamente cuando empezó este dolor?**
meh pooeh-deh deh-*seer* ehs-peh-*see*-fee-kah-mehn-teh kooahn-doh ehm-peh-*soh* ehs-teh doh-*lohr*
Can you tell me specifically when this pain began?

Mr. Manuel: **Pues, a ver, creo que empezó hace dos semanas, más o menos.**
poo*ehs* ah bvehr *kreh*-oh keh ehm-peh-*soh ah*-seh dohs seh-*mah*-nahs mahs oh *meh*-nohs
Well, let's see, I think it began two weeks ago, more or less.

Dr. Billess: **¿Hay unas cosas que mejoren o empeoren el dolor?**
ahy *oo*-nahs *koh*-sahs keh meh-*Hoh*-rehn oh ehm-peh-*oh*-rehn ehl doh-*lohr*
Are there any things that seem to lessen or worsen the pain?

Mr. Manuel: **Me parece que hay algunos movimientos que lo empeoren.**
meh pah-*reh*-seh keh ahy ahl-*goo*-nohs moh-bvee-mee*ehn*-tohs key loh ehm-peh-*oh*-rehn
It seems that there are certain movements that make it worse.

También me hace sentir mejor cuando aplico la almohadilla de calefacción a mi estomago.
tahm-bvee*ehn* meh *ah*-seh sehn-*teer* meh-*Hohr* koo*ahn*-doh ah-*plee*-koh lah ahl-moh-ah-*dee*-yah deh kah-leh-fahk-see*ohn* ah mee ehs-*toh*-mah-goh
Also I feel better when I put the heating pad on my stomach.

Dr. Billess: **Déjame ver. Voy a examinar el estómago. Por favor levante su camisa.**
deh-Hah-meh bvehr bvohy ah ehk-sah-mee-*nahr* ehl ehs-*toh*-mah-goh poh fah-*bvohr* leh-*bvahn*-teh soo kah-*mee*-sah
Let me see. I'm going to examine your stomach. Please lift up your shirt.

Mr. Manuel: **Bien.**
bvee*ehn*
Fine.

Book IV

Spanish at Work

Following are some of the most common questions doctors ask when interviewing their patients:

✔ *Do you have a fever?* **¿Tiene fiebre?** (te*eeh*-neh fee*eeh*-breh)

✔ *Are you sneezing a lot?* **¿Estornuda mucho?** (ehs-tohr-*noo*-dah *moo*-choh)

✔ *Do you have a cough?* **¿Tiene tos?** (tee*eh*-neh tohs)

✔ *How long have you been feeling like this?* **¿Hace cuánto tiempo que se siente mal?** (*ah*-seh koo*ahn*-toh tee*ehm*-poh keh seh see*ehn*-teh mahl)

✔ *Are you sleeping any more or less than usual?* **¿Duerme más o menos que lo normal?** (doo*ehr*-meh mahs oh *meh*-nohs keh loh nohr-*mahl*)

✔ *Where do you feel the pain?* **¿Dónde siente el dolor?** (*dohn*-deh see*ehn*-teh ehl doh-*lohr*)

✔ *Are there any medications that you take regularly?* **¿Hay algunas medicaciones que toma regularmente?** (ahy ahl-*goo*-nahs meh-dee-kah-see*ohn*-ehs keh *toh*-mah reh-goo-lahr-*mehn*-teh)

✔ *Do you have any problems with your digestion?* **¿Tiene un problema con la digestión?** (tee*eh*-neh oon proh-*bvleh*-mah kohn lah dee-Hehs-tee*ohn*)

✔ *Do you smoke?* **¿Usted fuma?** (oos-*tehd foo*-mah)

✔ *Is there any history of cancer in your family?* (Fill in any illness/disease.) **¿Hay una historia de cáncer en su familia?** (ahy *oo*-nah ees-*toh*-reeah deh *kahn*-sehr ehn soo fah-*mee*-leeah)

✔ *Do you ever feel dizzy?* **¿Tiene mareos a veces?** (tee*eh*-neh mah-*reh*-ohs ah *bveh*-sehs)

✔ *Are you constipated?* **¿Está estreñido/a?** (ehs-*tah* ehs-treh-*nyee*-doh/dah)

✔ *Do you have diarrhea?* **¿Tiene diarrea?** (tee*eh*-neh deeah-*rreh*-ah)

In the case of an accident, instead of asking *What's wrong?* you may want to ask *What happened?*:

✔ *What happened?* **¿Qué ocurrió?** (keh oh-koo-rree*oh*)

✔ *When did this happen?* **¿Cuándo ocurrió?** (koo*ahn*-doh oh-koo-rree*oh*)

✔ *Are you feeling any pain?* **¿Siente algún dolor?** (see*eh*-teh ahl-*goon* doh-*lohr*)

✔ *Where does it hurt?* **¿Dónde le duele?** (*dohn*-deh leh doo*eh*-leh)

✔ *Do you hurt anywhere else?* **¿Le duele en otra parte del cuerpo?** (leh doo*eh*-leh ehn *oh*-trah *pahr*-teh dehl koo*ehr*-poh)

✔ *Do you feel dizzy?* **¿Se siente mareado/a?** (seh see*ehn*-teh mah-reh-*ah* doh/dah)

Examining Your Patient

After the patient has had a chance to talk, you're ready to get down to business, check her vital signs, and take a closer look by performing a physical exam. In the following sections, we show you how to talk your patient through a standard physical examination, including taking her blood pressure and temperature, requesting a urine sample or blood sample (if necessary), and ordering x-rays.

Taking a patient's blood pressure and temperature

In most offices, the nurse or a medical assistant ushers the patient to an examination room and immediately takes the patient's blood pressure and temperature. If this job falls to you, you need to tell the patient what you're doing and instruct her on what she needs to do; check out the following dialogue for an example conversation.

Talkin' the Talk

The medical assistant Laurie weighs Mrs. López and takes her temperature and blood pressure while keeping Mrs. López informed of what she's doing.

Laurie: **Buenas tardes, Sra. López.**
bvoo*eh*-nahs *tahr*-dehs seh-*nyoh*-rah *loh*-pehs
Good afternoon, Mrs. López.

Mrs. López: **Buenas tardes.**
bvoo*eh*-nahs *tahr*-dehs
Good afternoon.

Laurie: **Por favor suba a la báscula. Necesito averiguar cuanto pesa.**
pohr fah-*bvohr* soo-bvah ah lah *bvahs*-koo-lah neh-seh-*see*-toh ah-bveh-ree-goo*ahr* koo*ahn*-toh *peh*-sah
Please step up on the scale. I need to get your weight.

Book IV

Spanish at Work

Mrs. López: **Bien.**
bvee*ehn*
Fine.

Laurie jots down Mrs. López's weight, and Mrs. López steps off the scale.

Laurie: **Vamos a la tercera sala a la derecha.**
bvah-mohs ah lah tehr-*seh*-rah *sah*-lah ah lah deh-*reh*-chah
We're going to the third room on the right.

After arriving in the examination room:

Por favor siéntese en esta mesa.
pohr fah-*bvohr* see*ehn*-teh-seh ehn *ehs*-tah *meh*-sah
Please take a seat on this table.

Necesito tomar su temperatura.
neh-seh-*see*-toh toh-*mahr* soo tehm-peh-rah-*too*-rah
I need to take your temperature.

Por favor ponga este termómetro en la boca.
pohr fah-*bvohr pohn*-gah *ehs*-teh tehr-*moh*-meh-troh ehn lah *bvoh*-kah
Please put this thermometer in your mouth.

After getting her temperature:

Ahora necesito tomar su presión de la sangre.
ah-*oh*-rah neh-seh-*see*-toh toh-*mahr* soo preh-see*ohn* deh lah *sahn*-greh
Now I need to take your blood pressure.

Por favor remánguese la camisa.
pohr fah-*bvohr* reh-*mahn*-geh-seh lah kah-*mee*-sah
Please roll up your shirt sleeve.

After getting her blood pressure:

Gracias. El médico llegará pronto.
grah-seeahs ehl *meh*-dee-koh yeh-gah-*rah prohn*-toh
Thanks. The doctor will be here soon.

Sra. López: **Gracias.**
grah-seeahs
Thanks.

Say "aah": The physical exam

During a physical exam, you're usually giving the patient a quick overall inspection to check for any obvious physical signs of illness. You may examine the patient's ears, nose, and throat; listen to her heart and breathing; and take a closer look at any body parts that show evidence of trauma or where the patient reports feeling pain. (The list of Spanish names for body parts in Table 1-2 near the beginning of the chapter comes in very handy here.)

- *I am going to examine you.* **Voy a examinarlo.** (bvohy ah ehk-sah-mee-*nahr*-loh)

- *Please sit up on the bed.* **Por favor, siéntese en la mesa.** (pohr fah-*bvohr* see*ehn*-teh-seh ehn lah *meh*-sah)

- *Sit upright.* **Siéntese derecho.** (see*ehn*-teh-seh deh-*reh*-choh)

- *Lift your head.* **Levante la cabeza.** (leh-*bvahn*-teh lah kah-*bveh*-sah)

- *Lower your head.* **Baje la cabeza.** (*bvah*-Heh lah kah-*bveh*-sah)

- *Turn your head to the left.* **Voltee la cabeza hacia la izquierda.** (bvohl-*teh*-eh lah kah-*bveh*-sah ah-seeah lah ees-kee*ehr*-dah)

- *Turn your head to the right.* **Voltee la cabeza hacia la derecha.** (bvohl-*teh*-eh lah kah-*bveh*-sah *ah*-sehah lah deh-*reh*-chah)

- *I am going to examine your ears.* **Voy a examinar sus orejas.** (bvoy ah ehk-sah-mee-*nahr* soos oh-*reh*-Hahs)

- *I am going to examine your nose.* **Voy a examinar su nariz.** (bvoy ah ehk-sah-mee-*nahr* soo nah-*rees*)

- *Open your mouth.* **Abra la boca.** (*ah*-bvrah lah *bvoh*-kah)

- *Say "aah."* **Diga "aaa."** (*dee*-gah aaah)

- *Close your mouth.* **Cierre la boca.** (see*eh*-rreh lah *bvoh*-kah)

- *Stick out your tongue.* **Saque la lengua.** (*sah*-keh lah *lehn*-gooah)

- *Lift your arm.* **Levante su brazo.** (leh-*bvahn*-teh soo *bvrah*-soh)

- *Bend your elbow.* **Doble el codo.** (*doh*-bvleh ehl *koh*-doh)

- *Tell me if it hurts.* **Dígame si duele.** (*dee*-gah-meh see doo*eh*-leh)

- *Make a fist.* **Haz un puño.** (ahs oon *poo*-nyoh)

- *Hold my finger.* **Agarre mi dedo.** (ah-*gah*-rreh mee *deh*-doh)

- *Tighten!* **¡Apriete!** (ah-pree*eh*-teh)

- *Lift your leg.* **Levante la pierna.** (leh-*bvahn*-teh lah pee*ehr*-nah)

- *Bend it.* **Dóblela.** (*doh*-bvleh-lah)

- *Extend it.* **Estírela.** (eh-*stee*-reh-lah)

- *Move your leg.* **Mueva su pierna.** (moo*eh*-bvah soo pee*ehr*-nah)

- *Forward.* **Adelante.** (ah-deh-*lahn*-teh)

- *Backward.* **Atrás.** (ah-*trahs*)

- *Lift your foot.* **Levante el pie.** (leh-*bvahn*-teh ehl pee*eh*)

- *Push hard.* **Haga fuerza, empuje.** (*ah*-gah foo*ehr*-sah, ehm-*poo*-Heh)

- *Bend your toes.* **Doble los dedos.** (*doh*-bvleh lohs *deh*-dohs)

- *Now I am going to examine your chest.* **Ahora, voy a examinar su pecho.** (ah-*oh*-rah bvoy ah ehk-sah-mee-*nahr* soo *peh*-choh)

- *I am going to listen to your heart.* **Voy a escuchar el corazón.** (bvoy ah ehs-koo-*char* ehl koh-rah-*sohn*)

- *Don't talk.* **No hable.** (noh *ah*-bvleh)

- *Take a deep breath.* **Respire profundamente.** (rehs-*pee*-reh proh-foon-dah-*mehn*-teh)

- *Hold it.* **Deténgalo.** (deh-*tehn*-gah-loh)

- *Let it out.* **Exhale.** (ehk-*sah*-leh)

- *Relax.* **Descanse.** (dehs-*kahn*-seh)

- *I am going to listen to your lungs.* **Voy a escuchar los pulmones.** (bvoy ah ehs-koo-*chahr* lohs pool-*moh*-nehs)

- *Breathe through your mouth.* **Respire con la boca abierta.** (rehs-*pee*-reh kohn lah *bvoh*-kah ah-bvee*ehr*-tah)

- *Again.* **Otra vez.** (*oh*-trah bvehs)

- *Breathe.* **Respire.** (rehs-*pee*-reh)

- *Breathe regularly.* **Respire normalmente.** (rehs-*pee*-reh nohr-mahl-*mehn*-teh)

- *Does it hurt to breathe?* **¿Le duele respirar?** (leh doo*eh*-leh rehs-pee-*rahr*)

- *Cough!* **¡Tosa!** (*toh*-sah)

- *Please lie down.* **Acuéstese, por favor.** (ah-koo*ehs*-teh-seh pohr fah-*bvohr*)

- *Turn onto your side.* **Voltéese de lado.** (bvohl-*teh*-eh-seh deh *lah*-doh)

- *Now I am going to examine your abdomen.* **Ahora, voy a examinar su abdomen/vientre.** (ah-*oh*-rah bvoy ah ehk-sah-mee-*nahr* soo ahbv-*doh*-mehn/bvee*ehn*-treh)

✔ *I am going to examine your genitalia.* **Voy a examinar los genitales.** (bvoy ah ehk-sah-mee-*nahr* lohs Heh-nee-*tah*-lehs)

✔ *I have finished the exam.* **Terminé la examinación.** (tehr-mee-*neh* lah ehk-sah-mee-nah-see*ohn*)

✔ *Do you have any questions?* **¿Tiene alguna pregunta?** (tee*eh*-neh ahl-*goo*-nah preh-*goon*-tah)

Explaining the Diagnosis and Treatment

After you've examined the patient, you're ready to deliver your diagnosis and treatment plan or refer the patient to a specialist. In the following sections, we offer Spanish translations of the most common illnesses and treatments and a quick reference guide for referring patients to other departments and specialists.

Delivering your diagnosis

Delivering your diagnosis is relatively easy as long as you know the Spanish equivalent for the condition or illness your patient has. Simply use one of the following expressions followed by the name of the illness or condition in Table 1-3:

✔ *You have. . .* **Tiene. . .** (tee*eh*-neh)

✔ *You suffer from. . .* **Padece de. . .** (pah-*deh*-seh deh)

Table 1-3	Common Illnesses and Conditions	
English	*Spanish*	*Pronunciation*
abrasion	**la abrasión**	lah ah-bvrah-see*ohn*
AIDS	**la SIDA**	lah *see*-dah
anemia	**la anemia**	lah ah-*neh*-mee-ah
arthritis	**la artritis**	lah ahr-*tree*-tees
bacterial infection	**la infección bacteriana**	lah een-fec-see*ohn* bvahk-teh-ree*ah*-nah

(continued)

Table 1-3 *(continued)*

English	Spanish	Pronunciation
bladder infection	**la infección de la vejiga**	lah een-fec-see*ohn* deh lah bveh-*Hee*-gah
bone fracture	**la fractura de un hueso**	lah frak-*too*-rah deh oon oo*eh*-soh
botulism	**el botulismo**	ehl bvoh-too-*lees*-moh
bronchitis	**la bronquitis**	lah bvrohn-*kee*-tees
bruise	**el moretón**	ehl moh-reh-*tohn*
cancer	**el cáncer**	ehl *kahn*-sehr
cellulitis	**la celulitis**	lah seh-loo-*lee*-tees
cerebral palsy	**la parálisis cerebral**	lah pah-*rah*-lee-sees seh-reh-*bvrahl*
chicken pox	**la varicela**	lah bvah-ree-*seh*-la
cholera	**el cólera**	ehl *koh*-leh-rah
cirrhosis	**la cirrosis**	lah see-*rroh*-sees
cold	**el catarro**	ehl kah-*tah*-rroh
	el resfriado	ehl rehs-free*ah*-doh
concussion	**la concusión**	lah kohn-koo-see*ohn*
cystic fibrosis	**la fibrosis cística**	lah fee-*bvroh*-sees *sees*-tee-kah
dermatitis	**la dermatitis**	lah dehr-mah-*tee*-tees
diabetes	**la diabetes**	lah dee-ah-*bveh*-tehs
diphtheria	**la difteria**	lah deef-*teh*-reeah
dysentery	**la disentería**	lah dee-sehn-teh-*ree*-ah
emphysema	**el enfisema**	ehl ehn-fee-*seh*-mah
encephalitis	**la encefalitis**	lah ehn-seh-fah-*lee*-tees
epilepsy	**la epilepsia**	lah eh-pee-*lehp*-seeah
fever	**la fiebre**	lah fee*eh*-bvreh
gallstones	**los cálculos en la vesícula**	lohs *kahl*-koo-lohs ehn lah veh-*see*-koo-lah
heart disease	**la enfermedad del corazón**	lah ehn-fehr-meh-*dahd* dehl koh-rah-*sohn*
hemophilia	**la hemofilia**	lah eh-moh-*fee*-leeah
hepatitis A, B, C	**la hepatitis A, B, C**	lah eh-pah-*tee*-tees ah bveh seh

English	Spanish	Pronunciation
high blood pressure	**la alta presión san-guínea**	lah *ahl*-tah preh-see*ohn* sahn-*gee*-nehah
high cholesterol	**el colesterol alto**	ehl koh-lehs-teh-*rohl ahl*-toh
HIV	**VIH**	veh ee *ah*-cheh
hyperthyroidism	**el hipertiroidismo**	ehl ee-pehr-tee-rohee-*dees*-moh
hypoglycemia	**la hipoglicemia**	lah ee-poh-glee-*seh*-meeah
infection	**la infección**	lah een-fehk-see*ohn*
influenza	**la influenza**	lah een-floo*ehn*-sah
kidney stones	**los cálculos en los riñones**	lohs *kahl*-koo-lohs ehn lohs ree-*nyoh*-nehs
laceration (cut)	**la laceración**	lah lah-sehr-ah-see*ohn*
leukemia	**la leucemia**	lah lehoo-*seh*-mee-ah
lupus	**el lupus**	ehl *loo*-poos
Lyme disease	**la enfermedad de Lyme**	lah ehn-fehr-meh-*dahd* deh lyme
malnutrition	**la malnutrición**	lah mahl-noo-tree-see*ohn*
measles	**el sarampión**	ehl sah-rahm-pee-*ohn*
meningitis	**la meningitis**	lah meh-neen-*Hee*-tees
multiple sclerosis	**la esclerosis múltiple**	lah ehs-kleh-*roh*-sees *mool*-tee-pleh
mumps	**las paperas**	lahs pah-*peh*-rahs
muscular dystrophy	**la distrofia muscular**	lah dees-*troh*-feeah moos-koo-*lahr*
osteoporosis	**la osteoporosis**	lah ohs-teh-oh-poh-*roh*-sees
pneumonia	**la pulmonía**	lah pool-moh-*nee*-ah
polio	**la polio**	lah *poh*-leeoh
pregnancy	**el embarazo**	ehl ehm-bah-*rah*-soh
psoriasis	**la soriasis**	lah soh-ree*ah*-sees
rheumatic fever	**la fiebre reumática**	lah fee*eh*-bvreh rehoo-*mah*-tee-kah
scarlet fever	**la escarlatina**	lah ehs-kahr-lah-*tee*-nah
smallpox	**la viruela**	lah bvee-roo*eh*-lah

(continued)

Table 1-3 *(continued)*

English	Spanish	Pronunciation
STDs	**las enfermedades venéreas**	lahs ehn-fehr-meh-*dah*-dehs veh-*neh*-reh-ahs
tetanus	**el tétano**	ehl *teh*-tah-noh
thrombosis	**la trombosis**	lah trohm-*bvoh*-sees
tonsillitus	**la amigdalitis**	lah ah-meeg-dah-*lee*-tees
tuberculosis	**la tuberculosis**	lah too-bvehr-koo-*loh*-sees
typhoid	**la tifoidea**	lah tee-fohee-*deh*-ah
ulcers	**las úlceras**	lahs *ool*-seh-rahs
vertigo	**el vértigo**	ehl *bvehr*-tee-goh
viral infection	**la infección viral**	lah een-fehk-see*ohn* bvee-*rahl*
West Nile virus	**el virus del Nilo Occidental**	ehl *bvee*-roos dehl *nee*-loh ohk-see-dehn-*tahl*
whooping cough	**la tos ferina, la tos convulsiva**	lah tohs feh-*ree*-nah, lah tohs kohn-bvool-*see*-bvah

Recommending treatment

Because treatments can vary so much depending on the illness or condition, we can't possibly provide you with all the phrases you need to deal with every scenario. You can, however, survive the most common situations with the following phrases (refer to Book I, Chapter 2 for dates, times, and numbers, which come in very handy at this stage):

- ✔ *I'll write you a prescription for the medication you need.* **Yo escribiré una receta para la medicación que usted necesita.** (yoh eh-scree-bee-*reh* *oo*-nah reh-*seh*-tah *pah*-rah lah meh-dee-kah-see*ohn* keh oos-*tehd* neh-seh-*see*-tah)

- ✔ *Here is the prescription for the medication you need.* **Aquí está la receta para la medicación que usted necesita.** (ah-*kee* ehs-*tah* lah reh-*seh*-tah *pah*-rah lah meh-dee-kah-see*ohn* keh oos-*tehd* neh-seh-*see*-tah)

- ✔ *I need to give you a vaccination/shot.* **Yo necesito darle una vacunación/ inyección.** (yoh neh-seh-*see*-toh *dahr*-leh *oo*-nah bvah-koo-nah-see*ohn*/ een-yehk-see*ohn*

✔ *Apply this ointment three times a day.* **Aplique este ungüento tres veces al día.** (ah-*plee*-keh *ehs*-teh oon-goo*ehn*-toh trehs *bveh*-sehs ahl *dee*-ah)

✔ *Keep this area clean and dry.* **Mantenga esta área limpia y seca.** (mahn-*tehn*-gah *ehs*-tah *ah*-reh-ah *leem*-peeah ee *seh*-kah)

✔ *Keep your leg elevated when possible.* **Mantenga su pierna elevada cuando sea posible.** (mahn-*tehn*-gah soo peee*ehr*-nah eh-leh-*bvah*-dah koo*ahn*-doh *seh*-ah poh-*see*-bvleh)

✔ *Get plenty of rest.* **Descanse bastante.** (dehs-*kahn*-seh bvah-*stahn*-teh)

✔ *Stay off your feet.* **Manténgase fuera de sus pies.** (mahn-*tehn*-gah-seh foo*eh*-rah deh soos pee*ehs*)

✔ *Drink plenty of fluids.* **Tome líquidos en abundancia.** (*toh*-meh *lee*-kee-dohs ehn ah-bvoon-*dahn*-seeah)

✔ *Take your medicine with food.* **Tome su medicación con la comida.** (*toh*-meh soo meh-dee-kah-seee*ohn* kohn lah koh-*mee*-dah)

✔ *Apply ice to reduce the swelling.* **Aplique hielo para reducir la hinchazón.** (ah-*plee*-keh eee*eh*-loh *pah*-rah reh-doo-*seer* lah een-chah-*sohn*)

✔ *Use a heating pad.* **Utilice una almohadilla de calefacción.** (oo-tee-*lee*-seh *oo*-nah ahl-mohah-*dee*-yah deh kah-leh-fahk-seee*ohn*)

✔ *Take a pain reliever when needed.* **Tome una calmante cuando sea necesario.** (*toh*-meh *oo*-nah kahl-*mahn*-teh koo*ahn*-doh *seh*-ah neh-seh-*sah*-reeoh)

✔ *I will need to stitch this up.* **Yo necesitaré coser la herida.** (yoh neh-seh-see-tah-*reh* koh-*sehr* lah eh-*ree*-dah)

✔ *We will have to run some additional tests.* **Tendremos que hacer unas pruebas adicionales.** (tehn-*dreh*-mohs keh *ah*-sehr *oo*-nahs proo*eh*-bvahs ah-dee-seeoh-*nah*-lehs)

Referring patients to specialists

Book IV

Spanish at Work

Patients often require additional diagnostic procedures and treatment options that you may not be able to provide. In cases such as these, you can refer the patient to a doctor who specializes in a certain field of medicine, as listed in Table 1-4. Use the following phrase followed by whichever area the doctor specializes in:

Necesita ver un especialista en . . . (neh-seh-*see*-tah bvehr oon ehs-peh-seeah-*lees*-tah ehn) (*You need to see a specialist in . . .*)

Table 1-4	Medical Specialties	
English	*Spanish*	*Pronunciation*
cardiology	**la cardiología**	lah kahr-deeoh-loh-*Hee*-ah
dermatology	**la dermatología**	lah dehr-mah-toh-loh-*Hee*-ah
endocrinology	**la endocrinología**	lah ehn-doh-kree-noh-loh-*Hee*-ah
gastroenterology	**la gastroenterología**	lah gah-stroh-ehn-teh-roh-loh-*Hee*-ah
geriatrics	**la geriatría**	lah Heh-reeah-*tree*-ah
gynecology	**la ginecología**	lah Hee-neh-koh-loh-*Hee*-ah
hematology	**la hematología**	lah eh-mah-toh-loh-*Hee*-ah
internal medicine	**la medicina interna**	lah meh-dee-*see*-nah een-*tehr*-nah
nephrology	**la nefrología**	lah neh-froh-loh-*Hee*-ah
neurology	**la neurología**	lah nehoo-roh-loh-*Hee*-ah
nutrition	**la nutrición**	lah noo-tree-see*ohn*
obstetrics	**la obstetricia**	lah ohb-steh-*tree*-seeah
oncology	**la oncología**	lah ohn-coh-loh-*Hee*-ah
ophthalmology	**la oftalmología**	lah ohf-tahl-moh-loh-*Hee*-ah
orthopedics	**la ortopedia**	lah ohr-toh-*peh*-deeah
pediatrics	**la pediatría**	lah peh-deeah-*tree*-ah
pneumology	**la neumología**	lah nehoo-moh-loh-*Hee*-ah
psychiatry	**la psiquiatría**	lah see-keeah-*tree*-ah
psychology	**la psicología**	lah see-koh-loh-*Hee*-ah
radiology	**el radiólogo**	ehl rah-dee*oh*-loh-goh
surgery	**la cirujía**	lah see-roo-*Hee*-ah

Chapter 2

Spanish for Law Enforcement Professionals

As more and more immigrants arrive in the United States, the streets are becoming increasingly multilingual. Spanish is particularly dominant and may often be the language of choice in certain neighborhoods. As a law enforcement professional, you need to protect and serve regardless of race, ethnicity, or language. You can perform your duties much more easily and effectively if you know the language.

In this chapter, we bring you up to speed on the basics of speaking to and understanding people who speak Spanish, including victims, suspects, criminals, and even colleagues. Here, we provide some general terminology that's likely to apply to various situations, along with language suitable for specific common scenarios.

Breaking the Ice with Common Words and Phrases

One of your primary jobs is to communicate with the people you serve . . . even if you happen to be serving them warrants. This process usually involves establishing rapport with the people you're speaking with, collecting information from them, and making them feel safe and secure. In the following sections, we cover some basic language that applies to most situations, so you can manage your initial encounters.

Introducing yourself

Assuming you wear one, a uniform can do wonders to introduce you as a law enforcement officer without requiring that you utter a single word. In most situations, however, you need to introduce yourself and explain a little about what you're doing at the scene. The following phrases can help:

✔ *Good morning/afternoon/evening, my name is Officer [name].* **Buenos días/tardes/ noches, me llamo Agente [Smith].** (boo*eh*-nohs *dee*-ahs/ *tahr*-dehs/*noh*-chehs meh *yah*-moh ah-*Hehn*-teh [Smith])

✔ *I am a police officer.* **Soy un policía.** (sohy oon poh-lee-*see*-ah)

✔ *I need to speak with you.* **Necesito hablar con usted.** (neh-seh-*see*-toh ah-*blahr* cohn oos-*tehd*)

✔ *Come here, please.* **Venga aquí, por favor.** (*bvehn*-gah ah-*kee* pohr fah-*bvohr*)

✔ *I am here to help.* **Estoy aquí para ayudar.** (ehs-*tohy* ah-*kee* pah-rah ah-yoo-*dahr*)

Gathering basic information

You may not realize it, but much of your job consists of gathering information from the people you interact with on a daily basis. You need to know who they are, where they live, how to get in contact with them in the future, where they work, and how they may be related to other people involved in the situation.

Pretend you're a reporter. In most cases, you want to know *who, what, when, where,* and *why.* In the following sections, we help you establish the *who* and the *where.* Later in this chapter, we help you sort out the *what.* For the *when,* check out Book I, Chapter 2, which discusses dates and time. Establishing *why* usually requires an intermediate to advanced understanding of Spanish.

The most basic information you need to collect consists of the person's name, address, and phone number. You may also need the person's Social Security or driver's license number. The following dialogue walks you through an sample info-gathering conversation.

Talkin' the Talk

 Officer Johnny Law gathers some very basic information from María, who called to file a crime report.

Officer Law: **¿Cómo se llama?**
koh-moh seh *yah*-mah
What is your name?

María: **Me llamo María Sánchez.**
meh *yah*-moh mah-*ree*-ah *sahn*-chehs
My name is Maria Sanchez.

Officer Law: **¿Me lo deletrea, por favor?**
meh loh deh-leh-*treh*-ah pohr fah-*bvohr*
Can you please spell that for me?

María: **Claro. Es m-a-r-i-a s-a-n-ch-e-z.**
klah-roh ehs *eh*-meh ah *eh*-reh ee ah *eh*-seh ah
eh-neh cheh ah seh-tah.
Of course. It's m-a-r-i-a -s-a-n-c-h-e-z.

Officer Law: **¿Qué es su dirección?**
keh ehs soo dee-rehk-see*ohn*
What is your address?

María: **Mi dirección es número trescientos cuatro en la calle Main.**
mee dee-rehk-see*ohn* ehs *noo*-meh-roh
treh-see*ehn*-tohs koo*ah*-troh ehn lah *kah*-yeh Main
My address is 304 Main St.

Officer Law: **¿Hace cuánto tiempo vive en esta dirección?**
ah-seh koo*ahn*-toh tee*ehm*-poh *bvee*-bveh ehn
ehs-tah dee-rehk-see*ohn*
How long have you lived at this address?

María: **Hace dos meses.**
ah-seh dohs *meh*-sehs
For two months.

Officer Law: **¿Qué es su número de teléfono?**
keh ehs soo *noo*-meh-roh deh teh-*leh*-foh-noh
What is your phone number?

Book IV

Spanish at Work

María:	**Mi número es cinco-ocho-seis-tres-dos-uno-uno.**
	mee *noo*-meh-roh ehs *seen*-koh *oh*-choh *seh*ees trehs dohs *oo*-noh *oo*-noh
	My number is 586-3211.

Finding out what someone does for a living

You can begin to discover a great deal about a person you're talking to by finding out what the person does for a living. Ask the following question and then consult Table 2-1 for answers you're likely to hear.

¿Qué empleo tiene usted? (keh ehm-*pleh*-oh tee*eh*-neh oos-*tehd*) *(What is your occupation?)*

Table 2-1	Common Jobs/Careers	
English	*Spanish*	*Pronunciation*
I am a (an) . . .	**Yo soy un/una . . .**	yoh sohy oon/*oo*-nah
baker	**panadero/a**	pah-nah-*deh*-roh/rah
banker	**banquero/a**	bahn-*keh*-roh/rah
business owner	**propietario/a**	proh-peeeh-*tah*-reeoh/ah
butcher	**carnicero/a**	kahr-nee-*seh*-roh/rah
carpenter	**carpintero/a**	kahr-peen-teh-roh/rah
cashier	**cajero/a**	kah-H*eh*-roh/rah
construction worker	**obrero/a de la construcción**	oh-*breh*-roh/rah deh lah *koh*-strook-see*ohn*
cook	**cocinero/a**	kohn-see-*neh*-roh/rah
dancer	**bailador/a**	bahee-lah-*dohr*/ah
dishwasher	**lavaplatos**	lah-bvah-*plah*-tohs
doctor	**doctór/a**	dohk-*tohr*/ah
domestic worker	**empleado/a doméstico/a**	ehm-leh-*ah*-doh doh-*mehs*-tee-koh/kah
electrician	**electricista**	ee-lehk-tree-*sees*-tah
employee	**empleado/a**	ehm-pleh-*ah*-doh/dah
engineer	**ingeniero/a**	een-Hehn-ee*eh*-roh/rah
gardener	**jardinero/a**	Hahr-dee-*neh*-roh/rah

English	Spanish	Pronunciation
janitor	**conserje**	kohn-*sehr*-Heh
landscaper	**paisajista**	pahee-sah-*Hees*-tah
manager (restaurant, store)	**gerente**	Heh-*rehn*-teh
manager (team)	**entrenador/a**	ehn-trehn-ah-*dohr*/ah
mechanic	**mecánico/a**	meh-*kah*-nee-koh/kah
musician	**músico/a**	*moo*-see-koh/kah
nurse	**enfermero/a**	ehn-fehr-*meh*-roh/rah
painter	**pintor/a**	peen-*tohr*/ah
plumber	**plomero/a**	ploh-*meh*-roh/rah
reporter	**periodista**	peh-reeoh-*dees*-tah
roofer	**techador/a**	teh-chah-*dohr*/ah
salesperson	**vendedor/a**	bvehn-deh-*dohr*/ah
teacher	**maestro/a**	mah-*ehs*-troh/trah
technician	**técnico/a**	*tehk*-nee-koh/kah
waiter/waitress	**mesero/a**	meh-*seh*-roh/rah
worker	**trabajador/a**	trah-bah-Hah-*dohr*/ah
workman (laborer)	**obrero/a**	oh-*breh*-roh/rah

Finding out who's related to whom and how

When you arrive on the scene, you're likely to be dealing with two or more people who may be related. How they're related is one of the first things you need to find out. The following questions can come in handy:

- *Are you related to him/her?* **¿Es él/ella pariente suyo?** (ehs ehl/*eh*-yah pah-ree*ehn*-teh *soo*-yoh)

- *What kinship is he/she to you?* **¿Qué parentesco tiene él/ella con usted?** (keh pah-rehn-*tehs*-koh tee*eh*-neh ehl/*eh*-yah kohn oos-*tehd*)

- *Are you married?* **¿Están ustedes casados?** (ehs-*tahn* oos-*teh*-dehs kah-*sah*-dohs)

After you've asked the appropriate question, check out Table 2-2 for answers you're likely to hear.

Table 2-2	Family Relations and Friends	
English	*Spanish*	*Pronunciation*
boyfriend/girlfriend	**novio/a**	*noh*-bveeoh/ah
brother/sister	**hermano/a**	ehr-*mah*-noh/nah
brother/sister-in-law	**cuñado/a**	koo-*nyah*-doh/dah
cousin	**primo/a**	*pree*-moh/mah
daughter-in-law	**nuera**	noo*eh*-rah
ex-husband/wife	**ex-esposo/a**	ehks-ehs-*poh*-soh/sah
father	**padre**	*pah*-dreh
father/mother-in-law	**suegro/a**	soo*eh*-groh/grah
friend	**amigo/a**	ah-*mee*-goh/gah
godson/daughter	**ahijado/a**	ah-ee-*Hah*-doh/dah
grandfather/grandmother	**abuelo/a**	ah-*bvooeh*-loh/lah
grandson/daughter	**nieto/a**	nee-*eh*-toh/tah
husband/wife	**esposo/a**	ehs-*poh*-soh/sah
mother	**madre**	*mah*-dreh
nephew/niece	**sobrino/a**	soh-*bree*-noh/nah
son/daughter	**hijo/a**	ee-Hoh/Hah
son-in-law	**yerno**	*yehr*-noh
stepbrother/sister	**hermanastro/a**	ehr-mah-*nahs*-troh/trah
stepfather	**padrastro**	pah-*drahs*-troh
stepmother	**madrastra**	mah-*drahs*-trah
stepson/daughter	**hijastro/a**	ee-*Hahs*-troh/trah
uncle/aunt	**tío/a**	*tee*-oh/ah

Establishing locations

When speaking to possible witnesses, suspects, and other parties of interest, you often have to establish where something happened, where somebody is, where you need to meet someone, or where a person must go at some future time. One of the best ways to establish a location is to refer to actual locations, such as a home or apartment, a store, a restaurant, or a gas station. Here are some questions you may ask to determine where an event occurred:

✔ *Where did that happen?* **¿Dónde ocurrió eso?** (*dohn*-deh oh-koo-rree*oh eh*-soh)

✔ *Where were you at the time?* **¿Dónde estaba usted cuando ocurrió?** (*dohn*-deh ehs-*tah*-bvah oos-*tehd* kooan-doh oh-koo-rreeoh)

✔ *Where are you going now?* **¿Adónde va usted ahora?** (ah-*dohn*-deh bvah oos-*tehd* ah-*oh*-rah)

✔ *Where do they live?* **¿Dónde viven ellos?** (*dohn*-deh *bvee*-bvehn *eh*-yohs)

Table 2-3 reveals the names of locations that people commonly refer to.

Table 2-3	Common Locations	
English	*Spanish*	*Pronunciation*
the apartment	**el apartamento**	ehl ah-pahr-tah-*mehn*-toh
the bakery	**la panadería**	ehl pah-nah-deh-*ree*-ah
the bank	**el banco**	ehl *bvahn*-koh
the bar	**el bar**	ehl bvahr
the block	**la cuadra**	lah kooah-drah
the clothing store	**la tienda de ropa**	lah teeehn-dah deh roh-pah
the condominium	**el condominio**	lah kahn-doh-*mee*-neeoh
the dance club	**la discoteca**	lah dees-koh-*teh*-kah
the downtown	**el centro**	ehl *sehn*-troh
the east side	**al este**	ahl *ehs*-teh
the grocery store	**el mercado**	ehl mehr-*kah*-doh
the home	**la casa**	lah *kah*-sah
the meat store	**la carnicería**	lah kahr-nee-seh-*ree*-ah
the north side	**al norte**	ahl *nohr*-teh
the park	**el parque**	ehl *pahr*-keh
the pharmacy	**la farmacia**	lah fahr-*mah*-seeah
the restaurant	**el restaurante**	ehl rehs-tahooh-*rahn*-teh
the river	**el río**	ehl *ree*-oh
the south side	**al sur**	ahl soor
the sport club	**el club deportivo**	ehl cloob deh-pohr-*tee*-voh
the stadium	**el estadio**	ehl ehs-*tah*-deeoh
the store (small)	**la tienda**	lah teeehn-dah
the street	**la calle**	lah *kah*-yeh
the subway	**el metro**	ehl *meh*-troh
the supermarket	**el supermercado**	ehl soo-pehr-mehr-*kah*-doh
the west side	**al oeste**	ahl oh-*ehs*-teh

Book IV

Spanish at Work

You're also likely to give directions or have to interpret directions given to you in Spanish. For more about directions, see Book I, Chapter 4.

Dealing with Traffic Violations

Whenever you have to pull somebody over for speeding or some other traffic violation, you usually have to gather some basic information, as discussed earlier in this chapter, along with some more-specific details. In addition, you need to inform the person why you pulled them over. The following sections can get you through most routine traffic stops.

Pulling over a driver

When you need to stop a driver who committed a traffic violation (or for whatever reason), you may need to issue some commands to protect yourself, the person you're pulling over, and others in the area. Following are some common commands:

- ✔ *Pull over!* **¡Pare en el acotamiento!** (*pah*-reh ehn ehl ah-koh-tah-mee*ehn*-toh)

- ✔ *Stop the vehicle!* **¡Pare el vehículo!** (*pah*-reh ehl bveh-*ee*-koo-loh)

- ✔ *Turn off your engine!* **¡Pare el motor!** (*pah*-reh ehl moh-*tohr*)

- ✔ *Stay inside the vehicle!* **¡Quédese en el vehículo!** (*keh*-deh-seh ehn ehl bveh-*ee*-koo-loh)

- ✔ *Keep your hands on the steering wheel!* **¡Quédese con las manos en el volante!** (*keh*-deh-seh kohn lahs *mah*-nohs ehn ehl bvoh-*lahn*-teh)

Requesting a driver's information

License, registration, and proof of insurance . . . asking for these three items sounds so easy until you pull over a driver who doesn't speak your language. If you're lucky, someone else in the car is bilingual in English and can translate for you. If not, the following phrases should be enough to get what you need:

- ✔ *May I see your driver's license?* **¿Puedo ver su licencia para conducir?** (poo*eh*-doh bvehr soo lee-*sehn*-seeah *pah*-rah kohn-doo-*seer*)

- ✔ *May I see your vehicle registration?* **¿Puedo ver su permiso de circulación?** (poo*eh*-doh bvehr soo pehr-*mee*-soh deh seer-koo-lah-see*ohn*)

✔ *Do you have insurance?* **¿Tiene usted seguro de automóvil?** (tee*eh*-neh oos-*tehd* seh-*goo*-roh deh ahoo-toh-*moh*-bveel)

✔ *What is the name of your insurance company?* **¿Cómo se llama la compañía de seguros?** (*koh*-moh seh *yah*-mah lah kohm-pah-*nyee*-ah deh seh-*goo*-rohs)

✔ *What is the phone number of your insurance company?* **¿Qué es el número de teléfono de la compañía de seguros?** (keh ehs ehl *noo*-meh-roh deh teh-*leh*-foh-noh deh lah kohm-pah-*nyee*-ah deh seh-*goo*-rohs)

✔ *What is the name of your insurance agent?* **¿Cómo se llama el agente de seguros?** (*koh*-moh seh *yah*-mah ehl ah-*Hehn*-teh deh seh-*goo*-rohs)

If the driver is unable to produce a driver's license, you may be dealing with someone who recently arrived in the United States and doesn't have a license. In cases like these, you probably need to ask additional questions, such as the following:

✔ *Are you a United States citizen?* **¿Es usted ciudadano/a de los Estados Unidos?** (ehs oos-*tehd* seeoo-dah-*dah*-noh/ah deh lohs ehs-*tah*-dohs oo-*nee*-dohs)

✔ *What country are you from?* **¿De qué país es usted?** (deh keh pah*ees* ehs oos-*tehd*)

Explaining why you stopped the driver

At some point in your conversation with the driver, you need to inform her why you stopped her and perhaps issue a warning or a ticket for a traffic violation. The following phrases can help you get your point across:

✔ *You were driving too fast.* **Usted estaba manejando demasiado rápido.** (oos-*tehd* ehs-*tah*-bvah mah-neh-*Hahn*-doh deh-mah-see*ah*-doh *rah*-pee-doh)

✔ *You didn't stop at the red light.* **Se pasó una luz roja.** (seh pah-*soh* oo-nah loos *roh*-Hah)

✔ *You didn't stop at the stop sign.* **Se pasó el señal de stop.** (seh pah-*soh* ehl seh-*nyahl* deh stohp)

✔ *You were driving dangerously.* **Usted estaba manejando peligrosamente.** (oos-*tehd* ehs-*tah*-bvah mah-neh-*Hahn*-doh peh-lee-groh-sah-*mehn*-teh)

✔ *You made an illegal turn.* **Usted giró ilegalmente.** (oos-*tehd* hee-*roh* ee-leh-gahl-*mehn*-teh)

Book IV

Spanish at Work

✔ *You were going the wrong way down a one-way street.* **Usted se metió en contra-dirección por una calle de sentido único.** (oos-*tehd* seh meh-tee*oh* ehn *kohn*-trah dee-rehk-see*ohn* pohr *oo*-nah *kah*-yeh deh sehn-*tee*-doh *oo*-nee-koh)

✔ *I have to give you a ticket for the traffic violation.* **Tengo que darle una multa por la infracción de tráfico.** (*tehn*-goh keh *dahr*-leh *oo*-nah *mool*-tah pohr lah een-frahk-see*ohn* deh *trah*-fee-koh)

✔ *Please sign here.* **Firme aquí, por favor.** (*feer*-meh ah-*kee* pohr fah-*bvohr*)

Interviewing Witnesses

Before you can resolve disagreements and other issues or solve a crime, you almost always need to gather information from the people involved, along with anyone who may have seen what happened — your witnesses. In the following sections, we introduce you to key questions you need to ask as well as words and phrases that can help you understand the answers you're likely to hear in response.

Keep it simple and focus on the facts. Otherwise, you're likely to be overwhelmed in trying to process all the information. In addition, when possible, ask yes/no questions and other questions that can be answered with only a word or a short phrase.

Asking some opening questions

Your first order of business usually consists of identifying possible suspects. The following questions can help you narrow your list:

✔ *Did you see what happened?* **¿Vió usted que ocurrió?** (bvee*oh* oos-*tehd* keh oh-koo-rree*oh*)

✔ *Can you describe the people involved?* **¿Puede describir las personas involucradas?** (poo*eh*-deh dehs-kree-*bveer* lahs pehr-*soh*-nahs een-bvoh-loo-*krah*-dahs)

✔ *Are you willing to testify in court?* **¿Está usted dispuesto/a a testificar ante un tribunal?** (ehs-*tah* oos-*tehd* dees-poo*ehs*-toh/tah ah tehs-tee-fee-*kahr* ahn-teh oon tree-boo-nahl)

Asking "What happened?"

Asking *What happened?* **¿Qué ocurrió?** (keh oh-koo-rree*oh*) is likely to over-whelm you with a lot more information than you need and certainly more Spanish than you may be able to handle. To figure out what happened, take more control over the discussion. Here are some questions that can help:

- *Are you hurt?* **¿Está usted herido/a?** (ehs-*tah* oos-*tehd* eh-*ree*-doh/dah)

- *Is anybody hurt?* **¿Hay alguién herido?** (ay ahl-gee*ehn* eh-*ree*-doh)

- *Did he/she hit you?* **¿Le pegó él/ella?** (leh peh-g*oh* ehl/*eh*-yah)

- *Was something stolen from you?* **¿Fue algo robado de usted?** (foo*eh* *ahl*-goh roh-*bah*-doh deh oos-*tehd*)

- *Have you been drinking alcohol?* **¿Ha tomado alcohol?** (ah toh-*mah*-doh ahl-koh-*ohl*)

- *Have you been taking drugs?* **¿Ha tomado drogas?** (ah toh-*mah*-doh *droh*-gahs)

- *Have you taken any medication?* **¿Ha tomado algún medicamento?** (ah toh-*mah*-doh ahl-*goon* meh-dee-kah-*mehn*-toh)

- *Was a weapon used? A gun? A knife?* **¿Fue usado un arma? ¿Una pistola? ¿Un cuchillo?** (foo*eh* oo-*sah*-doh oon *ahr*-mah *oo*-nah pees-*toh*-lah oon koo-*chee*-yoh)

- *Is there damage to your property?* **¿Hay daño a su propiedad?** (ay *dah*-nyoh ah soo proh-pee*eh*-*dahd*)

- *Did you argue with the suspect?* **¿Discutó con el/la sospechoso/a?** (dees-koo-*toh* kohn ehl/lah sohs-peh-*choh*-soh/sah)

- *Did you physically fight with the suspect?* **¿Luchó usted con el/la sospechoso/a?** (loo-*choh* oos-*tehd* kohn ehl/lah sohs-peh-*choh*-soh/sah)

Table 2-4 lists the names of some of the most common crimes and misde-meanors to help you gain a clearer understanding of what your witnesses are reporting.

Table 2-4	Common Crimes and Misdemeanors	
English	*Spanish*	*Pronunciation*
the assault	**el asalto**	ehl ah-*sahl*-toh
the attack	**el ataque**	ehl ah-*tah*-keh

(continued)

Table 2-4 *(continued)*

English	Spanish	Pronunciation
the vandalism	**el vandalismo**	ehl bvahn-dah-*lees*-moh
the identity theft	**el robo de identidad**	ehl *roh*-boh deh ee-dehn-tee-dahd
the murder	**el asesinato**	ehl ah-seh-see-*nah*-toh
the rape	**la violación**	lah bveeoh-lah-see*ohn*
the robbery/theft	**el robo**	ehl *roh*-boh
the shoplifting	**el hurto en las tiendas**	ehl *oor*-toh ehn lahs tee*ehn*-dahs
the shooting	**el ataque con disparos**	ehl ah-*tah*-keh kohn dees-*pah*-rohs
the stabbing	**el apuñalamiento**	ehl ah-poo-nyah-lah-mee*ehn*-toh

Getting a suspect's description

If you're extremely lucky, the suspect has remained at the scene, and your witnesses can point him out. But how often does that happen? In most cases, you need to get a description of the suspect from one or more witnesses. Here are some initial questions that can help:

- *Do you know the suspect?* **¿Conoce al sospechoso?** (koh-*noh*-seh ahl sohs-peh-*choh*-soh)

- *What is the suspect's complete name?* **¿Qué es el nombre completo del sospechoso?** (keh ehs ehl *nohm*-breh kohm-*pleh*-toh dehl sohs-peh-*choh*-soh)

- *Where does the suspect live?* **¿Dónde vive el sospechoso?** (*dohn*-deh *bvee*-bveh ehl sohs-peh-*choh*-soh)

- *Can you tell me the suspect's phone number?* **¿Puede usted decirme el número de teléfono del sospechoso?** (poo*eh*-deh oos-*tehd* deh-*seer*-meh ehl *noo*-meh-roh deh teh-*leh*-foh-noh dehl sohs-peh-*choh*-soh)

If the person doesn't know the suspect, you need to take down a description of the person. Ask the following questions, and use the physical traits in Table 2-5 to interpret the answers:

- *Is the suspect a man or a woman?* **¿Es el sospechoso un hombre o una mujer?** (ehs ehl sohs-peh-*choh*-soh oon *ohm*-bvreh oh *oo*-nah moo-*Hehr*)

- *What nationality is the suspect?* **¿De qué nacionalidad es el sospechoso?** (deh keh nah-seeoh-nah-lee-*dahd* ehs ehl sohs-peh-*cho*-soh)

✔ *How tall is the suspect?* **¿Qué mide el sospechoso?** (keh *mee*-deh ehl sohs-peh-*choh*-soh)

✔ *Approximately how much does the suspect weigh?* **Aproximadamente, ¿cuánto pesa el sospechoso?** (ah-proh-ksee-mah-dah-*mehn*-teh koo*ahn*-toh *peh*-sah ehl sohs-peh-*choh*-soh)

✔ *Approximately how old is the suspect?* **Aproximadamente, ¿cuántos años tiene el sospechoso?** (ah-proh-ksee-mah-dah-*mehn*-teh koo*ahn*-tohs *ah*-nyohs tee*eh*-neh ehl sohs-peh-*choh*-soh)

✔ *What color is the suspect's hair?* **¿De qué color es el pelo del sospechoso?** (deh keh koh-*lohr* ehs ehl *peh*-loh dehl sohs-peh-*choh*-soh)

✔ *Is the suspect's hair long, medium, or short?* **¿Es el pelo del sospechoso largo, mediano, o corto?** (ehs ehl *peh*-loh dehl sohs-peh-*choh*-soh *lahr*-goh meh-dee*ah*-noh oh *kohr*-toh)

✔ *What color are the suspect's eyes?* **¿De qué color son los ojos del sospechoso?** (deh keh koh-*lohr* sohn lohs *oh*-Hohs dehl sohs-peh-*choh*-soh)

✔ *Does the suspect have a mustache or beard?* **¿Tiene el sospechoso bigote o barba?** (tee*eh*-neh ehl sohs-peh-*choh*-soh bvee-*goh*-teh oh *bvahr*-bvah)

✔ *Does the suspect have any tattoos? Where?* (For a complete list of body parts, see Book IV, Chapter 1.) **¿Tiene el sospechoso algún tatuaje? ¿Dónde?** (tee*eh*-neh ehl sohs-peh-*choh*-soh ahl-*goon* tah-too-*ah*-Heh *dohn*-deh)

Table 2-5	**Physical Traits**	
English	*Spanish*	*Pronunciation*
dark skin	**piel oscura**	pee*ehl* ohs-*koo*-rah
light skin	**piel clara**	pee*ehl klah*-rah
Nationalities		
African American	**negro/a**	*neh*-groh/grah
Cuban	**cubano/a**	koo-*bvah*-noh/nah
European	**europeo/a**	ehoo-roh-*peh*-oh/ah
Latino	**latino/a**	lah-*tee*-noh/nah
Mexican American	**estadounidense de origen mejicano**	ehs-tah-doh-oo-nee-*dehn*-seh deh oh-*ree*-Hehn meh-Hee-*kah*-noh
Mexican	**mejicano/a**	meh-Hee-kah-noh/nah
Mexican, U.S.-born	**pocho/a**	poh-choh
	moreno/a	moh-reh-noh

(continued)

Table 2-5 (continued)

English	Spanish	Pronunciation
Puerto Rican	puertorriqueño/a	pooehr-toh-rree-*keh*-nyoh/nyah
U.S.	estadounidense	ehs-tah-doh-oo-nee-*dehn*-seh
U.S., Mexican-born	chicano/a	chee-kah-noh/nah
Height		
very tall	muy alto/a	mooy *ahl*-toh
tall	alto/a	*ahl*-toh/tah
medium height	de mediana estatura	deh meh-dee*ah*-nah ehs-tah-*too*-rah
short	bajo/a	*bvah*-Hoh/Hah
very short	muy bajo/a	mooy *bvah*-Hoh/Hah
Body type/shape		
skinny	flaco	*flah*-koh
thin	delgado	dehl-*gah*-doh
medium	mediano	meh-dee*ah*-noh
fat	gordo	*gohr*-doh
	panzón	pahn-*sohn*
muscular	musculoso	moos-koo-*loh*-soh
Approximate age		
old	viejo	bvee*eh*-Hoh
young	joven	*Hoh*-bvehn
teenager/adolescent	adolescente	ah-doh-leh-*sehn*-teh
middle-aged man	hombre maduro	*ohm*-bvreh mah-*doo*-roh
middle-aged woman	mujer madura	moo-*Hehr* mah-*doo*-rah
Hair color		
black	negro	*neh*-groh
blond	rubio	*roo*-bvee-oh
brown	café	kah-*feh*
brunette	moreno	moh-*reh*-noh
gray	canoso	kah-*noh*-soh
red	rojo	*roh*-Hoh
	pelirrojo	peh-lee-*roh*-Hoh

English	Spanish	Pronunciation
Hair style/type		
bald	**pelón**	peh-*lohn*
braids	**trenzas**	*trehn*-sahs
curly	**pelo rizado**	*peh*-loh ree-*sah*-doh
long	**pelo largo**	*peh*-loh *lahr*-goh
short	**pelo corto**	*peh*-loh *kohr*-toh
pony tail	**cola/cola de caballo**	*koh*-lah/*koh*-lah deh kah-*bvah*-yoh
straight	**pelo lacio**	*peh*-loh *lah*-seeoh
wavy	**pelo ondulado**	*peh*-loh ohn-doo-*lah*-doh
Mustache/beard		
beard	**barba**	*bvahr*-bvah
goatee	**perilla**	peh-*ree*-yah
mustache	**bigote**	bvee-*goh*-teh
sideburns	**patillas**	pah-*tee*-yahs
clean shaven	**bien afeitado**	bvee*ehn* ah-fehee-*tah*-doh

Taking a Suspect into Custody

Apprehending a suspect is probably the most dangerous aspects of your job. Communicating clearly and assertively is the key to ensuring that the suspect does nothing to endanger you, himself, or anyone else in the vicinity. Following are translations of some of the most common commands you're likely to issue when apprehending a suspect:

- ✔ *Police officer, stop!* **Soy un policía, ¡alto!** (sohy oon poh-lee-*see*-ah *ahl*-toh)

- ✔ *Don't move!* **¡No se mueva!** (noh seh moo*eh*-bvah)

- ✔ *Hands up!* or *Hands on your head!* **¡Manos arriba! ¡Manos en la cabeza!** (*mah*-nohs ah-*rree*-bvah *mah*-nohs ehn lah kah-*bveh*-sah)

- ✔ *Drop the weapon!* **¡Suelte el arma!** (soo*ehl*-teh ehl *ahr*-mah)

- ✔ *Lie face down on the ground!* **¡Acuéstese cara abajo!** (ah-koo*ehs*-teh-seh *kah*-rah ah-*bvah*-Hoh)

- ✔ *Turn around!* **¡Voltéese!** (bvohl-*teh*-eh-seh)

Book IV

Spanish at Work

✔ *Put your hands behind your back!* **¡Ponga las manos detrás de la espalda!** (*pohn*-gah lahs *mah*-nohs deh-*trahs* deh lah ehs-*pahl*-dah)

✔ *Spread your legs!* **¡Extienda las piernas!** (eks-tee*ehn*-dah lahs pee*ehr*-nahs)

✔ *Don't talk!* **¡No hable!** (noh *ah*-bvleh)

✔ *I am going to search you. Do you have anything dangerous in your pockets?* **Voy a registrarlo. ¿Tiene algo peligroso en sus bolsillos?** (bvoy ah reh-Hees-*trahr*-loh tee*eh*-neh *ahl*-goh peh-lee-*groh*-soh ehn soos bvohl-*see*-yohs)

✔ *You're under arrest.* **Usted está arrestado.** (oos-*tehd* ehs-*tah* ah-rrehs-*tah*-doh)

After taking the suspect into custody, you need to inform them of their *Miranda rights* — their rights to remain silent and have a lawyer:

You have the right to remain silent. **Usted tiene el derecho de guardar silencio/mantener silencio.** (oos-*tehd* tee*eh*-neh ehl deh-*reh*-choh deh gooahr-*dahr* see-*lehn*-seeoh/mahn-teh-*nehr* see-*lehn*-seeoh)

Anything you say can and may be used against you in the court of law. **Lo que diga puede ser usado en su contra.** (loh keh *dee*-gah poo*eh*-deh sehr oo-*sah*-doh ehn soo *kohn*-trah)

You have the right to an attorney and to have an attorney with you during questioning. **Tiene el derecho a un abogado y tenerlo presente durante la interrogacion.** (tee*eh*-neh ehl deh-*reh*-choh ah oon ah-bvoh-*gah*-doh ee-teh-*nehr*-loh preh-*sehn*-teh doo-*rahn*-teh lah een-teh-reh-gah-see*ohn*)

If you cannot afford to hire an attorney, one will be appointed for you before any questioning if you desire. **Si no tiene dinero para conseguir un abogado, uno le será designado antes de cualquier pregunta, si usted desea.** (see noh tee*eh*-neh dee-*neh*-roh *pah*-rah kohn-seh-*geer* oon ah-bvoh-*gah*-doh *oo*-noh leh seh-*rah* deh-seeg-*nah*-doh *ahn*-tehs deh kooahl-kee*ehr* preh-*goon*-tah see oos-*tehd* deh-*seh*-ah)

Do you understand? **¿Entiende usted?** (ehn-tee*ehn*-deh oos-*tehd*)

Do you wish to talk? **¿Quiere hablar?** (kee*eh*-reh ah-*bvlahr*)

Have the suspect and a witness sign and date a printed copy of the Miranda rights (in Spanish) when you get back to the station.

Chapter 3

Spanish for Educators and Administrators

As more and more immigrants from Spanish-speaking countries arrive in the United States, schools around the country have struggled to accommodate the influx of students from homes in which the first language is Spanish. As a teacher or school administrator, you want to help these students learn English as quickly as possible, but in the meantime, you may need to pick up a little Spanish in order to ease the transition.

This chapter is for teachers, school administrators, and staff who interact with Spanish-speaking students and their families. It covers everything from admissions to dealing with students in and out of the classroom and communicating with parents.

Admitting New Students

When a student shows up to enroll in your school, she and her parents may feel completely lost. Unless they've enrolled in school before, they may be unaware of the type of information and documentation they need to bring with them, and you may be completely at a loss when it comes to asking questions and gathering information.

Fortunately, you can handle most situations by being prepared in advance — by having the required forms translated into Spanish. In the following sections, we provide a couple of basic forms along with common words and phrases to use during the enrollment process.

Leading parents through the enrollment process

Although you can certainly gather much of the information you need from the forms provided in this chapter, you still need to greet the parents and perhaps the student and lead them through the enrollment process. Book I, Chapters 3 and 4 can be useful in bringing you up to speed on greeting Spanish-speakers and engaging them in some small talk.

Talkin' the Talk

Mrs. Muñoz has shown up at school to register her child for the upcoming school year. Mr. Kissle, a parent helping out during the enrollment period, greets Mrs. Muñoz, who doesn't speak very much English, and leads her through the process.

Mr. Kissle: **Buenos días. ¿Cómo puedo ayudarle?**
bvoo*eh*-nohs *dee*-ahs *koh*-moh pooo*eh*-doh
ah-yoo-*dahr*-leh
Good day. How may I help you?

Mrs. Muñoz: **Quisiera matricular a mi hijo/a.**
kee-see*eh*-rah mah-tree-koo-*lahr* ah mee ee-Hoh/Hah
I would like to enroll my child.

Mr. Kissle: **Siéntense, por favor.**
see*eh*-tehn-seh pohr fah-*bvohr*
Please have a seat.

Mrs. Muñoz: **Gracias.**
grah-seeahs
Thank you.

Mr. Kissle: **Necesitamos hacer una copia del Acta de Nacimiento, y la Tarjeta de Seguro Social de su hijo.**
neh-seh-see-*tah*-mohs ah-*sehr* oo-nah *koh*-peeah dehl *ahk*-tah deh nah-see-mee*eh*-toh ee lah tahr-*Heh*-tah deh seh-*goo*-roh soh-see*ahl* deh soo ee-Hoh

We need to make a copy of your child's birth certificate and Social Security card.

También necesita tener una prueba de residencia en el distrito.
tahm-bvee*ehn* neh-seh-*see*-tah teh-*nehr* oo-nah proo*eh*-bvah deh reh-see-*dehn*-seeah ehn ehl dees-*tree*-toh
Also, you need to show proof of residency in the district.

Mrs. Muñoz: **Está bien. Aquí tengo el Acta de Nacimiento y su Tarjeta de Seguro Social.**
ehs-*tah* bvee*ehn* ah-*kee* tehn-goh ehl *ahk*-tah deh nah-see-mee*ehn*-toh ee soo tahr-*Heh*-tah deh seh-*goo*-roh soh-see*ahl*
Fine. Here I have the birth certificate and Social Security card.

También tengo el Expediente de Vacunas.
tahm-bee*ehn tehn*-goh ehl ehks-peh-dee*ehn*-teh deh bvah-*koo*-nahs
I also have the certificate of vaccinations.

Mr. Kissle: **Excelente. Haré una fotocopia de esos documentos ahora mismo.**
ehk-kseh-*lehn*-teh ah-*reh* oo-nah foh-toh-*koh*-peeah deh *eh*-sohs doh-koo-*mehn*-tohs ah-*oh*-rah *mees*-moh
Fine. I will make a photocopy of those documents right now.

¿Tiene un recibo de un servicio público para la prueba de residencia?
tee*eh*-neh oon reh-*see*-bvoh deh oon sehr-*bvee*-seeoh *poo*-bvlee-koh *pah*-rah lah proo*eh*-bvah deh reh-see-*dehn*-seeah
Do you have a public utilities' receipt to show proof of residency?

Mrs. Muñoz: **No, hoy no traigo. ¿Puedo traerlo otro día?**
noh ohy noh trah*ee*-goh poo*eh*-doh trah*ehr*-loh *oh*-troh *dee*-ah
No, I didn't bring one today. Can I bring it another day?

Mr. Kissle: **Claro que sí. Sería perfectamente bien. Dentro de una semana sería lo mejor.**
klah-roh keh see seh-*ree*-ah pehr-fehk-tah-*mehn*-teh bvee*ehn dehn*-troh deh *oo*-nah seh-*mah*-nah seh-*ree*-ah loh meh-*Hohr*
Yes, of course. That would be perfectly fine. Within a week would be best.

Mrs. Muñoz: **Bien. ¿Hay algo más?**
bvee*ehn* ahy *ahl*-goh mahs
Okay. Is there anything else?

Mr. Kissle: **Sí. Necesita rellenar la Hoja de Matrícula y el Historial de Salud.**
see neh-seh-*see*-tah reh-yeh-*nahr* lah *oh*-Hah deh mah-*tree*-koo-lah ee ehl ees-toh-ree*ahl* deh sah-*lood*
Yes. You need to fill out this enrollment form and a health history form.

    También hay una forma de información que necesitamos en el caso de una emergencia.
tahm-bvee*ehn* ahy *oo*-nah *fohr*-mah deh een-fohr-mah-see*ohn* keh neh-seh-see-*tah*-mohs ehn ehl *kah*-soh deh *oo*-nah eh-mehr-*Hehn*-seeah
Also, there is an emergency information form in the case of an emergency.

Mrs. Muñoz: **Claro. No problema.**
klah-roh noh proh-*bvleh*-mah
Of course. No problem.

Mr. Kissle: **Aquí están las formas necesarias.**
ah-*kee* ehs-*tahn* lahs *fohr*-mahs neh-seh-*sah*-reeahs
Here are the necessary forms.

    Usted puede sentarse en la mesa allí para escribir.
oos-*tehd* poo*eh*-deh sehn-*tahr*-seh ehn lah *meh*-sah ah-*yee pah*-rah ehs-kree-*bveer*
You can sit at the table there to write.

    ¿Necesita un bolígrafo?
neh-seh-*see*-tah oon bvoh-*lee*-grah-foh
Do you need a pen?

Mrs. Muñoz: **Sí, por favor.**
see pohr fah-*bvohr*
Yes, please.

Mr. Kissle: **Aquí está un bolígrafo.**
ah-*kee* ehs-*tah* oon bvoh-*lee*-grah-foh
Here is a pen.

**Pregúnteme si hay algo que no entiende o si tiene
alguna pregunta.**
preh-*goon*-teh-me see ahy *ahl*-goh keh noh
ehn-tee*ehn*-deh oh see tee*eh*-neh ahl-*goo*-nah
preh-*goon*-tah
*Ask me if there is anything that you don't understand
or if you have any questions.*

Mrs. Muñoz: **Gracias.**
grah-seeahs
Thank you.
After some time:

Perdón, aquí están las formas completadas.
pehr-*dohn* ah-*kee* ehs-*tahn* lahs *fohr*-mahs
kohm-pleh-*tah*-dahs
Excuse me, here are the completed forms.

Mr. Kissle: **Gracias. ¿Firmó usted todas las formas?**
grah-seeahs feer-*moh* oos-*tehd toh*-dahs lahs
fohr-mahs
Thank you. Did you sign all of the forms?

Mrs. Muñoz: **Sí.**
see
Yes.

Mr. Kissle: **Bien. Entonces eso es todo lo que necesitamos.**
bvee*ehn* ehn-*tohn*-sees *eh*-soh ehs *toh*-doh loh keh
neh-seh-see-*tah*-mohs
Good. Then that is everything that we need.

**Aquí está una copia del calendario para la escuela y
la lista de lo que necesitará su hijo/a para la clase.**
ah-*kee* ehs-*tah* oo-nah *koh*-peeah dehl
kah-lehn-*dah*-reeoh *pah*-rah lah ehs-koo*eh*-lah ee lah
lees-tah deh loh keh neh-seh-see-tah-*rah* soo ee-Hoh/
Hah *pah*-rah lah *klah*-seh

Book IV

**Spanish
at Work**

Here is a copy of the school calendar and the list of what your child will need for class.

Muchas gracias por haber venido. Ha sido un placer conocerlos.
moo-chahs grah-seeahs pohr ah-bvehr bveh-nee-doh ah see-doh oon plah-sehr koh-noh-sehr-lohs
Thank you so much for coming. It has been a pleasure to meet you both (all).

Mrs. Muñoz: **Igualmente, gracias. Adiós.**
ee-guahl-mehn-teh grah-seeahs ah-deeohs
Likewise, thank you. Good-bye.

Gathering personal and contact information

Whenever students show up to enroll in your school, you have a standard form they need to complete for passing on all the relevant data, including the student's name, address, and phone number; contact information for the parents; the student's birthday and grade level; and so on. If you don't have a Spanish edition of your enrollment form, you can use the basic form shown in Figure 3-1.

You probably need parents to submit the necessary forms by a certain date, so be very specific. For more about dates, months, and days of the week, refer to Book I, Chapter 2.

Requesting medical and emergency contact information

Forms are also an excellent tool for gathering medical and emergency contact information, which most schools are required to have on file. If you don't have Spanish editions of medical forms, consider using the form in Figure 3-2.

Hoja de Matrícula (*Student Enrollment Form*)
Sección 1: A ser llenado por el padre o tutor del estudiante (*Section 1: To be completed by the student's parent or guardian*)

Nombre del padre o tutor: Apellido, nombre, inicial del segundo nombre
(*Parent/Guardian Name: Last, First, M.I.*)

Casa Teléfono (*Home Telephone Number*)	**Trabajo Teléfono** (*Work Telephone Number*)
Dirección del padre o tutor (*Parent/Guardian Address*)	**Ciudad/Estado/Código postal** (*City/State/Zip Code*)

Nombre del estudiante: Apellido, nombre, inicial del segundo nombre
(*Student Name: Last, First, M.I.*)

Fecha de nacimiento (*Birthdate*) **Mes** (*Month*) _____ **Día** (*Day*) _____ **Año** (*Year*) _____	**Sexo** (*Gender*) **Hombre** (*Male*) _____ **Hembra** (*Female*) _____
Número de Seguro Social (*Social Security Number*)	**Grado, en la fecha de hoy** (*Grade, as of today's date*)
Escuela a la que asistió por última (*School Last Attended*)	**Teléfono** (*Phone Number*)
Dirección (*Address*)	**Ciudad/Estado/Código postal** (*City/State/Zip Code*)

Necesidades especiales – opcional (*Special Needs – optional*)

Motivo de la solicitud: Esto no afecta su aceptación (*Reason for Request: This does not affect your acceptance*)

Checibía El Estudiante Servicios Especiales en la Escuela Anterior? (*Did Student Receive Special Services in Previous School?*)

Sí (*Yes*) _____ **No** (*No*) _____

Programa (*Program*): _____

Hermanos y hermanas que van a la escuela (*Brothers and Sisters in School*)

1. **Nombre** (*Name*): _____ **Escuela** (*School*): _____ **Grado** (*Grade*): _____

1. **Nombre** (*Name*): _____ **Escuela** (*School*): _____ **Grado** (*Grade*): _____

1. **Nombre** (*Name*): _____ **Escuela** (*School*): _____ **Grado** (*Grade*): _____

¿Cree que su hijo califica para recibir almuerzos gratis o a precio reducido?
(*Do you believe your child qualifies for free or reduced price lunch?*)

No (*No*) _____ **Sí** (*Yes*) _____ **No sé** (*Don't Know*) _____

Sección 2: Verificación de información del padre o tutor (*Section 2: Parent/guardian verification of information*)

Por este medio verifico que la información anterior es verdadera y correcta a mi mejor saber y entender.
(*I hereby verify that the above information is true and correct to the best of my knowledge and belief.*)

Firma – Padre/Tutor (*Signature – Parent/Guardian*): _____

Fecha (*Date*): **Mes** (*Month*) _____ **Día** (*Day*) _____ **Año** (*Year*) _____

Figure 3-1:
Enrollment form for Spanish-speaking students.

Información Medical y de Emergencia (*Student Medical/Emergency Contact Form*)

Nombre del estudiante: Apellido, nombre, inicial del segundo nombre
(*Student Name: Last, First, M.I.*)

Estudiante apodo *Student Nickname*	**Grado** *Grade Level*	**Nombre del profesor** *Teacher's Name*

Fecha de nacimiento (*Birthdate*)

Mes (*Month*) _____ **Día** (*Day*) _____ **Año** (*Year*) _____

Sexo (*Gender*)

Hombre (*Male*) _____ **Hembra** (*Female*) _____

Dirección (*Address*)

Ciudad/Estado/Código postal (*City/State/Zip Code*)

Padres casa teléfono (*Parents Home Telephone Number*)

Trabajo teléfono (*Work Telephone Number*)

En caso de emergencia, contacto (*In Case of Emergency, Contact*)

Nombre (*Name*): _____ **Relación** (Relationship): _____ **Teléfono** (Phone): _____

Nombre (*Name*): _____ **Relación** (Relationship): _____ **Teléfono** (Phone): _____

Nombre (*Name*): _____ **Relación** (Relationship): _____ **Teléfono** (Phone): _____

Inmunizaciones: Consultar con elmédico de su niño (*Immunizations:Consult your child's doctor*)

Type	DTP	Td	IPV (Polio)	Hepatitis B	MMR	Chickenpox
1st dose						
2nd dose						
3rd dose						
4th dose						
5th dose						

Doctor nombre (*Doctor Name*)

Doctor teléfono (*Doctor Telephone Number*)

Condiciones médicas (*Medical Conditions*)

Alergias (*Allergies*)

Medicamentos (Medications)

Nombre (*Name*): _____ **Dosis** (*Dose*): _____ **Tiempo** (*Time*): _____

Nombre (*Name*): _____ **Dosis** (*Dose*): _____ **Tiempo** (*Time*): _____

Nombre (*Name*): _____ **Dosis** (*Dose*): _____ **Tiempo** (*Time*): _____

Si su niño se enferma o lesionada, la escuela tratará de llamar al padre/madre o tutor en casa o en el trabajo. Si no se puede llegar a la escuela tratará de llamar a uno de los contactos de emergencia antes mencionadas. En caso de accidente grave o lesión/enfermedad, 911 serán llamados en caso necesario.

(*If your child becomes ill or injured, the school will attempt to call the parent/guardian at home or at work. If you cannot be reached the school will attempt to call one of the emergency contacts listed above. In case of serious accident/injury/illness, 911 will be called if necessary.*)

Firma – Padre/Tutor (*Signature – Parent/Guardian*): _____

Fecha (*Date*): **Mes** (*Month*) _____ **Día** (*Day*) _____ **Año** (*Year*) _____

Figure 3-2:
Medical and
emergency
contact
information
form.

Keeping students safe and attending to their medical needs is very important. For terminology dealing with health and medical issues, check out Book IV, Chapter 1.

Describing required school supplies

Prior to the first day of school, letting parents know what school supplies their children are likely to need is always a good idea. You can draw up a list of common supplies by using the words shown in Table 3-1.

Table 3-1	School Supplies	
English	*Spanish*	*Pronunciation*
ballpoint pen	**un bolígrafo**	oon bvoh-*lee*-grah-foh
book	**un libro**	oon *lee*-bvroh
backpack	**una mochila**	*oo*-nah moh-*chee*-lah
calculator	**una calculadora**	*oo*-nah kahl-koo-lah-*doh*-rah
colored pencils	**unos lápices de colores**	*oo*-nohs *lah*-pee-sehs de koh-*loh*-rehs
crayons	**unos crayones**	*oo*-nohs krah-*yoh*-nehs
dictionary	**un diccionario**	oon dee-ksee-oh-*nah*-reeoh
eraser	**una goma de borrar**	*oo*-nah *goh*-mah deh bvoh-rrahr
folder	**una carpeta**	*oo*-nah kahr-*peh*-tah
glue stick	**una barra de pegamento**	*oo*-nah *bvah*-rrah de peh-gah-*mehn*-toh
markers	**unos marcadores**	*oo*-nohs mahr-kah-*doh*-rehs
paper	**papel**	pah-*pehl*
wide-ruled	**con líneas**	kohn *lee*-neh-ahs
unruled	**sin líneas**	seen *lee*-neh-ahs
graph	**cuadriculado**	kooah-dree-koo-*lah*-doh
pen	**una pluma**	*oo*-nah *ploo*-mah
	un bolígrafo	oon bvoh-*lee*-grah-foh
pencil	**un lápiz**	oon *lah*-pees
ruler	**una regla**	*oo*-nah *reh*-glah
school supplies	**los útiles escolares**	lohs *oo*-tee-lehs ehs-koh-*lah*-rehs

(continued)

Table 3-1 *(continued)*

English	Spanish	Pronunciation
scissors	**unas tijeras**	*oo*-nahs tee-*Heh*-rahs
textbook	**un libro de texto**	oon *lee*-broh deh *tehks*-toh
three-ring binder	**una carpeta de tres anillos**	*oo*-nah kahr-*peh*-tah deh trehs ah-*nee*-yohs

Communicating with Students

Without being entirely aware of it, you probably bark out more orders and commands in a single day than any four-star general has issued in his entire career. If you didn't, anarchy would reign supreme, and your students wouldn't learn a thing.

Your Spanish-speaking students need your leadership just as much, so be prepared to give direction in Spanish as well as English. The following sections provide words and phrases to issue commands and instructions wherever you happen to be — in the classroom or cafeteria, in the gym or on the playground, in or on the way to the bathroom, and even on the bus.

When a teacher speaks with a student, he should use the **tú** (too) (informal *you*) form of commands and address to show familiarity. On the other hand, a student should use the **Ud.** or **usted** (oos-*tehd*) (formal *you*) when speaking to a teacher to show respect for authority.

Interacting in the classroom

Unless you speak Spanish at about an intermediate level, you probably won't be able to communicate effectively with a student who speaks very little English. You may get by with both of you speaking some degree of Spanglish or with the assistance of an ESL (English as a Second Language) specialist. Brushing up on some common commands and expressions, however, can help you maintain order and manage standard interactions:

✔ *Be quiet.* **Silencio.** (see-*lehn*-seeoh)

✔ *Behave!* **¡Compórtate!** (kohm-*pohr*-tah-teh)

↙ *Bring your book to class every day.* **Trae tu libro a la clase todos los días.** (*trah*-eh too *lee*-bvroh ah lah *klah*-seh *toh*-dohs lohs *dee*-ahs)

↙ *Close your book.* **Cierra tu libro.** (seee*eh*-rrah too *lee*-bvroh)

↙ *Correct your assignment.* **Haz las correcciones a tu tarea.** (ahs lahs koh-rreh-ksee*oh*-nehs ah too tah-*reh*-ah)

↙ *Go to the principal's office.* **Vete a la oficina del director/de la directora.** (*bveh*-teh ah lah oh-fee-*see*-nah dehl dee-rek-*tohr*/deh lah dee-rek-*tohr*-ah)

↙ *Great job!* **¡Buen trabajo!** (bvoo*ehn* trah-*bvah*-Hoh)

↙ *Hand me your assignment.* **Dame la tarea.** (*dah*-meh lah tah-*reh*-ah)

↙ *Ask your parents to sign this paper and return it to me.* **Pide a tus padres a firmar este papel y devuélvemelo.** (*pee*-deh ah toos *pah*-drehs ah feer-*mahr eh*-steh pah-*pehl* ee deh-bvoo*ehl*-bveh-meh-loh)

↙ *Don't bother others.* **No molesta a los demás.** (noh moh-*lehs*-tah ah lohs deh-*mahs*)

↙ *Leave the classroom.* **Vete de la clase.** (*bveh*-teh deh lah *klah*-seh)

↙ *No chewing gum.* **No se permite el chicle.** (noh seh pehr-*mee*-teh ehl *chee*-kleh)

↙ *No talking.* **No habla.** (noh *ah*-bvlah)

↙ *Pay attention.* **Presta atención.** (*prehs*-tah ah-tehn-see*ohn*)

↙ *Please be seated.* **Por favor siéntate.** (pohr fah-*bvohr* seee*ehn*-tah-teh)

↙ *Put that away, right now.* **Guárdalo, ahora mismo.** (goo*ahr*-dah-loh ah-*oh*-rah *mees*-moh)

↙ *Speak up.* **Habla más alto.** (*ah*-bvlah mahs *ahl*-toh)

↙ *Tomorrow, we are having a test on this material.* **Mañana, hay un examen sobre esta material.** (mah-*nyah*-nah ahy oon eh-*ksah*-mehn *soh*-bvreh *eh*-stah mah-teh-ree*ahl*)

↙ *Turn around.* **Voltéate.** (bvohl-*teh*-ah-teh)

↙ *You need to arrive at _____ o'clock or you'll be marked tardy.* **Necesitas llegar a las _____ o te anotaré tarde.** (neh-seh-*see*-tahs yeh-*gahr* ah lahs _____ oh teh ah-noh-tah-*reh* tahr-deh)

↙ *You need to turn in your homework assignments on time.* **Necesitas entregar la tarea a tiempo.** (neh-seh-*see*-tah ehn-treh-*gahr* lah tah-*reh*-ah ah teee*ehm*-poh)

Book IV

Spanish at Work

Giving instructions for the cafeteria or lunchroom

Lunchtime is always a little more relaxed than in the classroom — at least for the students. As a teacher, you need to keep order to ensure that everyone in the cafeteria or lunchroom has a safe and enjoyable dining experience. Following are some common phrases that can help you achieve that:

✔ *Have a seat and wait until it's your turn.* **Siéntate y espera hasta que te toca a ti.** (see*ehn*-tah-teh ee ehs-*peh*-rah *ahs*-tah keh teh *toh*-kah ah tee)

✔ *Now you can get in line.* **Ahora puedes ponerte en la cola.** (ah-*oh*-rah poo*eh*-dehs poh-*nehr*-teh en la *koh*-lah)

✔ *Don't cut.* **No cólete.** (noh koh-*leh*-teh)

✔ *Stand in line here.* **Haz una cola aquí.** (ahs *oo*-nah *koh*-lah ah-*kee*)

✔ *Have your money ready to pay the cashier.* **Está listo con su dinero a pagar al cajero.** (ehs-*tah lees*-toh kohn soo dee-*neh*-roh ah pah-*gahr* ahl kah-*Heh*-roh)

✔ *Don't bother others while they're eating.* **No molesta a los demás mientras comen.** (noh moh-*lehs*-tah ah lohs deh-*mahs* mee*ehn*-trahs *koh*-mehn)

✔ *Keep your voice down.* **Habla con la voz baja.** (*ah*-bvlah kohn lah bvohs *bvah*-Hah)

✔ *Stay at your table until you're dismissed.* **Quédate en la mesa hasta que estás despedido.** (*keh*-dah-teh ehn lah *meh*-sah *ahs*-tah keh ehs-*tahs* dehs-peh-*dee*-doh)

✔ *Now you may return to your classroom.* **Ahora puedes regresr a tu sala de clase.** (ah-*oh*-rah poo*eh*-dehs reh-greh-*sahr* ah too *sah*-lah deh *klah*-seh)

Supervising students in the gym or on the playground

Even the most well-behaved class can become a little rambunctious during gym class or recess, and that's perfectly acceptable. However, you want to keep your students' enthusiasm down to a dull roar for the benefit of everyone involved, which means you have to keep the channels of communication open between you and all of your students, regardless of the languages they speak. Here are some phrases you're likely to need whether you're supervising in the gym or on the jungle gym:

✔ *Come here.* **Ven aquí.** (bvehn ah-*kee*)

✔ *Wait your turn.* **Espera tu turno.** (ehs-*peh*-rah too *toor*-noh)

✔ *Play nicely.* **Llévate bien con los demás.** (*yeh*-bvah-teh bvee*ehn* kohn lohs deh-*mahs*)

✔ *Stop!* **¡Alto!** (*ahl*-toh)

✔ *No hitting.* **No pega.** (noh *peh*-gah)

✔ *Stand in a circle.* **Ponte a pie en un círculo.** (*pohn*-teh ah pee*eh* ehn oon *seer*-koo-loh)

Asking about the restroom

In addition to teaching, you usually have to deal with the essentials, like using the restroom, so familiarize yourself with the following common expressions:

✔ *Whoever needs to go to the restroom, raise your hand.* **Los que necesitan ir al baño, levánten las manos.** (lohs keh neh-seh-*see*-tahn eer ahl *bvah*-nyoh leh-*bvahn*-tehn lahs *man*-nohs)

✔ *Who needs to go to the restroom?* **¿Quién necesita ir al baño?** (kee*ehn* neh-seh-*see*-tah eer ahl *bvah*-nyoh)

✔ *I need to go to the restroom.* **Yo necesito ir al baño.** (yoh neh-seh-*see*-toh eer ahl *bvah*-nyoh)

✔ *Wash your hands after using the restroom.* **Lava las manos después de ir al baño.** (*lah*-bvah lahs *mah*-nohs dehs-poo*ehs* deh eer ahl *bvah*-nyoh)

Getting kids on the bus safely

When the buses are picking up or dropping off students, safety becomes the number one issue, and that means maintaining order. If you're pulling bus duty, brush up on the following phrases:

✔ *Stay in line.* **Quédate en la cola.** (*keh*-dah-teh ehn lah *koh*-lah)

✔ *Remain inside until your bus arrives.* **Quédate dentro de la escuela hasta que el autobús llega.** (*keh*-dah-teh *dehn*-troh deh lah ehs-koo*eh*-lah *ahs*-tah keh ehl ahoo-toh-*boos* yeh-gah)

✔ *Stay on the sidewalk.* **Quédate en la acera.** (*keh*-dah-teh ehn lah ah-*seh*-rah)

✔ *No pushing.* **No empuja.** (noh ehm-*poo*-Hah)

✔ *No running.* **No corre.** (noh *koh*-rreh)

✔ *Stay off the grass.* **No pisa el césped.** (noh *pee*-sah ehl *sehs*-pehd)

✔ *Step this way.* **Pasa por aquí.** (*pah*-sah pohr ah-*kee*)

✔ *Step back.* **Retrocede.** (reh-troh-*seh*-deh)

Communicating with Parents

When you have students, you (hopefully) have parents interested in how their children are doing in school. As you're already well aware, keeping parents in the loop can have a positive influence on a student's success, so you want to keep parents engaged.

In the following sections, we show you how to keep parents involved by communicating with them early and whenever necessary to get their children on track and enable them to fulfill their full potential.

Adjusting to cultural differences

Hispanic cultures hold the schools, teachers, and other school personnel in very high regard and consider any question about their expertise and authority disrespectful. This view stems from the fact that the Catholic Church traditionally ran all schools in these cultures. They may be unaccustomed to the typical U.S. school's practice of calling home to report incidents that occur at school, because they expect that the school knows how best to handle the situation and will do what is necessary. They're always very polite and willing to listen to any comments or suggestions that the school has for their child, but they don't expect to be asked for their input. They may also not be used to the requests for their attendance at conferences (to discuss grades and so on) but will graciously oblige. Education is very important to them; they'll comply with the U.S. way of doing things, but keeping these points in mind may help you interact more consciously.

You probably send a whole lot of printed information home with your students. When dealing with Spanish-speaking students, however, your calendars and letters probably go unread. Most studies show that even if you translate every piece of information you send home with your students, very few Spanish-speaking parents read all of it or even some of it. Depending on the district you teach in, many of your English-speaking parents probably don't read it either. In any event, try to keep written communication to a minimum.

Dealing with common issues

Unfortunately, you're usually contacting parents because their child is misbehaving or doing poorly in class. When these common scenarios present themselves, you need to know some common phrases to tell parents exactly what's going on.

Calling parents at home

The following phrases can come in very handy when you first call a student's home and someone picks up the phone or the answering machine prompts you to leave a message:

- *Hello, I am [name's] teacher.* **Hola, soy el/la maestro/a de [name].** (*oh*-lah sohy ehl/lah mah*ehs*-troh/trah deh [name])

- *I need to speak with [name's] mother or father.* **Necesito hablar con la madre o el padre de [name].** (neh-seh-*see*-toh ah-*bvlahr* kohn lah *mah*-dreh oh ehl *pah*-dreh deh [name])

- *[Name] is misbehaving in class.* **[Name] no está portándose bien en la clase.** ([Name] noh ehs-*tah* pohr-*tahn*-doh-seh bvee*ehn* ehn lah *klah*-seh)

- *[Name]is having difficulty in [subject].* **[Name] tiene dificultad en la clase de [subject].** ([Name] tee*eh*-neh dee-fee-kool-*tahd* ehn lah *klah*-seh deh [subject])

  Table 3-2 later in the chapter provides a list of subjects.

- *I need you to come into the school to speak with me.* **Necesito que ustedes vengan a la escuela para hablar conmigo.** (neh-seh-*see*-toh keh oos-*tehd*-ehs *bvehn*-gahn ah lah ehs-koo*eh*-lah *pah*-rah ah-*bvlahr* kohn-*mee*-goh)

- *Which day is best for you?* **¿Qué día es mejor para ustedes?** (keh *dee*-ah ehs meh-*Hohr pah*-rah oos-*tehd*-ehs)

- *What time could you come?* **¿A qué hora pudieran venir?** (ah keh *oh*-rah poo-dee*eh*-rahn bveh-*neer*)

Discussing classroom problems

If you're calling about specific behavioral issues, you probably want to refer to those issues so that the parents can speak with their child. The following list translates the most common issues into Spanish.

- *Talks too much* **Habla demasiado** (*ah*-bvlah deh-mah-see*ah*-doh)

- *Disturbs the class* **Disturba a la clase** (dees-*toor*-bvah ah lah *klah*-seh)

- *Doesn't pay attention* **No presta atención** (noh *prehs*-tah ah-tehn-see*ohn*)

✔ *Doesn't study enough* **No estudia bastante** (noh ehs-*too*-deeah bvahs-*tahn*-teh)

✔ *Doesn't turn in the homework* **No entrega la tarea** (noh ehn-*treh*-gah lah tah-*reh*-ah)

✔ *Is argumentative with the teacher* **Es discutidor/a con el/la maestro/a** (ehs dees-koo-tee-*dohr*/ah kohn ehl/lah mah*ehs*-troh/trah)

✔ *Is argumentative with other students* **Es discutidor/a con los demás estudiantes** (ehs dees-koo-tee-*dohr*/ah kohn lohs deh-*mahs* ehs-too-dee*ahn*-tehs)

✔ *Sleeps during class* **Duerme durante la clase** (dooehr-meh doo-*rahn*-teh lah *klah*-seh)

During your conversation with the parents, you may need to refer to the particular classes or subjects listed in Table 3-2.

Table 3-2	School Subjects	
English	**Spanish**	**Pronunciation**
algebra	**el álgebra**	ehl *ahl*-Heh-bvrah
art	**el arte**	ehl *ahr*-teh
band	**la banda**	lah *bvahn*-dah
biology	**la biología**	lah bvee-oh-loh-*Hee*-ah
calculus	**el cálculo**	ehl *kahl*-koo-loh
chemistry	**la química**	lah *kee*-mee-kah
computer science	**la informática**	lah een-fohr-*mah*-tee-kah
earth science	**la geología**	lah Heh-oh-loh-*Hee*-ah
English	**el inglés**	ehl een-*glehs*
geography	**la geografía**	lah Heh-oh-grah-*fee*-ah
geometry	**la geometría**	lah Heh-oh-meh-*tree*-ah
health	**la salud**	lah sah-*lood*
history	**la historia**	lah ees-*toh*-reeah
industrial arts	**las artes industriales**	lahs ahr-tehs een-doos-tree*ah*-lehs
mathematics	**las matemáticas**	lahs mah-teh-*mah*-tee-kahs
music	**la música**	lah *moo*-see-kah

English	Spanish	Pronunciation
penmanship	**la caligrafía**	lah kah-lee-grah-*fee*-ah
physical education/gym	**la educatión física**	lah eh-doo-kah-see*ohn fee*-see-kah
physics	**la física**	lah *fee*-see-kah
science	**la ciencia**	lah see*ehn*-seeah
social studies	**los estudios sociales**	lohs ehs-*too*-deeohs soh-see*ah*-lehs
speech	**el discurso**	ehl dees-*koor*-soh
spelling	**la ortografía**	lah ohr-toh-grah-*fee*-ah
trigonometry	**la trigonometría**	lah tree-goh-noh-meh-*tree*-ah
writing	**la escritura**	lah ehs-kree-*too*-rah

Chapter 4

Spanish for Banking and Financing

. . . .

In This Chapter

⮑ Exploring common banking expressions and terminology

⮑ Talking through common transactions

⮑ Dealing with problems

. . . .

If you're in the banking biz, you're likely to have at least a few Spanish-speaking customers (or want to expand your business by accommodating this typically underserved segment of the market).

The first order of business is to have all of your forms and slips (for deposits, withdrawals, and transfers) translated into Spanish — or add Spanish to make your current forms bilingual. This tactic enables you to gather most of the information you need by simply handing the form to the person and asking him to complete it. This chapter includes words and phrases that can help in translating the forms, but you probably want to have your forms translated professionally.

In this chapter, we give you enough Spanish to manage an average workday — whether you're a banker, teller, or loan officer. We show you how to navigate various situations and manage common transactions when dealing with your Spanish-speaking customers.

Brushing Up on Banker-Speak

When dealing with customers on a daily basis, you're probably not conscious of the fact that you use plenty of specialized financial words and phrases both during your initial greetings and as you assist customers with their transactions.

In the following sections, we reveal some of the most common words and phrases you need, along with verbs to describe the financial transactions and activities.

Mastering the meet and greet

Greeting people warmly isn't only common courtesy but also good business. Book I, Chapter 3 provides everything you need to know to greet people properly in Spanish. After the greeting, however, you need to get down to business. The following phrases can come in very handy during your initial greeting:

- ✔ *Welcome to our bank.* **Bienvenido/a(s) a nuestro banco.** (bveeehn-bveh-*nee*-doh(s)/dah(s) ah noo*eh*-stroh *bvahn*-koh)

- ✔ *How may I help you?* **¿Cómo puedo ayudarle?** (*koh*-moh poo*eh*-doh ah-yoo-*dahr*-leh)

- ✔ *What is your name?* **¿Cómo se llama?** (*koh*-moh seh *yah*-mah)

- ✔ *Thank you for waiting.* **Gracias por esperar.** (*grah*-see-ahs pohr ehs-peh-*rahr*)

- ✔ *I'll be right with you.* **Le atenderé pronto.** (leh ah-tehn-deh-*reh prohn*-toh)

- ✔ *Somebody will be right with you.* **Alguien le atenderé pronto.** (ahl-gee*ehn* leh ah-tehn-deh-*reh prohn*-toh)

- ✔ *With whom is your appointment?* **¿Con quién es su cita?** (kohn kee*ehn* ehs soo *see*-tah)

- ✔ *Come this way.* **Pase por aquí.** (*pah*-seh pohr ah-*kee*)

- ✔ *Wait here.* **Espere aquí.** (ehs-*peh*-reh ah-*kee*)

- ✔ *You need to speak with . . .* **Necesita hablar con . . .** (neh-seh-*see*-tah ah-*bvlahr* kohn)

Requesting identification

Whenever you're processing a transaction, particularly for a customer you don't know very well yet, you need to ask for identification:

- ✔ *You need identification.* **Necesita identificación.** (neh-seh-*see*-tah ee-dehn-tee-fee-kah-see*ohn*)

- ✔ *You need photo identification.* **Necesita identificación con foto.** (neh-seh-*see*-tah ee-dehn-tee-fee-kah-see*ohn* kohn *foh*-toh)

- ✔ *You need two forms of identification.* **Necesita dos formas de identificación.** (neh-seh-*see*-tah dohs *fohr*-mahs deh ee-dehn-tee-fee-kah-see*ohn*)

✔ *We accept a . . .* **Aceptamos un/una . . .** (ah-sehp-*tah*-mohs oon/*oo*-nah)

- *driver's license* **licencia de conducir** (lee-*sehn*-seeah deh kohn-doo-*seer*)

- *Social Security card* **Tarjeta de Seguro Social** (tahr-*Heh*-tah deh seh-*goo*-roh soh-see*ahl*)

- *Military I.D.* **identificación militar** (ee-dehn-tee-fee-kah-see*ohn* mee-lee-*tahr*)

- *Passport* **pasaporte** (pah-sah-*pohr*-teh)

- *Residence card* **tarjeta de residencia** (tahr-H*eh*-tah deh reh-see-*dehn*-seeah)

✔ *We don't accept this identification.* **No aceptamos esta identificación.** (noh ah-sehp-*tah*-mohs *ehs*-tah ee-dehn-tee-fee-kah-see*ohn*)

Getting a handle on bank vocab

Although you may be able to get by with pointing to items in the bank and handing the customer the form she needs to fill out and a pen to fill it out with, referring to these items by name is often more efficient. Table 4-1 provides a list of stuff you're likely to find in a bank or other financial institution along with Spanish translations of their names.

Table 4-1	Common Bank Items	
English	*Spanish*	*Pronunciation*
account	**la cuenta**	lah koo*ehn*-tah
account statement	**el extracto de cuenta**	ehl ehks-*trahk*-toh deh koo*ehn*-tah
ATM card	**la tarjeta ATM**	lah tar-*Heh*-tah ah teh *eh*-meh
ATM	**el cajero electrónico**	ehl kah-*Heh*-roh ee-lehk-*troh*-nee-koh
application	**la aplicación**	lah ah-plee-kah-see*ohn*
bank charges	**las comisiones**	lahs koh-mee-see*ohn*-ehs
bank	**el banco**	ehl *bvahn*-koh
branch	**la sucursal**	lah soo-koor-*sahl*
cashier	**el/la cajero/a**	ehl/lah kah-*Heh*-roh/rah

(continued)

Table 4-1 *(continued)*

English	Spanish	Pronunciation
cash machine	el cajero automático	ehl kah-*Heh*-roh ahoo-toh-*mah*-tee-koh
cents	los centavos	lohs sehn-*tah*-bvohs
change	el cambio	ehl *kahm*-bveeoh
check	el cheque	ehl *cheh*-keh
checkbook	la libreta de cheques	lah lee-*bvreh*-tah deh *cheh*-kehs
checking account	la cuenta de cheque	lah koo*ehn*-tah deh *cheh*-keh
credit card	la tarjeta de crédito	lah tar-*Heh*-tah de *kreh*-dee-toh
customer	el/la cliente	ehl/lah klee*ehn*-teh
customer service	el servicio al cliente	ehl sehr-*bvee*-seeoh ahl klee*ehn*-teh
debit card	la tarjeta de débito	lah tar-*Heh*-tah deh *deh*-bvee-toh
deposit	el depósito	ehl dee-*poh*-see-toh
deposit slip	la hoja de depósito	lah *oh*-Hah deh dee-*poh*-see-toh
dollars	los dólares	lohs *doh*-lah-rehs
interest rate	el interés	ehl een-teh-*rehs*
loan	el préstamo	ehl *prehs*-tah-moh
loan officer	el/la director/a de préstamo	ehl/lah dee-rehk-*tohr*/ah deh *prehs*-tah-moh
manager	el/la director/a	ehl/lah dee-rehk-*tohr*/ah
money	el dinero	ehl dee-*neh*-roh
money order	el giro postal	ehl *Hee*-roh pohs-*tahl*
mortgage	el préstamo hipotecario	ehl *prehs*-tah-moh ee-poh-teh-*kah*-reeoh
	la hipoteca	lah ee-poh-*teh*-kah
pen	el bolígrafo	ehl bvoh-*lee*-grah-foh
	la pluma	lah *ploo*-mah
principal	el préstamo principal	ehl *prehs*-tah-moh preen-see-*pahl*

English	Spanish	Pronunciation
safety deposit box	la caja de seguridad	lah *kah*-Hah deh seh-goo-ree-*dahd*
savings account	la cuenta de ahorros	lah koo*ehn*-tah deh ah-*oh*-rrohs
savings bank	la caja de ahorros	lah *kah*-Hah deh ah-*oh*-rrohs
signature	la firma	lah *feer*-mah
transfer	la transferencia	lah trahns-feh-*rehn*-seeah
teller window	la ventanilla	lah bvehn-tah-*nee*-yah

Describing routine customer needs

Although financial institutions toss around a great deal of specialized terminology, customers usually perform only a very limited range of activities, including cashing a check, depositing money, and making a withdrawal. To prepare, brush up on the following verbs used to describe the most common transactions.

- ✔ *Borrow* **pedir un préstamo** (peh-de*er* oon *prehs*-tah-moh)
- ✔ *Cancel a bank account* **cancelar una cuenta** (kahn-seh-*lahr* oo-nah koo*ehn*-tah)
- ✔ *Change money* **cambiar moneda** (kahm-bvee-*ahr* moh-*neh*-dah)
- ✔ *Make a deposit* **ingresar dinero** (een-greh-*sahr* dee-*neh*-roh)
- ✔ *Open a bank account* **abrir una cuenta** (ah-bv*reer* oo-nah koo*ehn*-tah)
- ✔ *Transfer money* **hacer una transferencia** (hah-*sehr* oo-nah trahns-feh-*rehn*-seeah)
- ✔ *Withdraw money* **retirar dinero** (reh-tee-*rahr* dee-*neh*-roh)

Giving customers common instructions

During the course of a typical transaction, you usually need the customer to do something — show you identification, sign a check or a piece of paper, give you his account number, and so on. Use the following commands to tell your customers what to do:

Book IV

Spanish at Work

- ✔ *Fill out this form.* **Llene este formulario.** (*yeh*-neh *ehs*-teh fohr-moo-*lah*-reeoh)

- ✔ *Follow me.* **Sígame.** (*see*-gah-meh)

- ✔ *Give me . . .* **Deme . . .** (*deh*-meh)

- ✔ *Give me your account number, please.* **Deme su número de cuenta, por favor.** (*deh*-meh soo *noo*-meh-roh deh koo*ehn*-tah pohr fah-*bvohr*)

- ✔ *Listen to me.* **Escúcheme.** (ehs-*koo*-cheh-meh)

- ✔ *Look here.* **Mire aquí.** (*mee*-reh ah-*kee*)

- ✔ *Show me.* **Enséñeme.** (ehn-*seh*-nyeh-meh)

- ✔ *Sign here.* **Firme aquí.** (*feer*-meh ah-*kee*)

- ✔ *Sit here.* **Siéntese aquí.** (see*ehn*-teh-seh ah-*kee*)

- ✔ *Take it.* **Tómelo.** (*toh*-meh-loh)

- ✔ *Tell me.* **Dígame.** (*dee*-gah-meh)

- ✔ *Wait a moment.* **Espere un momento.** (ehs-*peh*-reh oon moh-*mehn*-toh)

- ✔ *Write it.* **Escríbalo.** (ehs-*kree*-bvah-loh)

Processing Common Transactions

On an average day, you're likely to deal with a host of different transaction types, but in most cases, customers simply want to take money out or put money in. In the following sections, we show you how to deal with the most common transaction types.

Opening an account

When a customer shows up at your establishment for the first time, she usually needs to open an account before she's able to perform any other transactions. Whenever you encounter a customer you don't know, you may want to ask whether she has an account with the bank:

> *Do you have an account with us?* **¿Tiene una cuenta con nosotros?** (tee*ehn*-eh *oo*-nah koo*ehn*-tah kohn noh-*soh*-trohs)

If the person answers **sí** (see) *(yes)*, you can then ask for her account number:

> *What is your account number?* **¿Cuál es su número de cuenta?** (koo*ahl* ehs soo *noo*-meh-roh deh koo*ehn*-tah)

If the person answers **no** (noh) *(no)*, you can follow up by asking whether she wants to open an account:

> *Do you want to open an account?* **¿Quiere abrir una cuenta?** (keee*eh*-reh ah-*bvreer oo*-nah koo*oehn*-tah)

The following dialogue walks you through a typical account-opening.

Talkin' the Talk

Mrs. Escobar has arrived at the bank for the first time and needs to open an account. The bank teller, Brian, leads Mrs. Escobar through the process.

Brian: **Bienvenida a nuestro banco.**
bveeehn-bveh-*nee*-dah ah nooeh-stroh *bahn*-koh
Welcome to our bank.

Mrs. Escobar: **Buenas tardes.**
bvooeh-nahs *tahr*-dehs
Good afternoon.

Brian: **Me llamo Brian. ¿Cómo puedo ayudarle?**
meh yah-moh *bvree*-ahn *koh*-moh pooeh-doh ah-yoo-*dahr*-leh
My name is Brian, how may I help you?

Mrs. Escobar: **Quiero abrir una cuenta.**
keeeeh-roh ah-*bvreer oo*-nah kooehn-tah
I would like to open an account.

Brian: **¿Qué tipo de cuenta?**
keh *tee*-poh deh kooehn-tah
What type of account?

Mrs. Escobar: **Una cuenta de cheque.**
oo-nah kooehn-tah deh *cheh*-keh
A checking account.

Brian: **Se necesita depositar un mínimo de veinticinco dólares para abrir una cuenta de cheque.**
seh neh-seh-*see*-tah deh-poh-see-*tahr* oon *mee*-nee-moh deh bveheen-tee-*seen*-koh *doh*-lah-rehs *pah*-rah ah-*bvreer oo*-nah kooehn-tah deh *cheh*-keh
A minimum deposit of $25 is required to open a new checking account.

Book IV

Spanish at Work

¿**Tiene esa cantidad con usted?**
tee*ehn*-eh *eh*-sah kahn-tee-*dahd* kohn oos-tehd
Do you have that amount with you?

Mrs. Escobar: **Sí.**
see
Yes.

Brian: **Yo puedo ayudarle. ¿Cómo se llama?**
yoh pooeh-doh ah-yoo-*dahr*-leh *koh*-moh seh
yah-mah
I can help you. What is your name?

Mrs. Escobar: **María.**
mah-*ree*-ah
María.

Brian: **¿Qué es su apellido?**
keh ehs soo ah-peh-*yee*-doh
What is your last name?

Mrs. Escobar: **Escobar.**
ehs-koh-*bvahr*
Escobar.

Brian: **¿Cuál es su dirección?**
koo*ahl* ehs soo dee-rehk-see*ohn*
What is your address?

Mrs. Escobar: **4321 Main Street.**
koo*ah*-troh trehs dohs oo-noh Main Street
4321 Main Street.

Brian: **¿Cuál es su número de teléfono?**
koo*ahl* ehs soo *noo*-meh-roh deh teh-*leh*-foh-noh
What is your telephone number?

Mrs. Escobar: **212-253-1188.**
dohs oo-*noh* dohs dohs seen-*koh* trehs oo-noh
oo-noh *oh*-choh *oh*-choh
212-253-1188.

Brian: **¿Cuál es su fecha de nacimiento?**
koo*ahl* ehs soo *feh*-chah deh nah-see-mee*ehn*-toh
What is your date of birth?

Mrs. Escobar: **Es el veinte de enero de mil novecientos ochenta y cuatro.**
ehs ehl *bveh*een-teh deh eh-*neh*-roh deh meel noh-bveh-see*ehn*-tohs oh-*chehn*-tah ee koo*ah*-troh
It's January 20, 1984.

Brian: **Necesitamos hacer una copia de su tarjeta de Seguro Social.**
neh-seh-see-*tah*-mohs ah-*sehr* oo-nah *koh*-peeah deh soo tahr-*Heh*-tah deh seh-*goo*-roh soh-see*ahl*
I need to make a copy of your Social Security card.

Mrs. Escobar: **Está bien. Aquí tengo la tarjeta de la Seguro Social.**
ehs-*tah* beee*ehn* ah-*kee tehn*-goh lah tahr-*Heh*-tah deh seh-*goo*-roh soh-see*ahl*
Fine. Here I have the Social Security card.

Brian: **¿Cuánto quiere depositar en su cuenta?**
koo*ah*n-toh keee*eh*-reh deh-poh-see-*tahr* ehn soo koo*ehn*-tah
How much would you like to deposit into your account?

Mrs. Escobar: **Tengo cien dólares a depositar.**
tehn-goh see*ehn doh*-lah-rehs ah deh-poh-see-*tahr*
I have $100 to deposit.

Brian: **Aquí está una tarjeta con el número de su cuenta.**
ah-*kee* ehs-*tah* oo-nah tahr-*Heh*-tah kohn ehl *noo*-meh-roh deh soo koo*ehn*-tah
Here is a card with your account number on it.

Aquí está el recibo que demuestra la cantidad depositada en su cuenta.
ah-*kee* ehs-*tah* ehl reh-*see*-bvoh keh deh-moo*ehs*-trah lah kahn-tee-*dahd* deh-poh-see-*tah*-dah ehn soo koo*ehn* tah
Here is the receipt showing the amount deposited into your account.

Aquí hay unos cheques provisionales.
ah-*kee* ahy *oo*-nohs *cheh*-kehs proh-bvee-seeoh-*nah*-lehs
Here are some temporary checks.

Recibirá sus cheques oficiales por correo dentro de dos semanas.
reh-see-bvee-*rah* soos *cheh*-kehs oh-fee-see*ah*-lehs pohr koh-*rreh*-oh *dehn*-troh deh dohs seh-*mah*-nahs
You'll receive your official checks in the mail within two weeks.

Mrs. Escobar: **Gracias.**
grah-seeahs
Thank you.

Brian: **¿Hay algo más en que puedo ayudarle hoy?**
ahy *ahl*-goh mahs ehn keh poo*eh*-doh ah-yoo-*dahr*-leh ohy
Is there anything else I can help you with today?

Mrs. Escobar: **No, eso es todo.**
noh *eh*-soh ehs *toh*-doh
No, that's all.

Brian: **Gracias por escoger nuestro banco. Adiós.**
grah-seeahs pohr ehs-koh-H*eh*r noo*ehs*-troh *bvahn*-koh ah-dee*ohs*
Thank you for choosing our bank. Good-bye.

Mrs. Escobar: **Adiós**
ah-dee*ohs*
Good-bye.

Cashing checks

One of the most frequent transactions consists of cashing checks for your customers, especially on the typical Friday payday. Following are phrases that can help you process these transactions:

✔ *Do you want to cash the check?* **¿Quiere cambiar el cheque?** (kee*eh*-reh kahm-bvee*ahr* ehl *cheh*-keh)

✔ *Do you have an account with us?* **¿Tiene una cuenta con nosotros?** (tee*eh*-neh *oo*-nah koo*ehn*-tah kohn noh-*soh*-trohs)

✔ *What is your account number?* **¿Cuál es su número de cuenta?** (koo*ahl* ehs soo *noo*-meh-roh deh koo*ehn*-tah)

- *Please sign the check on the back.* **Firme el cheque por detrás por favor.** (*feer*-meh ehl *cheh*-keh pohr deh-*trahs* pohr fah-*bvohr*)

- *Write your account number on the back of the check.* **Escriba su número de cuenta por detrás.** (ehs-*kree*-bvah soo *noo*-meh-roh deh koo*ehn*-tah pohr deh-*trahs*)

If you can't cash the check for whatever reason, you need to tell your customer and explain why. See "Addressing Common Problems" later in this chapter for details.

Accepting deposits

If you're lucky, a customer presents you with a deposit slip, complete with his account number and type (savings or checking) and his name, when he shows up with money or cash to deposit into his account. If you're not so lucky, the following phrases can come in very handy:

- *How much do you want to deposit?* **¿Cuánto quiere depositar?** (koo*ahn*-toh kee*eh*-reh deh-poh-see-*tahr*)

- *Do you want to deposit a check?* **¿Quiere depositar un cheque?** (kee*eh*-reh deh-poh-see-*tahr* oon *cheh*-keh)

- *Do you want to deposit cash?* **¿Quiere depositar dinero?** (kee*eh*-reh deh-poh-see-*tahr* dee-*neh*-roh)

- *Please fill out this deposit slip.* **Por favor llene la hoja de depósito.** (pohr fah-*bvohr* yeh-neh lah *oh*-Hah deh deh-*poh*-see-toh)

- *Do you want this deposited into checking?* **¿Quiere depositarlo a la cuenta de cheque?** (kee*eh*-reh deh-poh-see-*tahr*-loh ah lah koo*ehn*-tah deh *cheh*-keh)

- *Do you want this deposited into savings?* **¿Quiere depositarlo a la cuenta de ahorros?** (kee*eh*-reh deh-poh-see-*tahr*-loh ah lah koo*ehn*-tah deh ah-*oh*-rrohs)

If the customer is depositing one or more checks, you may need him to sign the checks and write his account number on them. See the previous section for details about cashing checks.

Book IV

Spanish at Work

Processing withdrawals

When a customer shows up to pull some money out of his account, the easiest option is to hand him a withdrawal slip and instruct him to fill it out. If the customer speaks only Spanish, however, you may need to provide some additional instruction and obtain some additional information:

✔ *Please fill out this withdrawal slip.* **Por favor llene esta hoja de retiro.** (pohr fah-*bvohr* yeh-neh *ehs*-tah *oh*-Hah deh reh-*tee*-roh)

✔ *Do you want to withdraw the money from savings or checking?* **¿Quiere retirar el dinero de su cuenta de ahorros o su cuenta de cheque?** (kee*eh*-reh reh-tee-*rahr* ehl dee-*neh*-roh deh soo koo*ehn*-tah deh ah-*oh*-rrohs oh soo koo*ehn*-tah deh *cheh*-keh)

✔ *How much money do you want to take out?* **¿Cuánto dinero quiere retirar?** (koo*ahn*-toh dee-*neh*-roh kee*eh*-reh reh-tee-*rahr*)

✔ *Make a check out to yourself.* **Escriba un cheque a si mismo.** (ehs-*kree*-bvah oon *cheh*-keh ah see *mees*-moh)

✔ *Make the check out for cash.* **Escriba el cheque para efectivo.** (ehs-*kree*-bvah ehl *cheh*-keh *pah*-rah eh-fehk-*tee*-bvoh)

✔ *You don't have that much money in your account.* **No tiene los fondos disponibles en su cuenta.** (noh tee*eh*-neh lohs *fohn*-dohs dees-poh-*nee*-bvlehs ehn soo koo*ehn*-tah)

Handling transfers

Transferring money from one account to another is typically a no-brainer. All you need to know is how much, the account to transfer from, and the account to transfer to. If the customer presents you with a completed transfer slip, you're good to go. If she doesn't, you need to know how to ask for the information you need. Check out the following dialogue for a guide.

Talkin' the Talk

 Mr. Sanchez arrives at the bank to transfer $300 from his savings to his checking account. The bank teller, Bridgette, leads Mr. Sanchez through the transfer and processes the transaction.

Bridgette: **Bienvenido a nuestro banco.**
bveeehn-bveh-*nee*-doh ah noo*eh*-stroh *bvahn*-koh
Welcome to our bank.

¿Cómo puedo ayudarle?
koh-moh poo-*eh*-doh ah-yoo-*dahr*-leh
How may I help you?

Mr. Sanchez   **Quisiera transferir dinero.**
kee-see*eh*-rah trahns feh-*reer* dee-*neh*-roh
I would like to transfer some money.

Bridgette: **¿Cuál es su número de cuenta?**
koo*ahl* ehs soo *noo*-meh-roh deh koo*ehn*-tah
What is your account number?

Mr. Sanchez: **123-456789.**
oo-noh dohs trehs koo*ah*-troh *seen*-koh *seh*ees
see*eh*-teh *oh*-choh noo*eh*-bveh
123-456789.

Bridgette: **¿Cuánto dinero quisiera transferir?**
koo*ahn*-toh dee-*neh*-roh kee-see*eh*-rah
trahns-feh-*reer*
How much money would you like to transfer?

Mr. Sanchez: **Trescientos dólares.**
treh-see*eh*n-tohs *doh*-lah-rehs
$300.

Bridgette: **¿De cuál cuenta — de cheque o de ahorros?**
deh koo*ahl* koo*ehn*-tah deh *cheh*-keh oh deh
ah-*oh*-rrohs
From which account — checking or savings?

Mr. Sanchez: **De la cuenta de ahorros.**
deh lah koo*ehn*-tah deh ah-*oh*-rrohs
From savings.

Bridgette: **¿A cuál cuenta?**
ah koo*ahl* koo*ehn*-tah
To which account?

Mr. Sanchez: **A la cuenta de cheque.**
ah lah koo*ehn*-tah deh *cheh*-keh
To checking.

Bridgette: **Yo transferí trescientos dólares de su cuenta de ahorros a su cuenta de cheque.**
yoh trahns-feh-*ree* treh-see*eh*n-tohs doh-*lah*-rehs deh
soo koo*ehn*-tah deh ah-*oh*-rrohs ah soo koo*ehn*-tah
deh cheh-keh
*I transferred $300 from your savings account to your
checking account.*

Book IV

**Spanish
at Work**

Este es su recibo.
ehs-teh ehs soo reh-*see*-bvoh
This is your receipt.

¿Hay algo más hoy?
ahy *ahl*-goh mahs ohy
Is there anything else today?

Mr. Sanchez: **No, gracias.**
noh *grah*-seeahs
No, thank you.

Bridgette: **Gracias por su visita.**
grah-see*ahs* pohr soo bvee-*see*-tah
Thank you for your visit.

Addressing Common Problems

As you know, you spend a good deal of your day answering questions and solving problems. Perhaps the customer shows up with a check you can't cash, is trying to deal with an overdraw issue, or needs help understanding a discrepancy between what's on her bank statement and what she has written in her check register. Although we obviously can't script the infinite number of scenarios you may encounter, the following sections reveal phrases that apply to common scenarios.

Offering help

If a customer looks confused or lost, you may need to offer assistance. Here are some phrases to start the conversation on the right foot:

- ✔ *Do you need help?* **¿Necesita ayuda?** (neh-seh-*see*-tah ah-*yoo*-dah)
- ✔ *What is the problem?***¿Cuál es el problema?** (koo*ahl* ehs ehl proh-*bvleh*-mah)
- ✔ *What do you want?***¿Qué quiere?** (keh kee*eh*-reh)
- ✔ *What do you need?***¿Qué necesita?** (keh neh-seh-*see*-tah)
- ✔ *I'm sorry.* **Lo siento.** (loh see*ehn*-toh)
- ✔ *I'll see what I can do.* **Yo veré lo que puedo hacer.** (yoh bveh-*reh* loh keh poo*eh*-doh ah-*sehr*)

Explaining problems cashing checks

Here are some handy phrases for clarifying why you can't cash a customer's check; see "Cashing checks" earlier in this chapter for more on check cashing:

✔ *We can't cash this check.* **No podemos cambiar este cheque.** (noh poh-*deh*-mohs kahm-bvee*ahr* ehs-teh *cheh*-keh)

✔ *We can't cash your check unless you have an account with us.* **No podemos cambiar su cheque a menos que usted tenga una cuenta con nosotros.** (noh poh-*deh*-mohs kahm-bvee*ahr* soo *cheh*-keh ah *meh*-nohs keh oos-tehd *tehn*-gah *oo*-nah koo*ehn*-tah kohn noh-*soh*-trohs)

✔ *We deposited the check, but the funds will not be available until [day of week].* **Depositamos el cheque pero no tendrá fondos disponibles hasta que [day of week].** (deh-poh-see-*tah*-mohs ehl *cheh*-keh *peh*-roh noh tehn-*drah fohn*-dohs dees-poh-*nee*-bvlehs *ahs*-tah keh [day of week])

See Book I, Chapter 2 for days of the week and dates.

✔ *We can't cash the check unless you have a photo ID.* **No podemos cambiar el cheque a menos que usted tenga una identificación con foto.** (noh poh-*deh*-mohs kahm-bvee*ahr* chl *cheh*-keh ah *meh*-nohs keh oos-tehd *tehn*-gah *oo*-nah ee-dehn-tee-fee-kah-see*ohn* kohn *foh*-toh)

✔ *You don't have enough money in your account to cash this check.* **Usted no tiene los fondos disponibles en su cuenta para cambiar este cheque.** (oos-tehd noh tee*eh*-neh lohs *fohn*-dohs dees-poh-*nee*-bvlehs ehn soo koo*ehn*-tah *pah*-rah kahm-bvee*ahr* ehs-teh *cheh*-keh)

✔ *We can't accept this signature.* **No podemos aceptar esta firma.** (noh poh-*deh*-mohs ah-sehp-*tahr* ehs-tah *feer*-mah)

✔ *This check is invalid.* **Este cheque no es válido.** (*ehs*-teh *cheh*-keh noh ehs *bvah*-lee-doh)

Explaining other problems

Use the following phrases to describe other issues that customers commonly encounter:

✔ *Your account is overdrawn.* **Su cuenta está en discubierto.** (soo koo*ehn*-tah ehs-*tah* ehn dees-koo-bvee*ehr*-toh)

✔ *You don't have enough money in your account.* **No tiene los fondos disponibles en su cuenta.** (no tee*eh*-neh lohs *fohn*-dohs dees-poh-*nee*-bvlehs ehn soo koo*ehn*-tah)

Book IV

Spanish at Work

✔ *I can't help you because your name isn't on the account.* **No puedo ayudarle porque usted no tiene su nombre en la cuenta.** (noh poo*eh*-doh ah-yoo-*dahr*-leh *pohr*-keh oos-*tehd* noh tee*eh*-neh soo *nohm*-bvreh ehn lah koo*ehn*-tah)

✔ *I need more information.* **Necesito más información.** (neh-seh-*see*-toh mahs een-foh-mah-see*ohn*)

✔ *The funds aren't available.* **No tiene fondos disponibles.** (noh tee*eh*-neh *fohn*-dohs dees-poh-*nee*-bvlehs)

Chapter 5

Spanish in the Office

- -

In This Chapter

⌐ Gathering information from prospective employees

⌐ Describing compensation and benefits

⌐ Referring to buildings, office equipment, and furniture

⌐ Providing some basic training

- -

Depending on the type of business you run and its location, you may have a considerable number of highly qualified Spanish-speaking individuals in your workforce. Hiring these individuals can benefit your business in more ways than one. Of course, every business can benefit by hiring qualified and highly motivated individuals of any nationality, but Spanish-speakers can also make your business more culturally diverse and enable you to tap into unserved and underserved markets in your area.

This chapter is primarily for management, human resources personnel, and trainers in office environments. It addresses situations including interviewing Spanish-speaking job candidates; explaining compensation and benefits; describing buildings, office equipment, and supplies; and training new hires on common tasks.

Depending on what industry you're in, checking out the other chapters in Book IV may give you additional helpful vocabulary related to your workplace. For more strategies and tips on how to make your company, store, or office more culturally diverse and more appealing to the increasingly multicultural marketplace, check out *Cross-Cultural Selling For Dummies* by Michael Soon Lee and Ralph R. Roberts (Wiley).

Interviewing Job Candidates

The first step in introducing Spanish-speaking employees to your workplace is to have candidates complete an application before you then interview the most qualified applicants. The following sections show you how.

Prior to hiring any Spanish-speaking employees, consult your attorney to be sure you have any required notices posted and that you're in compliance with all federal and state labor laws. For more information, consider visiting the U.S. Department of Labor Web site at www.dol.gov.

Having candidates complete an application

One of the easiest ways to gather information about job candidates is to have them fill out a job application. Make sure the application is as detailed as you need it to be. The more information you can gather in writing, the less you need to acquire during interviews. Figure 5-1 provides a fairly basic job application to get you started.

You can simply hand the form to the applicant and say something like:

> *Please complete this application.* **Por favor, complete esta solicitud.**
> (pohr fah-*bvohr* kohm-*pleh*-teh *ehs*-tah soh-lee-see-*tood)*

Solicitud de Empleo *(Job Application)*	**Fecha** *(Date)*:
Nombre: Apellido, nombre, inicial del segundo nombre *(Name: Last, First, M.I.)*	

Dirección *(Address)*	**Ciudad/Estado/Código postal** *(City/State/Zip Code)*
Casa teléfono *(Home Telephone Number)*	**Número de teléfono celular** *(Cell Phone Number)*
Fecha de nacimiento *(Birthdate)* **Mes** *(Month)* _____ **Día** *(Day)* _____ **Año** *(Year)* _____	**Número de seguro social** *(Social Security Number)*
Posición deseada *(Position Sought)*	**Fecha de inicio deseada** *(Desired Start Date)*
Tiempo completo/parcial *(Full Time/Part Time)* ____ **Completo** ____ **Parcial**	**Cambio deseado** *(Desired Shift – Morning, Day, Night)* ____ **Mañana** ____ **Día** ____ **Noche**

Días que pueda trabajar *(Days You Can Work)*

____ **Lunes** *(Monday)* ____ **Martes** *(Tuesday)* ____ **Miércoles** *Wednesday* ____ **Jueves** *Thursday*

____ **Viernes** *Friday* ____ **Sábado** *Saturday* ____ **Domingo** *Sunday*

Historia de Empleo *(Employment History)*

Patrón *(Employer)*	**Teléfono** *(Telephone)*	**Empleo** *(Position)*	**Razón para abandonar** *(Reason for Leaving)*

¿Podemos entrar en contacto con su empleador actual? *(May we contact your present employer?)*

____ **Sí** ____ **No**

Educación *(Education)*

Escuela *(School)*	**Ubicación** *(Location)*	**Fechas** *(Dates)*	**Graduado** *(Graduate)*
			____ **Sí** ____ **No**
			____ **Sí** ____ **No**
			____ **Sí** ____ **No**

Especial de Formación/Habilidades *(Special Training/Skills)*

1. _____

2. _____

3. _____

Dos referencias, no familiares o empleadores anteriores *(Two References – Not Relatives or Previous Employers))*

1. _____

2. _____

Figure 5-1:
Use this job application to gather basic information.

Identifying skills

Hopefully, your applicants provide sufficient detail on their job applications to enable you to match their skills with specific job-related tasks. If you're still not sure, you may need to gather this information during the initial interview. You may want to ask the following question, filling in the task (from Table 5-1) that you need to know whether the person can perform:

Are you able to . . . ? **¿Puede usted . . . ?** (poo*eh*-deh oos-*tehd*)

Table 5-1	Common Office-Related Tasks	
English	*Spanish*	*Pronunciation*
clean	**limpiar**	leem-pee*ahr*
file documents	**archivar**	ahr-chee-*bvahr*
manage money	**administrar el dinero**	ahd-meen-ees-*trahr* ehl dee-*neh*-roh
manage others	**dirigir a los demás**	dee-ree-*heer* ah lohs deh-*mahs*
organize projects	**organizar proyectos**	ohr-gah-nee-*sahr* proh-*yehk*-tohs
operate a computer	**manejar una computadora**	mah-neh-*Hahr* oo-nah kohm-poo-tah-*doh*-rah
do computer programming	**programar computadoras**	proh-grah-*mahr* kohm-poo-tah-*doh*-rahs
do data entry	**entrar datos**	ehn-*trahr* dah-tohs
manage a database	**manejar una base de datos**	mah-neh-*hahr* oo-nah *bvah*-seh deh *dah*-tohs
use a presentation program	**usar un programa de presentación**	oo-*sahr* oon proh-*grah*-mah deh preh-sehn-tah-see*ohn*
create a spreadsheet	**crear una hoja de cálculo**	kreh-*ahr* oo-nah *oh*-Hah deh *kahl*-koo-loh
type	**escribir a máquina**	ehs-kree-*bveer* ah *mah*-kee-nah
do word processing	**manejar el procesamiento de textos**	mah-neh-*Hahr* ehl proh-seh-sah-mee*ehn*-toh deh *tehks*-tohs

Checking previous positions

Applicants who've had previous work experience are typically eager to list that on their applications, so make sure you have a space on your application form for "previous positions." Table 5-2 lists common office positions along with their Spanish equivalents to enable you to decipher the job applications you're reviewing.

Table 5-2	Common Office Positions	
English	*Spanish*	*Pronunciation*
the assistant	**el/la asistente/a**	ehl/lah ah-sees-*tehn*-teh/tah
the boss	**el/la patrón/a**	ehl/lah pah-*trohn*/ah
the cashier	**el/la cajero/a**	ehl/lah kah-*Heh*-roh/rah
the cleaner	**el/la limpiador/a**	ehl/lah leem-peeah-*dohr*/ah
the clerk	**el/la oficinista**	ehl/lah oh-fee-see-*nee*-stah
the data processor	**el/la proccsador/a de datos**	ehl/lah pro-seh-sah-*dohr*/ah deh *dah*-tohs
the driver	**el/la conductor/a**	ehl/lah kohn-dook-*tohr*/ah
the inspector	**el/la inspector/a**	ehl/lah een-spehk-*tohr*/ah
the janitor	**el/la conserje**	ehl/lah kohn-*sehr*-Heh
the operator	**el/la operador/a**	ehl/lah oh-peh-rah-*dohr*/ah
programmer	**el/la programador/a**	ehl/lah proh-grah-mah-*dohr*/ah
receptionist	**el/la recepcionista**	ehl/lah reh-kehp-seeohn-*ees*-tah
salesperson	**el/la vendedor/a**	ehl/lah bvehn-deh-*dohr*/ah
secretary	**el/la secretario/a**	ehl/lah sehk-reh-*tah*-reeoh/ah
technician	**el/la técnico/a**	ehl/lah *tehk*-nee-koh/kah
temp	**el/la temporero/a**	ehl/lah tehm-poh-*reh*-roh/rah
worker	**el/la obrero/a**	ehl/lah oh-*bvreh*-roh/rah

Book IV

Spanish at Work

Asking some key questions

Situational interviews — in which you place the interviewee in a situation and then evaluate what she would do and why — are all the rage. If the interviewee speaks little or no English (and your Spanish is no better), however, you can do better by sticking with very simple, direct questions that result in very simple, direct answers, as demonstrated in the following dialogue.

Talkin' the Talk

 Barry has invited Carmen to an interview for a position as an office assistant. After the usual greetings and pleasantries, Barry asks Carmen some very basic questions.

Barry	**¿Ha usted trabajado en una oficina antes?**
	ah oos-*tehd* trah-bvah-*Hah*-doh ehn *oo*-nah oh-fee-*see*-nah *ahn*-tehs
	Have you worked in an office before?

Carmen	**No. Generalmente he trabajado de limpiadora.**
	noh Heh-neh-rahl-*mehn*-teh eh trah-bvah-*Hah*-doh deh leem-peeah-*dohr*-ah
	No. I've done mostly cleaning.

Barry	**Este trabajo requiere que usted limpia un poco, pero también necesita escribir a máquina y archivar. ¿Puede hacer eso?**
	ehs-teh trah-*bvah*-Hoh reh-keee*eh*-reh keh oos-*tehd* *leem*-peeah oon *poh*-koh *peh*-roh tahm-bvee*ehn* neh-seh-*see*-tah ehs-kree-*bveer* ah *mah*-kee-nah ee ahr-chee-*bvahr* poo*eh*-deh ah-*sehr eh*-soh
	This job requires some cleaning, but I also need you to do some typing and filing. Can you do that?

Carmen	**Sí, no habría ningún problema con eso.**
	see noh ah-*bvree*-ah neen-*goon* proh-*bvleh*-mah kohn *eh*-soh
	Yes, that wouldn't be a problem.

Barry	**¿También puede usted preparar un paquete para enviar y llevarlo al correo?**
	tahm-bveee*ehn* poo*eh*-deh oos-*tehd* preh-pah-*rahr* oon pah-*keh*-teh *pah*-rah ehn-bveea*hr* ee yeh-*bvahr*-loh ahl koh-*rreh*-oh
	Are you also able to prepare packages and take them to the post office?

Carmen	**Sí, puedo hacer eso para usted.**
	see poo*eh*-doh ah-*sehr eh*-soh *pah*-rah oos-*tehd*
	Yes, I can do that for you.

| Barry | **¿Tiene una licencia de conducir?** |
| | teee*eh*-neh oo-nah lee-*sehn*-seeah deh kohn-doo-*seer* |

Do you have a driver's license?

Carmen   **Sí, aquí está mi licencia de conducir.**
see ah-*kee* ehs-*tah* mee lee-*sehn*-seeah deh
kohn-doo-*seer*
Yes, here is my driver's license.

Barry   **¿Puedo contar con usted estar aquí todos los días a tiempo?**
poo*eh*-doh kohn-*tahr* kohn oos-*tehd* ehs-*tahr* ah-*kee*
toh-dohs lohs *dee*-ahs ah tee*ehm*-poh
Can I rely on you to show up for work every day on time?

Carmen   **Claro que sí. Tengo muchas ganas de trabajar.**
klah-roh keh see *tehn*-goh *moo*-chahs *gah*-nahs deh
trah-bvah-*Hahr*
Yes, of course. I'm eager to work.

Barry   **¿Puede empezar el próximo lunes?**
poo*eh*-deh ehm-peh-*sahr* ehl *prohk*-see-moh *loo*-nehs
Can you begin working this coming Monday?

Carmen   **Sería mejor para mí empezar el lunes siguiente.**
seh-*ree*-ah meh-*Hohr* *pah*-rah mee ehm-peh-*sahr* ehl
loo-nehs see-gee*ehn*-teh
It would be better for me to start the following Monday.

Barry   **Está bien.**
ehs-*tah* bvee*ehn*
That is fine.

Por favor venga a mi oficina a las ocho de la mañana el lunes siguiente este lunes.
pohr fah-*bvohr* bvehn-gah ah mee oh-fee-*see*-nah ah
lahs *oh*-choh deh lah mah-*nyah*-nah ehl *loo*-nehs
see-gee*ehn*-teh *eh*-steh *loo*-nehs
Please report to me at eight o'clock in the morning on the Monday following this Monday.

Carmen   **Gracias. Hasta aquel entonces.**
grah-seeahs ah-stah ah-*kehl* ehn-*tohn*-sehs
Thank you. I'll see you then.

Checking a candidate's availability

After you have determined that a candidate has the knowledge, skills, and experience required for a particular opening, you need to find out whether the applicant can work the required days, shifts, and numbers of hours per week. The following yes/no questions can help you extract the necessary information:

- ✔ *Can you work Monday through Friday?* **¿Puede usted trabajar lunes a viernes?** (poo*eh*-deh oos-*tehd* trah-bvah-*Hahr loo*-nehs ah bvee*ehr*-nehs)

- ✔ *Are you willing to work weekends?* **¿Está usted dispuesto/a a trabajar durante los fines de semana?** (eh-*stah* oos-*tehd* dees-poo*ehs*-toh/tah ah trah-bvah-*Hahr* doo-*rahn*-teh lohs *fee*-nehs deh seh-*mah*-nah)

- ✔ *Can you work mornings?* **¿Puede usted trabajar durante la mañana?** (poo*eh*-deh oos-*tehd* trah-bvah-*Hahr* doo-*rahn*-teh lah mah-*nyah*-nah)

- ✔ *Can you work days?* **¿Puede usted trabajar durante el día?** (poo*eh*-deh oos-*tehd* trah-bvah-*Hahr* doo-*rahn*-teh ehl *dee*-ah)

- ✔ *Can you work nights?* **¿Puede usted trabajar durante la noche?** (poo*eh*-deh oos-*tehd* trah-bvah-*Hahr* doo-*rahn*-teh lah *noh*-cheh)

- ✔ *Can you start working today?* **¿Puede empezar hoy?** (poo*eh*-deh ehm-peh-*sahr* ohy)

- ✔ *Can you start working next week?* **¿Puede empezar la próxima semana?** (poo*eh*-deh ehm-peh-*sahr* lah *prohk*-see-mah seh-*mah*-nah)

- ✔ *Can you start working two weeks from today?* **¿Puede empezar en dos semanas?** (poo*eh*-deh ehm-peh-*sahr* ehn dohs seh-*mah*-nahs)

Explaining Compensation and Benefits

At some point in the hiring process, or perhaps the first day your new employee shows up for work, you have to provide some orientation and review your compensation package and benefits. The following sections bring you up to speed on the basics.

Laying out your pay rate

Hopefully, your personnel are eager to work, but they're probably even more eager to get paid! To avoid any confusion, make sure your employees know two things about their pay — how much they're getting paid and when.

When you're talking about how much and when, numbers, dates, and days of week come in very handy. Refer to Book I, Chapter 2 to brush up on the basics.

How much?

When describing how much your employees are earning, you usually have to specify your pay rate — a dollar amount per hour, week, month, or year. You may want to begin with a phrase such as:

- *You'll be earning* . . . **Usted ganará** . . . (oos-*tehd* gah-nah-*rah*)

- *We will be paying you* . . . **Nosotros le pagaremos** . . . (noh-*soh*-trohs leh pah-gah-*reh*-mohs)

And then follow up with a description of the pay rate, as in the following examples:

- *Minimum wage* **salario mínimo** (sah-*lah*-reeoh *mee*-nee-moh)

- *$8 per hour* **ocho dólares por hora** (*oh*-choh *doh*-lah-rehs pohr *oh*-rah)

- *$250 per week* **doscientos cincuenta dólares por semana** (doh-seee*ehn*-tohs seen-koo*ehn*-tah *doh*-lah-rehs pohr seh-*mah*-nah)

- *$20,000 per year* **Veinte mil dólares por año** (bveh*een*-teh meel *doh*-lah-rehs pohr *ah*-nyoh)

- *Time and a half for overtime* **Sueldo normal más una mitad por horas sobre cuarenta horas la semana** (soo*ehl*-doh nohr-*mahl* mahs *oo*-nah mee-*tahd* pohr *oh*-rahs *soh*-bvreh kooah-*rehn*-tah *oh*-rahs lah seh-*mah*-nah)

When?

Telling people when they can expect to get paid is fairly easy if you know the days of the week and times of day covered in Book I, Chapter 2. Here are some examples:

- *You receive a paycheck every Friday at the end of your shift.* **Recibirá un cheque de sueldo todos los viernes cuando termina su turno.** (reh-see-bvee-*rah* oon *cheh*-keh deh soo*ehl*-doh *toh*-dohs lohs bvee*ehr*-nehs koo*ahn*-doh tehr-*mee*-nah soo *toor*-noh)

- *Pick up your paycheck at the office every other Friday.* **Recoja su cheque de sueldo en la oficina dos viernes al mes.** (reh-*koh*-Hah soo *cheh*-keh deh soo*ehl*-doh ehn lah oh-fee-*see*-nah dohs bvee*ehr*-nehs ahl mehs)

- *We mail your paycheck to you every other Wednesday.* **Nosotros le mandaremos su cheque de sueldo por correo dos miércoles al mes.** (noh-*soh*-trohs leh mahn-dah-*reh*-mohs soo *cheh*-keh deh soo*ehl*-doh pohr koh-*rreh*-oh dohs meee*ehr*-koh-lehs ahl mehs)

Describing lunchtimes and breaks

You can avoid confusion by specifying upfront exactly when employees can take breaks and eat their lunches. Here are some sample phrases:

- ✔ *You have two breaks and a lunch hour every day.* **Tiene dos descansos y un almuerzo de una hora todos los días.** (tee*eh*-neh dohs dehs-*kahn*-sohs ee oon ahl-moo*ehr*-soh deh *oo*-nah *oh*-rah *toh*-dohs lohs *dee*-ahs)

- ✔ *Breaks last fifteen minutes.* **Los descansos duran quince minutos.** (lohs dehs-*kahn*-sohs *doo*-rahn *keen*-seh mee-*noo*-tohs)

- ✔ *Your breaks are at 10:30 a.m. and 2:30 p.m.* **Sus descansos son a las diez y media de la mañana y a las dos y media de la tarde.** (soos dehs-*kahn*-sohs sohn ah lahs dee*ehs* ee *meh*-deeah deh lah mah-*nyah*-nah ee ah lahs dohs ee *meh*-deeah deh lah *tahr*-deh)

- ✔ *You have a half hour for lunch.* **Tiene media hora de almuerzo.** (tee*eh*-neh *meh*-deeah *oh*-rah deh ahl-moo*ehr*-soh)

Explaining vacations and sick days

Explaining vacation days and sick days can become fairly complex, especially if you're hiring a new employee later in the year. In the following sections, we provide some basic phrases to get you started, but you may have to improvise quite a bit if your situation is more involved.

Vacation days

Explaining vacation days depends a great deal on how your vacation day benefits are structured. Some companies, for example, allocate vacation days in weeks, while at other companies employees may earn a day for every month they work. Here are some example explanations for different situations:

- ✔ *You earn one vacation day for every 30 days you work.* **Usted gana un día de vacación por cada treinta días que trabaja.** (oos-*tehd gah*-nah oon *dee*-ah deh bvah-kah-see*ohn* pohr *kah*-dah treh*een*-tah *dee*ahs keh trah-*bvah*-Hah)

- ✔ *You receive two weeks vacation per year.* **Usted recibe dos semanas de vacación por año.** (oos-*tehd* reh-*see*-bveh dohs seh-*mah*-nahs deh bvah-kah-see*ohn* pohr *ah*-nyoh)

- ✔ *After working here five years, you receive three weeks vacation per year.* **Después de trabajar aquí por cinco años, recibirá tres semanas de vacación por año.** (dehs-poo*ehs* deh trah-bvah-*Hahr* ah-*kee* pohr *seen*-koh *ah*-nyohs reh-see-bvee-*rah* trehs seh-*mah*-nahs deh bvah-kah-see*ohn* pohr *ah*-nyoh)

✔ *For this year, you earn four days vacation. When you work a full year, you'll have two weeks vacation per year.* **Por este año, ganará cuatro días de vacación. Cuando trabaja un año completo, tendrá dos semanas de vacación por año.** (pohr *eh*-steh *ah*-nyoh gah-nah-*rah* koo*ah*-troh *dee*-ahs deh bvah-kah-see*ohn* koo*ahn*-doh trah-*bvah*-Hah oon *ah*-nyoh kohm-*pleh*-toh tehn-*drah* dohs seh-*mah*-nahs deh bvah-kah-see*ohn*-ehs pohr *ah*-nyoh)

✔ *Please let us know your vacation plans at least one month prior to taking a vacation.* **Favor de informarnos de sus planes por lo menos un mes antes de tomar una vacación.** (fah-*bvohr* deh een-fohr-*mahr*-nohs deh soos *plah*-nehs pohr loh *meh*-nohs oon mehs *ahn*-tehs deh toh-*mahr* oo-nah bvah-kah-see*ohn*)

Sick days

Providing days off for illnesses and family illness is essential. Equally important is informing all of your employees of these important benefits. Following are some sample phrases that you can customize by plugging in the correct numbers when necessary:

✔ *You can take off up to five days per year for illness.* **Puede tomar hasta cinco días por año para enfermedad.** (poo*eh*-deh toh-*mahr* ahs-tah *seen*-koh *dee*-ahs pohr *ah*-nyoh *pah*-rah ehn-fehr-meh-*dahd*)

✔ *By law, you can take up to 12 weeks off after having a baby.* **Según la ley, se puede tomar hasta doce semanas después de dar a luz.** (seh-*goon* lah leh seh poo*eh*-deh toh-*mahr* ahs-tah doh-*seh* seh-mah-*nahs* dehs-poo*ehs* deh dahr ah loos)

✔ *We will keep your job until you return.* **Conservaremos su trabajo hasta que vuelva.** (kohn-sehr-bvah-*reh*-mohs soo trah-*bvah*-Hoh *ahs*-tah keh bvoo*ehl*-bvah)

✔ *We will pay you for up to four weeks after having a baby.* **Le pagaremos hasta cuatro semanas después de dar a luz** (leh pah-gah-*reh*-mohs *ahs*-tah coo*ah*-troh seh-*mah*-nahs dehs-poo*ehs* deh dahr ah loos

✔ *You can take off up to two days per year for any family illness.* **Puede tomar hasta dos días por año para una enfermedad en la familia.** (poo*eh*-deh toh-*mahr* ahs-tah dohs *dee*-ahs pohr *ah*-nyoh *pah*-rah oo-nah ehn-fehr-meh-*dahd* ehn lah fah-*mee*-leeah)

✔ *Any sick days you don't use carry over to the next year.* **Los días de enfermedad que no usa acumulan al próximo año.** (lohs *dee*-ahs deh ehn-fehr-meh-*dahd* keh noh oo-sah ah-koo-*moo*-lahn ahl *prohk*-see-moh *ah*-nyoh)

✔ *Unused sick days don't carry over to the next year.* **Los días de enfermedad que no usa no acumulan al próximo año.** (lohs *dee*-ahs deh ehn-fehr-meh-*dahd* keh noh oo-sah noh ah-koo-*moo*-lahn ahl *prok*-see-moh *ah*-nyoh)

Book IV

Spanish at Work

✔ *Sick days are only to be used if you or a family member is ill.* **Solamente se puede usar los días de enfermedad si usted o su familia esté enfermo.** (soh-lah-*mehn*-teh seh poo*eh*-deh *oo*-sahr lohs *dee*-ahs deh ehn-fehr-meh-*dahd* see oos-*tehd* oh soo fah-*mee*-leeah ehs-*teh* ehn-*fehr*-moh)

Discussing health insurance and pension

As medical costs soar and Social Security benefits become iffier and iffier, health insurance and pension plans are growing in importance for workers. Assuming you offer health insurance or a pension plan, you need to know how to communicate these valuable benefits to all of your employees.

Health insurance

Following are some phrases for explaining your health insurance benefits and plans:

✔ *You must work here for three months before you are eligible for health insurance.* **Tiene que trabajar aquí por tres meses antes de reunir los requisitos necesarios para recibir el seguro médico.** (tee*eh*-neh keh trah-bvah-*Hahr* ah-*kee* pohr trehs *meh*-sehs *ahn*-tehs deh *reh*oo-neer lohs reh-kee-*see*-tohs neh-seh-*sah*-reeohs *pah*-rah reh-see-*bveer* ehl seh-*goo*-roh *meh*-dee-koh

✔ *Our health insurance plan costs you $125 per month to cover only you.* **Nuestro plan de seguro médico cuesta ciento veinticinco dólares cada mes para usted solo/a.** (noo*es*-troh plahn deh seh-*goo*-roh *meh*-dee-koh koo*ehs*-tah see*ehn*-toh bveheen-tee-*seen*-koh *doh*-lah-rehs *kah*-dah mehs *pah*-rah oos-*tehd soh*-loh/lah)

✔ *To cover you and your family, the cost is $167 per month.* **Para asegurar a toda su familia, cuesta ciento sesenta y siete dólares cada mes.** (*pah*-rah ah-seh-goo-*rahr* ah *toh*-doh soo fah-*mee*-leeah koo*ehs*-tah see*ehn*-toh seh-*sehn*-tah ee see*eh*-teh *doh*-lah-rehs *kah*-dah mehs)

✔ *We pay more than half the cost of your health insurance.* **Nosotros pagamos más que la mitad de la costa del seguro médico.** (noh-*soh*-trohs pah-*gah*-mohs mahs keh lah mee-*tahd* deh lah *kohs*-tah dehl seh-*goo*-roh *meh*-dee-koh)

✔ *The payment is taken out of your paycheck.* **Nosotros sacamos la costa del seguro médico de su cheque de sueldo.** (noh-*soh*-trohs sah-*kah*-mohs lah *kohs*-tah dehl seh-*goo*-roh *meh*-dee-koh deh soo *cheh*-keh deh soo*ehl*-doh)

- ✔ *You'll receive medical insurance cards two weeks after you make your first payment.* **Recibirá sus tarjetas de seguro médico dos semanas después de hacer el primero pago.** (reh-see-bvee-*rah* soos tahr-*Heh*-tahs deh seh-*goo*-roh *meh*-dee-koh dohs seh-*mah*-nahs dehs-poo*ehs* deh ah-*sehr* ehl pree-*meh*-roh *pah*-goh)

- ✔ *Dental coverage is included.* **Seguro dental está incluido.** (seh-*goo*-roh dehn-*tahl* ehs-*tah* een-kloo*ee*-doh)

Pension plan

To describe pension plan benefits, warm up with the following statements:

- ✔ *You can contribute some of your pay to a retirement savings plan.* **Usted puede contribuir parte de su sueldo a un plan de jubilación.** (oos-*tehd* poo*eh*-deh kohn-tree-bvoo*eer pahr*-teh deh soo soo*ehl*-doh a oon plahn deh Hoo-bvee-lah-see*ohn*)

- ✔ *For every dollar you contribute, up to $100 per month, we add a dollar to your account.* **Para cada dólar que usted contribuya, hasta cien dólares por mes, nosotros contribuiríamos un dólar a su cuenta.** (*pah*-rah *kah*-dah *doh*-lahr keh oos-*tehd* kohn-tree-*bvoo*-yah *ahs*-tah see*ehn doh*-lah-rehs pohr mehs noh-*soh*-trohs kohn-tree-bvoo*eer*-*ee*-ah-mohs oon *doh*-lahr ah soo koo*ehn*-tah)

- ✔ *If you take the money out of the account before you have worked here for five years, you'll lose some of the money we have added.* **Si usted efectue un reintegro antes de trabajar aquí por cinco años, perdería una parte del dinero que nosotros contribuiríamos.** (see oos-*tehd* eh-*fehk*-tooeh oon reheen-*teh*-groh *ahn*-tehs deh trah-bvah-*Hahr* ah-*kee* pohr *seen*-koh *ah*-nyohs pehr-deh-*ree*-ah *oo*-nah *pahr*-teh dehl dee-*neh*-roh keh noh-*soh*-trohs kohn-tree-bvoo*ee*-*ree*-ah-mohs)

- ✔ *If you take money out of the account before age 59 ½, you'll have to pay taxes and a penalty.* **Si usted efectue un reintegro antes de cumplir cincuenta y nueve y medio años, tendría que pagar impuestos y una sanción.** (see oos-*tehd* eh-*fehk*-tooeh oon reheen-*teh*-groh *ahn*-tehs deh koom-*pleer* seen-koo*ehn*-tah ee noo*eh*-bveh ee *meh*-deeoh *ah*-nyohs tehn-*dree*-ah keh pah-*gahr* eem-poo*ehs*-tohs ee *oo*-nah sahn-see*ohn*)

Book IV

Spanish at Work

Describing Buildings, Furniture, Equipment, and Supplies

As you're conversing with colleagues and co-workers, you need to be able to refer to the various buildings, equipment, and other stuff that comprises your business and fills the space. In the following sections, we show you the

Spanish names for the most common places and items you find in a business office.

Buildings, hangouts, and other key areas

You can often avoid the challenge of giving directions (see Book I, Chapter 8), by simply telling a person where to go — the copy room, the fifth floor, the office, the storage room, the mail room, and so on. (Check out Book I, Chapter 2 for ordinal numbers to help you name specific floors.) Table 5-3 lists common buildings and other key areas within a building or office that you may need to refer to along with their Spanish names.

Table 5-3	Buildings and Other Key Areas	
English	**Spanish**	**Pronunciation**
branch office	**la sucursal**	lah soo-koor-*sahl*
break room	**la sala de descanso**	lah *sah*-lah deh dehs-*kahn*-soh
building	**el edificio**	ehl eh-dee-*fee*-seeoh
copy room	**la sala de copias**	lah *sah*-lah deh *koh*-peeahs
department	**el departamento**	ehl deh-pahr-tah-*mehn*-toh
division	**la división**	lah dee-bvee-see*ohn*
elevator	**el ascensor**	ehl ah-sehn-*sohr*
entrance	**la entrada**	lah ehn-*trah*-dah
escalator	**la escalera mecánica**	lah ehs-kah-*leh*-rah meh-*kah*-nee-kah
exit	**la salida**	lah sah-*lee*-dah
floor	**el piso**	ehl *pee*-soh
loading dock	**la zona de carga y descarga**	lah *soh*-nah deh *kahr*-gah ee dehs-*kahr*-gah
lobby	**el vestíbulo**	ehl bvehs-*tee*-bvoo-loh
mailroom	**la sala de correos**	lah *sah*-lah deh koh-*rree*-ohs
office	**la oficina**	lah oh-fee-*see*-nah
plant	**la fábrica**	lah *fah*-bvree-kah
restroom	**el baño**	ehl *bvah*-nyoh
shop	**el taller**	ehl tah-*yehr*

English	Spanish	Pronunciation
stairway	**la escalera**	lah ehs-kah-*leh*-rah
storage room	**el cuarto de almacenamiento**	ehl koo*ahr*-toh deh ahl-mah-seh-nah-mee*ehn*-toh
store	**la tienda**	lah tee*ehn*-dah
warehouse	**el almacén**	ehl ahl-mah-*sehn*

Office furniture, equipment, and supplies

Every office is packed with a collection of the usual furniture, equipment, and supplies — everything from desks and chairs to photocopiers, fax machines, paper, and staples. The following sections introduce you to the terms you need to refer to just about everything you can expect to find in an office.

Furniture

You can easily discuss types of office furniture in a few words:

- *the chair* **la silla** (lah *see*-yah)
- *the desk lamp* **la lámpara de escritorio** (lah *lahm*-pah-rah deh ehs-kree-*toh*-reeoh)
- *the desk* **el escritorio** (ehl ehs-kree-*toh*-reeoh)
- *the filing cabinet* **el fichero** (ehl fee-*cheh*-roh)
- *the supply cabinet* **la vitrina** (lah bvee-*tree*-nah)
- *the waste basket* **el bote de basura** (ehl *bvoh*-teh deh bvah-*soo*-rah)

Equipment

Office equipment can vary a great deal but typically consists of one or more items (usually more) listed in Table 5-4.

Table 5-4	Common Office Equipment	
English	**Spanish**	**Pronunciation**
camera	**la cámara**	lah *kah*-mah-rah
cellphone	**el teléfono celular**	ehl teh-*leh*-foh-noh seh-loo-*lahr*
coffeemaker	**la cafetera**	lah kah-feh-*teh*-rah

(continued)

Table 5-4 *(continued)*

English	Spanish	Pronunciation
computer	**la computadora**	lah kohm-poo-tah-*doh*-rah
fax machine	**la máquina de fax**	lah *mah*-kee-nah deh fahks
hole punch	**la perforadora**	lah pehr-foh-rah-*doh*-rah
laptop computer	**la computadora portátil**	lah kohm-poo-tah-*doh*-rah pohr-*tah*-teel
pencil sharpener	**el sacapuntas**	ehl sah-kah-*poon*-tahs
photocopier	**la fotocopiadora**	lah foh-toh-koh-peeah-*doh*-rah
printer	**la impresora**	lah eem-preh-*soh*-rah
projector	**el proyector**	ehl proh-yehk-*tohr*
scissors	**las tijeras**	lahs tee-*Heh*-rahs
stapler	**la grapadora**	lah grah-pah-*doh*-rah
staple remover	**el sacagrapas**	ehl sah-kah-*grah*-pahs
telephone	**el teléfono**	ehl teh-*leh*-foh-noh
water cooler	**el enfriador de agua**	ehl ehn-freeah-*dohr* deh *ah*-gooah

Supplies

Before sending your assistant on an errand to the supply cabinet, brush up on the Spanish names for various office supplies, listed in Table 5-5.

Table 5-5   Common Office Supplies

English	Spanish	Pronunciation
adhesive tape	**la cinta adhesiva**	lah *seen*-tah ahd-eh-*see*-bvah
appointment book	**la agenda de entrevistas**	lah ah-*Hehn*-dah deh ehn-treh-*bvees*-tahs
calendar	**el calendario**	ehl kah-lehn-*dah*-reeoh
copy paper	**papel de fotocopiadora**	pah-*pehl* deh foh-toh-koh-peeah-*doh*-rah
envelopes	**sobres**	*soh*-bvrehs
erasers	**gomas de borrar**	*goh*-mahs de bvoh-*rrahr*
file folders	**carpetas**	kahr-*peh*-tahs
glue	**pegamento**	peh-gah-*mehn*-toh

English	Spanish	Pronunciation
ink cartridge	**un cartucho de tinta**	un kahr-*too*-choh deh *teen*-tah
markers	**marcadores**	mahr-kah-*doh*-rehs
notepads	**libretas**	lee-*bvreh*-tahs
paper	**papel**	pah-*pehl*
paper clips	**sujetapapeles**	soo-Heh-tah-pah-*peh*-lehs
pens	**bolígrafos**	bvoh-*lee*-grah-fohs
pencils	**lápices**	*lah*-pee-sehs
rubber bands	**ligas**	*lee*-gahs
stamps	**sellos**	*seh*-yohs
staples	**grapas**	*grah*-pahs

Training New Hires

The key to clear communication in an office setting is to keep it as simple as possible, at least until you have a pretty good grasp of Spanish or your Spanish-speaking employees have picked up enough English to understand most of what you have to say.

In the following sections, we provide you with some useful expressions, including some very basic questions to ask, and then provide you with basic commands you can issue to delegate tasks.

Mastering some useful expressions

Before you begin communicating with Spanish speaking workers, brush up on the following expressions:

- *What do you need?* **¿Qué necesita usted?** (keh neh-seh-*see*-tah oos-*tehd*)
- *Did you understand?* **¿Comprendió usted?** (kohm-prehn-dee*oh* oos-*tehd*)
- *Speak more slowly, please.* **Hable más despacio, por favor.** (*ah*-bvleh mahs dehs-*pah*-seeoh pohr fah-*bvohr*)
- *Please repeat.* **Repita, por favor.** (reh-*pee*-tah pohr fah-*bvohr*)
- *Again.* **De nuevo.** (deh noo*eh*-bvoh)

Issuing basic commands

Delegating tasks may be one of the most difficult jobs in an office setting, especially if you don't speak the language of the people who are supposed to be performing those tasks. In the following sections, we show you how to issue basic commands that are common in the office.

Most of the commands we present in the following sections consist of the imperative form of a verb. You can then add one or more nouns from earlier sections in this chapter to tell the employee what you want them to apply the action to. For example, *Bring the . . .* would be **Traiga el** or **la . . .**, which you can then follow with the word for *envelopes*, *stamps*, or whatever else you need the person to bring:

- *Come here.* **Venga aquí.** (*bvehn*-gah ah-*kee*)
- *Do it now.* **Hágalo ahora.** (*ah*-gah-loh ah-*oh*-rah)
- *Bring . . .* **Traiga . . .** (*trah*ee-gah)
- *Move . . .* **Mueva . . .** (moo*eh*-bvah)
- *Fill . . .* **Llene . . .** (*yeh*-neh)
- *Empty . . .* **Vacíe . . .** (bvah-*see*eh)
- *Open . . .* **Abra . . .** (*ah*-bvrah)
- *Close . . .* **Cierre . . .** (see*eh*-rreh)
- *Prepare . . .* **Prepare . . .** (preh-*pah*-reh)
- *Use . . .* **Use . . .** (*oo*-seh)
- *Do this . . .* **Haga eso . . .** (*ah*-gah *eh*-soh)
- *Please order . . .* **Por favor, pida . . .** (pohr fah-*bvohr pee*-dah)
- *Help . . .* **Ayude . . .** (ah-*yoo*-deh)
- *Find . . .* **Encuentre . . .** (ehn-koo*ehn*-treh)
- *Count . . .* **Cuente . . .** (koo*ehn*-teh)
- *Print . . .* **Imprima . . .** (eem-*pree*-mah)
- *Copy . . .* **Haga una copia . . .** (*ah*-gah *oo*-nah *koh*-peeah)
- *Staple . . .* **Engrape . . .** (ehn-*grah*-peh)
- *File . . .* **Archive . . .** (ahr-*chee*-bveh)
- *Paste . . .* **Pegue . . .** (*peh*-geh)
- *Count . . .* **Cuente . . .** (koo*ehn*-teh)

- *Type . . .* **Escriba a máquina . . .** (ehs-*kree*-bvah ah *mah*-kee-nah)

- *Mail . . .* **Envíe por correo . . .** (ehn-*bvee*eh pohr koh-*rreh*-oh)

- *E-mail . . .* **Envíe por correo electrónico . . .** (ehn-*bvee*eh pohr koh-*rreh*-oh eh-lehk-*troh*-nee-koh)

- *Deliver . . .* **Entregue . . .** (ehn-*treh*-geh)

For commands dealing with janitorial duties, such as mopping floors and emptying trash cans, refer to Book IV, Chapter 6.

Giving directions

Telling a co-worker where to go can be fairly easy, assuming you simply need to refer to a building or a particular area of the building (covered in "Buildings, hangouts, and other key areas" earlier in this chapter). (If you want to tell them to go certain other places, you're on your own.) If you need to be more specific, the following commands (or some variation of them) can come in handy:

- *Go up the stairs.* **Suba las escaleras.** (*soo*-bvah lahs ehs-kah-*leh*-rahs)

- *Go down the stairs.* **Baje las escaleras.** (*bvah*-Heh lahs ehs-kah-*leh*-rahs)

- *Use the elevator.* **Use el ascensor.** (*oo*-seh ehl ahs-sehn-*sohr*)

- *Turn to the right.* **Doble a la derecha.** (*doh*-bvleh ah lah deh-*reh*-chah)

- *Turn to the left.* **Doble a la izquierda.** (*doh*-bvleh ah lah ees-kee*ehr*-dah)

- *Straight ahead.* **Derecho.** (deh-*reh*-choh)

Laying down the rules

As an employer or supervisor, part of your job is to inform and remind employees of the rules. The following commands should help you cover the basics:

- *Be on time.* **Sea puntual.** (*seh*-ah poon-too*ahl*)

- *Don't leave early.* **No salga temprano.** (noh *sahl*-gah tehm-*prah*-noh)

- *No smoking.* **No fumar.** (no foo-*mahr*)

- *Park in the employee parking lot.* **Aparque en el estacionamiento de empleados.** (ah-*pahr*-keh ehn ehl ehs-tah-seeoh-nah-mee*ehn*-toh deh ehm-pleh-*ah*-dohs)

- *Report problems to your supervisor.* **Informe los problemas a su supervisor.** (een-*fohr*-meh lohs proh-*bvleh*-mahs ah soo soo-pehr-bvee-*sohr*)

Chapter 6

Spanish for Hotel and Restaurant Managers

As a hotel or restaurant manager, you may need to deal with Spanish on two fronts — when dealing with guests and with employees. With guests, you have to master the usual pleasantries — meeting and greeting new guests, providing them with a few basic instructions and directions, and explaining what you offer and how much you charge.

Dealing with employees can be more of a challenge, because you need to get a handle on a specialized vocabulary. If you manage a restaurant, for example, you need to know words for common kitchen equipment, utensils, and ingredients. If you're managing a hotel, on the other hand, you need to brush up on terminology for items found in most hotel rooms, cleaning equipment and supplies, and laundry room items.

This chapter provides the basic lexicon of words and phrases you need to communicate with Spanish-speaking guests, patrons, and employees, including housekeeping staff, laundry-room attendants, and kitchen workers.

Greeting Guests and Patrons

When Spanish-speaking guests who speak little English arrive at your establishment, you need to provide them with a warm greeting and know at least the basics of checking them in or seating them at a table. The following sections bring you up to speed in a hurry and can function as a quick refresher when Spanish-speakers arrive.

Mastering the meet and greet

Whenever guests arrive at your establishment, you should smile sincerely to show that you're happy to see them and then express a warm greeting, as explained in Book I, Chapter 3. Remember to use a formal greeting initially. Shift to an informal greeting in the future only if your guests address you in a more familiar way.

Regardless of how Spanish or Hispanic your guests may "look," don't automatically assume that they're foreigners or they prefer speaking Spanish. If two or more guests show up, listen to hear whether they're speaking Spanish to one another. If they are, you may want to greet them in Spanish. Otherwise, let them greet you first. If they greet you in English, speak English to them until they tell you otherwise or you feel that you're not understanding one another. You can then say something like the following:

> **Yo hablo un poco español. ¿Preferiría que yo hable en español?** (yoh *ah*-bvloh oon *poh*-koh ehs-pah-*nyohl* preh-feh-reh-*ree*-ah keh yoh *ah*-bvleh ehn ehs-pah-*nyohl*) *I speak a little Spanish. Would you prefer I speak in Spanish?*

Asking a few key questions

Before you can provide your guests with service, you need to gather some information about them by asking a few key questions. If you're just learning Spanish, try to ask *yes/no* **(sí/no)** questions as much as possible to avoid eliciting answers that that you're probably not going to understand.

The following questions can help you gather the most essential information:

- ✔ *Are you alone or with others?* **¿Está solo/a o hay otros con usted?** (ehs-*tah* soh-loh/lah oh ahy *oh*-trohs kohn oos-*tehd*)

- ✔ *How many people are in your group?* **¿Cuántos hay en su grupo?** (koo*ahn*-tohs ahy ehn soo *groo*-poh)

- ✔ *Do you have a reservation?* **¿Tiene una reservación?** (tee*eh*-neh *oo*-nah reh-sehr-bvah-see*ohn*)

✔ *What name did you give for the reservation?* **¿Qué apellido dieron para la reservación?** (keh ah-peh-*yee*-doh dee*eh*-rohn *pah*-rah lah reh-sehr-bvah-see*ohn*)

✔ *How many rooms do you need?* **¿Cuántas habitaciones necesita?** (koo*ahn*-tahs ah-bvee-tah-see*oh*-nehs neh-seh-*see*-tah)

✔ *Would you prefer a smoking or nonsmoking room/table?* **¿Preferiría una habitación/mesa de fumar o no fumar?** (preh-feh-ree-*ree*-ah *oo*-nah ah-bvee-tah-see*ohn*/*meh*-sah deh foo-*mahr* oh noh foo-*mahr*)

Unfortunately for some guests, you may be unable to provide service if all your rooms are booked or reservations are taken. In such cases, you need to explain what's going on:

✔ *I'm sorry, but all our rooms are occupied.* **Lo siento, pero todas las habitaciones están ocupadas.** (loh see*ehn*-toh *peh*-roh *toh*-dahs lahs ah-bvee-tah-see*ohn*-ehs ehs-*tahn* oh-koo-*pah*-dahs)

✔ *I'm sorry, you need to make a reservation in advance.* **Lo siento, es necesario reservar una habitación de antemano.** (loh see*ehn*-toh ehs neh-seh-*sah*-reeoh reh-sehr-*bvahr* oo-nah ah-bvee-tah-see*ohn* deh ahn-teh-*mah*-noh)

Explaining room rates, check-in times, and more

When guests are registering for a room at your hotel or motel, you need to explain your room rates and check-in/check-out times, obtain a credit card number, and perhaps have them sign a registry. Following are some phrases that can get you through the check-in process; see Book I, Chapter 2 for more information on numbers and times:

✔ *The room costs $45 dollars per day.* **La habitación cuesta cuarenta y cinco dólares por día.** (lah ah-bvee-tah-see*ohn* koo*ehs*-tah kooah-*rehn*-tah ee *seen*-koh *doh*-lah-rehs pohr *dee*-ah)

✔ *Your room will be available at 2:00 p.m.* **La habitación estará disponible a las dos de la tarde.** (lah ah-bvee-tah-see*ohn* ehs-tah-*rah* dees-poh-*nee*-bvleh ah lahs dohs deh lah *tahr*-deh)

✔ *You must check out of your room before 11:00 a.m.* **Hay que irse de la habitación antes de las once de la mañana.** (ahy keh *eer*-seh deh lah ah-bvee-tah-see*ohn* *ahn*-tehs deh lahs *ohn*-seh deh lah mah-*nyah*-nah)

Book IV

Spanish at Work

✔ *May I please have your credit card for the registration (check in)?* **Por favor, ¿Puedo tener su tarjeta de crédito para la registración?** (pohr fah-*bvohr* pooe*h*-doh teh-*nehr* soo tahr-*Heh*-tah deh *kreh*-dee-toh *pah*-rah lah reh-Hees-trah-see*ohn*)

✔ *Please sign in here.* **Por favor, firme aquí.** (pohr fah-*bvohr feer*-meh ah-*kee*)

✔ *You'll be staying in room number 317.* **Su habitación es el número trescientos diecisiete.** (soo ah-bvee-tah-see*ohn* ehs ehl *noo*-meh-roh trehs-seee*hn*-tohs deee*h*-see-seee*h*-teh)

✔ *Here are the keys for your room.* **Aquí están las llaves para la habitación.** (ah-*kee* ehs-*tahn* lahs *yah*-bvehs *pah*-rah lah ah-bvee-tah-see*ohn*)

✔ *This card gets you into your room.* **Esta tarjeta abre la puerta de su habitación.** (*ehs*-tah tahr-*Heh*-tah *ah*-bvreh lah pooe*hr*-tah deh soo ah-bvee-tah-see*ohn*)

✔ *Do you need help with your luggage?* **¿Necesita ayuda con su equipaje?** (neh-seh-*see*-tah ah-*yoo*-dah kohn soo eh-kee-*pah*-Heh)

Showing your guests to their table or room

After you've made your way through the preliminaries, you're ready to show your guests to their table or room, or at least provide some directions. If you need to give directions, refer to Book I, Chapter 8. Otherwise, use one of the following statements prior to ushering your guests to their table or room:

✔ *Please follow me.* **Por favor, sígame.** (pohr fah-*bvohr see*-gah-meh)

✔ *[Name] will take you to your table/room.* **[Name] lo(s)/la(s) llevará a su mesa/habitación.** ([Name] loh(s)/lah (s) yeh-bvah-*rah* ah soo *meh*-sah/ah-bvee-tah-see*ohn*)

When giving directions to specific rooms or areas, the terms in Table 6-1 can come in handy.

Table 6-1	Areas in a Hotel	
English	*Spanish*	*Pronunciation*
bathroom	**el baño**	ehl *bvah*-nyoh
elevator	**el ascensor**	ehl ah-sehn-*sohr*
exercise room	**la sala de ejercicio**	lah *sah*-lah deh eh-Hehr-*see*-seeoh
first floor	**la planta baja**	lah *plahn*-tah *bvah*-Hah

English	Spanish	Pronunciation
second floor	**el primer piso**	ehl *pree*-mehr *pee*-soh
third floor	**el segundo piso**	ehl seh-*goon*-doh *pee*-soh
game room	**la sala de juegos**	lah *sah*-lah deh Hoo*eh*-gohs
ice machine	**la máquina de hielo**	lah *mah*-kee-nah deh ee*eh*-loh
lobby	**el vestíbulo**	ehl bvehs-*tee*-bvoo-loh
lounge	**el bar**	ehl bvahr
restaurant	**el restaurante**	ehl rehs-tahoo-*rahn*-teh
snack machine	**la máquina de tentempiés**	lah *mah*-kee-nah deh tehn-tehm-pee*ehs*
swimming pool	**la piscina**	lah pee-*see*-nah

The following dialogue presents a typical hotel check-in.

Talkin' the Talk

Mr. and Mrs. Esposa have arrived at the Motel Getaway with their two children and need to reserve a room. Greg, the motel's manager, greets the Esposas, asks Mr. Esposa a few questions, and then directs them to their room.

Greg: **Bienvenidos al Motel Getaway.**
Bvee*ehn*-bveh-*nee*-dohs ahl moh-*tehl* Getaway
Welcome to Motel Getaway.

Me llamo Greg — ¿cómo puedo servirles?
meh *yah*-moh greg *koh*-moh poo*eh*-doh sehr-*bveer*-lehs
My name is Greg — how may I help you?

Mr. Esposa: **Mi familia quisiera una habitación por la noche.**
mee fah-*mee*-leeah kee-see*eh*-rah *oo*-nah ah-bvee-tah-see*ohn* pohr lah *noh*-cheh
My family would like a room for tonight.

Greg: **¿Cuántas personas hay en su grupo?**
koo*ahn*-tahs pehr-*soh*-nahs ahy ehn soo *groo*-poh
How many people are in your group?

Mr. Esposa: **Somos cuatro.**
soh-mohs koo*ah*-troh
Four.

Greg: **¿Está alguién del grupo bajo de doce años de edad?**
ehs-*tah* ahl-gee*ehn* dehl *groo*-poh *bvah*-Hoh deh
doh-seh *ah*-nyos deh eh-*dahd*
Is anyone in your group under 12 years old?

Mr. Esposa: **Sí, nuestros dos hijos.**
see noo*ehs*-trohs dohs *ee*-Hohs
Yes, both of our children.

Greg: **¿Quieren una habitación con dos camas de matrimonio?**
kee*eh*-rehn *oo*-nah ah-bvee-tah-see*ohn* kohn dohs
kah-mahs deh mah-tree-*moh*-neeoh
Would you like a room with two double beds?

Mr. Esposa: **Sí, eso sería perfecto.**
see *eh*-soh seh-*ree*-ah pehr-*fehk*-toh
Yes, that would be perfect.

Greg: **¿Necesitarán un catre?**
neh-seh-see-tah-*rahn* oon *kah*-treh
Will you need a roll-out cot?

Mr. Esposa: **No, gracias, no es necesario.**
noh *grah*-seeahs noh ehs neh-seh-*sah*-reeoh
No, thank you, that isn't necessary.

Greg: **¿Quieren una habitación con fumar o no fumar?**
kee*eh*-rehn *oo*-nah ah-bvee-tah-see*ohn* kohn
foo-*mahr* oh noh foo-*mahr*
Would you like a smoking or a nonsmoking room?

Mr. Esposa: **No fumar.**
noh foo-*mahr*
Nonsmoking.

Greg: **¿Puedo ver la tarjeta de crédito que quiere usar?**
poo*eh*-doh bvehr lah tahr-*Heh*-tah deh *kreh*-dee-toh
keh kee*eh*-reh oo-*sahr*
May I see the credit card that you want to use?

Mr. Esposa: **Sí, aquí está.**
see ah-*kee* ehs-*tah*
Yes, here it is.

Greg: **Gracias.**
grah-seeahs
Thank you.

Handing back the card:

Aquí está su tarjeta de crédito y dos llaves para la habitación. Están en la habitación número 202 que tiene una vista a la piscina.
ah-*kee* ehs-*tah* soo tahr-*Heh*-tah deh *kreh*-dee-toh ee dohs *yah*-bvehs *pah*-rah lah ah-bvee-tah-see*ohn* ehs-*tahn* ehn lah ah-bvee-tah-see*ohn* noo-meh-roh dohs-seee*ehn*-tohs dohs keh teee*eh*-neh *oo*-nah *bvees*-tah ah lah pee-*see*-nah
Here is your credit card and two room keys. You'll be in room 202 overlooking the swimming pool.

Pueden llegar a su habitación subiendo estas escaleras o por el ascensor.
poo*eh*-dehn yeh-*gahr* ah soo ah-bvee-tah-see*ohn* soo-bvee*ehn*-doh *ehs*-tahs ehs-kah-*leh*-rahs oh pohr ehl ah-sehn-*sohr*
You can reach your room by going up these stairs or using the elevator.

O se puede conducir alrededor del hotel y aparcar al norte.
oh seh poo*eh*-deh kohn-doo-*seer* ahl-reh-deh-*dohr* dehl oh-*tehl* ee ah-pahr-*kahr* ahl *nohr*-teh
Or you can drive around and park on the north side of the building.

Mr. Esposa: **Gracias. ¿Cuándo tenemos que irnos por la mañana?**
grah-seeahs koo*ahn*-doh teh-*neh*-mohs keh *eer*-nohs pohr lah mah-*nyah*-nah
Thank you. When do we need to check out?

Greg: **Tienen que irse por las once de la mañana para evitar una cobra de otro día.**
teee*eh*-nehn keh *eer*-seh pohr lahs *ohn*-seh deh lah mah-*nyah*-nah *pah*-rah eh-bvee-*tahr* oo-nah *koh*-bvrah deh *oh*-troh *dee*-ah
You must check out by 11:00 a.m. to avoid getting charged for another day.

Mr. Esposa: **Gracias.**
grah-seeahs
Thank you.

Book IV

Spanish at Work

Greg:	Gracias, y por favor marquee 0 en el teléfono en la habitación si haya algo que necesitan.
	grah-seeahs ee pohr fah-bvohr mahr-keh seh-roh ehn ehl teh-leh-foh-noh ehn lah ah-bvee-tah-seeohn see ah-yah ahl-goh keh neh-seh-see-tahn
	Thank you, and please dial 0 on the phone in your room if you need anything.

Training the Housekeeping Staff

Training housekeeping staff can be relatively easy even if your trainee speaks only Spanish. You can simply show the person where you store all the supplies and how to go from room to room to perform the required cleaning. Being able to speak a little Spanish, however, can make your training sessions run much more smoothly and help you deal with any questions that may come up.

The following sections provide you with the vocabulary and some basic phrases to help you navigate your initial training sessions.

For words and phrases you need to interview job candidates and describe the compensation and benefits that come with the job, refer to Book IV, Chapter 5.

Stocking the cart

At the beginning or end of each shift, room attendants need to stock their carts with various cleaning supplies and clean linens. You can instruct the attendant as follows, referring to the items in Table 6-2.

Necesita abastecer el carrito con las siguientes suministros.
(neh-seh-*see*-tah ah-bvahs-teh-*sehr* ehl kah-*rree*-toh kohn lahs see-gee*ehn*-tehs soo-mee-*nees*-trohs) (*You must stock your cart with the following supplies.*)

Table 6-2	Room and Cleaning Supplies	
English	*Spanish*	*Pronunciation*
bars of soap	**jabón**	Hah-*bvohn*
coffee cups	**tazas**	*tah*-sahs
coffee	**café**	kah-*feh*

English	Spanish	Pronunciation
conditioner	**acondicionador**	ah-kohn-dee-seeohn-ah-*dohr*
cream	**crema**	*kreh*-mah
drinking glasses	**vasos**	*bvah*-sohs
dust cloths	**trapos**	*trah*-pohs
facial tissue	**pañuelos de papel**	pah-nyoo*eh*-lohs deh pah-*pehl*
light bulbs	**bombillas**	bvohm-*bvee*-yahs
linens	See Table 6-3	
notepads	**libretas**	lee-*bvreh*-tahs
paper towels	**toallas de papel**	toh-*ah*-yahs deh pah-*pehl*
pens	**plumas**	*ploo*-mahs
room supplies	**suministros para la habitación**	soo-mee-*nees*-trohs *pah*-rah lah ah-bvee-tah-see*ohn*
shampoo	**champú**	cham-*poo*
sugar	**azúcar**	ah-*soo*-kahr
sugar substitute	**substituto de azúcar**	soobv-stee-*too*-toh deh ah-*soo*-kahr
toilet bowl cleaner	**limpiador para el inodoro**	leem-peeah-*dohr pah*-rah ehl ee-noh-*doh*-roh
toilet paper	**papel higiénico**	pah-*pehl* ee-Hee*eh*-nee-koh
toothpaste	**crema dental**	*kreh*-mah dehn-*tahl*
trash bags	**bolsas para la basura**	*bohl*-sahs *pah*-rah lah bah-*soo*-rah

Having a checklist of items (including required quantities) in Spanish on each cart can save you loads of time having to train or retrain room attendants.

Cleaning rooms

Telling someone how to clean a hotel room is more involved than it sounds, but the following phrases cover just about everything.

A picture is worth a thousand words — demonstrating the procedures and products described in this list can help get you the results you want.

✔ *Leave your cleaning cart outside the room.* **Deja el carrito fuera de la habitación.** (*deh*-Hah ehl kah-*rree*-toh foo*eh*-rah deh lah ah-bvee-tah-see*ohn*)

Book IV

Spanish at Work

✔ *Use this to clean like this.* **Use esto para limpiar así.** (*oo*-seh *ehs*-toh *pah*-rah leem-pee*ahr* ah-*see*)

✔ *Open the drapes and windows.* **Abra las cortinas y las ventanas.** (*ah*-bvrah lahs kohr-*tee*-nahs ee *lahs* bvehn-*tah*-nahs)

✔ *Dust all furniture and surfaces with a rag, like this.* **Quite el polvo de todos los muebles y superficies con un trapo, así.** (*kee*-teh ehl *pohl*-bvoh deh *toh*-dohs lohs moo*eh*-bvlehs ee soo-pehr-*fee*-seeehs kohn oon *trah*-poh ah-*see*)

✔ *Clean all glass surfaces with this cleaning solution and paper towel.* **Limpie todas las superficies de vidrio con esta solución limpiadora y toallas de papel.** (*leem*-peeeh *toh*-dahs lahs soo-pehr-*fee*-seeehs deh *bvee*-dreeoh kohn *ehs*-tah soh-loo-see*ohn* leem-peeah-*doh*-rah ee toh-*ah*-yahs deh pah-*pehl*)

✔ *Put this solution on any spots on the carpet and then wipe it off with a rag like this.* **Ponga esta solución limpiadora en cualquier mancha que haya en la alfombra y luego límpiela con un trapo así.** (*pohn*-gah *ehs*-tah soh-loo-see*ohn* leem-peeah-*doh*-rah ehn kooahl-kee*ehr mahn*-chah keh *ah*-yah ehn lah ahl-*fohm*-bvrah ee loo*eh*-goh *leem*-peeeh-lah kohn oon *trah*-poh ah-*see*)

✔ *Vacuum the carpet.* **Pase la aspiradora por la alfombra.** (*pah*-seh lah ahs-pee-rah-*doh*-rah pohr lah ahl-*fohm*-bvrah)

✔ *Don't throw away any books, newspapers, or magazines.* **No tire a la basura ningunos libros, periódicos, ni revistas.** (noh *tee*-reh ah lah bvah-*soo*-rah neen-*goo*-nohs *lee*-bvrohs peh-reeoh-dee-kohs nee reh-*bvees*-tahs)

✔ *Fold the guests' clothing and put it here.* **Doble la ropa de los huéspedes y póngala aquí.** (*doh*-bvleh lah *roh*-pah deh lohs ooehs-peh-dehs ee *pohn*-gah-lah ah-*kee*)

✔ *Check the lights and replace any burned-out light bulbs.* **Cheque las luces y cambie cualquier bombilla quemada.** (*cheh*-keh lahs *loo*-sehs ee *kahm*-bveeeh kooahl-kee*ehr* bvohm-*bvee*-yah keh-*mah*-dah)

✔ *Take out all the trash.* **Saque toda la basura.** (*sah*-keh *toh*-dah lah bvah-*soo*-rah)

 Having a checklist of cleaning activities you expect the attendant to perform in each room is always a good idea. Demonstrate exactly how you want your trainee to perform each cleaning activity in the first room and then have the attendant clean one or two rooms on her own under your supervision.

Cleaning bathrooms

Although bathrooms tend to be small, they generally have more items in them that need cleaning, so you need some very specialized language. Here are some phrases that can come in handy when training a room attendant:

✔ *Remove all used towels and the bathmat.* **Saque todas las toallas usadas y el tapete.** (*sah*-keh *toh*-dahs lahs toh-*ah*-yahs oo-*sah*-dahs ee ehl tah-*peh*-teh)

✔ *Scrub the toilet with this brush and cleaning solution.* **Friegue el inodoro con este cepillo y solución limpiadora.** (free*eh*-geh ehl een-oh-*doh*-roh kohn *ehs*-teh seh-*pee*-yoh ee soh-loo-see*ohn* leem-peeah-*doh*-rah)

✔ *Take everything off the sink before cleaning it.* **Quite todos los artículos de encima del lavabo antes de limpiarlo.** (*kee*-teh *toh*-dohs lohs ahr-*tee*-koo-lohs deh ehn-*see*-mah dehl lah-*bvah*-bvoh *ahn*-tehs deh leem-pee*ahr*-loh)

✔ *Scrub the sink with a sponge and this cleaning product and then rinse it like this.* **Friegue el lavabo con una esponja y este producto limpiador y después enjuáguelo así.** (free*eh*-geh ehl lah-*bvah*-bvoh kohn *oo*-nah ehs-*pohn*-Hah ee *ehs*-teh proh-*dook*-toh leem-peeah-*dohr* ee dehs-poo*ehs* ehn-Hoo*ah*-geh-loh ah-*see*)

✔ *Scrub the shower with a sponge and this cleaning product and then rinse it like this.* **Friegue la ducha con una esponja y este producto limpiador y después enjuáguelo así.** (free*eh*-geh lah *doo*-chah kohn *oo*-nah ehs-*pohn*-Hah ee *ehs*-teh proh-*dook*-toh leem-peeah-*dohr* ee dehs-poo*ehs* ehn-Hoo*ah*-geh-loh ah-*see*)

✔ *Clean the shower curtain like this.* **Limpie la cortina de la ducha así** (*leem*-peeeh lah kohr-*tee*-nah deh lah *doo*-chah ah-*see*)

✔ *Mop the floor.* **Friegue el suelo.** (free*eh*-geh ehl soo*eh*-loh)

✔ *Clean the mirror.* **Limpie el espejo.** (*leem*-peeeh ehl ehs-*peh*-Hoh)

Changing beds

Guests can get very particular about their beds and how they expect them to be made, so demonstrating exactly how you want the attendant to make a bed is key. You can use the following phrases to offer some basic instructions:

✔ *Remove all the bedding.* **Quite toda la ropa de la cama.** (*kee*-teh *toh*-dah lah *roh*-pah deh lah *kah*-mah)

✔ *Make the bed. I'll show you how.* **Arregle la cama. Yo le demostraré.** (ah-*rreh*-gleh lah *kah*-mah yoh leh deh-mohs-trah-*reh*)

✔ *Tuck in the sheet like this.* **Meta la sábana debajo del colchón así.** (*meh*-tah lah *sah*-bvah-nah deh-*bvah*-Hoh dehl kohl-*chohn* ah-*see*)

✔ *Fold the top sheet like this.* **Doble la sábana de encima así.** (*doh*-bvleh lah *sah*-bvah-nah deh ehn-*see*-mah ah-*see*)

Table 6-3 presents additional bed-related vocabulary.

Book IV

Spanish at Work

Table 6-3		Bedding
English	*Spanish*	*Pronunciation*
bed	**la cama**	lah *kah*-mah
bedspread	**el cubrecama**	ehl koo-bvreh-*kah*-mah
blanket	**la manta**	lah *mahn*-tah
bottom sheet	**la sábana de abajo**	lah *sah*-bvah-nah deh ah-*bvah*-Hoh
mattress pad	**la cubierta del colchón**	lah koo-bvee*ehr*-tah dehl kohl-*chohn*
pillowcase	**la funda**	lah *foon*-dah
pillow	**la almohada**	lah ahl-moh-*ah*-dah
top sheet	**la sábana de encima**	lah *sah*-bvah-nah deh ehn-*see*-mah

Restocking rooms and bathrooms

No room cleaning is complete until the room is fully restocked with all the necessities and any courtesy items you decide to provide for your guests — tissues, toilet paper, those little bars of soap, coffee, cups and glasses, and so on. Refer to Table 6-1 earlier in the chapter for a list of these items. You can then use those words in the following phrases to instruct your attendee to check and restock those items:

✔ *Check the . . .* **Cheque el/la . . .** (*cheh*-keh ehl/lah)

✔ *Every room should have . . .* **Todas las habitaciones deben de tener . . .** (*toh*-dahs lahs ah-bvee-tah-see*oh*-nehs *deh*-bvehn deh teh-*nehr*)

✔ *The bathroom should have . . .* **El baño debe de tener . . .** (ehl *bvah*-nyoh *deh*-bveh deh teh-*nehr*)

Training the Laundry Room Staff

If your motel or hotel has a laundry room, you need to train the laundry room attendants on how to sort items, operate the washing machines and dryers, press and fold the linens and other items, and complete other basic tasks. Demonstrating how to complete these tasks can take a huge burden off how much Spanish you need to pick up, but knowing a few key words and phrases can make your job easier.

Table 6-4 lists Spanish words and English equivalents for naming many of the items you're likely to find in *the laundry room* — **la lavandería** (lah lah-bvahn-deh-*ree*-ah). The sections that follow introduce you to phrases and expressions you can use to describe various common tasks.

Table 6-4	Laundry Room Items and Equipment	
English	*Spanish*	*Pronunciation*
basket	**la canasta**	lah kah-*nahs*-tah
bath towels	**las toallas**	lahs toh-*ah*-yahs
blankets	**las mantas**	lahs *mahn*-tahs
bleach	**la lejía**	lah leh-*Hee*-ah
button (clothes)	**el botón**	ehl bvoh-*tohn*
conveyor belt	**la cinta transportadora**	lah *seen*-tah trahns-pohr-tah-*doh*-rah
cycle (wash/rinse/dry)	**el programa**	ehl proh-*grah*-mah
detergent	**el detergente**	ehl deh-tehr-*Hehn*-teh
dial (control)	**el indicador**	ehl een-dee-kah-*dohr*
dryer	**la secadora**	lah seh-kah-*doh*-rah
fabric softener	**el suavizante**	ehl sooah-bvee-*sahn*-teh
guest's clothing	**la ropa de los huéspedes**	lah *roh*-pah deh lohs oo*ehs*-peh-dehs
iron	**la plancha**	lah *plahn*-chah
linen presser	**la planchadora**	lah plahn-chah-*doh*-rah
linens (bed)	**la ropa de cama**	lah *roh*-pah deh *kah*-mah
linens (table)	**la mantelería**	lah mahn-teh-leh-*ree*-ah
lint filters	**los filtros**	lohs *feel*-trohs
machine	**la máquina**	lah *mah*-kee-nah
napkins	**las servilletas**	lahs sehr-bvee-*yeh*-tahs
pillow cases	**las fundas**	lahs *foon*-dahs
plastic bags	**las bolsas de plástico**	lahs *bvohl*-sahs deh *plahs*-tee-koh
sheets	**las sábanas**	lahs *sah*-bvah-nahs
stains	**las manchas**	lahs *mahn*-chahs
tablecloths	**los manteles**	lohs mahn-*teh*-lehs

(continued)

Book IV

Spanish at Work

Table 6-4 *(continued)*

English	Spanish	Pronunciation
table linen ironer	**la planchadora de mantelería**	lah plahn-chah-*doh*-rah deh mahn-teh-leh-*ree*-ah
towel folder	**la dobladora de toallas**	lah doh-bvlah-*doh*-rah deh toh-*ah*-yahs
uniforms	**los uniformes**	lohs oo-nee-*fohr*-mehs
washcloths	**las toallitas (para lavarse)**	lahs toh-ah-*yee*-tahs (*pah*-rah lah-*bvahr*-seh)
washing machine	**la máquina de lavar**	lah *mah*-kee-nah deh lah-*bvahr*
water	**el agua**	ehl *ah*-gooah
cold water	**el agua fría**	ehl *ah*-gooah *free*-ah
hot water	**el agua caliente**	ehl *ah*-gooah kah-lee*ehn*-teh
warm water	**el agua tibia**	ehl *ah*-gooah *tee*-bveeah

Operating the washing machines

Washing machines tend to have different controls and settings, so we can't cover all the variations you're likely to encounter. But we can provide you with some basics to help you step a trainee through the process:

- ✔ *Sort the laundry by category.* **Divida la ropa por categoría.** (dee-*bvee*-dah lah *roh*-pah pohr kah-teh-goh-*ree*-ah)

- ✔ *Put items with tears or holes in this basket.* **Ponga la ropa con roturas o agujeros en esta canasta.** (*pohn*-gah lah *roh*-pah kohn roh-*too*-rahs oh ah-goo-*Heh*-rohs ehn *ehs*-tah kah-*nahs*-tah)

- ✔ *Place sheets in this pile.* **Ponga las sábanas en esta pila.** (*pohn*-gah lahs *sah*-bvah-nahs ehn *ehs*-tah *pee*-lah)

- ✔ *Use this product on any stains.* **Use este producto en cualquier manchas.** (*oo*-seh *ehs*-teh proh-*dook*-toh ehn kooahl-kee*ehr mahn*-chahs)

- ✔ *Put the clothes in the machine up to here.* **Ponga la ropa en la máquina hasta aquí.** (*pohn*-gah lah *roh*-pah ehn lah *mah*-kee-nah *ah*-stah ah-*kee*)

- ✔ *Wash in hot/cold/warm water.* **Lave la ropa en agua caliente/fría/tibia.** (*lah*-bveh lah *roh*-pah ehn *ah*-gooah kah-lee*ehn*-teh/*free*-ah/*tee*-bveeah)

✔ *Measure the detergent/bleach/fabric softener.* **Mida el detergente/la lejía/el suavizante de telas.** (*mee*-dah ehl deh-tehr-*Hehn*-teh/lah leh-*Hee*-ah/ehl sooah-bvee-*sahn*-teh deh *teh*-lahs)

✔ *Add detergent/bleach/fabric softener here.* **Agregue el detergente/la lejía/el suavizante de telas aquí.** (ah-*greh*-geh ehl deh-tehr-*Hehn*-teh/lah leh-*Hee*-ah/ehl sooah-bvee-*sahn*-teh deh *teh*-lahs ah-*kee*)

✔ *Set the wash cycle.* **Seleccione el programa de lavado.** (seh-lehk-see*oh*-neh ehl proh-*grah*-mah deh lah-*bvah*-doh)

✔ *Select the water level.* **Seleccione la cantidad de agua.** (seh-lehk-see*oh*-neh lah kahn-tee-*dahd* deh *ah*-gooah)

✔ *Set the timer.* **Ponga el reloj.** (*pon*-gah ehl reh-*loh*)

✔ *Close the door/lid.* **Cierre la puerta/tapa.** (see*eh*-rreh lah poo*ehr*-tah/*tah*-pah)

✔ *Press the dial to start the machine.* **Apriete el indicador para encender la máquina.** (ah-pree*eh*-teh ehl een-dee-*kah*-dohr *pah*-rah ehn-sehn-*dehr* lah *mah*-kee-nah)

✔ *Push the dial in./Pull the dial out.* **Empuje el indicador./Jale el indicador.** (ehm-*poo*-Heh ehl een-dee-kah-*dohr*/*Hah*-leh ehl een-dee-kah-*dohr*)

✔ *Turn the dial.* **Gire el indicador.** (*Hee*-reh ehl een-dee-kah-*dohr*)

✔ *Remove the items from the machine.* **Saque los artículos de la máquina.** (*sah*-keh lohs ahr-*tee*-koo-lohs deh lah *mah*-kee-nah)

✔ *Place the clean items in a basket, like this.* **Ponga los artículos limpios en una canasta, así.** (*pohn*-gah lohs ahr-*tee*-koo-lohs *leem*-peeohs ehn *oo*-nah kah-*nahs*-tah ah-*see*)

Operating the dryers

Dryers are usually a little easier to operate, so training someone on how to use one is easier, too. The following phrases can help:

✔ *Load the clean laundry into the dryer.* **Ponga la ropa limpia en la secadora.** (*pohn*-gah lah *roh*-pah *leem*-peeah ehn lah seh-kah-*doh*-rah)

✔ *Set the temperature.* **Seleccione la temperatura.** (seh-lehk-see*oh*-neh lah tehm-peh-rah-*too*-rah)

✔ *Set the timer.* **Ponga el reloj.** (*pohn*-gah ehl reh-*loh*)

✔ *Press this button to start the machine.* **Apriete este botón para encender la máquina.** (ah-pree*eh*-teh *ehs*-teh bvoh-*tohn* *pah*-rah ehn-sehn-*dehr* lah *mah*-kee-nah)

Book IV

Spanish at Work

✔ *Remove all items from the dryer.* **Saque todos los artículos de la secadora.** (*sah*-keh *toh*-dohs lohs ahr-*tee*-koo-lohs deh lah seh-kah-*doh*-rah)

✔ *Be careful. This is very hot.* **Tenga cuidado. Esto está muy caliente.** (*tehn*-gah kooee-*dah*-doh *ehs*-toh ehs-*tah* moo*eee* kah-lee*ehn*-teh)

✔ *Clean out the lint filter after each load, like this.* **Limpie el filtro después de cada lavado, así.** (*leem*-pee*eh* ehl *feel*-troh dehs-poo*ehs* deh *kah*-dah lah-*bvah*-doh ah-*see*)

✔ *Place the items in a basket, like this.* **Ponga los artículos en una canasta, así.** (*pohn*-gah lohs ahr-*tee*-koo-lohs ehn *oo*-nah kah-*nahs*-tah ah-*see*)

Pressing and folding items

Training laundry room staff on how to fold items varies, depending on what you have to fold, how you like it folded, and whether you do everything by hand or have machines that help with some of the work. The following general phrases, however, can come in handy during training:

✔ *Put the corners together like this.* **Ponga juntas las puntas, así.** (*pohn*-gah *Hoon*-tahs lahs *poon*-tahs ah-*see*)

✔ *Fold the sheets like this.* **Doble las sábanas, así.** (*doh*-bvleh lahs *sah*-bvah-nahs ah-*see*)

✔ *Feed a corner into the machine, like this.* **Introduzca una punta en la máquina, así.** (een-troh-*doos*-kah *oo*-nah *poon*-tah ehn lah *mah*-kee-nah ah-*see*)

✔ *Use the guides to feed the item into the machine.* **Use los guías para introduzca los artículos en la máquina.** (*oo*-seh lohs *gee*-ahs *pah*-rah een-troh-*doos*-kah lohs ahr-*tee*-koo-lohs ehn lah *mah*-kee-nah)

✔ *Stack the folded items.* **Apile los artículos doblados.** (ah-*pee*-leh lohs ahr-*tee*-koo-lohs doh-*bvlah*-dohs)

✔ *Wrap the guests' clothing like this.* **Envuelva la ropa de los huéspedes, así.** (ehn-bvoo*ehl*-bveh lah *roh*-pah deh lohs oo*ehs*-peh-dehs ah-*see*)

✔ *Put these items in a plastic bag.* **Ponga estos artículos en una bolsa de plástico.** (*pohn*-gah *ehs*-tohs ahr-*tee*-koo-lohs ehn *oo*-nah *bvohl*-sah deh *plahs*-tee-koh)

Managing Spanish in the Kitchen

Kitchens are complicated affairs, especially when you're trying to train someone in another language. The reason it's such a challenge is that you have to learn a ton of words — not only for all the kitchen equipment and utensils you're likely to encounter but also for ingredients and all the specialized activities, such as chopping, dicing, sautéing, mixing, blending, baking, frying, and so on. And that doesn't even touch on all the prep work and cleanup.

Mastering kitchen Spanish would require a book in itself, but in the following sections, we introduce you to some basic words and phrases to help you communicate effectively with your kitchen staff.

Kitchen equipment and utensils

Although you may be able to cook a decent entrée on the stove with a frying pan and a wooden spoon, you usually need other equipment and utensils in a professional kitchen. Table 6-5 introduces you to the Spanish words for the most common items:

Table 6-5	Kitchen Equipment and Utensils	
English	*Spanish*	*Pronunciation*
appliance	**el aparato elcctrodoméstico**	ehl ah-pah-*rah*-toh eh-lehk-troh-doh-*mehs*-tee-koh
baking pan	**la cacerola**	lah kah-seh-*roh*-lah
blender	**el batidor**	ehl bvah-tee-*dohr*
bowl	**el tazón**	ehl tah-*sohn*
bread slicer	**la máquina rebanadora**	lah *mah*-kee-nah reh-bvah-nah-*doh*-rah
chopper	**la picadora**	lah pee-kah-*doh*-rah
colander	**el colador**	ehl koh-lah-*dohr*
cooking utensil	**los utensilios**	lohs oo-tehn-*see*-leeohs
deep fryer	**la freidora**	lah frehee-*doh*-rah
fork	**el tenedor**	ehl teh-neh-*dohr*
freezer	**el congelador**	ehl kohn-Heh-lah-*dohr*
frying pan	**la sartén**	lah sahr-*tehn*
grater	**el rallador**	ehl rah-yah-*dohr*
knife	**el cuchillo**	ehl koo-*chee*-yoh
meat slicer	**la máquina de cortar fiambre**	lah *mah*-kee-nah deh kohr-*tahr* fee*ahm*-bvreh
metal tray	**la bandeja de metal**	lah bvahn-*deh*-Hah deh meh-*tahl*

(continued)

Table 6-5 *(continued)*

English	Spanish	Pronunciation
mixer	**la batidora**	lah bvah-tee-*doh*-rah
oven	**el horno**	ehl *ohr*-noh
peeler	**el pelapapas**	ehl peh-lah-*pah*-pahs
pot	**la olla**	lah *oh*-yah
refrigerator	**el refrigerador**	ehl reh-free-Heh-rah-*dohr*
rolling pin	**el rodillo**	ehl roh-*dee*-yoh
sifter	**el tamiz**	ehl tah-*mees*
spatula	**la espátula**	lah ehs-*pah*-too-lah
spoon	**la cuchara**	lah koo-*chah*-rah
stove	**la estufa**	lah ehs-*too*-fah
strainer	**el escurridor**	ehl ehs-koo-rree-*dohr*
toaster	**el tostador**	ehl tohs-tah-*dohr*
whisk	**el batidor manual**	ehl bvah-tee-*dohr* mah-noo*ahl*

Cooking and baking activities

A variety of activities occur in a kitchen over an average workday — chopping, mixing, slicing, dicing, mincing, whipping, frying, broiling, baking, and so on. By brushing up on the Spanish verbs that describe these activities, you can start issuing commands and instructions that really get your kitchen staff cooking. Table 6-6 gives you some verbs that apply to kitchen duties.

Table 6-6	**Kitchen Activities**	
English	Spanish	Pronunciation
add	**añada**	ah-*nyah*-dah
bake	**cocínelo en el horno**	koh-*see*-neh-loh ehn ehl *ohr*-noh
beat	**bata**	*bvah*-tah
boil	**hierva**	ee*ehr*-bvah
braise	**estofe**	ehs-*toh*-feh
broil	**áselo a la parrilla**	*ah*-seh-loh ah lah pah-*rree*-yah

English	Spanish	Pronunciation
chop	pique	*pee*-keh
cook	cocine	koh-*see*-neh
crumble	desmigaje	dehs-mee-*gah*-Heh
cut	corte	*kohr*-teh
dice	córtelo en dados	*kohr*-teh-loh ehn *dah*-dohs
fry	fría	*free*-ah
garnish	guarnezca	gooahr-*nehs*-kah
grate	ralle	*rah*-yeh
grill	asar a la parilla	ah-*sahr* ah lah pah-*ree*-yah
heat	cocine	koh-*see*-neh
knead	amase	ah-*mah*-seh
marinate	marine	mah-*ree*-neh
measure	mida	*mee*-dah
melt	funda	*foon*-dah
mix	mezcle	*mehs*-kleh
peel	pele	*peh*-leh
rinse	enjuague	ehn-Hoo*ah*-geh
roast	ase	*ah*-seh
roll out	estírelo con el rodillo	ehs-*tee*-reh-loh kohn ehl roh-*dee*-yoh
separate	separe	seh-*pah*-reh
shred	ralle	*rah*-yeh
slice (bread)	córtelo en rebanadas	*kohr*-teh-loh ehn reh-bvah-*nah*-dahs
slice (cheese, meat)	córtelo en lonchas	*kohr*-teh-loh ehn *lohn*-chahs
slice (cake, pizza)	córtelo en trozos	*kohr*-teh-loh ehn *troh*-sohs
slice (melon)	córtelo en rajas	*kohr*-teh-loh ehn *rah*-Hahs
squeeze	exprima	ehks-*pree*-mah
steam	cocínelo al vapor	koh-*see*-neh-loh ahl bvah-*pohr*
toss salad/stir	remueva	reh-moo*eh*-bvah
wash	lave	*lah*-bveh
whip	bata	*bvah*-tah

Common kitchen ingredients and measurements

When you're asking your kitchen staff to follow recipes, you need to be able to refer to the most basic ingredients and explain how much of each ingredient to add. Table 6-7 provides a list of the most common *ingredients* — **ingredientes** (een-greh-dee*ehn*-tehs) — and spices — **especias** (ehs-*peh*-seeah) — and Table 6-8 lists measurements.

Table 6-7	Common Ingredients	
English	*Spanish*	*Pronunciation*
breadcrumbs	**las migas de pan**	lahs *mee*-gahs deh pahn
butter	**la mantequilla**	lah mahn-teh-*kee*-yah
cream	**la crema**	lah *kreh*-mah
curry powder	**el curry**	ehl *koo*-ree
egg	**el huevo**	ehl oo*eh*-bvoh
egg whites	**las claras**	lahs *klah*-rahs
egg yolks	**las yemas**	lahs *yeh*-mahs
fish	**el pescado**	ehl pehs-*kah*-doh
flour	**la harina**	lah ah-*ree*-nah
fruit	**la fruta**	lah *froo*-tah
lemon	**el limón**	ehl lee-*mohn*
meat	**la carne**	lah *kahr*-neh
milk	**la leche**	lah *leh*-cheh
mint	**la menta**	lah *mehn*-tah
oil	**el aceite**	ehl ah-*seh*ee-teh
paprika	**la paprika**	lah pah-*pree*-kah
parsley	**el perejil**	ehl peh-reh-*Heel*
pepper	**la pimienta**	lah pee-mee*ehn*-tah
salt	**el sal**	ehl sahl
seasoning	**el condimento**	ehl kohn-dee-*mehn*-toh
shrimp	**el camarón**	ehl kah-mah-*rohn*
sugar	**el azúcar**	ehl ah-*soo*-kahr
vegetable	**la verdura**	lah bvehr-*doo*-rah

Table 6-8	Cooking Measurements	
English	*Spanish*	*Pronunciation*
a cup	**una taza**	*oo*-nah *tah*-sah
a half	**un/a medio/a**	*oon*/nah *meh*-deeoh/ah
an ounce	**una onza**	*oo*-nah *ohn*-sah
a pound	**una libra**	*oo*-nah *lee*-bvrah
a quarter	**un/a cuarto/a**	*oon* /nah koo*ahr*-toh /tah
a tablespoon	**una cucharada**	*oo*-nah koo-chah-*rah*-dah
a teaspoon	**una cucharadita**	*oo*-nah koo-chah-rah-*dee*-tah
a third	**un/a tercer/a**	*oon*/nah tehr-*sehr*/ah

Book IV

Spanish at Work

Chapter 7

Spanish for Builders, Mechanics, and Factory Workers

. . . .

In This Chapter

✔ Giving your tools Spanish names

✔ Referring to heavy machinery and other equipment

✔ Issuing common orders and requests on the job

✔ Describing common controls and activities

. . . .

For many workers, *on the job* means "on the job site," complete with a truck, van, or garage packed with tools and other equipment. These are the workers who run the factories, build homes and other structures, and repair everything from home appliances and automobiles to the various machines that lighten the workload and make everyone a little more comfortable.

In this chapter, we bring you up to speed on terms used in manufacturing, construction, and mechanical repairs — particularly the tools, machinery, and equipment and the action words that describe how to use them.

Brushing Up on the Tools of the Trade

You wouldn't show up for work without your tools, so you shouldn't show up without the words used to refer to your tools. In Table 7-1, we list the most common tools you're likely to find at a worksite along with their Spanish equivalents.

Table 7-1	Tools, Equipment, and Related Terms	
English	*Spanish*	*Pronunciation*
ax	**el hacha**	ehl *ah*-chah
bolt	**el perno**	ehl *pehr*-noh
cart	**la carretilla**	lah kah-rreh-*tee*-yah
cast	**el molde**	ehl *mohl*-deh
caulking gun	**la pistola de sellador**	lah pees-*toh*-lah de seh-yah-*dohr*
chain	**la cadena**	lah kah-*deh*-nah
chisel	**el cincel**	ehl seen-*sehl*
circular saw	**el serrucho circular**	ehl seh-*rroo*-choh seer-koo-*lahr*
clamp	**el sujetador**	ehl soo-Heh-tah-*dohr*
compressor	**el compresor de aire**	ehl kohm-preh-*sohr* deh *ahee*-reh
cordless drill	**el taladro a pilas**	ehl tah-*lah*-droh ah *pee*-lahs
drill	**el taladro**	ehl tah-*lah*-droh
earplugs	**tapones de oídos**	tah-*poh*-nehs deh oh*ee*-dohs
electricity	**la electricidad**	lah eh-lehk-tree-see-*dahd*
extension cord	**el cordón eléctrico**	ehl kohr-*dohn* eh-*lehk*-tree-koh
filter	**el filtro**	ehl *feel*-troh
flashlight	**la linterna**	lah leen-*tehr*-nah
fuel	**el combustible**	ehl kohm-bvoos-*tee*-bvleh
gas	**el gas**	ehl gahs
gasoline	**la gasolina**	lah gah-soh-*lee*-nah
generator	**el generador**	ehl Heh-neh-rah-*dohr*
gloves	**guantes**	goo*ahn*-tehs
glue	**el pegamento/la cola**	ehl peh-gah-*mehn*-toh/lah *koh*-lah
goggles	**anteojos**	ahn-teh-*oh*-Hohs
hacksaw	**la sierra para metales**	lah see*eh*-rrah *pah*-rah meh-*tah*-lehs
hammer	**el martillo**	ehl mahr-*tee*-yoh
hoist	**el montacargas**	ehl mohn-tah-*kahr*-gahs
hook	**el gancho**	ehl *gahn*-choh
hose	**la manguera**	lah man-*geh*-rah

English	Spanish	Pronunciation
hydraulic	**hidráulico**	ee-*drah*oo-lee-koh
jack	**el gato**	ehl *gah*-toh
kerosene	**la parafina**	lah pah-rah-*fee*-nah
ladder	**la escala**	lah ehs-*kah*-lah
level	**el nivel**	ehl nee-*bvehl*
machine	**la máquina**	lah *mah*-kee-nah
measuring tape	**la cinta de medir**	lah *seen*-tah de meh-*deer*
nail	**el clavo**	ehl *klah*-bvoh
nail gun	**la pistola clavadora**	lah pees-*toh*-lah klah-bvah-*doh*-rah
nut	**la tuerca**	lah too*ehr*-kah
paint	**la pintura**	lah peen-*too*-rah
paintbrush	**la brocha**	lah *bvroh*-chah
Phillips screwdriver	**el destornillador de cruz**	ehl dehs-toh-mee-yah-*dohr* deh kroos
pick	**el pico**	ehl *pee*-koh
pliers	**tenazas**	teh-*nah*-sahs
pneumatic	**neumático**	nehoo-*mah*-tee-koh
pulley	**la polea**	lah poh-*leh*-ah
rope	**la soga/la cuerda/la cordel**	lah *soh*-gah/lah koo*ehr*-dah/lah kohr-*dehl*
safety glasses	**gafas de seguridad**	*gah*-fahs deh seh-goo-ree-*dahd*
sandpaper	**el papel de lija**	ehl pah-*pehl* deh lee-Hah
saw	**la sierra**	lah see*eh*-rrah
sawhorse	**el caballete**	ehl kah-bah-*yeh*-teh
scaffold	**el andamio**	ehl ahn-*dah*-meeoh
scale	**la báscula**	lah *bvahs*-koo-lah
scraper	**el raspador**	ehl rahs-pah-*dohr*
screw	**el tornillo**	ehl tohr-*nee*-yoh
screwdriver	**el atornillador**	ehl ah-tohr-nee-yah-*dohr*
shed	**el cobertizo**	ehl koh-bvehr-*tee*-soh
shovel	**la pala**	lah *pah*-lah

(continued)

Table 7-1 *(continued)*

English	Spanish	Pronunciation
staple	**la grapa**	lah *grah*-pah
tape	**la cinta**	lah *seen*-tah
tape measure	**la cinta para medir**	lah *seen*-tah *pah*-rah meh-*deer*
tool	**la herramienta**	lah eh-rrah-mee*ehn*-tah
toolbox	**la caja de herramientas**	lah *kah*-Hah deh eh-rrah-mee*ehn*-tahs
trash can	**el bote de basura**	ehl *bvoh*-teh deh bvah-*soo*-rah
utility knife	**la cuchilla**	lah koo-*chee*-yah
vise	**la prensa de tornillo**	lah *prehn*-sah deh tohr-*nee*-yoh
wheel	**la rueda**	lah roo*eh*-dah
wheelbarrow	**la carretilla**	lah kah-rreh-*tee*-yah
wire	**el alambre**	ehl ah-*lahm*-bvreh
worktable	**el tablero de trabajo**	ehl tah-*bvleh*-roh deh trah-*bvah*-Hoh
wrench	**la llave inglesa**	lah *yah*-bveh een-*gleh*-sah

Worksites, particularly in construction zones, often have their fair share of heavy-duty equipment, including bulldozers, backhoes, loaders, and graders. In Table 7-2, we bring on the heavy machinery, or at least the Spanish terms for it.

Table 7-2   Heavy Machinery

English	Spanish	Pronunciation
backhoe	**la retroexcavadora**	lah reh-troh-ehks-kah-bvah-*doh*-rah
bulldozer	**el bulldozer**	ehl bvool-*doh*-sehr
cement truck	**el camión hormigonero**	ehl kah-mee*ohn* ohr-mee-goh-*neh*-roh
compactor	**la compactadora**	lah kohm-pahk-tah-*doh*-rah
crane	**la grúa**	lah *groo*ah
dump truck	**el camión volquete**	ehl kah-mee*ohn* bvohl-*keh*-teh
flatbed truck	**el camión plataforma**	ehl kah-mee*ohn* plah-tah-*fohr*-mah

English	Spanish	Pronunciation
grader	**la niveladora**	lah nee-bveh-lah-*doh*-rah
hand compactor	**la compactadora manual**	lah kohm-pahk-tah-*doh*-rah mah-noo*ahl*
jackhammer	**el martillo neumático**	ehl mahr-*tee*-yoh nehoo-*mah*-tee-koh
loader	**la cargadora**	lah kahr-gah-*doh*-rah
pickup truck	**la camioneta**	lah kah-meeoh-*neh*-tah
power shovel	**la pala motorizada**	lah *pah*-lah moh-toh-ree-*sah*-dah
roller	**la aplandadora**	lah ah-plahn-dah-*doh*-rah
scraper	**la rastreadora**	lah rahs-treh-ah-*doh*-rah
trencher	**la excavadora**	lah ehks-kah-bvah-*doh*-rah
water tank truck	**el camión cisterna**	ehl kah-mee*ohn* sees-*tehr*-nah

Of course, whenever you've completed a job or are about to stop working for the day, you usually need a whole new set of tools — cleanup tools. You can find the Spanish names for these tools in Table 7-3.

Table 7-3	Cleaning Tools and Related Words	
English	Spanish	Pronunciation
broom	**la escoba**	lah ehs-*koh*-bvah
brush	**el cepillo**	ehl seh-*pee*-yoh
bucket	**el balde**	ehl *bvahl*-deh
debris	**los escombros**	lohs ehs-*kohm*-bvrohs
dumpster	**el basurero grande**	ehl bvah-soo-*reh*-roh *grahn*-deh
dustpan	**la pala de recoger basura**	lah *pah*-lah deh reh-koh-*Hehr* bvah-*soo*-rah
mop	**el trapeador**	ehl trah-peh-ah-*dohr*
water	**el agua**	ehl *ah*-gooah
rag	**el trapo**	ehl *trah*-poh
sponge	**la esponja**	lah ehs-*pohn*-Hah
towel	**la toalla**	lah toh-*ah*-yah
trash	**la basura**	lah bvah-*soo*-rah
trashbag	**la bolsa para basura**	lah *bvohl*-sah *pah*-rah bvah-*soo*-rah
vacuum cleaner	**la aspiradora**	lah ahs-pee-rah-*doh*-rah

Book IV

Spanish at Work

Using the Tools of the Trade

When you have a few Spanish terms for tools under your belt (your tool belt, that is), you're ready for some verbs that describe how to use those tools to actually perform tasks. Table 7-4 lists some common verbs that apply to using tools and performing other mechanical operations.

When training a new employee, you can often avoid having to use a great deal of Spanish by demonstrating the tasks you want the person to perform. This tactic improves the chances that he performs the task the way you want it done. Prior to giving a worker the go-ahead to work alone, supervise him as he completes the tasks and provide any necessary corrections. Check out Book IV, Chapter 5 for more on training employees in Spanish.

Table 7-4	Tool-Related Actions	
English	*Spanish*	*Pronunciation*
attach	**sujetar/fijar**	soo-Heh-*tahr*/fee-*Hahr*
bend	**doblar**	doh-*bvlahr*
bury	**enterrar**	ehn-teh-*rrahr*
close	**cerrar**	seh-*rrahr*
cover	**cubrir**	koo-*bvreer*
cut	**cortar**	kohr-*tahr*
dig	**excavar**	ehks-kah-*bvahr*
dig a trench	**atrincherar/zanjar**	ah-treen-cheh-*rahr*/sahn-*Hahr*
drill	**taladrar**	tah-lah-*drahr*
dump, to	**tirar**	tee-*rahr*
frame	**enmarcar**	ehn-mahr-*kahr*
glue	**pegar**	peh-*gahr*
grind	**moler/pulverizar**	moh-*lehr*/pool-bvehr-ee-*sahr*
hammer	**martillear**	mahr-tee-yeh-*ahr*
haul	**llevar/transportar**	yeh-*bvahr*/trahns-pohr-*tahr*
heat	**calentar**	kah-lehn-*tahr*
hold	**agarrar**	ah-gah-*rrahr*
level	**nivelar**	nee-bveh-*lahr*
loosen	**aflojar**	ah-floh-*Hahr*
lower	**bajar**	bvah-*Hahr*

English	Spanish	Pronunciation
mark	**marcar**	mahr-*kahr*
measure	**medir**	meh-*deer*
mix	**mezclar**	mehs-*klahr*
open	**abrir**	ah-*bvreer*
prep	**preparar**	preh-pah-*rahr*
pump	**bombear**	bvohm-bveh-*ahr*
raise	**levantar**	leh-bvahn-*tahr*
repair	**reparar/arreglar**	reh-pah-*rahr*/ah-rreh-*glahr*
rinse	**enjuagar**	ehn-Hooah-*gahr*
saw	**serrar**	seh-*rrahr*
screw	**atornillar**	ah-tohr-nee-*yahr*
seal	**sellar**	seh-*yahr*
smooth	**allanar/aplanar**	ah-yah-*nahr*/ah-plah-*nahr*
soak	**remojar**	reh-moh-*Hahr*
spray	**rociar**	roh-see*ahr*
spread	**extender/esparcir**	ehks-tehn-*dehr*/ehs-pahr-*seer*
sprinkle	**espolvorear**	ehs-pohl-bvohr-eh-*ahr*
straighten	**enderezar**	ehn-deh-rch-*sahr*
tape	**pegar**	peh-*gahr*
tie	**atar**	ah-*tahr*
tighten	**apretar**	ah-preh-*tahr*
turn	**voltear**	bvohl-teh-*ahr*
unscrew	**destornillar**	dehs-tohr-nee-*yahr*
wash	**lavar**	lah-*bvahr*
water down	**aguar/diluir**	ah-goo*ahr*/dee-loo*eer*
weld	**soldar**	sohl-*dahr*
wrap	**envolver**	ehn-bvohl-*bvehr*

Book IV

Spanish at Work

Issuing Common Commands

One of the best ways to train new employees is to allow them to assist you or another worker for a few days and simply observe how you perform various tasks. During this time, the new hire is likely to act as the designated gofer (as in "go for this" and "go for that"), so you need to know a few phrases to tell her what to do:

- *Bring me the . . .* **Tráigame el/la . . .** (*trah*ee-gah-meh ehl/lah)

- *Put this away.* **Devuélvalo a su sitio.** (deh-bvoo*ehl*-bvah-loh ah soo see-teeoh)

- *Sweep this area.* **Barra esta área.** (*bvah*-rrah *ehs*-tah *ah*-reh-ah)

- *Pick up all of the . . .* **Recoja todos/as los/las . . .** (reh-*koh*-Hah *toh*-dohs/dahs lohs/lahs)

- *Put the trash in the dumpster.* **Tire la basura en el basurero grande.** (*tee*-reh lah bvah-*soo*-rah ehn ehl bvah-soo-*reh*-roh *grahn*-deh)

- *Carry this over there.* **Lleve esto allá.** (*yeh*-bveh *ehs*-toh ah-*yah*)

- *Help me.* **Ayúdeme.** (ah-*yoo*-deh-meh)

- *Hold this like this.* **Agarre esto así.** (ah-*gah*-rreh *ehs*-toh ah-*see*)

- *Get the . . . out of my van.* **Saque el/la . . . de mi camioneta.** (*sah*-keh ehl/lah . . . deh mee kah-meeoh-*neh*-tah)

- *Use the . . .* **Use el/la . . .** (*oo*-seh ehl/lah)

- *Give me the . . .* **Déme el/la. . .** (*deh*-meh ehl/lah)

- *Move this over here.* **Ponga esto allí.** (*pohn*-gah *ehs*-toh ah-*yee*)

- *Stop.* **Pare.** (*pah*-reh)

- *Wait.* **Espere.** (ehs-*peh*-reh)

The following dialogue walks you through a sample on-the-job greeting and quick orientation.

Talkin' the Talk

Bill owns and manages a construction company that builds new homes. He has just hired a carpenter, Paco, who recently arrived from Mexico to work in the United States. When Paco reports for his first day at work, Bill greets him and provides a brief orientation session so Paco knows what to expect.

Bill:	**Buenos días, Paco.**
	bvoo*eh*-nohs *dee*-ahs *Pah*-koh
	Good morning, Paco.

Paco: **Buenos días.**
bvoo*eh*-nohs *dee*-ahs
Good morning.

Bill: **Desde que hoy es su primer día, vas a trabajar conmigo.**
dehs-deh keh ohy ehs soo pree-*mehr dee*-ah bvahs ah trah-bvah-*Hahr* kohn-*mee*-goh
Because this is your first day, you'll be working with me.

Paco: **Bien.**
bvee*ehn*
Okay.

Bill: **Trabajamos desde las ocho de la mañana hasta la puesta del sol con una hora de descanso para almorzar alrededor del mediodía.**
trah-bvah-*Hah*-mohs *dehs*-deh lahs *oh*-choh deh lah mah-*nyah*-nah *ahs*-tah lah poo*ehs*-tah dehl sohl kohn oo-nah *oh*-rah deh dehs-*kahn*-soh *pah*-rah ahl-mohr-*sahr* ahl-reh-deh-*dohr* dehl meh-deeoh-*dee*-ah
We work from 8:00 a.m. until sundown with a one-hour break for lunch at about noon.

Hoy vamos a enmarcar una casa.
ohy *bvah*-mohs ah ehn-mahr-*kahr* oo-nah *kah*-sah
Today we'll be framing a house.

Usted me ayudaría hoy para ver como lo haremos.
oos-*tehd* meh ah-yoo-dah-*ree*-ah ohy *pah*-rah bvehr *koh*-moh loh ah-*seh*-mohs
You'll assist me today to see how it's done.

Mañana, continuaremos, pero usted hará el trabajo, y yo le ayudaré.
mah-*nyah*-nah kohn-tee-nooah-*reh*-mohs *peh*-roh oos-*tehd* ah-*rah* ehl trah-*bvah*-Hoh ee yoh leh ah-yoo-dah-*reh*
Tomorrow, we'll continue, but you'll do the work, and I'll assist you.

Paco: **Me parece bien.**
meh pah-*reh*-seh bvee*ehn*
That sounds good.

Book IV

Spanish at Work

Upon arriving at the worksite:

Bill: **¿Tiene sus herramientas?**
teee*eh*-neh soos eh-rrah-mee*eh*n-tahs
Do you have your tools with you?

Paco: **Sí, las tengo en mi camión.**
see lahs *tehn*-goh ehn mee kah-mee*ohn*
Yes, I have them in my truck.

Bill: **Tráiga sus herramientas y póngalas en mi camioneta.**
*trah*ee-gah soos eh-rrah-mee*eh*n-tahs ee
pohn-gah-lahs ehn mee kah-meeoh-*neh*-tah
Go get your tools and put them in my van.

Usted vendrá en mi camioneta conmigo hoy.
oos-*tehd* bvehn-*drah* ehn mee kah-meeoh-*neh*-tah
kohn-*mee*-goh ohy
You'll drive with me today.

Communicating on the Factory Floor

Factory terminology can vary a great deal, depending on what you're manufacturing, the tools and equipment used in the manufacturing process, and how you package and ship items. Some terminology, however, is common to a wide variety of factories and situations you're likely to encounter, and we present this handy info in the following sections.

Referring to buttons and controls

When running standard machinery, operators typically need to press buttons, move levers, turn dials, and set timers, so master the following words:

- *the button* **el botón** (ehl bvoh-*tohn*)
- *the dial* **el cuadrante** (ehl kooah-*drahn*-teh)
- *the lever* **la palanca** (lah pah-*lahn*-kah)
- *the switch* **el interruptor** (ehl een-teh-rroop-*tohr*)
- *the timer* **el temporizador** (ehl tehm-poh-ree-sah-*dohr*)

Describing common actions

Some commands are primarily useful in a factory setting, including the following:

- ✔ *Press this button.* **Empuje este botón.** (ehm-*poo*-Heh *ehs*-teh bvoh-*tohn*)

- ✔ *Push this lever forward.* **Empuje esta palanca hacia delante.** (ehm-*poo*-Heh *ehs*-tah pah-*lahn*-kah *ah*-seeah deh-*lahn*-teh)

- ✔ *Pull this lever back.* **Arrastre esta palanca hacia atrás.** (ah-*rrahs*-treh *ehs*-tah pah-*lahn*-kah *ah*-seeah ah-*trahs*)

- ✔ *Press down with your foot.* **Empuje con su pie.** (ehm-*poo*-Heh kohn soo pee*eh*)

- ✔ *Turn this dial.* **Gire este cuadrante.** (*Hee*-reh *eh*-steh kooah-*drahn*-teh)

- ✔ *Set the timer.* **Ponga este temporizador.** (*pohn*-gah *eh*-steh tehm-poh ree-sah-*dohr*)

- ✔ *Turn on* . . . **Prenda** . . . (*prehn*-dah)

- ✔ *Turn off* . . . **Apague** . . . (ah-*pah*-geh)

- ✔ *Start* . . . **Empiece** . . . (ehm-pee*eh*-seh)

- ✔ *Stop* . . . **Pare** . . . (*pah*-reh)

- ✔ *Lift* . . . **Levante** . . . (leh-*bvahn*-teh)

- ✔ *Load* . . . **Cargue** . . . (*kahr*-geh)

- ✔ *Lower* . . . **Baje** . . . (*bvah*-Heh)

- ✔ *Mix* . . . **Mezcle** . . . (*mehs*-kleh)

- ✔ *Pull* . . . **Arrastre** . . . (ah-*rrahs*-treh)

- ✔ *Push* . . . **Empuje** . . . (ehm-*poo*-Heh)

- ✔ *Tighten* . . . **Apriete** . . . (ah-pree*eh*-teh)

- ✔ *Loosen* . . . **Afloje** . . . (ah-*floh*-Heh)

- ✔ *Unload* . . . **Descargue** . . . (dehs-*kahr*-geh)

Filling and emptying containers

Many factory workers spend a good part of their time filling, emptying, and packing containers. When you need to talk about containers, refer to the terminology listed in Table 7-5.

Book IV

Spanish at Work

Table 7-5	Common Containers	
English	*Spanish*	*Pronunciation*
bottle	**la botella**	lah bvoh-*teh*-yah
box	**la caja**	lah *kah*-Hah
bucket	**la cubeta**	lah koo-*bveh*-tah
canister	**el recipiente**	ehl reh-see-pee*ehn*-teh
container	**el contenedor**	ehl kohn-teh-neh-*dohr*
crate	**la caja para transporte**	lah *kah*-Hah *pah*-rah trahn-*spohr*-teh
jar	**la jarra**	lah *Hah*-rrah
pallet	**el soporte de madera**	ehl soh-*pohr*-teh deh mah-*deh*-rah
tank	**el tanque**	ehl *tahn*-keh
tray	**la bandeja**	lah bvahn-*deh*-Hah
tube	**el tubo**	ehl *too*-bvoh

Chapter 8

Spanish for Real Estate Professionals

I n the real estate biz, communicating effectively with clients is a key to success regardless of which language they prefer to speak. Fortunately, the property can do much of the talking for you, particularly when you're representing Spanish-speaking buyers. If you're representing the sellers, you probably need to know more Spanish so you can explain to the sellers what you're doing to sell their home for top dollar and as quickly as possible.

In this chapter, we introduce you to some of the key words and phrases you need to know to communicate effectively with Spanish-speaking clients, whether you're trying to sell to them or for them. We cover everything from setting up an appointment to describing neighborhoods, showing a home, and dealing with financial issues and the closing.

Consider investing more time and resources into giving your business a complete multicultural transformation. Have all of your forms, brochures, and other printed materials professionally translated into Spanish and offer a Spanish version of your Web site. You may also want to start looking for a bilingual assistant to answer the phones, interpret for you, and offer suggestions on how to make your business more appealing to your Spanish-speaking clientele. For additional details on how to give your business a multicultural makeover, check out *Cross-Cultural Selling For Dummies* by Michael Soon Lee and Ralph R. Roberts (Wiley).

Setting Appointments

Before you even begin to do the serious business of meeting your clients and selling their home or showing them homes they may be interested in buying, you need to set up an appointment. In the following sections, you pick up enough Spanish to do just that.

Use the following phrases to introduce yourself to new Spanish-speaking clients:

✔ *Hello, my name is [name].* **Hola, me llamo [name].** (*oh*-lah meh *yah*-moh [name])

✔ *I'm a real estate agent.* **Soy un agente de bienes raíces.** (*sohy* oon ah-*Hehn*-teh deh bvee*ehn*-ehs rah*ee*-sehs)

Check out Book I, Chapter 2 for a crash course in the numbers, dates, and times you need for setting up meetings.

Answering the phone

If you're just starting out in the business, you probably have to do your fair share of *floor time* — answering the phones while the other agents are out in the field. Be prepared to answer calls from Spanish-speakers by practicing the following phrases:

✔ *Hello.* **Hola.** (*oh*-lah)

✔ *How may I help you?* **¿Cómo puedo ayudarle?** (*koh*-moh poo*eh*-doh ah-yoo-*dahr*-leh)

✔ *Whom do you need to speak with?* **¿Con quién necesita hablar?** (kohn kee*ehn* neh-seh-*see*-tah ah-*bvlahr*)

✔ *Please wait.* **Favor de esperar.** (fah-*bvohr* deh ehs-peh-*rahr*)

✔ *Thank you for waiting.* **Gracias por esperar.** (*grah*-seeahs pohr ehs-peh-*rahr*)

✔ *He/she is unavailable.* **Él/Ella no está disponible ahora.** (ehl/*eh*-yah noh ehs-*tah* dees-poh-*nee*-bvleh ah-*oh*-rah)

✔ *I'll take a message.* **Tomaré un mensaje.** (toh-mah-*reh* oon mehn-*sah*-Heh)

✔ *What is your name?* **¿Cómo se llama usted?** (*koh*-moh seh *yah*-mah oos-*tehd*)

✔ *What is your phone number?* **¿Cuál es su número de teléfono?** (koo*ahl* ehs soo *noo*-meh-roh deh teh-*leh*-foh-noh)

✔ *When is a good time to call you?* **¿Cuándo es un buen tiempo llamar?** (koo*ahn*-doh ehs oon boo*ehn* tee*ehm*-poh yah-*mahr*)

✔ *I'll give him/her the message to call you back.* **Yo le daré el mensaje a llamarle.** (yoh leh dah-*reh* ehl mehn-*sah*-Heh ah yah-*mahr*-leh)

Calling a client

When calling a client, the person who answers may not be the person you need to speak with, so the conversation can get a bit complicated. Assuming the situation doesn't become too involved, the following phrases should be sufficient to get you on the right path:

✔ *Hello, my name is* . . . **Hola, me llamo. . .** (*oh*-lah meh *yah*-moh)

✔ *I'd like to speak with* . . . **Quisiera hablar con. . .** (kee-see*eh*-rah ah-*bvlahr* kohn)

✔ *I want to leave a message.* **Quiero dejar un mensaje.** (kee*eh*-roh deh-*Hahr* oon mehn-*sah*-Heh)

✔ *This message is for* . . . **Este mensaje es para** . . . (*eh*-steh mehn-*sah*-Heh ehs *pah*-rah)

✔ *Tell him/her I called.* **Dígale que llamé.** (*dee*-gah-leh keh yah-*meh*)

✔ *Tell him/her to call me.* **Dígale que me llame.** (*dee*-gah-leh keh meh *yah*-meh)

✔ *My telephone number is* . . . **Mi número de teléfono es** . . . (mee *noo*-meh-roh deh teh-*leh*-foh-noh ehs)

Gathering basic information

Before you can assist clients, you need to know a little bit about them and whether they're looking for a property to buy or have a property to sell. Put the following questions to work in gathering this basic information:

✔ *What is your name?* **¿Cómo se llama?** (*koh*-moh seh *yah*-mah)

✔ *What is your address?* **¿Cuál es su dirección?** (koo*ahl* ehs soo dee-rehk-see*ohn*)

✔ *What is your phone number?* **¿Cuál es su número de teléfono?** (koo*ahl* ehs soo *noo*-meh-roh deh teh-*leh*-foh-noh)

✔ *Do you want to buy a property?* **¿Quiere comprar una propiedad?**
(kee*eh*-reh kohm-*prahr* oo-nah proh-peeeh-*dahd*)

✔ *Do you want to sell a property?* **¿Quiere vender una propiedad?**
(kee*eh*-reh bvehn-*dehr* oo-nah proh-peeeh-*dahd*)

Agreeing on a meeting time and place

Early in your initial conversation, you need to agree on a time and place to officially meet and discuss details. Use the following phrases:

✔ *When do you want an appointment?* **¿Cuándo quiere una cita?**
(koo*ahn*-doh kee*eh*-reh *oo*-nah *see*-tah)

✔ *On which day would you like to meet?* **¿En cuál día quisiera reunirnos?**
(ehn koo*ahl* *dee*-ah kee-see*eh*-rah reh-oo-*neer*-nohs)

✔ *Which days are best?* **¿Cuáles días son mejores?** (koo*ah*-lehs *dee*-ahs sohn meh-*Hoh*-rehs)

✔ *What time is convenient for you?* **¿A qué hora es mejor para usted?** (ah keh *oh*-rah ehs meh-*Hohr* pah-rah oos-*tehd*)

✔ *Where do you want to meet?* **¿Dónde desea reunirnos?** (*dohn*-deh deh-*seh*-ah reh-oo-*neer*-nohs)

✔ *Do you want to come to the office?* **¿Quiere venir a la oficina?** (kee*eh*-reh bveh-*neer* ah lah oh-fee-*see*-nah)

✔ *Do you want me to come to your home?* **¿Quiere que yo venga a su casa?** (kee*eh*-reh keh yoh bvehn-gah ah soo kah-sah)

If you're running early or late, be sure to call ahead to let your client know:

✔ *I'll be early.* **Estaré temprano.** (ehs-tah-*reh* tehm-*prah*-noh)

✔ *I'll be late.* **Estaré tarde.** (ehs-tah-*reh* *tahr*-deh)

Understanding Your Clients

Conversing in Spanish requires more than just being able to rattle off a few well-practiced lines. It also requires that you tune into and understand what your clients are saying. Although we can't cover the infinite number of expressions you're likely to encounter, the following list gives you several phrases you're likely to hear when you're dealing with clients:

✔ *I want to make an appointment.* **Quiero hacer una cita.** (kee*eh*-roh ah-*sehr oo*-nah *see*-tah)

✔ *I want to cancel my appointment.* **Quiero cancelar mi cita.** (kee*eh*-roh kahn-seh-l*ahr* mee *see*-tah)

✔ *I need to change the appointment.* **Necesito cambiar la cita.** (neh-seh-*see*-toh kahm-bvee*ahr* lah *see*-tah)

✔ *I want to sell my house/property.* **Quiero vender mi casa/propiedad.** (kee*eh*-roh bvehn-*dehr* mee *kah*-sah/proh-peeeh-*dahd*)

✔ *I want to buy a house/property.* **Quiero comprar una casa/propiedad.** (kee*eh*-roh kohm-*prahr oo*-nah *kah*-sah/proh-peeeh-*dahd*)

✔ *What is your commission?* **¿Cuál es su comisión?** (koo*ahl* ehs soo koh-mee-see*ohn*)

✔ *How much does it cost?* **¿Cuánto cuesta?** (koo*ahn*-toh koo*eh*-stah)

✔ *I like it.* **Me gusta.** (meh *goo*-stah)

✔ *I don't like it.* **No me gusta.** (noh meh *goo*-stah)

✔ *It's too small.* **Es demasiado pequeño/a.** (ehs deh-mah-see*ah*-doh peh-*keh*-nyoh/nyah)

✔ *It's too big.* **Es demasiado grande.** (ehs deh-mah-see*ah*-doh *grahn*-deh)

In the following dialogue, you hear a real estate agent interview some searching buyers.

Talkin' the Talk

Mr. and Mrs. Vargas have dropped by Lakeside Realty to talk to an agent about purchasing a home for their family. Sarah greets the couple and sets up an appointment for them to look at a few houses Saturday afternoon.

Sarah: **Hola, me llamo Sarah.**
oh-lah meh *yah*-moh *sah*-rah
Hello, my name is Sarah.

Soy un agente de bienes raíces.
*soh*y oon ah-*Hehn*-teh deh bvee*ehn*-ehs rah-*ee*-sehs
I'm a real estate agent.

¿Cómo puedo ayudarle?
koh-moh poo*eh*-doh ah-yoo-*dahr*-leh
How may I help you?

Mrs. Vargas: **Me llamo Sancha, y este es mi esposo, Pedro.**
meh *yah*-moh *sahn*-chah ee *ehs*-teh ehs mee
ehs-*poh*-soh *peh*-droh
My name is Sancha, and this is my husband, Pedro.

Buscamos una casa para nuestra familia.
bvoos-*kah*-mohs *oo*-nah *kah*-sah *pah*-rah noo*ehs*-trah
fah-*mee*-leeah
We are looking for a home for our family.

Sarah: **Les puedo ayudar a encontrar una casa.**
lehs poo*eh*-doh ah-yoo-*dahr* ah ehn-kohn-*trahr*
oo-nah *kah*-sah
I can help you find a home.

¿Cuál es su presupuesto?
koo*ahl* ehs soo preh-soo-poo*ehs*-toh
What is your price range?

Mrs. Vargas: **Aproximadamente ciento sesenta mil dólares.**
ah-prohk-see-mah-dah-*mehn*-teh see*ehn*-toh
seh-*sehn*-tah meel *doh*-lah-rehs
About $160,000.

Sarah: **¿Preferirían un vecindario o un distrito escolar
específico?**
preh-feh-ree-*ree*-ahn oon bveh-seen-*dah*-reeoh oh
oon dees-*tree*-toh ehs-koh-*lahr* ehs-peh-*see*-fee-koh
*Would you prefer a specific neighborhood or school
district?*

Mrs. Vargas: **Sí. Preferiríamos que nuestros hijos fueran a las
escuelas de South Vernon.**
see preh-feh-ree-*ree*-ah-mohs keh noo*ehs*-trohs
ee-Hohs foo*eh*-rahn ah lahs ehs-koo*eh*-lahs deh South
Vernon
*Yes. We would prefer that our children went to the
South Vernon Schools.*

**También nos gustaría estar cerca de una tienda de
comestibles y un parque.**
tahm-bvee*ehn* nohs goos-tah-*ree*-ah ehs-*tahr*
sehr-kah deh *oo*-nah tee*ehn*-dah deh
koh-mehs-*tee*-bvlehs ee oon pahr-keh
*We would also like to be close to a grocery store and
park.*

Sarah: **¿Cuántas recámaras necesitan?**
koo*ahn*-tahs reh-*kah*-mah-rahs neh-seh-*see*-tahn
How many bedrooms do you need?

Mrs. Vargas: **Tres o cuatro.**
trehs o koo*ah*-troh
Three or four.

Sarah: **¿Cuántos cuartos de baño?**
koo*ahn*-tohs coo*ahr*-tohs deh *bvah*-nyoh
How many bathrooms?

Mrs. Vargas: **Dos.**
dohs
Two.

Sarah: **¿Tienen en cuenta unas casas que quieren mirar?**
tee*eh*-nehn ehn koo*ehn*-tah oo-nahs *kah*-sahs keh
kee*eh*-rehn mee-rahr
Do you know of any homes for sale that you want to look at?

Mrs. Vargas: **No.**
noh
No.

Sarah: **Encontraré unas casas que pienso que les van a gustar.**
ehn-kohn-trah-*reh* oo-nahs *kah*-sahs keh pee*ehn*-soh
keh lehs bvahn ah goos-*tahr*
I'll find some homes that I think you're going to like.

¿Qué días son mejores para ustedes mirar las casas?
keh *dee*-ahs sohn meh-*Hoh*-rehs *pah*-rah
oos-*tehd–*ehs mee-*rahr* lahs *kah*-sahs
What days are best for you to look at homes?

Mrs. Vargas: **Los lunes o sábados.**
lohs *loo*-nehs oh *sah*-bvah-dohs
Monday or Saturday.

Sarah: **¿A qué hora del día es mejor?**
ah keh *oh*-rah dehl *dee*-ah ehs meh-*Hohr*
What time of day is best?

Book IV

Spanish at Work

Mrs. Vargas: **Los lunes después de las cuatro de la tarde o a cualquier hora los sábados.**
lohs *loo*-nehs dehs-poo*ehs* deh lahs koo*ah*-troh deh lah *tahr*-deh oh ah koo*ahl*-keeehr *oh*-rah lohs *sah*-bvah-dohs
Monday evenings after 4:00 or anytime Saturday.

Sarah: **¿Tienen tiempo este sábado entre la una y las cuatro de la tarde?**
tee*eh*-nehn tee*ehm*-poh *ehs*-teh *sah*-bvah-doh *ehn*-treh lah *oo*-nah ee lahs koo*ah*-troh deh lah *tahr*-deh
Do you have time this Saturday from 1:00 until 4:00 in the afternoon?

Mrs. Vargas: **Eso sería perfecto.**
eh-soh seh-*ree*-ah pehr-*fek*-toh
That would be perfect.

Sarah: **Yo los puedo recoger.**
yoh lohs poo*eh*-doh reh-koh-*Hehr*
I can come by to pick you up.

¿Cuál es su dirección?
koo*ahl* ehs soo dee-rehk-see*ohn*
What is your address?

Mrs. Vargas: **Trece-trece Sandy Lane, apartamento número 117.**
treh-seh *treh*-seh Sandy Lane, ah-pahr-tah-*mehn*-toh *noo*-meh-roh see*ehn*-toh dee*eh*-see-see*eh*-teh
1313 Sandy Lane, Apartment 117.

Sarah: **Yo los recogeré a la una el sábado en su apartamento.**
yoh lohs reh-koh-Heh-*reh* ah lah *oo*-nah ehl *sah*-bvah-doh ehn soo ah-pahr-tah-*mehn*-toh
I'll pick you up at 1:00 on Saturday at your apartment.

Les llamaré a confirmar el viernes por la noche.
lehs yah-mah-*reh* ah kohn-feer-*mahr* ehl bvee*ehr*-nehs pohr lah *noh*-cheh
I'll call you on Friday night to confirm.

¿Cuál es su número de teléfono?
koo*ahl* ehs soo *noo*-meh-roh deh teh-*leh*-foh-noh
What is your phone number?

Mrs. Vargas: **321-522-1328.**
trehs dohs oo-*noh* seen-*koh* dohs dohs oo-*noh* trehs dohs oh-*choh*
321-522-1328.

Describing Homes

Whether you're listing homes or presenting them to prospective buyers, you need to know how to talk about their features, including the number and types of rooms, overall square footage, when the house was built, whether the home has a garage, and so forth. The following sections introduce you to the descriptive words and phrases you need.

When showing homes, ask questions before giving answers. Not everyone wants a huge house on a huge lot. For example, say a prospective buyer asks

> **¿De qué tamaño es el lote?** (deh keh tah-*mah*-nyoh ehs ehl *loh*-teh) *How big is the lot?*

Answer with a question like

> **¿Qué tamaño está buscando?** (keh tah-*mah*-nyoh ehs-*tah* bvoos-*kahn*-doh) *How big of a lot are you looking for?*

Based on the person's answer, you can then form a more appropriate response. For example, if the person wants a large lot, you may answer,

> **Este lote es muy grande.** (*ehs*-teh *loh*-teh ehs *mooee grahn*-deh) *This lot is very large.*

If the person doesn't want a large lot, however, your answer may be

> **El lote es promedio para esta área.** (ehl *loh*-teh ehs proh-*meh*-deeoh *pah*-rah ehs-*tah ah*-reh-ah) *The lot is average for this area.*

Describing the home's age, size, and style

Most people in the market for a home have a vague notion of whether they want a newer home or a classic model. They probably also have a style preference — single-family, ranch, two-story, bungalow, and so on — and size (in square feet). The following phrases can help you convey the age, style, and size of the home.

Age is pretty easy, so start with that. Use the following example and just plug in the required number from Book I, Chapter 2:

> *The house was built 15 years ago.* **La casa fue construida hace quince años.** (lah *kah*-sah foo*eh* kohn-stroo*ee*-dah *ah*-seh *keen*-seh *ah*-nyohs)

To describe the size of the home, take the same approach. Substitute the appropriate number from Book I, Chapter 2 in this example:

> *It's 2,000 square feet.* **Tiene dos mil pies cuadrados.** (tee*eh*-neh dohs meel pee*ehs* kooah-*drah*-dohs)

Table 8-1 list Spanish terms for some common house styles.

Table 8-1	Common Home Styles	
English	*Spanish*	*Pronunciation*
beach house	**una casa de playa**	*oo*-nah *kah*-sah deh *plah*-yah
brick house	**una casa de ladrillo**	*oo*-nah *kah*-sah deh lah-*dree*-yoh
bungalow	**un bungalow**	oon bvoon-*gah*-loh
cabin, hut	**una cabaña**	*oo*-nah kah-*bvah*-nah
colonial house	**una casa colonial**	*oo*-nah *kah*-sah koh-loh-nee*ahl*
condominium	**un condominio**	oon kohn-doh-*mee*-neeoh
contemporary house	**una casa contemporánea**	*oo*-nah *kah*-sah kohn-tehm-poh-*rah*-nee-ah
duplex	**un dúplex**	oon *doo*-plehks
farm house	**una casa de granja**	*oo*-nah *kah*-sah deh *grahn*-Hah
lower level	**una planta baja**	*oo*-nah *plahn*-tah *bvah*-Hah
mansion	**una mansión**	*oo*-nah mahn-see*ohn*
modern house	**una casa moderna**	*oo*-nah *kah*-sah moh-*dehr*-nah
one-story house	**una casa de una planta**	*oo*-nah *kah*-sah deh *oo*-nah *plahn*-tah
ranch house	**un rancho**	oon *rahn*-choh
single-family home	**una casa individual**	*oo*-nah *kah*-sah een-dee-bvee-doo*ahl*
two-story house	**una casa de dos plantas**	*oo*-nah *kah*-sah deh dohs *plahn*-tahs
upper level	**una planta alta**	*oo*-nah *plahn*-tah *ahl*-tah

Touring the various rooms

When you're preparing a listing or showing homes to prospective buyers, being able to refer to the various rooms by name is much more effective. Table 8-2 reveals the Spanish names for the rooms of a house.

Table 8-2	Rooms of a House	
English	*Spanish*	*Pronunciation*
attic	**el ático**	ehl *ah*-tee-koh
balcony	**el balcón**	ehl bvahl-*kohn*
basement	**el sótano**	ehl *soh*-tah-noh
bathroom	**el baño**	ehl *bvah*-nyoh
bedroom	**el dormitorio**	ehl dohr-mee-*toh*-reeoh
closet	**el armario**	ehl ahr-*mah*-reeoh
deck	**la terraza**	lah teh-*rrah*-sah
dining room	**el comedor**	ehl koh-meh-*dohr*
driveway	**el camino de entrada**	ehl kah-*mee*-noh deh chn-*trah*-dah
garage	**el garaje**	ehl gah-*rah*-Heh
half bath	**el medio baño**	ehl *meh*-deeoh *bvah*-nyoh
kitchen	**la cocina**	lah koh-*see*-nah
laundry room	**la lavandería**	lah lah-bvahn-deh-*ree*-ah
living room	**la sala**	lah *sah*-lah
room	**el cuarto**	ehl koo*ahr*-toh
yard	**el patio**	ehl *pah*-teeoh

Highlighting a home's amenities

Homes are often packed with features and other amenities that can make them more attractive to potential buyers. When listing or showing a home, don't forget to point out any of the special features it has; we've listed several in Table 8-3.

TIP

First time homeowners may not have a lot of furniture or appliances or money to spend on them. If you're dealing with first-time buyers, and the home is furnished, be sure to point it out:

The home is furnished. **La casa está amueblada.** (lah *kah*-sah eh-*stah* ah-mooeh-*bvlah*-dah)

Table 8-3	Appliances, Furnishings, and Special Features	
English	*Spanish*	*Pronunciation*
carpet	**alfombra**	ahl-*fohm*-bvrah
central air	**aire central**	*ahee*-reh sehn-*trahl*
dishwasher	**una lavadora de platos**	*oo*-nah lah-bvah-*doh*-rah deh *plah*-tohs
dryer	**una secadora**	*oo*-nah seh-kah-*doh*-rah
electric heating	**calefacción eléctrica**	kah-leh-fahk-see*ohn* eh-*lehk*-tree-kah
electric stove	**una estufa eléctrica**	*oo*-nah eh-*stoo*-fah eh-*lehk*-tree-kah
fireplace	**una chimenea**	*oo*-nah chee-meh-*neh*-ah
gas heating	**calefacción de gas**	kah-leh-fahk-see*ohn* deh gahs
gas stove	**una estufa de gas**	*oo*-nah eh-*stoo*-fah deh gahs
new roof	**un techo nuevo**	oon *teh*-choh noo-*eh*-bvoh
oil heating	**calefacción de aceite**	kah-leh-fahk-see*ohn* deh ah-*seh*ee-teh
refrigerator	**un refrigerador**	oon reh-free-Heh-rah-*dohr*
sprinkler system	**un sistema de regadío**	oon see-*steh*-mah deh reh-gah-*dee*oh
swimming pool	**una piscina**	*oo*-nah pee-*see*-nah
tile floors	**pisos en losa**	*pee*-sohs ehn *loh*-sah
washer	**una lavadora**	*oo*-nah lah-bvah-*doh*-rah
water heater	**un calentador de agua**	oon kah-lehn-tah-*dohr* deh *ah*-gooah
wood floors	**pisos en madera**	*pee*-sohs ehn mah-*deh*-rah

Location, location, location

In the world of real estate, location is crucial — both in terms of property values and standard of living. Location often determines the level of education and the distance you have to travel to secure your necessities and pursue your pleasures. Most homeowners are first going to wonder about the neighborhood's overall rating — good, bad, quiet, safe — so use one of the following phrases to describe its atmosphere and reputation:

- *This is a good neighborhood.* **Este es un vecindario bueno.** (*ehs*-teh ehs oon bveh-seen-*dah*-reeoh bvoo*eh*-noh)

- *This is a bad neighborhood.* **Este es un vecindario malo.** (*ehs*-teh ehs oon bveh-seen-*dah*-reeoh *mah*-loh)

- *This is a quiet neighborhood.* **Este es un vecindario tranquilo.** (*ehs*-teh ehs oon bveh-seen-*dah*-reeoh trahn-*kee*-loh)

- *This is a good location.* **Esta es una localización buena.** (*ehs*-tah ehs *oo*-nah loh-kah-lee-sah-see*ohn* bvoo*eh*-nah)

- *This is a safe neighborhood.* **Este es un vecindario seguro.** (*ehs*-teh ehs oon bveh-seen-*dah*-reeoh seh-*goo*-roh)

Proximity to schools, shopping, and other neighborhood offerings is often an important consideration for homeowners. If parks, schools, and shopping are nearby, be sure to point that out with the following phrase and the words listed in Table 8-4:

The property is close to . . . **La propiedad está cerca de . . .** (lah proh-peeeh-*dahd* ehs-*tah sehr*-kah deh)

Table 8-4	Neighborhood Offerings	
English	*Spanish*	*Pronunciation*
bay	**la bahía**	lah bvah-*ee*-ah
beach	**la playa**	lah *plah*-yah
city	**la ciudad**	lah seeoo-*dahd*
golf course	**el campo de golf**	ehl *kahm*-poh deh gohlf
grocery store	**la tienda de comestibles**	lah tee*ehn*-dah deh koh-mehs-*tee*-bvlehs
hospital	**el hospital**	ehl ohs-pee-*tahl*
lake	**el lago**	ehl *lah*-goh
park	**el parque**	ehl *pahr*-keh
school	**la escuela**	lah ehs-koo*eh*-lah
shopping mall	**el centro comercial**	ehl *sehn*-troh koh-mehr-see*ahl*

Book IV

Spanish at Work

If the property has a unique location relative to other properties on the same block, you can use one of the following phrases to describe the location:

✔ *a corner lot* **un terreno de esquina** (oon teh-*rreh*-noh deh ehs-*kee*-nah)

✔ *a cul-de-sac* **un callejón** (oon kah-yeh-*Hohn*)

Discussing the Financing and Purchase

When dealing with prospective home buyers, you eventually need to talk about money and lead the buyers through the process of presenting the seller with a purchase agreement. In the following sections, we get the preliminary money talk out of the way and then deal with the process of pitching an offer.

Don't be surprised if clients show a reluctance to discuss money matters, including financing and the down payment. They're likely to have a very different attitude toward these subjects than your other clients and may even prefer paying for the property with cash. Be prepared to spend more time discussing these matters with your Spanish-speaking clients. If possible, partner with a bilingual mortgage broker who is more accustomed to dealing with these situations.

Talking money

Prior to showing homes, you usually need to sit down with your clients and have a frank talk about finances, especially as the topic relates to how much home they can afford and whether they can afford homes within their targeted price range. Before you talk money, brush up on the following phrases:

✔ *Do you have a down payment?* **¿Tiene un pago inicial?** (tee*eh*-neh oon *pah*-goh ee-nee-see*ahl*)

✔ *Has your bank already preapproved you for a loan?* **¿Está pre-aprobado para una hipoteca?** (ehs-*tah* preh-ah-proh-*bvah*-doh *pah*-rah oo-nah ee-poh-*teh*-kah)

✔ *For how much money?* **¿Por cuánto dinero?** (pohr koo*ahn*-toh dee-*neh*-roh)

✔ *From which bank?* **¿De cuál banco?** (deh koo*ahl* *bvahn*-koh)

✔ *What is the telephone number?* **¿Cuál es el número de teléfono?** (koo*ahl* ehs ehl *noo*-meh-roh deh teh-*leh*-foh-noh)

✔ *What is your gross income?* **¿Cuál es su salario bruto?** (koo*ahl* ehs soo sah-*lah*-reeoh *bvroo*-toh)

✔ *How much do you have for a down payment?* **¿Cuánto tiene para el pago inicial?** (koo*ahn*-toh tee*eh*-neh *pah*-rah ehl *pah*-goh ee-nee-see*ahl*)

Later in the process, you probably need to explain the various costs involved and tell the buyers how much they can expect their monthly payment to be:

✔ *The interest rate is . . .* **La tasa de interés es . . .** (lah *tah*-sah deh een-teh-*rehs* ehs)

✔ *Your monthly payment will be . . .* **Su pago mensual será de . . .** (soo *pah*-goh mehn-soo*ahl* seh-*rah* deh)

Table 8-5 lists terms that involve fees, costs, and payments typical of real estate transactions.

Table 8-5	Real Estate Fees, Costs, and Payments	
English	*Spanish*	*Pronunciation*
association fee	**el costo de asociación**	ehl *kohs*-toh deh ah-soh-seeah-see*ohn*
closing cost	**el gasto de cierre**	ehl *gahs*-toh deh see*eh*-rreh
condo fees	**los costos de condominio**	lohs *kohs*-tohs deh kohn-doh-*mee*-neeoh
homeowner's insurance	**el seguro de un propietario de vivienda**	ehl seh-*goo*-roh deh oon proh-peeeh-*tah*-reeoh de bvee-bvee*ehn*-dah
minimum down payment	**la entrega inicial mínima**	lah ehn-*treh*-gah ee-nee-see-*ahl mee*-nee-mah
mortgage payment	**el pago de la hipoteca**	ehl *pah*-goh deh lah hee-poh-*teh*-kah
property tax	**el impuesto de la propiedad**	ehl eem-poo*ehs*-toh deh lah proh-peeeh-*dahd*

Book IV

Spanish at Work

Making a purchase offer

When your clients finally show some interest in one of the homes they've seen, you can begin discussing the purchase with them to determine whether they want to make an offer on it. During this time, the following phrases can be very useful:

✔ *Would you like to make an offer for the home?* **¿Quisieran hacer una oferta por la casa?** (kee-see*eh*-rahn ah-*sehr* oo-nah oh-*fehr*-tah pohr lah *kah*-sah)

✔ *How much money would you like to offer?* **¿Cuánto dinero quisieran ofrecer?** (koo*ahn*-toh dee-*neh*-roh kee-see*eh*-rahn oh-freh-*sehr*)

✔ *Is there anything you'd like the homeowner to fix before you buy the home?* **¿Hay unas cosas que quisiera que el dueño de la casa arregle antes de que comprara la casa?** (ahy oo-nahs *koh*-sahs keh kee-see*eh*-rah keh ehl doo*eh*-nyoh deh lah *kah*-sah ah-*rreh*-gleh *ahn*-tehs deh keh kohm-*prah*-rah lah *kah*-sah)

✔ *Do you want the homeowner to include anything else as part of the deal?* **¿Hay algo más que quiere que el dueño incluye como parte de la transacción?** (ahy *ahl*-goh mahs keh kee*eh*-reh keh ehl doo*eh*-nyoh een-*kloo*-yeh *koh*-moh *pahr*-teh deh lah trahn-sahk-see*ohn*)

✔ *When would you like to have an answer from the homeowner to your offer?* **¿Cuándo quisiera tener una respuesta del dueño a su oferta?** (koo*ahn*-doh kee-see*eh*-rah teh-*nehr* oo-nah rehs-poo*ehs*-tah dehl doo*eh*-nyoh ah soo oh-*fehr*-tah)

✔ *Please sign the purchase offer here.* **Favor de firmar la oferta de compra aquí.** (fah-*bvohr* deh feer-*mahr* lah oh-*fehr*-tah deh *kohm*-prah ah-*kee*)

✔ *I'll present your offer to the seller.* **Presentaré la oferta al vendedor.** (preh-sehn-tah-*reh* lah oh-*fehr*-tah ahl bvehn-deh-*dohr*)

After presenting the offer, you need to follow up with your clients to let them know where their offer stands:

✔ *The seller accepted your offer.* **El vendedor aceptó su oferta.** (ehl bvehn-deh-*dohr* ah-sehp-*toh* soo oh-*fehr*-tah)

✔ *The seller didn't accept your offer.* **El vendedor no aceptó su oferta.** (ehl bvehn-deh-*dohr* noh ah-sehp-*toh* soo oh-*fehr*-tah)

✔ *The seller has made a counteroffer.* **El vendedor ha hecho una contraoferta.** (ehl bvehn-deh-*dohr* ah *eh*-choh oo-nah kohn-trah-oh-*fehr*-tah)

✔ *The seller will consider the offer.* **El vendedor considerará su oferta.** (ehl bvehn-deh-*dohr* kohn-see-deh-rah-*rah* soo oh-*fehr*-tah)

HUD (U.S. Department of Housing and Urban Development) has a comprehensive English-Spanish glossary of home buying terms on its Web site. Visit www.hud.gov/buying/terms_eng-sp.cfm.

Navigating the Closing

Unless somebody decides to read every document word for word at the closing, it should proceed very smoothly with a shuffling of papers around the table for each party's signature. To make sure your client shows up at the right place at the right time and is prepared to close, provide the following instructions:

- ✔ *The closing date is . . .* **La fecha del cierre es . . .** (lah *feh*-chah dehl see*eh*-rreh ehs)

- ✔ *The closing is at . . .* **El cierre está en. . .** (ehl see*eh*-rreh ehs-*tah* ehn)

- ✔ *You need to bring identification.* **Usted necesita traer identificación.** (oos-*tehd* neh-seh-*see*-tah trah-*ehr* ee-dehn-tee-fee-kah-see*ohn*)

- ✔ *You need to bring your checkbook.* **Usted necesita traer su chequera.** (oos-*tehd* neh-seh-*see*-tah trah-*ehr* soo cheh-*keh*-rah)

- ✔ *Your lawyer can come to the closing.* **Su abogado puede venir al cierre.** (soo ah-bvoh-*gah*-doh poo*eh*-deh bveh-*neer* ahl see*eh*-rreh)

- ✔ *You may bring an interpreter.* **Puede traer un intérprete.** (poo*eh*-deh trah-*ehr* oon een-*tehr*-preh-teh)

- ✔ *Review the closing documents before the closing date.* **Examine los documentos antes de la fecha del cierre.** (ehk-sah-*mee*-neh lohs doh-koo-*mehn*-tohs *ahn*-tehs deh lah *feh*-chah dehl see*eh*-rreh)

- ✔ *Call me if you have any concerns.* **Llámeme si tenga cualquier preocupación.** (*yah*-mah-meh see *tehn*-gah kooahl-kee*ehr* preh-oh-koo-pah-see*ohn*)

- ✔ *Your lawyer may want to review the closing documents.* **Puede ser que su abogado quisiera examinar los documentos del cierre.** (poo*eh*-deh sehr keh soo ah-bvoh-*gah*-doh kee-see*eh*-rah ehk-sah-mee-*nahr* lohs doh-koo-*mehn*-tohs dehl see*eh*-rreh)

Table 8-6 lists some common commands that can come in handy when you're sitting around the closing table.

Book IV

Spanish at Work

Table 8-6	Closing Table Commands	
English	*Spanish*	*Pronunciation*
look here	**mire aquí**	*mee*-reh ah-*kee*
read this (carefully)	**lea esto (cuidadosamente)**	*leh*-ah *ehs*-toh (kooee-dah-doh-sah-*mehn*-teh)
show me	**enséñeme**	ehn-*seh*-nyeh-meh

(continued)

Table 8-6 (continued)

English	Spanish	Pronunciation
sign here	**firme aquí**	*feer*-meh ah-*kee*
sit here	**siéntese aquí**	see*ehn*-teh-seh ah-*kee*
tell him/her	**dígale**	*dee*-gah-leh
tell me	**dígame**	*dee*-gah-meh
write	**escriba**	eh-*skree*-bvah

Dealing with Sellers

With a few variations, you can use much of the vocab in the earlier sections of this chapter when representing the seller. You still need to set up an appointment, gather information, and reference the property and its features. When dealing with sellers, however, you need to know at least a few unique expressions, including the following:

✔ *Do you want to sell the property?* **¿Quiere vender la propiedad?** (kee*eh*-reh bvehn-*dehr* lah proh-peeeh-*dahd*)

✔ *Do you have a buyer?* **¿Tiene un comprador?** (tee*eh*-neh oon kohm-prah-*dohr*)

✔ *What is the lowest price you'll consider?* **¿Cuál es su precio más bajo?** (koo*ahl* ehs soo *preh*-seeoh mahs *bvah*-Hoh)

✔ *Are you in a hurry to sell?* **¿Tiene prisa vender?** (tee*eh*-neh *pree*-sah bvehn-*dehr*)

✔ *Similar properties have sold for about this much.* **Unas propiedades similares han vendido por aproximadamente esta cantidad.** (*oo*-nahs proh-peeeh-*dah*-dehs see-mee-*lah*-rehs ahn bvehn-*dee*-doh pohr ah-prohk-see-mah-dah-*mehn*-teh *ehs*-tah kahn-tee-*dahd*)

✔ *Someone wants to see your property.* **Alguien quiere ver su propiedad.** (ahl-gee*ehn* kee*eh*-reh bvehr soo proh-peeeh-*dahd*)

✔ *Someone wants to buy your property.* **Alguien quiere comprar su propiedad.** (ahl-gee*ehn* kee-*eh*-reh kohm-*prahr* soo proh-pee-eh-*dahd*)

✔ *He/she liked your property.* **Le gustó su propiedad.** (leh goos-*toh* soo proh-peeeh-*dahd*)

✔ *He/she made an offer.* **Él/Ella sometió una oferta.** (ehl/*eh*-yah soh-meh-tee*oh oo*-nah oh-*fehr*-tah)

✔ *This is the offer.* **Esta es la oferta.** (*ehs*-tah ehs lah oh-*fehr*-tah)

✔ *Do you accept the offer?* **¿Acepta usted la oferta?** (ah-*sehp*-tah oos-*tehd* lah oh-*fehr*-tah)

Book IV

Spanish at Work

Chapter 9

Spanish for Gardening and Landscaping

Whether you're a homeowner trying to landscape your property or an owner or manager of a landscaping company who needs to communicate with Spanish-speaking workers or customers, knowing some landscaping-related Spanish can help you get the job done right.

In this chapter, we introduce you to common landscaping terminology so that you can refer to plants and other landscape decor along with the tools and machinery required to get the job done. We also provide you with plenty of action words, phrases, and commands to describe common landscaping tasks, including preparing the ground, planting, fertilizing, watering, and cleaning up.

Brushing Up on the Tools of the Trade

Whether you're grading a pristine landscape, digging out overgrown shrubs, pruning trees, laying sod, or planting flowers, you're usually using one or more tools or instructing others to use the tools to do the job more easily and efficiently. When it comes to using tools, you can combine the following phrases with terms from Table 9-1:

✏ *Bring me the . . .* **Tráigame el/la . . .** (*trah*ee-gah-meh ehl/lah)

✏ *Use the . . .* **Use el/la. . .** (*oo*-seh ehl/lah)

✏ *Put away the . . .* **Guarde el/la . . .** (goo*ahr*-deh ehl/lah)

Table 9-1	Landscaping Tools and Related Terms	
English	*Spanish*	*Pronunciation*
aerator	**el abridor de hoyos**	ehl ah-bvree-*dohr* deh *oh*-yohs
ax	**el hacha**	ehl *ah*-chah
backhoe	**la excavadora**	lah eks-kah-bvah-*doh*-rah
broom	**la escoba**	lah ehs-*koh*-bvah
brush	**el cepillo**	ehl seh-*pee*-yoh
bucket	**la cubeta/el cubo**	lah koo-*bveh*-tah/ehl *koo*-bvoh
bulldozer	**la excavadora**	lah eks-kah-bvah-*doh*-rah
cart	**la carreta**	lah kah-*rreh*-tah
clippers	**las podadoras**	lahs poh-dah-*doh*-rahs
chainsaw	**la motosierra**	lah moh-toh-see*eh*-rrah
compactor	**el compactador**	ehl kohm-pahk-tah-*dohr*
edger	**el cortabordes**	ehl kohr-tah-*bvohr*-dehs
grass catcher	**el recogedor de cortada**	ehl reh-koh-Heh-*dohr* deh kohr-*tah*-dah
hedge clippers	**las podadoras**	las poh-dah-*doh*-rahs
hoe	**el azadón**	ehl ah-sah-*dohn*
hose (drip)	**la manguera chorreando**	lah mahn-*geh*-rah choh-rreh-*ahn*-doh
hose (soaker)	**la manguera de remojo**	lah mahn-*geh*-rah deh reh-*moh*-Hoh
lawn mower	**la cortadora de césped**	lah kohr-tah-*doh*-rah deh *sehs*-pehd
high-wheel	**la cortadora de ruedas altas**	lah kohr-tah-*doh*-rah deh roo*eh*-dahs *ahl*-tahs
power	**la cortadora de motor**	lah kohr-tah-*doh*-rah deh moh-*tohr*
push	**la cortadora manual**	lah kohr-tah-*doh*-rah mah-noo*ahl*
riding	**la cortadora con asiento**	lah kohr-tah-*doh*-rah kohn ah-see*ehn*-toh

English	Spanish	Pronunciation
lawn tractor	**el tractor para el césped**	ehl trahk-*tohr pah*-rah ehl *sehs*-pehd
leaf blower	**la sopladora de hojas**	lah soh-plah-*doh*-rah deh *oh*-Hahs
loppers	**las tijeras de mango largo**	lahs tee-*Heh*-rahs deh *mahn*-goh *lahr*-goh
mulcher	**el desmenusador**	ehl dehs-meh-noo-sah-*dohr*
pickaxe	**el pico**	ehl *pee*-koh
pitchfork	**la horca**	lah *ohr*-kah
plow	**el arado**	ehl ah-*rah*-doh
power rake	**el rastrillo de motor**	ehl rahs-*tree*-yoh deh moh-*tohr*
pruners	**las tijeras de podar**	lahs tee-*Heh*-rahs deh poh-*dahr*
rake	**el rastrillo**	ehl rahs-*tree*-yoh
roller	**el rodillo**	ehl roh-*dee*-yoh
rotary tiller	**la cultivadora rotatoria**	lah kool-tee-bvah-*doh*-rah roh-tah-*toh*-reeah
saw	**la sierra**	lah see*eh*-rrah
shovel/spade	**la pala**	lah *pah*-lah
spade (hand)	**la pala de mano**	lah pah-lah deh *mah*-noh
spreader (of seeds)	**la máquina de sembrar**	lah *mah*-kee-nah deh sehm-*bvrahr*
spreader	**el esparcidor/la bomba de asperjar**	ehl ehs-pahr-see-*dohr*/lah *bvohm*-bvah deh ahs-pehr-*Hahr*
sprinkler	**el aspersor**	ehl ahs-pehr-*sohr*
valve	**la válvula**	lah *bvahl*-bvoo-lah
watering can	**la regadera**	lah reh-gah-*deh*-rah
wheelbarrow	**la carretilla**	lah kah-rreh-*tee*-yah
wood chipper	**el trituradora**	ehl tree-too-rah-*doh*-rah

You also need to be aware of some of the Spanish words for the safety gear that protects you and your fellow workers on the job. Check out Table 9-2 for a quick primer.

Table 9-2	Safety Gear for Gardening	
English	*Spanish*	*Pronunciation*
boots	**las botas**	lahs *bvoh*-tahs
earplugs	**los tapones para los oídos**	lohs tah-*poh*-nehs *pah*-rah lohs oh*ee*-dohs
face shield/mask	**la máscara**	lah *mahs*-kah-rah
gloves	**los guantes**	lohs goo*ahn*-tehs
goggles	**los lentes de seguridad**	lohs *lehn*-tehs deh seh-goo-ree-*dahd*
hard hat	**el casco**	ehl *kahs*-koh
hat (for the sun)	**el sombrero**	ehl sohm-*bvreh*-roh
respirator	**la filtradora de aire**	lah feel-trah-*doh*-rah deh *ah*ee-reh

Commanding Your Crew

If you're just starting to acquire Spanish-speaking skills, you may want to ease yourself into the situation by paring down the verbal instructions and showing rather than telling your crew what you want them to do and how you want them to do it. To train your crew, combine the suitable phrases from the following list with actual demonstrations of landscaping tasks:

- ✔ *Follow me.* **Sígame.** (*see*-gah-meh)

- ✔ *Watch me do it.* **Obsérveme hacerlo.** (ohbv-*sehr*-bveh-meh ah-*sehr*-loh)

- ✔ *Let me show you how.* **Déjeme demostrar.** (*deh*-Heh-meh deh-mohs-*trahr*)

- ✔ *Do it like this.* **Hágalo así.** (*ah*-gah-loh ah-*see*)

- ✔ *Help me.* **Ayúdeme.** (ah-*yoo*-deh-meh)

- ✔ *Mow the grass in this area.* **Corte la hierba en esta área.** (*kohr*-teh lah ee*ehr*-bvah ehn *ehs*-tah *ah*-reh-ah)

- ✔ *Remove the weeds like this.* **Quite la mala hierba así.** (*kee*-teh lah *mah*-lah ee*ehr*-bvah ah-*see*)

- ✔ *Rake this area.* **Rastrille esta área.** (rahs-*tree*-yeh *ehs*-tah *ah*-reh-ah)

- ✔ *Blow the debris off the walks and driveways like this.* **Sople la basura de las aceras y la calzada así.** (*soh*-pleh lah bvah-*soo*-rah deh lahs ah-*seh*-rahs ee lah kahl-*sah*-dah ah-*see*)

✔ *Sweep up when you are done.* **Bárralo cuando termine con todo.** (*bvah*-rreh-loh koo*ahn*-doh tehr-*mee*-neh kohn *toh*-doh)

✔ *Stay off of this area.* **Quédese de esta área.** (*keh*-deh-seh deh *ehs*-tah *ah*-reh-ah)

✔ *Plant these plants here.* **Plante estas plantas aquí.** (*plahn*-teh *ehs*-tahs *plahn*-tahs ah-*kee*)

✔ *Trim the tree like this.* **Recorte el árbol así.** (reh-*kohr*-teh ehl *ahr*-bvohl ah-*see*)

✔ *Dig here like this.* **Cave aquí como esto.** (*kah*-bveh ah-*kee koh*-moh *ehs*-toh)

✔ *Clean up this area.* **Limpie esta área.** (*leem*-peeeh *ehs*-tah *ah*-reh-ah)

✔ *Place the trash in the dumpster.* **Tire la basura en el basurero.** (*tee*-reh lah bvah-*soo*-rah ehn lah bvah-soo-*reh*-roh)

✔ *Water these plants.* **Regue estas plantas.** (*reh*-geh *ehs*-tahs *plahn*-tahs)

✔ *Turn on the water.* **Prenda el agua.** (*prehn*-dah ehl *ah*-gooah)

✔ *Turn off the water.* **Apague el agua.** (ah-*pah*-geh ehl *ah*-gooah)

✔ *Start the machine like this.* **Encienda la máquina así.** (ehn-seee*ehn*-dah lah *mah*-kee-nah ah-*see*)

✔ *Turn off the machine like this.* **Apague la máquina así.** (ah-*pah*-geh lah *mah*-kee-nah ah-*see*)

When giving directions, you also need to point out any potential safety hazards, such as overhead power lines or buried power lines, gas lines, and water pipes. Following are some key phrases you need to master:

✔ *Don't dig where you see these markers.* **No cave donde se ve estos marcadores.** (noh *kah*-bveh *dohn*-deh seh bveh *ehs*-tohs mahr-kah-*doh*-rehs)

✔ *Don't cut down any of the marked trees.* **No corte los árboles marcados.** (noh *kohr*-the lohs *ahr*-bvoh-lehs mahr-*kah*-dohs)

✔ *Stay away from those power lines.* **Quédese lejos de las líneas eléctricas.** (*keh*-deh-seh *leh*-Hohs deh lahs *lee*-neh-ahs eh-*lehk*-tree-kahs)

✔ *Put on your safety glasses first.* **Póngase sus gafas de seguridad primero.** (*pohn*-gah-seh soos *gah*-fahs deh seh-goo-ree-*dahd* pree-*meh*-roh)

✔ *Turn off the power first.* **Apague la electricidad primero.** (ah-*pah*-geh lah eh-lehk-tree-see-*dahd* pree-*meh*-roh)

Book IV

Spanish at Work

Prepping the Ground for Planting

Every landscaper and gardener knows that one of the keys to a healthy landscape is to prepare the ground properly before planting anything. You need to ensure proper drainage, make sure the soil is the right consistency and has the right mix of nutrients, and put down any necessary landscaping fabric to control weeds.

In the following sections, we provide several commands and phrases to help you lead any Spanish-speaking workers through the process.

Grading the lot

A properly graded lot directs water away from any structures and prevents pools from developing during heavy rains. Make sure your workers grasp the basic concepts and grade the lot properly:

- ✔ *The ground needs to slope down away from the building.* **La tierra necesita bajar de la estructura.** (lah tee*eh*-rrah neh-seh-*see*-tah bvah-*Hahr* deh lah ehs-trook-*too*-rah)

- ✔ *Rain water must flow down away from the home.* **El agua de lluvia debe de fluir fuera de la casa.** (ehl *ah*-gooah deh *yoo*-bveeah *deh*-bveh deh floo-*eer* foo*eh*-rah deh lah *kah*-sah)

- ✔ *Level any areas that look high.* **Nivele cualquier área que parezca alta.** (nee-*bveh*-leh kooahl-kee*ehr* ah-reh-ah keh pah-*rehs*-kah *ahl*-tah)

- ✔ *Fill in areas that look low.* **Rellene cualquier área que parezca baja.** (reh-*yeh*-neh kooahl-kee*ehr* ah-reh-ah keh pah-*rehs*-kah *bvah*-Hah)

- ✔ *Clear all rocks and debris from the area.* **Limpie las piedras y la basura de la área.** (*leem*-pee*eh* lahs pee*eh*-drahs ee lah bvah-*soo*-rah deh lah *ah*-reh-ah)

- ✔ *Use the bulldozer to move any big rocks.* **Use la excavadora a trasladar cualquier piedra grande.** (*oo*-seh lah ehsk-kah-bvah-*doh*-rah ah trahs-lah-*dahr* kooahl-kee*ehr* pee*eh*-drah *grahn*-deh)

- ✔ *Dig up all the roots.* **Saque todas las raíces.** (*sah*-keh *toh*-dahs lahs rah*ee*-sehs)

- ✔ *Spray some water on the dirt to keep the dust down.* **Rocie la tierra con agua para controlar el polvo.** (*roh*-seee*eh* lah tee*eh*-rrah kohn *ah*-gooah *pah*-rah kohn-troh-*lahr* ehl *pohl*-bvoh)

Preparing the soil

Before you do any serious planting, you may need to till the soil and add a level of topsoil. Here are some directives you can use to instruct your crew:

- ✔ *Spread a layer of topsoil.* **Esparza un estrato de capa superior de suelo.** (ehs-*pahr*-sah oon ehs-*trah*-toh deh *kah*-pah soo-peh-ree*ohr* deh soo*eh*-loh)

- ✔ *Add compost here.* **Añada el abono aquí.** (ah-*nyah*-dah ehl ah-*bvoh*-noh ah-*kee*)

- ✔ *Add manure here.* **Añada el estiércol aquí.** (ah-*nyah*-dah ehl ehs-tee*ehr*-kohl ah-*kee*)

- ✔ *Till the soil before planting.* **Cultive la tierra antes de sembrarla.** (kool-*tee*-bveh lah tee*eh*-rrah *ahn*-tehs deh sehm-*bvahr*-lah)

- ✔ *Rake this area smooth first.* **Rastrille esta área liso primero.** (rahs-*tree*-yeh *ehs*-tah *ah*-reh-ah *lee*-soh pree-*meh*-roh)

Laying landscaping fabric and edging

In areas where weeds are likely to become a problem later, you want to lay down some landscaping fabric and edging before planting. Here are a couple of phrases that can help you provide the necessary direction:

- ✔ *Lay the fabric down here before planting.* **Despliegue la tela aquí antes de sembrar la tierra.** (dehs-plee*eh*-geh lah *teh*-lah ah-*kee ahn*-tehs deh sehm-*bvrahr* lah tee*eh*-rrah)

- ✔ *Make sure the fabric goes all the way to the edge here.* **Asegure que la tela llegue al borde aquí.** (ah-seh-*goo*-reh keh lah *teh*-lah *yeh*-geh ahl *bvohr*-deh ah-*kee*)

- ✔ *Use steel edging along here.* **Use el borde de fierro aquí.** (*oo*-seh ehl *bvohr*-deh deh fee*eh*-rroh ah-*kee*)

Book IV

Spanish at Work

Planting Trees, Shrubs, and Flowers

Planting sounds easy at first — dig a hole, stick the plant in it, and fill the hole back up with dirt. However, when you start to consider all the different types of plants and variations in how best to plant them, planting instructions become much more complex. We can't begin to deal with all the nuances of location, proper planting depths, and drainage considerations for each type of plant, but we can provide some basic instructions:

- *Dig the hole two feet deep and two feet wide.* **Cave el hoyo dos pies profundo y dos pies ancho.** (*kah*-bveh ehl *oh*-yoh dohs pee*ehs* proh-*foon*-doh ee dohs pee*ehs* *ahn*-choh)

- *The hole is too deep.* **El hoyo es demasiado profundo.** (ehl *oh*-yoh ehs deh-mah-see*ah*-doh proh-*foon*-doh)

- *Dig a little deeper.* **Cave el hoyo más profundo.** (*kah*-bveh ehl *oh*-yoh mahs proh-*foon*-doh)

- *Mix peat moss and fertilizer with the dirt before filling in the hole.* **Mezcle el sustrato orgánico y el fertilizante con la tierra antes de rellenar el hoyo.** (*mehs*-kleh ehl soos-*trah*-toh ohr-*gah*-nee-koh ee ehl fehr-tee-lee-*sahn*-teh kohn lah tee*eh*-rrah *ahn*-tehs deh reh-yeh-*nahr* ehl *oh*-yoh)

- *Make sure the roots are below the ground.* **Asegure que las raíces quedan debajo del suelo.** (ah-seh-*goo*-reh keh lahs rah*ee*-sehs *keh*-dahn deh-*bvah*-Hoh dehl soo*eh*-loh)

- Make sure the roots are level with the ground. **Asegure que las raíces están plano con el suelo.** (ah-seh-*goo*-reh keh lahs rah*ee*-sehs ehs-*tahn* *plah*-noh kohn ehl soo*eh*-loh)

- *Make sure the top of the roots are just above the ground.* **Asegure que la parte de arriba de las raíces queda encima del suelo.** (ah-seh-*goo*-reh keh lah *pahr*-teh deh ah-*rree*-bvah deh lahs rah*ee*-sehs *keh*-dah ehn-*see*-mah dehl soo*eh*-loh)

- *Fill back in with soil like this.* **Rellene el hoyo con la tierra así.** (reh-*yeh*-neh ehl *oh*-yoh kohn lah tee*eh*-rrah ah-*see*)

- *Water all the plants when you're done planting.* **Riegue todas las plantas después de plantarlas.** (ree*eh*-geh *toh*-dahs lahs *plahn*-tahs dehs-poo*ehs* deh plahn-*tahr*-lahs)

As you're directing the landscapers, refer to Table 9-3 for some additional words that are likely to come into play.

Table 9-3	Plants and Related Words	
English	*Spanish*	*Pronunciation*
annual	**la planta anual**	lah *plahn*-tah ah-noo*ahl*
ball	**la bola**	lah *bvoh*-lah
bed (of flowers)	**el arriate**	ehl ah-ree*ah*-teh
border	**el borde**	ehl *bvohr*-deh

English	Spanish	Pronunciation
bulb	**el bulbo**	ehl *bvool*-bvoh
bush	**el arbusto**	ehl ahr-*bvoos*-toh
flower	**la flor**	lah flohr
flower pot	**la maceta**	lah mah-*seh*-tah
flowering plant	**la planta que da flores**	lah *plahn*-tah keh dah *floh*-rehs
ground	**la tierra**	lah tee*eh*-rrah
ground cover	**las plantas de cobertura**	lahs *plahn*-tahs deh koh-bvehr-*too*-rah
hole	**el hoyo/el hueco**	ehl *oh*-yoh/ehl oo*eh*-koh
manure	**el estiércol**	ehl ehs-tee*ehr*-kohl
mulch	**el sustrato/la composta/ el mulchin**	ehl soos-*trah*-toh/lah kohm-*pohs*-tah/ehl mool-*cheen*
peat moss	**el sustrato orgánico**	ehl soos-*trah*-toh ohr-*gah*-nee-koh
perennial	**la planta perenne**	lah *plahn*-tah peh-*reh*-neh
planter	**la jardinera**	lah Hahr-dee-*neh*-rah
seeds	**las semillas**	lahs seh-*mee*-yahs
soil	**la tierra**	lah tee*eh*-rrah

Lawn Care Lingo

Unless you're living and working in desert areas, a good portion of your landscaping duties revolve around lawn care — laying sod, seeding, mowing, fertilizing, watering, and so on. In the following sections, we introduce some essential lawn care terminology for dealing with the most common lawn care tasks.

Mowing

From spring until fall, mowing becomes a weekly and sometimes biweekly chore, during which time the following phrases can come in very handy:

✔ *Cut the grass two inches tall.* **Corte la hierba a dos pulgadas.** (*kohr*-teh lah ee*ehr*-bvah ah dohs pool-*gah*-dahs)

✔ *Set the mower higher.* **Ajuste la segadura más alta.** (ah-*Hoos*-teh lah seh-gah-*doo*-rah mahs *ahl*-tah)

✔ *Set the mower lower.* **Ajuste la segadura más baja.** (ah-*Hoos*-teh lah seh-gah-*doo*-rah mahs *bah*-Hah)

✔ *Don't mow where we just planted seed.* **No corte la hierba donde acabamos de sembrar.** (noh *kohr*-teh lah ee*ehr*-bvah *dohn*-deh ah-kah-*bvah*-mohs deh sehm-*bvrahr*)

✔ *Attach the grass catcher to bag the clippings.* **Sujete la bolsa para recoger la hierba.** (soo-*Heh*-tah lah *bvohl*-sah *pah*-rah reh-koh-*Hehr* lah ee*ehr*-bvah)

✔ *Leave the clippings on the lawn.* **Deje la hierba cortada en el jardín.** (*deh*-Heh lah ee*ehr*-bvah kohr-*tah*-dah ehn ehl Hahr-*deen*)

✔ *Place the clippings in the mulch pile.* **Coloque la hierba cortada en el pilón orgánico.** (koh-*loh*-keh lah ee*ehr*-bvah kohr-*tah*-dah ehn ehl pee-*lohn* ohr-*gah*-nee-koh)

✔ *Be careful mowing near the flower beds.* **Tenga cuidado cortando la hierba cerca de los arrietes.** (*tehn*-gah kooee-*dah*-doh kohr-*tahn*-doh lah ee*ehr*-bvah *sehr*-kah deh lohs ah-rree*eh*-tehs)

✔ *Use the edger around the walkways.* **Use el cortabordes alrededor de las aceras.** (*oo*-seh ehl kohr-tah-*bvohr*-dehs ahl-reh-deh-*dohr* deh lahs ah-*seh*-rahs)

Watering

Nowadays, many people water with sprinkling systems, but you're still likely to encounter situations in which you need to instruct workers or property owners on when to water and how much:

✔ *Water this every day.* **Riegue esta parte todos los días.** (ree*eh*-geh *ehs*-tah *pahr*-teh *toh*-dohs lohs *dee*-ahs)

✔ *Water this every other day when it doesn't rain.* **Riegue esta parte cada dos días cuando no llueva.** (ree*eh*-geh *ehs*-tah *pahr*-teh *kah*-dah dohs *dee*-ahs koo*ahn*-doh noh yoo*eh*-bvah)

✔ *Water this very heavily.* **Riegue esta parte mucho.** (ree*eh*-geh *ehs*-tah *pahr*-teh *moo*-choh)

✔ *Water this lightly.* **Riegue esta parte poco.** (ree*eh*-geh *ehs*-tah *pahr*-teh *poh*-koh)

✔ *Keep this damp until the seeds sprout.* **Mantenga esta área húmeda hasta que las semillas broten.** (mahn-*tehn*-gah *ehs*-tah *ah*-reh-ah *oo*-meh-dah *ahs*-tah keh lahs seh-*mee*-yahs *bvroh*-tehn)

✔ *Don't water on days when it rains.* **No riegue en los días cuando llueva.** (noh ree*eh*-geh ehn lohs *dee*-ahs koo*ahn*-doh yoo*eh*-bvah)

Applying fertilizer and herbicides

Applying fertilizer, herbicides, and pesticides may be beneficial restoring a distressed lawn or maintaining a lawn's health, but you also need to address worker safety. The following expressions can help you ensure proper and safe applications:

- ✔ *Use fertilizer here.* **Use fertilizante aquí.** (*oo*-seh fehr-tee-lee-*sahn*-teh ah-*kee*)

- ✔ *Use the fertilizer spreader.* **Use el esparcidor de fertilizante.** (*oo*-seh ehl ehs-pahr-see-*dohr* deh fehr-tee-lee-*sahn*-teh)

- ✔ *Use this setting.* **Ajústelo así.** (ah-*Hoos*-teh-loh ah-*see*)

- ✔ *Don't use too much.* **No use demasiado.** (noh *oo*-seh deh-mah-see*ah*-doh)

- ✔ *Don't get this on your skin.* **Esto no debe de tocar el piel.** (*ehs*-toh noh *deh*-bveh deh toh-*kahr* ehl pee*ehl*)

- ✔ *Don't breathe the dust.* **No respire el polvo.** (noh rehs-*pee*-reh ehl *pohl*-bvoh)

- ✔ *Always wear a mask.* **Siempre usa una máscara.** (see*ehm*-preh *oo*-sah *oo*-nah *mahs*-kah-rah)

- ✔ *Wash your hands after use.* **Lávese las manos después de usar.** (*lah*-bvah-seh lahs *mah*-nohs dehs-poo*ehs* deh oo-*sahr*)

- ✔ *Spray this only on the weeds.* **Rocie esto solamente en las hierbas malas.** (*roh*-seeeh *ehs*-toh soh-lah-*mehn*-teh ehn lahs ee*ehr*-bvahs *mah*-lahs)

Aerating and dethatching

Aerating and dethatching not only give lawns a breath of fresh air but also give water and nutrients easier access to reaching the roots. When a lawn needs to be aerated or dethatched, use the following expressions:

- ✔ *Dethatch the lawn.* **Airee el césped.** (ahee-*reh*-eh el *sehs*-pehd)

- ✔ *Use the power rake.* **Use el rastrillo de motor.** (*oo*-seh el rah-*stree*-yoh deh moh-*tohr*)

- ✔ *Rake up the debris.* **Rastrille los escombros.** (rah-*stree*-yeh lohs ehs-*kohm*-brohs)

- ✔ *Aerate the lawn.* **Airee el jardín.** (ahee-*reh*-eh ehl Hahr-*deen*)

Spreading grass seed

For new or severely damaged lawns, you may need to seed or over-seed. Use the following expressions to provide direction:

- ✐ *Seed the area.* **Siembre el área.** (see*ehm*-bvreh el *ah*-reh-ah)

- ✐ *Scatter the seed with the mechanical spreader.* **Siembre las semillas con la máquina de sembrar.** (see*ehm*-bvreh lahs seh-*mee*-yahs kohn lah *mah*-kee-nah deh sem-*bvrahr*)

Laying sod

When laying sod, keeping it from drying out and laying it properly are the keys to success:

- ✐ *Keep the sod out of the sun.* **Guarde el celote en la sombra.** (goo*ahr*-deh ehl seh-*loh*-teh ehn lah *sohm*-bvrah)

- ✐ *Start here.* **Empiece aquí.** (ehm-pee*eh*-seh ah-*kee*)

- ✐ *Lay the sod parallel to the house.* **Coloque el celote paralelamente a la casa.** (koh-*loh*-keh ehl seh-*loh*-teh pah-rah-leh-lah-*mehn*-teh ah lah *kah*-sah)

- ✐ *Lay the sod perpendicular to the house.* **Coloque el celote perpendicularmente a la casa.** (koh-*loh*-keh ehl seh-*loh*-teh pehr-pehn-dee-koo-lahr-*mehn*-teh ah lah *kah*-sah)

- ✐ *Don't leave gaps.* **No deje ningún hueco entre las fajas del celote.** (noh *deh*-Heh neen-*goon* Hoo*eh*-koh *ehn*-treh lahs *fah*-Hahs dehl seh-*loh*-teh)

- ✐ *Lay the strips closer together.* **Coloque las tiras cerca el uno al otro.** (koh-*loh*-keh lahs *tee*-rahs *sehr*-kah ehl *oo*-noh ahl *oh*-troh)

- ✐ *Press the sod down with a drum roller when you're finished.* **Use el rodillo cuando haya terminado colocando el celote.** (*oo*-seh ehl roh-*dee*-yoh koo*ahn*-doh *ah*-yah tehr-mee-*nah*-doh koh-loh-*kahn*-doh ehl seh-*loh*-teh)

Book V
Appendixes

"I know it's a popular American expression, but you just don't say 'Hasta la vista, baby' to a nun."

In this book . . .

*P*icking up a new language requires a great deal of memorization. You need to memorize the vocabulary, of course, but you also need to memorize the various grammatical rules and verb conjugations. When your brain isn't quite up to the task of providing you with total recall, turn to these appendixes for quick reference. We also include a CD track listing.

Here are the contents of Book V at a glance:

Appendix A
Spanish Verbs

Regular Spanish Verbs

decidir: to decide
Present participle: decidiendo
Past Participle: decidido

Simple Tenses		Compound Tenses	
Singular	**Plural**	**Singular**	**Plural**
Present		*Present perfect*	
decido	decidimos	he decidido	hemos decidido
decides	decidís	has decidido	habéis decidido
decide	deciden	ha decidido	han decidido
Imperfect		*Pluperfect*	
decidía	decidíamos	había decidido	habíamos decidido
decidías	decidíais	habías decidido	habíais decidido
decidía	decidían	había decidido	habían decidido
Preterit		*Preterit perfect*	
decidí	decidimos	hube decidido	hubimos decidido
decidiste	decidisteis	hubiste decidido	hubisteis decidido
decidió	decidieron	hubo decidido	hubieron decidido
Future		*Future perfect*	
decidiré	decidiremos	habré decidido	habremos decidido
decidirás	decidirán	habras decidido	habréis decidido
decidirá	decidirán	habrá decidido	habrán decidido

Simple Tenses		Compound Tenses	
Singular	**Plural**	**Singular**	**Plural**
Conditional		*Conditional perfect*	
decidiría	decidiríamos	habría decidido	habríamos decidido
decidirías	decidiríais	habrías decidido	habríais decidido
decidiría	decidirían	habría decidido	habrían decidido
Present subjunctive		*Present perfect subjunctive*	
decida	decidamos	haya decidido	hayamos decidido
decidas	decidáis	hayas decidido	hayáis decidido
decida	decidan	haya decidido	hayan decidido
Imperfect subjunctive		*Pluperfect subjunctive*	
decidiera	decidiéramos	hubiera decidido	hubiéramos decidido
decidieras	decidierais	hubieras decidido	hubierais decidido
decidiera	decidieran	hubiera decidido	hubieran decidido
Imperative			
N/A	decidamos		
decide; no decidas	decidid; no decidáis		
decida	decidan		

admitir: to admit, to permit
Present participle: admitiendo
Past Participle: admitido

Simple Tenses		Compound Tenses	
Singular	**Plural**	**Singular**	**Plural**
Present		*Present perfect*	
admito	admitimos	he admitido	hemos admitido
admites	admitís	has admitido	habéis admitido

Simple Tenses		Compound Tenses	
Singular	**Plural**	**Singular**	**Plural**
admite	admiten	ha admitido	han admitido
Imperfect		*Pluperfect*	
admitía	admitíamos	había admitido	habíamos admitido
admitías	admitíais	habías admitido	habíais admitido
admitía	admitían	había admitido	habían admitido
Preterit		*Preterit perfect*	
admití	admitimos	hube admitido	hubimos admitido
admitiste	admitisteis	hubiste admitido	hubisteis admitido
admitió	admitieron	hubo admitido	hubieron admitido
Future		*Future perfect*	
admitiré	admitiremos	habré admitido	habremos admitido
admitirás	admitiréis	habrás admitido	habréis admitido
admitirá	admitirán	habrá admitido	habrán admitido
Conditional		*Conditional perfect*	
admitiría	admitiríamos	habría admitido	habríamos admitido
admitirías	admitiríais	habrías admitido	habríais admitido
admitiría	admitirían	habría admitido	habrían admitido
Present subjunctive		*Present perfect subjunctive*	
admita	admitamos	haya admitido	hayamos admitido
admitas	admitáis	hayas admitido	hayáis admitido
admita	admitan	haya admitido	hayan admitido
Imperfect subjunctive		*Pluperfect subjunctive*	
admitiera	admitiéramos	hubiera admitido	hubiéramos admitido

Simple Tenses		Compound Tenses	
Singular	**Plural**	**Singular**	**Plural**
admitieras	admitierais	hubieras admitido	hubierais admitido
admitiera	admitieran	hubiera admitido	hubieran admitido
Imperative			
N/A	admitamos		
admite; no admitas	admitid; no admitáis		
admita	admitan		

comprender: to understand
Present participle: comprendiendo
Past Participle: comprendido

Simple Tenses		Compound Tenses	
Singular	**Plural**	**Singular**	**Plural**
Present		*Present perfect*	
comprendo	comprendemos	he comprendido	hemos comprendido
comprendes	comprendéis	has comprendido	habéis comprendido
comprende	comprenden	ha comprendido	han comprendido
Imperfect		*Pluperfect*	
comprendía	comprendíamos	habías comprendido	habíamos comprendido
comprendías	comprendíais	habías comprendido	habíais comprendido
comprendía	comprendían	había comprendido	habían comprendido
Preterit		*Preterit perfect*	
comprendí	comprendimos	hube comprendido	hubimos comprendido

Simple Tenses		Compound Tenses	
Singular	**Plural**	**Singular**	**Plural**
comprendiste	comprendisteis	hubiste comprendido	hubisteis comprendido
comprendió	comprendieron	hubo comprendido	hubieron comprendido
Future		*Future perfect*	
comprenderé	comprenderemos	habré comprendido	habremos comprendido
comprenderás	comprenderéis	habrás comprendido	habréis comprendido
comprenderá	comprenderán	habrá comprendido	habrán comprendido
Conditional		*Conditional perfect*	
comprendería	comprenderíamos	habría comprendido	habríamos comprendido
comprenderías	comprenderíais	habrías comprendido	habríais comprendido
comprendería	comprenderían	habría comprendido	habrían comprendido
Present subjunctive		*Present perfect subjunctive*	
comprenda	comprendamos	haya comprendido	hayamos comprendido
comprendas	comprendáis	hayas comprendido	hayáis comprendido
comprenda	comprendan	haya comprendido	hayan comprendido
Imperfect subjunctive		*Pluperfect subjunctive*	
comprendiera	comprendiéramos	hubiera comprendido	hubiéramos comprendido

Simple Tenses		Compound Tenses	
Singular	**Plural**	**Singular**	**Plural**
comprendieras	comprendierais	hubieras comprendido	hubierais comprendido
comprendiera	comprendieran	hubiera comprendido	hubieran comprendido
Imperative			
N/A	comprendamos		
comprende; no comprendas	comprended; no comprendáis		
comprenda	comprendan		

escuchar: to listen (to)
Present participle: escuchando
Past Participle: escuchado

Simple Tenses		Compound Tenses	
Singular	**Plural**	**Singular**	**Plural**
Present		*Present perfect*	
escucho	escuchamos	he escuchado	hemos escuchado
escuchas	escucháis	has escuchado	habéis escuchado
escucha	escuchan	ha escuchado	han escuchado
Imperfect		*Pluperfect*	
escuchaba	escuchábamos	había escuchado	habíamos escuchado
escuchabas	escuchabais	habías escuchado	habíais escuchado
escuchaba	escuchaban	había escuchado	habían escuchado
Preterit		*Preterit perfect*	
escuché	escuchamos	hube escuchado	hubimos escuchado
escuchaste	escuchasteis	hubiste escuchado	hubisteis escuchado

Simple Tenses		Compound Tenses	
Singular	**Plural**	**Singular**	**Plural**
escuchó	escucharon	hubo escuchado	hubieron escuchado
Future		*Future perfect*	
escucharé	escucharemos	habré escuchado	habremos escuchado
escucharás	escucharéis	habrás escuchado	habréis escuchado
escuchará	escucharán	habrá escuchado	habrán escuchado
Conditional		*Conditional perfect*	
escucharía	escucharíamos	habría escuchado	habríamos escuchado
escucharías	escucharíais	habrías escuchado	habríais escuchado
escucharía	escucharían	habría escuchado	habrían escuchado
Present subjunctive		*Present perfect subjunctive*	
escuche	escuchemos	haya escuchado	hayamos escuchado
escuches	escuchéis	hayas escuchado	hayáis escuchado
escuche	escuchen	haya escuchado	hayan escuchado
Imperfect subjunctive		*Pluperfect subjunctive*	
escuchara	escucháramos	hubiera escuchado	hubiéramos escuchado
escucharas	escucharais	hubieras escuchado	hubierais escuchado
escuchara	escucharan	hubiera escuchado	hubieran escuchado
Imperative			
N/A	escuchemos		
escucha; no escuches	escuchad; no escuchéis		
escuche	escuchen		

felicitar: to congratulate
Present participle: felicitando
Past Participle: felicitado

Simple Tenses		Compound Tenses	
Singular	**Plural**	**Singular**	**Plural**
Present		*Present perfect*	
felicito	felicitamos	he felicitado	hemos felicitado
felicitas	felicitáis	has felicitado	habéis felicitado
felicita	felicitan	ha felicitado	han felicitado
Imperfect		*Pluperfect*	
felicitaba	felicitábamos	había felicitado	habíamos felicitado
felicitabas	felicitabais	habías felicitado	habíais felicitado
felicitaba	felicitaban	había felicitado	habían felicitado
Preterit		*Preterit perfect*	
felicité	felicitamos	hube felicitado	hubimos felicitado
felicitaste	felicitasteis	hubiste felicitado	hubisteis felicitado
felicitó	felicitaron	hubo felicitado	hubieron felicitado
Future		*Future perfect*	
felicitaré	felicitaremos	habré felicitado	habremos felicitado
felicitarás	felicitaréis	habrás felicitado	habréis felicitado
felicitará	felicitarán	habrá felicitado	habrán felicitado
Conditional		*Conditional perfect*	
felicitaría	felicitaríamos	habría felicitado	habríamos felicitado
felicitarías	felicitéis	habrías felicitado	habríais felicitado
felicitaría	felicitarían	habría felicitado	habrían felicitado
Present subjunctive		*Present perfect subjunctive*	
felicite	felicitemos	haya felicitado	hayamos felicitado
felicites	felicitéis	hayas felicitado	hayáis felicitado

Simple Tenses		Compound Tenses	
Singular	**Plural**	**Singular**	**Plural**
felicite	feliciten	haya felicitado	hayan felicitado
Imperfect subjunctive		*Pluperfect subjunctive*	
felicitara	felicitáramos	hubiera felicitado	hubiéramos felicitado
felicitaras	felicitarais	hubieras felicitado	hubierais felicitado
felicitara	felicitaran	hubiera felicitado	hubieran felicitado
Imperative			
N/A	felicitemos		
felicita; no felicites	felicitad; no felicitéis		
felicite	feliciten		

barrer: to sweep
Present participle: barriendo
Past Participle: barrido

Simple Tenses		Compound Tenses	
Singular	**Plural**	**Singular**	**Plural**
Present		*Present perfect*	
barro	barremos	he barrido	hemos barrido
barres	barréis	has barrido	habéis barrido
barre	barren	ha barrido	han barrido
Imperfect		*Pluperfect*	
barría	barríamos	había barrido	habíamos barrido
barrías	barríais	habías barrido	habíais barrido
barría	barrían	había barrido	habían barrido

Simple Tenses		Compound Tenses	
Singular	**Plural**	**Singular**	**Plural**
Preterit		*Preterit perfect*	
barrí	barrimos	hube barrido	hubimos barrido
barriste	barristeis	hubiste barrido	hubisteis barrido
barrió	barrieron	hubo barrido	hubieron barrido
Future		*Future perfect*	
barreré	barreremos	habré barrido	habremos barrido
barrerás	barreréis	habrás barrido	habréis barrido
barrerá	barrerán	habrá barrido	habrán barrido
Conditional		*Conditional perfect*	
barrería	barreríamos	habría barrido	habríamos barrido
barrerías	barreríais	habrías barrido	habríais barrido
barrería	barrerían	habría barrido	habrían barrido
Present subjunctive		*Present perfect subjunctive*	
barra	barramos	haya barrido	hayamos barrido
barras	barráis	hayas barrido	hayáis barrido
barra	barran	haya barrido	hayan barrido
Imperfect subjunctive		*Pluperfect subjunctive*	
barriera	barriéramos	hubiera barrido	hubiéramos barrido
barrieras	barrierais	hubieras barrido	hubierais barrido
barriera	barrieran	hubiera barrido	hubieran barrido
Imperative			
N/A	barramos		
barre; no barras	barred; no barráis		
barra	barran		

ganar: to gain, to earn, to win
Present participle: ganando
Past Participle: ganado

Simple Tenses		Compound Tenses	
Singular	**Plural**	**Singular**	**Plural**
Present		*Present perfect*	
gano	ganamos	he ganado	hemos ganado
ganas	ganáis	has ganado	habéis ganado
gana	ganan	ha ganado	han ganado
Imperfect		*Pluperfect*	
ganaba	ganábamos	había ganado	habíamos ganado
ganabas	ganabais	habías ganado	habíais ganado
ganaba	ganaban	había ganado	habían ganado
Preterit		*Preterit perfect*	
gané	ganamos	hube ganado	hubimos ganado
ganaste	ganasteis	hubiste ganado	hubisteis ganado
ganó	ganaron	hubo ganado	hubieron ganado
Future		*Future perfect*	
ganaré	ganaremos	habré ganado	habremos ganado
ganarás	ganaréis	habrás ganado	habréis ganado
ganará	ganarán	habrá ganado	habrán ganado
Conditional		*Conditional perfect*	
ganaría	ganaríamos	habría ganado	habríamos ganado
ganarías	ganaríais	habrías ganado	habríais ganado
ganaría	ganarían	habría ganado	habrían ganado
Present subjunctive		*Present perfect subjunctive*	
gane	ganemos	haya ganado	hayamos ganado
ganes	ganéis	hayas ganado	hayáis ganado

Simple Tenses		Compound Tenses	
Singular	**Plural**	**Singular**	**Plural**
gane	ganen	haya ganado	hayan ganado
Imperfect subjunctive		*Pluperfect subjunctive*	
ganara	ganáramos	hubiera ganado	hubiéramos ganado
ganaras	ganarais	hubieras ganado	hubierais ganado
ganara	ganaran	hubiera ganado	hubieran ganado
Imperative			
N/A	ganemos		
gana; no ganes	ganad; no ganéis		
gane	ganen		

heredar: to inherit
Present participle: heredando
Past Participle: heredado

Simple Tenses		Compound Tenses	
Singular	**Plural**	**Singular**	**Plural**
Present		*Present perfect*	
heredo	heredamos	he heredado	hemos heredado
heredas	heredáis	has heredado	habéis heredado
hereda	heredan	he heredado	han heredado
Imperfect		*Pluperfect*	
heredaba	heredábamos	había heredado	habíamos heredado
heredabas	heredabais	habías heredado	habíais heredado
heredaba	heredaban	había heredado	habían heredado
Preterit		*Preterit perfect*	
heredé	heredamos	hube heredado	hubimos heredado

Simple Tenses		Compound Tenses	
Singular	**Plural**	**Singular**	**Plural**
heredaste	heredasteis	hubiste heredado	hubisteis heredado
heredó	heredaron	hubo heredado	hubieron heredado
Future		*Future perfect*	
heredaré	heredaremos	habré heredado	habremos heredado
heredarás	heredaréis	habrás heredado	habréis heredado
heredará	heredarán	habrá heredado	habrán heredado
Conditional		*Conditional perfect*	
heredaría	heredaríamos	habría heredado	habríamos heredado
heredarías	heredaríais	habrías heredado	habríais heredado
heredaría	heredarían	habría heredado	habrían heredado
Present subjunctive		*Present perfect subjunctive*	
herede	heredemos	haya heredado	hayamos heredado
heredes	heredéis	hayas heredado	hayáis heredado
herede	hereden	haya heredado	hayan heredado
Imperfect subjunctive		*Pluperfect subjunctive*	
heredara	heredáramos	hubiera heredado	hubiéramos heredado
heredaras	heredarais	hubieras heredado	hubierais heredado
heredara	heredaran	hubiera heredado	hubieran heredado
Imperative			
N/A	heredemos		
hereda; no heredes	heredad; no heredéis		
herede	hereden		

insistir: to insist
Present participle: insistiendo
Past Participle: insistido

Simple Tenses		Compound Tenses	
Singular	**Plural**	**Singular**	**Plural**
Present		*Present perfect*	
insisto	insistimos	he insistido	hemos insistido
insistes	insistís	has insistido	habéis insistido
insiste	insisten	ha insistido	han insistido
Imperfect		*Pluperfect*	
insistía	insistíamos	había insistido	habíamos insistido
insistías	insistíais	habías insistido	habíais insistido
insistía	insistían	había insistido	habían insistido
Preterit		*Preterit perfect*	
insistí	insistimos	hube insistido	hubimos insistido
insististe	insististeis	hubiste insistido	hubisteis insistido
insistió	insistieron	hubo insistido	hubieron insistido
Future		*Future perfect*	
insistiré	insistiremos	habré insistido	habremos insistido
insistirás	insistiréis	habrás insistido	habréis insistido
insistirá	insistirán	habrá insistido	habrán insistido
Conditional		*Conditional perfect*	
insistiría	insistiríamos	habría insistido	habríamos insistido
insistirías	insistiríais	habrías insistido	habríais insistido
insistiría	insistirían	habría insistido	habrían insistido
Present subjunctive		*Present perfect subjunctive*	
insista	insistamos	haya insistido	hayamos insistido
insistas	insistáis	hayas insistido	hayáis insistido
insista	insistan	haya insistido	hayan insistido

Simple Tenses		Compound Tenses	
Singular	**Plural**	**Singular**	**Plural**
Imperfect subjunctive		*Pluperfect subjunctive*	
insistiera	insistiéramos	hubiera insistido	hubiéramos insistido
insistieras	insistierais	hubieras insistido	hubierais insistido
insistiera	insistieran	hubiera insistido	hubieran insistido
Imperative			
N/A	insistamos		
insiste; no insistas	insistid; no insistáis		
insista	insistan		

jurar: to take an oath, to swear
Present participle: jurando
Past Participle: jurado

Simple Tenses		Compound Tenses	
Singular	**Plural**	**Singular**	**Plural**
Present		*Present perfect*	
juro	juramos	he jurado	hemos jurado
juras	juráis	has jurado	habéis jurado
jura	juran	ha jurado	han jurado
Imperfect		*Pluperfect*	
juraba	jurábamos	había jurado	habíamos jurado
jurabas	jurabais	habías jurado	habíais jurado
juraba	juraban	había jurado	habían jurado
Preterit		*Preterit perfect*	
juré	juramos	hube jurado	hubimos jurado
juraste	jurasteis	hubiste jurado	hubisteis jurado
juró	juraron	hubo jurado	hubieron jurado

Simple Tenses		Compound Tenses	
Singular	**Plural**	**Singular**	**Plural**
Future		*Future perfect*	
juraré	juraremos	habré jurado	habremos jurado
jurarás	juraréis	habrás jurado	habréis jurado
jurará	jurarán	habrá jurado	habrán jurado
Conditional		*Conditional perfect*	
juraría	juraríamos	habría jurado	habríamos jurado
jurarías	juraríais	habrías jurado	habríais jurado
juraría	jurarían	habría jurado	habrían jurado
Present subjunctive		*Present perfect subjunctive*	
jure	juremos	haya jurado	hayamos jurado
jures	juréis	hayas jurado	hayáis jurado
jure	juren	haya jurado	hayan jurado
Imperfect subjunctive		*Pluperfect subjunctive*	
jurara	juráramos	hubiera jurado	hubiéramos jurado
juraras	jurarais	hubieras jurado	hubierais jurado
jurara	juraran	hubiera jurado	hubieran jurado
Imperative			
N/A	juremos		
jura; no jures	jurad; no juréis		
jure	juren		

limpiar: to clean
Present participle: limpiando
Past Participle: limpiado

Simple Tenses		Compound Tenses	
Singular	**Plural**	**Singular**	**Plural**
Present		*Present perfect*	
limpio	limpiamos	he limpiado	hemos limpiado
limpias	limpiáis	has limpiado	habéis limpiado
limpia	limpian	ha limpiado	han limpiado
Imperfect		*Pluperfect*	
limpiaba	limpiábamos	había limpiado	habíamos limpiado
limpiabas	limpiabais	habías limpiado	habíais limpiado
limpiaba	limpiaban	había limpiado	habían limpiado
Preterit		*Preterit perfect*	
limpié	limpiamos	hube limpiado	hubimos limpiado
limpiaste	limpiasteis	hubiste limpiado	hubisteis limpiado
limpió	limpiaron	hubo limpiado	hubieron limpiado
Future		*Future perfect*	
limpiaré	limpiaremos	habré limpiado	habremos limpiado
limpiarás	limpiaréis	habrás limpiado	habréis limpiado
limpiará	limpiarán	habrá limpiado	habrán limpiado
Conditional		*Conditional perfect*	
limpiaría	limpiaríamos	habría limpiado	habríamos limpiado
limpiarías	limpiaríais	habrías limpiado	habríais limpiado
limpiaría	limpiarían	habría limpiado	habrían limpiado
Present subjunctive		*Present perfect subjunctive*	
limpie	limpiemos	haya limpiado	hayamos limpiado
limpies	limpiéis	hayas limpiado	hayáis limpiado
limpie	limpien	haya limpiado	hayan limpiado

Simple Tenses		Compound Tenses	
Singular	**Plural**	**Singular**	**Plural**
Imperfect subjunctive		*Pluperfect subjunctive*	
limpiara	limpiáramos	hubiera limpiado	hubiéramos limpiado
limpiaras	limpiarais	hubieras limpiado	hubierais limpiado
limpiara	limpiaran	hubiera limpiado	hubieran limpiado
Imperative			
N/A	limpiemos		
limpia; no limpies	limpiad; no limpiéis		
limpie	limpien		

llevar: to wear, to take or carry away
Present participle: llevando
Past Participle: llevado

Simple Tenses		Compound Tenses	
Singular	**Plural**	**Singular**	**Plural**
Present		*Present perfect*	
llevo	llevamos	he llevado	hemos llevado
llevas	lleváis	has llevado	habéis llevado
lleva	llevan	ha llevado	han llevado
Imperfect		*Pluperfect*	
llevaba	llevábamos	había llevado	habíamos llevado
llevabas	llevabais	habías llevado	habíais llevado
llevaba	llevaban	había llevado	habían llevado
Preterit		*Preterit perfect*	
llevé	llevamos	hube llevado	hubimos llevado
llevaste	llevasteis	hubiste llevado	hubisteis llevado
llevó	llevaron	hubo llevado	hubieron llevado

Simple Tenses		Compound Tenses	
Singular	**Plural**	**Singular**	**Plural**
Future		*Future perfect*	
llevaré	llevaremos	habré llevado	habremos llevado
llevarás	llevaréis	habrás llevado	habréis llevado
llevará	llevarán	habrá llevado	habrán llevado
Conditional		*Conditional perfect*	
llevaría	llevaríamos	habría llevado	habríamos llevado
llevarías	llevaríais	habrías llevado	habríais llevado
llevaría	llevarían	habría llevado	habrían llevado
Present subjunctive		*Present perfect subjunctive*	
lleve	llevemos	haya llevado	hayamos llevado
lleves	llevéis	hayas llevado	hayáis llevado
lleve	lleven	haya llevado	hayan llevado
Imperfect subjunctive		*Pluperfect subjunctive*	
llevara	lleváramos	hubiera llevado	hubiéramos llevado
llevaras	llevarais	hubieras llevado	hubierais llevado
llevara	llevaran	hubiera llevado	hubieran llevado
Imperative			
N/A	llevemos		
lleva; no lleves	llevad; no llevéis		
lleve	lleven		

mudarse: to move (**mudarse de casa:** to change residences)
Present participle: mudándose
Past Participle: mudado

Simple Tenses		Compound Tenses	
Singular	**Plural**	**Singular**	**Plural**
Present		*Present perfect*	
me mudo	nos mudamos	me he mudado	nos hemos mudado
te mudas	os mudáis	te has mudado	os habéis mudado
se muda	se mudan	se ha mudado	se han mudado
Imperfect		*Pluperfect*	
me mudaba	nos mudábamos	me había mudado	nos habíamos mudado
te mudabas	os mudabais	te habías mudado	os habíais mudado
se mudaba	se mudaban	se había mudado	se habían mudado
Preterit		*Preterit perfect*	
me mudé	nos mudamos	me hube mudado	nos hubimos mudado
te mudaste	os mudasteis	te hubiste mudado	os hubisteis mudado
se mudó	se mudaron	se hubo mudado	se hubieron mudado
Future		*Future perfect*	
me mudaré	nos mudaremos	me habré mudado	nos habremos mudado
te mudarás	os mudaréis	te habrás mudado	os habréis mudado
se mudará	se mudarán	se habrá mudado	se habrán mudado
Conditional		*Conditional perfect*	
me mudaría	nos mudaríamos	me habría mudado	nos habríamos mudado
te mudarías	os mudaríais	te habrías mudado	os habríais mudado
se mudaría	se mudarían	se habría mudado	se habrían mudado

Simple Tenses		Compound Tenses	
Singular	**Plural**	**Singular**	**Plural**
Present subjunctive		*Present perfect subjunctive*	
me mude	nos mudemos	me haya mudado	nos hayamos mudado
te mudes	os mudéis	te hayas mudado	os hayáis mudado
se mude	se muden	se haya mudado	se hayan mudado
Imperfect subjunctive		*Pluperfect subjunctive*	
me mudara	nos mudáramos	me hubiera mudado	nos hubiéramos mudado
te mudaras	os mudarais	te hubieras mudado	os hubierais mudado
se mudara	se mudaran	se hubiera mudado	se hubieran mudado
Imperative			
N/A	mudémonos		
múdate; no te mudes	mudaos; no os mudéis		
múdese	múdense		

necesitar: to need
Present participle: necesitando
Past Participle: necesitado

Simple Tenses		Compound Tenses	
Singular	**Plural**	**Singular**	**Plural**
Present		*Present perfect*	
necesito	necesitamos	he necesitado	hemos necesitado
necesitas	necesitáis	has necesitado	habéis necesitado
necesita	necesitan	ha necesitado	han necesitado

Simple Tenses		Compound Tenses	
Singular	**Plural**	**Singular**	**Plural**
Imperfect		*Pluperfect*	
necesitaba	necesitábamos	había necesitado	habíamos necesitado
necesitabas	necesitabais	habías necesitado	habíais necesitado
necesitaba	necesitaban	había necesitado	habían necesitado
Preterit		*Preterit perfect*	
necesité	necesitamos	hube necesitado	hubimos necesitado
necesitaste	necesitasteis	hubiste necesitado	hubisteis necesitado
necesitó	necesitaron	hubo necesitado	hubieron necesitado
Future		*Future perfect*	
necesitaré	necesitaremos	habré necesitado	habremos necesitado
necesitarás	necesitaréis	habrás necesitado	habréis necesitado
necesitará	necesitarán	habrá necesitado	habrán necesitado
Conditional		*Conditional perfect*	
necesitaría	necesitaríamos	habría necesitado	habríamos necesitado
necesitarías	necesitaríais	habrías necesitado	habríais necesitado
necesitaría	necesitarían	habría necesitado	habrían necesitado
Present subjunctive		*Present perfect subjunctive*	
necesite	necesitemos	haya necesitado	hayamos necesitado
necesites	necesitéis	hayas necesitado	hayáis necesitado
necesite	necesiten	haya necesitado	hayan necesitado

Simple Tenses		Compound Tenses	
Singular	**Plural**	**Singular**	**Plural**
Imperfect subjunctive		*Pluperfect subjunctive*	
necesitara	necesitáramos	hubiera necesitado	hubiéramos necesitado
necesitaras	necesitarais	hubieras necesitado	hubierais necesitado
necesitara	necesitaran	hubiera necesitado	hubieran necesitado
Imperative			
N/A	necesitemos		
necesita; no necesites	necesitad; no necesitéis		
necesite	necesiten		

olvidar: to forget
Present participle: olvidando
Past Participle: olvidado

Simple Tenses		Compound Tenses	
Singular	**Plural**	**Singular**	**Plural**
Present		*Present perfect*	
olvido	olvidas	he olvidado	hemos olvidado
olvidas	olvidáis	has olvidado	habéis olvidado
olvida	olvidan	ha olvidado	han olvidado
Imperfect		*Pluperfect*	
olvidaba	olvidábamos	había olvidado	habíamos olvidado
olvidabas	olvidabais	habías olvidado	habíais olvidado
olvidaba	olvidaban	había olvidado	habían olvidado

Simple Tenses		Compound Tenses	
Singular	**Plural**	**Singular**	**Plural**
Preterit		*Preterit perfect*	
olvidé	olvidamos	hube olvidado	hubimos olvidado
olvidaste	olvidasteis	hubiste olvidado	hubisteis olvidado
olvidó	olvidaron	hubo olvidado	hubieron olvidado
Future		*Future perfect*	
olvidaré	olvidaremos	habré olvidado	habremos olvidado
olvidarás	olvidaréis	habrás olvidado	habréis olvidado
olvidará	olvidarán	habrá olvidado	habrán olvidado
Conditional		*Conditional perfect*	
olvidaría	olvidaríamos	habría olvidado	habríamos olvidado
olvidarías	olvidaríais	habrías olvidado	habríais olvidado
olvidaría	olvidarían	habría olvidado	habrían olvidado
Present subjunctive		*Present perfect subjunctive*	
olvide	olvidemos	haya olvidado	hayamos olvidado
olvides	olvidéis	hayas olvidado	hayáis olvidado
olvide	olviden	haya olvidado	hayan olvidado
Imperfect subjunctive		*Pluperfect subjunctive*	
olvidara	olvidáramos	hubiera olvidado	hubiéramos olvidado
olvidaras	olvidarais	hubieras olvidado	hubierais olvidado
olvidara	olvidaran	hubiera olvidado	hubieran olvidado
Imperative			
N/A	olvidemos		
olvida; no olvides	olvidad; no olvidéis		
olvide	olviden		

permitir: to permit
Present participle: **permitiendo**
Past Participle: **permitido**

Simple Tenses		Compound Tenses	
Singular	**Plural**	**Singular**	**Plural**
Present		*Present perfect*	
permito	permitimos	he permitido	hemos permitido
permites	permitís	has permitido	habéis permitido
permite	permiten	ha permitido	han permitido
Imperfect		*Pluperfect*	
permitía	permitíamos	había permitido	habíamos permitido
permitías	permitíais	habías permitido	habíais permitido
permitía	permitían	había permitido	habían permitido
Preterit		*Preterit perfect*	
permití	permitimos	hube permitido	hubimos permitido
permitiste	permitisteis	hubiste permitido	hubisteis permido
permitió	permitieron	hubo permitido	hubieron permitido
Future		*Future perfect*	
permitiré	permitiremos	habré permitido	habremos permitido
permitirás	permitiréis	habrás permitido	habréis permitido
permitirá	permitirán	habrá permitido	habrán permitido
Conditional		*Conditional perfect*	
permitiría	permitiríamos	habría permitido	habríamos permitido
permitirías	permitiríais	habrías permitido	habríais permitido
permitiría	permitirían	habría permitido	habrían permitido

Simple Tenses		Compound Tenses	
Singular	**Plural**	**Singular**	**Plural**
Present subjunctive		*Present perfect subjunctive*	
permita	permitamos	haya permitido	hayamos permitido
permitas	permitáis	hayas permitido	hayáis permitido
permita	permitan	haya permitido	hayan permitido
Imperfect subjunctive		*Pluperfect subjunctive*	
permitiera	permitiéramos	hubiera permitido	hubiéramos permitido
permitieras	permitierais	hubieras permitido	hubierais permitido
permitiera	permitieran	hubiera permitido	hubieran permitido
Imperative			
N/A	permitamos		
permite; no permitas	permitid; no permitáis		
permita	permitan		

quedarse: to remain or stay
Present participle: quedándose
Past Participle: quedado

Simple Tenses		Compound Tenses	
Singular	**Plural**	**Singular**	**Plural**
Present		*Present perfect*	
me quedo	nos quedamos	me he quedado	nos hemos quedado
te quedas	os quedáis	te has quedado	os habéis quedado
se queda	se quedan	se ha quedado	se han quedado

Simple Tenses		Compound Tenses	
Singular	**Plural**	**Singular**	**Plural**
Imperfect		*Pluperfect*	
me quedaba	nos quedábamos	me había quedado	nos habíamos quedado
te quedabas	os quedabais	te habías quedado	os habíais quedado
se quedaba	se quedaban	se había quedado	se habían quedado
Preterit		*Preterit perfect*	
me quedé	nos quedamos	me hube quedado	nos hubimos quedado
te quedaste	os quedasteis	te hubiste quedado	os hubisteis quedado
se quedó	se quedaron	se hubo quedado	se hubieron quedado
Future		*Future perfect*	
me quedaré	nos quedaremos	me habré quedado	nos habremos quedado
te quedarás	os quedaréis	te habrás quedado	os habréis quedado
se quedará	se quedarán	se habrá quedado	se habrán quedado
Conditional		*Conditional perfect*	
me quedaría	nos quedaríamos	me habría quedado	nos habríamos quedado
te quedarías	os quedaríais	te habrías quedado	os habríais quedado
se quedaría	se quedarían	se habría quedado	se habrían quedado
Present subjunctive		*Present perfect subjunctive*	
me quede	nos quedemos	me haya quedado	nos hayamos quedado

Simple Tenses		Compound Tenses	
Singular	**Plural**	**Singular**	**Plural**
te quedes	os quedéis	te hayas quedado	os hayáis quedado
se quede	se queden	se haya quedado	se hayan quedado
Imperfect subjunctive		*Pluperfect subjunctive*	
me quedara	nos quedáramos	me hubiera quedado	nos hubiéramos quedado
te quedaras	os quedarais	te hubieras quedado	os hubierais quedado
se quedara	se quedaran	se hubiera quedado	se hubieran quedado
Imperative			
N/A	quedémonos		
quédate; no te quedes	quedaos; no os quedéis		
quédese	quédense		

recibir: to receive
Present participle: recibiendo
Past Participle: recibido

Simple Tenses		Compound Tenses	
Singular	**Plural**	**Singular**	**Plural**
Present		*Present perfect*	
recibo	recibes	he recibido	hemos recibido
recibes	recibís	has recibido	habéis recibido
recibe	reciben	ha recibido	han recibido
Imperfect		*Pluperfect*	
recibía	recibíamos	había recibido	habíamos recibido
recibías	recibíais	habías recibido	habíais recibido
recibía	recibían	había recibido	habían recibido

Simple Tenses		Compound Tenses	
Singular	**Plural**	**Singular**	**Plural**
Preterit		*Preterit perfect*	
recibí	recibimos	hube recibido	hubimos recibido
recibiste	recibisteis	hubiste recibido	hubisteis recibido
recibió	recibieron	hubo recibido	hubieron recibido
Future		*Future perfect*	
recibiré	recibiremos	habré recibido	habremos recibido
recibirás	recibiréis	habrás recibido	habréis recibido
recibirá	recibirán	habrá recibido	habrán recibido
Conditional		*Conditional perfect*	
recibiría	recibiríamos	habría recibido	habríamos recibido
recibirías	recibiríais	habrías recibido	habríais recibido
recibiría	recibirían	habría recibido	habrían recibido
Present subjunctive		*Present perfect subjunctive*	
reciba	recibamos	haya recibido	hayamos recibido
recibas	recibáis	hayas recibido	hayáis recibido
reciba	reciban	haya recibido	hayan recibido
Imperfect subjunctive		*Pluperfect subjunctive*	
recibiera	recibiéramos	hubiera recibido	hubiéramos recibido
recibieras	recibierais	hubieras recibido	hubierais recibido
recibiera	recibieran	hubiera recibido	hubieran recibido
Imperative			
N/A	recibamos		
recibe; no recibas	recibid; no recibáis		
reciba	reciban		

subir: to go up, to climb, to get on (a bus, train, and so on)
Present participle: subiendo
Past Participle: subido

Simple Tenses		Compound Tenses	
Singular	**Plural**	**Singular**	**Plural**
Present		*Present perfect*	
subo	subimos	he subido	hemos subido
subes	subís	has subido	habéis subido
sube	suben	ha subido	han subido
Imperfect		*Pluperfect*	
subía	subíamos	había subido	habíamos subido
subías	subíais	habías subido	habíais subido
subía	subían	había subido	habían subido
Preterit		*Preterit perfect*	
subí	subimos	hube subido	hubimos subido
subiste	subisteis	hubiste subido	hubisteis subido
subió	subieron	hubo subido	hubieron subido
Future		*Future perfect*	
subiré	subiremos	habré subido	habremos subido
subirás	subiréis	habrás subido	habréis subido
subirá	subirán	habrá subido	habrán subido
Conditional		*Conditional perfect*	
subiría	subiríamos	habría subido	habríamos subido
subirías	subiríais	habrías subido	habríais subido
subiría	subirían	habría subido	habrían subido
Present subjunctive		*Present perfect subjunctive*	
suba	subamos	haya subido	hayamos subido
subas	subáis	hayas subido	hayáis subido
suba	suban	haya subido	hayan subido

	Simple Tenses	Compound Tenses	
Singular	**Plural**	**Singular**	**Plural**
Imperfect subjunctive		*Pluperfect subjunctive*	
subiera	subiéramos	hubiera subido	hubiéramos subido
subieras	subierais	hubieras subido	hubierais subido
subiera	subieran	hubiera subido	hubieran subido
Imperative			
N/A	subamos		
sube; no subas	subid; no subáis		
suba	suban		

temer: to fear
Present participle: temiendo
Past Participle: temido

	Simple Tenses	Compound Tenses	
Singular	**Plural**	**Singular**	**Plural**
Present		*Present perfect*	
temo	tememos	he temido	hemos temido
temes	teméis	has temido	habéis temido
teme	temen	ha temido	han temido
Imperfect		*Pluperfect*	
temía	temíamos	había temido	habíamos temido
temías	temíais	habías temido	habíais temido
temía	temían	había temido	habían temido
Preterit		*Preterit perfect*	
temí	temimos	hube temido	hubimos temido
temiste	temisteis	hubiste temido	hubisteis temido
temió	temieron	hubo temido	hubieron temido

Simple Tenses		Compound Tenses	
Singular	**Plural**	**Singular**	**Plural**
Future		*Future perfect*	
temeré	temeremos	habré temido	habremos temido
temerás	temeréis	habrás temido	habréis temido
temerá	temerán	habrá temido	habrán temido
Conditional		*Conditional perfect*	
temería	temeríamos	habría temido	habríamos temido
temerías	temeríais	habrías temido	habríais temido
temería	temerían	habría temido	habrían temido
Present subjunctive		*Present perfect subjunctive*	
tema	temamos	haya temido	hayamos temido
temas	temáis	hayas temido	hayáis temido
tema	teman	haya temido	hayan temido
Imperfect subjunctive		*Pluperfect subjunctive*	
temiera	temiéramos	hubiera temido	hubiéramos temido
temieras	temierais	hubieras temido	hubierais temido
temiera	temieran	hubiera temido	hubieran temido
Imperative			
N/A	temamos		
teme; no temas	temed; no temáis		
tema	teman		

usar: to use
Present participle: **usando**
Past Participle: **usado**

Simple Tenses		Compound Tenses	
Singular	**Plural**	**Singular**	**Plural**
Present		*Present perfect*	
uso	usamos	he usado	hemos usado
usas	usáis	has usado	habéis usado
usa	usan	ha usado	han usado
Imperfect		*Pluperfect*	
usaba	usábamos	había usado	habíamos usado
usabas	usabais	habías usado	habíais usado
usaba	usaban	había usado	habían usado
Preterit		*Preterit perfect*	
usé	usamos	hube usado	hubimos usado
usaste	usasteis	hubiste usado	hubisteis usado
usó	usaron	hubo usado	hubieron usado
Future		*Future perfect*	
usaré	usaremos	habré usado	habremos usado
usarás	usaréis	habrás usado	habréis usado
usará	usarán	habrá usado	habrán usado
Conditional		*Conditional perfect*	
usaría	usaríamos	habría usado	habríamos usado
usarías	usaríais	habrías usado	habríais usado
usaría	usarían	habría usado	habrían usado
Present subjunctive		*Present perfect subjunctive*	
use	usemos	haya usado	hayamos usado
uses	uséis	hayas usado	hayáis usado
use	usen	haya usado	hayan usado

Simple Tenses		Compound Tenses	
Singular	**Plural**	**Singular**	**Plural**
Imperfect subjunctive		*Pluperfect subjunctive*	
usara	usáramos	hubiera usado	hubiéramos usado
usaras	usarais	hubieras usado	hubierais usado
usara	usaran	hubiera usado	hubieran usado
Imperative			
N/A	usemos		
usa; no uses	usad; no uséis		
use	usen		

vender: to sell
Present participle: vendiendo
Past Participle: vendido

Simple Tenses		Compound Tenses	
Singular	**Plural**	**Singular**	**Plural**
Present		*Present perfect*	
vendo	vendemos	he vendido	hemos vendido
vendes	vendéis	has vendido	habéis vendido
vende	venden	ha vendido	han vendido
Imperfect		*Pluperfect*	
vendía	vendíamos	había vendido	habíamos vendido
vendías	vendíais	habías vendido	habíais vendido
vendía	vendían	había vendido	habían vendido
Preterit		*Preterit perfect*	
vendí	vendimos	hube vendido	hubimos vendido
vendiste	vendisteis	hubiste vendido	hubisteis vendido
vendió	vendieron	hubo vendido	hubieron vendido

Simple Tenses		Compound Tenses	
Singular	**Plural**	**Singular**	**Plural**
Future		*Future perfect*	
venderé	venderemos	habré vendido	habremos vendido
venderás	venderéis	habrás vendido	habréis vendido
venderá	venderán	habrá vendido	habrán vendido
Conditional		*Conditional perfect*	
vendería	venderíamos	habría vendido	habríamos vendido
venderías	venderíais	habrías vendido	habríais vendido
vendería	venderían	habría vendido	habrían vendido
Present subjunctive		*Present perfect subjunctive*	
venda	vendamos	haya vendido	hayamos vendido
vendas	vendáis	hayas vendido	hayáis vendido
venda	vendan	haya vendido	hayan vendido
Imperfect subjunctive		*Pluperfect subjunctive*	
vendiera	vendiéramos	hubiera vendido	hubiéramos vendido
vendieras	vendierais	hubieras vendido	hubierais vendido
vendiera	vendieran	hubiera vendido	hubieran vendido
Imperative			
N/A	vendamos		
vende; no vendas	vended; no vendáis		
venda	vendan		

Irregular Spanish Verbs

caer: to fall
Present participle: cayendo
Past Participle: caído

Simple Tenses		Compound Tenses	
Singular	**Plural**	**Singular**	**Plural**
Present		*Present perfect*	
caigo	caemos	he caído	hemos caído
caes	caéis	has caído	habéis caído
cae	caen	ha caído	han caído
Imperfect		*Pluperfect*	
caía	caíamos	había caído	habíamos caído
caías	caíais	habías caído	habíais caído
caía	caían	había caído	habían caído
Preterit		*Preterit perfect*	
caí	caímos	hube caído	hubimos caído
caíste	caísteis	hubiste caído	hubisteis caído
cayó	cayeron	hubo caído	hubieron caído
Future		*Future perfect*	
caeré	caeremos	habré caído	habremos caído
caerás	caeréis	habrás caído	habremos caído
caerá	caerán	habrá caído	habrán caído
Conditional		*Conditional perfect*	
caería	caeríamos	habría caído	habremos caído
caerías	caeríais	habrías caído	habríais caído
caería	caerían	habría caído	habrían caído

Simple Tenses		Compound Tenses	
Singular	**Plural**	**Singular**	**Plural**
Present subjunctive		*Present perfect subjunctive*	
caiga	caigamos	haya caído	hayamos caído
caigas	caigáis	hayas caído	hayáis caído
caiga	caigan	haya caído	hayan caído
Imperfect subjunctive		*Pluperfect subjunctive*	
cayera	cayéramos	hubiera caído	hubiéramos caído
cayeras	cayerais	hubieras caído	hubierais caído
cayera	cayeran	hubiera caído	hubieran caído
Imperative			
N/A	caigamos		
cae; no caigas	caed; no caigáis		
caiga	caigan		

creer: to believe
Present participle: creyendo
Past Participle: creído

Simple Tenses		Compound Tenses	
Singular	**Plural**	**Singular**	**Plural**
Present		*Present perfect*	
creo	creemos	he creído	hemos creído
crees	creéis	has creído	habéis creído
cree	creen	ha creído	han creído
Imperfect		*Pluperfect*	
creía	creíamos	había creído	habíamos creído
creías	creíais	habías creído	habíais creído
creía	creían	había creído	habían creído

Simple Tenses		Compound Tenses	
Singular	**Plural**	**Singular**	**Plural**
Preterit		*Preterit perfect*	
creí	creímos	hube creído	hubimos creído
creíste	creísteis	hubiste creído	hubisteis creído
creyó	creyeron	hubo creído	hubieron creído
Future		*Future perfect*	
creeré	creeremos	habré creído	habremos creído
creerás	creeréis	habrás creído	habréis creído
creerá	creerán	habrá creído	habrán creído
Conditional		*Conditional perfect*	
creería	creeríamos	habría creído	habríamos creído
creerías	creeríais	habrías creído	habríais creído
creería	creerían	habría creído	habrían creído
Present subjunctive		*Present perfect subjunctive*	
crea	creamos	haya creído	hayamos creído
creas	creáis	hayas creído	hayáis creído
crea	crean	haya creído	hayan creído
Imperfect subjunctive		*Pluperfect subjunctive*	
creyera	creyéramos	hubiera creído	hubiéramos creído
creyeras	creyerais	hubieras creído	hubierais creído
creyera	creyeran	hubiera creído	hubieran creído
Imperative			
N/A	creamos		
cree; no creas	creed; no creáis		
crea	crean		

dar: to give
Present participle: dando
Past Participle: dado

Simple Tenses		Compound Tenses	
Singular	**Plural**	**Singular**	**Plural**
Present		*Present perfect*	
doy	damos	he dado	hemos dado
das	dais	has dado	habéis dado
da	dan	ha dado	han dado
Imperfect		*Pluperfect*	
daba	dábamos	había dado	habíamos dado
dabas	dabais	habías dado	habíais dado
daba	daban	había dado	habían dado
Preterit		*Preterit perfect*	
di	dimos	hube dado	hubimos dado
diste	disteis	hubiste dado	hubisteis dado
dio	dieron	hubo dado	hubieron dado
Future		*Future perfect*	
daré	daremos	habré dado	habremos dado
darás	daréis	habrás dado	habréis dado
dará	darán	habrá dado	habrán dado
Conditional		*Conditional perfect*	
daría	daríamos	habría dado	habríamos dado
darías	daríais	habrías dado	habríais dado
daría	darían	habría dado	habrían dado
Present subjunctive		*Present perfect subjunctive*	
dé	demos	haya dado	hayamos dado
des	deis	hayas dado	hayáis dado
dé	den	haya dado	hayan dado

Simple Tenses		Compound Tenses	
Singular	**Plural**	**Singular**	**Plural**
Imperfect subjunctive		*Pluperfect subjunctive*	
diera	diéramos	hubiera dado	hubiéramos dado
dieras	dierais	hubieras dado	hubierais dado
diera	dieran	hubiera dado	hubieran dado
Imperative			
N/A	demos		
da; no des	dad; no deis		
dé	den		

decir: to say, to tell
Present participle: diciendo
Past Participle: dicho

Simple Tenses		Compound Tenses	
Singular	**Plural**	**Singular**	**Plural**
Present		*Present perfect*	
digo	decimos	he dicho	hemos dicho
dices	decís	has dicho	habéis dicho
dice	dicen	ha dicho	han dicho
Imperfect		*Pluperfect*	
decía	decíamos	había dicho	habíamos dicho
decías	decíais	habías dicho	habíais dicho
decía	decían	había dicho	habían dicho
Preterit		*Preterit perfect*	
dije	dijimos	hube dicho	hubimos dicho
dijiste	disteis	hubiste dicho	hubisteis dicho
dijo	dijeron	hubo dicho	hubieron dicho

Simple Tenses		Compound Tenses	
Singular	**Plural**	**Singular**	**Plural**
Future		*Future perfect*	
diré	diremos	habré dicho	habremos dicho
dirás	diréis	habrás dicho	habréis dicho
dirá	dirán	habrá dicho	habrán dicho
Conditional		*Conditional perfect*	
diría	diríamos	habría dicho	habríamos dicho
dirías	diríais	habrías dicho	habríais dicho
diría	dirían	habría dicho	habrían dicho
Present subjunctive		*Present perfect subjunctive*	
diga	digamos	haya dicho	hayamos dicho
digas	digáis	hayas dicho	hayáis dicho
diga	digan	haya dicho	hayan dicho
Imperfect subjunctive		*Pluperfect subjunctive*	
dijera	dijéramos	hubiera dicho	hubiéramos dicho
dijeras	dijerais	hubieras dicho	hubierais dicho
dijera	dijeran	hubiera dicho	hubieran dicho
Imperative			
N/A	digamos		
di; no digas	decid; no digáis		
diga	digan		

estar: to be
Present participle: estando
Past Participle: estado

Simple Tenses		Compound Tenses	
Singular	**Plural**	**Singular**	**Plural**
Present		*Present perfect*	
estoy	estamos	he estado	hemos estado
estás	estáis	has estado	habéis estado
está	están	ha estado	han estado
Imperfect		*Pluperfect*	
estaba	estábamos	había estado	habíamos estado
estabas	estabais	habías estado	habíais estado
estaba	estaban	había estado	habían estado
Preterit		*Preterit perfect*	
estuve	estuvimos	hube estado	hubimos estado
estuviste	estuvisteis	hubiste estado	hubisteis estado
estuvo	estuvieron	hubo estado	habremos estado
Future		*Future perfect*	
estaré	estaremos	habré estado	habremos estado
estarás	estaréis	habrás estado	habréis estado
estará	estarán	habrá estado	habrán estado
Conditional		*Conditional perfect*	
estaría	estaríamos	habría estado	habríamos estado
estarías	estaríais	habrías estado	habríais estado
estaría	estarían	habría estado	habrían estado
Present subjunctive		*Present perfect subjunctive*	
esté	estemos	haya estado	hayamos estado
estés	estéis	hayas estado	hayáis estado
esté	estén	haya estado	hayan estado

Simple Tenses		Compound Tenses	
Singular	**Plural**	**Singular**	**Plural**
Imperfect subjunctive		*Pluperfect subjunctive*	
estuviera	estuviéramos	hubiera estado	hubiéramos estado
estuvieras	estuvierais	hubieras estado	hubierais estado
estuviera	estuvieran	hubiera estado	hubieran estado
Imperative			
N/A	estemos		
está; no estés	estad; no estéis		
esté	estén		

hacer: to do, to make
Present participle: haciendo
Past Participle: hecho

Simple Tenses		Compound Tenses	
Singular	**Plural**	**Singular**	**Plural**
Present		*Present perfect*	
hago	hacemos	he hecho	hemos hecho
haces	hacéis	has hecho	habéis hecho
hace	hacen	ha hecho	han hecho
Imperfect		*Pluperfect*	
hacía	hacíamos	había hecho	habíamos hecho
hacías	hacíais	habíamos hecho	habíais hecho
hacía	hacían	había hecho	habían hecho
Preterit		*Preterit perfect*	
hice	hicimos	hube hecho	hubimos hecho
hiciste	hicisteis	hubiste hecho	hubisteis hecho
hizo	hicieron	hubo hecho	hubieron hecho

Simple Tenses		Compound Tenses	
Singular	**Plural**	**Singular**	**Plural**
Future		*Future perfect*	
haré	haremos	habré hecho	habremos hecho
harás	haréis	habrás hecho	habréis hecho
hará	harán	habrá hecho	habrán hecho
Conditional		*Conditional perfect*	
haría	haríamos	habría hecho	habríamos hecho
harías	haríais	habrías hecho	habríais hecho
haría	harían	habría hecho	habrían hecho
Present subjunctive		*Present perfect subjunctive*	
haga	hagamos	haya hecho	hayamos hecho
hagas	hagáis	hayas hecho	hayáis hecho
haga	hagan	haya hecho	hayan hecho
Imperfect subjunctive		*Pluperfect subjunctive*	
hiciera	hiciéramos	hubiera hecho	hubiéramos hecho
hicieras	hicierais	hubieras hecho	hubierais hecho
hiciera	hicieran	hubiera hecho	hubieran hecho
Imperative			
N/A	hagamos		
haz; no hagas	haced; no hagáis		
haga	hagan		

ir: to go
Present participle: yendo
Past Participle: ido

Simple Tenses		Compound Tenses	
Singular	**Plural**	**Singular**	**Plural**
Present		*Present perfect*	
voy	vamos	he ido	hemos ido
vas	vais	has ido	habéis ido
va	van	ha ido	han ido
Imperfect		*Pluperfect*	
iba	íbamos	había ido	habíamos ido
ibas	ibais	habías ido	habíais ido
iba	iban	había ido	habían ido
Preterit		*Preterit perfect*	
fui	fuimos	hube ido	hubimos ido
fuiste	fuisteis	hubiste ido	hubisteis ido
fue	fueron	hubo ido	hubieron ido
Future		*Future perfect*	
iré	iremos	habré ido	habremos ido
irás	iréis	habrás ido	habréis ido
irá	irán	habrá ido	habrán ido
Conditional		*Conditional perfect*	
iría	iríamos	habría ido	habríamos ido
irías	iríais	habrías ido	habríais ido
iría	irían	habría ido	habrían ido
Present subjunctive		*Present perfect subjunctive*	
vaya	vayamos	haya ido	hayamos ido
vayas	vayáis	hayas ido	hayáis ido
vaya	vayan	haya ido	hayan ido

Simple Tenses		Compound Tenses	
Singular	**Plural**	**Singular**	**Plural**
Imperfect subjunctive		*Pluperfect subjunctive*	
fuera	fuéramos	hubiera ido	hubiéramos ido
fueras	fuerais	hubieras ido	hubierais ido
fuera	fueran	hubiera ido	hubieran ido
Imperative			
N/A	vamos (no vayamos)		
ve; no vayas	id; no vayáis		
vaya	vayan		

leer: to read
Present participle: leyendo
Past Participle: leído

Simple Tenses		Compound Tenses	
Singular	**Plural**	**Singular**	**Plural**
Present		*Present perfect*	
leo	leemos	he leído	hemos leído
lees	leéis	has leído	habéis leído
lee	leen	ha leído	han leído
Imperfect		*Pluperfect*	
leía	leíamos	había leído	habíamos leído
leías	leíais	habías leído	habíais leído
leía	leían	había leído	habían leído
Preterit		*Preterit perfect*	
leí	leímos	hube leído	hubimos leído
leíste	leísteis	hubiste leído	hubisteis leído
leyo	leyeron	hubo leído	hubieron leído

Simple Tenses		Compound Tenses	
Singular	**Plural**	**Singular**	**Plural**
Future		*Future perfect*	
leeré	leeremos	habré leído	habremos leído
leerás	leeréis	habrás leído	habréis leído
leerá	leerán	habrá leído	habrán leído
Conditional		*Conditional perfect*	
leería	leeríamos	habría leído	habríamos leído
leerías	leeríais	habrías leído	habríais leído
leería	leerían	habría leído	habrían leído
Present subjunctive		*Present perfect subjunctive*	
lea	leamos	haya leído	hayamos leído
leas	leáis	hayas leído	hayáis leído
lea	lean	haya leído	hayan leído
Imperfect subjunctive		*Pluperfect subjunctive*	
leyera	leyéramos	hubiera leído	hubiéramos leído
leyeras	leyerais	hubieras leído	hubierais leído
leyera	leyeran	hubiera leído	hubieran leído
Imperative			
N/A	leamos		
lee; no leas	leed; no leáis		
lea	lean		

poder: to be able
Present participle: pudiendo
Past Participle: podido

Simple Tenses		Compound Tenses	
Singular	**Plural**	**Singular**	**Plural**
Present		*Present perfect*	
puedo	podemos	he podido	hemos podido
puedes	podéis	has podido	habéis podido
puede	pueden	ha podido	han podido
Imperfect		*Pluperfect*	
podía	podíamos	había podido	habíamos podido
podías	podéis	habías podido	habíais podido
podía	podían	había podido	habían podido
Preterit		*Preterit perfect*	
pude	pudimos	hube podido	hubimos podido
pudiste	pudisteis	hubiste podido	hubisteis podido
pudo	pudieron	hubo podido	hubieron podido
Future		*Future perfect*	
podré	podremos	habré podido	habremos podido
podrás	podréis	habrás podido	habréis podido
podrá	podrán	habrá podido	habrán podido
Conditional		*Conditional perfect*	
podría	podríamos	habría podido	habríamos podido
podrías	podríais	habrías podido	habríais podido
podría	podría	habría podido	habrían podido
Present subjunctive		*Present perfect subjunctive*	
pueda	podamos	haya podido	hayamos podido
puedas	podáis	hayas podido	hayáis podido
pueda	puedan	haya podido	hayan podido

Simple Tenses		Compound Tenses	
Singular	**Plural**	**Singular**	**Plural**
Imperfect subjunctive		_Pluperfect subjunctive_	
pudiera	pudiéramos	hubiera podido	hubiéramos podido
pudieras	pudierais	hubieras podido	hubierais podido
pudiera	pudieran	hubiera podido	hubieran podido
Imperative			
N/A	podamos		
puede; no puedas	poded; no podáis		
pueda	puedan		

poner: to put, to turn on (a light, TV, radio)
Present participle: poniendo
Past Participle: puesto

Simple Tenses		Compound Tenses	
Singular	**Plural**	**Singular**	**Plural**
Present		_Present perfect_	
pongo	ponemos	he puesto	hemos puesto
pones	ponéis	has puesto	habéis puesto
pone	ponen	ha puesto	han puesto
Imperfect		_Pluperfect_	
ponía	poníamos	había puesto	habíamos puesto
ponías	poníais	habías puesto	habíais puesto
ponía	ponían	había puesto	habían puesto
Preterit		_Preterit perfect_	
puse	pusimos	hube puesto	hubimos puesto
pusiste	pusisteis	hubiste puesto	hubisteis puesto
puso	pusieron	hubo puesto	hubieron puesto

Simple Tenses		Compound Tenses	
Singular	**Plural**	**Singular**	**Plural**
Future		*Future perfect*	
pondré	pondremos	habré puesto	habremos puesto
pondrás	pondréis	habrás puesto	habréis puesto
pondrá	pondrán	habrá puesto	habrán puesto
Conditional		*Conditional perfect*	
pondría	pondríamos	habría puesto	habríamos puesto
pondrías	pondríais	habrías puesto	habríais puesto
pondría	pondrían	habría puesto	habrían puesto
Present subjunctive		*Present perfect subjunctive*	
ponga	pongamos	haya puesto	hayamos puesto
pongas	pongáis	hayas puesto	hayáis puesto
ponga	pongan	haya puesto	hayan puesto
Imperfect subjunctive		*Pluperfect subjunctive*	
pusiera	pusiéramos	hubiera puesto	hubiéramos puesto
pusieras	pusierais	hubieras puesto	hubierais puesto
pusiera	pusieran	hubiera puesto	hubieran puesto
Imperative			
N/A	pongamos		
pon; no pongas	poned; no pongáis		
ponga	pongan		

querer: to want
Present participle: queriendo
Past Participle: querido

Simple Tenses		Compound Tenses	
Singular	**Plural**	**Singular**	**Plural**
Present		*Present perfect*	
quiero	queremos	he querido	hemos querido
quieres	queréis	has querido	habéis querido
quiere	quieren	ha querido	han querido
Imperfect		*Pluperfect*	
quería	queríamos	había querido	habíamos querido
querías	queríais	habías querido	habíais querido
quería	querían	había querido	habían querido
Preterit		*Preterit perfect*	
quise	quisimos	hube querido	hubimos querido
quisiste	quisisteis	hubiste querido	hubisteis querido
quiso	quisieron	hubo querido	hubieron querido
Future		*Future perfect*	
querré	querremos	habré querido	habremos querido
querrás	querréis	habrás querido	habréis querido
querrá	querrán	habrá querido	habréis querido
Conditional		*Conditional perfect*	
querría	querríamos	habría querido	habríamos querido
querrías	querríais	habrías querido	habríais querido
querría	querrían	habría querido	habrían querido
Present subjunctive		*Present perfect subjunctive*	
quiera	queramos	haya querido	hayamos querido
quieras	queráis	hayas querido	hayáis querido
quiera	quieran	haya querido	hayan querido

Simple Tenses		Compound Tenses	
Singular	**Plural**	**Singular**	**Plural**
Imperfect subjunctive		*Pluperfect subjunctive*	
quisiera	quisiéramos	hubiera querido	hubiéramos querido
quisieras	quisierais	hubieras querido	hubierais querido
quisiera	quisieran	hubiera querido	hubieran querido
Imperative			
N/A	queramos		
quiere; no quieras	quered; no queráis		
quiera	quieran		

saber: to know, to know how
Present participle: sabiendo
Past Participle: sabido

Simple Tenses		Compound Tenses	
Singular	**Plural**	**Singular**	**Plural**
Present		*Present perfect*	
sé	sabemos	he sabido	hemos sabido
sabes	sabéis	has sabido	habéis sabido
sabe	saben	ha sabido	han sabido
Imperfect		*Pluperfect*	
sabía	sabíamos	había sabido	habíamos sabido
sabías	sabíais	habías sabido	habíais sabido
sabía	sabían	había sabido	habían sabido
Preterit		*Preterit perfect*	
supe	supimos	hube sabido	hubimos sabido
supiste	supisteis	hubiste sabido	hubisteis sabido
supo	supieron	hubo sabido	hubieron sabido

Simple Tenses		Compound Tenses	
Singular	**Plural**	**Singular**	**Plural**
Future		*Future perfect*	
sabré	sabremos	habré sabido	habremos sabido
sabrás	sabréis	habrás sabido	habréis sabido
sabrá	sabrán	habrá sabido	habrán sabido
Conditional		*Conditional perfect*	
sabría	sabríamos	habría sabido	habríamos sabido
sabrías	sabríais	habrías sabido	habríais sabido
sabría	sabrían	habría sabido	habrían sabido
Present subjunctive		*Present perfect subjunctive*	
sepa	sepamos	haya sabido	hayamos sabido
sepas	sepáis	hayas sabido	hayáis sabido
sepa	sepan	haya sabido	hayan sabido
Imperfect subjunctive		*Pluperfect subjunctive*	
supiera	supiéramos	hubiera sabido	hubiéramos sabido
supieras	supierais	hubieras sabido	hubierais sabido
supiera	supieran	hubiera sabido	hubieran sabido
Imperative			
N/A	sepamos		
sabe; no sepas	sabed; no sepáis		
sepa	sepan		

salir: to go out, to leave
Present participle: saliendo
Past Participle: salido

Simple Tenses		Compound Tenses	
Singular	**Plural**	**Singular**	**Plural**
Present		*Present perfect*	
salgo	salimos	he salido	hemos salido
sales	salís	has salido	habéis salido
sale	salen	ha salido	han salido
Imperfect		*Pluperfect*	
salía	salíamos	había salido	habíamos salido
salías	salíais	habías salido	habíais salido
salía	salían	había salido	habían salido
Preterit		*Preterit perfect*	
salí	salimos	hube salido	hubimos salido
saliste	salisteis	hubiste salido	hubisteis salido
salió	salieron	hubo salido	hubieron salido
Future		*Future perfect*	
saldré	saldremos	habré salido	habremos salido
saldrás	saldréis	habrás salido	habréis salido
saldrá	saldrán	habrá salido	habrán salido
Conditional		*Conditional perfect*	
saldría	saldríamos	habría salido	habríamos salido
saldrías	saldríais	habrías salido	habríais salido
saldría	saldrían	habría salido	habrían salido
Present subjunctive		*Present perfect subjunctive*	
salga	salgamos	haya salido	hayamos salido
salgas	salgáis	hayas salido	hayáis salido
salga	salgan	haya salido	hayan salido

Simple Tenses		Compound Tenses	
Singular	**Plural**	**Singular**	**Plural**
Imperfect subjunctive		*Pluperfect subjunctive*	
saliera	saliéramos	hubiera salido	hubiéramos salido
salieras	salierais	hubieras salido	hubierais salido
saliera	salieran	hubiera salido	hubieran salido
Imperative			
N/A	salgamos		
sal; no salgas	salid; no salgis		
salga	salgan		

ser: to be
Present participle: siendo
Past Participle: sido

Simple Tenses		Compound Tenses	
Singular	**Plural**	**Singular**	**Plural**
Present		*Present perfect*	
soy	somos	he sido	hemos sido
eres	sois	has sido	habéis sido
es	son	ha sido	han sido
Imperfect		*Pluperfect*	
era	éramos	había sido	habíamos sido
eras	erais	habías sido	habíais sido
era	eran	había sido	habían sido
Preterit		*Preterit perfect*	
fui	fuimos	hube sido	hubimos sido
fuiste	fuisteis	hubiste sido	hubisteis sido
fue	fueron	hubo sido	hubieron sido

Simple Tenses		Compound Tenses	
Singular	**Plural**	**Singular**	**Plural**
Future		*Future perfect*	
seré	seremos	habré sido	habremos sido
serás	seréis	habrás sido	habréis sido
será	serán	habrá sido	habrán sido
Conditional		*Conditional perfect*	
sería	seríamos	habría sido	habríamos sido
serías	seríais	habrías sido	habríais sido
sería	serían	habría sido	habrían sido
Present subjunctive		*Present perfect subjunctive*	
sea	seamos	haya sido	hayamos sido
seas	seáis	hayas sido	hayáis sido
sea	sean	haya sido	hayan sido
Imperfect subjunctive		*Pluperfect subjunctive*	
fuera	fuéramos	hubiera sido	hubiéramos sido
fueras	fuerais	hubieras sido	hubierais sido
fuera	fueran	hubiera sido	hubieran sido
Imperative			
N/A	seamos		
sé; no seas	sed; no seáis		
sea	sean		

tener: to have
Present participle: teniendo
Past Participle: tenido

Simple Tenses		Compound Tenses	
Singular	**Plural**	**Singular**	**Plural**
Present		*Present perfect*	
tengo	tenemos	he tenido	hemos tenido
tienes	tenéis	has tenido	habéis tenido
tiene	tienen	ha tenido	han tenido
Imperfect		*Pluperfect*	
tenía	teníamos	había tenido	habíamos tenido
tenías	teníais	habías tenido	habíais tenido
tenía	tenían	había tenido	habían tenido
Preterit		*Preterit perfect*	
tuve	tuvimos	hube tenido	hubimos tenido
tuviste	tuvisteis	hubiste tenido	hubisteis tenido
tuvo	tuvieron	hubo tenido	hubieron tenido
Future		*Future perfect*	
tendré	tendremos	habré tenido	habremos tenido
tendrás	tendréis	habrás tenido	habréis tenido
tendrá	tendrán	habrá tenido	habrán tenido
Conditional		*Conditional perfect*	
tendría	tendríamos	habría tenido	habríamos tenido
tendrías	tendríais	habrías tenido	habríais tenido
tendría	tendrían	habría tenido	habrían tenido
Present subjunctive		*Present perfect subjunctive*	
tenga	tengamos	haya tenido	hayamos tenido
tengas	tengáis	hayas tenido	hayáis tenido
tenga	tengan	haya tenido	hayan tenido

Simple Tenses		Compound Tenses	
Singular	**Plural**	**Singular**	**Plural**
Imperfect subjunctive		*Pluperfect subjunctive*	
tuviera	tuviéramos	hubiera tenido	hubiéramos tenido
tuvieras	tuvierais	hubieras tenido	hubierais tenido
tuviera	tuvieran	hubiera tenido	hubieran tenido
Imperative			
N/A	tengamos		
ten; no tengas	tened; no tengáis		
tenga	tengan		

traer: to bring
Present participle: trayendo
Past Participle: traído

Simple Tenses		Compound Tenses	
Singular	**Plural**	**Singular**	**Plural**
Present		*Present perfect*	
traigo	traemos	he traído	hemos traído
traes	traéis	has traído	habéis traído
trae	traen	ha traído	han traído
Imperfect		*Pluperfect*	
traía	traíamos	había traído	habíamos traído
traías	traíais	habías traído	habíais traído
traía	traían	había traído	habían traído
Preterit		*Preterit perfect*	
traje	trajimos	hube traído	hubimos traído
trajiste	trajisteis	hubiste traído	hubisteis traído
trajo	trajeron	hubo traído	hubieron traído

Simple Tenses		Compound Tenses	
Singular	**Plural**	**Singular**	**Plural**
Future		*Future perfect*	
traeré	traeremos	habré traído	habremos traído
traerás	traeréis	habrás traído	habréis traído
traerá	traerán	habrá traído	habrán traído
Conditional		*Conditional perfect*	
traería	traeríamos	habría traído	habríamos traído
traerías	traeríais	habrías traído	habríais traído
traería	traerían	habría traído	habrían traído
Present subjunctive		*Present perfect subjunctive*	
traiga	traigamos	haya traído	hayamos traído
traigas	traigáis	hayas traído	hayáis traído
traiga	traigan	haya traído	hayan traído
Imperfect subjunctive		*Pluperfect subjunctive*	
trajera	trajéramos	hubiera traído	hubiéramos traído
trajeras	trajerais	hubieras traído	hubierais traído
trajera	trajeran	hubiera traído	hubieran traído
Imperative			
N/A	traigamos		
trae; no traigas	traed; no traigáis		
traiga	traigan		

venir: to come
Present participle: viniendo
Past Participle: venido

Simple Tenses		Compound Tenses	
Singular	**Plural**	**Singular**	**Plural**
Present		*Present perfect*	
vengo	venimos	he venido	hemos venido
vienes	venís	has venido	habéis venido
viene	vienen	ha venido	han venido
Imperfect		*Pluperfect*	
venía	veníamos	había venido	habíamos venido
venías	veníais	habías venido	habíais venido
venía	venían	había venido	habían venido
Preterit		*Preterit perfect*	
vine	vinimos	hube venido	hubimos venido
viniste	vinisteis	hubiste venido	hubisteis venido
vino	vinieron	hubo venido	hubieron venido
Future		*Future perfect*	
vendré	vendremos	habré venido	habremos venido
vendrás	vendréis	habrás venido	habréis venido
vendrá	vendrán	habrá venido	habrán venido
Conditional		*Conditional perfect*	
vendría	vendríamos	habría venido	habríamos venido
vendrías	vendríais	habrías venido	habríais venido
vendría	vendrían	habría venido	habrían venido
Present subjunctive		*Present perfect subjunctive*	
venga	vengamos	haya venido	hayamos venido
vengas	vengáis	hayas venido	hayáis venido
venga	vengan	haya venido	hayan venido

Simple Tenses		Compound Tenses	
Singular	**Plural**	**Singular**	**Plural**
Imperfect subjunctive		*Pluperfect subjunctive*	
viniera	viniéramos	hubiera venido	hubiéramos venido
vinieras	vinierais	hubieras venido	hubierais venido
viniera	vinieran	hubiera venido	hubieran venido
Imperative			
N/A	vengamos		
ven; no vengas	venid; no vengáis		
venga	vengan		

ver: to see
Present participle: viendo
Past Participle: visto

Simple Tenses		Compound Tenses	
Singular	**Plural**	**Singular**	**Plural**
Present		*Present perfect*	
veo	vemos	he visto	hemos visto
ves	veis	has visto	habéis visto
ve	ven	ha visto	han visto
Imperfect		*Pluperfect*	
veía	veíamos	había visto	habíamos visto
veías	veíais	habías visto	habíais visto
veía	veían	había visto	habían visto
Preterit		*Preterit perfect*	
vi	vimos	hube visto	hubimos visto
viste	visteis	hubiste visto	hubisteis visto
vio	vieron	hubo visto	hubieron visto

Simple Tenses		Compound Tenses	
Singular	**Plural**	**Singular**	**Plural**
Future		*Future perfect*	
veré	veremos	habré visto	habremos visto
verás	veréis	habrás visto	habréis visto
verá	verán	habrá visto	habrán visto
Conditional		*Conditional perfect*	
vería	veríamos	habría visto	habríamos visto
verías	veríais	habrías visto	habríais visto
vería	verían	habría visto	habrían visto
Present subjunctive		*Present perfect subjunctive*	
vea	veamos	haya visto	hayamos visto
veas	veáis	hayas visto	hayáis visto
vea	vean	haya visto	hayan visto
Imperfect subjunctive		*Pluperfect subjunctive*	
viera	viéramos	hubiera visto	hubiéramos visto
vieras	vierais	hubieras visto	hubierais visto
viera	vieran	hubiera visto	hubieran visto
Imperative			
N/A	veamos		
ve; no veas	ved; no veáis		
vea	vean		

Stem-Changing Spanish Verbs

The verb tables in this section use underline to point out the conjugations with stem changes; use these flags to help you remember which verbs change in which forms.

pedir (e to i): to ask for
Present participle: pidiendo
Past Participle: pedido

Simple Tenses		Compound Tenses	
Singular	**Plural**	**Singular**	**Plural**
Present		*Present perfect*	
pido	pedimos	he pedido	hemos pedido
pides	pedís	has pedido	habéis pedido
pide	piden	ha pedido	han pedido
Imperfect		*Pluperfect*	
pedía	pedíamos	había pedido	habíamos pedido
pedías	pedíais	habías pedido	habíais pedido
pedía	pedían	había pedido	habían pedido
Preterit		*Preterit perfect*	
pedí	pedimos	hube pedido	hubimos pedido
pediste	pedisteis	hubiste pedido	hubisteis pedido
pidió	pidieron	hubo pedido	hubieron pedido
Future		*Future perfect*	
pediré	pediremos	habré pedido	habremos pedido
pedirás	pediréis	habrás pedido	habréis pedido
pedirá	pedirán	habrá pedido	habrán pedido
Conditional		*Conditional perfect*	
pediría	pediríamos	habría pedido	habríamos pedido
pedirías	pediríais	habrías pedido	habríais pedido
pediría	pedirían	habría pedido	habrían pedido
Present subjunctive		*Present perfect subjunctive*	
pida	pidamos	haya pedido	hayamos pedido
pidas	pidáis	hayas pedido	hayáis pedido
pida	pidan	haya pedido	hayan pedido

Simple Tenses		Compound Tenses	
Singular	**Plural**	**Singular**	**Plural**
Imperfect subjunctive		*Pluperfect subjunctive*	
pidiera	pidiéramos	hubiera pedido	hubiéramos pedido
pidieras	pidierais	hubieras pedido	hubierais pedido
pidiera	pidieran	hubiera pedido	hubieran pedido
Imperative			
N/A	pidamos		
pide; no pidas	pedid; no pidáis		
pida	pidan		

perder (e to ie): to lose
Present participle: perdiendo
Past Participle: perdido

Simple Tenses		Compound Tenses	
Singular	**Plural**	**Singular**	**Plural**
Present		*Present perfect*	
pierdo	perdemos	he perdido	hemos perdido
pierdes	perdéis	has perdido	habéis perdido
pierde	pierden	ha perdido	han perdido
Imperfect		*Pluperfect*	
perdía	perdíamos	había perdido	habíamos perdido
perdías	perdíais	habías perdido	habíais perdido
perdía	perdían	había perdido	habían perdido
Preterit		*Preterit perfect*	
perdí	perdimos	hube perdido	hubimos perdido
perdiste	perdisteis	hubiste perdido	hubisteis perdido
perdió	perdieron	hubo perdido	hubieron perdido

Simple Tenses		Compound Tenses	
Singular	**Plural**	**Singular**	**Plural**
Future		*Future perfectperder*	
perderé	perderemos	habré perdido	habremos perdido
perderás	perderéis	habrás perdido	habréis perdido
perderá	perderán	habrá perdido	habrán perdido
Conditional		*Conditional perfect*	
perdería	perdíamos	habría perdido	habríamos perdido
perderías	perderíais	habrías perdido	habríais perdido
perdería	perderían	habría perdido	habrían perdido
Present subjunctive		*Present perfect subjunctive*	
<u>pierda</u>	perdamos	haya perdido	hayamos perdido
<u>pierdas</u>	perdáis	hayas perdido	hayáis perdido
<u>pierda</u>	<u>pierdan</u>	haya perdido	hayan perdido
Imperfect subjunctive		*Pluperfect subjunctive*	
perdiera	perdiéramos	hubiera perdido	hubiéramos perdido
perdieras	perdierais	hubieras perdido	hubierais perdido
perdiera	perdieran	hubiera perdido	hubieran perdido
Imperative			
N/A	perdamos		
<u>pierde</u>; no <u>pierdas</u>	perded; no perdáis		
<u>pierda</u>	<u>pierdan</u>		

dormir (o to ue or u): to sleep
Present participle: durmiendo
Past Participle: dormido

Simple Tenses		Compound Tenses	
Singular	**Plural**	**Singular**	**Plural**
Present		*Present perfect*	
duermo	dormimos	he dormido	hemos dormido
duermes	dormís	has dormido	habéis dormido
duerme	duermen	ha dormido	han dormido
Imperfect		*Pluperfect*	
dormía	dormíamos	había dormido	habíamos dormido
dormías	dormíais	habías dormido	habíais dormido
dormía	dormían	había dormido	habían dormido
Preterit		*Preterit perfect*	
dormí	dormimos	hube dormido	hubimos dormido
dormiste	dormisteis	hubiste dormido	hubisteis dormido
durmió	durmieron	hubo dormido	hubieron dormido
Future		*Future perfect*	
dormiré	dormiremos	habré dormido	habremos dormido
dormirás	dormiréis	habrás dormido	habréis dormido
dormirá	dormirán	habrá dormido	habrán dormido
Conditional		*Conditional perfect*	
dormiría	dormiríamos	habría dormido	habríamos dormido
dormirías	dormiríais	habrías dormido	habríais dormido
dormiría	dormirían	habría dormido	habrían dormido
Present subjunctive		*Present perfect subjunctive*	
duerma	durmamos	haya dormido	hayamos dormido
duermas	durmáis	hayas dormido	hayáis dormido
duerma	duerman	haya dormido	hayan dormido

Simple Tenses		Compound Tenses	
Singular	**Plural**	**Singular**	**Plural**
Imperfect subjunctive		*Pluperfect subjunctive*	
durmiera	durmiéramos	hubiera dormido	hubiéramos dormido
durmieras	durmierais	hubieras dormido	hubierais dormido
durmiera	durmieran	hubiera dormido	hubieran dormido
Imperative			
N/A	durmamos		
duerme; no duermas	dormid; no durmáis		
duerma	duerman		

jugar (u to ue): to play (a game or sport)
Present participle: jugando
Past Participle: jugado

Simple Tenses		Compound Tenses	
Singular	**Plural**	**Singular**	**Plural**
Present		*Present perfect*	
juego	jugamos	he jugado	hemos jugado
juegas	jugáis	has jugado	habéis jugado
juega	juegan	ha jugado	han jugado
Imperfect		*Pluperfect*	
jugaba	jugábamos	había jugado	habíamos jugado
jugabas	jugabaís	habías jugado	habíais jugado
jugaba	jugaban	había jugado	hubieron jugado
Preterit		*Preterit perfect*	
jugué	jugamos	hube jugado	hubimos jugado
jugaste	jugasteis	hubiste jugado	hubisteis jugado
jugó	jugaron	hubo jugado	hubieron jugado

Simple Tenses		Compound Tenses	
Singular	**Plural**	**Singular**	**Plural**
Future		*Future perfect*	
jugaré	jugaremos	habré jugado	habremos jugado
jugarás	jugaréis	habrás jugado	habréis jugado
jugará	jugarán	habrá jugado	habrán jugado
Conditional		*Conditional perfect*	
jugaría	jugaríamos	habría jugado	habríamos jugado
jugarías	jugaríais	habrías jugado	habríais jugado
jugaría	jugarían	habría jugado	habrían jugado
Present subjunctive		*Present perfect subjunctive*	
<u>juegue</u>	juguemos	haya jugado	hayamos jugado
<u>juegues</u>	juguéis	hayas jugado	hayáis jugado
<u>juegue</u>	<u>jueguen</u>	haya jugado	hayan jugado
Imperfect subjunctive		*Pluperfect subjunctive*	
jugara	jugáramos	hubiera jugado	hubiéramos jugado
jugaras	jugarais	hubieras jugado	hubierais jugado
jugara	jugaran	hubiera jugado	hubieran jugado
Imperative			
N/A	juguemos		
<u>juega</u>; no <u>juegues</u>	jugad; no juguéis		
<u>juegue</u>	<u>jueguen</u>		

Spelling-Changing Spanish Verbs

The verb tables in this section use underline to indicate the conjugations with spelling changes; use these markers to help you remember which verbs change in which forms.

escoger (soft g to j): to choose
Present participle: escogiendo
Past Participle: escogido

Simple Tenses		Compound Tenses	
Singular	**Plural**	**Singular**	**Plural**
Present		*Present perfect*	
<u>escojo</u>	escogemos	he escogido	hemos escogido
escoges	escogéis	has escogido	habéis escogido
escoge	escogen	ha escogido	han escogido
Imperfect		*Pluperfect*	
escogía	escogíamos	había escogido	habíamos escogido
escogías	escogíais	habías escogido	habíais escogido
escogía	escogían	había escogido	habían escogido
Preterit		*Preterit perfect*	
escogí	escogimos	hube escogido	hubimos escogido
escogiste	escogisteis	hubiste escogido	hubisteis escogido
escogió	escogieron	hubo escogido	hubieron escogido
Future		*Future perfect*	
escogeré	escogeremos	habré escogido	habremos escogido
escogerás	escogeréis	habrás escogido	habréis escogido
escogerá	escogerán	habrá escogido	habrán escogido
Conditional		*Conditional perfect*	
escogería	escogeríamos	habría escogido	habríamos escogido
escogerías	escogeríais	habrías escogido	habríais escogido
escogería	escogerían	habría escogido	habrían escogido

Simple Tenses		Compound Tenses	
Singular	**Plural**	**Singular**	**Plural**
Present subjunctive		*Present perfect subjunctive*	
escoja	escojamos	haya escogido	hayamos escogido
escojas	escojáis	hayas escogido	hayáis escogido
escoja	escojan	haya escogido	hayan escogido
Imperfect subjunctive		*Pluperfect subjunctive*	
escogiera	escogiéramos	hubiera escogido	hubiéramos escogido
escogieras	escogierais	hubieras escogido	hubierais escogido
escogiera	escogieran	hubiera escogido	hubieran escogido
Imperative			
N/A	escojamos		
escoge; no escojas	escoged; no escojáis		
escoja	escojan		

distinguir (hard gu to g): to distinguish
Present participle: distinguiendo
Past Participle: distinguido

Simple Tenses		Compound Tenses	
Singular	**Plural**	**Singular**	**Plural**
Present		*Present perfect*	
distingo	distinguimos	he distinguido	hemos distinguido
distingues	distinguís	has distinguido	habéis distinguido
distingue	distinguen	ha distinguido	han distinguido

Simple Tenses		Compound Tenses	
Singular	**Plural**	**Singular**	**Plural**
Imperfect		*Pluperfect*	
distinguía	distinguíamos	había distinguido	habíamos distinguido
distinguías	distinguíais	habías distinguido	habíais distinguido
distinguía	distinguían	había distinguido	habían distinguido
Preterit		*Preterit perfect*	
distinguí	distinguimos	hube distinguido	hubimos distinguido
distinguiste	distinguisteis	hubiste distinguido	hubisteis distinguido
distinguió	distinguieron	hubo distinguido	hubieron distinguido
Future		*Future perfect*	
distinguiré	distinguiremos	habré distinguido	habremos distinguido
distinguirás	distinguiréis	habrás distinguido	habréis distinguido
distinguirá	distinguirán	habrá distinguido	habrán distinguido
Conditional		*Conditional perfect*	
distinguiría	distinguiríamos	habría distinguido	habríamos distinguido
distinguirías	distinguiríais	habrías distinguido	habríais distinguido
distinguiría	distinguirían	habría distinguido	habrían distinguido
Present subjunctive		*Present perfect subjunctive*	
<u>distinga</u>	<u>distingamos</u>	haya distinguido	hayamos distinguido
<u>distingas</u>	<u>distingáis</u>	hayas distinguido	hayáis distinguido
<u>distinga</u>	<u>distingan</u>	haya distinguido	hayan distinguido

Simple Tenses		Compound Tenses	
Singular	**Plural**	**Singular**	**Plural**
Imperfect subjunctive		*Pluperfect subjunctive*	
distinguiera	distinguiéramos	hubiera distinguido	hubiéramos distinguido
distinguieras	distinguierais	hubieras distinguido	hubierais distinguido
distinguiera	distinguieran	hubiera distinguido	hubieran distinguido
Imperative			
N/A	<u>distingamos</u>		
distingue; no <u>distingas</u>	distinguid; no <u>distingáis</u>		
<u>distinga</u>	<u>distingan</u>		

delinquir (hard qu to c): to commit a crime, to break the law
Present participle: delinquiendo
Past Participle: delinquido

Simple Tenses		Compound Tenses	
Singular	**Plural**	**Singular**	**Plural**
Present		*Present perfect*	
<u>delinco</u>	delinquimos	he delinquido	hemos delinquido
delinques	delinquís	has delinquido	habéis delinquido
delinque	delinquen	ha delinquido	han delinquido
Imperfect		*Pluperfect*	
delinquía	delinquíamos	había delinquido	habíamos delinquido
delinquías	delinquiías	habías delinquido	habíais delinquido
delinquía	delinquían	había delinquido	habían delinquido

Simple Tenses		Compound Tenses	
Singular	**Plural**	**Singular**	**Plural**
Preterit		*Preterit perfect*	
delinquí	delinquimos	hube delinquido	hubimos delinquido
delinquiste	delinquisteis	hubiste delinquido	hubisteis delinquido
delinquió	delinquieron	hubo delinquido	hubieron delinquido
Future		*Future perfect*	
delinquiré	delinquiremos	habré delinquido	habremos delinquido
delinquirás	delinquiréis	habrás delinquido	habréis delinquido
delinquirá	delinquirán	habrá delinquido	habrán delinquido
Conditional		*Conditional perfect*	
delinquiría	delinquiríamos	habría delinquido	habríamos delinquido
delinquirías	delinquiríais	habrías delinquido	habríais delinquido
delinquiría	delinquirían	habría delinquido	habrían delinquido
Present subjunctive		*Present perfect subjunctive*	
<u>delinca</u>	<u>delincamos</u>	haya delinquido	hayamos delinquido
<u>delincas</u>	<u>delincáis</u>	hayas delinquido	hayáis delinquido
<u>delinca</u>	<u>delincan</u>	haya delinquido	hayan delinquido
Imperfect subjunctive		*Pluperfect subjunctive*	
delinquiera	delinquiéramos	hubiera delinquido	hubiéramos delinquido
delinquieras	delinquierais	hubieras delinquido	hubierais delinquido
delinquiera	delinquieran	hubiera delinquido	hubieran delinquido
Imperative			
N/A	<u>delincamos</u>		
delinque; no <u>delincas</u>	delinquid; no <u>delincáis</u>		
<u>delinca</u>	<u>delincan</u>		

convencer (c to z): to convince
Present participle: convenciendo
Past Participle: convencido

Simple Tenses		Compound Tenses	
Singular	**Plural**	**Singular**	**Plural**
Present		*Present perfect*	
convenzo	convencemos	he convencido	hemos convencido
convences	convencéis	has convencido	habéis convencido
convence	convencen	ha convencido	han convencido
Imperfect		*Pluperfect*	
convencía	convencíamos	había convencido	habíamos convencido
convencías	convencíais	habías convencido	habíais convencido
convencía	convencían	había convencido	habían convencido
Preterit		*Preterit perfect*	
convencí	convencimos	hube convencido	hubimos convencido
convenciste	convencisteis	hubiste convencido	hubisteis convencido
convenció	convencieron	hubo convencido	hubieron convencido
Future		*Future perfect*	
convenceré	convenceremos	habré convencido	habremos convencido
convencerás	convenceréis	habrás convencido	habréis convencido
convencerá	convencerán	habrá convencido	habrán convencido
Conditional		*Conditional perfect*	
convencería	convenceríamos	habría convencido	habríamos convencido
convencerías	convenceríais	habrías convencido	habríais convencido
convencería	convencerían	habría convencido	habrían convencido

Simple Tenses		Compound Tenses	
Singular	**Plural**	**Singular**	**Plural**
Present subjunctive		*Present perfect subjunctive*	
<u>convenza</u>	<u>convenzamo</u>	haya convencido	hayamos convencido
<u>convenzas</u>	<u>convenzáis</u>	hayas convencido	hayáis convencido
<u>convenza</u>	<u>convenzan</u>	haya convencido	haya convencido
Imperfect subjunctive		*Pluperfect subjunctive*	
convenciera	convenciéramos	hubiera convencido	hubiéramos convencido
convencieras	convencierais	hubieras convencido	hubierais convencido
convenciera	convencieran	hubiera convencido	hubieran convencido
Imperative			
N/A	<u>convenzamos</u>		
convence; no <u>convenzas</u>	convenced; no <u>convenzáis</u>		
<u>convenza</u>	<u>convenzan</u>		

tocar (hard c to qu): to play (an instrument)
Present participle: tocando
Past Participle: tocado

Simple Tenses		Compound Tenses	
Singular	**Plural**	**Singular**	**Plural**
Present		*Present perfect*	
toco	tocamos	he tocado	hemos tocado
tocas	tocáis	has tocado	habéis tocado
toca	tocan	ha tocado	han tocado

Simple Tenses		Compound Tenses	
Singular	**Plural**	**Singular**	**Plural**
Imperfect		*Pluperfect*	
tocaba	tocábamos	había tocado	habíamos tocado
tocabas	tocabais	habías tocado	habíais tocado
tocaba	tocaban	había tocado	habían tocado
Preterit		*Preterit perfect*	
toqué	tocamos	hube tocado	hubimos tocado
tocaste	tocasteis	hubiste tocado	habisteis tocado
tocó	tocaron	hubo tocado	hubieron tocado
Future		*Future perfect*	
tocaré	tocaremos	habré tocado	habremos tocado
tocarás	tocaréis	habrás tocado	habréis tocado
tocará	tocarán	habrá tocado	habrán tocado
Conditional		*Conditional perfect*	
tocaría	tocaríamos	habría tocado	habríamos tocado
tocarías	tocaríais	habrías tocado	habríais tocado
tocaría	tocarían	habría tocado	habrían tocado
Present subjunctive		*Present perfect subjunctive*	
toque	toquemos	haya tocado	hayamos tocado
toques	toquéis	hayas tocado	hayáis tocado
toque	toquen	haya tocado	hayan tocado
Imperfect subjunctive		*Pluperfect subjunctive*	
tocara	tocáramos	hubiera tocado	hubiéramos tocado
tocaras	tocarais	hubieras tocado	hubierais tocado
tocara	tocaran	hubiera tocado	hubieran tocado

Simple Tenses		Compound Tenses	
Singular	**Plural**	**Singular**	**Plural**
Imperative			
N/A	<u>toquemos</u>		
toca; no <u>toques</u>	tocad; no <u>toquéis</u>		
<u>toque</u>	<u>toquen</u>		

cruzar (z to c): to cross
Present participle: cruzando
Past Participle: cruzado

Simple Tenses		Compound Tenses	
Singular	**Plural**	**Singular**	**Plural**
Present		_Present perfect_	
cruzo	cruzamos	he cruzado	hemos cruzado
cruzas	cruzáis	has cruzado	habéis cruzado
cruza	cruzan	ha cruzado	han cruzado
Imperfect		_Pluperfect_	
cruzaba	cruzábamos	había cruzado	habíamos cruzado
cruzabas	cruzabais	habías cruzado	habíais cruzado
cruzaba	cruzaban	había cruzado	habían cruzado
Preterit		_Preterit perfect_	
<u>crucé</u>	cruzamos	hube cruzado	hubimos cruzado
cruzaste	cruzasteis	hubiste cruzado	hubisteis cruzado
cruzó	cruzaron	hubo cruzado	hubieron cruzado
Future		_Future perfect_	
cruzaré	cruzaremos	habré cruzado	habremos cruzado
cruzarás	cruzaréis	habrás cruzado	habréis cruzado
cruzará	cruzarán	habrá cruzado	habrán cruzado

Simple Tenses		Compound Tenses	
Singular	**Plural**	**Singular**	**Plural**
Conditional		*Conditional perfect*	
cruzaría	cruzaríamos	habría cruzado	habríamos cruzado
cruzarías	cruzaríais	habrías cruzado	habríais cruzado
cruzaría	cruzarían	habría cruzado	habrían cruzado
Present subjunctive		*Present perfect subjunctive*	
<u>cruce</u>	<u>crucemos</u>	haya cruzado	hayamos cruzado
<u>cruces</u>	<u>crucéis</u>	hayas cruzado	hayáis cruzado
<u>cruce</u>	<u>crucen</u>	haya cruzado	hayan cruzado
Imperfect subjunctive		*Pluperfect subjunctive*	
cruzara	cruzáramos	hubiera cruzado	hubiéramos cruzado
cruzaras	cruzarais	hubieras cruzado	hubierais cruzado
cruzara	cruzaran	hubiera cruzado	hubieran cruzado
Imperative			
N/A	<u>crucemos</u>		
cruza; no <u>cruces</u>	cruzad; no <u>crucéis</u>		
<u>cruce</u>	<u>crucen</u>		

pagar (g to gu): to pay (for)
Present participle: pagando
Past Participle: pagado

Simple Tenses		Compound Tenses	
Singular	**Plural**	**Singular**	**Plural**
Present		*Present perfect*	
pago	pagamos	he pagado	hemos pagado
pagas	pagáis	has pagado	habéis pagado

Simple Tenses		Compound Tenses	
Singular	**Plural**	**Singular**	**Plural**
paga	pagan	ha pagado	han pagado
Imperfect		*Pluperfect*	
pagaba	pagábamos	había pagado	habíamos pagado
pagabas	pagabais	habías pagado	habíais pagado
pagaba	pagaban	había pagado	habían pagado
Preterit		*Preterit perfect*	
pagué	pagamos	hube pagado	hubimos pagado
pagaste	pagasteis	hubiste pagado	hubisteis pagado
pagó	pagaron	hubo pagado	hubieron pagado
Future		*Future perfect*	
pagaré	pagaremos	habré pagado	habremos pagado
pagarás	pagaréis	habrás pagado	habréis pagado
pagará	pagarán	habrá pagado	habrán pagado
Conditional		*Conditional perfect*	
pagaría	pagaríamos	habría pagado	habríamos pagado
pagarías	pagaríais	habrías pagado	habríais pagado
pagaría	pagarían	habría pagado	habrían pagado
Present subjunctive		*Present perfect subjunctive*	
pague	paguemos	haya pagado	hayamos pagado
pagues	paguéis	hayas pagado	hayáis pagado
pague	paguen	haya pagado	hayan pagado
Imperfect subjunctive		*Pluperfect subjunctive*	
pagara	pagáramos	hubiera pagado	hubiéramos pagado
pagaras	pagarais	hubieras pagado	hubierais pagado
pagara	pagaran	hubiera pagado	hubieran pagado

Simple Tenses		Compound Tenses	
Singular	**Plural**	**Singular**	**Plural**
Imperative			
N/A	paguemos		
paga; no pagues	pagad; no paguéis		
pague	paguen		

Appendix B
Spanish-English Mini Dictionary

● ●

A

a menudo: a meh-*noo*-doh = often

a pie: ah pee*eh* = walking (literally: on foot)

a rayas: ah *rah*-yahs = striped

a sus órdenes: a soos *ohr*-dehn-ehs = at your service

a veces: ah *bveh*-sehs = sometimes

abeja (f): ah-*bveh*-hah = bee

abogado/a (m, f): ah-bvoh-*gah*-doh/dah = lawyer

abrazarse: ah-bvrah-*sahr*-seh = to hug each other

abrigo (m): ah-*bvree*-goh = coat

abril (m): ah-*bvreel* = April

abrir: ah-*bvreer* = to open

abrocharse: ah-bvroh-*chahr*-seh = to fasten

absurdo: ahbv-*soor*-doh = absurd

abuela (f): ah-bvoo*eh*-lah = grandmother

abuelo (m): ah-bvoo*eh*-loh = grandfather

abuelos (m): ah-*bveh*-lohs = grandparents

aburrido: ah-bvoo-*rree*-doh = boring

aburrir: ah-bvoo-*rreer* = to bore

aburrirse: ah-bvoo-*rreer*-seh = to become bored

acabar de: ah-kah-*bvahr* deh = to have just

acercarse: ah-sehr-*kahr*-seh = to approach, to near

aconsejar: ah-kohn-seh-*Hahr* = to advise

acordar (ue): ah-kohr-*dahr* = to agree

acostar (ue): ah-kohs-*tahr* = to put to bed

acostarse (ue): ah-kohs-*tahr*-seh = to go to bed

actor (m): ahk-*tohr* = actor

actriz (f): ahk-*trees* = actress

actuar: ahk-too*ahr* = to act

adelante: ah-deh-*lahn*-teh = in front, ahead

adiós: ah-dee*ohs* = good bye

aduana (f): ah-doo*ah*-nah = customs

aeropuerto (m): ah-eh-roh-poo*ehr*-toh = airport

afeitarse: ah-fehee-*tahr*-seh = to shave

afortunado: ah-fohr-too-*nah*-doh = fortunate

afuera: ah-foo*eh*-rah = outside

agencia (f): ah-Hehn-*see*ah = agency

agosto (m): ah-*gohs*-toh = August

agua (m): *ah*-gooah = water

aguacate (m): ah-gooah-*kah*-teh = avocado

ahora: ah-*oh*-rah = now

ahora mismo: ah-*hoh*-rah *mees*-moh = right now

ahorrar: ah-hoh-*rrahr* = to save

ajedrez (m): ah-*Heh*-drehs = chess

ají (m): ah-*Hee* = hot pepper (South America)

ajo (m): *ah*-Hoh = garlic

al fin: ahl feen = finally

alarma (f): ah-*lahr*-mah = alarm

alcalde (m, f): ahl-*kahl*-deh = mayor

alegrarse (de): ah-leh-*grahr*-seh (deh) = to be glad, to be happy

alegre: ah-*leh*-greh = happy

alegremente: ah-leh-greh-*mehn*-teh = happily

alemán/alemana (m,f): ah-leh-*mahn*/nah = German

alfombra (f): ahl-*fohm*-bvrah = rug

algodón (m): ahl-goh-*dohn* = cotton

algún: ahl-*goon* = some

allá: ah-*yah* = over there

allí: ah-*yee* = there

almacén (m): ahl-mah-*sehn* = department store

almorzar (ue): ahl-mohr-*sahr* = to eat lunch

almuerzo (m): ahl-moo*ehr*-soh = lunch

alrededor de: ahl-reh-deh-*dohr* de = around

alto: *ahl*-toh = tall; high

amable: ah-*mah*-bvleh = nice

amar: ah-*mahr* = to love

amarillo: ah-mah-*ree*-yoh = yellow

añadir: ah-nyah-*deer* = to add

andar: ahn-*dahr* = to walk

año (m): *ah*-nyoh = year

antes (de): *ahn*-tehs (deh) = before

apagar: ah-pah-*gahr* = to turn off

aparecer: ah-pah-reh-*sehr* = to appear

aplaudir: ah-plahoo-*deer* = to applaud

aplicar(se): ah-plee-*kahr*(seh) = to apply (oneself)

aprender: ah-prehn-*dehr* = to learn

apresurarse: ah-preh-soo-*rahr*-seh = to hurry

apretado: ah-preh-*tah*-doh = tight

aprobar (un examen): ah-proh-*bahr* (oon ehk-*sah*-mehn) = to pass (a test)

aquel, aquella: ah-*kehl*, ah-*keh*-yah = that

aquél, aquélla: ah-*kehl*, ah-*keh*-yah = that one

aquellos, aquellas: ah-*keh*-yohs, ah-*keh*-yahs = those

aquéllos, aquéllas: ah-*keh*-yohs, ah-*keh*-yahs = those ones

aquí: ah-*kee* = here

aretes (m): ah-*reh*-tehs = earrings

arreglar: ah-rreh-*glahr* = to repair

arroz (m): ah-*rrohs* = rice

ascensor (m): ah-sehn-*sohr* = elevator

asegurarse de: ah-seh-goo-*rahr*-seh deh = to make sure

asesor/a (m, f): ah-seh-*sohr*/rah = consultant

asiento (m): ah-see*ehn*-toh = seat

asistir: ah-sees-*teer* = to attend

asombrado: ah-sohm-*bvrah*-doh = astonished, surprised, amazed

aspiradora: ahs-pee-rah-*doh*-rah = vacuum cleaner

asustado: ah-soos-*tah*-doh = frightened

atacar: ah-tah-*kahr* = to attack

atentamente: ah-tehn-tah-*mehn*-teh = sincerely yours

atractivo: ah-trahk-*tee*-bvoh = attractive

atroz: ah-*trohs* = atrocious

atún (m): ah-*toon* = tuna

auditorio (m): ahoo-dee-*toh*-reeoh = auditorium

aumento (m): ahoo-*mehn*-toh = raise

aumento de sueldo (m): ahoo-*mehn*-toh deh soo*ehl*-doh = raise (of salary)

auto (m): *ah*oo-toh = car (South America)

autopista (f): ahoo-toh-*pees*-tah = freeway

avenida (f): ah-bveh-*nee*-dah = avenue

avergonzado: ah-bvehr-gohn-*sah*-doh = embarrassed, ashamed

avergonzarse de: ah-bvehr-gohn-*sahr*-seh deh = to be ashamed of

avión (m): *ah*-bveeohn = plane

ayer: ah-*yehr* = yesterday

ayudar: ah-yoo-*dahr* = to help

azul: ah-*sool* = blue

B

bailar: bvahee-*lahr* = to dance

bajo: *bvah*-Ho = short, low, under

balcón (m): bvahl-*kohn* = balcony

baloncesto (m): bvah-lohn-*sehs*-toh = basketball

bañar: bvah-*nyahr* = to bathe (someone)

bañarse: bvah-*nyahr*-seh = to bathe oneself

bañera (f): bah-*nyeh*-rah = bathtub

baño (m): *bvah*-nyoh = bathroom

banquero/a (m, f): bvahn-*keh*-roh/rah = banker

barco (m): *bvahr*-koh = boat

barrio (m): *bvah*-rreeoh = neighborhood

basta: *bvahs*-tah = enough

bastante: bvahs-*tahn*-teh = quite; enough

basura (f): bvah-*soo*-rah = garbage

bate (m): *bvah*-teh = bat

batir: bvah-*teer* = to beat, whip, whisk

beber: bveh-*bvehr* = to drink

bebida (f): bveh-*bvee*-dah = drink

bello: *bveh*-yoh = beautiful

besar: bveh-*sahr* = to kiss

biblioteca (f): bvee-bvleeoh-*teh*-kah = library

bicicleta (f): bvee-see-*kleh*-tah = bicycle

bigote (m): bvee-*goh*-teh = moustache

bistec (m): bvees-*tehk* = steak

blanco: *bvlahn*-koh = white

boca (f): *bvoh*-kah = mouth

boda (f): *bvoh*-dah = wedding

boleto (m): bvoh-*leh*-toh = ticket

bolsillo (m): bvohl-*see*-yoh = pocket

bonito: bvoh-*nee*-toh = pretty

botella (f): bvoh-*teh*-yah = bottle

brazo (m): *bvrah*-soh = arm

brevemente: bvreh-bveh-*mehn*-teh = briefly

brillo: *bvree*-yoh = shine

brócoli (m): *bvroh*-koh-lee = broccoli

bronceador (m): bvrohn-seh*ah*-dohr = suntan lotion

broncearse: bvrohn-seh-*ahr*-seh = to tan

bueno: bvoo*eh*-noh = good

bulevar (m): bvoo-leh-*bvahr* = boulevard

burlarse (**de**): bvoor-*lahr*-seh (deh) = to make fun of

buscar: bvoos-*kahr* = to search, to look for

C

caballo (m): kah-*bvah*-yoh = horse

caber: kah-*bvehr* = to fit

cabeza (f): kah-*bveh*-sah = head

caer: cah-*ehr* = to fall

café (m): kah-*feh* = coffee

caja (f): *kah*-Hah = box

cajero/a (m, f): kah-*Heh*-roh/rah = cashier

caliente: kah-lee*ehn*-teh = hot [temperature]

calificar: kah-lee-fee-*kahr* = to grade (papers, exams, and so on)

callarse: kah-*yahr*-seh = to be silent

calle (f): *kah*-yeh = street

calor (m): kah-*lohr* = heat

cama (f): *kah*-mah = bed

cámara de video (f): *kah*-mah-rah deh bvee-*deh*-oh = video camera

camarero/a (m, f): kah-mah-*reh*-roh/rah = waiter (waitress)

camarón (m): kah-mah-*rohn* = shrimp

camarote (m): kah-mah-*roh*-teh = cabin (stateroom)

cambiar: kahm-bvee*ahr* = to change

camino (m): kah-*mee*-noh = road

camisa (f): kah-*mee*-sah = shirt

camiseta (f): kah-mee-*seh*-tah = t-shirt

campo (m): *kahm*-poh = countryside, field

cancelar: kah-seh-*lahr* = to cancel

canción (f): kahn-see*ohn* = song

cansado: kahn-*sah*-doh = tired

cansarse: kahn-*sahr*-seh = to become tired

cantar: kahn-*tahr* = to sing

caries (f): *kah*-reeehs = cavity

cariño (m): kah-*ree*-nyoh = affection

caro: *kah*-roh = expensive

carrera (f): kah-*rreh*-rah = race; profession

carro (m): *kah*-rroh = car (Mexico)

carta (f): *kahr*-tah = letter

cartel (m): kahr-*tehl* = sign

cartera (f): kahr-*teh*-rah = wallet

cartero/a (m, f): kahr-*teh*-roh/rah = postal worker

casa (f): *kah*-sah = house

casarse: kah-*sahr*-seh = to get married

cascada (f): kahs-*kah*-dah = waterfall

casi: *kah*-see = almost

cebollas (f): seh-*bvoh*-yahs = onions

cena (f): *seh*-nah = supper

centro comercial (m): *sehn*-troh coh-mehr-see-*ahl* = shopping mall

cepillarse: seh-pee-*yahr*-seh = to brush (hair, teeth)

cerámica (f): seh-*rah*-mee-kah = ceramic

cerca (de): *sehr*-kah (deh) = near (to)

cereales (m): seh-reh-*ah*-lehs = cereals

cereza (f): seh-*reh*-sah = cherry

cero (m): *seh*-roh = zero

cerrado: seh-*rrah*-doh = closed

cerrar: seh-*rrahr* = to close

cerveza (f): sehr-*bveh*-sah = beer

césped (m): *sehs*-pehd = lawn

champán (m): chahm-*pahn* = champagne

chaqueta (f): chah-*keh*-tah = jacket

cheque (m): *cheh*-keh = check

chico: *chee*-koh = little; small

chile (m): *chee*-leh = hot pepper (Mexico and Guatemala)

chiste (m): *chees*-teh = joke

chofer (m): choh-*fehr* = driver

cielo (m): see*eh*-loh = sky

ciencia (f): seeehn-*seeah* = science

cierto: see*ehr*-toh = certain, sure

cine (m): *see*-neh = cinema

ciruela (f): see-roo-*eh*-lah = plum

cirugía (f): see-roo-*Hee*ah = surgery

cirujano (m): see-roo-*hah*-noh = surgeon

cita (f): *see*-tah = appointment, date

ciudad (f): seeoo-*dahd* = city

claro: *klah*-roh = light

cobre (m): *koh*-bvreh = copper

coche (m): *koh*-cheh = car

cochecito (m): koh-cheh-*see*-toh = baby carriage

cocina (f): koh-*see*-nah = kitchen

cocinar: koh-see-*nahr* = to cook

cocinero/a (m, f): koh-see-*neh*-rah = cook

coco (m): *koh*-koh = coconut

código postal (m): *koh*-dee-goh pohs-*tahl* = postal code [ZIP code]

coger: koh-*hehr* = to catch

colgar: kohl-*gahr* = to hang; to hang up

collar (m): koh-*yahr* = necklace

colocar: koh-loh-*kahr* = to place (something)

colocarse: koh-loh-*kahr*-seh = to place oneself; to get a job

comedor (m): koh-meh-*dohr* = dining room

comenzar (ie): koh-mehn-*sahr* = to begin

comer: koh-*mehr* = to eat

comida (f): koh-*mee*-dah = dinner

cómo: *koh*-moh = how

compañero/a (m, f): kohm-pah-*nyeh*-roh/rah = friend

compartir: kohm-pahr-*teer* = to share

completamente: kohm-pleh-tah-*mehn*-teh = completely

comportamiento (m): kohm-pohr-tah-mee*ehn*-toh = behavior

comprar: kohm-*prahr* = to buy

computadora (f): kohm-poo-tah-*doh*-rah = computer

computadora portátil (f): lah kohm-poo-tah-*doh*-rah pohr-*tah*-teel = laptop computer

concesión (f): kohn-seh-*see*ohn = dealership

concienzudo: kohn-seeehn-*soo*-doh = conscientious

concluir: kohn-clu*eer* = to conclude

conducir: kohn-doo-seer = to steer, to drive

confianza (f): kohn-fee*ahn*-sah = confidence

conocer: koh-noh-*sehr* = to know (to be acquainted with)

conseguir (i): kohn-seh-*geer* = to get, obtain

consejo (m): kohn-*seh*-hoh = advice

consentir (ie): kohn-sehn-*teer* = to consent

construir: kohn-stroo*eer* = to build

contar: kohn-*tahr* = count

contento: kohn-*tehn*-toh = content; satisfied

contestar: kohn-tehs-*tahr* = to answer

continuar: kohn-tee-nooo*ahr* = to continue

contratar: kohn-trah-*tahr* = to hire

contribuir: kohn-tree-boo*eer* = to contribute

convencer: kohn-bvehn-*sehr* = to convince

conveniente: kohn-bveh-nee*ehn*-teh = fitting

conviene: kohn-bvee*eh*-neh = it is advisable that

copiar: koh-pee*ahr* = to copy, cheat

corazón (m): koh-rah-*sohn* = heart

corregir (i): koh-rreh-*heer* = to correct

correo (m): koh-*rreh*-oh = mail; post

correo electrónico (m): koh-*rreh*-oh eh-lehk-*troh*-nee-koh = e-mail

correr: koh-*rrehr* = to run

corrida de toros (f): koh-*rree*-dah deh *toh*-rohs = bullfight

cortar: kohr-*tahr* = to cut

cortés (cortesa): kohr-*tehs*, kohr-*teh*-sah = courteous

cortesía (f): kohr-teh-*seeah* = courtesy

cosa (f): *koh*-sah = thing

costar: kohs-*tahr* = to cost (as in price)

crecer: kreh-*sehr* = to grow

creer: kreh-*ehr* = to disbelieve

crucero (m): kroo-*seh*-roh = cruise

cuadra (f): koo*ah*-drah = block

cuál(es): koo*ahl*, koo-ah-lehs = which, what

cuándo: koo*ahn*-doh = when

cuánto: koo*ahn*-toh = how much

cuarto (m): koo*ahr*-toh = fourth

cuarto (m): koo*ahr*-toh = quarter

cuarto (m): koo*ahr*-toh = room

cubrir: koobv-*reer* = to cover

cuchara (f): koo-*chah*-rah = spoon

cuello (m): koo*eh*-yoh = neck

cuenta (f): koo*ehn*-tah = account

cuenta bancaria (f): koo*ehn*-tah bvahn-kah-*reeah* = bank account

cuerpo (m): koo*ehr*-poh = body

cuidado (m): kooee-*dah*-doh = care

cumpleaños (m): koom-plee*ah*-nyohs = birthday

cuñada (f): koo-*nyah*-dah = sister-in-law

cuñado (m): koo-*nyah*-doh = brother-in-law

curioso: koo-ree*oh*-soh = curious

D

dar: dahr = to give

dar un paseo: dahr oon pah-*sehoh* = to take a walk

dato (m): *dah*-toh = data

de: deh = from

de antemano: deh ahn-teh-*mah*-noh = beforehand, in advance

de buena gana: deh bvoo*eh*-nah *gah*-nah = willingly

de nuevo: deh noo*eh*-bvoh = again

de repente: deh reh-*pehn*-teh = suddenly

de retraso: deh reh-*trah*-soh = late (in arriving)

de vez en cuando: deh bvehs ehn koo*ahn*-doh = from time to time

deber: deh-*bvehr* = to have to

débil: *deh*-bveel = weak

débito (m): *deh*-bvee-toh = debit

decidir: deh-see-*deer* = to decide

décimo (m): *deh*-see-moh = tenth

decir: deh-*seer* = to tell, say

dedo (f): *deh*-doh = finger

dedo del pie (m): *deh*-doh dehl pee*eh* = toe

defender: deh-fehn-*dehr* = to defend

dejar (el trabajo): deh-*hahr* (ehl trah-*bvah*-hoh) = to quit (work)

delante (de): deh-*lahn*-teh (deh) = in front of

delgado: dehl-*gah*-doh = thin

delicioso: deh-lee-see*oh*-soh = delicious

demasiado/a (m, f): deh-mah-see*ah*-doh/dah = rather, too, too much

demostrar: deh-mohs-*trahr* = to demonstrate

dentista (m): dehn-*tees*-tah = dentist

dentro (de): *dehn*-troh (deh) = inside (of)

deporte (m): deh-*pohr*-teh = sport

deportivo: deh-pohr-*tee*-bvoh = sporty

deprimido: deh-pree-*mee*-doh = depressed

derecha (f): deh-*reh*-chah = right

derecho (m): deh-*reh*-choh = straight

derramar: deh-rrah-*mahr* = to spill

desafortunadamente: deh-sah-fohr-too-nah-dah-*mehn*-teh = unfortunately

desayunarse: deh-sah-yoo-*nahr*-seh = to have breakfast

desayuno (m): deh-sah-*yoo*-noh = breakfast

descansar: dehs-kahn-*sahr* = to rest

desconocido/a (m, f): dehs-kohn-oh-*see*-doh/dah = stranger

describir: dehs-kree-*bveer* = to describe

descubrir: dehs-koobv-*reer* = to discover

descuidado: dehs-kooee-*dah*-doh = untidy

desde: *dehs*-deh = from, since

desear: deh-seh*ahr* = to desire, to wish, to want

desenfrenadamente: deh-sehn-freh-nah-dah-*mehn*-teh = unrestrainedly

desfile (m): dehs-*fee*-leh = parade

desmayarse: dehs-mah-*yahr*-seh = to faint

despacio: dehs-*pah*-seeoh = slowly

despedir(se) (i): dehs-peh-*deer* (seh) = to say goodbye

despertar(se) (ie): dehs-pehr-*tahr* (seh) = to wake up

después: dehs-poo*ehs* = after

destruir: dehs-troo*eer* = to destroy

desvestirse (i): dehs-bvehs-*teer*-seh = to get undressed

devolver (ue): deh-bvol-*bvehr* = to return

día (m): *dee*ah = day

diario (m): dee*ah*-reeoh = newspaper

dibujo (m): dee-*bvoo*-Hoh = drawing; pattern

diccionario (m): deek-seeohn-*ah*-reeoh = dictionary

diciembre (m): dee-see*ehm*-bvreh = December

diente (m): dee*ehn*-teh = tooth

difícil: dee-*fee*-seel = difficult

dinero (m): dee-*neh*-roh = money

dirección (f): dee-rehk-see-*ohn* = address

discutir: dees-koo-*teer* = to discuss, to debate

disponible: dees-poh-*nee*-bvleh = available

distinguir: dees-teen-*geer* = to distinguish

distribuir: dees-tree-bvoo*eer* = to distribute

divertido: dee-bvehr-*tee*-doh = amusing; funny

divertirse (ie): dee-bvehr-*teer*-seh = to have fun

doblar: doh-*bvlahr* = to turn

doce: *doh*-seh = twelve

doler (ue): doh-*lehr* = to hurt

dolor (m): doh-*lohr* = pain

dolor de muelas (m): doh-*lohr* deh moo*eh*-lahs = toothache

domingo (m): doh-*meen*-goh = Sunday

¿dónde?: *dohn*-deh = where

dormir (ue): dohr-*meer* = to sleep

dormirse (ue): dohr-*meer*-seh = to fall asleep

dos: dohs = two

ducharse: doo-*chahr*-seh = to take a shower

duda (f): *doo*-dah = doubt

dudar: doo-*dahr* = to doubt

dudoso: doo-*doh*-soh = doubtful

dulce: *dool*-seh = sweet

durante: doo-*rahn*-teh= during

durazno (m): doo-*rahs*-noh = peach

E

edificio (m): eh-dee-*fee*-seeoh = building

eficiente: eh-fee-seee*ehn*-teh = efficient

egoísta: eh-goh*ees*-tah = selfish

ejercicio (m): eh-hehr-*see*-seeoh = exercise

el: ehl = the

él: ehl = he

elegante: eh-leh-*gahn*-teh = elegant

elegir (i): eh-leh-*Heer* = to elect

ella: *eh*-yah = she

ellos, ellas: *eh*-yohs, *eh*-yahs = they

embotellada: ehm-bvoh-teh-*yah*-dah = bottled

emocionado: eh-moh-seeoh-*nah*-doh = excited

empezar: ehm-peh-*sahr* = to begin; to start

empleo (m): ehm-*pleh*-oh = job

empujar: ehm-poo-*hahr* = to push

en: ehn = in, on, at

en seguida: ehn seh-*gee*-dah = immediately

en taxi: ehn *tahk*-see = by taxi

en vez de: ehn vehs deh = instead of

encantado: ehn-kahn-*tah*-doh = delighted

encantador: ehn-kahn-tah-*dohr* = enchanting

encender (ie): ehn-sehn-*dehr* = to light

encontrar: ehn-kohn-*trahr* = to find

encontrarse (ue): ehn-kohn-*trahr*-seh = to meet, be located

encuesta (f): ehn-*kooehs*-tah = survey

enemigo (m): eh-neh-*mee*-goh = enemy

enero (m): eh-*neh*-roh = January

enfadado: ehn-fah-*dah*-doh = angry

enfadar: ehn-fah-*dahr* = to anger, irritate

enfadarse (con): ehn-fah-*dahr*-seh (kohn) = to get angry, annoyed (with)

enfermero/a (m, f): ehn-fehr-*meh*-roh/ rah = nurse

enfermo/a (m, f): ehn-*fehr*-moh = sick person

enfrente (de): ehn-*frehn*-teh (deh) = in front (of)

engañar: ehn-gah-*nyahr* = to deceive

engañarse: ehn-gah-*nyahr*-seh = to be mistaken

enojado: eh-noh-*Hah*-do = angry, mad

enojarse: eh-noh-*Hahr*-seh = to become angry

ensalada (f): ehn-sah-*lah*-dah = salad

enseñar: ehn-seh-*nyahr* = to teach

entender (ie): ehn-tehn-*dehr* = to understand

entero (m): ehn-*teh*-roh = whole

entonces: ehn-*tohn*-sehs = then

entradas (f): ehn-*trah*-dahs = hors d'oeuvres

entre: *ehn*-treh = between

entrenador/a (m, f): ehn-treh-nah-*dohr*/ rah= coach

entrevista (f): ehn-treh-*bvees*-tah = interview

enviar: ehn-bvee*ahr* = to send

envolver (ue): ehn-bvohl-*bvehr* (oo-eh) = to wrap up

equipaje (m): eh-kee-*pah*-Heh = baggage

equipo (m): eh-*kee*-poh = team

equivocarse: eh-kee-bvoh-*kahr*-seh = to make a mistake, to be mistaken

escaparate (m): ehs-kah-pah-*rah*-teh = store window

escena (f): ehs-*seh*-nah = scene

escoger: ehs-koh-*hehr* = to choose

esconder: ehs-kohn-*dehr* = to hide (something)

esconder(se): ehs-kohn-*dehr*(seh) = to hide (oneself)

escribir: ehs-kree-*bveer* = to write

escritor/a (m, f): ehs-kree-*tohr*/rah = writer

escuchar: ehs-koo-*chahr* = to listen; to hear

escuela (f): ehs-*kooeh*-lah = school

escultura (f): ehs-kool-*too*-rah = sculpture

ese, esa: *eh*-seh, *eh*-sah = that

ése, ésa: *eh*-seh, *eh*-sah = that one

esencial: eh-sehn-see*ahl* = essential

esos, esas: *eh*-sohs, *eh*-sahs = those

ésos, ésas: *eh*-sohs, *eh*-sahs = those ones

español (m): ehs-pah-*nyohl* = Spanish (language)

español/a (m, f): ehs-pah-*nyohl*/ah = Spanish (person)

esparcir: ehs-pahr-*seer* = to spread out

especial: ehs-peh-see*ahl* = special

especialmente: ehs-peh-seeahl-*mehn*-teh = especially

espectáculo (m): eh-spehk-*tah*-koo-loh = show

esperar: ehs-peh-*rahr* = to wait, to hope

espinaca (f): ehs-pee-*nah*-kah = spinach

esposo/a (m, f): ehs-*poh*-soh/sah = spouse

esquí (m): ehs-*kee* = ski

esquiar: ehs-kee*ahr* = to ski

esquina (f): ehs-*kee*-nah = corner

estación (m): ehs-tah-see*ohn* = station

estacionamiento (m): ehs-tah-seeoh-nah-mee*ehn*-toh = parking

estadio (m): ehs-*tah*-deeoh = stadium

estado (m): ehs-*tah*-doh = state

estallar: ehs-tah-*yahr* = to break out

estar: ehs-*tahr* = to be

este, esta: *ehs*-teh, *ehs*-tah = this

éste, ésta: *ehs*-teh, *ehs*-tah = this one

estómago (m): ehs-*toh*-mah-goh = stomach

estos, estas: *ehs*-tohs, *ehs*-tahs = these

éstos, éstas: *ehs*-tahs = these ones

estrecho: ehs-*treh*-choh = narrow

estreñimiento (m): ehs-treh-nyee-mee*ehn*-toh = constipation

estupendo: ehs-too-*pehn*-doh = stupendous

evidente: eh-bvee-*dehn*-teh = evident

exacto: ehk-*sahk*-toh = exact

examinar: ehk-sah-mee-*nahr* = to test, examine

excelente: ehk-seh-*lehn*-teh = excellent

excesivo: ehk-seh-*see*-bvoh = excessive

exigir: ehk-see-*Heer* = to require, to demand

expedir (i): ehks-peh-*deer* = to dispatch, issue

explicación (f): ehks-plee-*kah*-seeohn = explanation

explicar: ehks-plee-*kahr* = to explain

exposición (f): ehks-poh-*see*-seeohn = exhibit

extraer: ehks-trah-*ehr* = to extract

extranjero: ehks-trahn-*Heh*-roh = foreign

extraño: ehks-*trah*-nyoh = strange

F

fábrica (f): *fah*-bvree-kah = factory

fácil: *fah*-seel = easy

falda (f): *fahl*-dah = skirt

familia (f): fah-*mee*-leeah = family

famoso: fah-*moh*-soh = famous

farmacia (f): fahr-*mah*-seeah = pharmacy

fastidiado: fahs-tee-dee*ah*-doh = bothered

fe (f): feh = faith

febrero (m): feh-*bvreh*-roh = February

fecha (f): *feh*-chah = date

felicidad (f): feh-lee-see-*dahd* = happiness

feliz: feh-*lees* = happy

feo: *feh*-oh = ugly

feroz: *feh*-rohs = ferocious

ferozmente: feh-rohs-*mehn*-teh = ferociously

festín (m): fehs-*teen* = feast

fiarse de: fee*ahr*-seh deh = to trust

fideo (m): fee-*de*-oh = pasta

fiebre (f): fee*eh*-bvreh = fever

fiesta (f): fee*ehs*-tah = party

fijarse (en): fee-*Hahr*-seh (ehn) = to notice

finalmente: fee-nahl-*mehn*-teh = finally

firmar: feer-*mahr* = to sign

físico: *fee*-see-koh = physical

flaco: *flah*-koh = skinny

flojera (f): floh-*Heh*-rah = weakness, laziness

flojo: *floh*-Hoh = loose, slack, lazy

folleto (m): foh-*yeh*-toh = brochure

fortaleza (f): fohr-tah-*leh*-sah = fort

fotografiar: foh-toh-grah-fee*ahr* = to photograph

fotógrafo/a (m, f): foh-*toh*-grah-foh/fah = photographer

franqueza: frah-*keh*-sah = frankness

frecuentemente: freh-kooehn-teh-*mehn*-teh = frequently

fresa (f): *freh*-sah = strawberry (Mexico, Central America, and Spain)

fresco: *frehs*-koh = cool

frío: *free*oh = cold

fruta (f): *froo*-tah = fruit

frutilla (f): froo-*tee*-yah = strawberry (from Colombia to the South Pole)

fuera: foo*eh*-rah = outside

furioso: foo-ree*oh*-soh = furious

fútbol (m): *foot*-bvohl = soccer

G

gabinete (m): gah-bvee-*neh*-teh = cabinet (government)

galletas (f): gah-*yeh*-tahs = cookies; crackers

ganar: gah-*nahr* = to earn, win

ganga (f): *gahn*-gah = bargain

ganso (m): *gan*-soh = goose

garantía (f): gah-rahn-*tee*ah = warranty

garganta (f): gahr-*gahn*-tah = throat

gastar: gah-*stahr* = to spend

gastos (m): *gahs*-tohs = expenses

gato (m): *gah*-toh = cat

generoso: Heh-neh-*roh*-soh = generous

genial: Heh-nee*ahl* = pleasant

gerente (m, f): Heh-*rehn*-teh = manager

gimnasio (m): Heem-*nah*-seeoh = gym

globo (m): *gloh*-bvoh = balloon, globe

gordo: *gohr*-doh = fat

grabación (f): grah-bvah-see*ohn* = tape recording

gracias: *grah*-seeahs = thank you

grande: *grahn*-deh = big; large

gris: grees = grey

gritar: gree-*tahr* = to scream

guantera (f): gooahn-*teh*-rah = glove compartment

guapo: goo*ah*-poh = pretty, good-looking

guayaba (f): gooah-*yah*-bvah = guava

guerra (f): *geh*-rrah = war

guía (m, f) *ghee*ah = guide

guiar: gee-*ahr* = to guide

guisante (m): gee-*sahn*-teh = pea

gustar: goos-*tahr* = to like

H

habituar: ah-bvee-too*ahr* = to accustom

hablador: ah-bvlah-*dohr* = talkative

hablar: ah-*bvlahr* = to talk, speak

hace (+ time): *ah*-seh = ago

hacer ejercicio: *ah*-sehr eh-Hehr-*see*-seeoh = to exercise

hacer: ah-*sehr* = to make, to do

hacerse: ah-*sehr*-seh = to become

hambre: *ahm*-bvreh = hunger

hay: ahy = there is, are

hecho a mano: *eh*-choh ah *mah*-noh = hand made

helado (m): eh-*lah*-doh = ice cream

helar (ie): eh-*lahr* = to freeze

herencia (f): ehr-*ehn*-seeah = inheritance

hermana (f): ehr-*mah*-nah = sister

hermano (m): ehr-*mah*-noh = brother

hígado (m): *ee*-gah-doh = liver

higo (m): *ee*-goh = fig

hija (f): *ee*-Hah = daughter

hijo (m): *ee*-Hoh = son

hijos (m): *ee*-Hohs = children

hombre (m): *ohm*-bvreh = man

hombro (m): *ohm*-bvroh = shoulder

hora (f): *oh*-rah = hour

horrible: hoh-*rree*-bvleh = horrible

hospedar: ohs-peh-*dahr* = to house

hoy: ohy = today

hoy (en) día: ohy (ehn) *dee*ah = nowadays

huachinango (m): ooah-chee-*nahn*-goh = red snapper

hueso (m): oo*eh*-soh = bone

huéspedes (m): oo*ehs*-peh-dehs = guests

huevo (m): oo*eh*-bvoh = egg

I

identificación (f): ee-dehn-tee-fee-kah-see*ohn* = identification

idioma (m): ee-dee*oh*-mah = language

iglesia (f): ee-*gleh*-seeah = church

imperativo: eem-peh-rah-*tee*-bvoh = imperative

impermeable (m): eem-pehr-meh-*ah*-bleh = raincoat

importante: eem-pohr-*tahn*-teh = important

imposible: eem-poh-*see*-bvleh = impossible

imprimir: eem-pree-*meer* = to print

improbable: eem-proh-*bvah*-bvleh = improbable

impuesto (m): eem-poo*ehs*-toh = tax

incluido: een-kloo*ee*-doh = included

incluir: een-kloo*eer* = to include

increíble: een-kreh*ee*-bvleh = incredible

indispensable: een-dees-pehn-*sah*-bvleh = indispensable

infeliz: een-feh-*lees* = unhappy

ingeniero/a (m, f): een-Heh-nee*eh*-roh/rah = engineer

inglés (m): een-*glehs* = English (language)

inglés/a (m, f): een-*glehs*/ah = English (person)

ingrediente (m): een-greh-dee*ehn*-teh = ingredient

ingresar: een-greh-*sahr* = to deposit

injusto: een-*Hoo*-stoh = unfair

inmigración (f): een-mee-grah-see*ohn* = immigration

inodoro: ee-noh-*doh*-roh = without a smell

insistir: een-sees-*teer* = to insist

institución de beneficencia (f): een-stee-too-see*ohn* deh bveh-neh-fee-*sehn*-seeah = charity organization

inteligente: een-teh-lee-*Hehn*-teh = intelligent

interesante: een-teh-reh-*sahn*-teh = interesting

intestino (m): een-tehs-*tee*-noh = bowel; intestine; gut

invierno (m): een-bvee*ehr*-noh = winter

ir: eer = to go

ir de compras: eer deh *kohm*-prahs = to go shopping

irónico: ee-*roh*-nee-koh = ironic

irritado: ee-rree-*tah*-doh = irritated

irse: *eer*-seh = to go away

isla (f): *ees*-lah = island

izquierda: ees-kee*ehr*-dah = left

J

jardín (m): Hahr-*deen* = garden

jarrón (m): Hah-*rrohn* = vase

jefe (m): *Heh*-feh = boss

joven: *Hoh*-bvehn = young

jueves (m): Hoo*eh*-bvehs = Thursday

juez (m, f): Hoo*ehs* = judge

jugar (ue): Hoo-*gahr* = to play

jugar (ue) a las damas: Hoo-*gahr* ah lahs *dah*-mahs = to play checkers

jugo (m): Hoo-goh = juice

juguete (m): Hoo-*geh*-teh = toy

julio (m): Hoo-leeoh = July

junio (m): Hoo-neeoh = June

junto: Hoon-toh = together

justo: Hoos-toh = fair

juzgar: Hoos-*gahr* = to judge

L

la: lah = the; her, it

ladrar: lah-*drahr* = to bark

lago (m): *lah*-goh = lake

lamentable: lah-mehn-*tah*-bvleh = regrettable

lamentar: lah-mehn-*tahr* = to regret

lana (f): *lah*-nah = wool

langostino (m): lahn-gohs-*tee*-noh = prawn

lápiz (m): *lah*-pees = pencil

largo: *lahr*-goh = long

las: lahs = the; them

lástima (f): *lahs*-tee-mah = pity; shame

lavar: lah-*bvahr* = to wash

lavarse: lah-*bvahr*-seh = to wash oneself

le: leh = to him, to her, to you formal

leal: leh-*ahl* = loyal

lección (f): lehk-see*ohn* = lesson

leche (f): *leh*-cheh = milk

lechuga (f): leh-*choo*-gah = lettuce

leer: leh-*ehr* = to read

lejos: *leh*-Hohs = far

lentamente: lehn-tah-*mehn*-teh = slowly

les: lehs = to them, to you plural

levantar: leh-bvahn-*tahr* = to raise (something)

levantarse: leh-bvahn-*tahr*-seh = to get up

ley (f): *leh* = law

libra (f): *lee*-bvrah = pound

libre: *lee*-bvreh = free

libro (m): *lee*-bvroh = book

ligero: lee-*Heh*-roh = light, swift

limón (m): lee-*mohn* = lemon

limpiar: leem-pee*ahr* = to clean

línea (f): *lee*-neh-ah = line

lisonjeado: lee-sohn-Heh-*ah*-doh = flattered

listo: *lees*-toh = ready

llamar: yah-*mahr* = to call

llamarse: yah-*mahr*-seh = to be called, to call oneself

llave (f): *yah*-bveh = key

llegar: yeh-*gahr* = to arrive

llevar: yeh-*bvahr* = to wear

llorar: yoh-*rahr* = to cry

llover (ue): yoh-*bvehr* = to rain

lluvia (f): *yoo*-bveeah = rain

lo: loh = him, it

lodo (m): *loh*-doh = mud

los: lohs = the, them

luego: loo*eh*-goh = later

lugar (m): loo-*ghar* = place

lujoso: loo-*Hoh*-soh = luxurious

luna (f): *loo*-nah = moon

lunes (m): *loo*-nehs = Monday

M

madera (f): mah-*deh*-rah = wood

madre (f): *mah*-dreh = mother

madrina (f): mah-*dree*-nah = godmother

magnífico: mahg-*nee*-fee-koh = magnificent

maleta (f): mah-*leh*-tah = luggage; suitcase

malo: *mah*-loh = bad

mañana (f): mah-*nyah*-nah = morning

mañana (f): mah-*nyah*-nah = tomorrow

mandar: mahn-*dahr* = to command, to order, to send

manejar: mah-neh-*Hahr* = to drive, to operate, to manage

manga (f): *mahn*-gah = sleeve

mango (m): *mahn*-goh = mango

mantel (m): mahn-*tehl* = tablecloth

mantequilla (f): mahn-teh-*kee*-yah = butter

manzana (f): mahn-*sah*-nah = apple

mapa (m): *mah*-pah = map

maquillarse: mah-kee-*yahr*-seh = to put on makeup

máquina (f): *mah*-kee-nah = machine

mar (m): mahr = sea

maravilloso: mah-rah-bvee-*yoh*-soh = marvelous

marcar: mahr-*kahr* = to mark; to dial; to punch in the number

marcharse: mahr-*chahr*-seh = to go away

marea (f): mah-*reh*-ah = tide

mareo (m): mah-*reh*-oh = dizziness

maridos (m): mah-*ree*-dohs = married couple

mariposa (f): mah-ree-*poh*-sah = butterfly

marisco (m): mah-*rees*-koh = seafood

marrón: mah-*rrohn* = brown

martes (m): *mahr*-tehs = Tuesday

marzo (m): *mahr*-soh = March

más: mahs = more

más tarde: mahs *tahr*-deh = later

masticar: mahs-tee-*kahr* = to chew

materialista: mah-teh-reeah-*lees*-tah = materialistic

matrícula (f): mah-*tree*-koo-lah = tuition

mayo (m): *mah*-yoh = May

me: meh = me, to me

medicina (f): meh-dee-*see*-nah = medicine

médico/a (m, f): *meh*-dee-koh/kah = physician; doctor

medio (m): *meh*-deeoh = half

medio baño (m): *meh*-deeoh *bvah*-nyoh = half-bathroom (a bathroom with no shower or tub)

mediodía (m): meh-deeoh-*dee*-ah = noon

medir (i): meh-*deer* = to measure

mejor: meh-*Hohr* = best

melón (m): meh-*lohn* = melon

memorizar: meh-moh-ree-*sahr* = to memorize

menos: *meh*-nohs = less

mensajero/a (m, f): mehn-sah-*Heh*-roh/rah = messenger

mentir: mehn-*teer* = to lie

merecer: meh-reh-*sehr* = to deserve

mes (m): mehs = month

mesa (f): *meh*-sah = table

metro (m): *meh*-troh = subway

mezclar: mehs-*klahr* = to mix

mi(s): mee(s) = my

mientras: mee*ehn*-trahs = while

miércoles (m): mee*ehr*-koh-lehs = Wednesday

mil (m): meel = one thousand

milla (f): *mee*-yah = mile

millón (m): mee-*yohn* = one million

minuto (m): mee-*noo*-toh = minute

mío/a(s) (m, f, pl.): *mee*-oh(s)/ah(s) = mine

mirar: mee-*rahr* = to look at, to watch

mismo: *mees*-moh = same

mochila (f): moh-*chee*-lah = backpack

moda (f): *moh*-dah = style

moderno: moh-*dehr*-noh = modern

mojado: moh-*Hah*-doh = wet

moneda (f): moh-*neh*-dah = coin

montaña (f): mohn-*tah*-nyah = mountain

mora (f): *moh*-rah = blackberry

morado: moh-*rah*-doh = purple

moreno: moh-*reh*-noh = dark-haired

morir (ue): moh-*reer* = to die

mostaza: mohs-*tah*-sah = mustard

mostrar (ue): mohs-*trahr* = to show

mucho: *moo*-choh = a lot; much

mueble (m): moo*eh*-bvleh = furniture

mujer (f): moo-*Hehr* = woman

muñeca (f): moo-*nyeh*-kah = wrist

muñeco de nieve (m): moo-*nyeh*-koh deh nee*eh*-bveh = snowman

museo (m): moo-*seh*-oh = museum

música clásica (f): *moo*-see-kah *klah*-see-kah = classical music

muslo (m): *moos*-loh = thigh

muy: *moo*ee = very

N

nacer: nah-*sehr* = to be born

nada: *nah*-dah = nothing

nadar: nah-*dahr* = to swim

nadie: *nah*-deeeh = nobody, no one

naipe (m): *nah*ee-peh = card (playing)

naranja (f): nah-*rahn*-Hah = orange

nariz (f): nah-*rees* = nose

natación (f): nah-tah-see*ohn* = swimming

natural: nah-too-*rahl* = natural

necesario: neh-seh-*sah*-reeoh = necessary

necesitar: neh-seh-see-*tahr* = to need

negar (ie): neh-*gahr* = to deny

negro: *neh*-groh = black

nevar (ie): neh-*bvahr* = to snow

ni . . . ni: nee . . . nee = neither . . . nor

nieta (f): nee*eh*-tah = granddaughter

nieto (m): nee*eh*-toh = grandson

niña (f): *nee*-nyah = girl

ningún: neen-*goon* = none

niño (m): *nee*-nyoh = boy

no: noh = no, not

noche (f): *noh*-cheh = night

nos: nohs = us, to us, ourselves

nosotros: noh-*soh*-trohs = we, us

noticias (f): noh-*tee*-seeahs = news

novela (f): noh-*bveh*-lah = novel

noveno: noh-*bveh*-noh = ninth

noviembre (m): noh-bvee*ehm*-bvreh = November

novio/a (m,f): *noh*-bveeoh/ah = boyfriend/girlfriend

nube (f): *noo*-bveh = cloud

nuera (f): noo*eh*-rah = daughter-in-law

nuestro/a (s): noo*ehs*-troh(s)/trah(s) = our (ours)

nuevo: noo*eh*-bvoh = new

número (m): *noo*-meh-roh = number

nunca: *noon*-kah = never

O

o: oh = or

obedecer: oh-bveh-deh-*sehr* = to obey

obvio: *ohb*-bveeoh = obvious

octavo: ohk-*tah*-bvoh = eighth

octubre (m): ohk-*too*-bvreh = October

ocupado: oh-koo-*pah*-doh = occupied; busy

ofrecer: oh-freh-*sehr* = to offer, give

oír: oh*eer* = to hear

ojalá que . . .: oh-Hah-*lah* keh = if only . . .

ojo (m): *oh*-Hoh = eye

oler: oh-*lehr* = to smell

olla (f): *oh*-yah = pot

olvidar: ohl-bvee-*dahr* = to forget

olvidarse (de): ohl-bvee-*dahr*-seh (deh)= to forget about

once: *ohn*-seh = eleven

oponer: oh-poh-*nehr* = to oppose

optimista: ohp-tee-*mees*-tah = optimistic

ordenar: ohr-deh-*nahr* – to order (command)

ordinario: ohr-dee-*nah*-reeoh = ordinary

oreja (f): oh-*reh*-Hah = ear

orgulloso: ohr-goo-*yoh*-soh = proud

orina (f): oh-*ree*-nah = urine

oro (m): *oh*-roh = gold

os: ohs = you, to you, yourselves

oscuro: ohs-*koo*-roh = dark

otoño (m): oh-*toh*-nyoh = autumn

otro: *oh*-troh = another

P

paciencia (f): pah-see*ehn*-seeah = patience

padre (m): *pah*-dreh = father

padrino (m): pah-*dree*-noh = godfather

pagado: pah-*gah*-doh = paid for

pagar: pah-*gahr* = to pay

país (m): pah*ees* = country

pájaro (m): *pah*-Hah-roh = bird

palabra (f): pah-*lah*-bvrah = word

palomitas de maíz (f): pah-loh-*mee*-tahs deh mah*ees* = popcorn

panadero/a (m, f): pah-nah-*deh*-roh/rah = baker

pantalla (f): pahn-*tah*-yah = screen

pantalones (m): pahn-tah-*loh*-nehs = trousers

pantorrilla (f): pahn-toh-*rree*-yah = calf

papas (f): *pah*-pahs = potatoes

papas fritas (f): *pah*-pahs *free*-tahs = potato chips

papaya (f): pah-*pah*-yah = papaya

papel (m): pah-*pehl* = paper, role

paquete (m): pah-*keh*-teh = package

para: *pah*-rah = for

parar: pah-*rahr* = to stop (something)

pararse: pah-*rahr*-seh = to stop oneself

parecer: pah-reh-*sehr* = to seem

parque (m): *pahr*-keh = park

partido (m): pahr-*tee*-doh = (sports) game

pasado: pah-*sah*-doh = past, last

pasaporte (m): pah-sah-*pohr*-teh = document; paper; passport

pasar: pah-*sahr* = to spend (time)

pasearse: pah-seh*ahr*-seh = to go for a walk

paseo (m): pah-*seh*-oh = walk

pasillo (m): pah-*see*-yoh = aisle

pastel (m): pahs-*tehl* = cake

patín: pah-*teen* = skate

pato (m): *pah*-toh = duck

peaje (m): peh-*ah*-Heh = toll

pecho (m): *peh*-choh = chest

pedir (i): peh-*deer* = to ask for

peinarse: peh-*nahr*-seh = to comb one's hair

pelar: peh-*lahr* = to peel

pelea (f): peh-*leh*-ah = fight

película (f): peh-*lee*-koo-lah = movie, film

peligroso: peh-lee-*groh*-soh = dangerous

pelo (m): *peh*-loh = hair

pensar: pehn-*sahr* = to think

peor: peh-*ohr* = worse

pequeño: peh-*keh*-nyoh = small

pera (f): *peh*-rah = pear

perder: pehr-*dehr* = to lose

perezoso: peh-reh-*soh*-soh = lazy

perfeccionar: pehr-fehk-seeoh-*nahr* = to perfect

perfecto: pehr-*fehk*-toh = perfect

periódico (m): peh-ree*oh*-dee-koh = newspaper

perla (f): *pehr*-lah = pearl

permitir: pehr-mee-*teer* = to permit

pero: *peh*-roh = but

perro (m): *peh*-rroh = dog

pescado (m): pehs-*kah*-doh = fish (to eat)

pescar: pehs-*kahr* = to fish

pesimista: peh-see-*mees*-tah = pessimistic

peso: *peh*-soh = weight

pez (m): pehs = fish (live)

picante: pee-*kahn*-teh = hot [flavor]

pie (m): pee*eh* = foot

pierna (f): pee*ehr*-nah = leg

piloto/a (m,f): pee-*loh*-toh/tah = pilot

piña (f): *pee*-nyah = pineapple

pintar: peen-*tahr* = to paint

pintura (f): peen-*too*-rah = painting

piscina (f): pees-*see*-nah = swimming pool

piso (m): *pee*-soh = floor

planchar: plahn-*chahr* = to iron

plátano (m): *plah*-tah-noh = banana

plato (m): *plah*-toh = plate

platos (m): *plah*-tohs = dishes

playa (f): *plah*-yah = beach

plaza (f): *plah*-sah = square

plomo (m): *ploh*-moh = lead

pobre: *poh*-bvreh = poor

poco (m): *poh*-koh = a bit; a small amount

poder (ue): poh-*dehr* = to be able to, can

pollo (m): *poh*-yoh = chicken

polvo (m): *pohl*-bvoh = dust

poner (la mesa): poh-*nehr* (lah *meh*-sah) = to set (the table)

ponerse: poh-*nehr*-seh = to put (something on), to become, to place oneself

popular: poh-poo-*lahr* = popular

por: pohr = for, per

por ciento: pohr see*ehn*-toh = percent

por consiguiente: pohr kohn-see-gee*ehn*-teh = consequently

por favor: pohr fah-*bvohr* = please

¿por qué?: *pohr* keh = why

por supuesto: pohr soo-poo*ehs*-toh = of course

porcentaje (m): pohr-sehn-*tah*-Heh = percentage

porción (f): pohr-see*ohn* = portion

porque: *pohr*-keh = because

posible: poh-*see*-bvleh = possible

potable: poh-*tah*-bvleh = drinkable

precio (m): *preh*-seeoh = price

precioso: preh-see*oh*-soh = gorgeous; beautiful; lovely

preferible: preh-feh-*ree*-bvleh = preferable

preferir (ie): preh-feh-*reer* = to prefer

preguntar: preh-goon-*tahr* = to ask (a question)

preocuparse (de): preoh-koo-*pahr*-seh (deh) = to worry (about)

presión sanguínea (f): preh-see*ohn* sahn-*gee*-neh-ah = blood pressure

prestar: preh-*stahr* = to borrow

prestar atención: prehs-tahr ah-tehn-see*ohn* = to pay attention

prima (f): *pree*-mah = cousin [female]

primavera (f): pree-mah-*bveh*-rah = spring

primero: pree-*meh*-roh = first

primo (m): *pree*-moh = cousin [male]

probable: proh-*bvah*-bvleh = probable

probador (m): proh-bvah-*dohr* = fitting room

probar(se): proh-*bvahr*(seh) = to try (on)

producir: proh-doo-*seer* = to produce

producto lácteo (m): proh-*dook*-toh *lahk*-tehoh = dairy product

profundamente: pro-foon-dah-*mehn*-teh = deeply

prohibir: proh-hee-*bveer* = to forbid

prometer: proh-meh-*tehr* = to promise

pronto: *prohn*-toh = right away, soon

pronunciar: proh-noon-see*ahr* = to pronounce

propietario/a (m, f): proh-peeeh-*tah*-reeoh/ah = proprietor, owner

propio: *proh*-peeoh = [one's] own

próximo: *prohk*-see-moh = next

proyecto (m): proh-*yehk*-toh = project

puerto (m): *pooehr*-toh = port

puesto (m): *pooehs*-toh = job, position

pulir: poo-*leer* = to polish

pulmón (m): pool-*mohn* = lung

pura: *poo*-rah = pure

Q

que: keh = that, than

¿qué?: keh = what

quedarse: keh-*dahr*-seh = to stay

quejarse (de): keh-*hahr*-seh (deh) = to complain (of, about)

quemadura (f): keh-mah-*doo*-rah = burn

queso (m): *keh*-soh = cheese

¿quién?: kee*ehn* = who, whom

química (f): *kee*-mee-kah = chemistry

quinto: *keen*-toh = fifth

quitar(se): keeh-*tahr*(seh) = to remove, to take off

R

receta (f): reh-*seh*-tah = prescription, recipe

recibo (m): reh-*see*-bvoh = receipt

reclamar: reh-klah-*mahr* = to demand

recordar: reh-kohr-*dahr* = to remember

reembolsar: reh-ehm-bvol-*sahr* = to refund

refresco (m): reh-*frehs*-koh = soft drink

refriarse: reh-free*ahr*-seh = to catch a cold

regalo (m): reh-*gah*-loh = gift

régimen (m): *reh*-gee-mehn = diet

regla (f): *reh*-glah = rule, ruler

reglamentos (m, pl.): rehg-lah-*mehn*-tohs = regulations

regresar: reh-greh-*sahr* = to return

reino (m): reh*ee*-noh = kingdom

reír: reh*eer* = to laugh

relámpagos: reh-*lahm*-pah-gohs = lightning

repetir: reh-peh-*teer* = to repeat

reservación (f): reh-sehr-bvah-see*ohn* = reservation

responder: rehs-pohn-*dehr* = to answer

respuesta (f): rehs-poo*ehs*-tah = answer

restaurante (m): rehs-tahoo-*rahn*-teh = restaurant

retiro: reh-*tee*-roh = withdrawal

reunión (f): rehoo-nee*ohn* = meeting

reunirse: rehoo-*neer*-seh = to meet

riñón (m): ree-*nyohn* = kidney

río (m): *ree*-oh = river

robar: roh-*bvahr* = to steal; to rob

robo (m): *roh*-bvoh = robbery

rojo: *roh*-Hoh = red

romper: rohm-*pehr* = to break

rosado: roh-*sah*-doh = pink

roto: *roh*-toh = broken, shattered

rótulo (m): *roh*-too-loh = label

ruido (m): roo*ee*-doh = noise

ruinas (f): roo*ee*-nahs = ruins

ruta (f): *roo*-tah = road, route

S

sábado (m): *sah*-bvah-doh = Saturday

saco (m): *sah*-koh = bag

sagaz: *sah*-gahs = astute, wise

sala (f): *sah*-lah = living room

salado: sah-*lah*-doh = salty

saldo (m): *sahl*-doh = balance

salir: sah-*leer* = to leave

saltar: sahl-*tahr* = to jump

saludable: sah-loo-*dah*-bvleh = healthy

sandía (f): sahn-*dee*-ah = watermelon

sangre (f): *sahn*-greh = blood

secar(se): seh-*kahr*(seh) = to dry (oneself)

seco: *seh*-koh = dry

sed: sehd = thirst

seda (f): *seh*-dah = silk

seguir: seh-*gheer* = to follow

segundo (m): seh-*goon*-doh = second

selva (f): *sehl*-bvah = rainforest

semana (f): seh-*mah*-nah = week

señal (f): seh-*nyahl* = sign

señalar: seh-nyah-*lahr* = to signal

sentir (ie): sehn-*teer* = to be sorry, to regret

septiembre (m): sehp-teee*hm*-breh = September

séptimo: *sehp*-tee-moh = seventh

ser: sehr = to be

sexto: *sehks*-toh = sixth

siempre: seee*hm*-preh = always

siguiente: see-geee*hm*-teh = next

sirviente/a (m, f): seer-*bveeehn*-teh/tah = servant

sol (m): sohl = sun

sonar (ue): soh-*nahr* = to ring

sorprendido: sohr-prehn-*dee*-doh = surprised

sorpresa (f): sohr-*preh*-sah = surprise

subterráneo: soobv-teh-*rrah*-neh-oh = underground

suelo (m): soo*eh*-loh = ground

suelto: soo*ehl*-toh = loose

suerte (f): soo*ehr*-teh = luck

suéter (m): soo*eh*-tehr = sweater

suficiente: soo-fee-*seeehn*-teh = enough

sugerir (ie): soo-Heh-*reer* = to suggest

supermercado (m): soo-pehr-mehr-*kah*-doh = supermarket

suprimir: soo-pree-*meer* = to suppress

T

tabla (f): *tah*-bvlah = board [wood]

tal vez: tahl bvehs = perhaps

talla (f): *tah*-yah = size (of a person)

tamaño (m): tah-*mah*-nyoh = size (of a place or object)

también: tahm-bvee*ehn* = also, too

tampoco: tahm-*poh*-koh = neither; not . . . either

tarde (f): *tahr*-deh = afternoon, late

tarjeta (f): tahr-*Heh*-tah = card

teatro (m): teh-*ah*-troh = theater

teclado (m): teh-*klah*-doh = keyboard

tele (f): *teh*-leh = TV (colloquial)

televisión (f): teh-leh-bvee-see*ohn* = television

tempestad (f): tehm-pehs-*tahd* = storm

temprano: tehm-*prah*-noh = early

tener (ie): teh-*nehr* = to have

tercero: tehr-*seh*-roh = third

terminar: tehr-mee-*nahr* = to finish

tía (f): *tee*-ah = aunt

tiempo (m): teee*hm*-poh = time

tiempo (m): teee*hm*-poh = weather

tienda (f): tee*ehn*-dah = store

tierra (f): tee*eh*-rrah = land

timbre (m): *teem*-breh = bell

tintorería (f): teen-toh-reh-*ree*ah = dry cleaner

tío (m): *tee*oh = uncle

típica: *tee*-pee-kah = typical

título (m): tee-*too*-loh = degree

tobillo (m): toh-*bvee*-yoh = ankle

todavía: toh-dah-*bvee*-ah = yet; still

todos (los domingos): *toh*-dohs (lohs doh-*meen*-gohs) = every (Sunday)

tomar el sol: toh-*mahr* ehl sohl = to sunbathe

toronja (f): toh-*rohn*-Hah = grapefruit

torpe: *tohr*-peh = clumsy

tos (f): tohs = cough

trabajador: trah-bvah-Hah-*dohr* = hard-working

traducir: trah-doo-*seer* = to translate

traer: trah-*ehr* = to bring

tráfico (m): *trah*-fee-koh = traffic

tragar: trah-*gahr* = to swallow

traje de baño (m): *tra*-Heh deh *bvah*-nyoh = swimsuit

tranquilo: trahn-*kee*-loh = quiet

tratar de: trah-*tahr* deh = to try to

tren (m): trehn = train

tronar (ue): troh-*nahr* = to thunder

trozo (m): *troh*-soh = piece

trucha (f): *troo*-chah = trout

truenos (m): troo*eh*-nohs = thunder

U

un rato: oon *rah*-toh = awhile

uniforme (m): oo-nee-*fohr*-meh = uniform

uva (f): *oo*-bvah = grape

V

vaciar: bvah-see*ahr* = to empty

valer: bvah-*lehr* = to be worth

vecindario (m): bveh-seen-*dah*-reeoh = neighborhood

vehículo (m): bveh-*ee*-koo-loh = vehicle

vender: bvehn-*dehr* = to sell

venir: bveh-*neer* = to come

venta (f): *bvehn*-tah = sale

ver: bvehr = to see

verano (m): bveh-*rah*-noh = summer

verdad (f): bvehr-*dahd* = truth

verde: *bvehr*-deh = green

vestir (i): bvehs-*teer* = to clothe

viajar: bveeah-*Hahr* = to travel

viaje (m): bvee*ah*-Heh = trip

viajero/a (m,f): bveeah-*Heh*-roh/rah = traveler

vida (f): *bvee*-dah = life

vidrio (m): *bvee*-dreeoh = glass

viernes (m): bvee*ehr*-nehs = Friday

vino (m): *bvee*-noh = wine

violeta: bveeoh-*leh*-tah = violet; purple

violín (m): bveeoh-*leen* = violin

víspera (f): *bvees*-peh-rah = eve

vivir: bvee-*bveer* = to live

volar: bvoh-*lahr* = to fly

volver (ue): bvohl-*bvehr* = to return

votar: bvoh-*tahr* = to vote

voz (f): bvohs = voice

vuelta (f): bvoo*ehl*-tah = lap

vuelto (m): *bvoo*oehl-toh = change (as in money back)

vuestro(s): *bvoo*oehs-troh = your, yours

Y

ya: yah = already

yerno (m): *yehr*-noh = son-in-law

Z

zanahoria (f): sah-nah-*oh*-reeah = carrot

Appendix C

English-Spanish Mini Dictionary

● ●

A

a bit/small amount: **poco** (*poh*-koh)

a lot/much: **mucho** (*moo*-choh)

abolish: **abolir** (ah-bvoh-*leer*)

absurd: **absurdo** (ahbv-*soor*-doh)

accompany: **acompañar** (ah-kohm-pah-*nyahr*)

account: **cuenta** (koo*ehn*-tah) f

accustom: **habituar** (ah-bvee-too*ahr*)

act: **actuar** (ahk-too*ahr*)

actor: **actor** (ahk-*tohr*) m

actress: **actriz** (ahk-*trees*)

add: **añadir** (ah-nyah-*deer*)

address: **dirección** (dee-rehk-see*ohn*) f

advice: **consejo** (kohn-*seh*-hoh) m

advise: **aconsejar** (ah-kohn-seh-*Hahr*)

affection: **cariño** (kah-*ree*-nyoh) m

after: **después** (dehs-poo*ehs*)

afternoon (p.m.): **tarde** (*tahr*-deh) f

afterward: **después** (dehs-poo*ehs*)

again: **de nuevo** (deh noo*eh*-bvoh)

agency: **agencia** (ah-*Hehn*-seeah) f

ago: **hace + (time)** (*ah*-seh + (time))

agree on: **acordar (ue)** (ah-kohr-*dahr*)

airport: **aeropuerto** (ah-eh-roh-poo*ehr*-toh) m

aisle: **pasillo** (pah-*see*-yoh) m

alarm: **alarma** (ah-*lahr*-mah)

all: **todo** (*toh*-doh)

almost: **casi** (*kah*-see)

already: **ya** (yah)

also/too: **también** (tahm-bvee*ehn*)

always: **siempre** (see*ehm*-preh)

amusing/funny: **divertido** (dee-bvehr-*tee*-doh)

anger/irritate: **enfadar** (ehn-fah-*dahr*)

angry: **enojado** (eh-noh-*Hah*-doh)

ankle: **tobillo** (toh-*bvee*-yoh) m

another: **otro** (*oh*-troh)

answer: **respuesta** (rehs-poo*ehs*-tah) f

answer: **contestar** (kohn-tehs-*tahr*); **responder** (rehs-pohn-*dehr*)

appear: **aparecer** (ah-pah-reh-*sehr*)

applaud: **aplaudir** (ah-plahoo-*deer*)

apple: **manzana** (mahn-*sah*-nah) f

apply (oneself): **aplicar(se)** (ah-plee-*kahr* (seh))

appointment/date: **cita** (*see*-tah) f

approach/near: **acercarse** (ah-sehr-*kahr*-seh)

April: **abril** (ah-*bvreel*) m

arm: **brazo** (*bvrah*-soh) m

around: **alrededor de** (ahl-reh-deh-*dohr* deh)

arrive: **llegar** (yeh-*gahr*)

as: **tan** (tahn)

ask (a question): **preguntar** (preh-goon-*tahr*)

ask for: **pedir (i)** (peh-*deer*)

astonished/surprised/amazed: **asombrado** (ah-sohm-*bvrah*-doh)

astute/wise: **sagaz** (sah-*gahs*)

at least: **por lo menos** (pohr loh *meh*-nohs)

at the disposition: **a las órdenes** (a lahs *ohr*-dehn-ehs)

atrocious: **atroz** (ah-*trohs*)

attack: **atacar** (ah-tah-*kahr*)

attend: **asistir** (ah-sees-*teer*)

attractive: **atractivo** (ah-trahk-*tee*-bvoh)

auditorium: **auditorio** (ahoo-dee-toh-ree*oh*) m

August: **agosto** (ah-*gohs*-toh) m

aunt: **tía** (*tee*-ah) f

autumn: **otoño** (oh-*toh*-nyoh) m

available: **disponible** (dees-poh-*nee*-bvleh)

avenue: **avenida** (ah-bveh-*nee*-dah) f

avocado: **aguacate** (ah-gooah-*kah*-teh) m

awhile: **un rato** (oon *rah*-toh)

B

baby carriage: **cochecito** (koh-cheh-*see*-toh) m

backpack: **mochila** (moh-*chee*-lah) f

bad: **malo** (*mah*-loh)

bag: **saco** (*sah*-koh) f

baggage: **equipaje** (eh-kee-*pah*-Heh) f

baker: **panadero/a** (pah-nah-*deh*-roh/rah) m, f

balance (of an account): **saldo** (*sahl*-doh) m

balcony: **balcón** (bvahl-*kohn*) m

balloon: **globo** (*gloh*-bvoh) m

banana: **plátano** (*plah*-tah-noh) m

bank: **banco** (*bvahn*-koh) m

bank account: **cuenta bancaria** (koo*ehn*-tah bahn-*kah*-reeah) f

banker: **banquero/a** (bvahn-*keh*-roh/rah) m, f

bargain: **ganga** (gahn-gah) f

bark: **ladrar** (lah-*drahr*)

basketball: **baloncesto** (bvah-lohn-*sehs*-toh) m

bat: **bate** (*bvah*-teh) m

bathe (someone): **bañar** (bvah-*nyahr*)

bathe oneself: **bañarse** (bvah-*nyahr*-seh)

bathroom: **baño** (*bvah*-nyoh) m

bathtub: **bañera** (bvah-*nyeh*-rah) f

be: **estar** (ehs-*tahr*); **ser** (sehr)

be able to: **poder (ue)** (poh-*dehr*)

be ashamed of: **avergonzarse de** (ah-bvehr-gohn-*sahr*-seh deh)

be born: **nacer** (nah-*sehr*)

be glad/happy: **alegrarse** (ah-lehg-*rahr*-seh)

be hungry: **tener hambre** (teh-*nehr* ahm-*bvreh*)

be lucky: **tener suerte** (teh-*nehr* soo*ehr*-teh)

be mistaken: **engañarse** (ehn-gah-*nyahr*-seh); **equivocarse** (eh-kee-bvoh-*kahr*-seh)

beach: **playa** (*plah*-yah) f

beautiful: **bello** (*bveh*-yoh)

because: **porque** (*pohr*-keh)

become: **hacerse** (ah-*sehr*-seh)

become angry: **enojarse** (eh-noh-*Hahr*-seh)

become annoyed: **enfadarse** (ehn-fah-*dahr*-seh)

become bored: **aburrirse** (ah-bvoo-*rreer*-seh)

become tired: **cansarse** (kahn-*sahr*-seh)

bed: **cama** (*kah*-mah) f

bee: **abeja** (ah-*bveh*-Hah) f

beer: **cerveza** (sehr-*bveh*-sah) f

before: **antes (de)** (*ahn*-tehs (deh))

beforehand/in advance: **de antemano** (deh ahn-teh-*mah*-noh)

begin: **comenzar (ie)** (koh-mehn-*sahr*)

begin/start: **empezar** (ehm-peh-*sahr*)

behavior: **comportamiento** (kohm-pohr-tah-mee*ehn*-toh) m

bell: **timbre** (*teem*-bvreh) m

best: **lo mejor/el mejor/la mejor/los mejores/las mejores** (loh meh-*Hohr*/ehl meh-*Hohr*/lah meh-*Hohr*/lohs-*Hohr*-ehs/lahs meh-*Hohr*-ehs)

better: **mejor** (meh-*Hohr*)

between: **entre** (*ehn*-treh)

bicycle: **bicicleta** (bvee-see-*kleh*-tah) f

big/large: **grande** (*grahn*-deh)

bill: **billete** (bvee-*yeh*-teh) m

bird: **pájaro** (*pah*-Hah-roh) m

birthday: **cumpleaños** (koom-plee*ah*-nyohs) m

black: **negro** (*neh*-groh)

blackberry: **mora** (*moh*-rah) f

block: **cuadra** (koo*ah*-drah) f

blood: **sangre** (*sahn*-greh) f

blood pressure: **presión sanguínea** (preh-see*ohn* sahn-*ghee*-neh-ah) f

blue: **azul** (ah-*sool*)

board [wood]: **tabla** (*tah*-bvlah) f

boat: **barco** (*bvahr*-koh) m

body: **cuerpo** (koo*ehr*-poh) m

bone: **hueso** (oo*eh*-soh) m

book: **libro** (*lee*-bvroh) m

bore: **aburrir** (ah-bvoo-*rreer*)

boring: **aburrido** (ah-bvoo-*rree*-doh)

borrow: **prestar** (preh-*stahr*)

boss: **jefe** (*Heh*-feh) m

bothered: **fastidiado** (fahs-tee-dee*ah*-doh)

bottle: **botella** (bvoh-*teh*-yoh) f

bottled: **embotellado** (ehm-bvoh-teh-*yah*-dah)

boulevard: **bulevar** (bvoo-leh-*bvahr*) m

bowel/intestine/gut: **intestino** (een-tehs-*tee*-noh) m

box: **caja** (*kah*-Hah) f

boy : **niño** (*nee*-nyoh) m

boyfriend: **novio** (*noh*-bveeoh) m

bracelet: **pulsera** (pool-*seh*-rah) f

break out: **estallar** (ehs-*tah*-yahr)

break: **romper** (rohm-*pehr*)

breakfast: **desayuno** (deh-sah-*yoo*-noh)

briefly: **brevemente** (bvreh-bveh-*mehn*-teh)

bring: **traer** (trah-*ehr*)

broccoli: **brócoli** (*bvroh*-koh-lee) m

brochure: **folleto** (foh-*yeh*-toh) m

broken/shattered: **roto** (*roh*-toh)

brother: **hermano** (ehr-*mah*-noh) m

brother-in-law: **cuñado** (koo-*nyah*-doh) m

brown: **marrón** (mah-*rrohn*)

brush (hair): **cepillarse el pelo** (seh-pee-*yahr*-seh ehl *peh*-loh)

brush (teeth): **cepillarse los dientes** (seh-pee-*yahr*-seh lohs dee*ehn*-tehs)

build: **construir** (kohn-stroo*eer*)

building: **edificio** (eh-dee-*fee*-seeoh) m

bull: **toro** (*toh*-roh) m

bullfight: **corrida de toros** (koh-*rree*-dah deh *toh*-rohs) f

burn: **quemadura** (keh-mah-*doo*-rah) f

bus: **autobús** (ahoo-toh-*bvoos*) m

but: **pero** (*peh*-roh)

butter: **mantequilla** (mahn-teh-*kee*-yah) f

buy: **comprar** (kohm-*prahr*)

by taxi: **en taxi** (ehn *tahk*-see)

C

cabin (stateroom): **camarote** (kah-mah-*roh*-teh) m

cabinet (in government): **gabinete** (gah-bee-*neh*-teh) m

cake: **pastel** (pahs-*tehl*) m

calf: **pantorrilla** (pahn-toh-*rree*-yah) f

call: **llamar** (yah-*mahr*)

call oneself/be called: **llamarse** (yah-*mahr*-seh)

calmly: **tranquilamente** (trahn-kee-lah-*mehn*-teh)

cancel: **cancelar** (kahn-seh-*lahr*)

candy: **dulces** (*dool*-sehs) m

car: **carro** (*kah*-rroh) m

card (playing): **naipe** (*nah*ee-peh) m

card: **tarjeta** (tahr-*Heh*-tah) f

care: **cuidado** (kooee-dah-doh) m

carrot: **zanahoria** (sah-nah-*oh*-reeah) f

cashier: **cajero/a** (kah-*Heh*-roh/rah) m, f

cat: **gato** (*gah*-toh) m

catch: **coger** (koh-*Hehr*)

catch a cold: **refriarse** (reh-free*ahr*-seh)

cathedral: **catedral** (kah-teh-*drahl*) m

cavity: **caries** (*kah*-reeehs) f

celebrate: **celebrar** (seh-leh-*bvrahr*)

ceramic: **cerámica** (seh-*rah*-mee-kah) f

cereal: **cereal** (seh-reh-*ahl*) m

certain, sure: **cierto** (see*ehr*-toh)

champagne: **champána** (chahm-*pahn*) m

change (as in money): **cambio** (*kahm*-bveeoh) m

change: **cambiar** (kahm-bvee*ahr*)

chauffer: **chófer** (*choh*-fehr) m, f

check: **cheque** (*cheh*-keh) m

cheese: **queso** (*keh*-soh) m

chemistry: **química** (*kee*-mee-kah) f

cherry: **cereza** (seh-*reh*-sah) f

chess: **ajedrez** (ah-Heh-*drehs*) m

chest: **pecho** (*peh*-choh) m

chew: **masticar** (mahs-tee-*kahr*)

chicken: **pollo** (*poh*-yoh) m

children: **hijos** (*ee*-Hohs)

choose: **escoger** (ehs-koh-*Hehr*)

Christmas: **Navidad** (nah-bvee-*dahd*) f

church: **iglesia** (ee-*gleh*-seeah) f

cinema: **cine** (*see*-neh) m

city: **ciudad** (seeoo-*dahd*) f

class: **clase** (*klah*-seh) f

classical music: **música clásica** (*moo*-see-kah *klah*-see-kah) f

clean: **limpiar** (leem-pee*ahr*)

climb: **subir** (soo-*bveer*)

close: **cerrar** (seh-*rrahr*)

closed: **cerrado** (seh-*rrah*-doh)

clothe: **vestir (i)** (*bvehs*-teer)

cloud: **nube** (*noo*-bveh) f

clumsy: **torpe** (*tohr*-peh)

coach: **entrenador/a** (ehn-treh-nah-*dohr*/ah) m, f

coat: **abrigo** (ah-*bvree*-go) m

coconut: **coco** (*koh*-koh) m

coffee: **café** (kah-*feh*) m

coin: **moneda** (moh-*neh*-dah) f

cold: **frío** (*free*oh)

color: **color** (koh-*lohr*) m

comb one's hair: **peinarse** (pehee-*nahr*-seh)

come: **venir** (bveh-*neer*)

command/order: **mandar** (mahn-*dahr*)

companion: **compañero/a** (kohm-pah-*nyeh*-roh/rah) m, f

complain (about, of): **quejarse (de)** (keh-*Hahr*-seh (deh))

completely: **completamente** (kohm-pleh-tah-*mehn*-teh)

computer: **computadora** (kohm-poo-tah-*doh*-rah) f

conclude: **concluir** (kohn-klu*eer*)

confidence: **confianza** (kohn-fee*ahn*-sah) f

conger eel: **congrio** (*kohn*-greeoh) m

conscientious: **concienzudo** (kohn-seeehn-*soo*-doh)

conscientiously: **concienzudamente** (kohn-seeehn-soo-dah-*mehn*-teh)

consent: **consentir (ie)** (kohn-sehn-*teer*)

consequently: **por consiguiente** (pohr kohn-see-gee*ehn*-teh)

constipation: **estreñimiento** (ehs-treh-nyee-mee*ehn*-toh) m

consultant: **consultor/a** (kohn-sool-*tohr*/ah) m, f

content/satisfied: **contento** (kohn-*tehn*-toh)

continue: **continuar** (kohn-tee-noo*ahr*)

contribute: **contribuir** (kohn-tree-bvoo*eer*)

convince: **convencer** (kohn-bvehn-*sehr*)

cook: **cocinero/a** (koh-see-*neh*-roh/rah) m, f

cook: **cocinar** (koh-see-*nahr*)

cookies/crackers: **galletas** (gah-*yeh*-tahs) f

cool: **fresco** (*frehs*-koh)

copper: **cobre** (*koh*-bvreh) m

copy/cheat: **copiar** (koh-pee*ahr*)

corner: **esquina** (ehs-*kee*-nah) f

correct: **corregir (i)** (koh-rreh-*Heer*)

cost: **costar** (kohs-*tahr*)

cotton: **algodón** (ahl-goh-*dohn*) m

cough: **tos** (tohs) f

count: **contar** (kohn-*tahr*)

country: **país** (pah*ees*) m

countryside/field: **campo** (*kahm*-poh) m

courteous: **cortés** (kohr-*tehs*)

courtesy: **cortesía** (kohr-teh-*seeah*) f

cousin [female]: **prima** (*pree*-mah) f

cousin [male]: **primo** (*pree*-moh) m

cover: **cubrir** (koobv-*reer*)

cruise: **crucero** (kroo-*seh*-roh) m

cry: **llorar** (yoh-*rahr*)

cure: **curar** (koo-*rahr*)

curious: **curioso** (koo-ree*oh*-soh)

customs: **aduana** (ah-doo*ah*-nah) f

cut: **cortar** (kohr-*tahr*)

D

dairy product: **producto lácteo** (proh-*dook*-toh *lahk*-teh-oh) m

dance: **bailar** (bvahee-*lahr*)

dangerous: **peligroso** (peh-lee-*groh*-soh)

dark: **oscuro** (ohs-*koo*-roh)

dark-haired: **moreno** (moh-*reh*-noh)

data: **dato** (*dah*-toh) m

date: **fecha** (*feh*-chah) f

daughter: **hija** (*ee*-Hah) f

daughter-in-law: **nuera** (noo*eh*-rah) f

day: **día** (*dee*-ah) m

dealership: **concesión** (kohn-seh-see*ohn*) f

debit: **débito** (*deh*-bvee-toh) m

deceive: **engañar** (ehn-gah-*nyahr*)

December: **diciembre** (dee-see*ehm*-bvreh) m

decide: **decidir** (deh-see-*deer*)

deeply: **profundamente** (proh-foon-dah-*mehn*-teh)

defend: **defender** (deh-fehn-*dehr*)

degree: **título** (*tee*-too-loh) m

delicious: **delicioso** (deh-lee-see*oh*-soh)

delighted: **encantado** (ehn-kahn-*tah*-doh)

demand: **exigir** (ehk-see-*Heer*)

demonstrate: **demostrar** (deh-mohs-*trahr*)

dentist: **dentista** (dehn-*tees*-tah) m, f

deny: **negar (ie)** (neh-*gahr*)

department store: **almacén** (ahl-mah-*sehn*) m

deposit: **ingresar** (een-greh-*sahr*)

depressed: **deprimido** (deh-pree-*mee*-doh)

describe: **describir** (dehs-kree-*bveer*)

deserve: **merecer** (meh-reh-*sehr*)

desire/wish/want: **desear** (deh-seh-*ahr*)

destroy: **destruir** (dehs-troo*eer*)

dial a phone: **marcar** (mahr-*kahr*)

dictionary: **diccionario** (deek-seeoh-*nah*-reeoh) m

die: **morir (ue)** (moh-*reer*)

diet: **régimen** (*reh*-gee-mehn) m

difficult: **difícil** (dee-*fee*-seel)

dining room: **comedor** (koh-meh-*dohr*) m

dinner: **cena** (*seh*-nah) f

disbelieve: **dudar** (doo-*dahr*)

discover: **descubrir** (dehs-koo-*bveer*)

discuss/debate: **discutir** (dees-koo-*teer*)

disease: **enfermedad** (ehn-fehr-meh-*dahd*) f

dishes: **platos** (*plah*-tohs) m

displeased: **disgustado** (dees-goos-*tah*-doh)

distinguish: **distinguir** (dees-teen-*geer*)

distribute: **distribuir** (dees-tree-bvoo*eer*)

dizziness: **mareo** (mah-*reh*-oh) m

do: **hacer** (ah-*sehr*)

doctor: **médico** (*meh*-dee-koh) m

document: **documento** (doh-koo-*mehn*-toh) m

document/passport: **pasaporte** (pah-sah-*pohr*-teh) m

dog: **perro** (*peh*-rroh) m

dollar: **dólar** (*doh*-lahr) m

doubt: **duda** (*doo*-dah) f

doubt: **dudar** (doo-*dahr*)

doubtful: **dudoso** (doo-*doh*-soh)

downtown: **centro** (*sehn*-troh) m

drawing/pattern: **dibujo** (dee-*bvoo*-Hoh) m

dress oneself: **vestirse (i)** (bvehs-*teer*-seh)

drink: **bebida** (bve-*bvee*-dah) f

drink: **beber** (bveh-*bvehr*)

drinkable: **potable** (poh-*tah*-bvleh)

drive: **conducir** (kohn-doo-*seer*)

driver: **chófer** (choh-*fehr*) m, f

dry (oneself): **secar(se)** (seh-*kahr*(seh))

dry: **seco** (*seh*-koh)

dry cleaner: **tintorería** (teen-toh-reh-*ree*ah) f

duck: **pato** (*pah*-toh) m

during: **durante** (doo-*rahn*-teh)

dust: **polvo** (*pohl*-bvoh) m

E

ear: **oreja** (oh-*reh*-Hah) f

early: **temprano** (tehm-*prah*-noh)

earn: **ganar** (gah-*nahr*)

earrings: **aretes** (ah-*reh*-tehs) m

easy: **fácil** (*fah*-seel)

eat: **comer** (koh-*mehr*)

eat breakfast: **desayunar** (dehs-ah-yoo-*nahr*)

eat lunch: **almorzar (ue)** (ahl-mohr-*sahr*)

educate: **educar** (eh-doo-*kahr*)

efficient: **eficiente** (eh-fee-see*ehn*-teh)

egg: **huevo** (oo*eh*-bvoh) m

eight: **ocho** (*oh*-choh)

eighteen: **dieciocho (diez y ocho)** (deeeh-see-*oh*-choh)

eighth: **octavo** (ohk-*tah*-bvoh)

eighty: **ochenta** (oh-*chehn*-tah)

elect: **elegir (i)** (eh-leh-*Heer*)

elegant: **elegante** (eh-leh-*gahn*-teh)

elevator: **ascensor** (ah-sehn-*sohr*) m

eleven: **once** (*ohn*-seh)

e-mail: **correo electrónico** (koh-*rreh*-oh eh-lehk-*troh*-nee-koh)

embarrassed/ashamed: **avergonzado** (ah-bvehr-gohn-*sah*-doh)

empty: **vaciar** (bvah-see*ahr*)

enchanting: **encantador** (ehn-kahn-tah-*dohr*)

end: **poner fin a** (poh-*nehr* feen ah)

enemy: **enemigo/a** (eh-neh-*mee*-goh/gah) m,f

engineer: **ingeniero/a** (een-Heh-nee*eh*-roh/rah) m, f

English (language): **el inglés** (ehl een-*glehs*) m

English (person) **inglés/a** (een-*glehs*/sah) m, f

enough: **bastante** (bvahs-*tahn*-teh)

especially: **especialmente** (ehs-peh-seeahl-*mehn*-teh)

essential: **esencial** (eh-sehn-see*ahl*)

eve: **víspera** (*bvees*-peh-rah) f

every: **cada** (*kah*-dah)

every (Sunday): **todos (los domingos)** (*toh*-dohs (lohs doh-*meen*-gohs))

everybody: **todo el mundo** (*toh*-doh ehl *moon*-doh)

evident: **evidente** (eh-bvee-*dehn*-teh)

exact: **exacto** (ehk-*sahk*-toh)

excellent: **excelente** (ehk-seh-*lehn*-teh)

excessive: **excesivo** (ehk-seh-*see*-bvoh)

excited: **emocionado** (eh-moh-seeoh-*nah*-doh)

exercise: **hacer ejercicio** (ah-*sehr* eh-Hehr-*see*-seeoh)

exercises: **ejercicios** (eh-Hehr-*see*-seeohs) m

exhibit: **exposición** (ehks-poh-see-see*ohn*) f

expenses: **gastos** (*gahs*-tohs) m

expensive: **caro** (*kah*-roh)

explain: **explicar** (ehks-plee-*kahr*)

explanation: **explicación** (ehks-plee-kah-see*ohn*) f

extract: **extraer** (ehks-trah-*ehr*)

eye: **ojo** (*oh*-Hoh) m

F

factory: **fábrica** (*fah*-bvree-kah) f

faint: **desmayarse** (dehs-mah-*yahr*-seh)

fair: **justo** (*Hoos*-toh)

faith: **fe** (feh) f

fall asleep: **dormirse (ue)** (dohr-*meer*-seh)

fall: **caer** (cah-*er*)

family: **familia** (fah-*mee*-leeah) f

famous: **famoso** (fah-*moh*-soh)

far (from): **lejos (de)** (*leh*-Hohs (deh))

fast: **rápido** (*rah*-pee-doh)

fasten: **abrochar** (ah-bvroh-*chahr*)

fat: **gordo** (*gohr*-doh)

father: **padre** (*pah*-dreh) m

feast: **festín** (fehs-*teen*) m

February: **febrero** (feh-*bvreh*-roh) m

feed: **alimentar** (ah-lee-mehn-*tahr*)

ferocious: **feroz** (feh-*rohs*)

ferociously: **ferozmente** (feh-rohs-*mehn*-teh)

fever: **fiebre** (fee*eh*-bvreh) f

fifteen: **quince** (*keen*-seh)

fifth: **quinto** (*keen*-toh)

fifty: **cincuenta** (seen-koo*ehn*-tah)

fig: **higo** (*ee*-goh) m

fight: **pelea** (peh-*leh*-ah) f

film: **película** (peh-*lee*-koo-lah) f

finally: **finalmente** (fee-nahl-*mehn*-teh)

find: **encontrar (ue)** (ehn-kohn-*trahr*)

finger: **dedo** (*deh*-doh) m

finish: **terminar** (tehr-mee-*nahr*)

firefighter: **bombero/a** (bvohm-*bveh*-roh/
rah) m, f

first: **primero** (pree-*meh*-roh)

fish (live)= **pez** (pehs) m

fish (to eat): **pescado** (pehs-*kah*-doh) m

fish: **pescar** (pehs-*kahr*)

fit: **caber** (kah-*bvehr*)

fitting: **apropriado** (ah-proh-pree*ah*-doh)

fitting room: **probador** (proh-bvah-*dohr*) m

five: **cinco** (*seen*-koh)

flattered: **lisonjeado**
(lee-sohn-Heh-*ah*-doh)

floor: **piso** (*pee*-soh) m

flower: **flor** (flohr) f

fluently: **fluidamente**
(flooee-dah-*mehn*-teh)

fly: **volar** (bvoh-*lahr*)

follow: **seguir (i)** (seh-*geer*)

foot: **pie** (pee*eh*) m

for: **para** (*pah*-rah)

for/per/through: **por** (pohr)

forbid: **prohibir** (proh-hee-*bveer*)

foreign: **extranjero** (ehks-trahn-*Heh*-roh)

forget: **olvidar** (ohl-bvee-*dahr*)

forget about: **olvidarse (de)** (ohl-bvee-
dahr-seh (deh))

forgive: **perdonar** (pehr-doh-*nahr*)

fort: **fortaleza** (fohr-tah-*leh*-sah) f

fortunate: **afortunado**
(ah-fohr-too-*nah*-doh)

forty: **cuarenta** (kooah-*rehn*-tah)

four: **cuatro** (koo*ah*-troh)

fourteen: **catorce** (kah-*tohr*-seh)

fourth: **cuarto** (koo*ahr*-toh)

frankness: **franqueza** (frahn-*keh*-sah) f

free: **libre** (*lee*-bvreh)

freeway: **autopista** (ahoo-toh-*pees*-tah) f

freeze: **helar (ie)** (eh-*lahr*)

frequently: **frecuentemente**
(freh-kooehn-teh-*mehn*-teh)

Friday: **viernes** (bvee*ehr*-nehs) m

friend: **amigo/a** (ah-*mee*-goh/gah) m, f

frightened: **asustado** (ah-soos-*tah*-doh)

from time to time: **de vez en cuando**
(deh bvehs ehn koo*ahn*-doh)

from/of: **de** (deh)

from/since: **desde** (*dehs*-deh)

fruit: **fruta** (*froo*-tah) f

furious: **furioso** (foo-ree*oh*-soh)

furniture: **mueble** (moo*eh*-bvleh) m

future: **futuro** (foo-*too*-roh) m

G

gamble: **jugar** (Hoo-*gahr*)

game (board): **juego** (Hoo*eh*-goh) m

game (sport): **partido** (pahr-*tee*-doh) m

garbage: **basura** (bvah-*soo*-rah) f

garden: **jardín** (Hahr-*deen*) m

garlic: **ajo** (*ah*-Hoh) m

generous: **generoso** (Heh-neh-*roh*-soh)

German (language): **el alemán** (ehl
ah-leh-*mahn*) m

German (person): **alemán/a** (ah-leh-*mahn*/ah) m, f

get/obtain: **conseguir (i)** (kohn-seh-*geer*)

get up: **levantarse** (leh-bvahn-*tahr*-seh)

gift: **regalo** (reh-*gah*-loh) m

girl: **niña** (*nee*-nyah) f

give: **dar** (dahr)

glass: **vidrio** (*bvee*-dreeoh) m

glove compartment: **guantera** (gooahn-*teh*-rah) f

go: **ir** (eer)

go away: **irse** (*eer*-seh)

go out: **salir** (sah-*leer*)

go shopping: **ir de compras** (eer deh *kohm*-prahs)

go to bed: **acostarse (ue)** (ah-kohs-*tahr*-seh)

godfather: **padrino** (pah-*dree*-noh) m

godmother: **madrina** (mah-*dree*-nah) f

gold: **oro** (*oh*-roh) m

good: **bueno** (bvoo*eh*-noh)

good-bye: **adiós** (ah-dee*ohs*)

goose: **ganso** (gan-soh) m

gorgeous/beautiful/lovely: **precioso** (preh-see*oh*-soh)

government: **gobierno** (goh-bvee*ehr*-noh) m

governor: **gobernador** (goh-bvehr-nah-*dohr*) m

grade (papers, exams, and so on): **calificar** (cah-lee-fee-*kahr*)

grade: **nota** (*noh*-tah) f

granddaughter: **nieta** (nee*eh*-tah) f

grandfather: **abuelo** (ah-bvoo*eh*-loh) m

grandmother: **abuela** (ah-bvoo*eh*-lah) f

grandparents: **abuelos** (ah-*bveh*-lohs) m

grandson: **nieto** (nee*eh*-toh) m

grape: **uva** (*oo*-bvah) f

grapefruit: **toronja** (toh-*rohn*-Hah) f

green: **verde** (*bvehr*-deh)

grey: **gris** (grees)

ground: **suelo** (soo*eh*-loh) m

grow: **crecer** (kreh-*sehr*)

guava: **guayaba** (gooah-*yah*-bvah) f

guest: **huésped** (oo*ehs*-pehd) m

guide: **guía** (*ghee*ah) m, f

guide: **guiar** (gee*ahr*)

gym: **gimnasio** (Heem-*nah*-seeoh) m

H

hair: **pelo** (*peh*-loh) m

half: **medio** (*meh*-deeoh) m

half-bathroom (a bathroom with no shower or tub): **medio baño** (*meh*-deeoh *bvah*-nyoh) m

handmade: **hecho a mano** (*eh*-choh ah *mah*-noh)

hang/hang up: **colgar** (kohl-*gahr*)

happily: **alegremente** (ah-lehg-reh-*mehn*-teh)

happiness: **felicidad** (feh-lee-see-*dahd*) f

happy: **alegre** (ah-*leh*-greh)

hard-working: **trabajador** (trah-bah-Hah-*dohr*)

have: **tener (ie)** (teh-*nehr*)

have breakfast: **desayunar** (deh-sah-yoo-*nahr*)

have fun: **divertirse (ie)** (dee-bvehr-*teer*-seh)

have just (completed): **acabar de** (ah-kah-*bvahr* deh)

have to: **deber** (deh-*behr*); **tener que** (teh-*nehr* keh)

he: **él** (ehl)

head: **cabeza** (kah-*bveh*-sah) f

healthy: **saludable** (sah-loo-dah-bvleh)

hear: **oír** (oh*eer*)

heart: **corazón** (koh-rah-*sohn*) m

heat: **calor** (kah-*lohr*) m

help: **ayudar** (ah-yoo-*dahr*)

her: **su(s)** (soo(s))

her/it: **la** (lah)

here: **aquí** (ah-*kee*)

hide (oneself): **esconder(se)**
(ehs-kohn-*dehr*(seh))

hide (something): **esconder**
(ehs-kohn-dehr)

him/it: **lo** (loh)

hire: **contratar** (kohn-trah-*tahr*)

his: **su(s)** (soo(s))

hit: **pegar** (peh-*gahr*)

home: **casa** (*kah*-sah) f

homeless: **los sin techo** (lohs seen
teh-choh)

homework: **tarea** (tah-*reh*-ah) f

honesty: **honestidad** (oh-nehs-tee-*dahd*) f

honeymoon: **luna de miel** (*loo*-nah deh
mee*ehl*) f

hope: **esperar** (ehs-peh-*rahr*)

hope: **esperanza** (ehs-peh-*rahn*-sah) f

horrible: **horrible** (hoh-*rree*-bvleh)

hors d'oevres: **entradas** (ehn-*trah*-dahs) f

horse: **caballo** (kah-*bvah*-yoh) m

hot [flavor]: **picante** (pee-*kahn*-teh)

hot [temperature]: **caliente**
(kah-lee*ehn*-teh)

hot pepper (Mexico and Guatemala)**:**
chile (*chee*-leh) m

hot pepper (South America)**: ají** (ah-*Hee*) m

hour: **hora** (*oh*-rah) f

house: **casa** (*kah*-sah) f

house: **hospedar** (ohs-peh-*dahr*)

how: **cómo** (*koh*-moh)

how much: **cuánto** (koo*ahn*-toh)

hug each other: **abrazarse**
(ah-bvrah-*sahr*-seh)

hundred: **cien(to)** (see*ehn*(toh))

hunger: **hambre** (*ahm*-bvreh) m

hurry: **apresurarse** (ah-preh-soo-*rahr*-seh)

hurt: **doler (ue)** (doh-*lehr*)

I

I: **yo** (yoh)

ice cream: **helado** (eh-*lah*-doh) m

identification: **identificación** (ee-dehn-
tee-fee-kah-see*ohn*) f

if only . . .: **ojalá que . . .** (oh-hah-*lah* keh)

immediately: **en seguida** (ehn seh-*gee*-dah)

immigration: **inmigración** (een-mee-grah-
see*ohn*) f

imperative: **imperativo**
(eem-peh-rah-*tee*-bvoh)

important: **importante** (eem-pohr-*tahn*-teh)

impossible: **imposible** (eem-poh-*see*-bvleh)

improbable: **improbable**
(eem-proh-*bvah*-bvleh)

impulsively: **impulsivamente**
(eem-pool-see-bvah-*mehn*-teh)

in/on/at: **en** (ehn)

in front (of): **enfrente (de)** (ehn-*frehn*-teh
(deh))

in front/ahead: **adelante** (ah-deh-*lahn*-teh)

incident: **incidente** (een-see-*dehn*-teh) m

include: **incluir** (een-kloo*eer*)

included: **incluido** (een-kloo*ee*-doh)

incredible: **increíble** (een-kreh*ee*-bvleh)

indispensable: **indispensable**
(een-dees-pehn-*sah*-bvleh)

influential: **influyente** (een-floo-*yehn*-teh)

ingredient: **ingrediente** (een-greh-
dee*ehn*-teh) m

inheritance: **herencia** (ehr-*ehn*-seeah) f

inside (of): **dentro (de)** (*dehn*-troh (deh))

insist: **insistir** (een-sees-*teer*)

inspire: **inspirar** (een-spee-*rahr*)

instead of: **en vez de** (ehn vehs deh)

instruction: **instrucción** (een-strook-see*ohn*) f

intelligent: **inteligente** (een-teh-lee-*hehn*-teh)

interesting: **interesante** (een-teh-reh-*sahn*-teh)

interview: **entrevista** (ehn-treh-*bvees*-tah) f

invite: **invitar** (een-bvee-*tahr*)

iron: **planchar** (plahn-*chahr*)

ironic: **irónico** (ee-*roh*-nee-koh)

irritated: **irritado** (ee-rree-*tah*-doh)

island: **isla** (*ees*-lah) f

it is advisable that: **conviene que** (kohn-bvee*eh*-neh keh)

J

jacket: **chaqueta** (chah-*keh*-tah) f

January: **enero** (eh-*neh*-roh) m

job: **empleo** (ehm-*pleh*-oh) m

joke: **chiste** (*chees*-teh) m

judge: **juez** (Hoo*ehs*) m, f

judge: **juzgar** (Hoos-*gahr*)

juice: **jugo** (*Hoo*-goh) m

July: **julio** (*Hoo*-leeoh) m

jump: **saltar** (sahl-*tahr*)

June: **junio** (*Hoo*-neeoh) m

K

keep going: **seguir** (seh-*gheer*)

key: **llave** (*yah*-bveh) f

keyboard: **teclado** (tehk-*lah*-doh) m

kidney: **riñón** (ree-*nyohn*) m

kingdom: **reino** (*rehee*-noh) m

kiss: **besar** (bveh-*sahr*)

kitchen: **cocina** (koh-*see*-nah) f

know (be acquainted with): **conocer** (koh-noh-*sehr*)

know (a fact): **saber** (sah-*bvehr*)

L

lake: **lago** (*lah*-goh) m

land: **tierra** (tee*eh*-rrah) f

language: **idioma** (ee-dee*oh*-mah) m

lap: **vuelta** (bvoo*ehl*-tah) f

laptop computer: **computadora portátil** (kohm-poo-tah-*doh*-rah pohr-*tah*-teel) f

last: **último** (*ool*-tee-moh)

late (in arriving): **de retraso** (deh reh-*trah*-soh)

later: **más tarde** (mahs *tahr*-deh)

laugh: **reír** (reh*eer*)

law: **ley** (leh) f

lawn: **césped** (*sehs*-pehd) m

lawyer: **abogado/a** (ah-bvoh-*gah*-doh/dah) m, f

lazy: **flojo** (*floh*-Hoh)

lead: **plomo** (*ploh*-moh) m

learn: **aprender** (ah-prehn-*dehr*)

leave: **salir** (sah-*leer*)

left: **izquierda** (ees-kee*ehr*-dah) f

leg: **pierna** (pee*ehr*-nah) f

lemon: **limón** (lee-*mohn*) m

less: **menos** (*meh*-nohs)

lesson: **lección** (lehk-see*ohn*) f

letter: **carta** (*kahr*-tah) f

lettuce: **lechuga** (leh-*choo*-gah) f

library: **biblioteca** (bvee-bvleeoh-*teh*-kah) f

lie: **mentir (ie)** (mehn-*teer*)

life: **vida** (*bvee*-dah) f

light: **claro** (*klah*-roh)

light/swift: **ligero** (lee-*Heh*-roh)

light: **encender (ie)** (ehn-*sehn*-dehr)

lightening: **relámpago** (reh-*lahm*-pah-goh) m

like: **gustar** (goos-*tahr*)

line: **línea** (*lee*-neh-ah) f

listen (to)/to hear: **escuchar** (ehs-koo-*chahr*)

little/small: **pequeño** (peh-*keh*-nyoh)

live: **vivir** (bvee-*bvee*r)

liver: **hígado** (*ee*-gah-doh) m

living room: **sala** (*sah*-lah) f

long: **largo** (*lahr*-goh)

look at: **mirar** (mee-*rahr*)

loose: **suelto** (soo*ehl*-toh)

loose/slack/lazy: **flojo** (*floh*-hoh)

lose: **perder** (pehr-*dehr*)

lottery: **lotería** (loh-teh-*ree*-ah) f

love: **amar** (ah-*mahr*)

low: **bajo** (*bvah*-Hoh)

loyal: **leal** (leh-*ahl*)

luck: **suerte** (soo*ehr*-teh) f

luggage/suitcase: **maleta** (mah-*leh*-tah) f

lunch: **almuerzo** (ahl-moo*ehr*-soh) m

lung: **pulmón** (pool-*mohn*) *m*

luxurious: **lujoso** (loo-*Hoh*-soh)

M

machine: **máquina** (*mah*-kee-nah) f

magazine: **revista** (reh-*bvees*-tah) f

magnificent: **magnífico** (mahg-*nee*-fee-koh)

mail/post: **correo** (koh-*rreh*-oh) m

make/do: **hacer** (ah-*sehr*)

make fun of: **burlarse (de)** (bvoor-*lahr*-seh (deh))

make sure: **asegurarse** (ah-seh-goo-*rahr*-seh)

mall: **centro commercial** (*sehn*-troh koh-mehr-see*ahl*) m

man: **hombre** (*ohm*-bvreh) m

manage/operate/drive: **manejar** (mah-neh-*Hahr*)

manager: **gerente** (Heh-*rehn*-teh) m, f

mango: **mango** (*mahn*-goh) m

map: **mapa** (*mah*-pah) m

marathon: **maratón** (mah-rah-*tohn*) m

March: **marzo** (*mahr*-soh) m

mark/dial/punch in the number: **marcar** (mahr-*kahr*)

married couple: **maridos** (mah-*ree*-dohs) m

marry/get married: **casarse** (kah-*sahr*-seh)

marvelous: **maravilloso** (mah-rah-bvee-*yoh*-soh)

mass: **masa** (*mah*-sah) f

materialistic: **materialista** (mah-teh-reeah-*lees*-tah)

May: **mayo** (*mah*-yoh) m

mayor: **alcalde** (ahl-*kahl*-deh) m, f

me/to me/for me/: **me** (meh)

meal: **comida** (koh-*mee*-dah) f

measure: **medir (i)** (meh-*deer*)

medicine: **medicina** (f) (meh-dee-*see*-nah)

meet: **reunirse** (rehoo-*neer*-seh)

meeting: **reunión** (rehoo-nee*ohn*) f

melon: **melón** (meh-*lohn*) m

memorize: **memorizer** (meh-moh-ree-*sahr*)

merchant: **comerciante** (koh-mehr-see-*ahn*-teh) m, f

merry: **feliz** (feh-*lees*)

messenger: **mensajero/a** (mehn-sah-*Heh*-roh/rah) m, f

midnight: **medianoche** (meh-deeah-*noh*-cheh) f

mile: **milla** (*mee*-yah) f

milk: **leche** (*leh*-cheh) f

million: **millón** (mee-*yohn*) m

mine: **mío, mía, míos, mías** (*mee*-oh, *mee*-ah, *mee*-ohs, *mee*-ahs)

minute: **minuto** (mee-*noo*-toh) m

mistake: **error** (eh-*rrohr*) m

mistake/be mistaken: **equivocarse** (eh-kee-bvoh-*kahr*-seh)

mix: **mezclar** (mehs-*klahr*)

modern: **moderno** (moh-*dehr*-noh)

Monday: **lunes** (*loo*-nehs) m

money: **dinero** (dee-*neh*-roh) m

month: **mes** (mehs) m

moon: **luna** (*loo*-nah) f

more: **más** (mahs)

morning (a.m.): **mañana** (mah-*nyah*-nah) f

mother: **madre** (*mah*-dreh) f

mountain: **montaña** (mohn-*tah*-nyah) f

moustache: **bigote** (bvee-*goh*-teh) m

mouth: **boca** (*bvoh*-kah) f

movie/film: **película** (peh-*lee*-koo-lah) f

movies: **cine** (*see*-neh) m

much: **mucho** (*moo*-choh)

mud: **lodo** (*loh*-doh) m

museum: **museo** (moo-*seh*-oh) m

mustard: **mostaza** (mohs-*tah*-sah) f

my: **mi(s)** (mee(s))

N

narrow: **estrecho** (ehs-*treh*-choh)

natural: **natural** (nah-too-*rahl*)

near (to): **cerca (de)** (*sehr*-kah (deh))

necessary: **necesario** (neh-seh-*sah*-reeoh)

neck: **cuello** (koo*eh*-yoh) m

necklace: **collar** (koh-*yahr*) m

need: **necesitar** (neh-seh-see-*tahr*)

neighborhood: **vecindario** (bveh-seen-*dah*-reeoh) m

neither . . . nor: **ni . . . ni** (nee . . . nee)

neither/not . . . either: **tampoco** (tahm-*poh*-koh)

never: **nunca** (*noon*-kah)

new: **nuevo** (noo*eh*-bvoh)

news: **noticias** (noh-*tee*-seeahs) f

newspaper: **periódico** (peh-ree*oh*-dee-koh) m

next: **próximo** (*prohk*-see-moh)

nice: **amable** (ah-*mah*-bvleh)

night: **noche** (*noh*-cheh) f

nine: **nueve** (noo*eh*-bveh)

nineteen: **diecinueve (diez y nueve)** (dee*eh*-see-noo*eh*-bveh)

ninety: **noventa** (noh-*bvehn*-tah)

ninth: **noveno** (noh-*bveh*-noh)

no/not: **no** (noh)

nobody/no one: **nadie** (*nah*-deeeh)

noise: **ruido** (roo*ee*-doh)

none: **ningún** (neen-*goon*)

noon: **mediodía** (meh-deeoh-*dee*ah) m

nose: **nariz** (nah-*rees*) f

nothing: **nada** (*nah*-dah)

notice: **observer** (ohbv-sehr-*bvahr*)

novel: **novela** (noh-*bveh*-lah) f

November: **noviembre** (noh-bvee*ehm*-bvreh) m

now: **ahora** (ah-*oh*-rah)

nowadays: **hoy en día** (ohy ehn *dee*ah)

number: **número** (*noo*-meh-roh) m

nurse: **enfemero/a** (ehn-fehr-*meh*-roh/rah) m, f

O

obey: **obedecer** (oh-bveh-deh-*sehr*)

obvious: **obvio** (*ohbv*-bveeoh)

occupied/busy: **ocupado** (oh-koo-*pah*-doh)

October: **octubre** (ohk-*too*-bvreh) m

of: **de** (deh)

of course: **por supuesto** (pohr soo-poo*ehs*-toh)

offer/give: **ofrecer** (oh-freh-*sehr*)

office: **oficina** (oh-fee-*see*-nah) f

often: **a menudo** (a meh-*noo*-doh)

one: **un/uno/una** (oon/*oo*-noh/*oo*-nah)

one million: **millón** (mee-*yohn*) m

one thousand: **mil** (meel) m

one's own: **propio** (*proh*-peeoh)

onion: **cebolla** (seh-*bvoh*-yah) f

open: **abrir** (ah-*bvreer*)

opportunity: **oportunidad** (oh-pohr-too-nee-*dahd*) f

oppose: **oponer** (oh-poh-*nehr*)

optimistic: **optimista** (ohp-tee-*mees*-tah)

or: **o** (oh)

orange: **naranja** (nah-*rahn*-Hah) f

order (command): **ordenar** (ohr-deh-*nahr*)

order (request): **pedir** (peh-*deer*)

ordinary: **ordinario** (ohr-dee-*nah*-reeoh)

other: **otro** (*oh*-troh)

our, ours: **nuestro/nuestra/nuestros/ nuestras** (noo*ehs*-troh/noo*ehs*-trah/ noo*ehs*-trohs/noo*ehs*-trahs)

outside: **afuera** (ah-foo*eh*-rah)

over there: **allá** (ah-*yah*)

P

package: **paquete** (pah-*keh*-teh) m

paid for: **pagado** (pah-*gah*-doh)

pain: **dolor** (doh-*lohr*) m

paint: **pintar** (peen-*tahr*)

painting: **pintura** (peen-*too*-rah) f

papaya: **papaya** (pah-*pah*-yah) f

paper/role: **papel** (pah-*pehl*) m

parade: **desfile** (dehs-*fee*-leh) m

park: **parque** (*pahr*-keh) m

parking: **estacionamiento** (ehs-tah-seeoh-nah-mee*ehn*-toh) m

participate (in): **participar (en)** (pahr-tee-see-*pahr* (ehn))

party: **fiesta** (fee*ehs*-tah) f

pass (a test): **aprobar (un examen)** (ah-proh-*bvahr* (oon ehk-*sah*-mehn))

passport: **pasaporte** (pah-sah-*pohr*-teh) m

pasta: **fideo** (fee-*de*-oh) m

patience: **paciencia** (pah-see*ehn*-seeah)

pay: **pagar** (pah-*gahr*)

pay attention: **prestar atención** (prehs-*tahr* ah-tehn-see*ohn*)

pea: **guisante** (gee-*sahn*-teh) m

peace: **paz** (pahs) f

peach: **durazno** (doo-*rahs*-noh) m

pear: **pera** (*peh*-rah) f

pearl: **perla** (*pehr*-lah) f

peel: **pelar** (peh-*lahr*)

pencil: **lápiz** (*lah*-pees) m

percent: **por ciento** (pohr see*ehn*-toh)

percentage: **porcentaje** (pohr-sehn-*tah*-Heh) m

perfect: **perfecto** (pehr-*fehk*-toh)

perfect: **perfeccionar** (pehr-fehk-seeoh-*nahr*)

perhaps: **tal vez** (tahl bvehs)

permit: **permitir** (pehr-mee-*teer*)

person: **persona** (pehr-*soh*-nah) f

pessimistic: **pesimista** (peh-see-*mees*-tah)

pharmacy: **farmacia** (fahr-*mah*-seeah) f

photograph: **fotografiar**
(foh-toh-grah-fee*ahr*)

photographer: **fotógrafo/a**
(foh-*toh*-grah-foh/fah) m, f

physical: **físico** (*fee*-see-koh)

physician/doctor: **médico/a** (*meh*-dee-koh/
kah) m, f

piece: **trozo** (*troh*-soh) m

pilot: **piloto/a** (pee-*loh*-toh/tah) m, f

pilot: **pilotar** (pee-loh-*tahr*)

pineapple: **piña** (*pee*-nyah) f

pink: **rosado** (roh-*sah*-doh)

pity/shame: **lástima** (*lahs*-tee-mah) f

place (something): **colocar**
(koh-loh-*kahr*)

place: **lugar** (loo-*ghar*) m

place one's self/get a job: **colocarse**
(koh-loh-*kahr*-seh)

plane: **avión** (ah-bvee*ohn*) m

plate: **plato** (*plah*-toh) m

play (a sport): **jugar (ue)** (Hoo-*gahr*)

play checkers: **jugar (ue) a las damas**
(Hoo-*gahr* ah lahs *dah*-mahs)

pleasant: **genial** (Heh-nee*ahl*)

please: **por favor** (pohr fah-*bvohr*)

please: **complacer** (kohm-plah-*sehr*)

plum: **ciruela** (see-roo*eh*-lah) f

pocket: **bolsillo** (bvohl-*see*-yoh) m

police officer: **policía** (poh-lee-*see*ah) m, f

polish: **pulir** (poo-*leer*)

poor: **pobre** (*poh*-bvreh)

popcorn: **palomitas de maíz**
(pah-loh-*mee*-tahs deh mah*ees*) f

popular: **popular** (poh-poo-*lahr*)

port: **puerto** (poo*ehr*-toh) m

portion: **porción** (pohr-see*ohn*) f

possible: **posible** (poh-*see*-bvleh)

postal code [ZIP code]: **código postal**
(*koh*-dee-goh pohs-*tahl*) m

postal worker: **cartero/a** (kahr-*teh*-roh/
rah) m, f

pot: **olla** (*oh*-yah) f

potato chips: **papas fritas**
(*pah*-pahs *free*-tahs) f

potatoes: **papas** (*pah*-pahs) f

pound: **libra** (*lee*-bvrah) f

prawn: **langostino** (lahn-gohs-*tee*-noh) m

prefer: **preferir (ie)** (preh-feh-*reer*)

preferable: **preferible**
(preh-feh-*ree*-bvleh)

prepare (oneself): **preparar(se)**
(preh-pah-*rahr*(seh))

prescription: **receta** (reh-*seh*-tah) f

present: **regalo** (reh-*gah*-loh) m

president: **presidente** (preh-see-*dehn*-
teh) m, f

pretty: **bonito** (bvoh-*nee*-toh)

pretty/good-looking: **guapo** (goo*ah*-poh)

price: **precio** (*preh*-see*oh*) m

print: **imprimir** (eem-pree-*meer*)

probable: **probable** (proh-*bvah*-bvleh)

produce: **producir** (proh-doo-*seer*)

project: **proyecto** (proh-*yehk*-toh)

promise: **prometer** (proh-meh-*tehr*)

pronounce: **pronunciar**
(proh-noon-see*ahr*)

proprietor: **propietario/a** (proh-peeeh-
tah-reeoh/ah) m, f

proud: **orgulloso** (ohr-goo-*yoh*-soh)

pure: **pura** (*poo*-rah)

purple: **morado** (moh-*rah*-doh)

push: **empujar** (ehm-poo-*hahr*)

put: **poner** (poh-*nehr*)

put on makeup: **maquillarse**
(mah-kee-*yahr*-seh)

put something on one's self: **ponerse**
(poh-*nehr*-seh)

put to bed: **acostar (ue)** (ah-kohs-*tahr*)

Q

quarter: **cuarto** (koo*ahr*-toh) m

question: **pregunta** (preh-*goon*-tah) f

quickly: **rápidamente**
(rah-pee-dah-mehn-teh)

quiet: **tranquilo** (trahn-*kee*-loh)

quit (work): **dejar (el trabajo)** (deh-*hahr*
(ehl trah-*bvah*-Hoh))

quite/enough: **bastante** (bvahs-*tahn*-teh)

R

race: **carrera** (kah-*rreh*-rah) f

racecar: **auto de carreras** (*ahoo*-toh deh
kah-*rreh*-rahs) m

rain: **llover (ue)** (yoh-*bvehr*)

rain: **lluvia** (*yoo*-bveeah) f

raincoat: **impermeable** (eem-pehr-meh-
ah-bvleh) m

rainforest: **selva** (*sehl*-bvah) f

raise (of salary): **aumento (de sueldo)**
(ahoo-*mehn*-toh (deh soo*ehl*-doh)) m

raise (something): **levantar**
(leh-bvahn-*tahr*)

rather/too/too much: **demasiado/a**
(deh-mah-see*ah*-doh/dah) m, f

react: **reaccionar** (reh-ahk-seeoh-*nahr*)

read: **leer** (leh-*ehr*)

ready: **listo** (*lees*-toh)

receipt: **recibo** (m) (reh-*see*-bvoh)

receive: **recibir** (reh-see-*bveer*)

reception: **recepción** (reh-sehp-see*ohn*) f

recipe: **receta** (reh-*seh*-tah) f

record: **grabar** (grah-*bvahr*)

red: **rojo** (*roh*-Hoh)

red snapper: **huachinango**
(ooah-chee-*nahn*-goh) m

refund: **reembolsar** (reh-ehm-bvol-*sahr*)

regret: **lamentar** (lah-mehn-*tahr*)

regrettable: **lamentable**
(lah-mehn-*tah*-bvleh)

regulations: **reglamento**
(rehg-lah-*mehn*-toh) m

remain: **quedarse** (keh-*dahr*-seh)

remember: **recordar** (reh-kohr-*dahr*)

remove/take off: **quitar(se)**
(kee-*tahr*(seh))

repair: **arreglar** (ah-rreh-*glahr*)

repeat: **repetir** (reh-peh-teer)

request: **pedir** (peh-*deer*)

require/demand: **exigir** (ehk-see-*Heer*)

research: **investigación** (een-bvehs-tee-
gah-see*ohn*) f

reservation: **reservación** (reh-sehr-bvah-
see-*ohn*) f

respectfully: **respetuosamente**
(rehs-peh-toooh-sah-*mehn*-teh)

responsible: **responsable**
(rehs-pohn-*sah*-bvleh)

rest: **descansar** (deh-kahn-*sahr*)

restaurant: **restaurante**
(rehs-tahoo-*rahn*-teh) m

return (someone from someplace):
volver (ue) bvol-*bvehr*)

return, (something to someone):
devolver (ue) (deh-bvol-*bvehr*)

rice: **arroz** (ah-*rros*) m

right: **derecha** (deh-*reh*-chah)

right away/soon: **pronto** (*prohn*-toh)

right now: **ahora mismo** (ah-*Hoh*-rah
mees-moh)

ring: **sonar (ue)** (soh-*nahr*)

river: **río** (*ree*-oh) m

road: **camino** (kah-*mee*-noh) m

road/route: **ruta** (*roo*-tah) f

robbery: **robo** (*roh*-boh) m

room: **cuarto** (koo*ahr*-toh) m

rug: **alfombra** (ahl-*fohm*-bvrah) f

ruins: **ruinas** (roo*ee*-nahs) f

rule/ruler: **regla** (*reh*-glah) f

run: **correr** (koh-*rrehr*)

S

safari: **safari** (sah-*fah*-ree) m

sail: **navegar** (nah-bveh-*gahr*)

salad: **ensalada** (ehn-sah-*lah*-dah) f

sale: **venta** (*bvehn*-tah) f

salesperson: **dependiente** (deh-pehn-dee*ehn*-teh) m, f

salty: **salado** (sah-*lah*-doh)

same: **mismo** (*mees*-moh)

Saturday: **sábado** (*sah*-bvah-doh) m

save: **ahorrar** (ah-Hoh-*rrahr*)

say/tell: **decir** (deh-*seer*)

say good-bye: **despedir(se) (i)** (dehs-peh-*deer*(seh))

scene: **escena** (ehs-*seh*-nah) f

school: **escuela** (ehs-koo*eh*-lah) f

science: **ciencia** (see*ehn*-see*ah*) f

scientific: **científico** (see*ehn*-*tee*-fee-koh)

scream: **gritar** (gree-*tahr*)

screen: **pantalla** (pahn-*tah*-yah) f

sculpture: **escultura** (ehs-kool-*too*-rah) f

sea: **mar** (mahr) m

seafood: **marisco** (mah-*rees*-koh) m

search/look for: **buscar** (bvoos-*kahr*)

seat: **asiento** (ah-see*ehn*-toh) m

second: **segundo** (seh-*goon*-doh) m

see: **ver** (bvehr)

seem: **parecer** (pah-reh-*sehr*)

selfish: **egoísta** (eh-goh*ees*-tah)

sell: **vender** (bvehn-*dehr*)

send: **enviar** (ehn-bvee*ahr*); **expedir (i)** (ehks-peh-*deer*); **mandar** (mahn-*dahr*)

September: **septiembre** (sehp-tee*ehm*-bvreh) m

servant: **sirvienta** (seer-bveeehn-tah) f

serve: **servir (i)** (sehr-*bveer*)

set (the table): **poner (la mesa)** (poh-*nehr* (lah *meh*-sah))

seven: **siete** (see*eh*-teh)

seventeen: **diecisiete (diez y siete)** (deeeh-see-see*eh*-teh)

seventh: **séptimo** (*sehp*-tee-moh)

seventy: **setenta** (seh-*tehn*-tah)

share: **compartir** (kohm-pahr-*teer*)

shave: **afeitarse** (ah-fehee-*tahr*-seh)

she: **ella** (*eh*-yah)

shelter: **dar refugio** (dahr reh-*foo*-Heeoh)

shine: **brillo** (*bvree*-yoh)

shirt: **camisa** (kah-*mee*-sah) f

shop: **ir de compras** (eer deh *kohm*-prahs)

shopping mall: **centro comercial** (*sehn*-troh koh-mehr-see*ahl*) m

short/below: **bajo** (*bvah*-Hoh)

shoulder: **hombro** (*ohm*-bvroh) m

show: **espectáculo** (eh-spehk-*tah*-koo-loh) m

show: **mostrar (ue)** (mohs-*trahr*)

shower: **ducharse** (doo-*chahr*-seh)

showing: **exposición** (ehks-poh-see-see*ohn*) f

shrimp: **camarón** (kah-mah-*rohn*) m

sick person: **enfermo/a** (ehn-*fehr*-moh/ah) m, f

sign: **señal** (seh-*nyahl*) f

sign: **firmar** (feer-*mahr*)

signal: **señalar** (seh-nyah-*lahr*)

silence: **callarse** (kah-*yahr*-seh)

silk: **seda** (*seh*-dah) f

sincerely yours: **atentamente** (ah-tehn-tah-*mehn*-teh)

sing: **cantar** (kahn-*tahr*)

sister: **hermana** (ehr-*mah*-nah) f

sister-in-law: **cuñada** (koo-*nyah*-dah) f

six: **seis** (*seh*ees)

sixteen: **dieciséis (diez y seis)** (deeeh-see-*seh*ees)

sixth: **sexto** (*sehks*-toh)

sixty: **sesenta** (seh-*sehn*-tah)

size (of a person): **talla** (*tah*-yah) f

size (of a place or object): **tamaño** (tah-*mah*-nyoh) m

skate: **patín** (pah-*teen*) m

ski: **esquí** (ehs-*kee*) m

ski: **esquiar** (ehs-kee*ahr*)

skinny: **flaco** (*flah*-koh)

skirt: **falda** (*fahl*-dah) f

sky: **cielo** (see*eh*-loh) m

sleep: **dormir (ue)** (dohr-*meer*)

sleeve: **manga** (*mahn*-gah) f

slowly: **despacio** (dehs-*pah*-seeoh)

small: **pequeño** (peh-*keh*-nyoh)

small amount: **poco (m)** (*poh*-koh)

smell: **oler** (oh-*lehr*)

snow: **nevar (ie)** (neh-*bvahr*)

snowman: **muñeco de nieve** (moo-*nyeh*-koh deh neee*eh*-bveh) m

soccer: **fútbol** (*foot*-bvohl) m

soft drink: **refresco** (reh-*frehs*-koh) m

some: **algún** (ahl-*goon*)

sometimes: **a veces** (ah *bveh*-sehs)

son: **hijo** (*ee*-Hoh) m

song: **canción** (kahn-see*ohn*) f

son-in-law: **yerno** (*yehr*-noh) m

soon: **pronto** (*prohn*-toh)

Spain: **España** (ehs-*pah*-nyah)

Spanish (language): **el español** (ehl ehs-pah-*nyohl*) m

Spanish (person): **español/a** (ehs-pah-*nyohl*/ah) m, f

speak/talk: **hablar** (ah-*bvlahr*)

special: **especial** (ehs-peh-see*ahl*)

spend (money): **gastar** (gah-*stahr*)

spend (time): **pasar** (pah-*sahr*)

spill: **derramar** (deh-rrah-*mahr*)

spinach: **espinaca** (ehs-pee-*nah*-kah) f

spoon: **cuchara** (koo-*chah*-rah) f

sport: **deporte** (deh-*pohr*-teh) m

sporty: **deportivo** (deh-pohr-*tee*-bvoh)

spouse: **esposo/a** (eh-*spoh*-soh/sah) m, f

spread out: **esparcir** (ehs-pahr-*seer*)

spring: **primavera** (pree-mah-*bveh*-rah) f

square: **plaza** (*plah*-sah) f

stadium: **estadio** (ehs-*tah*-deeoh) m

state: **estado** (ehs-*tah*-doh) m

station: **estación** (ehs-tah-see*ohn*) f

stay: **quedarse** (keh-*dahr*-seh)

steak: **bistec** (bees-*tehk*) m

steal/rob: **robar** (roh-*bvahr*)

stomach: **estómago** (ehs-*toh*-mah-goh) m

stop (something): **parar** (pah-*rahr*)

stop oneself: **pararse** (pah-*rahr*-seh)

store: **tienda** (tee*ehn*-dah) f

store window: **escaparate** (ehs-kah-pah-*rah*-teh) m

storm: **tempestad** (tehm-pehs-*tahd*) f

straight: **derecho** (deh-*reh*-choh)

strange: **extraño** (ehks-*trah*-nyoh)

stranger: **desconocido/a** (dehs-kohn-oh-*see*-doh/dah) m, f

strawberry (from Colombia to the South Pole): **frutilla** (froo-*tee*-yah) f strawberry (Mexico, Central America, and Spain): **fresa** (*freh*-sah) f

street: **calle** (*kah*-yeh) f

striped: **a rayas** (ah *rah*-yahs)

study: **estudiar** (ehs-too-dee*ahr*)

stupendous: **estupendo** (ehs-too-*pehn*-doh)

style: **moda** (*moh*-dah) f

subway: **metro** (*meh*-troh) m

suddenly: **de repente** (deh reh-*pehn*-teh)

suggest: **sugerir (ie)** (soo-Heh-*reer*)

suitcase: **maleta** (mah-*leh*-tah) f

summer: **verano** (bveh-*rah*-noh) m

sun: **sol** (sohl) m

sunbathe: **tomar el sol** (toh-*mahr* ehl sohl)

Sunday: **domingo** (doh-*meen*-goh) m

suntan lotion: **bronceador** (bvrohn-seh-ah-*dohr*) m

supermarket: **supermercado** (soo-pehr-mehr-*kah*-doh) m

supper: **cena** (*seh*-nah) f

suppress/omit: **suprimir** (soo-pree-*meer*)

surf: **hacer surf** (ah-*sehr* soorf)

surgeon: **cirujano/a** (see-roo-*Hah*-noh/ nah) m, f

surgery: **cirugía** (see-roo-*Hee*-ah) f

surprise: **sorpresa** (sohr-*preh*-sah) f

surprised: **sorprendido** (sohr-prehn-*dee*-doh)

survey: **encuesta** (ehn-koo*ehs*-tah)

swallow, to: **tragar** (trah-*gahr*)

sweater: **suéter** (soo*eh*-tehr) m

sweet: **dulce** (*dool*-seh)

swim: **nadar** (nah-*dahr*)

swimming: **natación** (nah-tah-see*ohn*) f

swimming pool: **piscina** (pees-*see*-nah) f

swimsuit: **traje de baño** (*trah*-Heh deh *bah*-nyoh) m

T

table: **mesa** (*meh*-sah) f

tablecloth: **mantel** (mahn-*tehl*) m

take: **tomar** (toh-*mahr*)

take a cruise: **hacer un crucero** (ah-*sehr* oon kroo-*seh*-roh)

take a trip: **hacer un viaje** (ah-*sehr* oon bvee*ah*-Heh)

talk/speak: **hablar** (ah-*bvlahr*)

talkative: **hablador** (ah-bvlah-*dohr*)

tall/: **alto** (*ahl*-toh)

tan: **broncearse** (bvrohn-seh*ahr*-seh)

tape recording: **grabación** (grah-bah-see*ohn*) f

tax: **impuesto** (eem-poo*ehs*-toh) m

taxi: **taxi** (*tahk*-see) m

teach: **enseñar** (ehn-seh-*nyahr*)

team: **equipo** (eh-*kee*-poh) m

t-shirt: **camiseta** (kah-mee-*seh*-tah) f

television: **televisión** (teh-leh-bvee-see*ohn*) f

tell/say: **decir** (deh-*seer*)

ten: **diez** (dee*ehs*)

tenth: **décimo** (*deh*-see-moh)

test: **examinar** (ehk-sah-mee-*nahr*)

thank you: **gracias** (*grah*-seeahs)

that (over there): **aquel/aquella** (ah-*kehl*/ah-*keh*-yah)

that (there): **ese/esa** (*eh*-seh/eh-*sah*)

that one (over there): **aquél/aquélla** (ah-*kehl*/ah-*keh*-yah)

that one (there): **ése/ésa** (*eh*-seh/*eh*-sah)

that/than: **que** (keh)

the: **el/la/los/las** (ehl/lah/lohs/lahs)

theater: **teatro** (teh*ah*-troh) m

their: **su(s)** (soo(s))

then: **entonces** (ehn-*tohn*-sehs)

there is/are: **hay** (ahy)

these: **estos/estas** (*ehs*-tohs/*ehs*-tahs)

these ones: **éstos/éstas** (*ehs*-tohs/
ehs-tahs)

they: **ellos/ellas** (*eh*-yohs/*eh*-yahs)

thigh: **muslo** (*moos*-loh) m

thin: **delgado** (dehl-*gah*-doh)

thing: **cosa** (*koh*-sah) f

think: **pensar (ie)** (pehn-*sahr*)

third: **tercero** (tehr-*seh*-roh)

thirst: **sed** (sehd) f

thirteen: **trece** (*treh*-seh)

thirty: **treinta** (*treh*een-tah)

this: **este/esta** (*ehs*-teh/*ehs*-tah)

this one: **éste/ ésta** (*ehs*-teh/*ehs*-tah)

those (over there): **aquellos/aquellas**
(ah-*keh*-yohs/ah-*keh*-yahs)

those (there) : **esos/esas** (*eh*-sohs/*eh*-sahs)

those ones (over there): **aquéllos/aquéllas**
(ah-*keh*-yohs/ah-*keh*-yahs)

those ones (there)= **ésos/ésas** (*eh*-sos/
eh-sahs)

thousand: **mil** (meel) m

three: **tres** (trehs)

throat: **garganta** (gahr-*gahn*-tah) f

through: **por** (pohr)

thunder: **truenos** (troo*eh*-nohs)

thunder: **tronar (ue)** (troh-*nahr*)

Thursday: **jueves** (Hoo*eh*-bvehs) m

ticket: **boleto** (bvoh-*leh*-toh) m

tide: **marea** (mah-*reh*-ah) f

tight: **apretado** (ah-preh-*tah*-doh)

time: **tiempo** (tee*ehm*-poh)

tired: **cansado** (kahn-*sah*-doh)

to: **a** (ah)

to or for him/her/you (formal): **le** (leh)

to or for them/you (formal, plural): **les**
(lehs)

today: **hoy** (ohy)

toe: **dedo del pie** (*deh*-doh dehl pee*eh*) m

together: **junto** (*Hoon*-toh)

toll: **peaje** (peh-*ah*-Heh) m

tomorrow: **mañana** (mah-*nyah*-na)

tooth: **diente** (dee*ehn*-teh) m

toothache: **dolor de muelas** (doh-*lohr*
deh moo*eh*-lahs) m

toy: **juguete** (Hoo-*geh*-teh) m

traffic: **tráfico** (*trah*-fee-koh) m

train: **tren** (trehn) m

translate: **traducir** (trah-doo-*seer*)

travel: **viajar** (bveeah-*Hahr*)

traveler: **viajero/a** (bveeah-*Heh*-roh/rah)
m, f

trip: **viaje** (bvee*ah*-Heh) m

trousers: **pantalones** (pahn-tah-*loh*-
nehs) m

trout: **trucha** (*troo*-chah) f

trust: **fiarse en** (fee*ahr*-seh)

truth: **verdad** (bvehr-*dahd*) f

try: **probar** (proh-*bvahr*)

Tuesday: **martes** (*mahr*-tehs) m

tuition: **matrícula** (mah-*tree*-koo-lah) f

tuna: **atún** (ah-*toon*) m

turn: **doblar** (doh-*bvlahr*)

turn off: **apagar** (ah-pah-*gahr*)

TV: **tele** (*teh*-leh) f

twelve: **doce** (*doh*-seh)

twenty: **veinte** (*bveh*een-teh)

two: **dos** (dohs)

typical: **típica** (*tee*-pee-kah)

U

ugly: **feo** (*feh*-oh)

uncle: **tío** (*tee*-oh) m

underground: **subterráneo** (soobv-teh-*rrah*-neh-oh)

understand: **entender (ie)** (ehn-tehn-*dehr*)

undress: **desvestirse (i)** (dehs-bvehs-*teer*-seh)

unfair: **injusto** (een-*Hoos*-toh)

unfortunately: **desafortunadamente** (deh-sah-fohr-too-nah-dah-*mehn*-teh)

unhappy: **infeliz** (een-feh-*lees*)

uniform: **uniforme** (oo-nee-*fohr*-meh) m

unjust: **injusto** (een-*Hoos*-toh)

unrestrainedly: **desenfrenadamente** (dehs-ehn-freh-nah-dah-*mehn*-teh)

untidy: **descuidado** (dehs-kooee-*dah*-doh)

until: **hasta** (*ahs*-tah)

urine: **orina** (oh-*ree*-nah) f

us/to us/ourselves: **nos** (nohs)

V

vacuum cleaner: **aspiradora** (ahs-pee-rah-*doh*-rah) f

vase: **jarrón** (Hah-*rrohn*) m

vehicle: **vehículo** (bveh-*ee*-koo-loh) m

very: **muy** (*mooee*)

video camera: **cámara de video** (*kah*-mah-rah deh bvee-*deh*-oh) f

violet/purple: **violeta** (bveeoh-*leh*-tah)

violin: **violín** (bveeoh-*leen*) m

vocabulary: **vocabulario** (bvoh-kah-bvoo-*lah*-reeoh) m

voice: **voz** (bvohs) f

volleyball: **voleibol, volibol** (bvoh-lee-*bvohl*) m

vote: **votar** (bvoh-*tahr*)

W

wait: **esperar** (ehs-peh-*rahr*)

waiter (waitress): **camarero/a** (kah-mah-*reh*-roh/rah) m, f

wake up: **despertarse (ie)** (dehs-pehr-*tahr*-seh)

walk: **andar** (ahn-*dahr*)

walk: **paseo** (pah-*seh*-oh) m

walk (take a walk): **dar un paseo** (dahr oon pah-*seh*-oh); **pasearse** (pah-seh-*ahr*-seh)

walking (on foot): **a pie** (ah pee*eh*)

wallet: **cartera** (kahr-*teh*-rah) f

want: **querer (ie)** (keh-*rehr*)

war: **guerra** (*gheh*-rrah) f

warranty: **garantía** (gah-rahn-*tee*-ah) m

wash: **lavar** (lah-*bvahr*)

wash oneself: **lavarse** (lah-*bvahr*-seh)

watch/look at: **mirar** (mee-*rahr*)

water: **agua** (*ah*-gooah) m

waterfall: **cascada** (kahs-*kah*-dah) f

watermelon: **sandía** (sahn-*dee*-ah) f

we/us: **nosotros** (noh-*soh*-trohs)

weak: **débil** (*deh*-bveel)

weakness/laziness: **flojera** (floh-*Heh*-rah) f

wear: **llevar** (yeh-*bvahr*)

weather: **tiempo** (tee*ehm*-poh) m

wedding: **boda** (*bvoh*-dah) f

Wednesday: **miércoles** (mee*ehr*-koh-lehs) m

week: **semana** (seh-*mah*-nah) f

weight: **peso** (*peh*-soh)

well: **bien** (bvee*ehn*)

wet: **mojado** (moh-*Hah*-doh)

what: **¿qué?** (keh)

when: **¿cuándo?** (koo*ahn*-doh)

where (to):**¿adónde?** (ah-*dohn*-deh)

where: **¿dónde?** (*dohn*-deh)

which/what: **¿cuál(es)?** (koo*ahl* (ehs)

while: **mientras** (mee*ehn*-trahs)

white: **blanco** (*bvlahn*-koh)

who/whom: **¿quién?** (kee*ehn*)

whole: **entero** (ehn-*teh*-roh)

why? **¿por qué?** (pohr keh)

wide: **ancho** (*ahn*-choh)

willingly: **de buena gana** (deh bvoo*eh*-nah *gah*-nah)

win: **ganar** (gah-*nahr*)

wine: **vino** (m) (*bvee*-noh)

winter: **invierno** (een-bvee*ehr*-noh) m

with: **con** (kohn)

withdrawal: **retiro** (reh-*tee*-roh) m

without: **sin** (seen)

without a smell: **inodoro** (ee-noh-*doh*-roh)

woman: **mujer** (moo-*Hehr*) f

wood: **madera** (mah-*deh*-rah) f

wool: **lana** (*lah*-nah) f

word: **palabra** (pah-*lah*-bvrah) f

work: **trabajar** (trah-bvah-*Hahr*)

world: **mundo** (*moon*-doh) m

worry (about): **preocuparse (de)** (preoh-koo-*pahr*-seh (deh))

worse: **peor** (peh-*ohr*)

worth: **valer** (bvah-*lehr*)

wrap up: **envolver (ue)** (ehn-bvohl-*bvehr*)

wrist: **muñeca** (moo-*nyeh*-kah) f

write: **escribir** (ehs-kree-*bveer*)

writer: **escritor/a** (ehs-kree-*tohr*/rah) m, f

Y

year: **año** (*ah*-nyoh) m

yellow: **amarillo** (ah-mah-*ree*-yoh)

yesterday: **ayer** (*ah*-yehr)

yet/still: **todavía** (toh-dah-*bvee*ah)

you: **tú/Ud./vosotros/Uds.** (too/oos-*tehd*/bvoh-*soh*-trohs/oos-*tehd*-ehs)

you/to you/yourselves, yourself: **os** (ohs); **te** (teh)

young: **joven** (*Hoh*-bvehn)

your/yours: **tu(s)** (too(s)); **vuestro(s)** (bvoo*ehs*-troh(s))

Z

zero: **cero** (*seh*-roh)

Appendix D

About the CD

● ●

What You'll Find on the CD

The following is a list of tracks that appear on this book's audio CD. Note that this is an audio-only CD. It'll play in any standard CD player or in your computer's CD-ROM drive.

Track 1: Introduction and Pronunciation Guide

Track 2: Formal Greeting

Track 3: Two Different Greetings

Track 4: Formal Introduction

Track 5: Informal Greeting

Track 6: The Verb *To Be*

Track 7: Finding a Bathroom

Track 8: Talking about the Weather

Track 9: Talking about Work

Track 10: Making a Restaurant Reservation

Track 11: Bartering at the Vegetable Stand

Track 12: Buying Clothes

Track 13: Haggling at an Outdoor Market

Track 14: Greetings on the Telephone

Track 15: Making a Collect Call

Track 16: Getting Information at a Hotel

Track 17: Talking to a Doctor's Receptionist

Track 18: Explaining Symptoms to a Doctor

Track 19: Talking to the Police

Track 20: Signing in at the Doctor's Office

Track 21: Gathering Insurance Information

Track 22: Asking Questions of a Patient

Track 23: Gathering Police Information

Track 24: Enrolling a Child at School

Track 25: Making an Account Transfer

Track 26: Interviewing an Applicant

Track 27: Welcoming Guests at a Hotel

Track 28: Greeting a New Employee

Customer Care

If you have trouble with the CD, please call Wiley Product Technical Support at 877-762-2974. Outside the United States, call 317-572-3993. You can also contact Wiley Product Technical Support at `http://support.wiley.com`. Wiley Publishing will provide technical support only for installation and other general quality control items.

To place additional orders or to request information about other Wiley products, please call 877-762-2974.

Index

• F •

• *M* •

• *W* •

Notes

Notes

Notes

Notes

Wiley Publishing, Inc.
End-User License Agreement

READ THIS. You should carefully read these terms and conditions before opening the software packet(s) included with this book "Book". This is a license agreement "Agreement" between you and Wiley Publishing, Inc. "WPI". By opening the accompanying software packet(s), you acknowledge that you have read and accept the following terms and conditions. If you do not agree and do not want to be bound by such terms and conditions, promptly return the Book and the unopened software packet(s) to the place you obtained them for a full refund.

1. **License Grant.** WPI grants to you (either an individual or entity) a nonexclusive license to use one copy of the enclosed software program(s) (collectively, the "Software") solely for your own personal or business purposes on a single computer (whether a standard computer or a workstation component of a multi-user network). The Software is in use on a computer when it is loaded into temporary memory (RAM) or installed into permanent memory (hard disk, CD-ROM, or other storage device). WPI reserves all rights not expressly granted herein.

2. **Ownership.** WPI is the owner of all right, title, and interest, including copyright, in and to the compilation of the Software recorded on the physical packet included with this Book "Software Media". Copyright to the individual programs recorded on the Software Media is owned by the author or other authorized copyright owner of each program. Ownership of the Software and all proprietary rights relating thereto remain with WPI and its licensers.

3. **Restrictions on Use and Transfer.**

   (a) You may only (i) make one copy of the Software for backup or archival purposes, or (ii) transfer the Software to a single hard disk, provided that you keep the original for backup or archival purposes. You may not (i) rent or lease the Software, (ii) copy or reproduce the Software through a LAN or other network system or through any computer subscriber system or bulletin-board system, or (iii) modify, adapt, or create derivative works based on the Software.

   (b) You may not reverse engineer, decompile, or disassemble the Software. You may transfer the Software and user documentation on a permanent basis, provided that the transferee agrees to accept the terms and conditions of this Agreement and you retain no copies. If the Software is an update or has been updated, any transfer must include the most recent update and all prior versions.

4. **Restrictions on Use of Individual Programs.** You must follow the individual requirements and restrictions detailed for each individual program in the "About the CD" appendix of this Book or on the Software Media. These limitations are also contained in the individual license agreements recorded on the Software Media. These limitations may include a requirement that after using the program for a specified period of time, the user must pay a registration fee or discontinue use. By opening the Software packet(s), you agree to abide by the licenses and restrictions for these individual programs that are detailed in the "About the CD" appendix and/or on the Software Media. None of the material on this Software Media or listed in this Book may ever be redistributed, in original or modified form, for commercial purposes.

5. **Limited Warranty.**

   (a) WPI warrants that the Software and Software Media are free from defects in materials and workmanship under normal use for a period of sixty (60) days from the date of purchase of this Book. If WPI receives notification within the warranty period of defects in materials or workmanship, WPI will replace the defective Software Media.

   (b) WPI AND THE AUTHOR(S) OF THE BOOK DISCLAIM ALL OTHER WARRANTIES, EXPRESS OR IMPLIED, INCLUDING WITHOUT LIMITATION IMPLIED WARRANTIES OF MERCHANTABILITY AND FITNESS FOR A PARTICULAR PURPOSE, WITH RESPECT TO THE SOFTWARE, THE PROGRAMS, THE SOURCE CODE CONTAINED THEREIN, AND/OR THE TECHNIQUES DESCRIBED IN THIS BOOK. WPI DOES NOT WARRANT THAT THE FUNCTIONS CONTAINED IN THE SOFTWARE WILL MEET YOUR REQUIREMENTS OR THAT THE OPERATION OF THE SOFTWARE WILL BE ERROR FREE.

   (c) This limited warranty gives you specific legal rights, and you may have other rights that vary from jurisdiction to jurisdiction.

6. **Remedies.**

   (a) WPI's entire liability and your exclusive remedy for defects in materials and workmanship shall be limited to replacement of the Software Media, which may be returned to WPI with a copy of your receipt at the following address: Software Media Fulfillment Department, Attn.: *Spanish All-in-One For Dummies*, Wiley Publishing, Inc., 10475 Crosspoint Blvd., Indianapolis, IN 46256, or call 1-877-762-2974. Please allow four to six weeks for delivery. This Limited Warranty is void if failure of the Software Media has resulted from accident, abuse, or misapplication. Any replacement Software Media will be warranted for the remainder of the original warranty period or thirty (30) days, whichever is longer.

   (b) In no event shall WPI or the author be liable for any damages whatsoever (including without limitation damages for loss of business profits, business interruption, loss of business information, or any other pecuniary loss) arising from the use of or inability to use the Book or the Software, even if WPI has been advised of the possibility of such damages.

   (c) Because some jurisdictions do not allow the exclusion or limitation of liability for consequential or incidental damages, the above limitation or exclusion may not apply to you.

7. **U.S. Government Restricted Rights.** Use, duplication, or disclosure of the Software for or on behalf of the United States of America, its agencies and/or instrumentalities "U.S. Government" is subject to restrictions as stated in paragraph (c)(1)(ii) of the Rights in Technical Data and Computer Software clause of DFARS 252.227-7013, or subparagraphs (c)(1) and (2) of the Commercial Computer Software - Restricted Rights clause at FAR 52.227-19, and in similar clauses in the NASA FAR supplement, as applicable.

8. **General.** This Agreement constitutes the entire understanding of the parties and revokes and supersedes all prior agreements, oral or written, between them and may not be modified or amended except in a writing signed by both parties hereto that specifically refers to this Agreement. This Agreement shall take precedence over any other documents that may be in conflict herewith. If any one or more provisions contained in this Agreement are held by any court or tribunal to be invalid, illegal, or otherwise unenforceable, each and every other provision shall remain in full force and effect.

USINESS, CAREERS & PERSONAL FINANCE

counting For Dummies, 4th Edition*
3-0-470-24600-9

okkeeping Workbook For Dummies†
3-0-470-16983-4

mmodities For Dummies
8-0-470-04928-0

ing Business in China For Dummies
8-0-470-04929-7

E-Mail Marketing For Dummies
978-0-470-19087-6

Job Interviews For Dummies, 3rd Edition*†
978-0-470-17748-8

Personal Finance Workbook For Dummies*†
978-0-470-09933-9

Real Estate License Exams For Dummies
978-0-7645-7623-2

Six Sigma For Dummies
978-0-7645-6798-8

Small Business Kit For Dummies,
2nd Edition*†
978-0-7645-5984-6

Telephone Sales For Dummies
978-0-470-16836-3

USINESS PRODUCTIVITY & MICROSOFT OFFICE

cess 2007 For Dummies
8-0-470-03649-5

cel 2007 For Dummies
8-0-470-03737-9

fice 2007 For Dummies
8-0-470-00923-9

tlook 2007 For Dummies
8-0-470-03830-7

PowerPoint 2007 For Dummies
978-0-470-04059-1

Project 2007 For Dummies
978-0-470-03651-8

QuickBooks 2008 For Dummies
978-0-470-18470-7

Quicken 2008 For Dummies
978-0-470-17473-9

Salesforce.com For Dummies,
2nd Edition
978-0-470-04893-1

Word 2007 For Dummies
978-0-470-03658-7

DUCATION, HISTORY, REFERENCE & TEST PREPARATION

rican American History For Dummies
8-0-7645-5469-8

gebra For Dummies
8-0-7645-5325-7

gebra Workbook For Dummies
8-0-7645-8467-1

t History For Dummies
8-0-470-09910-0

ASVAB For Dummies, 2nd Edition
978-0-470-10671-6

British Military History For Dummies
978-0-470-03213-8

Calculus For Dummies
978-0-7645-2498-1

Canadian History For Dummies, 2nd Edition
978-0-470-83656-9

Geometry Workbook For Dummies
978-0-471-79940-5

The SAT I For Dummies, 6th Edition
978-0-7645-7193-0

Series 7 Exam For Dummies
978-0-470-09932-2

World History For Dummies
978-0-7645-5242-7

OOD, GARDEN, HOBBIES & HOME

ridge For Dummies, 2nd Edition
78-0-471-92426-5

oin Collecting For Dummies, 2nd Edition
78-0-470-22275-1

ooking Basics For Dummies, 3rd Edition
78-0-7645-7206-7

Drawing For Dummies
978-0-7645-5476-6

Etiquette For Dummies, 2nd Edition
978-0-470-10672-3

Gardening Basics For Dummies*†
978-0-470-03749-2

Knitting Patterns For Dummies
978-0-470-04556-5

Living Gluten-Free For Dummies†
978-0-471-77383-2

Painting Do-It-Yourself For Dummies
978-0-470-17533-0

EALTH, SELF HELP, PARENTING & PETS

nger Management For Dummies
78-0-470-03715-7

nxiety & Depression Workbook
or Dummies
78-0-7645-9793-0

ieting For Dummies, 2nd Edition
78-0-7645-4149-0

og Training For Dummies, 2nd Edition
78-0-7645-8418-3

Horseback Riding For Dummies
978-0-470-09719-9

Infertility For Dummies†
978-0-470-11518-3

Meditation For Dummies with CD-ROM,
2nd Edition
978-0-471-77774-8

Post-Traumatic Stress Disorder For Dummies
978-0-470-04922-8

Puppies For Dummies, 2nd Edition
978-0-470-03717-1

Thyroid For Dummies, 2nd Edition†
978-0-471-78755-6

Type 1 Diabetes For Dummies*†
978-0-470-17811-9

Separate Canadian edition also available
Separate U.K. edition also available

 WILE

INTERNET & DIGITAL MEDIA

AdWords For Dummies
978-0-470-15252-2

Blogging For Dummies, 2nd Edition
978-0-470-23017-6

Digital Photography All-in-One Desk Reference For Dummies, 3rd Edition
978-0-470-03743-0

Digital Photography For Dummies, 5th Edition
978-0-7645-9802-9

Digital SLR Cameras & Photography For Dummies, 2nd Edition
978-0-470-14927-0

eBay Business All-in-One Desk Reference For Dummies
978-0-7645-8438-1

eBay For Dummies, 5th Edition*
978-0-470-04529-9

eBay Listings That Sell For Dummies
978-0-471-78912-3

Facebook For Dummies
978-0-470-26273-3

The Internet For Dummies, 11th Edition
978-0-470-12174-0

Investing Online For Dummies, 5th Edition
978-0-7645-8456-5

iPod & iTunes For Dummies, 5th Editi
978-0-470-17474-6

MySpace For Dummies
978-0-470-09529-4

Podcasting For Dummies
978-0-471-74898-4

Search Engine Optimization For Dummies, 2nd Edition
978-0-471-97998-2

Second Life For Dummies
978-0-470-18025-9

Starting an eBay Business For Dumm 3rd Edition†
978-0-470-14924-9

GRAPHICS, DESIGN & WEB DEVELOPMENT

Adobe Creative Suite 3 Design Premium All-in-One Desk Reference For Dummies
978-0-470-11724-8

Adobe Web Suite CS3 All-in-One Desk Reference For Dummies
978-0-470-12099-6

AutoCAD 2008 For Dummies
978-0-470-11650-0

Building a Web Site For Dummies, 3rd Edition
978-0-470-14928-7

Creating Web Pages All-in-One Desk Reference For Dummies, 3rd Edition
978-0-470-09629-1

Creating Web Pages For Dummies, 8th Edition
978-0-470-08030-6

Dreamweaver CS3 For Dummies
978-0-470-11490-2

Flash CS3 For Dummies
978-0-470-12100-9

Google SketchUp For Dummies
978-0-470-13744-4

InDesign CS3 For Dummies
978-0-470-11865-8

Photoshop CS3 All-in-One Desk Reference For Dummies
978-0-470-11195-6

Photoshop CS3 For Dummies
978-0-470-11193-2

Photoshop Elements 5 For Dummie
978-0-470-09810-3

SolidWorks For Dummies
978-0-7645-9555-4

Visio 2007 For Dummies
978-0-470-08983-5

Web Design For Dummies, 2nd Editi
978-0-471-78117-2

Web Sites Do-It-Yourself For Dumm
978-0-470-16903-2

Web Stores Do-It-Yourself For Dumm
978-0-470-17443-2

LANGUAGES, RELIGION & SPIRITUALITY

Arabic For Dummies
978-0-471-77270-5

Chinese For Dummies, Audio Set
978-0-470-12766-7

French For Dummies
978-0-7645-5193-2

German For Dummies
978-0-7645-5195-6

Hebrew For Dummies
978-0-7645-5489-6

Ingles Para Dummies
978-0-7645-5427-8

Italian For Dummies, Audio Set
978-0-470-09586-7

Italian Verbs For Dummies
978-0-471-77389-4

Japanese For Dummies
978-0-7645-5429-2

Latin For Dummies
978-0-7645-5431-5

Portuguese For Dummies
978-0-471-78738-9

Russian For Dummies
978-0-471-78001-4

Spanish Phrases For Dummies
978-0-7645-7204-3

Spanish For Dummies
978-0-7645-5194-9

Spanish For Dummies, Audio Set
978-0-470-09585-0

The Bible For Dummies
978-0-7645-5296-0

Catholicism For Dummies
978-0-7645-5391-2

The Historical Jesus For Dummies
978-0-470-16785-4

Islam For Dummies
978-0-7645-5503-9

Spirituality For Dummies, 2nd Edition
978-0-470-19142-2

NETWORKING AND PROGRAMMING

NET 3.5 For Dummies
470-19592-5

For Dummies
19109-5

Dummies, 2nd Edition
35-8

ng For Dummies, 4th Edition

Java For Dummies, 4th Edition
978-0-470-08716-9

Microsoft® SQL Server™ 2008 All-in-One Desk Reference For Dummies
978-0-470-17954-3

Networking All-in-One Desk Reference For Dummies, 2nd Edition
978-0-7645-9939-2

Networking For Dummies, 8th Edition
978-0-470-05620-2

SharePoint 2007 For Dummies
978-0-470-09941-4

Wireless Home Networking For Dummies, 2nd Edition
978-0-471-74940-0

PERATING SYSTEMS & COMPUTER BASICS

Mac For Dummies, 5th Edition
8-0-7645-8458-9

Laptops For Dummies, 2nd Edition
8-0-470-05432-1

Linux For Dummies, 8th Edition
8-0-470-11649-4

MacBook For Dummies
8-0-470-04859-7

**Mac OS X Leopard All-in-One
Desk Reference For Dummies**
8-0-470-05434-5

Mac OS X Leopard For Dummies
978-0-470-05433-8

Macs For Dummies, 9th Edition
978-0-470-04849-8

PCs For Dummies, 11th Edition
978-0-470-13728-4

Windows® Home Server For Dummies
978-0-470-18592-6

Windows Server 2008 For Dummies
978-0-470-18043-3

**Windows Vista All-in-One
Desk Reference For Dummies**
978-0-471-74941-7

Windows Vista For Dummies
978-0-471-75421-3

Windows Vista Security For Dummies
978-0-470-11805-4

PORTS, FITNESS & MUSIC

Coaching Hockey For Dummies
8-0-470-83685-9

Coaching Soccer For Dummies
8-0-471-77381-8

Fitness For Dummies, 3rd Edition
8-0-7645-7851-9

Football For Dummies, 3rd Edition
8-0-470-12536-6

GarageBand For Dummies
978-0-7645-7323-1

Golf For Dummies, 3rd Edition
978-0-471-76871-5

Guitar For Dummies, 2nd Edition
978-0-7645-9904-0

**Home Recording For Musicians
For Dummies, 2nd Edition**
978-0-7645-8884-6

**iPod & iTunes For Dummies,
5th Edition**
978-0-470-17474-6

Music Theory For Dummies
978-0-7645-7838-0

Stretching For Dummies
978-0-470-06741-3

Get smart @ dummies.com®

- **Find a full list of Dummies titles**
- **Look into loads of FREE on-site articles**
- **Sign up for FREE eTips e-mailed to you weekly**
- **See what other products carry the Dummies name**
- **Shop directly from the Dummies bookstore**
- **Enter to win new prizes every month!**

Separate Canadian edition also available
Separate U.K. edition also available